THREADS of POWER

Edited by Emma Cormack and Michele Majer

THREADS *of* POWER

Lace from the Textilmuseum St. Gallen

Published by Bard Graduate Center, New York
Distributed by Yale University Press, New Haven and London

This catalogue is published in conjunction with the exhibition *Threads of Power: Lace from the Textilmuseum St. Gallen*, organized by Bard Graduate Center and the Textilmuseum St. Gallen, and held at Bard Graduate Center Gallery from September 16, 2022, to January 1, 2023.

Catalogue editors: Emma Cormack and Michele Majer
Exhibition curators: Emma Cormack, Ilona Kos, and Michele Majer
Project manager: Emma Cormack
Book designer: Laura Grey
Managing editor: Katherine Atkins
Copyeditor: Florence Grant
Manager of photographic rights and reproductions: Alexis Mucha

A previous iteration of *Threads of Power: Lace from the Textilmuseum St. Gallen* was titled *Lace and Status: The Collection of Historical Lace in the Textilmuseum St. Gallen*. It was curated by Barbara Karl and was on display at the Textilmuseum St. Gallen from October 26, 2018, to February 10, 2019.

Published by Bard Graduate Center, New York, and distributed by Yale University Press, New Haven and London.

Chapter 1 was translated and expanded from Barbara Karl, "Die Spitze der Gesellschaft: Luxus, Macht, Kontrolle in der Frühen Neuzeit," in *160. Neujahrsblatt HVSG (2020) Der Status uns seine Symbole*, ed. Arman Weidenmann and Clemens Müller (Schwellbrunn, Switzerland: FormatOst, 2020), 55–65.

Chapter 4 was translated and expanded from Frieda Sorber, "Antwerpen und Brüssel: Zwei Zentren der Spitzenherstellung und des Spitzenhandels 1550–1750," in *Historische Spitzen: Die Leopold-Iklé-Sammlung im Textilmuseum St. Gallen*, ed. Textilmuseum St. Gallen and Iklé-Frischknecht-Stiftung (Stuttgart, Germany: Arnoldsche, 2018), 23–31.

Chapter 14 was translated and expanded from Anne Wanner-Jean-Richard, "'Das Alte auf eine neue Weise tun—das ist Innovation,'" in *Historische Spitzen: Die Leopold-Iklé-Sammlung im Textilmuseum St. Gallen*, ed. Textilmuseum St. Gallen and Iklé-Frischknecht-Stiftung (Stuttgart, Germany: Arnoldsche, 2018), 10–22.

This book is set in FreightTextPro

Production by Booklabs, London

Printed in China by C&C Offset Printing Co., Ltd.

Library of Congress Control Number: 2022940720
ISBN: 978-0-300-26349-7
A catalogue record for this book is available from the British Library.

First edition
10 9 8 7 6 5 4 3 2

Cover: Detail of *punto in aria* needle-lace border fragment, Venice, second quarter of the 18th century. Textilmuseum St. Gallen, Acquired from the Estate of John Jacoby, 1954, 00063. Cat. 37.

Endpapers: Detail of *point de France* needle-lace border, France, 1695–1710. Textilmuseum St. Gallen, Acquired from the Estate of John Jacoby, 1954, 01231. Cat. 86.

Frontispiece: Nicolas de Larmessin III, "Habit de la Lingère," from *Les Costumes Grotesques*, 1695. Engraving. Cooper Hewitt, Smithsonian National Design Museum, New York, Museum purchase through gift of Mrs. Samuel W. Bridgham, 1949-38-9.

Generous support for *Threads of Power: Lace from the Textilmuseum St. Gallen* has been provided by the Coby Foundation with additional support from the Zurich Silk Association, Lenore G. Tawney Foundation, Consulate General of Switzerland in New York, Switzerland Tourism, Forster Rohner AG, Tobias Forster, AKRIS, and other donors to Bard Graduate Center.

 THE COBY FOUNDATION, LTD.

This project is supported in part by the National Endowment for the Arts.

Special thanks to the Finger Lakes Lace Guild and the New England Lace Group.

TABLE *of* CONTENTS

Director's Foreword

Bard Graduate Center is pleased to present *Threads of Power: Lace from the Textilmuseum St. Gallen* and welcome the Textilmuseum's world-class collection of historical lace to New York. This important exhibition is organized in collaboration with the Textilmuseum, where an earlier iteration titled *Lace and Status: The Collection of Historical Lace in the Textilmuseum St. Gallen* was on view from October 26, 2018, to February 10, 2019. In addition to marking the American debut of approximately 150 significant objects from their collection, *Threads of Power* is the first large-scale installation in New York in more than forty years to trace the development of European lace, illuminating its integral role in fashion from the sixteenth to the twenty-first century, and to emphasize the contribution of countless women—whose names are now unknown—to the creation of this luxury textile. In bringing the exhibition to Bard Graduate Center, we have extended its original chronology to the twenty-first century and incorporated chemical lace, which has been a hallmark of the Swiss textile industry since the late nineteenth century. This expanded focus highlights the strong connections between St. Gallen firms and the US market. Using this exceptional collection as a guide, our exploration of the history of lace is enhanced by painted portraits, garments, books, and photographs from North American institutions and private lenders, allowing *Threads of Power* to take a broad view of European lace production and consumption over six centuries.

This richly illustrated volume, which accompanies the exhibition, is the first major English-language publication in more than fifteen years to address the subject of both historical and contemporary lace from a variety of cultures and geographic regions. Featuring new research, this catalogue presents sixteen chapters inclusive of an interview with leading designers at two prominent St. Gallen textile companies and covers a wide range of topics related to the making, selling, and wearing of lace; lace in the Spanish Americas in the seventeenth and eighteenth centuries; lace in portraiture; the vogue for collecting antique lace among museums, manufacturers, and individuals; and the mechanization of the lace industries in the nineteenth and twentieth centuries. We thank Laura Beltrán-Rubio, Denis Bruna, Amalia Descalzo Lorenzo, Annina Dosch, Tobias Forster, Paula Hohti, Barbara Karl, Ilona Kos, Martin Leuthold, Kenna Libes, Mariselle Meléndez, James Middleton, Lesley Ellis Miller, Catherine Örmen, Hans

Handmade Chantilly bobbin-lace flounce, France or Belgium, third quarter of the 19th century. Silk. Textilmuseum St. Gallen, Acquired from the Estate of John Jacoby, 1954, 00484. Cat. 127.

Schreiber, Frieda Sorber, Femke Speelberg, Annabel Bonnin Talbot, Anne Wanner-JeanRichard, Emily Zilber, and translators Patricia Cabral, Andrew Horsfield, and Nils Schott for their contributions to this catalogue.

Bard Graduate Center associate curator Emma Cormack and assistant professor Michele Majer have brilliantly guided this project over the last two years. As project manager, Emma was responsible for overseeing all aspects of the exhibition and catalogue, and as co-curators and co-editors, she and Michele have produced a visually rich and intellectually engaging exhibition and publication.

The realization of *Threads of Power* is the outcome of a successful collaboration with the Textilmuseum St. Gallen. We are obliged to each member of the museum's team for their dedication to the project and their indefatigable assistance throughout its development. First and foremost, we owe a special debt of gratitude to Ilona Kos, who is co-curator of the exhibition and curator and head of collections and library at the Textilmuseum. Her expert knowledge of the collection and guiding vision for the contemporary section of the installation were fundamental in shaping its implementation. It is thanks to her steadfast efforts and fruitful and collegial working relationship with Emma and Michele that the exhibition is a reality. We are likewise very appreciative of the Textilmuseum's interim director, Stefan Aschwanden, and newly appointed director, Mandana Roozpeikar, for their enthusiasm and facilitation of the collection's debut in New York. The research undertaken by Barbara Karl, curator of the Textilmuseum's *Lace and Status* exhibition, provided us with the fundamental groundwork for the installation in New York, and we are grateful for her ongoing feedback and encouragement. The exhibition and this publication have relied heavily on the comprehensive study of the Textilmuseum's historical lace holdings that Thessy Schoenholzer Nichols conducted in 2018–19. Annina Dosch, collections assistant at the Textilmuseum, has been integral to the development of this project, and her skillful coordination of all matters related to the objects in the exhibition was invaluable. Likewise essential to this publication is the beautiful work by photographer Michael Rast, whose artful eye captured the technical intricacies and elegance of the hundreds of lace objects in the Textilmuseum's collection illustrated in this volume. The careful presentation of the lace in the exhibition is thanks to the expert work and coordination of Sarah Obrecht, the project's conservator. We are thankful for Silvia Gross, who, as the head of communication and education at the Textilmuseum, worked with Bard Graduate Center's team to connect audiences in New York and St. Gallen. We are equally grateful for the opportunity to work alongside other members of the Textilmuseum's talented team, including Christine Freydl-Kuster, collections assistant; Angela Graf, responsible for the Textilmuseum's shop and visitor services; Claudia Merfert, textile conservator; Debora Messerli, librarian; Maria Weber, who operates the hand-embroidery machine (constructed ca. 1889) on display in the Textilmuseum's galleries; and Pia Zweifel, head of visitor services and administration.

We owe an immense debt of gratitude to the Swiss lenders and individuals who generously agreed to participate in *Threads of Power*, among them Tobias Forster, Hans Schreiber, and Miriam Rüthemann, Forster Rohner AG; Fabio Di Silvio, Jakob Schlaepfer AG; Albert Kriemler and Sophie Feneberg, Akris Prêt-à-Porter AG; and Gwen Aubry and Lisa Fässler Hofstetter, Bischoff Textil AG. We thank these contributors for opening their archives and sharing the rich textile history of St. Gallen with our New York audiences.

We are equally obliged to the numerous lenders in North America for their cooperation, support, and generosity. Among those individuals and institutions we would like to thank for their efforts are Brooke L. Clement and Erin McKeen, Barack Obama Presidential Library; Titi Halle and Martina D'Amato, Cora Ginsburg, LLC; Christoph Heinrich and Jorge Rivas Pérez, Denver Art Museum; David R. Daly, Longfellow House - Washington's Headquarters National Historic Site; Max Hollein, Elizabeth Cleland, Clara Goldman, David Pullins, Elizabeth Randolph, Allison Rudnick, Femke Speelberg, Anna Yanofsky, and Elizabeth Zanis, the Metropolitan Museum of Art; Valerie Steele and Sonia Dingilian, the Museum at FIT; Joanna Groarke and Stephen Sinon, New York Botanical Garden; Timothy Rub and Kristina Haugland, Philadelphia Museum of Art; Josh Basseches, Alexandra Palmer, and Chris Paulocik, Royal Ontario Museum; Pamela Franks, Diane Hart, and Kevin M. Murphy, Williams College Museum of Art; as well as Eliza Bolen and Mayer Campbell, Oscar de la Renta; and private lenders Elaine J. Condon, Donna Ghelerter, Jane M. Gincig, Patricia L. Kalayjian, Martin Leuthold, and Ruben Toledo.

The significant contributions of Elena Kanagy-Loux, whose specially commissioned bobbin-lace collar welcomes visitors to the exhibition, have been central to the curatorial thinking around this project. We extend our deep gratitude for her willingness to engage with the material as both a lacemaker and a lace scholar and for facilitating collaborative programming that invites audiences to consider the lives and work of lacemakers in the past.

We are fortunate to have a highly talented team at Bard Graduate Center whose collective efforts, led by Emma Cormack and Michele Majer, helped realize this publication and the exhibition and its related programming. This volume's elegant design is all thanks to the creative vision of Laura Grey. Under the direction of Daniel Lee and Katherine Atkins, Florence Grant and Helen Polson expertly managed the complex task of readying catalogue and exhibition texts for publication. Alexis Mucha skillfully sourced the hundreds of images illustrated here. Marina Asenjo coordinated all aspects of the production of this volume.

Ian Sullivan created the beautiful exhibition design for *Threads of Power*, which sensitively showcases the objects and their contextual material. Eric Edler handled the exhibition's assembly and installation with Alexander Gruen and Bard Graduate Center's crew, aided by Tae Smith and Samantha Wood. Andrew Kircher, Jen Ha, Olivia Kalin, Laura Minsky, Carla Repice, Nadia Rivers, and Rachael Schwabe organized the broad range of public programming and tours related to the exhibition, activating the objects on view for our visitors.

Benjamin Krevolin, Ruth Epstein, Minna Lee, Maddy Warner, and Daniel Zimmer contributed to the successful fundraising for all facets of this project and the organization of its related events at Bard Graduate Center. Amy Estes handled all aspects of marketing and communications for *Threads of Power*, alongside Ema Furusho and Maggie Walter, and Laura Grey and Jocelyn Lau designed the in-gallery visuals, interpretation, and printed materials related to the exhibition. Our visitor services team of Ben James and Bree Klauser welcomed guests to the exhibition.

Jesse Merandy and Julie Fuller, working with Emma Cormack, created the *Threads of Power* digital components that invited and enabled online visitors to experience the exhibition. Librarians Heather Topcik, Anna Helgeson, and Sebastian Moya were instrumental in acquiring materials and assisting the curatorial team with research throughout the project. Bard Graduate Center finance and administration, including Tim Ettenheim, Mohammed Alam, Samantha Baron, Miao Chen, and Rita Niyazova, supported all aspects of the project's development and realization. James Congregane, Chandler Small, and the security and facilities teams dependably managed the upkeep of Bard Graduate Center buildings and the safety of our visitors.

Key to the Bard Graduate Center mission is the integration of teaching and exhibitions, and this project has benefited greatly from student participation. Members of Michele Majer's fall 2021 Threads of Power seminar, including Mary Adeogun, Antonia Anagnostopoulos, Grace Billingslea, Ariana Bishop, Caroline Elenowitz-Hess, Emily Harvey, Kenna Libes, Isabella Margi, Samuel Snodgrass, Maura Tangum, and Zoe Volpa, collaborated with the co-curators and Jesse Merandy to create in-gallery digital interactives that supplement exhibition themes. Equally important to the realization of this exhibition and publication was the work of Bard Graduate Center Gallery exhibitions assistants, including MA and PhD students Grace Billingslea, Julia Carabatsos, Nicholas de Godoy Lopes, Noah Dubay, Emily Harvey, Kenna Libes, Louise Lui, Isabella Margi, Jeremy Reeves, Genny Schiel, and Samuel Snodgrass, and students in Bard Graduate Center's Teen Program, Hope Dworkin and Crys Pereira. The exhibition was enhanced by the fall 2022 season of Bard Graduate Center's *Fields of the Future* podcast exploring lace in Yoruba fashion and culture, which was skillfully developed and produced by Mary Adeogun. We are immensely thankful for these students' input and expertise and for their role as valuable collaborators on this project.

I have saved the final words of gratitude for our sponsors. Among them are respected patrons Tobias Forster and his late wife, Yvonne, whose friendship and passion for textile research, design, and innovation have been critical to this project.

We are grateful for the outstanding leadership of Ward E. Mintz and the Coby Foundation, Kathleen Nugent Mangan and the Lenore G. Tawney Foundation, and we deeply appreciate the sponsorship of Alexis Schwarzenbach and the Zurich Silk Association, Divine Bonga and Switzerland Tourism, the Consulate General of Switzerland in New York, Forster Rohner AG, and Akris.

Special thanks go to the Finger Lakes Lace Guild and the New England Lace Group. This project is supported in part by the National Endowment for the Arts.

Without these sponsors, this thorough investigation of lace and its dynamic history would not have been possible.

In organizing *Threads of Power*, we have had the pleasure of interacting with numerous lace historians, contemporary lacemakers, and lace enthusiasts, all of whom are thrilled at the opportunity to see and study so many significant pieces of historical lace in one space. We hope that they and other visitors will learn from and find inspiration in this project's compelling objects and narratives.

Susan Weber
Director and Founder, Bard Graduate Center

Editors' Note

Throughout the process of curating *Threads of Power: Lace from the Textilmuseum St. Gallen* and editing this exhibition catalogue, we have been confronted with two overarching questions: what constitutes lace and, by extension, how it is defined. In *Lace: A History* (1983), Santina Levey, former curator in the department of textiles at the Victoria and Albert Museum, London, and one of the foremost authorities on this subject, who we have relied on extensively for this project, states that "lace is versatile fabric for which there is no single comprehensive definition." This nonwoven fabric encompasses needle and bobbin laces but also other techniques, "such as macramé, knitting, knotting, [and] crochet."[1] Although many different types of openwork textiles with a lacelike appearance have been produced around the world since antiquity, we have necessarily confined ourselves to the forms of lace that are on view in the *Threads of Power* exhibition at the Bard Graduate Center Gallery and discussed in this publication. These comprise handmade needle and bobbin lace, machine-made lace that replicates bobbin lace, and the so-called "chemical lace" made on an embroidery machine that closely resembles needle lace.

The success of Swiss embroidery manufacturers' endeavors beginning in the late nineteenth century to create a textile that mimicked traditional handmade lace was acknowledged in the early twentieth century by French writers on lace, who used various terms to designate these products, including "la broderie brûlée de Saint Gall" (burnt embroidery of St. Gall; 1906), "dentelles mécaniques" (mechanical laces; 1907), "la dentelle au métier suisse" (lace [made on] a Swiss loom; 1914), and "dentelles chimiques" (chemical laces; 1922).[2] The US fashion press referred to St. Gallen chemical lace using English terms such as "machine embroideries" (1909), "St. Gall lace" (1921), and "guipure" lace (1946, 1963).[3] In 1892 the St. Gallen Kaufmännische Directorium (the city's entrepreneurial association) used the term *Aetzstickerei* (etched embroidery), and in 1914 Charles Wetter-Rüesch (1857–1921) referred to *Aetzspitze* (etched lace), while recalling his experimentation and eventual success in developing the chemical-lace production process in the early 1880s (SEE CHAP. 14).[4] The voided spaces resulting from dissolving the ground led to the identification of these textiles as "lace" in the fashion press. Even today, many clients of the leading St. Gallen manufacturers refer to these fabrics as lace.

Lace terminology is—and has been—notoriously inconsistent and therefore confusing. In the eighteenth century, for example, point d'Angleterre referred to bobbin lace made in Brussels, and in the nineteenth century *gros point de Venise* was used to refer to seventeenth-century Venetian lace, although the descriptor was never used at that time. Drawing on the expertise of lace scholars including Levey, Pat Earnshaw, and Patricia Wardle as a foundation, the glossary in this volume, compiled by Kenna Libes, incorporates terms used by the contributing authors who write about lace in Europe and the Spanish Americas from the sixteenth to the twenty-first century.

We are pleased to echo Susan Weber's acknowledgment of our many talented project collaborators and would like to express our own deepest gratitude to Ilona Kos, Katherine Atkins, Laura Grey, Alexis Mucha, Ian Sullivan, Elena Kanagy-Loux, and Brooklyn Lace Guild. Their determined efforts, ongoing encouragement, and unfailing humor made this project a pleasure to work on. Finally, we would like to extend very special thanks to Colin Bain, Dodie Sorrell, Spencer Majer, Anna Cormack, Maddie Staurseth, Earl Martin, Laura Microulis, and our other friends and family who have endured years of talk about lace and lacemakers and have offered us invaluable support—intellectual, moral, and culinary.

1   Santina Levey, *Lace: A History* (London: Victoria and Albert Museum; Leeds, UK: W. S. Maney & Son, 1983), 1.
2   L. Deshairs, "L'Éxposition de dentelles anciennes et modernes," *Art et Décoration* 20 (1906): 64–65; Marguerite Charles, *Dentelles françaises et étrangères: Les broderies et les dentelles* (Paris, 1907), 136–37; Émile Bayard, *L'art de reconnaître les dentelles, les guipures, etc.* (Paris: R. Roger et F. Chernoviz, 1914), 233–34, 136–37; and *Le Moniteur de la maille*, no. 493 (October 1922): 1228.
3   "Fashion: Forecasts of the Spring Modes," *Vogue*, February 4, 1909, 179; "Undergarments: Crepe Satin Attains New Importance in High Grade Silk Line—Novel Shade of Cyclamen Introduced in Complete Set; St. Gall Lace on Crepe De Chine," *Women's Wear*, February 8, 1921, 27; "Merchandising, Millinery and Accessories Fabrics: Embroideries, Laces Improve for 1947: Lacy Embroideries and 'Guipure' Venises in Swiss Collection Forster Willi & Co," *Women's Wear Daily*, November 29, 1946, 21; and "Fashion: Night Matters—Twill and Lace," *Vogue*, October 1, 1963, 182–83.
4   Kaufmännisches Directorium, *Bericht des Kaufm. Directoriums, Handel, Industrie & Geldverhältnisse des Kantons St. Gallen im jarhe 1891* (St. Gallen, Switzerland: Zollukofer'schen Buchdruckerei, 1892), 16–17; and Charles Wetter-Ruesch, "Die Erfindung der Atztechnik 1882/83," in *Schweizerische Landesausstellung in Bern 1914: Die Stickerei-Industrie. Eine Schilderung der Ausstellung verbunden mit einer Darlegung geschichtlicher Entwicklung und der gesamten Organisation dieser Industrie*, ed. E. A. Steiger-Züst (Zurich: Art Institut Orell Füssli, 1915), 36.

Threads of Power

Emma Cormack and Michele Majer

On January 18, 2009, as Barack Obama was sworn in as the first Black president of the United States, Michelle Obama stood by his side wearing a now-famous matching lace coat and dress, a scene documented in thousands of photographs taken of the historic event. For many Americans, these images of the smiling couple walking in the parade and details of the soon-to-be First Lady's ensemble are easily recalled (FIG. I.1). Insight into the sartorial choices of the wealthy and powerful has long been a source of public fascination, and the media coverage of the First Lady's clothing that frigid January day was no different. Designed by the late Cuban American designer Isabel Toledo (1960–2019) and constructed from a chartreuse wool guipure made by Swiss textile manufacturer Forster Rohner, the ensemble embodied the historic significance of the day (FIG. I.2).

For Toledo, the lace, which she described as "fragile to the eye, but strong and sturdy," came first.[1] In her memoir, she recalls drawing inspiration directly from it:

> Quite honestly, it all started with the fabric. The textile itself began to weave the magic that followed. I have always allowed textiles to lead the way to a new vision, and this time was no different—except the results were staggering. This was a felted wool lace and reminded me of floating islands connected by one strong and sturdy thread. The empty spaces gave me the ability to play with the illusion of light escaping from beneath. . . . I love lace in any form because for me, it is one of the most modern as well as ancient textiles. . . . With that tiny lemongrass lace swatch, I had found my voice and was immediately inspired to start designing.[2]

The sheath dress and matching coat are lined in cream-colored silk that is visible beneath the lace (FIGS. I.3 AND I.4). For warmth during the outdoor swearing-in ceremony, Toledo backed the lace with sewn-in layers of pashmina and "cloudlike" silk netting. The resulting garment is elegant and modern, and the streamlined cut of the silhouette draws attention to the intricacy of the fabric. Toledo's creation for Michelle Obama constitutes a recent example in the long tradition of employing lace on the body as a status symbol.

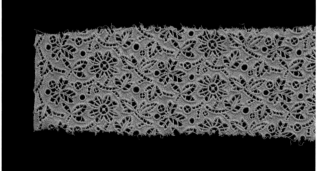

Emma Cormack and Michele Majer

Connections between power and handmade lace in Europe can be traced back to its sixteenth-century origins; royalty and nobility, political leaders, and the upper classes utilized this luxurious textile to convey authority and wealth. Lace embellished headwear, collars, sleeves, and hems, as is evident from portraits painted between the sixteenth and eighteenth centuries, and served as a material indicator of elevated social standing. Handmade lace was an expensive and labor-intensive commodity, whose production required immense skill and time. Only in the nineteenth century did advances in mechanization make lace more widely available to consumers.

The type of fabric that Toledo used—made on embroidery machines and often referred to as "Swiss lace," "guipure lace," or "chemical lace"—is produced in and around St. Gallen, a city in eastern Switzerland that boasts a long history of textile production.[3] Located on the southwestern edge of Lake Constance, St. Gallen sits approximately 2,300 feet above sea level with a humid climate that provided fertile ground for successful linen production beginning in the early modern period (FIG. I.5). By 1910, thanks to various machine innovations by Swiss manufacturers in the late nineteenth century, the regional textile industry employed approximately seventy thousand people, and machine embroidery constituted a significant portion of Swiss exports (FIGS. I.6–8).[4] However, severely affected by World War I, the industry faced a crisis from which it would not fully recover until the postwar period.[5]

Today St. Gallen is home to many textile manufacturing companies, among them Forster Rohner and Jakob Schlaepfer, both established in 1904, and Bischoff Textil, founded in 1927. These firms design and manufacture high-quality custom lace and embroidery for couture houses including Prada, Dior, Oscar de la Renta, Chanel, Yves Saint Laurent, Akris, and Givenchy (SEE CHAP. 16). The city is also home to the Textilmuseum St. Gallen, which houses a world-class collection of historical lace (FIG. I.9). Established in 1878 as the St. Gallen Industry and Trade Museum, the institution served to educate and inspire local designers and manufacturers in the late nineteenth and early twentieth centuries during the high point of the Swiss embroidery industry. It is

FIG. I.1 (OPPOSITE, TOP RIGHT)
President Barack Obama and First Lady Michelle Obama at the 2009 Presidential Inauguration Parade, January 20, 2009. Courtesy Barack Obama Presidential Library, Chicago.

FIG. I.2 (OPPOSITE, TOP LEFT)
Isabel Toledo (designer) and Forster Rohner AG (textile manufacturer), 2009 Presidential Inauguration ensemble worn by First Lady Michelle Obama, United States and St. Gallen, Switzerland, ca. 2008. Felted wool lace, silk radzimir, and silk netting. Courtesy Barack Obama Presidential Library, Chicago, FL2011.1a–b. Cat. 172.

FIG. I.3 (OPPOSITE, BOTTOM LEFT)
Forster Rohner AG, guipure fragment used for Isabel Toledo's 2009 Presidential Inauguration ensemble for First Lady Michelle Obama, 2008. Forster Rohner AG. Cat. 174.

FIG. I.4 (OPPOSITE, BOTTOM RIGHT)
Ruben Toledo, sketch and swatch of Isabel Toledo–designed 2009 Presidential Inauguration ensemble for First Lady Michelle Obama, 2008. Ink on paper and felted wool lace. Ruben Toldeo, courtesy Ruben and Isabel Toledo Archives. Cat. 173.

FIG. I.5 (BELOW)
Jacob Christoph Stauder, *View from Rosenberg*, 1675 (?). Oil on canvas. Historisches und Völkerkundemuseum St. Gallen, G_2878.

primarily thanks to the ambitious collecting practices of Leopold Iklé (1838–1922), head of the St. Gallen–based Iklé Frères textile manufacturing company, that the Textilmuseum's collection of more than five thousand examples of historical lace rivals holdings at other major institutions around the world.

The collection includes a variety of significant hand- and machine-made lace from a period spanning the early sixteenth century to the twentieth century. From small trimmings and edgings (FIG. I.10) to large-scale pieces such as a twelve-foot-long gold needle-lace panel made around 1700 (FIG. I.11) and a bobbin-lace coverlet (ca. 1625–50) likely commissioned for the wedding of Philip IV of Spain and Mariana of Austria (FIG. I.12), the collection showcases representative examples of fashions in European lace throughout history. This rich collection was the focus of the Textilmuseum's exhibition *Lace and Status: The Collection of Historical Lace in the Textilmuseum St. Gallen* (2018–19), curated by Barbara Karl.[6] The exhibition, which featured more than 160 highlights from the historical lace collection, examined styles worn at the royal courts in Spain and France in the seventeenth and eighteenth centuries, respectively (FIG. I.13), and has been adapted and expanded for presentation at Bard Graduate Center in 2022. Marking the American debut of approximately 150 pieces of lace from the Textilmuseum's collection, *Threads of Power* is the first large-scale lace exhibition in New York in forty years, and this accompanying catalogue constitutes the first English-language publication in more than fifteen years to trace the history of European lace in fashion from its origins to the present.

The title is intended to evoke the power associated with those at the top of the social hierarchy in Europe, who were the primary consumers of lace for most of the past five centuries, whose lace-bedecked portraits are featured in the galleries, and whose great wealth enabled the purchase of exquisite objects like those on display from the Textilmuseum. It also alludes to the actual and symbolic connections between makers, merchants, manufacturers, and wearers. These "threads" have connected women and men across geography and time. Lightweight and eminently portable, lace has been an internationally traded luxury commodity since its emergence as a textile in its own right. In the seventeenth century, bobbin lace made in Flanders and needle lace made in Italy traveled to many other countries in Europe, and in the eighteenth century, large quantities of lace were shipped across the Atlantic to eager consumers in the Spanish Americas. During the nineteenth and twentieth centuries, women in the United States constituted an important market for both hand- and machine-made lace from Britain, France, and Switzerland, and today, manufacturers in St. Gallen depend on global sales for their continued success.

These threads also link past and present. In the second half of the nineteenth century, the vogue among fashionable women for antique lace that often complemented their revival-style toilettes combined the historical and the contemporary in a single garment

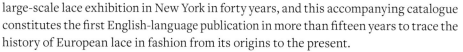

FIG. I.6 (ABOVE)
Wehrli brothers, photograph of a man and a woman at work in an embroidery factory, St. Gallen, Switzerland, ca. 1905. Swiss National Library, Federal Archives of Historic Monuments: Archives Photoglob-Wehrli, EAD-WEHR-752-A.

FIG. I.7 (OPPOSITE, TOP)
Saurer Schiffli embroidery machines from 1905 operated with pantographs, ca. 1910. Private collection.

FIG. I.8 (OPPOSITE, BOTTOM)
Women and men working in the Jacob Rohner factory, St. Gallen, Switzerland, ca. 1905. Private collection.

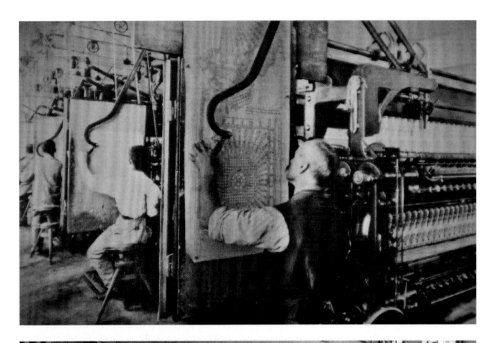

Introduction

and distinguished the very wealthy, who could afford old, "real" lace, from the merely comfortable, who wore newly made machine goods. Further, lace passed down through generations would have underscored familial ties to those who bought and originally wore these pieces and reaffirmed their descendants' status. At the turn of the twentieth century, historical Venetian lace—the most expensive lace at the height of its popularity in the third quarter of the seventeenth century—was acquired by affluent American collectors and made available for study to Italian immigrant women who had recently arrived in the United States. While the collectors acquired the social and cultural prestige conferred by these prized objects, the working-class women who reproduced them using the same techniques, types of tools, and materials as their anonymous predecessors forged an embodied link with these early lacemakers and used their handwork skills to assert pride in their country of birth even as they became American citizens (SEE CHAP. 13).

The early lace objects on display in the exhibition connect the visitor with both wearers and makers. However, while the contemporary portraits in the galleries (many of known sitters) evoke the physical presence and appearance of the elite men and women who wore lace collars, cuffs, caps, and lappets reflecting their rank and social visibility, identified lacemakers are pictorially absent here and in the larger visual record. These socially invisible and inadequately remunerated female workers, who could not afford the products of their time-consuming labor, are relegated to representation in genre paintings

FIG. I.9
Textilmuseum St. Gallen, Switzerland.
Schweizerisches Nationalmuseum.

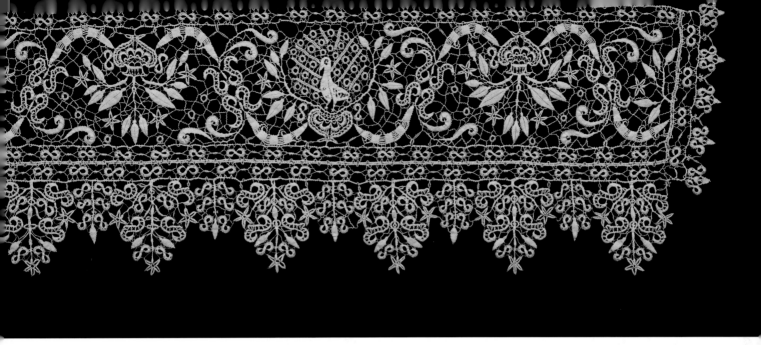

rather than individualized likenesses. It is through the material evidence of their consummate skills that we aim to recover and celebrate the physical presence of these women.

Contemporary Connections

The first object visitors to *Threads of Power* encounter at Bard Graduate Center is a specially commissioned piece that upsets this historical divide between luxurious lace and the anonymous hands that created it (FIGS. I.14 AND I.15). The artist is New York–based lacemaker Elena Kanagy-Loux, who boasts a background in textile arts and fashion design and notably created a bobbin-lace collar for Ruth Bader Ginsburg (1933–2020) on the twenty-fifth anniversary of her investiture to the US Supreme Court. Kanagy-Loux's interest and expertise in historical lace developed during a four-month grant-funded study of traditional handmade techniques in which she worked with and learned from lacemakers in over a dozen European countries.[7] The bobbin-lace collar that she designed and created for *Threads of Power* is deliberately displayed alongside a photograph of her wearing the piece, a juxtaposition that aims to underscore that the layered assertions of status conveyed through portraits were largely inaccessible to early lacemakers.

The collar was inspired by iconography that Kanagy-Loux noticed in several examples of historical lace from around the world illustrating the Old Testament story of the widow Judith beheading Assyrian general Holofernes.[8] It was an early Italian example in the Metropolitan Museum of Art's collection that initially caught Kanagy-Loux's eye (FIG. I.16). The story is told in *punto in aria*, with an inscription on the upper border that

FIG. I.10

Bobbin-lace border with scalloped edge, Venice, first quarter of the 17th century. Linen. Textilmuseum St. Gallen, Acquired from the Estate of John Jacoby, 1954, 01010. Cat. 24.

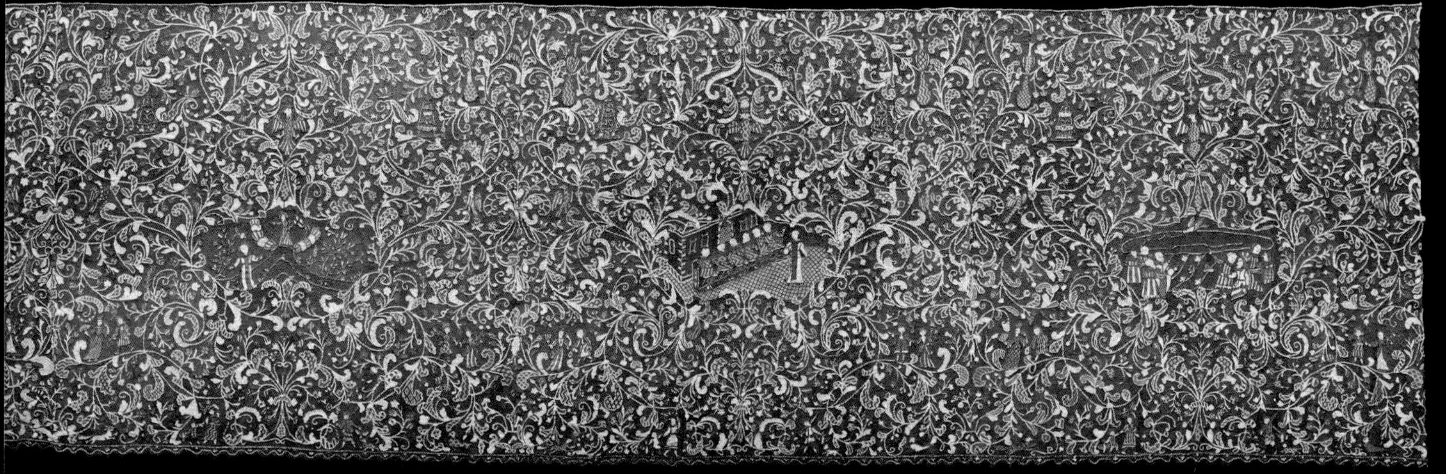

FIG. I.11 (TOP)

Golden needle-lace panel with religious scenes, possibly an antependium (altar frontal) or trimming for an alb, Flanders, Southern Netherlands; France; or Italy, ca. 1695–1710. Linen, silk, and metal threads with silk core. Textilmuseum St. Gallen, Acquired from the Estate of John Jacoby, 1954, 00816. Cat. 50.

FIG. I.12 (BOTTOM)

Bobbin-lace coverlet, perhaps made for the 1649 wedding of Philip IV (1605–1655) and Mariana of Austria (1634–1696), probably Italy, 1625–50. Linen and glass beads. Textilmuseum St. Gallen, Gift of the Iklé-Frischknecht Foundation, 2006, 52093. Cat. 65.

FIG. I.13 (TOP, RIGHT)
Installation of the exhibition *Lace and Status* at the Textilmuseum St. Gallen, 2018–19. Textilmuseum St. Gallen.

FIG. I.14A,B (ABOVE)
Elena Kanagy-Loux, in-process Judith and Holofernes bobbin-lace collar and scallop detail, United States, 2022. Silk. Textilmuseum St. Gallen, 76004. Cat. 1.

identifies the needle-lace figures as Judith, Holofernes, and Judith's servant, Abra.[9] This piece shares many characteristics with a seventeenth-century border in the collection of the Textilmuseum St. Gallen (FIG. I.17); both consist of several scenes divided into squares separated by decorative foliate borders and bear an inscription on the upper border.[10] Notable differences between the two include the composition of the large-scale flowers and plants in the background and the presence of elaborately worked arches on the lower edge of the Textilmuseum's piece. Many of the other examples to which Kanagy-Loux was drawn depict the same scene following Judith's deadly act: in an English example dating to the mid-1600s, rendered in twisted buttonhole stitch, Judith and her maid lower Holofernes's head into a bag (FIG. I.18). The lacemaker added human hair to each of the three figures' heads, and blood, represented by what was likely once red silk now faded to pink, pours from Holofernes's neck. Again, oversized foliate motifs fill the background behind the canopied bed and Judith (who is still holding her sword), their forms delineated by raised outlines made of bundles of threads.

Although most of the surviving examples of this subject are needle lace, Kanagy-Loux intentionally crafted her collar in bobbin lace, which is her specialty, in a style inspired by the work of twentieth-century makers. These include bobbin-lace pieces by Wiener Werkstätte textile artist Vally Wieselthier (1895–1945; FIG. I.19); as well as work by Margarete Naumann (1881–1946), who created "Margaretenspitze" macramé lace in the early twentieth century; and bobbin lace made by Czech lacemaker Luba Krejci (b. 1925) in the 1960s.[11] The form of Kanagy-Loux's piece evokes the pronounced scallops of Genoese bobbin-lace collars of the seventeenth century (FIG. I.20), and the decision to use red silk instead of the traditional white linen or blonde silk is a deliberate one—the dash of red at the wearer's neck is at once a nod to the striking colorful accents of the historical pieces and a reminder of Holofernes's ultimate fate.

FIG. I.15 (OPPOSITE)
Elena Kanagy-Loux, Judith and Holofernes bobbin-lace collar, commissioned by Bard Graduate Center for *Threads of Power: Lace from the Textilmuseum St. Gallen*, United States, 2022. Silk. Textilmuseum St. Gallen, 76004. Cat. 1.

FIG. I.16 (BOTTOM)
Punto in aria needle-lace border depicting Judith and Holofernes, Venice, 16th–17th century. Linen. The Metropolitan Museum of Art, New York, Purchase by subscription, 1909, 09.68.90.

FIG. I.17 (TOP)
Needle-lace border depicting Judith and Holofernes, probably Italy for the Portuguese market, 1600–25. Linen. Textilmuseum St. Gallen, Gift of Leopold Iklé, 1904, 00040. Cat. 40.

Threads of Power in the Gallery

Presented on three floors of Bard Graduate Center's Gallery, *Threads of Power* is arranged chronologically and thematically. Following the display of Kanagy-Loux's commissioned lace collar, the ground floor serves as an introduction to the two main types of lace that emerged in the late sixteenth and early seventeenth centuries: needle and bobbin lace. Textilmuseum objects in this gallery dating from about 1600 include samplers, borders, inserts, a cap and bonnet, a set of collar and cuffs, and a cushion cover, all of which incorporate some combination of cutwork, reticella, and needle and bobbin lace. The object groupings elucidate techniques and terminology, the marketing of lace, and the significant contribution of early modern pattern books and botanical books, on loan from the Metropolitan Museum of Art and the New York Botanical Garden, to the development of lace design (FIG. I.21). Contextualizing these pieces are reproduction images of bobbin-lace makers, a Parisian stall selling lace accessories, a female lace peddler, and female sitters adorned with oversized ruffs and spreading collars (FIG. I.22; SEE FIGS. 9.9 AND 10.18).

Significant examples of seventeenth- and eighteenth-century ecclesiastical lace occupy the first gallery on the second floor (SEE FIG. I.11). Although the exhibition focuses on lace and fashion, the church was an important and enthusiastic consumer of lace, much of which was produced in convents in the early modern period. Incorporated into vestments and used in the form of altar cloths during the liturgy, lace communicated the material and spiritual splendor of the church.

In the following two galleries, Italian, Flemish, and French needle- and bobbin-lace collars, cravat ends, lappets, cap backs, sleeve ruffles, stomachers, and a rare surviving *frelange* headdress dating to about 1700 (SEE FIG. 10.3) attest to the lavish consumption of this expensive textile among elites in Spain and France between 1600 and 1800, when these two countries dominated Europe politically, economically, and culturally. Also considered is the use of lace by affluent men and women in the Spanish American colonies (SEE CHAPS. 6–8). As in the first gallery, portraits as well as two *robes à la française* and an embroidered man's court suit from the eighteenth century enhance the visitor's appreciation of these garments on the body and underscore the integral role that lace played in the completion of a fashionable ensemble (FIGS. I.23–25).

A selection of nineteenth- and early twentieth-century hand- and machine-made lace objects on the third floor transition the visitor into an overview of chemical-lace production and fashion during the twentieth and twenty-first centuries in the two main galleries. Large-scale reproductions of turn-of-the-century photographs showing men and women in factories convey the re-gendering of lace production that occurred with mechanization. Early twentieth-century fashion photographs, sketches, sample books, couture garments spanning 1949 to 2021, and samples of twenty-first-century 3D-printed silicone lace illustrate the past and ongoing creativity and innovations of leading St. Gallen manufacturers, attuned to changing demands in a worldwide market. A key object in this last gallery is the dress-and-coat ensemble designed by Isabel Toledo for Michelle Obama for the 2009 presidential inauguration.

Expanding and Contextualizing
Threads of Power

Divided into five sections, the sixteen chapters in this publication reflect the geographic and chronological spread of the exhibition while adding significantly to its presentation in the galleries. "The Emergence of Lace in Early Modern Europe," "Fashion and Lace in Spain and the Americas, 1500–1800," "The Dominance of France, 1660–1790," "Mechanization and Revivalism in the Lace Industries, 1800–1925," and "Innovations in Lace, 1900 to Today" chart this five-century relationship between lace and fashion. In their investigations of the many facets of this narrative, the authors draw on a wide range of visual and textual primary sources and highlight Textilmuseum objects. Across this long history of changing production and consumption, several "threads" emerge: issues of gender in the making, selling, and wearing of lace and the primary role of untold thousands of now

FIG. I.18 (TOP)
Needle-lace panel depicting Judith and Holofernes, England, mid-1600s. Linen, silk, and human hair. Museum of Applied Arts and Sciences, Sydney, Gift of Christian R. Thornett, 1966, A5535.

FIG. I.19 (BOTTOM)
Vally Wieselthier for the Wiener Werkstätte, bobbin-lace insert for a curtain panel, designed 1919, made 1922. Linen. Cooper-Hewitt, Smithsonian Design Museum, New York, Museum purchase from General Acquisitions Endowment Fund, 2018-4-1-3.

unknown female lacemakers; lace as a material signifier of status, class, and race, and the enactment of sumptuary laws, particularly in the early modern period, to ensure the exclusivity of this textile and dissuade extravagant expenditure; the importance of design, whether for hand- or machine-made lace; the international trade in this commodity; and the wearing, collecting, and dealing of antique lace.

The first part introduces the reader to the early history of lace in Europe from the mid-sixteenth to the mid-eighteenth century. "Lace and Status: Luxury, Power, and Control in Early Modernity" by Barbara Karl provides an overview of the emergence of

FIG. I.20
Artist unknown, *Princess Elizabeth, Queen of Bohemia and Electress Palatine*, 1613. Oil on panel. © National Portrait Gallery, London, NPG 5529.

needle and bobbin lace as sought-after textiles that accessorized men's and women's dress in increasing quantities and elaborate forms. Drawing on examples from the Textilmuseum's collection, Karl examines the role that lace "occupied amid relationships between economy, politics, and social structures." She establishes the lace industry's reliance on the expert skills of low-paid female workers who operated outside the guild system that strictly regulated other textile trades and discusses the leading centers of production in Italy, the Southern Netherlands, and France, which would become renowned for particular types of lace; the contribution of well-known artists who created designs for lace; and the association of lace with princely power and the frequent, if ineffective, passing of sumptuary laws.

Early textile pattern books with designs for lace published between the mid-sixteenth and early seventeenth centuries are the subject of "Putting a Name to a Lace: Fashion, Fame, and the Production of Printed Textile Pattern Books" by Femke Speelberg. The author focuses on publications by notable artists and designers who were knowledgeable about the art of lacemaking, a factor that contributed to their success; almost all were published in Italy. Authors include a woman known as "RM," whose book featured "not only the first known image of a woman making bobbin lace but also the first reference to the designer of the patterns," as well as Matteo Pagano, Federico Vinciolo, Isabella Catanea Parasole, and Bartolomeo Danieli. Particularly relevant to the importance of women as lacemakers and the association of lace with feminine skill and virtue at the upper levels of society is the presence of Parasole's name on the title page of her books, identifying her as the designer and "stak[ing] a humble yet significant claim" for the "thousands of (now) nameless" lacemakers working in Europe at this time. Her name appears in conjunction with a presumed portrait medallion of Elisabeth of Bourbon that "seems to blend the characteristics of both the artist and her dedicatee." These publications were not only highly influential and widespread at the turn of the seventeenth century, but their patterns would be reproduced by Italian lacemakers following the unification of the country in 1870 and a revival of the glory days of Italian lacemaking.

Paula Hohti's chapter, "'Monstrous Ruffs' and Elegant Trimmings: Lace and Lacemaking in Early Modern Italy," examines the increasing demand for lace in the

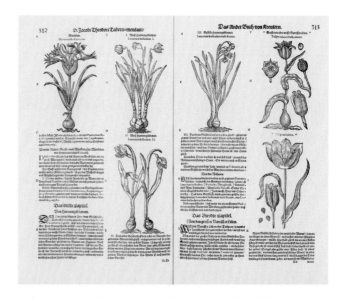

FIG. I.21 (TOP)
Jacobus Theodorus Tabermontanus, *Neuw vollkommentlich Kreuterbuch, mit schönen unnd künstlichen Figuren . . .* Published by Paul Jacobi; Johann Dreutels, Frankfurt, 1625. The LuEsther T. Mertz Library, New York Botanical Garden, f QK41.T42 1625 t.2-3. Cat. 38.

FIG. I.22 (BOTTOM)
Nicolaes Maes, *The Lacemaker*, ca. 1656. Oil on canvas. The Metropolitan Museum of Art, New York, the Friedsam Collection, Bequest of Michael Friedsam, 1931, 32.100.5.

sixteenth and seventeenth centuries, primarily but not exclusively among wealthy elites, which prompted often-flouted sumptuary laws. In the concomitant commercialization of lace production, convents and charitable institutions were instrumental (as they were in all the major lacemaking countries from the early modern period through the nineteenth century). A recurring refrain from founders of these institutions and many social commentators, which would persist until the ultimate decline of the European handmade lace industry following World War I, was that lacemaking taught young women a useful skill, providing them with a source of income and preventing them from falling into idleness or an immoral lifestyle. However, as Hohti observes, these lacemakers had no say in what they produced or the amount they were paid for their work; rather, their supervisors (or other intermediaries) negotiated commissions with merchants who sold the finished pieces—a practice that characterized the organization of the European handmade lace industries until the early twentieth century.

It is worth noting here that in the mid-seventeenth century, *point de Venise*, a needle lace defined by swirling sculptural flowers and leaves, became the most sought-after throughout Europe, and it was the lace initially copied by government-sponsored French workshops after the establishment of that industry in 1665. Further, the technical excellence of point de Venise and the beauty of its flowing designs were widely acknowledged and admired in the late nineteenth and early twentieth centuries, when it was purchased by dealers and collectors, worn by wealthy women, and used as inspiration during the revival of handmade lace in Italy and by the manufacturers of chemical lace in St. Gallen (FIG. I.26; SEE FIG. 1.2).

The last chapter in this section, "Antwerp, a Center of Lacemaking and Lace Dealing, 1550–1750" by Frieda Sorber, foregrounds this city as one of the most important centers of the European lace industry in the sixteenth and seventeenth centuries and the rise of Brussels in the eighteenth century. Drawing extensively on the archives housed in Antwerp's Museum Plantin-Moretus, Sorber describes the already well-organized network of suppliers, lacemakers, and male and female merchants (notably, the Plantin daughters) that existed in mid-sixteenth-century Antwerp as well as the international reach of the lace trade that would continue to expand in the following two centuries. Sorber also highlights Margaretha von der Marck, a German aristocrat, who used her social connections to sell lace—some of it acquired in Antwerp—and other luxury goods to her sister and high-ranking clients and friends in Munich, Florence, and elsewhere in Europe. In the eighteenth century, Brussels took the lead in the Flemish lace trade, and probably its most spectacular production was an entire dress of bobbin lace made for Empress Maria Theresa in 1744. Recorded in two full-length portraits, this gown conveys the literal and figurative threads that connected this powerful female ruler with the many unidentified female workers who were her subjects and who toiled for months to create this one-of-a-kind offering from the city of Brussels to the Austro-Hungarian monarch. Although the industry in Antwerp declined at the end of the eighteenth century, its lacemakers continued to produce trims and other goods for the Dutch market well into the nineteenth century.

Amalia Descalzo Lorenzo's chapter, "The Triumph of Lace: Spanish Portraiture in the Sixteenth and Seventeenth Centuries," opens the second part, which focuses on

Spain and its American colonies between 1500 and 1800. Spain's political, economic, cultural, and territorial power under the Habsburg monarchs is on full view in the painted representations of its rulers and nobles arrayed in costly silks, velvets, and lace, communicating their enormous wealth and elevated social position. The black garments that dominated the distinctive Spanish court fashions of this time provided the perfect foil for the lace-trimmed *lechuguilla* (a heavily starched ruff collar of oversized proportions), the *valona llana* (a spreading collar that extended over the shoulders and upper chest), prominent cuffs, and other lace accessories. Repeated attempts to curb the voracious appetite for the most expensive Flemish and Italian laces among consumers outside the court through pragmatic sanctions proved ineffectual; as portraits by Velázquez show, those of lesser status were equally eager to acquire and be depicted in this desirable textile, according to their means.

A predilection across class and race in the Spanish colonies for opulent attire in which lace featured prominently is a consistent theme in the following three chapters: "'A Desire of Being Distinguished by an Elegant Dress Is Universal': Clothing, Status, and Convenience in Eighteenth-Century Spanish America" by Mariselle Meléndez; "'A Prodigious Excess': Lace in New Spain and Peru, ca. 1600–1800" by James Middleton; and "'Covered in Much Fine Lace': Dress in the Viceroyalty of New Granada" by Laura

FIG. I.23 (LEFT)

Woman's dress (*robe à la française*) with matching stomacher and petticoat, France, ca. 1755–60. Chinese export brocaded silk satin, trimmed with silk chenille looped fringe. Philadelphia Museum of Art, Purchased with the John D. McIlhenny Fund, the John T. Morris Fund, the Elizabeth Wandell Smith Fund, and with funds contributed by Mrs. Howard H. Lewis and Marion Boulton Stroud, 1988, 1988-83-1a–c. Cat. 91.

FIG. I.24 (RIGHT)

Man's silk-embroidered court suit with needle-lace *jabot*, France, 1780–90. Silk and linen. Textilmuseum St. Gallen, Acquired from the Estate of John Jacoby, 1954, 21500. Cat. 104.

Beltrán-Rubio. Seventeenth- and eighteenth-century portraits, accounts by travelers to these regions, inventories, and wills attest to the extravagant use of rich silks, metallic galloons, and lace that came from both Europe and Asia and highlight the access that consumers in America had to global trade networks. Further, all three authors note that an appreciation of domestically produced fine fabrics among Indigenous people predated the arrival of the Spanish and point to the visual affinity between European lace and the openwork textiles that had long been made in Peru, for example. Additionally, the time-consuming labor involved in the creation of both enhanced their aesthetic appeal and social currency.

Although European fashions were quickly transmitted to the Spanish colonies, they were not unreservedly copied. At the viceregal courts and throughout Spanish American society, variations, adaptations, and regional preferences, especially among women, characterized dress. At the same time, Indigenous women in Peru incorporated lace into the *pollera*, a flounced skirt that was part of an ensemble completely distinct from European modes. Similarly, the lace-covered dance clothing worn by Indigenous men for festivals, while based on shirts and trousers introduced by European missionaries, constituted a local interpretation of recently adopted garments and textiles.

FIG. I.25
François Hubert Drouais, *Marie Rinteau, Called Mademoiselle de Verrières*, 1761. Oil on canvas. The Metropolitan Museum of Art, New York, the Jules Bache Collection, 1949, 49.7.47. Cat. 80.

As in the European context, Spanish American portraiture conveyed wealth and status; Beltrán-Rubio observes that these "retratos de ostentación" (portraits of ostentation) focus on details of dress, including lace, and sumptuous interiors as "essential element[s] in the performance of . . . elite identities" in the Viceroyalty of New Granada. In the specifically Spanish American context, however, there was an almost obsessive recording of both social and racial identity that was communicated by skin color and dress in *casta* paintings that represented white, Indigenous, Black, and multiracial men, women, and children. These and other images illustrate the widespread consumption of lace across socioeconomic groups in the Spanish Americas (SEE FIG. 7.19).

The two chapters in the third part, "The Dominance of France, 1660–1790," present a close look at the French lace industry between its establishment in 1665 and its precipitous decline at the time of the French Revolution in 1789. In "Lace, an Economic Factor in France during the Reign of Louis XIV," Denis Bruna considers how a textile as delicate as lace "could be at the center of a tough commercial conflict marked by royal decrees, secret agents, coded letters, condemnations, and the poaching of workers." For

Louis XIV and his ambitious finance minister, Jean-Baptiste Colbert, creating and robustly supporting a domestic lace industry was part of their greater agenda to enrich the royal coffers, expand the French luxury economy, and glorify the king. Their endeavor involved luring lacemakers from Venice and Flanders, setting up manufactories in specific towns, and commissioning designs from leading artists employed by the crown. Its success resulted in the development of *point de France*, a light needle lace with small-scale symmetrical designs that, in the late seventeenth century, superseded point de Venise as the most fashionable type of lace (SEE FIG. 10.11A).

Lesley Ellis Miller's chapter, "Lace *à la Mode* in France, ca. 1690–1790," delves into the production, consumption, marketing, and distribution of lace over this century-long period. Using portraits of male and female sitters in fashionable and court dress as "snapshots" and drawing on archival sources to contextualize these images, Miller examines the religious and charitable institutions that played a role in the training and employment of lacemakers, as they had since the sixteenth century, and the livelihoods of this female workforce; the importance of acquiring good designs, which was a key factor for a successful merchant; the range of prices that depended on the quality of the lace and the time it took to produce (up to a year); lace retailers, from those with elegant shops in the center of Paris selling high-end inventory to hawkers and peddlers who dealt in inexpensive accessories and trimmings; and the national and international lace markets. Like other contributors to this publication, Miller emphasizes that the purchase of lace was much more than just an enjoyable shopping expedition—its consumption was a social imperative. In her conclusion, Miller reiterates that although men participated in the lace economy as wearers and sellers, it was women who "proved skilled, ill-remunerated makers; shrewd, capable merchants; and conspicuous, thoughtful consumers."

The fourth part, "Mechanization and Revivalism in the Lace Industries, 1800–1925," addresses the rise and rapid expansion of the machine-made lace industry in the nineteenth century; the vogue for wearing antique lace as a marker of status by affluent women, particularly after midcentury; the practice of collecting historical pieces by wealthy individuals and manufacturers who used them as design inspiration; and the revival of handmade lace by Italian immigrant women in New York.

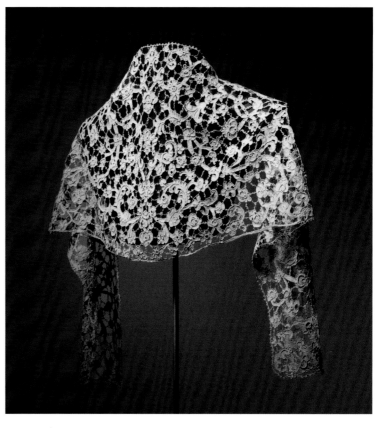

FIG. I.26

Point de Venise needle-lace mantelet or *frelange*, Italy, ca. 1700. Linen. Textilmuseum St. Gallen, Acquired from the Estate of John Jacoby, 1954, 01180. Cat. 72.

Emma Cormack and Michele Majer

In "Fashion and the Lace Industries in France, Belgium, and England, 1800–1900," we begin with a brief summary of lace and the fashionable female silhouette during this period and provide an overview of both the hand- and machine-made lace industries in these three countries with particular emphasis on the most significant innovations in machine technology; the organization of these industries and the increasing presence of men in factories as operators of lace machines; and the marketing and dissemination of lace on a much wider scale than previously, such as in the large department stores that flourished from the 1850s onward. The chapter ends with a consideration of the lacemaker as a cultural icon and a reassuring symbol of what was perceived as acceptable feminine labor and domestic virtue in the face of mechanization's irreversible encroachment into this traditionally female domain (FIG. I.27).

In "Ahead of the Curve: A. Blackborne & Co. and the Late Nineteenth-Century British Lace Industry," Annabel Bonnin Talbot focuses on the father-and-son, London-based lace business that rose to prominence in the second half of the century and whose impressive antique lace collection forms the basis of the holdings of the Bowes Museum in County Durham, England. As successful merchants of handmade lace, the Blackbornes took an early interest in historical pieces, and Anthony Blackborne parlayed his connoisseurship of antique lace into a position of authority and influence among his elite private clients, museum curators, and other lace specialists. Talbot cites contemporary periodicals, international exhibition reports, and other primary sources that trace the firm's growing renown and its success as a major player in this lucrative business. Additionally, Anthony's son Arthur actively supported the study of historical models by contemporary designers and manufacturers to improve the quality of their products. Talbot also draws our attention to the mutually reinforcing relationship between the seemingly separate worlds of commerce and museums, whereby merchants like the Blackbornes benefited from their association with these institutions, while museums enriched their collections with high-quality objects.

The revival and transferal of hand lacemaking techniques is the subject of Emily Zilber's chapter, "Italy to New York: Making Historic Textiles Modern at the Scuola d'Industrie Italiane." Zilber situates the establishment of the Scuola at the Richmond Hill Settlement House in Greenwich Village in 1905 within the larger context of the lace revival in Italy and issues of national identity, women's handwork, and female patronage. She also examines the workings of this charitable organization for recently arrived Italian immigrant women, founded by lawyer and immigration advocate Gino Speranza and arts patron Florence Colgate, who would marry in 1909. Zilber highlights their motivations and goals; the romanticized presentation of the Scuola workshop conditions in contemporary magazines and journals; its day-to-day operations; the rift that appeared among the financial supporters in 1910, who disagreed on whether the Scuola was to provide welfare or function as a solvent business; and the factors that led to its closure in 1927. The author also emphasizes the importance of collecting and collections in this story. The Scuola's founders and board members, who made available their own historical pattern books and textiles to the students, had close links to museums and relied on these institutions to validate their collections and the mission of the Scuola.

In "A Source of Inspiration: The Leopold Iklé Collection in St. Gallen," Anne Wanner-JeanRichard and Ilona Kos present an overview of Iklé Frères, an international firm that enjoyed great success as a manufacturer of machine-made lace and embroidery at the turn of the twentieth century. The company operated against the backdrop of innovations in the mechanized production of embroidery in eastern Switzerland, including the process that would come to be known as "chemical lace" (FIG. I.28). Wanner-JeanRichard and Kos stress Iklé's enthusiasm for collecting historical examples of embroidery and lace, many of which he donated to what is now the Textilmuseum St. Gallen between 1904 and 1908. Iklé's personal passion for historical textiles and his commercial enterprise illuminate the overlapping relationships between the acquisition of historical models, design education, manufacturing, and the formation of museum collections.

A final chapter, "Fashion and Lace since 1900," by Catherine Örmen and an interview with Tobias Forster and Hans Schreiber of Forster-Rohner AG and Martin Leuthold of Jakob Schlaepfer AG constitute the last part of this publication. Touching on the main stylistic trends of the twentieth and early twenty-first centuries, Örmen highlights the ways in which lace was and continues to be incorporated into the fashionable female silhouette by leading couturiers as well as innovations in machine-lace technology and the introduction of synthetic materials like nylon, which revolutionized lingerie. From Jacques Doucet and Callot Sœurs at the turn of the twentieth century to Gabrielle Chanel and Madeleine Vionnet in the 1920s and 1930s, Christian Dior in the 1950s, Yves Saint Laurent in the 1960s, Christian Lacroix in the 1980s, and Jean Paul Gaultier in the 2010s, designers have used lace creatively and extensively—as discreet embellishment, as the lining of a coat, and as the main fabric of a dress—exploring its qualities

FIG. I.27
"Point d'Alençon École Dentellière"
postcard, ca. 1900. Private collection.

20   Emma Cormack and Michele Majer

to reveal and conceal the female body. Throughout this period, Calais and St. Gallen firms have been the main suppliers of lace for many couture houses, whose designers often work closely with manufacturers. In addition to casting light on this important relationship between manufacturer and client, the interview with Forster, Schreiber, and Leuthold offers detailed insights into the design process, manufacturing techniques, and marketing strategies of these world-renowned firms, whose creations are on view in the exhibition.

Conclusion

Although to many among the general public lace may seem an outdated interest that conjures images of old family heirlooms stored away in the attic, a thriving global community of scholars, collectors, teachers, and artists engaged with its history and traditional lacemaking techniques proves otherwise. The last two years of the pandemic have only expanded this interconnected web; from all over the world, lectures, workshops, classes, and programming streamed online have brought lacemakers and lace enthusiasts alike together. In contrast to their predecessors whose work served primarily to adorn the wealthy and powerful, many of today's lacemakers are using the medium to comment on issues of gender and identity, community, religion and ritual, and the relationship of the past to the present. As curators of *Threads of Power*, it has been our great honor and pleasure to work with the Textilmuseum's collection and lace

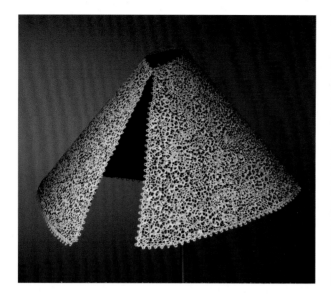

objects from other lenders. In showcasing these historical and contemporary pieces, we hope to bring a renewed attention to and appreciation of this "most modern" yet "ancient" textile and its multilayered significance over the last five centuries (FIGS. I.29 AND I.30).

FIG. I.29 (LEFT)

Bobbin tape lace, mounted as a collar, Italy, 1690–1725. Linen. Textilmuseum St. Gallen, Gift of Leopold Iklé, 1905, 00524. Cat. 82.

FIG. I.30 (RIGHT)

Jakob Schlaepfer AG, hypertube guipure collar, St. Gallen, Switzerland, ca. 2021. Silicone. Private collection. Cat. 195.

1   Isabel Toledo, *The Roots of Style: Weaving Together Life, Love & Fashion* (New York: New American Library, 2012), 338.

2   Toledo, *Roots of Style*, 337–38, 340.

3   For a history of the region's textile production, see Cornel Dora, ed., *Textiles St. Gallen: Tausend Jahre Tradition, Technologie und Trends/A Thousand Years of Tradition, Technology and Trends*, exh. cat. (St. Gallen, Switzerland: Amt für Kultur, 2004).

4   The American market was of particular importance; between 1864 and 1906, sales of goods there increased from CHF 352,277 to CHF 92.42 million. By 1914 embroidery constituted 15 percent of all Swiss exports. Ibid., 72.

5   Eric Häusler and Caspar Meili, "Swiss Embroidery: Erfolg und Krise der Schweizer Stickerei-Industrie 1865–1929," *Neujahrsblatt: Historischer Verein des Kantons St. Gallen* 155 (2015): 11–12, https://www.hvsg.ch/pdf/neujahrsblaetter/hvsg_neujahrsblatt_2015.pdf.

6   Textilmuseum St. Gallen and Iklé-Frischknecht-Stiftung, eds., *Historische Spitzen: Die Leopold-Iklé-Sammlung im Textilmuseum St. Gallen* (Stuttgart, Germany: Arnoldsche, 2018).

7   Elena Kanagy-Loux, "The Disconnected Web: Making Lace by Hand in a Modern World" (MA thesis, New York University, 2018).

8   Needle-lace examples include those in the collections of the Museum of Fine Arts, Boston (43.272); the Fitzwilliam Museum, Cambridge, England (T.11-1938); the Metropolitan Museum of Art, New York (09.68.92); and the Cooper Hewitt, Smithsonian Design Museum, New York (1950-121-27-a), as well as the only depiction rendered in bobbin lace: a section of the coverlet in the collection of the Royal Museum of Art and History, Brussels (D.2543.00; SEE FIG. 4.6).

9   The inscription is in Portuguese, despite the object's probable Italian origin: "ABRA E IVDIQVE E ALEVA / RAN / ES / E COMO / IVDIQVE OV MATOV / DE / NOI / TE / ESTANDO / DVRMINDO F (for e) POSV A CABESA / NA / TORE" (Abra and Judith and Holofernes and how Judith killed him at night being asleep and placed the head on the tower). Translation by Edith Appleton Standon, 1952. The Metropolitan Museum of Art, New York, 09.68.90, https://www.metmuseum.org/art/collection/search/218029. This piece was donated to the Metropolitan Museum of Art in 1909 by Arthur Blackborne (SEE CHAP. 12).

10   The inscription on the Textilmuseum's border reads, "Foumatou de noite estando durmindo e po sua cabesa natore judi ve" (He was killed in the night when he slept and his head placed on the tower, Judith sees [. . .]). Translated in Leopold Iklé and Emil Wild, *Industrie- und Gewerbemuseum St. Gallen: Textilsammlung Iklé, Katalog* (Zurich: Orell Füssli, 1908), 137. The panel scenes show, from left to right, soldiers, the decapitated Holofernes under a canopy, Judith with Holofernes's head, Judith and her maid, Judith on the tower, soldiers again, the tower with the head of Holofernes, and, finally, a seated figure.

11   See, for example, a piece of bobbin lace made in the 1960s by Luba Krejci in the collection of the University of Wisconsin–Madison (2017.06.012).

THE EMERGENCE OF LACE
IN EARLY MODERN EUROPE

1 Lace and Status: Luxury, Power, and Control in Early Modernity

Barbara Karl

I N TODAY'S FASHION INDUSTRY, trends change several times a year and are accessible to broad swaths of the population, but in the early modern period, from the sixteenth to the eighteenth century, fashion was primarily a concern of the elites. Apparel befitting one's rank was an integral part of demonstrating power at royal courts in Europe, and laws governing luxury and clothing regulated the market. Wearing lace was both a fashion statement and a demonstration of status, wealth, and power—a point many painted portraits make emphatically clear. This essay sheds light on the production, distribution, and use of lace, drawing on examples from the collection of historical lace in the Textilmuseum St. Gallen.

The Collection

The Textilmuseum St. Gallen boasts one of the world's finest collections of historical lace, rivaling those of the Victoria and Albert Museum in London and the Metropolitan Museum of Art in New York. The Textilmuseum's collection offers a representative overview of European lace production over the last six centuries. The development of the handmade lace industry began in the mid-sixteenth century with important production centers located in northern Italy, France, and the Netherlands.[1] Until around 1800, fine handmade lace was an exclusive luxury good that shaped European fashion. The rise of an affluent middle class during the Industrial Revolution fed demand for luxury items, which in turn drove technological innovation, including the development of machine-made lace and mechanical embroidery mimicking historical handmade lace (SEE CHAP. 14). In the nineteenth century, as lace became more affordable for larger sections of the population, the machine-made lace industry saw a downright boom (SEE CHAP. 11). The starting point for these new machine-produced imitations was handmade bobbin lace and needle lace developed in northern Italy, in Venice and Milan, and in the Southern Netherlands, likely around Antwerp, in the second half of the sixteenth century. Over the course of the nineteenth century, constant innovation fueled the development of machine-aided processes that perfectly replicated the handmade products created centuries earlier.

Mechanized production allowed for the manufacturing of these textiles in considerably larger quantities at much lower prices than their handmade counterparts, all of which supported an ever-expanding worldwide market.[2] This growing market demanded increasing numbers of novel designs for rapidly changing fashions, and designers found inspiration in historical models from all over the world. This was particularly true in eastern Switzerland, where, starting in 1863, the entrepreneurial association Kaufmännische Directorium and individual manufacturers in St. Gallen collected lace and other textiles to serve as production models for the expanding local embroidery industry.[3] The Directorium merged their collection, drawing school, and pattern room to promote production of and trade in embroideries, which ultimately led to the creation of the Textilmuseum St. Gallen in 1878 (then called the Museum of Industry and Trade) and its unique holdings.[4]

Eastern Switzerland emerged as the most important center of industrially manufactured embroidery in the second half of the nineteenth century. It was there that the famous chemical lace known as "St. Gall lace" was developed (SEE CHAP. 14).[5] The

FIG. 1.1
Iklé Frères and Co., book with chemical-lace samples, St. Gallen, Switzerland, 1900–30. Paper, cardboard, leather, and cotton. Textilmuseum St. Gallen, STI IKL 4. Cat. 143.

fact that manufacturers were in constant need of new designs to follow fashion and meet market demand was one of the guiding motivations behind the Textilmuseum St. Gallen's founding. The museum acquired an extensive collection that was accessible to those working in the region's embroidery and lace industries, providing inspiration and functioning as a training facility in textile design. The role that historical models played in inspiring local industry is clear when comparing the samples preserved in company pattern books with their handmade historical counterparts (**FIGS. 1.1–4; SEE FIG. 14.19**). Given the specialization of the local textile industry, historical lace formed an important component of the collection, and in its mission, the museum followed the example of the Victoria and Albert Museum (then called the South Kensington Museum), founded after the Great Exhibition of 1851. The first museum of this kind on the continent was the Museum of Applied Art (MAK; then called the Imperial Royal Austrian Museum of Art and Industry), which opened in Vienna in 1863. The Textilmuseum St. Gallen was among the museums that opened in the second half of the nineteenth century that sought to promote collaboration between art and industry with the goal of improving design for mass-produced goods.[6]

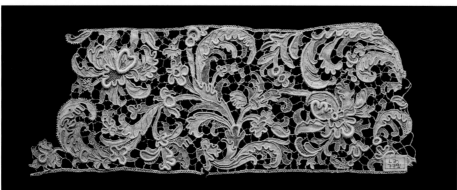

FIG. 1.2 (TOP)

Iklé Frères and Co., book with chemical-lace samples, St. Gallen, Switzerland, 1900–30. Paper, cardboard, leather, and cotton. Textilmuseum St. Gallen, STI IKL 1. Cat. 141.

FIG. 1.3 (CENTER)

Point de Venise needle-lace border, Orne, France; or Venice, third quarter of the 17th century. Linen. Textilmuseum St. Gallen, Gift of Leopold Iklé, 1904, 01143. Cat. 139.

FIG. 1.4 (BOTTOM)

Point de Venise needle-lace border, Venice or France, ca. 1690. Linen. Textilmuseum St. Gallen, Gift of Leopold Iklé, 1905, 01144. Cat. 140.

Like museums, manufacturers also collected textiles as models for their own production. One of the best-known among these was Leopold Iklé (1838–1922). The scion of a Hamburg merchant family, Iklé founded and led the Iklé Frères embroidery firm in St. Gallen together with his brothers. An avid collector of historical textiles, he donated important parts of his collection to the Textilmuseum St. Gallen between 1904 and 1908. The lace from his collection and from that of his nephew John Jacoby (1869–1953) forms the core of the museum's holdings in historical lace.[7]

Luxury Produced by Women

All types of lace are characterized by openwork effects in various shapes and sizes. Unlike other textiles such as embroidery, lace has no base fabric and is instead built up by combining threads using different techniques. These patterned combinations of threads form holes that constitute the design. "Lace" is the umbrella term for various decorative textile techniques, including, for example, bobbin lace, needle lace, knitted lace, and crocheted lace.[8] The techniques of handmade lace production developed in early modern Italy, specifically in Venice, Genoa, and Milan, starting in the late fifteenth century, and they quickly spread across much of the European continent.[9]

Needlework was an integral part of upper-class women's education. Printed books containing patterns, some of which were even edited by women, provided inspiration for artisanal activity starting in the sixteenth century (SEE CHAP. 2). The books, which often included dedications to women of a high social status (thus revealing one facet of their intended audience), were used by traveling women who actively taught the techniques. One such teacher was the anonymous author "RM" of the *Nüw Modelbüch von allerley gattungen Däntelschnür*, which was published by Christoph Froschauer (ca. 1490–1564)—one of the most important printers of the Reformation—in Zurich around 1561 (SEE FIG. 2.8). In the preface, the female lacemaker who authored the book writes that the art of producing lace had come from Italy and spread to Switzerland in the 1530s.[10] The then increasingly popular and influential technique of printing with moveable type distributed the patterns across Europe in the form of these pattern books.[11] Botanical books and herbals, which were often rich in flower illustrations, constituted another category of printed sources for needleworkers. Embroidery designers of the late sixteenth and seventeenth centuries looked to these publications for inspiration, and it is likely that they also served as reference for lace designs that incorporated natural motifs.[12] The phenomenon of textile pattern books and herbals was part of wider efforts in sixteenth-century Europe to endow things with order, which is apparent in biological and zoological publications as well as the establishment of cabinets of curiosities and art in princely and scholarly circles.[13]

The majority of the lace in the Textilmuseum's collection is bobbin and needle lace. Most of this lace is made with linen thread, particularly the early examples that date from the late fifteenth century through the sixteenth and seventeenth centuries; fewer are made of silk and metal thread in gold and silver. These lacemaking techniques emerged from embroidery and braiding in late fifteenth-century Italy.[14] Although there were other forms of nonwoven openwork that both predated these types of lace and coexisted with them, the further development of needle and bobbin techniques is among the most important textile achievements of early modern Europe. Many earlier technological advances in textile refinement, such as weaving or dyeing techniques, had been imported to Europe from Asia during the Middle Ages. The techniques associated with lace production became mechanized comparatively early (knitting, for instance, starting around 1600) and were important vectors of the Industrial Revolution in Europe (**SEE CHAP. 11**).[15]

A derivation of embroidery, needle lace represents a development from so-called cutwork, in which sections of warp and/or weft were selectively removed from the woven fabric. This process "opened up" the fabric ground, and then the edges of the voided areas were reinforced and decorated with buttonhole stitches made using a needle and thread (**FIGS. 1.5–7**). Soon, the embroidery was liberated from the textile ground and was worked freely in the "air" (*punto in aria*). During this process, a parchment mat supported the textile structure and was then removed after completion (**FIG. 1.8**).

Bobbin lace was also exclusively produced by women and developed from braiding, a technique that first arose as decoration for the borders and seams of white undergarments or towels.[16] Soon bobbin lace was fashioned independently from a textile base, and while working, the lacemaker would affix the threads to a pillow (**FIG. 1.9**). With the help of bobbins and pins that secured them, the threads were crossed, interlaced, or twisted, and a great variety of patterns emerged, which decorated cushions and other textiles for the home, as well as garments worn by men and women.

These important technical innovations are all the more remarkable for the fact that from the beginning, they were made by women who produced lace in their homes, far from the tightly regulated guilds of weavers or dyers. On the one hand, women of high social status belonging to the small upper classes produced for their own consumption (**FIG. 1.10**). Only they had the financial means to afford what could be expensive materials, and only they had the luxury of time. On the other hand, lower-class women produced lace for the upper-class market to generate much-needed supplementary income. Increasing demand gradually gave rise to a home industry that was supported, in certain regions, by tens of thousands of lower-class women who produced, depending on period and region, high-quality needle or bobbin lace. In eastern Switzerland, too, the home industry was an important economic component, yet it focused largely on embroidery.[17]

The production of lace in Europe from the sixteenth through the eighteenth centuries mostly took place in convents or, via the putting-out system, in the home. Employers provided women and girls with material and tools and then marketed the completed lace at a profit. Given the calculable basic costs and high profits, this was an extremely

FIG. 1.5 (OPPOSITE, LEFT)
Sampler with openwork and needle lace, western Europe, first third of the 17th century. Linen. Textilmuseum St. Gallen, Gift of Leopold Iklé, 1908, 20138. Cat. 6.

FIG. 1.6 (OPPOSITE, CENTER)
Sampler with openwork and needle lace, Italy, 1630–70. Linen. Textilmuseum St. Gallen, Gift of Leopold Iklé, 1908, 20135. Cat. 7.

FIG. 1.7 (OPPOSITE, RIGHT)
Sampler with openwork and needle lace, England, 17th century. Linen. Textilmuseum St. Gallen, Acquired from the Estate of John Jacoby, 1954, 20120. Cat. 8.

FIG. 1.8 (BELOW)
Unfinished *punto in aria* needle-lace border, Italy, ca. 1700. Parchment, paper, and linen. Textilmuseum St. Gallen, Gift of Leopold Iklé, 1905, 01256. Cat. 3.

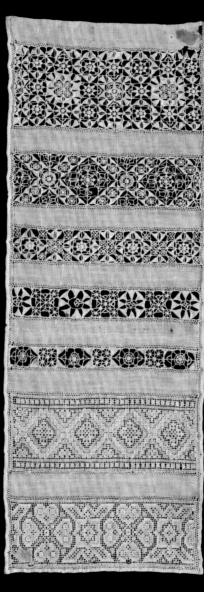
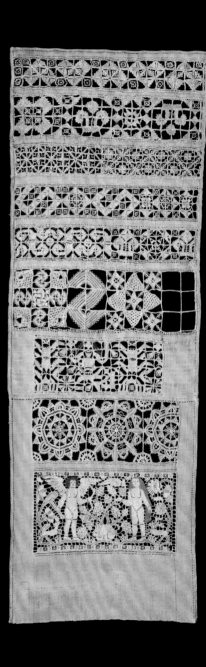

FIG. 1.9 (OPPOSITE)
Lace pillow with bobbins and in-process torchon lace, Lauterbrunnen, Switzerland, 1897. Cotton, paper, metal, and wood. Textilmuseum St. Gallen, 40017. Cat. 5.

FIG. 1.10 (ABOVE)
RM, detail of the title page from *Nüw Modelbüch von allerley gattungen Däntelschnür*, ca. 1561. Woodcut, published by Christoph Froschauer, Zurich. Zentralbibliothek Zürich, RaP 108_page 5.

lucrative business model. Working conditions were frequently difficult. Depending on the season, daylight was limited, and women were often employed in naturally damp environments, since fine linen thread is easier to manipulate in high humidity.[18] Despite its often precarious nature, though, this activity did allow women to earn a regular additional income for the family, apart from the husband's. As was argued at the time, lacemaking also protected women from idleness and vice.[19]

Lace, Fashion, and Power

Throughout the entire early modern period, lace was a luxury good. It proved that the master of the house could afford to purchase expensive linen thread for his wife to create lace at her own leisure. However, lace made in elite homes for personal use did not satisfy the growing consumer demand. Items produced by professional lacemakers working in the putting-out system for the wider market could be extremely expensive (especially the more elaborate laces) and were mostly of better quality than those created by elite women. Only a few could afford accessories of this kind. Moreover, sumptuary laws governed the use of ostentatious apparel and further limited access to valuable clothing and jewelry.

Unlike today, fashion in Europe at the time did not express the individuality of the wearer. It was one of the ways in which the powerful imposed social order and hierarchy, as is evident, for example, in the portrait of Isabella Clara Eugenia, daughter of King Philip II of Spain (FIGS. 1.11 AND 1.12). She is wearing a silk dress with gold decorations and a huge lace collar, all items subject to sumptuary legislation and reserved for the elite. Clothing thus expressed identification with a particular social group. Society was structured according to a pyramidal system, with the nobility and the clergy at the top. In St. Gallen, although the majority of the population was officially prohibited from wearing expensive imported and even homemade lace, some disobeyed and were fined. The city archives include mandates governing acceptable apparel; surviving documents from the seventeenth century prohibit the wider population from wearing lace, but in the eighteenth century, rules were gradually relaxed, an indication of the increasing wealth and influence of the middle classes.[20] As a mandate from 1611 dictates, "lace and all other precious work on the ruffs, whether they are smooth or not, and also on the shirts and the cuffs in front on the sleeves is completely forbidden: and especially on shirts, cuffs as well as on ruffs, whether they are smooth or not, no precious whitework may be made, whether it is made for a groom or a bride or not, except for a hemstitch and a seam." Violating these regulations resulted in "a fine of ten pfennigs."[21] In the nineteenth century, mechanization further lowered the cost of producing lace and made it a commodity accessible to a wider audience (SEE CHAP. 11).[22]

In the early modern period, the more valuable the piece of lace, the more noble its wearer. Lace was a sign of status and influence, as is evident in portraits of high-ranking

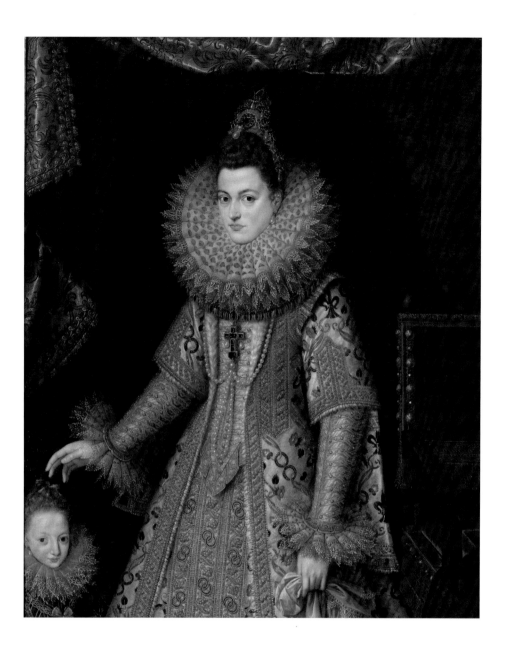

sitters painted between the late sixteenth century and the end of the eighteenth century. The fashion for wearing lace spread from centers of power like Madrid and Paris to regional courts across Europe and beyond. The most prominent political actors of the time, including Philip II of Spain, and Louis XIV of France a century later, as well as their wives and daughters, displayed and shaped this taste. For most of the period between 1550 and 1650, the dominant European power was Spain, and from approximately the mid-seventeenth century to the French Revolution, it was France and the court at Versailles (SEE CHAPS. 9 AND 10).

FIG. 1.11

Frans Pourbus the Younger, *Portrait of Infanta Isabella Clara Eugenia,* 1599–1600. Oil on canvas. Williams College Museum of Art, Williamstown, Massachusetts, Gift of Prentis Cobb Hale, Jr., 64.31. Cat. 51.

Barbara Karl

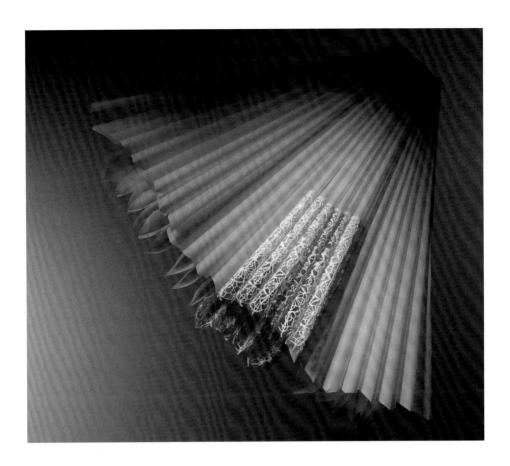

Representation and Status

Strengthened by the skillfully arranged marital alliances of the Habsburg dynasty governing Spain, the Southern Netherlands, and Austria, Spain's sphere of influence spanned the globe. This hegemonic position was reflected in the arts and in courtly fashion, which other European elites were eager to copy. The main features of Spanish court fashion for women are illustrated by the portrait of Isabella Clara Eugenia and include tightly fitting doublets and rigid hoop skirts. Men also wore doublets as well as breeches and semicircular capes (*herreruelos*) that covered the shoulders. Both sexes wore ruffs (millstone collars) of various widths, and expensive lace in linen, silk, gold, and silver embellished all these items of clothing (SEE CHAP. 5).[23]

When Spain's power reached its political and cultural apex between the mid-sixteenth and mid-seventeenth centuries, white lace accessories became indispensable and valuable components of ensembles worn by royalty and other elites. Lace soon adorned the wide collars and cuffs of courtiers, the altars of the most important cathedrals, and the tables of the most splendid palaces in Europe. Black was one of the most important and most expensive fashionable colors of the Spanish *siglo de oro* (Golden Age) and provided a stark contrast to trimmings of white lace. While white represented purity

FIG. 1.12

Bobbin-lace border mounted as a millstone collar, northern Europe, 1580–1620. Linen. Textilmuseum St. Gallen, Gift of Leopold Iklé, 1904, 00679. Cat. 52.

FIG. 1.13
Needle-lace cover or chalice cover,
Italy, ca. 1700. Silk and metal threads
with silk core. Textilmuseum St.
Gallen, Gift of Leopold Iklé, 1908,
23963. Cat. 29.

Barbara Karl

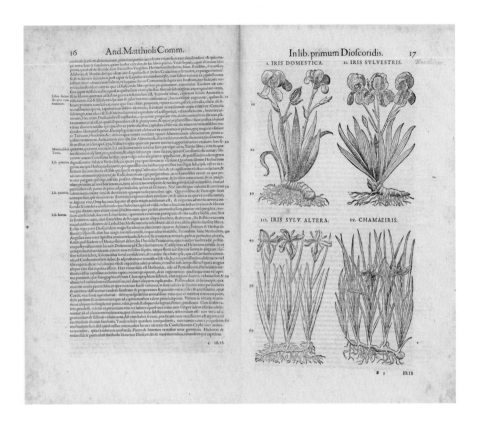

and cleanliness, black underscored the strict attitude of the courtly body and reflected the rigid protocol at the court.[24]

From the sixteenth century on, northern Italy and, somewhat later, the Southern Netherlands established themselves as centers of professional lace production and of trade in such products. Politically, both regions were largely under Spanish influence. The Dutch city of Antwerp (SEE CHAP. 4) and the Italian city of Milan, both important hubs, were part of the Spanish empire; Genoa, another lacemaking center, was an important ally.

Spanish fashion was influenced by a variety of factors including historical and contemporary dynastic relations, dominions, and protocol.[25] Via trade routes and marriages, fashions in lace became popular at the Spanish court, which set the standard for the other European courts. The Netherlands, for instance, was an important center of the exclusive trade in flowers, of book printing, and of the emerging natural sciences. It is thus not surprising that in the 1630s, exotic floral patterns were increasingly making their way into lace designs all over Europe (FIGS. 1.13 AND 1.14). This also included floral and foliate patterns inspired by plants imported from Asia or by the colorful Indian cottons that were then a novelty in Europe. Due to European colonial expansion across the globe, Iberian courtly fashions spread as far as the Americas (SEE CHAPS. 6–8) and Asia.

Expensive lace accessories were worn by both sexes. In the seventeenth century in particular, men's clothes were often more richly adorned with lace than women's. Men wore lace at the neck and on their gloves, doublets, boots, and sashes; and like women, they also carried decorated handkerchiefs. As a fashion accessory and status symbol, lace, mostly white, adorned Europe's most powerful men, whose apparel, until the French Revolution, was often ostentatious and extravagant (FIGS. 1.15 AND 1.16).

In the first half of the seventeenth century, Spain was permanently weakened by armed conflict, in particular the Dutch War of Independence (1568–1648) and the Thirty Years' War (1618–48). As a result, France gained the advantage to become the most powerful country in western Europe. This shift was also reflected in fashion.

FIG. 1.14
Pietro Andrea Mattioli, *Opera quae extant omnia: Hoc est, Commentarii in VI. libros Pedacii Dioscoridis Anazarbei De medica materia. . . .*, 1598. Published by Nicolaus Bassaeus, Frankfurt. The LuEsther T. Mertz Library, New York Botanical Garden, f QK 99 D5 M3 1598. Cat. 35.

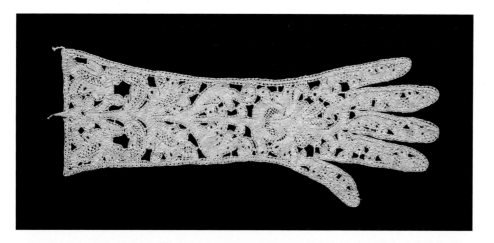

FIG. 1.15

Upper part of a bobbin-lace glove, probably Lombardy, Italy, second half of the 17th century. Linen. Textilmuseum St. Gallen, Gift of Leopold Iklé, 1904, 00223. Cat. 54.

FIG. 1.16

Punto in aria needle-lace cuff, Venice, ca. 1650, reworked in the 19th century. Linen. Textilmuseum St. Gallen, Acquired from the Estate of John Jacoby, 1954, 00065. Cat. 53.

Endowed with power and vision embodied in the creation of Versailles (constructed from 1661 to 1715), King Louis XIV (1638–1715) set the standard of taste for the courts of Europe. In the second half of the seventeenth century, Venice celebrated its last great innovation in the field of making: *gros point de Venise*. This technique is considered the pinnacle of lacemaking in the early modern period. The generous, heavy floral decor, which gives the impression of three-dimensionality, dominated contemporary court fashion. A young Louis XIV wears this style in a 1665 marble portrait by Gian Lorenzo Bernini (**FIGS. 1.17–20**). As is often the case for successful innovations, this lace in the Venetian style was soon imitated in other production centers, particularly in France, which makes it difficult today to attribute geographical origins to this and other laces (**FIG. 1.21**).

The young Louis XIV celebrated himself as the Sun King, and Versailles was the center of politics and fashion. The arts were as much at his service in this endeavor as was France's centrally controlled mercantilist economy under the direction of his powerful finance minister, Jean-Baptiste Colbert (1619–1683; **SEE CHAP. 9**).[26] The silk fabric manufactories in Lyon and the French lacemaking regions were closely associated with the court, which systematically supported and controlled them.[27] King Louis XIV enticed Italian lacemakers with concessions and financing and settled them in France. This gave rise to new production sites in France, which subsequently became a center of innovation for European lace production. Lace in the gros point de Venise style was gradually displaced by the more intricate *point de France* (**FIG. 1.22**). The most important artists at Louis XIV's court created designs for lace, including Jean Bérain (1640–1711), who played a central role in shaping contemporary style. Bérain created ornamental and decorative paintings as well as designs for furniture, tapestries, carpets, and goldwork.[28]

The king wore French lace in the point de France style, as is evident in royal portraits such as Hyacinthe Rigaud's depiction of Louis XIV from 1701 (**FIG. 1.23**). Courtly Europe followed the standard set by the French court, and lace in the French style was not only worn in other regions of Europe but soon produced there as well. This transfer of knowledge was still largely ensured by the female lacemakers and dealers creating this luxury good.[29]

FIG. 1.17
Gian Lorenzo Bernini, *Bust of Louis XIV, King of France and Navarre*, 1665. Marble. Musée national des châteaux de Versailles et de Trianon, Versailles, MV2040.

The history of lace is not a straightforward success story; it has been dependent on ever-changing fashions and industry fluctuations. In the second half of the seventeenth century, for example, delicate cotton fabrics imported from East India (Bengal) came into fashion in Europe. Often richly embroidered, they were light, bright white, and easy to wash. These delicate fabrics increasingly competed with both the heavy gros point de Venise lace and the delicate point de France lace. As a result, the turn of the eighteenth century saw a crisis in the lace industry during which many lace producers lost their jobs. The response to this new competition was the advent of lace whose lightness imitated the Indian cottons (SEE FIG. 4.25). More delicate than lace had ever been, this textile was immensely successful, and its production required extreme skill on the part of the female lacemakers, especially the bobbin lacemakers, the best of whom underwent years of training.[30]

Over the course of the seventeenth and eighteenth centuries, European lace production continued to professionalize because as middle classes grew, so did demand, and codes governing luxury items and dress were relaxed. Production remained in the hands of women; so did at least a portion of sales (SEE CHAP. 4).[31] Networks of specially trained women working at home satisfied the demand of the upper classes and produced light,

FIG. 1.18 (LEFT)
Philibert Bouttats, *Portrait of Louis XIV, King of France*, 1664/after 1731. Engraving on paper, published by Nicolaes Visscher I. Rijksmuseum, Amsterdam, RP-P-1910-2286.

FIG. 1.19 (RIGHT, TOP)
Point plat de Venise needle lace mounted as cravat ends, Venice, ca. 1690, reworked at the end of the 19th century. Linen and cotton. Textilmuseum St. Gallen, Acquired from the Estate of John Jacoby, 1954, 01226.1-2. Cat. 75.

FIG. 1.20 (RIGHT, BOTTOM)
Point de Venise needle-lace *rabat*, probably Alençon, France; or Venice, ca. 1670. Linen. Textilmuseum St. Gallen, Gift of the Estate of Isador Grauer, 1983, 03914. Cat. 78.

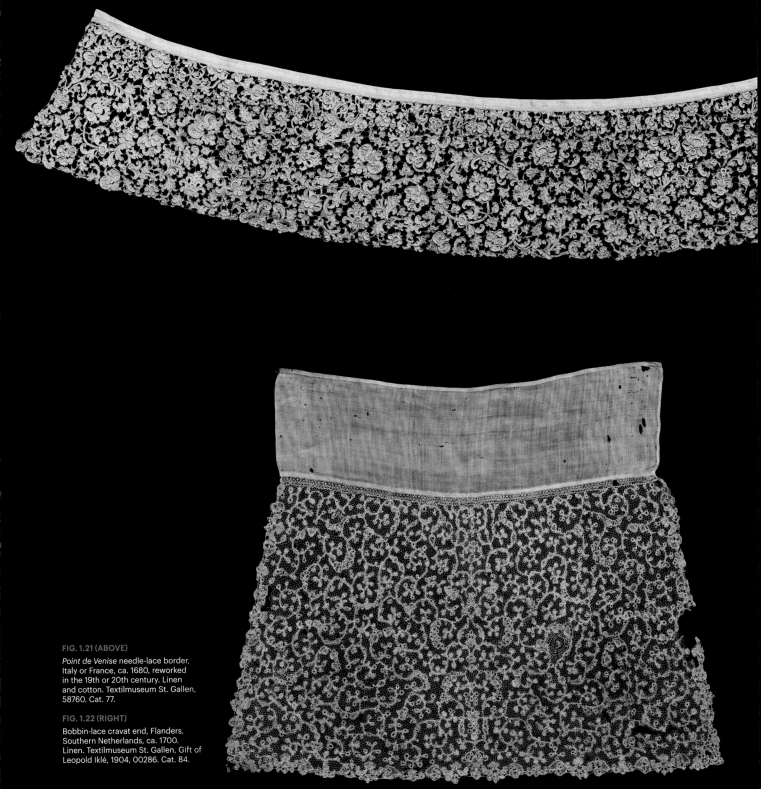

FIG. 1.21 (ABOVE)

Point de Venise needle-lace border,
Italy or France, ca. 1680, reworked
in the 19th or 20th century. Linen
and cotton. Textilmuseum St. Gallen,
58760. Cat. 77.

FIG. 1.22 (RIGHT)

Bobbin-lace cravat end, Flanders,
Southern Netherlands, ca. 1700.
Linen. Textilmuseum St. Gallen, Gift of
Leopold Iklé, 1904, 00286. Cat. 84.

Barbara Karl

refined, and expensive lace. In the eighteenth century, for example, a high-quality bonnet with lappets required a year's time from conception to completion and was priced accordingly. The material, the finest linen thread, added to the cost. The labor of women working at home in the textile sector was an important economic factor throughout the time period in question throughout Europe. The same is true for comparable developments in the field of embroidery production in eastern Switzerland beginning in the mid-eighteenth century.[32]

Fashions at the French court, and thus at other European courts, changed ever more quickly, which boosted the production of luxury textiles in silk and fine linen. Lace production spread geographically. Certain towns drew notoriety for producing specific kinds of lace (for example, Alençon and Valenciennes in France or Mechlin, Brussels, and Binche in the Southern Netherlands). As mentioned above, however, it is difficult to attribute lace to individual centers of production because successful styles were quickly copied elsewhere. In the designs of the first half of the eighteenth century, valuable lace and silk fabrics cross-fertilized, especially since they were often worn in combination. During the 1720s, the famous Lyon silk industry incorporated lace motifs into its designs, and lacemakers in turn translated the plant motifs of silk fabrics into bobbin- and needle-lace techniques (**FIG. 1.24**).[33] The French court remained the most important arbiter of fashion, especially the late eighteenth-century style icon Queen Marie-Antoinette (1755–1793; **FIGS. 1.25 AND 1.26**). Already in the 1780s, however, a trend toward simplification emerged in patterns and textiles. This is readily apparent in the designs of both silks and lace, which increasingly showed more ground and fewer and smaller motifs.

The church was yet another important consumer of lace. Textiles are an essential part of Christian religious rites (**FIG. 1.27**). The clergy, whose fashions were modeled (often with some delay) on those of the court, discovered lace early on. The church also benefited from the industry financially, and a significant amount of lace was produced by nuns in convents. Innumerable lace items used in churches were manufactured specifically for that purpose; religious symbolism such as monograms of Christ and depictions of saints suggests custom productions. Luxurious textiles including lace belonging to the courtly elites often made their way into church institutions as donations.[34]

FIG. 1.23 (OPPOSITE)
Hyacinthe Rigaud, *Louis XIV, King of France*, 1701. Oil on canvas. Musée du Louvre, Paris, INV7492.

FIG. 1.24 (ABOVE)
Lace-patterned silk, France, ca. 1720–25. Silk. Cora Ginsburg, LLC. Cat. 90.

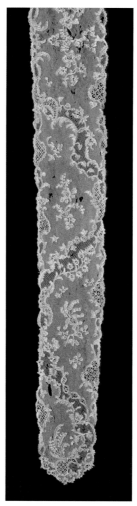

The French Revolution (1789–99), which brought down the ancien régime and rejected and destroyed much of what was associated with it, threw the centers of French luxury textile production into crisis. The production of lace continued, but in much smaller quantities. As mechanization processes developed in the textile sector, much of the associated hand labor, such as spinning, was replaced, and tens of thousands of women lost their livelihood. Through the introduction of new machinery, the techniques employed in lacemaking and costs of goods were affected. Thanks to declining prices, the absence of sumptuary legislation, and a growing middle class, lace—and lacelike products such as chemical lace—became available to an increasing number of consumers over the course of the nineteenth century (SEE CHAPS. 11 AND 14). Although the home-based female workforce was reduced, many women continued; in eastern Switzerland, for example, embroideries that were used to create chemical lace were often finished at home by women and girls.[35]

FIG. 1.25 (TOP, LEFT)
Christian Friedrich Fritzsch (after Franz Xaver Wagenschön), *Portrait of the Archduchess Marie Antoinette, Later Queen of France*, 1770–74. Engraving on paper. Rijksmuseum, Amsterdam, RP-P-1910-2121.

FIG. 1.26 (TOP, RIGHT)
Point d'Angleterre or Brussels needle-lace lappet, Brussels, Southern Netherlands, ca. 1770. Linen. Textilmuseum St. Gallen, Acquired from the Estate of John Jacoby, 1954, 00736. Cat. 138.

FIG. 1.27 (OPPOSITE)
Needle-lace chasuble, Venice, 1650–75. Linen, silk, and silver threads. Textilmuseum St. Gallen, 51480. Cat. 44.

Conclusion

The Textilmuseum St. Gallen's extensive collection offers an overview of lace development in early modern Europe, elucidating the role this exclusive luxury textile occupied amid relationships between economy, politics, and social structures. For consumers, about whom we know much more than we do about the producers, high-quality handmade lace was for three centuries a sign of status and an integral component of courtly representation that communicated wealth and power. This use of lace is a stark contrast to the often rather humble and precarious environment in which female lacemakers worked. Lace was manufactured almost exclusively by women, and they were also often responsible for its trade and sale. This widespread involvement meant that these women were the most important innovators of the early modern lace industry; they developed, created, and sustained lace production beyond the reach of guild regulations for an elite market. This domestic work enriched the economy of entire European regions in significant ways, offering hundreds of thousands of women an income and involvement in an industry that changed as various techniques were mechanized in the late eighteenth and nineteenth centuries.

This chapter emerged following the *Lace and Status* exhibition at the Textilmuseum St. Gallen (October 2018–February 2019). I would like to thank the staff at the museum, especially Christine Freydl, Silvia Gross, and Ilona Kos, as well as Cornel Dora, Silvio Frigg, Ulrike Ganz, Dorothee Guggenheimer, and Stefan Sonderegger, for allowing me to consult books and other documents while preparing for the exhibition and to put them on display. Thanks also to Emma Cormack, Florence Grant, Michele Majer, and Arman Weidemann for their valuable editorial work on this chapter.

This chapter (including quotations unless otherwise noted) was translated from the German by Nils Schott.

1   The beginnings of lacemaking techniques emerged in the late 15th and early 16th centuries in the form of decorated edges worn on veils, sleeve cuffs, and at the neck. For a comprehensive history of lace from its origins to 1914, see Santina M. Levey, *Lace: A History* (Leeds, UK: W. S. Maney & Son; London: Victoria and Albert Museum, 1983). See also Fanny Bury Palliser, *History of Lace* (London: S. Low, Son, & Marston, 1865); Marie Risselin-Steenbrugen, *Trois siècles de dentelles aux Musées royaux d'art et d'histoire* (Brussels: Musées royaux d'art et d'histoire, 1980).
2   For a discussion of the textile industries in eastern Switzerland in the late 19th and early 20th centuries, see Peter Röllin, *Stickerei-Zeit: Kultur und Kunst in St. Gallen, 1870–1930* (St. Gallen, Switzerland: Verlagsgemeinschaft St. Gallen, 1989); Cornel Dora, ed., *Textiles St. Gallen: Tausend Jahre Tradition, Technologie und Trends/A Thousand Years of Tradition, Technology and Trends* (St. Gallen, Switzerland: Amt für Kultur, 2004); and Eric Häusler and Caspar Meili, "Swiss Embroidery: Erfolg und Krise der Schweizer Stickerei-Industrie 1865–1929," *Neujahrsblatt: Historischer Verein des Kantons St. Gallen* 155 (2015): 11–101.
3   This "merchant directorate" was founded in the 15th century as a merchant guild under the name Gesellschaft zum Notenstein. For a

history of manufacturing in St. Gallen, see Hans Rudolf Leuenberger, *500 Jahre Kaufmännische Corporation St. Gallen, 1466–1966* (St. Gallen, Switzerland: Kaufmännisches Directorium, Zollikofer, 1966).
4   Heinrich Bendel, *Erster Bericht über das St. Gallische Industrie- und Gewerbemuseum 1878* (St. Gallen, Switzerland: Zollikofer'sche Buchdruckerei, 1879), 2, 3.
5   Chemical lace is also known as guipure. In this process, a base fabric is embroidered and then treated in a chemical bath, dissolving the base and leaving behind the embroidered threads that constitute the pattern design. Friedrich Schöner, *Spitzen: Enzyklopädie der Spitzentechniken* (Leipzig, Germany: Fachbuchverlag, 1982), 304.
6   John Physick, *The Victoria and Albert Museum: The History of Its Building* (Oxford: Phaidon, 1982), 19–23, 37–39; and Barbara Mundt, *Die deutschen Kunstgewerbemuseen im 19. Jahrhundert* (Munich, Germany: Prestel, 1974), 36–40.
7   Textilmuseum St. Gallen and Iklé-Frischknecht-Stiftung, eds., *Historische Spitzen: Die Leopold-Iklé-Sammlung im Textilmuseum St. Gallen* (Stuttgart, Germany: Arnoldsche, 2018); and Anne Wanner-JeanRichard, Marianne Gächter-Weber, and Cordula Kessler-Loerischer, eds., *Leopold Iklé: Ein leidenschaftlicher Sammler* (St. Gallen, Switzerland: Textilmuseum St. Gallen, 2002).
8   Tina Frauberger, *Handbuch der Spitzenkunde: Technisches und Geschichtliches über die Näh-, Klöppel- und Maschinenspitzen* (Leipzig, Germany: Verlag Seemann, 1894), 11–16.
9   On the history of lace, see especially Levey, *Lace*; and Anne Kraatz, *Die Kunst der Spitze: Textiles Filigran* (Frankfurt, Germany: Propyläen, 1989). Videos aid in understanding lacemaking techniques. The Textilmuseum commissioned several films as part of the 2018–19 *Lace and Status* exhibition, including demonstrations of needle lace and bobbin lace: "Die Spitzen der Gesellschaft: Fertigung von Nadelspitze," YouTube, April 16, 2019, https://www.youtube.com/watch?v=BktY2qalcU0; and "Die Spitzen der Gesellschaft: Klöppeln," YouTube, April 16, 2019, https://www.youtube.com/watch?v=6umvIoPhvnA.

10   RM, *Nüw Modelbüch von allerley gattungen Däntelschnür* (Zurich: Christoph Froschauer, ca. 1561). Zentralbibliothek Zürich, RaP. https://www.e-rara.ch/zuz/content/zoom/1658135.

11   Femke Speelberg, "Fashion & Virtue: Textile Patterns and the Print Revolution, 1520–1620," *Metropolitan Museum of Art Bulletin* 73, no. 2 (Fall 2015).

12   Andrew Morrall, "Regaining Eden: Representations of Nature in Seventeenth-Century English Embroidery," in *English Embroidery from The Metropolitan Museum of Art, 1580–1700: 'Twixt Art and Nature,* ed. Andrew Morrall and Melinda Watt (New York: Bard Graduate Center for Studies in the Decorative Arts, Design, and Culture, 2008), 79–80. Eventually, 18th-century silk designers looked to botanical illustrations for inspiration as well. Deborah E. Kraak, "Eighteenth-Century English Floral Silks," *Magazine Antiques* (June 1998): 842–48. See also Brian W. Ogilvie, *The Science of Describing: Natural History in Renaissance Europe* (Chicago: University of Chicago Press, 2006).

13   On the establishment of 16th- and 17th-century cabinets of curiosities, see Oliver Impey and Arthur MacGregor, eds., *The Origins of Museums: The Cabinet of Curiosities in Sixteenth- and Seventeenth-Century Europe* (London: House of Stratus, 2001).

14   Frauberger, *Handbuch der Spitzenkunde,* 56–177.

15   For further reading about the trajectory of the machine-made knitting and lace industries, see William Felkin, *History of the Machine-Wrought Hosiery and Lace Manufactures* (London: Longmans, Green, 1867); and Pat Earnshaw, *Embroidered Machine Nets: Limerick and Worldwide* (Guildford, UK: Gorse Publications, 1993).

16   Frauberger, *Handbuch der Spitzenkunde,* 131–77.

17   On the eastern Swiss embroidery industry, see "Aufschwung und Blüte der Stickerei" and "Arbeit und Leben in der Stickerei," in Albert Tanner, *Das Schiffchen fliegt, die Maschine rauscht: Weber, Sticker und Fabrikanten in der Ostschweiz* (Zurich: Unionsverlag, 1985), 99–131, 132–80.

18   Pat Earnshaw, *The Identification of Lace* (Princes Risborough, UK: Shire Publications, 1980), 82.

19   See Speelberg, "Fashion & Virtue"; Marie Risselin-Steenebrugen, "Martine et Catherine Plantin: Leur rôle dans la fabrication et le commerce de la lingerie et des dentelles au XVIe siècle," *Revue belge d'archeologie et d'histoire d'art* 26, nos. 3–4 (1957): 169–88.

20   The archives include, for example, Mandatenbuch, 1638–95, vol. 547, 2:1100–1101 (1678), 2:1134–36 (1682), Municipal Archive St. Gallen; Mandatenbuch, 1695–1794, vol. 548, 3:453–55 (1761), 3:569–83 (1769).

21   "Mandate and order of the Lord Mayor. And of the small and large councils of the city of St. Gallen, concerning Christian churchgoing and attendance at sermons: to put a stop to dissolute or wasteful living as well as excessive pomp and costliness at banquets, at weddings and in dress." (Mandat und Anordnung des Herrn Bürgermeister. Und der Klein- und Grossräte der Stadt St. Gallen, betreffend den christlichen Kirchgang und den Besuch der Predigten: Zur Abstellung des liederlichen oder verschwenderischen Lebens sowie der übermässigen Pracht und Kostspieligkeit

bei Festmählern, bei Hochzeiten und in der Bekleidung. Ferner ist gesetzt, dass Spitze und alle andere kostbare Arbeit an den Krausen, ob sie glatt sind oder nicht, und auch an den Hemden und den Manschetten vorn an den Aermeln ganz verboten ist: und namentlich an Hemden, Manschetten wie auch an Krausen, sie seien glatt oder nicht, keine kostbare Weissarbeit gemacht werden darf, ob sie für einen Bräutigam oder eine Braut gemacht wird oder nicht, ausser einen Hohlsaum und einer Naht. Bei Busse an zehn Pfennig.) Vadianische Sammlung der Ortsbürgergemeinde, S 1962 A (K6), Kantonsbibliothek Vadiana St. Gallen. I thank Dorothee Guggenheimer for making her transcriptions available to me. Author's translation.

22   Earnshaw, *Embroidered Machine Nets,* 3.

23   Amalia Descalzo, "Spanish Male Costume in the Habsburg Period," and Amalia Descalzo and Carmen Bernis, "Spanish Female Costume in the Habsburg Period," in *Spanish Fashion at the Courts of Early Modern Europe,* 2 vols., ed. José Luis Colomer and Amalia Descalzo (Madrid: Centro de Estudios Europa Hispánica, 2014), 15–76.

24   José Luis Colomer, "Black and the Royal Image," in Colomer and Descalzo, *Spanish Fashion,* 77–112.

25   For more on these issues, see the chapters in "Spanish Court Dress," in Colomer and Descalzo, *Spanish Fashion,* 15–208.

26   Peter Burke, *The Fabrication of Louis XIV* (New Haven, CT: Yale University Press, 1992).

27   Levey, *Lace,* 35–37.

28   Jean Bérain, *Décorations intérieures: Style Louis XIV composées par Jean Bérain/lithographiées par Arnout Père* (Paris: A. Morel et Cie, éditeurs, 1864).

29   For a discussion of women involved in the Flemish lace trade specifically, see Risselin-Steenebrugen, "Martine et Catherine Plantin"; and Risselin-Steenebrugen, *Trois siècles de dentelles,* 245–49. SEE ALSO CHAP. 4.

30   Levey, *Lace,* 43–45, 72.

31   Risselin-Steenebrugen, "Martine et Catherine Plantin," 181–82, 185, 187; and Peter Neu, *Margaretha von der Marck (1527–1599): Landesmutter, Geschäftsfrau und Händlerin, Katholikin* (Enghien, Belgium: Arenberg Stiftung, 2013).

32   Tanner, *Das Schiffchen fliegt,* 57, 79; Röllin, *Stickerei-Zeit,* 35–40; and Dora, *Textiles St. Gallen,* 60–79.

33   Levey, *Lace,* 68–70; and Santina M. Levey, "Lace and Lace-Patterned Silks: Some Comparative Illustrations," in *Studies in Textile History: In Memory of Harold B. Burnham,* ed. V. Gervers (Toronto: Royal Ontario Museum, 1977), 184–201.

34   Pauline Johnstone, *High Fashion in the Church: The Place of Church Vestments in the History of Art from the Ninth to the Nineteenth Century* (Leeds, UK: Maney, 2002), 2, 107. See also Silvio Tomasini and Thessy Schönholzer Nichols, *Merletti a Gandino: La collezione in oro, argento e lino del Museo della Basilica* (Gandino, Italy: Museo della Basilica di Gandino, 2012).

35   "Arbeit und Leben der Heirmarbeiter," in Tanner, *Das Schiffchen fliegt,* 57–98.

2 Putting a Name to a Lace: Fashion, Fame, and the Production of Printed Textile Pattern Books

Femke Speelberg

I N 1931, TWO YEARS BEFORE HE PUBLISHED his *Bibliographie der Modelbücher*, Arthur Lotz (active ca. 1909–1940) wrote a short article on the lace books of the Italian artist Bartolomeo Danieli (active 1610–1643; FIG. 2.1).[1] Lotz deemed these works to be of considerable importance, not simply for their rarity and beauty but also because they offered tangible insight into the artistic personality of their maker. In this respect, they formed a sharp contrast to "the mass of nameless artists and artisans that could hardly be separated from one another," which had defined the field up to that moment. With this statement, Lotz did not imply that there were no names at all attached to earlier publications containing textile patterns but rather that—unlike Danieli—few of the people involved in their production were actually professionals active in the textile trade.[2]

Danieli's four lace books were published between 1610 and 1641. They marked the end of the thriving tradition of publishing textile patterns on the Italian peninsula, which had begun about a century earlier with Giovanni Antonio Tagliente's *Essempio di recammi* (Venice, 1527).[3] As the title and illustrations on the frontispiece of this booklet suggest, its designs were primarily intended for application in needlework and weaving (FIG. 2.2). While the latter required a specific format of annotation to successfully translate a printed pattern into the right combination of warp and weft, most designs for sewing and embroidery were—akin to drawing and writing—essentially linear in nature.[4] This was one of the main reasons why the writing master Tagliente (ca. 1465–1528) could transition from publishing works on mathematics, reading, writing, and calligraphy to the new genre of the textile pattern book.[5] The models did not necessitate

FIG. 2.1
Bartolomeo Danieli, *Vari disegni di merletti*. Published by Agostino Parisini and Giovanni Battista Negroponte, Bologna, 1639. Etching. The Metropolitan Museum of Art, New York, Harris Brisbane Dick Fund, 1937, 37.47.2(11). Cat. 30.

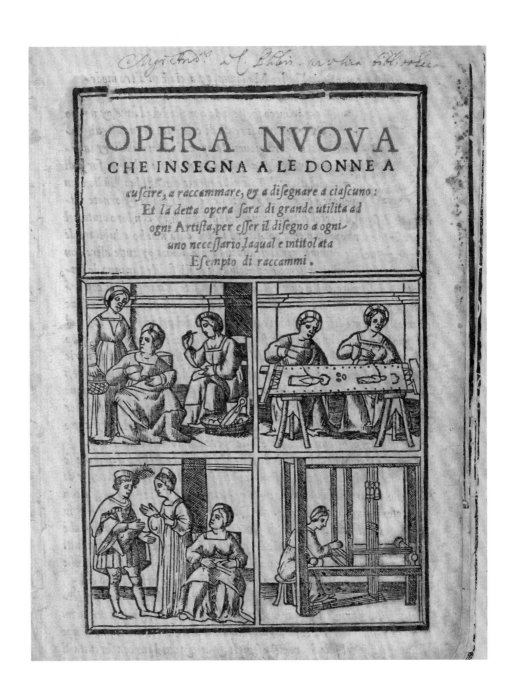

a professional background, nor indeed any practical knowledge of the techniques that would be used for their execution in needle and thread. Most important, according to Tagliente, was the "varieta di bellisimi esempli" (variety of beautiful examples).[6] In his written explanation, he emphasized that these could be found anywhere and also unabashedly admitted to using several patterns designed by other "eccellentissimi maestri" (excellent masters).[7] Other publishers similarly interpreted the relative open-endedness of embroidery templates as an invitation to creatively gather content from a variety of sources. Not only did they harvest from other pattern books, but they also copied local and foreign (ornament) prints and frequently recycled blocks that had been used in other publications.[8] In most cases, the subject matter of these prints and blocks warranted their reuse in the textile pattern book format, but there are occasional examples of plates that seem entirely out of place. A full-page illustration of a coffered ceiling might be counted among the strangest of these outliers.[9]

In line with Tagliente's professional background, his original contributions to his pattern book focused on the letters of the alphabet, calligraphic scripts and flourishes, and the closely related art of designing *groppi* (motifs and patterns in knotwork; FIG. 2.3). This focus is evident in the fact that his explanatory text chiefly discusses the design of such knotwork patterns and largely ignores the subject matter of the other plates included in the booklet.[10] However, the principles Tagliente outlined for learning how to draw and ultimately design such patterns—by beginning with single, simple shapes and expanding one's vocabulary from there on—could easily be transposed to any of his other subjects.[11] Thus, four pages of individual motifs of flowers, animals, and objects form a preamble to a large figurative composition of *Orpheus Playing to the Animals*. These exercises make clear that the ultimate goal of Tagliente's *Essempio di recammi* (and most other pattern books) was not to teach how to embroider or weave but instead to offer instruction on how to compose designs for application in these art forms.[12] Rather than exposing the "secrets" of needlework to the world, the publication thus infused the widely and often domestically practiced craft of textile decoration with workshop practices found, for example, in the more exalted environment of a painter's studio. In line with this idea, the Italian author Tommaso Garzoni (1549–1589) emphasized the importance of *disegno* (the art of designing) as part of the embroiderer's profession: "the embroiderer, with a kind of disegno, works a thousand fantasies which are taught by books belonging specifically to that trade."[13] Accordingly, the word "disegno" also echoes emphatically throughout Tagliente's text, and a few decades later, the block-cutter-turned-printer-publisher Matteo Pagano (1515–1588) described needlework as "Dipingendo con Lago, come Apelle" (painting with the needle, just like Apelles).[14]

FIG. 2.3
Giovanni Antonio Tagliente, *Essempio di recammi*. Published by Giovanni Antonio di Nicolini da Sabio e i Fratelli, Venice, 1530 (3rd ed.). Woodcut and letterpress. The Metropolitan Museum of Art, New York, Harris Brisbane Dick Fund, 1935, 35.75.3(33).

Given this emphasis on designing over making, it is perhaps not surprising that, in those rare cases where we have some insight into who actually designed the patterns for these booklets, the artists can often be identified as painters. For example, in his *Ein new Modelbuch* (Zwickau, 1524), the publisher Johannes Schönsperger the Younger (active 1510–1530) included a series of patterns that closely relate to the workshop style of Lucas Cranach the Elder (1472–1553; FIG. 2.4).[15] In addition, Arthur Lotz has demonstrated the role played by the illuminator Narcissus Renner (ca. 1502–after 1535) in supplying designs for several textile pattern books published during the 1530s by Christian Egenolff (1502–1555) and Johann Schwartzenberger (active 1530s), respectively.[16] It is noteworthy, however, that neither of these artists is explicitly mentioned on the title pages or in the publisher's introductions, signaling that their involvement as designers did not contribute in any significant manner to the marketability of these booklets.[17] Most early textile pattern books are therefore principally known under the name of their publisher(s), which—alongside the shop address or street sign—formed the most crucial information to facilitate sales.

An exception to this rule is formed by the few instances in which the initiative for publication came from an artist rather than a publisher. As a writing master, Giovanni Antonio Tagliente can be classified under this category. The German *Formschneider* (block cutter) Hans Hoffman (active 1550s) represents another example. The tone of the introduction to his *New Modelbüch* (Strasbourg, 1556) and the frequent use of his initials and artist's device (FIG. 2.5) make clear that he perceived the booklet as a vehicle of self-promotion. Ironically, however, in the two later editions of the publication, all references to his authorship were erased, indicating that Hoffman did not achieve the fame he had sought. That his patterns were nevertheless deemed as *nutzlich* (useful), as he had boasted, is evidenced by the fact that they were reprinted as late as 1597.[18]

The same fate of anonymity did not befall the majority of artists who tried their hand at publishing textile pattern books dedicated more specifically to designs for lace. Several factors can be identified that contributed to this perceived shift in status. The timing of their introduction, for one, was fortuitous. Even though both needle and bobbin lace had been practiced in various countries throughout Europe for several decades at least, the first pattern books dedicated specifically to these techniques were not issued until the second half of the sixteenth century.[19] By this time, the publishing world itself had undergone important changes. A notable development was the growing interest in the authorial voice. Peter Burke has argued, for example, that the frequent inclusion of frontispiece portraits and biographical prefaces in the literary world illustrates the rise of the (proto-historiographical) assumption that information about the writer helps us to better understand or appreciate their work.[20] For the art world, the second edition of *Vite de' piu eccellenti architetti, pittori, et scultori italiani*

(Florence, 1568) by Giorgio Vasari (1511–1574) can be considered a watershed moment in this respect. Not only did it bring to life three generations of artists by placing their œuvres in a biographical narrative, but it literally put a face to their names by opening the majority of the entries with a portrait of the artist.[21] After this moment, the inclusion of portraits became a common feature in treatises on art and architecture and other trade-specific publications. Of note, for example, is the prominent placement of the portrait of the Spanish tailor Juan de Alcega (active 1578–1599) on the title page to his *Libro de Geometría, Práctica y Traça* (Madrid, 1580; FIG. 2.6). As Evelyn Lincoln has argued, the combination of text and portrait in such publications formed an important vehicle of self-fashioning for the author.[22] Burke has further suggested that, more than simply illustrating the rising cult of the individual, such representations had as much to do with the desire to belong to a certain group and bestowed on authors a sense of authority through their adherence to a collective identity.[23]

The notion that a certain level of specialized knowledge was required to create (designs for) needle and bobbin lace—as opposed to the previously discussed models for embroidery—may further have impressed upon publishers the urgency of revealing the identities of their collaborators. Thus, the title page of the earliest-known lace book to appear north of the Alps contains not only the first known image of a woman making bobbin lace but also the first reference to the designer of the patterns (FIG. 2.7).[24] Unfortunately, the choice was made to use initials (RM) rather than the full name of the author. Lotz has suggested that the printer-publisher Christoph Froschauer (ca. 1490–1564) might have done so because the author was a woman and publishing a woman's work was still rather unorthodox at the time.[25] However, in this case, it made a lot of sense because the woman in question not only was a skilled lacemaker herself but also had over twelve years of experience in teaching lacemaking to young girls and women from in and around Zurich. Her technical knowledge and edificatory inclination shine through in the written introduction and also come to the fore in the short explanatory titles given

FIG. 2.6

Juan de Alcega, detail of the title page from *Libro de Geometría, Práctica y Traça*. Published by Guillermo Drouy, Madrid, 1589. Woodcut. The Metropolitan Museum of Art, New York, Rogers Fund, transferred from the Library, 41.7.

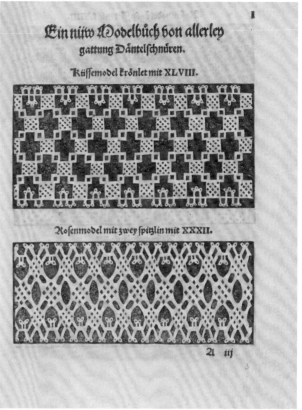

to each pattern (FIG. 2.8). The relative obscurity of "Frau RM" (active mid-sixteenth century) might indicate that, like many women in the early modern period, she operated in the gray zone between institutional professionalism and the sphere of the "amateur."[26] Yet it is quite possible that in her day, through her laces and work as a teacher, she had become something of a local celebrity, in which case the initials on the title page might have sufficed to convey her identity to a local audience of buyers. While history—at least for the time being—has forgotten that name, she should almost certainly be placed on par with her better-known successors Isabella Catanea Parasole (ca. 1565/1570–ca. 1625), Rosina Helena Fürst (1642–1709), and Margaretha Helm (1659–1742).[27]

The acknowledgment of RM's contribution is nevertheless an important step forward, especially if we consider that, only four years earlier, the brothers Giovanni Battista (active 1546–1602) and Marchio Sessa (active 1506–1563) published *Le pompe* (Venice, 1557), the first and arguably most important lace book to be issued during the sixteenth century, without naming the artist who designed its patterns (FIG. 2.9).[28] Based on the impresa printed on the title page and the vocabulary of shapes used in the lace patterns, Lotz has suggested that they might have been the work of Pagano. Throughout his career, Pagano showed great dedication to the genre of the textile pattern book. During the 1530s, he cut blocks for several booklets issued by the Venetian

FIG. 2.7 (LEFT)
RM, title page from *Nüw Modelbüch von allerley gattungen Däntelschnür*, published by Christoph Froschauer, Zurich, ca. 1561. Woodcut. Zentralbibliothek Zürich, RaP 108_page 5.

FIG. 2.8 (RIGHT)
RM, *Nüw Modelbüch von allerley gattungen Däntelschnür*, published by Christoph Froschauer, Zurich, ca. 1561. Woodcut. Zentralbibliothek Zürich, RaP 108_page 9.

publisher Nicolò Zoppino (1478/1480–1544), before publishing under his own name from 1542 onward. Excluding *Le pompe* and the subsequent *Libro secondo*, he issued seven distinct pattern books in multiple editions between 1542 and 1568, bringing his output to at least thirty-two publications.[29] Pagano's activities offer valuable insight into the market for these booklets. In certain years, as many as four distinct pattern books were printed on his presses, and intervals without publications in this area were invariably followed by greater activity in the following year(s). Barring examples of exceptional popularity, it seems it took anywhere from one to three years for a specific edition to go out of stock, after which a new edition would be printed.[30] Demand for Pagano's books, in particular, may also have been influenced by contemporary trends in fashion, as he was the first publisher to offer pattern books dedicated to specific techniques, including *punto tagliato* (cutwork) and *punti in aere* (embroidered patterns on a minimal textile ground; FIG. 2.10). The specificity of these patterns strongly suggests the involvement of a skilled professional. Whether that person was Pagano himself, or whether he instead worked closely with a (group of) skilled practitioner(s) to translate their designs into print by way of his woodblocks and presses, remains unclear.

The Venetian artist Federico Vinciolo (active ca. 1587–1599) might be considered the first celebrity lacemaker who also published his designs. Most likely invited to come to France by Queen Catherine de Medici (1519–1589) herself, he filled several books with lace designs, which were published in Paris between 1587 and 1623.[31] As Lotz has

FIG. 2.9

Matteo Pagano (?), *Le pompe: Opera Nova*. Published by Giovanni Battista and Marchio Sessa, Venice, 1557. Woodcut. The Metropolitan Museum of Art, New York, Harris Brisbane Dick Fund, 1937, 37.74(1–31).

56   Femke Speelberg

noted, the choice of Paris as the place of publication marked a notable shift. Previous French pattern books had been published almost exclusively in Lyon, and up to that moment—unlike today—the capital had contributed little to the worlds of fashion and textile design.[32] With the French court now more permanently settled in and around Paris, much changed in this respect. An engraving by Abraham Bosse (1602/1604–1676), made around 1638, shows just how central fashion had become to Parisian life during the period that Vinciolo was active in France. It depicts a gallery of shops within the Palais de la Cité, where—next to books—two stands were dedicated entirely to the sale of fashionable accessories, including a large selection of lace ruffs, borders, and hand-kerchiefs (FIG. 2.11). According to the text below the image, the people represented are aspiring courtiers and chevaliers, there to display their savoir faire of the latest styles worn at court by making (or feigning to indulge in) such fashionable purchases.[33] In a similar vein, in her discussion of Giacomo Franco's *Habiti delle donne venetiane* (Venice, ca. 1591–1610), Ann Rosalind Jones has pointed out that lace accessories formed an excellent means to distinguish oneself but could also be used to assimilate with the higher

FIG. 2.10

La Gloria et l'Honore di Ponti Tagliati, E Ponti in Aere. Published by Matteo Pagano, Venice, 1556. Woodcut. The Metropolitan Museum of Art, New York, Harris Brisbane Dick Fund, 1929, 29.59.1(1–32).

Within the etching, text on banner: A GALERIE DV PALAIS.

Inscription below image (four columns):

Tout ce que l'Art humain a jamais inuenté
Pour mieux charmer les sens par la galanterie,
Et tout ce qu'ont dupas la grace et la beauté,
Se descouure a nos yeux dans cette Gallerie.
Bosse in. et fe.

Jcy les Caualiers les plus aduantureux
En lisant les Romans s'animent à combatre ;
Et de leur passion les Amans languoureux
Flattent les mouuemens par des vers de Theatre.

Jcy faisant semblant d'acheter deuant tous
Des gands, des Euantails, du ruban, des danteles ;
Les adroits Courtisans se donnent rendez-vous,
Et pour se faire aimer, galantisent les Belles.

Jcy quelque Lingere à faute de succez
A vendre abondamment, de colere se picque
Contre des Succeaneurs qui parlant de procez
Empeschent les Chalands d'aborder sa Boutique.
le Blond le ieune excud Auec Priuilege du Roy.

classes by literally "dressing up." In his book, Franco (1550–1620) intended to show how Venetian women of different classes dressed for a variety of occasions, but without reading the accompanying descriptions, it proves virtually impossible to distinguish between the *dogaressa*, the wife of a merchant, and a notorious courtesan (FIGS. 2.12 AND 2.13). All are depicted wearing a very similar "uniform of lace."[34]

The concept of upward mobility through dress also played a part in the choice of women from the French royal family as the dedicatees of Vinciolo's pattern books. His first book, for example, was dedicated to the reigning Queen Louise of Lorraine (1555–1601) and included her portrait as well as that of her husband, King Henry III (1551–1589; FIGS. 2.14 AND 2.15). The presentation of the queen as the primary reader or user of Vinciolo's booklet spoke to the general prestige and authority of the work. In addition, it offered the wider category of "secondary readers"—who arguably formed its true target

FIG. 2.11

Abraham Bosse, *Galerie du Palais.* Published by Jean I Le Blond, Paris, ca. 1638. Etching. The Metropolitan Museum of Art, New York, Rogers Fund, 1922, 22.67.16.

audience—an ideal, living embodiment of the qualities to which they themselves could aspire.[35] The inclusion of contemporary (female) dedicatees can therefore be seen as an important pendant to mythological heroines such as Arachne, Penelope, and Lucretia, who were frequently invoked in textile pattern books to inspire virtuous behavior.[36] While the dedicatees are often credited with similar virtues, an additional function they fulfilled in the context of the pattern books was undoubtedly that of fashion icons. Queen Louise in particular formed a perfect spokesperson for Vinciolo's work, as she is consistently portrayed wearing a lace ruff or collar according to the latest fashions. For his second book, Vinciolo and his publisher Jean Le Clerc (1560–1621/22) found a welcome successor in the sister of King Henry IV (1553–1610), Catherine de Bourbon (1559–1604; FIG. 2.16).[37] In turn, her niece Elisabeth of Bourbon (1602–1644) became the dedicatee of Isabella Catanea Parasole's *Fiori d'ogni virtu* (Rome, 1610), later republished as the *Teatro delle Nobili et Virtuose Donne* (Rome, 1616; SEE FIG. 2.22).[38]

Aside from Vinciolo's French publications, the most important contributions to the genre of lace pattern books were all created in Italy. Their extreme popularity is illustrated by the great number of publications that were issued during the last decade of the century. The year 1591, in particular, is marked by an unusually high number of new pattern books, the most important of which were the first three installments to the *Corona delle Nobili et Virtuose Donne* by Cesare Vecellio (1521–1601). The dedications in the three books—all to Viena Vendramina Nani (second half of the sixteenth century), the wife of one of the nine procurators of San Marco—are signed and dated by Vecellio on January 20, January 24, and June 15, respectively, indicating that they were all part of one concentrated campaign.[39] Vecellio was no stranger to large-scale productions, as he had recently completed work on the costume book *De gli habiti antichi et moderni di diversi*

FIG. 2.12 (LEFT)
Giacomo Franco, "The Wife of a Merchant" from *Habiti delle Donne Venetiane*. Published by the author, Venice, ca. 1591–1610. Engraving. The Metropolitan Museum of Art, New York, Harris Brisbane Dick Fund, 1934, 34.68.

FIG. 2.13 (RIGHT)
Giacomo Franco, "The Notorious Courtisan" from *Habiti delle Donne Venetiane*. Published by the author, Venice, ca. 1591–1610. Engraving. The Metropolitan Museum of Art, New York, Harris Brisbane Dick Fund, 1934, 34.68.

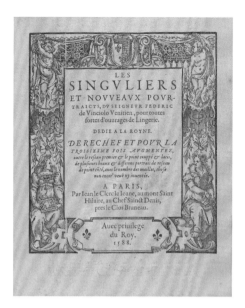

parti del mondo (Venice, 1590), which contained 420 illustrations depicting habits of dress from all over Europe as well as parts of Africa and Asia (FIG. 2.17). His lace books are characterized by their consistency in form and presentation, and they set the standard for all other pattern books that were issued in the following years. Like Vinciolo, he presented his patterns in white on a dark ground but adjusted the format of his booklets to that of an oblong quarto (FIGS. 2.18 AND 2.19). The popularity of Vecellio's *Corona* is illustrated by the numerous direct copies by publishers such as Matteo Florimi (active 1581–1613) and Giovanni Bazachi (active ca. 1590–ca. 1650), and it also undoubtedly formed the inspiration for the Roman publications of Isabella Catanea Parasole (FIG. 2.20).[40] The similarity of her first two books, *Specchio* and *Studio delle virtuose donne* (Rome, 1595; 1597), to those of Vecellio can be considered as one of the main reasons why her work was not given more accolades by Arthur Lotz in his *Bibliographie der Modelbücher*.[41] Even though his book engaged with women's work, the emancipation of women artists was not among his main priorities in 1933. However, the importance of Parasole's place in the world of printmaking has since been discussed by various authors, most prominently by Evelyn Lincoln, who published her feature article on Parasole's botanical and lace illustrations in 2001.[42] Frederika Jacobs has further proposed that Parasole was, in fact, one of the first female printmakers to create prints that were based on her own inventions, an element that also stood out to Lotz amid the sea of copies that were being issued by her male counterparts in this period.[43] The fact that Parasole could proudly sign the title pages of her books "Dissegnati da Isabetta Catanea Parasole" staked a humble yet significant claim for the hundreds if not thousands of (now) nameless women who were active in the field of lacemaking across Europe at the time.[44]

The lace-book genre reached its zenith in the early seventeenth century, when some of the most luxurious pattern books were printed. Most were notably larger than the

FIG. 2.14 (LEFT)
Federico de Vinciolo, title page from *Les Singuliers et Nouveaux Portraicts*. . . . Published by Jean Le Clerc, Paris, 1588 (3rd ed.). Woodcut and letterpress. The Metropolitan Museum of Art, New York, Rogers Fund, 1918, 18.68(1).

FIG. 2.15 (RIGHT)
Federico de Vinciolo, *Les Singuliers et Nouveaux Portraicts*. . . . Published by Jean Le Clerc, Paris, 1588 (3rd ed.). Woodcut and letterpress. The Metropolitan Museum of Art, New York, Rogers Fund, 1918, 18.68(4).

FIG. 2.16 (OPPOSITE)
Jan (Johannes) Wierix, *Portrait of Catherine de Bourbon*. Published by Paul de la Houve, Paris, 1600. Engraving. The Metropolitan Museum of Art, New York, Harris Brisbane Dick Fund, 1923, 23.28.3.

Joan. Wierx
sculpsit
1600.

Qui void ce beau portrait cette Auguste aparence
Void tout L'honeur du Monde et l'abregé de cieux
Cest le plaisir de l'ame, et le mirouer des yeux
Princesse des Vertus aufi bien que de France.

Auec priuil: du Roy

Paul. de la Houue
excudebat
au Palais

Catarina Borbonia Henrici IV Galliæ regis soror.

older publications, providing room to depict intricate lace designs true to scale. Cesare Vecellio, again, seems to have led the way in this development with the publication of his *Libro quinto* of the *Corona* (Venice, 1596), later published by Alessandro de' Vecchi (active 1570–1629) under the new title *Ornamento nobile* (Venice, 1620).[45] The book is largely dedicated to so-called *bavari*, which were a type of modesty cover worn by Venetian women to conceal their chest in situations when their low-cut dresses were not deemed appropriate (FIG. 2.21). Vecellio had treated the subject before, in the third installment of his *Corona*, but there the designs were presented in reduced size and with multiple patterns squeezed together on the small plates, making it more difficult to appreciate the intricacies of the individual designs.

Parasole followed Vecellio's example in the *Fiori d'ogni virtu* (Rome, 1610), which can be considered her absolute masterpiece (FIG. 2.22). The frontispiece added to the second edition of the book (Rome, 1616) by the publisher Mauritio Bona (active ca. 1609–ca. 1670) truly gave the work the sense of grandeur it deserved. Rather than a simple title description in letterpress, the lace book was graced with an elaborate engraving, possibly executed by the prolific engraver Francesco Villamena (ca. 1565–1624) after a design that had been made specifically for this book (FIG. 2.23).[46] The coat of arms, at top, refers to the young princess Elisabeth of Bourbon, whose likeness may also have been captured in the portrait medallion below, although the age of the woman depicted has raised questions in this respect. As Evelyn Lincoln has argued, the picture seems to blend characteristics

FIG. 2.17

Christoph Krieger after Cesare Vecellio, *De gli habiti antichi et moderni di diversi parti del mondo.* Published by Damiano Zenaro, Venice, 1590. Woodcut. The Metropolitan Museum of Art, New York, Rogers Fund, 1906, transferred from the Library, 21.36.146.

Ouurages de point Couppé.

B iij

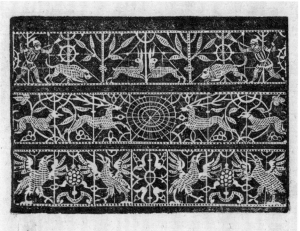

LAVORO DE PONTO INARIA.

FIG. 2.18 (TOP LEFT)

Federico de Vinciolo, *Les Singuliers et Nouveaux Portraicts.* . . . Published by Jean Le Clerc, Paris, 1588 (3rd ed.). Woodcut. The Metropolitan Museum of Art, New York. Rogers Fund, 1918, 18.68(10).

FIG. 2.19 (TOP RIGHT)

Cesare Vecellio, *Corona delle Nobili et Virtuose Donne: Libro I.* Published by the author, Venice, 1601 (8th ed.). Woodcut. The Metropolitan Museum of Art, New York, Rogers Fund, 1918, 18.67.2(8).

FIG. 2.20 (RIGHT)

Isabella Catanea Parasole, *Studio delle virtuose Dame.* Published by Antonio Fachetti, Rome, 1597. Woodcut and letterpress. The Metropolitan Museum of Art, New York, Harris Brisbane Dick Fund, 1918, 18.67.1(7).

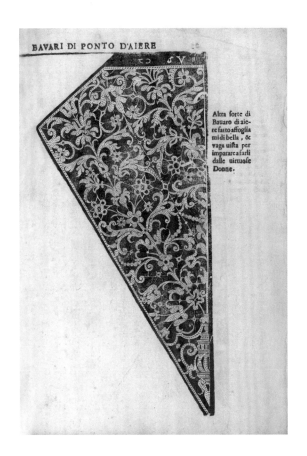

Altra forte di Bauaro di aie-re fatto affoglia mi di bella , & vaga uifta per imparare a farfi dalle uirtuofe Donne.

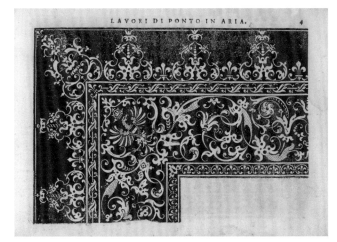

of both the artist and her dedicatee, leaving it up to the reader to decide whose face adorns this treasure book of lace designs.[47] Indeed, Parasole's book is the only textile pattern book to contain a portrait, and in that sense the only one that truly followed suit in the recent development of trade publications toward increased self-representation.[48] Yet for all its qualities, it was not Parasole's work, but that of her contemporary Bartolomeo Danieli (active 1610–1643), that stood out to Arthur Lotz in this respect. In all likelihood, this was not simply due to the fact that Danieli identified himself as a man of the trade on his title page but can also be attributed to Danieli's choice of the etching needle over the more traditional method of woodblock printing. Lotz greatly appreciated the sense of personality that shone through in Danieli's quintessential designs and the steadfast manner of his hand, signaling that his idea of self-expression was greatly influenced by the notion of the *peintre-graveur*, or artist-printmaker (FIG. 2.24).[49]

When Danieli stepped onto the scene with his first pattern book, he may have done so with the intention to rival the work of Parasole. He published the work in December 1610, nine months after Parasole had published her *Fiori d'ogni virtu*, with the very similar title *Fiore pretioso d'ogni virtu*, thus seemingly underlining that his work was slightly more precious and delicate than that of his Roman colleague.[50] It is unlikely, however, that he could have foreseen at the time that he would indeed ultimately have the final word. His subsequent publications turned out to be the only original lace designs to be published in Italy until the 1640s, when the genre as a whole disappeared for several decades. When textile pattern books began to be printed again from the late seventeenth

FIG. 2.21 (LEFT)
Cesare Vecellio, *Ornamento nobile . . . (Libro V of the Corona).* Published by Alessandro de' Vecchi, Venice, 1620 (2nd ed.). Woodcut and letterpress. The Metropolitan Museum of Art, New York, Harris Brisbane Dick Fund, 1933, 33.64.1(14).

FIG. 2.22 (RIGHT)
Isabella Catanea Parasole, *Teatro delle Nobili et Virtuose Donne. . . .* Published by Mauritio Bona, Rome, 1616 (2nd ed.). Woodcut and letterpress. The Metropolitan Museum of Art, New York. Rogers Fund, 1919, 19.51(12).

TEATRO DELLE NOBILI ET VIRTVOSE DONNE
DOVE SI RAPPRESENTANO
varij Diſegni di Lauori nouamente
Inuentati, et diſegnati da Eliſabetta
Catanea Paraſole Romana.

FIG. 2.23 (TOP)

Francesco Villamena (?), possibly after Rosato Parasole or Bernardino Parasole, frontispiece from *Teatro delle Nobili et Virtuose Donne. . . .* Published by Mauritio Bona, Rome 1616 (2nd ed.). Woodcut and letterpress. The Metropolitan Museum of Art, New York, Rogers Fund, 1919, 19.51(1).

FIG. 2.24 (BOTTOM)

Bartolomeo Danieli, *Vari disegni di merletti*. Published by Agostino Parisini and Giovanni Battista Negroponte, Bologna, 1639. Etching. The Metropolitan Museum of Art, New York, Harris Brisbane Dick Fund, 1937, 37.47.2(12). Cat. 30.

century onward, the majority were once again dedicated to embroidery, rather than lace. What had remained, however, was the notion that authors deserved recognition for their work. Most of the new textile pattern books therefore revealed the name of the artist responsible for the designs: a concept that even took hold in the domestic world of the eighteenth- and nineteenth-century amateur, as illustrated by the numerous surviving copybooks that are proudly adorned with a title page containing the name of their maker (FIG. 2.25).

FIG. 2.25
Mary Frances Matilda Wroughton, copy book of embroidery patterns, ca. 1830–35. Pen and ink and graphite. The Metropolitan Museum of Art, New York, Harris Brisbane Dick Fund, 1940, 40.48.3.

1   Arthur Lotz, *Bibliographie der Modelbücher: Beschreibendes Verzeichnis der Stick- und Spitzenmusterbücher des 16. und 17. Jahrhunderts* (Leipzig, Germany: Karl W. Hiersemann, 1933).
2   Arthur Lotz, "Die Spitzenmusterbücher des Bartolomeo Danieli," *Berliner Museen* 52, no. 3 (1931): 63–65.
3   Arthur Lotz, *Bibliographie der Modelbücher: Beschreibendes Verzeichnis der Stick- und Spitzenmusterbücher des 16. und 17. Jahrhunderts*, 2nd ed. (Stuttgart, Germany: Anton Hiersemann; London: Holland Press, 1963), cat. no. 64. All subsequent references to this work in this essay refer to the second edition.
4   As with modern examples, early modern weaving patterns are generally represented as a geometric pattern on a grid. They correspond to the drawdown (diagram of the weaving pattern). Information about the threading, tie-up, and treadling (diagrams of how to thread the loom, connect the treadles to the shafts of the loom, and operate the treadles for a specific pattern) is not given.
5   Lotz, *Bibliographie der Modelbücher*, 114; and Carmen Bambach, "Leonardo, Tagliente, and Dürer: 'La scienza del far di groppi,'" *Achademia Leonardi Vinci: Journal of Leonardo Studies & Bibliographie Vinciana* 4 (1991): 76. For a brief history of the emergence of the genre in English, see Femke Speelberg, "Fashion & Virtue: Textile Patterns and the Print Revolution, 1520–1620," *Metropolitan Museum of Art Bulletin* 73, no. 2 (Fall 2015); and for a full overview of the earliest surviving textile pattern books, see Lotz, *Bibliographie der Modelbücher*.
6   For these remarks, see the written instructions in Giovanni Antonio Tagliente, *Essempio di recammi*, 3rd ed. (Venice: Giovanni Antonio di Nicolini da Sabio e i Fratelli, 1530), the Metropolitan Museum of Art, New York, Harris Brisbane Dick Fund, 1935 (35.75.3(1–55)), at 35.75.3(50–55).
7   Ibid.
8   The Venetian printmaker Nicolò Zoppino, for example, included designs after Nicoletto da Modena (active ca. 1500–ca. 1520) and the Hopfer family in his pattern books. The German printmaker Johannes Sibmacher (1561–1611) copied grotesque designs published by the French printmaker Jacques Androuet du Cerceau (ca. 1510/20–1585/86), and Giovanni Ostaus (active ca. 1554–91) included designs by Heinrich Aldegrever (ca. 1502–1555/61) and Virgil Solis (1514–62) in his *La vera perfettione del disegno di varie sorti di recami*. Lotz, *Bibliographie der Modelbücher*, cat. nos. 32, 74, 96. Christian Egenolff (1502–1555) printed animal motifs in his pattern book, which he is known to have used in several of his *Kreuterbücher* as well. In turn, Giovanni Ostaus included several elegantly designed illustrations of mythological scenes and landscapes that had undoubtedly been conceived as book illustrations for a different

publication altogether. Lotz, *Bibliographie der Modelbücher*, cat. nos. 13, 96; and Evelyn Lincoln, "Models for Science and Craft: Isabella Parasole's Botanical and Lace Illustrations," in "Illustrations as Visual Resources," ed. William B. MacGregor and Louis Marchesano, special issue, *Visual Resources* 17, no. 1 (2001): 11, 14.
9   The plate appears in Matteo Pagano's *Trionfo di virtu* (Venice), first published in 1559. This pattern book is a composite of blocks deriving from the workshops of Giovanni Antonio Tagliente and Nicolò Zoppino, and the block of the coffered ceiling was likely first used by the latter in one of his textile pattern books published during the 1530s. Lotz, *Bibliographie der Modelbücher*, cat. nos. 64, 65, 68, 74, 79, 98; see also *Trionfo di virtu: Libro novo* (Venice: Matteo Pagano, 1563), 5r, the Metropolitan Museum of Art, New York, Harris Brisbane Dick Fund, 1937 (37.47.1(8)).
10   Carmen Bambach has suggested that Tagliente may have based his instructions on a lost text by Leonardo da Vinci (1452–1519), or a paraphrase after it. She also emphasized the fact that Tagliente spoke of little other than the knotwork designs in his text. Bambach, "Leonardo, Tagliente, and Dürer," 72–98.
11   Tagliente, *Essempio di recammi*, 35.75.3(50–55):
    Tutti gli famosi maestri, & illustri inventori de ogni arte et scienza conchiudono, che chiunque vuol dar cominciamento all' imparar di ciascuna honesta industria, & disciplina, come sarebbe a dire, uno vuol imparar leggere, imprima ha di mestieri dar principio a cognoscer la lettera A, & dopo la lettera B, & cosi dal principio per insin al fine bisogna sequire, Simelmente quelli che vogliono imparare a disegnare una figura intiera inanzi che egli si porga a tirar fuori detta figura intiera, gli fa bisogno imparare a disegnare uno occhio, una orecchia, una mano col braccio, un piede, una testa integra, & a poco, a poco tutte le membra del corpo humano, le quali sapendo ben disegnare, potra etiamdio trasportare, & lo corpo intero propotionatamente formare. Trovo ugualmente a pian piano passo esser bisogno seguir l'arte del disegnare con precetti in quella ammaestrevoli. (All the famous masters and illustrious inventors of any art and science conclude that whoever desires to begin to learn any form of honest industry or discipline, for example, one would like to learn how to read,

they have to start their undertaking first by knowing [learning] the letter A, and then the letter B, and so one must persist from beginning to end. Similarly, those who want to learn how to design a figure in its entirety, before they apply themselves to drawing out this entire figure, they will need to learn how to draw an eye, an ear, a hand with an arm, a foot, an entire head, and then little by little all the limbs of the human body, which once you know how to draw them well, you can move them [in place] and form the body in its entirety according to its proportions. I think it necessary to learn the art of designing by taking slow steps with precepts that are easy to learn.) Translation by the author.

12 The glossary manner in which various types of threads and stitches are mentioned, without further technical instruction, suggests that the booklet presupposes a certain body of ready knowledge and skill in its readers. The absence of subject-specific technical instruction is a pervasive phenomenon among early modern textile pattern books. This often leads to some confusion due to their modern classification in the category of so-called how-to books, or instruction manuals. In actuality, they have more in common with cookbooks, which offer a variety of recipes without explaining elementary techniques such as how to dice or what it means to sauté a vegetable.

13 Tommasso Garzoni, *La piazza universale di tutte le professioni del mondo* (1585; Venice: Giovanni Battista Somasco, 1587), 490–91, quoted in Lincoln, "Models for Science and Craft," 18.

14 For this phrase, see the closing address to the reader in Matteo Pagano, *Giardineto [sic] novo di punti tagliati et grapposi per exercitio & ornamento delle donne* (Venice: Matteo Pagano, 1554), the Metropolitan Museum of Art, New York, Rogers Fund, 1921 (21.15.1bis(1–48)), at 21.15.1bis(26).

15 Lotz, *Bibliographie der Modelbücher*, cat. no. 2.

16 Ibid., cat. nos. 8, 9, 12, 13, 15.

17 Renner's initials, "NR," were added to only a few of the woodblocks from which the designs were printed.

18 Lotz, *Bibliographie der Modelbücher*, cat. no. 22.

19 The first book dedicated to bobbin lace, *Le pompe*, was published by the brothers Sessa in Venice in 1557, followed by the *Libro secondo* in 1560. Christoph Froschauer published a lace book in Zurich in the early 1560s. Lotz, *Bibliographie der Modelbücher*, cat. nos. 23, 95, 100.

20 Peter Burke, "Reflections on the Frontispiece Portrait in the Renaissance," in *Bildnis und Image: Das Portrait zwischen Intention und Rezeption*, ed. Andreas Köster and Ernst Seidl (Cologne, Germany: Böhlau 1998), 160–61.

21 The idea for the portraits had already been in place before the publication of the first edition but could not be executed in time. The 1568 edition includes 144 portraits. In eight cases, Vasari chose to print an empty frame, emphasizing that veracity was preferred over the inclusion of fictive or generic portraits. The portraits were also published as a separate collection. The first edition of the *Ritratti* appears to have been issued in conjunction with the *Vite* in 1568, but subsequent editions were published independently, well into the 17th century. Laura Moretti and Sean Roberts, "From the *Vite* or the *Ritratti*? Previously Unknown Portraits from Vasari's *Libro de' disegni*," *I Tatti Studies in the Italian Renaissance* 21, no. 1 (2018): 105–6, 108–9.

22 Evelyn Lincoln, "The Jew and the Worms: Portraits and Patronage in a Sixteenth-Century How-to Manual," *Word & Image* 19, nos. 1 and 2 (January–June 2003): 86–99.

23 This idea is reflected in the contemporary interest in building collections of illustrious men and women through their representation in portraits, whether through paintings, coins and medals, or—importantly—print. Burke, "Reflections on the Frontispiece Portrait," 154; and Moretti and Roberts, "From the *Vite* or the *Ritratti*?," 113.

24 RM, *Nüw Modelbüch von allerley gattungen Däntelschnür*

(Zurich: Christoph Froschauer, ca. 1561); and Lotz, *Bibliographie der Modelbücher*, cat. no. 23.

25 Ibid.

26 Elizabeth Alice Honig, "The Art of Being 'Artistic': Dutch Women's Creative Practices in the 17th Century," *Woman's Art Journal* 22, no. 2 (Autumn 2001–Winter 2002): 31.

27 For a discussion of the latter two, see Moira Thunder, "Deserving Attention: Margaretha Helm's Designs for Embroidery in the Eighteenth Century," *Journal of Design History* 23, no. 4 (2010): 409–27.

28 Lotz, *Bibliographie der Modelbücher*, cat. no. 95.

29 Ibid., cat. nos. 80–82, 85–87, 98.

30 Based on a tabulation by the present author of his output between 1542 and 1560. The years 1543, 1550, 1554, and 1558 show the highest output of pattern books. No books were printed in the years 1545, 1547, 1552, and 1555.

31 Lotz, *Bibliographie der Modelbücher*, cat. nos. 110, 128, 147.

32 Ibid., cat. no. 110.

33 Sophie Join-Lambert and Maxime Préaud, eds., *Abraham Bosse, savant-graveur: Tours, vers 1604–1676*, exh. cat. (Paris: BnF; Tours, France: Musée des Beaux Arts de Tours 2004), cat. no. 158.

34 Ann Rosalind Jones, "Labor and Lace: The Crafts of Giacomo Franco's *Habiti delle donne venetiane*," *I Tatti Studies in the Italian Renaissance* 17, no. 2 (September 2014): 418.

35 Brian Richardson, *Women and the Circulation of Text in Renaissance Italy* (Cambridge: Cambridge University Press, 2020), 38, 40.

36 Speelberg, "Fashion & Virtue," 39–46.

37 Federico de Vinciolo, *Les secondes œuvres et subtiles inventions de lingerie* (Paris: Jean Le Clerc, 1594); and Lotz, *Bibliographie der Modelbücher*, cat. no. 128.

38 Ibid., cat. no. 143.

39 Ibid., cat. nos. 116–18.

40 Ibid., cat. nos. 123, 136.

41 Ibid., cat. nos. 129, 132.

42 Lincoln, "Models for Science and Craft."

43 Frederika Herman Jacobs, *Defining the Renaissance Virtuosa: Women Artists and the Language of Art History and Criticism* (Cambridge: Cambridge University Press, 1997), 18, 187; Lia Markey, "The Female Printmaker and the Culture of the Reproductive Print Workshop," in *Paper Museums: The Reproductive Print in Europe, 1500–1800*, ed. Rebecca Zorach and Elizabeth Rodini (Chicago: David and Alfred Smart Museum of Art; Chicago: University of Chicago Press, 2005), 51–74; and Lotz, *Bibliographie der Modelbücher*, cat. no. 129.

44 Jones, "Labor and Lace," 406, 407; and Tiziana Plebani, "I segreti e gli inganni dei libri di ricamo: Uomo con l'ago e donne virtuose," in "I liberi di colore nello spazio atlantico," ed. Federica Morelli and Clément Thibaud, special issue, *Quaderni storici* 50, no. 1 (April 2015): 212.

45 Lotz, *Bibliographie der Modelbücher*, cat. no. 120.

46 The preparatory drawing for this title page was recently rediscovered in the collection of the Metropolitan Museum of Art. While credit was previously given to the artist Andrea Lilio (Italian, ca. 1560–ca. 1635), the work is now thought to be designed by one of Isabella's family members, either Rosato Parasole (Italian, documented 1592–1622) or Bernardino Parasole (Italian, 1594?–before 1642). Furio Rinaldi, "The Roman Maniera: Newly Discovered Drawings," *Metropolitan Museum Journal* 52 (2017): 136–38.

47 Lincoln, "Models for Science and Craft," 44–46.

48 It is possible that the genre scenes depicted on the title pages of Rosina Helena Fürst's embroidery books, published from around 1666 onward, represent the Fürst family, but this is not entirely certain. Lotz, *Bibliographie der Modelbücher*, cat. nos. 60–62.

49 Lotz, "Die Spitzenmusterbücher des Bartolomeo Danieli," 65.

50 Lotz, *Bibliographie der Modelbücher*, cat. no. 144.

3 "Monstrous Ruffs" and Elegant Trimmings: Lace and Lacemaking in Early Modern Italy

Paula Hohti

L ACEMAKING BECAME AN IMPORTANT FORM of economic, social, and cultural activity in sixteenth- and seventeenth-century Italy. By the early sixteenth century, young women working in convents and charitable institutions were producing Italian lace commercially, and by the second half of the sixteenth century, the industry saw rapid growth in the production of both needle lace, created with a needle and single thread, and bobbin lace, made with multiple threads.[1] Surviving visual images and lace objects demonstrate the rich variety of fashionable lace that was produced by Italian lacemakers during the early modern period. These include a range of lace from narrow borders and edges of fine linen or silver and gold thread (FIGS. 3.1–4) to large and expertly worked pieces of lace that were formed into ruffs, collars, cuffs, and lace trimmings according to contemporary fashions (FIG. 3.5).

The quintessential accessory between the years 1560 and 1620 was the large ruff, which developed during the second half of the sixteenth century from a tiny frill or a small lace edging into an elaborate wired lace collar or a full ruff tied around the neck (FIG. 3.6). Round ruffs, embellished with many variations of beautiful points of Italian needle lace, became especially extravagant all over Europe and assumed at times such enormous proportions that some of them were called "millstones."[2] The abundant use of lace and its purely decorative function were often disapproved by moralists who regarded the fashion for "great and monstrous Ruffes . . . clogged with gold, silver, or silke lace of stately prince" as frivolous and wasteful.[3] The stunning quality and appearance of late Renaissance lace ruffs, worn by both men and women, and the skill of the contemporary lacemakers are evident in numerous portraits. A painting from 1640, representing Cosimo II de' Medici, Maria Maddalena d'Austria, and their son Ferdinando, provides an example of the types of elaborate collars and ruffs in fine needle lace worn by wealthy aristocratic men and women in the period (FIG. 3.7). Some rare examples of these types of ruffs have survived in European museums, including one in the Textilmuseum St. Gallen's collection (SEE FIG. 1.12) and another conserved in the Livrustkammaren, Stockholm (FIG. 3.8).

The increasing production and popularity of lace is visible not only in painted portraits but also in the large number of printed pattern books that laid out designs for needle and bobbin laces. According to Ann Rosalind Jones, over 110 of these books were printed for the first time between 1523 and 1600 in a number of towns that had achieved a level of expertise in book printing, including editions by Venetian and Roman printers such as Cesare Vecellio (1521–1601), Matteo Pagano (1515–1588), Giacomo Franco (1550–1620), and Isabella Catanea Parasole (ca. 1565/1570–ca. 1625; SEE CHAP. 2).[4] Surviving lace pieces suggest that the patterns were familiar to lacemakers. There are close resemblances, for example, between motifs in a *reticella* needle-lace border made around 1600 and designs in Cesare Vecellio's *Corona delle Nobili et Virtuose Donne* (1591; SEE FIG. 3.1; SEE ALSO FIG. 2.21).

The cultural significance of lace, and the laborious and time-consuming process of making lace accessories and trims, meant that thousands of women in Italy, both in the city and in the countryside, produced lace for the European fashion market by the seventeenth century.[5] These women played a key role in the development of lace in Europe, in terms of both technique and design.

(TOP TO BOTTOM)

FIG. 3.1
Reticella needle-lace insert, Italy, ca. 1600. Linen. Textilmuseum St. Gallen, Gift of Leopold Iklé, 1905, 00895. Cat. 11.

FIG. 3.2
Bobbin-lace border, Italy, probably Venice, 1600–20. Linen. Textilmuseum St. Gallen, Gift of Leopold Iklé, 1905, 01005. Cat. 20.

FIG. 3.3
Punto in aria needle-lace border, Venice, 1630–50, reworked in the 19th century. Linen and cotton. Textilmuseum St. Gallen, Acquired from the Estate of John Jacoby, 1954, 00079. Cat. 36.

FIG. 3.4
Bobbin-lace trimming, Milan, northern Europe, or western Europe, 1580–1620. Metal thread with silk core and gold sequins. Textilmuseum St. Gallen, Gift of Leopold Iklé, 1904, 00096.1-2. Cat. 15.

FIG. 3.5
Punto a fogliame needle-lace
collar and cuffs, Italy, ca. 1600,
reworked in the 19th century. Linen.
Textilmuseum St. Gallen, Gift of
Leopold Iklé, 1904, 00402.1-3.
Cat. 43.

Paula Hohti

FIG. 3.6
Anasttasio Fontebuoni, *Cosimo I de Medici, Grand Duke*, 1602–03. Oil on canvas. Palazzo Medici Riccardi, Prefettura, Florence.

Contemporary travelers noted the skill and creativity of Italian lacemakers. On his visit to Italy in 1594 and 1595, the Englishman Fynes Moryson (1566–1630) wrote that "women of Italy are curious workers with the needle, of whom other nations have learned to make the laces commonly called cutworkes."[6] But how did lacemaking evolve, who were the makers and wearers of lace, and how was lace production organized in Renaissance Italy? This essay focuses on the development of lace and lacemaking in Italy, outlining how the lace industry grew from a home-based occupation into a highly commercialized activity and investigating how and by whom lace was made and used and how fashion laces were regarded and regulated in society. The essay demonstrates that, although fine lace is often associated only with the wealthy high-ranking elites, making and wearing lace held economic and cultural importance at all levels of society.

Lace Production in Italy

Italian Renaissance lacemakers made two types of lace: bobbin lace, made on a cushion by twisting and braiding a number of threads wound on separate bobbins; and needle lace, made with a needle and thread and constructed by means of tiny stitches built up on top of guiding threads pinned onto a pattern. The two techniques were often combined in a single object to achieve the desired decorative effect. A linen lace collar in the collection of the Rijksmuseum, Amsterdam, for example, is made of reticella and *punto in aria* needle lace with a small interlaced bobbin border (FIG. 3.9).[7]

Bobbin laces made in Venice, Genoa, and Milan enjoyed a high international reputation in Europe during the sixteenth century. The female author of a pattern book, known by her initials "RM," published by Christoph Froschauer in Zurich around 1561, wrote that as far back as 1535 Venetian merchants had carried into Switzerland bobbin lace of "so lovely a quality" that Swiss women set out at once to copy it (SEE CHAP. 2).[8] Europeans admired above all Venetian needle lace, which became one of Italy's most expensive and prestigious foreign products, purchased and worn by men and women of the highest

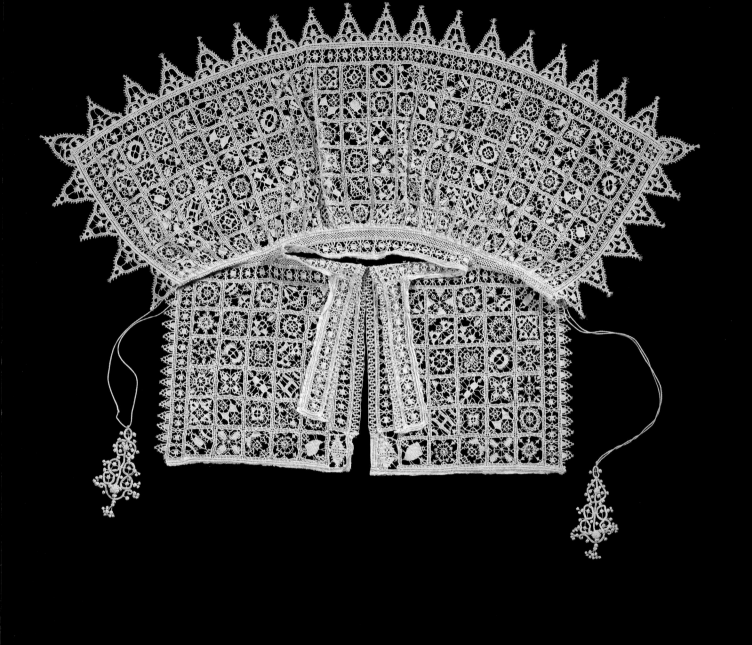

rank all over Europe.[9] Due to the level of technical sophistication, Venetian needle-lace production grew considerably during the sixteenth century and continued to dominate the markets during the seventeenth century. Praising the skills of Venetian needle-lace makers, one enthusiastic commentator, also Venetian, claimed that "there never was a nation which could dream of taking precedence to Venice in making needlepoint lace appreciated by the likes of emperors and princesses across the mountains."[10]

Most lace, unlike other textile crafts such as embroidery and sewing, was created by women who operated outside the formal guild system.[11] The division of female and male spheres within the art of lacemaking seems to have been relatively clear. White laces worked with linen thread used for edgings on linen collars, cuffs, napkins, and other linen items that were frequently laundered, such as those seen on the laundry line in a sixteenth-century mural painted by Alessandro Allori (1535–1607), were closely associated with "feminine works" (FIG. 3.10). Men were involved with the production of bobbin-made borders of precious-metal thread, which were traditionally made by the "passementiers" who belonged to the old professional guild.[12] The superb value and prestige of the glittering gold lace with which passementiers worked can be seen in the detail of another painting by Allori, which shows an unfinished border of gold bobbin lace on a cushion (FIG. 3.11).

FIG. 3.10
Alessandro Allori, *Women at Work around a Balcony*, 1587–90. Fresco. Palazzo Pitti, Florence.

The Makers of Lace

Lacemaking was associated originally with Venetian noblewomen who made needlework in their leisure time. Needle lace was regarded as a suitable pastime for elite women and a respected form of work because it could not be confused with "real" manual labor.[13] Many Italian editions of printed lace pattern books were dedicated to "virtuous" noblewomen, underscoring the close connection between aristocratic women and lacemaking. For

FIG. 3.11
Alessandro Allori, *Annunciation*,
1603. Oil on canvas. Accademia,
Florence.

"Monstrous Ruffs" and Elegant Trimmings

example, *Le pompe: Libro secondo*, published in 1560 in Venice, was addressed to "beautiful and virtuous women so that they can make all sorts of works, that is laces of diverse sort."[14]

Skilled women could create their lace designs by cutting out a page of the book and pinning or stitching it onto a parchment or linen backing, which provided the ground for the lacework. The design was then transferred onto the ground by pricking the pattern with pins and rubbing fine powder over the small holes so as to make the lines of the pattern visible on the ground fabric below.[15] Italian pattern books, such as the *Corona delle Nobili et Virtuose Donne* by Cesare Vecellio, also contain designs showing how to enlarge or reduce any pattern (**FIG. 3.12**).[16] A surviving lacework in the collection of the Museo del Merletto on the Venetian island of Burano shows an unfinished lace design prepared and begun on parchment (**FIG. 3.13**).

Venetian noblewomen were important patrons of lace. As several lace historians have shown, some of the most powerful women even set up schools in Venice for needle lace. In 1595, Morosina Morosini, the wife of Doge Marino Grimani, opened a workshop in the parish of Santa Fosca where 130 laceworkers were overseen by the *maestra* Catterina Gardin.[17]

Lace was made by elites as well as by women in more modest homes. Bobbin lace was seen as particularly suited for popular skill because it required simple, easily accessible tools that could either be purchased from the local market or made at home (pins, a cushion, a few bobbins, linen thread, and paper). The author of Froschauer's 1560 pattern book was a lacemaker and teacher of lacemaking and praised bobbin lace especially for the reason that women had quickly learned how to make it and the costs

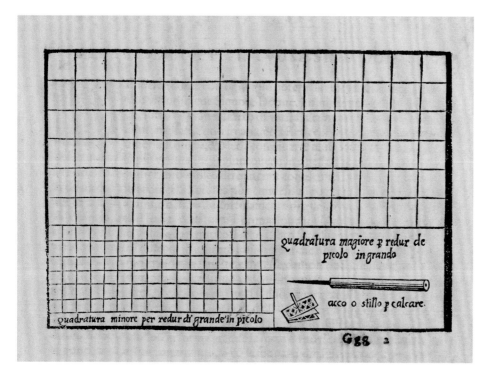

FIG. 3.12

Cesare Vecellio, *Corona delle Nobili et Virtuose Donne: Libro I*. Published by the author, Venice 1595, plate Ggg 3. The Newberry Library, Chicago, Case W 927.942 Special Collections.

Paula Hohti

of the materials were low: "Now you can buy a piece of lace at low-cost," she writes, "quickly put it on, and thus save many of the prior expenses."[18] The Textilmuseum St. Gallen collection includes a linen bobbin-lace insert that is similar to some of the designs in Froschauer's book and was probably intended for use on domestic textiles (FIG. 3.14).

Household inventories drawn up for non-elite homes from the late sixteenth and early seventeenth centuries in Italy testify to the presence of tools to make bobbin lace. A Florentine fishmonger's wife, for example, had a cushion to make bobbin lace, while the Venetian rag dealer Antonio Rossati's household goods, listed upon his death in 1555, included an unfinished small collar "worked with stitches and attached to a bob-bin-lace cushion."[19] Many also listed bobbin-made laceworks in the homes of Venetian artisans, such as collars and aprons with bobbin-made lace edgings. The wife of the Venetian mason Augustin Zorzi had two aprons made of cambric with "laces and trims of bobbin-lace"; the Venetian baker Maffio Truscardi had eleven *braccia* of bobbin-made lace trim for aprons as well as a woman's shirt made of home-woven linen with a collar and cuffs of bobbin lace; and a Venetian lime maker named Carlo del Iseppo had three handkerchiefs, all made of home-woven linen with bobbin edgings.[20]

Bobbin-made lace created in ordinary Italian homes could be produced for domestic use, but many women of the artisan classes and humble households took up lacemaking as a means of earning their living. According to the sixteenth-century author Federico Luigini, "the poor found benefit and income from the work while the rich, noble, and beautiful women also achieved honour."[21]

FIG. 3.13
Incomplete *punto Venezia* needle-lace border, Venice, ca. 1670. Signed "PAB Pietro Cupilli San Cassan Inv." Linen, ink, parchment, and linen canvas. Fondazione Musei Civici de Venezia.

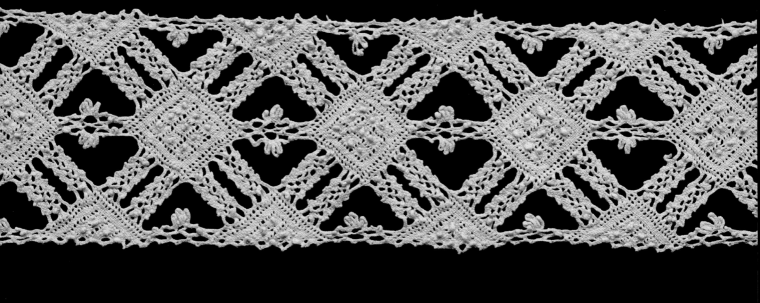

Lace in Convents and Charitable Institutions

As the demand for lace increased, laceworks began to be produced for sale on a greater scale, especially in convents and charitable institutions that were set up to house young orphan girls until their future was decided. In the 1590s Fynes Moryson recorded that in one of the institutions on Giudecca island in Venice, the Pia casa delle Cittelle (also known as Zitelle), the young girls "lived by the work of their hands."[22] By the second half of the seventeenth century, lacework in these Venetian institutions was often highly organized and commercialized. Noting the scale of lace production in Venetian religious and lay institutions, the French ambassador to Venice reported in 1671 to the French minister Jean-Baptiste Colbert (1619–1683) that "all the convents of the religious and all the poor families live off this work [of lacemaking] here."[23]

Convents and charitable institutions provided an important source of labor for the Italian lace industry. There were as many as thirty monasteries in sixteenth-century Venice, along with several charitable institutions that were established between 1520 and 1577 as temporary homes or protective shelters for the terminally ill, repentant prostitutes, women in dire conditions, and young orphan girls. Based on seventeenth-century documents, it has been calculated that there were as many as 2,500 nuns in Venetian convents alone.[24] Many of these women were engaged in lacemaking. The early eighteenth-century painting *Nuns at Work*, made by the follower of Alessandro Magnasco, presents a rare scene from an Italian convent where nuns, supervised by their mistress, are gathered to preform their daily tasks of spinning and lacework (**FIG. 3.15**).

Lacemaking was seen as especially suitable for poor girls living in charitable institutions because it kept them busy and therefore reduced allegedly dangerous idle time. Benedetto Palmi, the founder of the abovementioned Casa delle Cittelle, noted the social and moral benefits of needlework for the poor girls in the organization's house rules,

FIG. 3.14 (ABOVE)
Bobbin-lace insert, Italy, second half of the 16th century. Linen. Textilmuseum St. Gallen, Gift of Leopold Iklé, 1904, 00668. Cat. 27.

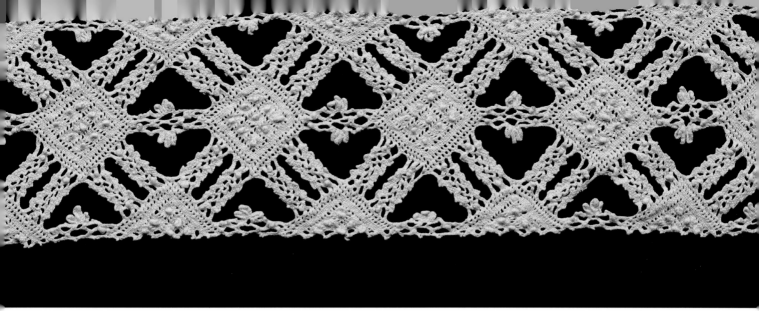

stating that "the continuous and diligent practice of obedience and needlework at which they attend in order to provide for themselves makes them women of worth, and banishes from this House idleness, root of every Evil."[25] Most institutions taught girls textile crafts, including lacemaking. A painting by Carlo Caliari (1570–1596), *The Foundation of the Casa del Soccorso* (1595), shows how the girls' supervisor has left her lace pillow for a moment and is showing a pupil how to make a stocking. Another girl is shown netting, a second is sewing, and a third is making bobbin lace (FIG. 3.16).

Women in convents and charitable institutions also carried out lace commissions from private citizens. Isabella Campagnol's research reveals how these commissions were often demanding and that some of the lace objects were so large and complex that work could take months or even years to complete. This fact is evident in a letter by the mid-seventeenth-century writer Arcangela Tarabotti (the author of the text *Inferno monacale*, or "Monastic Hell"), who was forced into a convent against her will, in which she laments that she is working on a "*punt'in aria* needle lace" that is driving her "crazy."[26]

Some of the lace made in convents and charitable hospitals was also produced for sale directly to merchants who bought lace either by unit or on specific commission on behalf of their customers. Sketches for a handkerchief with needlepoint lace dated between 1580 and 1590 probably illustrate some of the variations of lace designs that could be purchased through merchants (FIGS. 3.17 AND 3.18).

However, the women and girls making these lace pieces were not allowed to negotiate their commissions, sell their own work, or keep the profits of the sale. The daily work was assigned to each woman by the supervisors, or *maestre*, who were in full charge of the quality and the marketing of the resulting lace. It seems that, as a general rule, about two-thirds of the profit from the sale of lace was used to support the institutions themselves and one-third was set aside for the dowries of the young women who made the lace.[27]

FIG. 3.16 (LEFT)
Carlo Caliari, *The Foundation of the Casa del Soccorso* (altarpiece from the church of Santa Maria del Soccorso), 1595. Oil on canvas. Gallerie dell'Accademia, Venice, 400.

FIG. 3.17 (OPPOSITE, ABOVE)
Designs for handkerchiefs, Florence, 1580–90. Pen and ink on paper. Courtesy of Ministero per la cultura/ Archivio di Stato di Firenze, GM 143, cc. 555-556.

FIG. 3.18 (OPPOSITE, BELOW)
Bobbin-lace handkerchief, Italy, 17th century. Linen and silk. The Metropolitan Museum of Art, New York, Rogers Fund, 1939, 39.123.1.

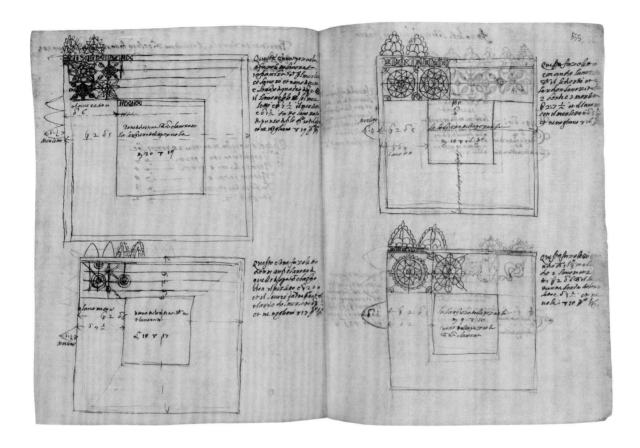

Consuming and Regulating Lace

Lace was a luxury product, and prices for fine pieces were high. Tarabotti noted that the cost of the lace produced for a noble customer was "no less than sixty ducats per braccio."[28] The convent of Sant'Anna also sold lace for very high prices, charging 360 ducats for a *braccio* of a border of very fine three-dimensional lace produced in the nunnery. Even the prices for secondhand lace works were high. In an auction organized in 1599 for the sale of the inheritance of Salutio Gnechi, a *cavaliere del doge*, seven ounces of "punto" (in aria) needle lace was priced at 1,115 lire, or 174 ducats.[29] This meant that a piece of fine lace of around 24 inches (60 centimeters) could be more valuable than the entire year's salary of a master artisan, and five times higher than the value of a lacemaker's yearly labor.[30]

Because of the luxury and cost associated with fashionable lace, its use in Italy was regulated by sumptuary laws. This was certainly the case in Venice as well as in other smaller Italian cities. Sumptuary laws issued in the Tuscan city of Lucca in 1595, for example, justified the need for regulations, lamenting that "it was not long ago when a prohibition was issued for certain embroidered collars for the high expense; today, they make collars of network with stitches on top of stitches . . . the prices of these have become intolerable."[31]

Such laws often gave specific guidelines regarding both the materials and the size of lace trims. Officials in Florence, where round lace ruffs had become popular in the early seventeenth century, published a sumptuary law in 1638 that stated that "no man or woman in the city of whatever condition" was allowed to use any other kind of lace in ruffs and collars than linen and that it was not to be wider than one and three-quarter inches (4.5 centimeters; one *soldo e mezzo di braccio*). Lace trims of silk, on the other hand, could be used for mantles and head coverings, as long as they did not exceed the width of eight *denari di braccio*, or a little less than seven-eighths of an inch (2 centimeters). The laws stipulated that none of these items could include lace made of gold thread.[32]

As these sumptuary laws suggest, lace was not an exclusive product of the Italian elites. Lace was made in a variety of qualities and was widely available ready-made from the city's street sellers as well as from local women who sold lace door to door at cheaper price points. Historian and curator Patricia Allerston's work suggests that street sellers often closely followed the latest fashion trends. She quotes a popular carnival song from the period, which urges passersby to purchase lace collars from a street seller because "they are of the latest style."[33] Some of the laces that were produced for broader consumption copied Genoese, Milanese, or Venetian laces (**FIG. 3.19**) or replaced precious materials with cheaper ones. For example, the bobbin insert referenced above (**SEE FIG. 3.14**) is similar in design to the gold lace worn by Eleonora of Toledo (1522–1562) in her portrait painted by Agnolo Bronzino (1503–1572) around 1560, but it is executed in linen (**FIG. 3.20**).

Documents that record offenses against sumptuary laws demonstrate that seventeenth-century Italian male artisans had a particular taste for lace ruffs and that men often broke these laws by wearing excessive amounts of lace.[34] For example, in March 1638, the specially appointed Florentine officials known as *birri*, who were stationed

FIG. 3.19 (BELOW)
Lace from Abbruzzo, copied from Genoese laces, 17th century, from Elisa Ricci, *Old Italian Lace*, vol. 2. London: W. Heinemann; Philadelphia, J. B. Lippincott, 1913. Archive.org, Getty Research Institute.

FIG. 3.20 (OPPOSITE)
Agnolo Bronzino, *Eleanora of Toledo*, ca. 1560. Oil on panel. Courtesy National Gallery of Art, Washington, DC, Samuel H. Kress Collection, 1961.9.7.

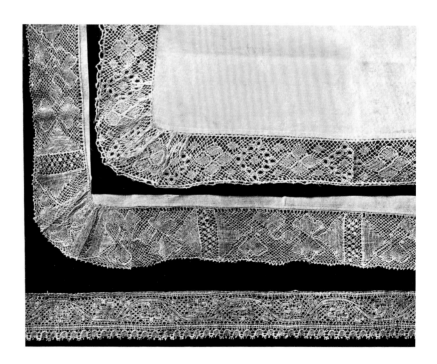

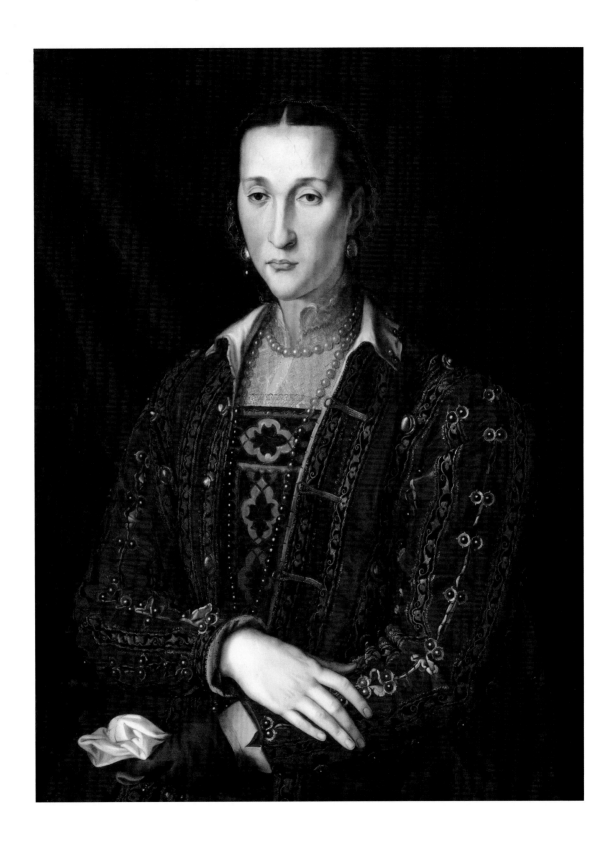

"Monstrous Ruffs" and Elegant Trimmings

in front of city taverns, marketplaces, piazze, and church entrances to ensure that clothing regulations were respected, confiscated a collar worn by a butcher named Nicolò because it was trimmed with lace that was too wide. Documentation of the court case is preserved in the Florentine state archives (FIG. 3.21).[35]

Household inventories confirm that lace was not only made for wealthy elites but also widely worn further down on the social scale. Data from Venice, Siena, and Florence between 1550 and 1650 show that many men and women had their clothing and accessories decorated with different types of bobbin-lace borders; fine lace cuffs and edgings of reticella; punto in aria needle lace of fine Venetian or Flemish linen thread; and fine gold lace that was attached to handkerchiefs, muffs, sleeves, and gowns. Some of these items are described as being in line with contemporary fashion. For example, the relatively modest Venetian innkeeper Giovanni Suster had among his possessions a small, delicate handkerchief edged with gold lace as well as three lace collars and cuffs, "all in current style."[36]

In the sixteenth and seventeenth centuries, wearing and making lace in Italy was an economically, socially, and culturally significant activity that cut across the social layers of the entire population. Not only was lace produced for and worn by all, but numerous Italian women—both noble and poor— worked in homes, cloisters, and hospitals in order to supply lace to European consumers, creating some of the most expensive and most desired textiles produced for the fashion markets in the early modern period.

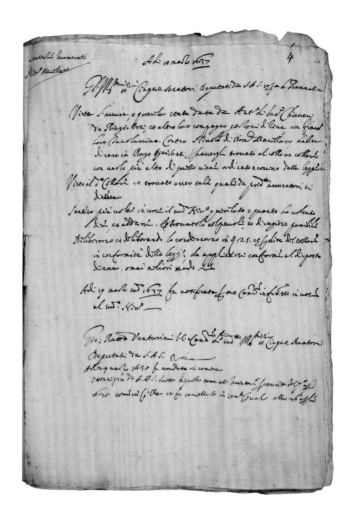

FIG. 3.21

Page from a sumptuary law case concerning a Florentine butcher, 1683. Pen and ink on paper. Courtesy of Ministero per la cultura/Archivio di Stato di Firenze, Pratica segreta, b. 176 (March 10, 1638): fol. 4r.

1 This research has been carried out as part of the Refashioning the Renaissance project. It has received funding from the European Research Council (ERC) under the European Union's Horizon 2020 research and innovation program (grant agreement no. 726195). For the development of fashion in lace, see Ann Rosalind Jones, "Labor and Lace: The Crafts of Giacomo Franco's *Habiti delle donne venetiane*," *I Tatti Studies in the Italian Renaissance* 17, no. 2 (September 2014): 412–15; and Anne Kraatz, *Lace: History and Fashion*, trans. Pat Earnshaw (New York: Rizzoli, 1989), 42–46. For the origins of lace as fashion, see Lidia Sciama, "Lacemaking in Venetian Culture," in *Dress and Gender: Making and Meaning*, ed. Ruth Barnes and Joanne B. Eicher (New York: Berg, 1997), 127.

2 Pat Earnshaw, *Lace in Fashion: From the Sixteenth to the Twentieth*

Centuries (London: B. T. Batsford, 1985), 15. For the fashion for ruffs and regional variations in styles, see Kraatz, *Lace*, 18; Santina M. Levey, *Lace: A History* (Leeds, UK: W. S. Maney & Son; London: Victoria and Albert Museum, 1983), 1; and Sciama, "Lacemaking," 128. The growing importance of lace accessories can be traced by comparing portraits by Palma il Vecchio (ca. 1480–1528), Titian (d. 1576), and Peter Paul Rubens (1577–1640) from the late 15th century to the late 16th and early 17th centuries. Initially, narrow lace edgings decorate the necklines and cuffs of women's shifts and men's shirts; by the end of this period, large separate lace collars, ruffs, and cuffs with elaborate designs are prominent.

3 Quoted in Levey, *Lace*, 12.

4 Jones, "Labor and Lace," 404. These books can be used to

reconstruct the development of lace from geometric cutwork with a gridlike structure to free-flowing patterns and *punto in aria*, or true needle-lace, technique. Levey, *Lace*, 21.

5   Isabella Campagnol, "Invisible Seamstresses: Feminine Works in Venetian Convents from the Fifteenth to the Eighteenth Century," in *Women and the Material Culture of Needlework and Textiles, 1750–1950*, ed. Maureen D. Goggin and Beth F. Tobin (Farnham, UK: Routledge, 2009), 168; and Kraatz, *Lace*, 7.

6   Quoted in Levey, *Lace*, 9.

7   For the basic lace techniques and terms, and for the origins and development of bobbin and needle lace, see Levey, *Lace*; Elisa Ricci, *Old Italian Lace*, 2 vols. (London: William Heinemann; Philadelphia: J. B. Lippincott Company, 1913); and for bobbin lace in particular, Lena Dahrén, "Printed Pattern Books for Early Modern Bobbin-Made Borders and Edgings," *Konsthistorisk tidskrift* 82, no. 3 (2013): 169–90.

8   Quoted in Ricci, *Old Italian Lace*, 1:24. For bobbin lace produced in Genoa and Milan, see Ricci, *Old Italian Lace*, 1:90.

9   See, for example, Kraatz, *Lace*, 12.

10   Quoted in Patricia Allerston, "An Undisciplined Activity? Lace Production in Early Modern Venice," in *Shadow Economies and Irregular Work in Urban Europe: 16th to Early 20th Centuries*, ed. Thomas Buchner and Philip R. Hoffmann-Rehnitz (Vienna: Lir Verlag, 2011), 64–65.

11   Kraatz, *Lace*, 18; and Campagnol, "Invisible Seamstresses," 179.

12   Dahrén, "Printed Pattern Books," 180.

13   For the early connections between needle lace and noble-women, see Jones, "Labor and Lace," 403; Campagnol, "Invisible Seamstresses," 168–69; and Ricci, *Old Italian Lace*, 1:134. The question whether lacemaking was initially an aristocratic pastime or whether it was in origin a "popular skill" has been debated; see Sciama, "Lacemaking," 130.

14   Dahrén, "Printed Pattern Books," 176: "Dove le belle et virtuose donne potranno fare ogni sorte di lavoro, cioè merli de diverse sorte, cavezzi, colari, maneghetti, & tutte quelle cose che le piaceranno" (Where beautiful and virtuous women will be able to do all sorts of work, that is, laces of different sorts, bands, collars, cuffs, & all those things that they will like.) Many other pattern books had similar dedications, such as that of Cesare Vecellio. Levey, *Lace*, 9.

15   Jones, "Labor and Lace," 405.

16   Ricci, *Old Italian Lace*, 1:255.

17   Levey, *Lace*, 9. For noblewomen's patronage of lace, see Jones, "Labor and Lace," 403; and Campagnol, "Invisible Seamstresses."

18   Jones, "Labor and Lace," 409. For the quotation, see RM, *New Pattern Book of All Kinds of Bobbin Laces* (1561), ed. and trans. Helen Hough (Arlington, TX: James G. Collins and Associates, 2018), 3, Internet Archive, https://archive.org/details/NewModelbook1561/mode/2up. For the original edition, see RM, *Nüw Modelbüch von allerley gattungen Däntelschnür* (Zurich: Christoph Froschauer, 1561), available online from the Zentralbibliothek Zürich, https://www.e-rara.ch/doi/10.3931/e-rara-5463.

19   Inventory of the fishmonger Tommaso di Salvadore Mariti, 1620, 12r, Magistrato dei pupilli, no. 2717, Archivio di stato di Firenze (hereafter abbreviated ASF): "Un tombola da far trine"; Inventory of the Venetian rag dealer Antonio Rossati, 1555, 12r, Cancelleria inferiore, Miscellanea, no. 39, 44 (1555), Archivio di stato di Venezia (hereafter abbreviated ASV): "Uno bavaro strazado e lavorado a ponto in tombola usado."

20   Inventory of the mason Augustin Zorzi, 1650, 1v, Giudici e petizion, Inventari, no. 361, 107, ASV: "Dette (traverse) sottile una di musolo con cordelle e merli, e doi di cambra con merli e cordelle a mazzette in tutto n. 3"; Inventory of the baker Maffio Truscardi, 1645, 1r–1v, Giudici e petizion, Inventari, no. 359, 93, ASV: "Brazza de cordella a mazzette da traverse largo n. 11" and "Camise da donna

de tella fatte in casa nove con suoi cavezzi, a mazzette et ago n. 35"; Inventory of the lime maker Carlo del q. Iseppo, 1620, 4v, Giudici e petizion, Inventari, no. 347, 89, ASV: "Tre facioli da man de tella fata in casa con merli a macete e gasi usadi."

21   Quoted in Dahrén, "Printed Pattern Books," 179n41.

22   Quoted in Allerston, "An Undisciplined Activity?," 67.

23   Ibid., 65–66.

24   Campagnol, "Invisible Seamstresses," 169–75; and Jones, "Labor and Lace," 407.

25   Quoted in Campagnol, "Invisible Seamstresses," 175. Venetian society was concerned that idleness might lead young women to immoral and indecent behavior. Sciama, "Lacemaking," 131.

26   Quoted in Campagnol, "Invisible Seamstresses," 172–73.

27   Sciama, "Lacemaking," 132; Allerston, "An Undisciplined Activity?," 68; Campagnol, "Invisible Seamstresses," 172; and Jones, "Labor and Lace," 409.

28   Quoted in Campagnol, "Invisible Seamstresses," 173.

29   For these examples, see Campagnol, "Invisible Seamstresses," 173; and Jones, "Labor and Lace," 408–11.

30   This valuation is based on lacemakers' estimated daily pay of as low as between 10 and 13 soldi and a little over 1 lira for an ordinary master artisan. For salaries of 16th-century artisans, see Paula Hohti, *Artisans, Objects and Everyday Life in Renaissance Italy: The Material Culture of the Middling Class* (Amsterdam: Amsterdam University Press, 2020), 155–59; and for estimated lacemakers' salaries, see Jones, "Labor and Lace," 406.

31   Quoted in Luigi Fumi, "La moda del vestire in Lucca dal secolo XIV al XIX," *Bollettino dell'Istituto Storico Artistico Orvietano* 54, no. 60 (2002–4): 554: "Non e molto che si fece prohibitone di certi collari lavorati, per la molta spesa che erano; hora si fanno collari di rete con punte e altri lavori sopra dette punte, che per quanto intendiamo, sono venuti a un prezzo intollerabile."

32   *Riforma, e Prammatica sopra l'uso delle perle, gioie, vestire, et altro per la Città & Contado di Firenze* (Florence: Massi e Landi, 1638), B3, 48v, and A4, 49r. I thank Michele Robinson for the translation of these documents.

33   Allerston, "An Undisciplined Activity?," 70, referring to Giovanni Croce, "Da Buranelle," in *Mascarate piacevoli et ridicolose per il carnevale a 4, 5, 6, 7 et otto voci: Di Giovanni Croce chiozotto; Libro primo* (Venice: Giacomo Vincenzi, 1590).

34   Paula Hohti, "Dress, Dissemination and Innovation: Artisan Fashions in Sixteenth- and Early Seventeenth-Century Italy," in *Fashioning the Early Modern: Dress, Textiles, and Innovation in Europe, 1500–1800*, ed. Evelyn Welch (Oxford: Oxford University Press/Pasold, 2017), 163.

35   "Un collare con merlo piu alto," quoted and translated in Michele Robinson, "Dirty Laundry: Caring for Clothing in Early Modern Italy," *Costume* 55, no. 1 (2021): 12. For the original, see Pratica segreta, b. 176 (March 10, 1638), fol. 4r, ASF. For the activities of Pratica segreta, see Giulia Calvi, "Abito, genere, cittadinanza nella Toscana moderna (secoli XVI–XVII)," *Quaderni storici* 110 (2002): 477–503.

36   Inventory of the innkeeper Giovanni Suster, 1634, 9v, Giudice di Petizion, Inventari, no. 360, 25, ASV: "Tre collari di tella da baston con merli fiamenghi, et tre para de maneghetti compagni il tutto alla moda," and 12v: "Un faciol de seda con merlo d'oro vechio." For Venetian punto in aria, see the inventory of the clothes seller Isach, 1634, 1r, Giudice di Petizion, Inventari, no. 354, 37, ASV: "Traverssa mussolo con lavor d'aiere." Further examples of lace among artisanal population can be found in the forthcoming online database, published online in 2022 by the Refashioning the Renaissance Project, https://refashioningrenaissance.eu/database/.

4 Antwerp, a Center of Lacemaking and Lace Dealing, 1550–1750

Frieda Sorber

S INCE THE EARLIEST DAYS OF LACE PRODUCTION in early modern Europe, the Southern Netherlands—which constituted most of modern-day Belgium and Luxembourg (including Antwerp and Brussels) from the sixteenth to the eighteenth century—played an important role in the development and commercialization of this luxury textile. The Flemish lace trade relied on makers, dealers, and consumers of various social classes and was largely concentrated in Antwerp and the surrounding region. Archival records that survive in a number of repositories shed light on early production and trade during this period. These include the important Plantin archives housed at Antwerp's Museum Plantin-Moretus, which, along with other documents preserved in the city's archives, elucidate the scope of an industry that at its height stretched from the Southern Netherlands to other European countries and overseas to clients in the Spanish Americas. This transmission of Flemish lace goods and lacemaking techniques helped solidify the region's reputation for high-quality needle and bobbin laces.

Plantin, Wholesale and Retail Lace Dealers in Mid-Sixteenth-Century Antwerp

September 1, 1567, was an important landmark in the life of Martine Plantin (FIG. 4.1): the fifteen-year-old girl spent her first day managing the shop that her father had rented in 1565 in Antwerp's Tapissierspand, the hall of the tapestry makers, which was at that time the equivalent of today's luxurious shopping malls.[1] Martine bought some blue paper (no doubt to wrap parcels of lace and lingerie) and sold half an ell and one-sixteenth of "breynaet" bobbin lace.[2] Her father, Christophe Plantin (ca. 1520–1589), and mother, Jeanne Rivière (ca. 1520–1596), had emigrated to Antwerp from France around 1550, when the city was a thriving metropolis comparable to Paris or London.[3] Christophe established himself as a book printer, publisher, and seller, quickly developing friendly relations with leading humanists and scientists of his day and publishing their books.[4] The couple had five daughters: Marguerite (1547–1594), Martine (1550–1616), Catherine (1553–1622), Madeleine (1557–1599), and Henriette (1561/1562–1640), all of whom are depicted on the right wing of Jacob de Backer's *Last Judgement* triptych, painted around 1580 (FIG. 4.2). The Plantin daughters received an excellent education; Madeleine acted as one of the editors of a polyglot Bible (among the most famous of Plantin's publications) when she was thirteen.[5] But Plantin was far more than a publisher with international connections; the book trade was often all but overshadowed by his other commercial activities.[6]

The Plantins also traded in luxury goods including pearls, precious stones, linens, embroidery, and lace.[7] This last facet of the Plantin business was often the domain of Jeanne, but Christophe, Martine, and Catherine appear often in the business records, which, exceptionally, have survived.[8] These papers, letters, and

FIG. 4.1
Peter Paul Rubens, *Portrait of Martine Plantin*, 1633. Oil on panel. Collectie Stad Antwerpen, Museum Plantin-Moretus, MPM.V.IV.052.

books that record sales, commissions, and production span the years 1556 to 1583 and, for the early history of bobbin and needle lace, constitute a unique source of information.[9]

The documents cover a very important period in Antwerp's history. By the early sixteenth century, the city had replaced Bruges as the commercial and artistic hub of the Southern Netherlands. At the same time, the political center of the Netherlands had moved from Mechlin to Brussels. Antwerp had attracted a large number of immigrants, and by midcentury, the population of the city is said to have included approximately 30 percent foreigners, most of whom were merchants or specialized craftsmen. Christophe Plantin must have been attracted to a city that held great promise for entrepreneurs. International contacts that extended far beyond the borders of western Europe opened up possibilities of marketing an increasing array of luxury products. It was in this climate that Plantin must have envisioned using his contacts in Paris to start dealing in lingerie and lace in his adopted city of Antwerp.[10]

The Plantin records contain the names of prominent Parisian lace dealers with whom Plantin did business. Pierre Gassen, who was referred to in numerous letters as "lingier de messieurs les frères du roy" (linens supplier to their highnesses the king's brothers), was the foremost.[11] Gassen would correspond with both Plantin and Catherine, who began communicating with him at age thirteen.[12] In the 1570s, linen and lace deals with Gassen would surpass 12,000 florins per year.[13] The business, which was conducted on the basis of mutual trust, was terminated in the 1580s for undocumented reasons. Another Parisian contact was the apothecary Pierre Porait, a friend from Plantin's youth. Martine sent him linen, embroidery, and lace and in return received "panaches, roses," and other luxury items made of feathers. She often referred to him in her letters and diaries as "mon oncle Maître Pierre Porait de Paris" (my uncle, Master Pierre Porait of Paris).[14] The Plantin sisters also supervised orders sent by the Parisian linen merchants Çayas and Nicolas Fournier. In addition to these Paris connections, Plantin also maintained close business contacts in Venice, Portugal, and Germany.[15]

Although business in Antwerp—including lace—boomed in the 1560s, the political and religious climate steadily grew worse. The Holy Roman emperor Charles V (1500–1558) was born in Flanders and was well liked, but his son Philip II (1527–1598) resided almost permanently in Spain and lost contact with his subjects in the Netherlands. This distance resulted in widespread discontent that culminated in the Spanish Fury, in which Habsburg armies violently destroyed Flemish cities and murdered their citizens. Spanish soldiers sacked Antwerp in 1576, which devastated parts of the city and sent many of its enterprising inhabitants, including lace merchants and lacemakers, to the Northern Netherlands (which would eventually be recognized as independent from Spain in 1648), Germany, France, and England.[16] Outbreaks of the plague and political troubles in France would bring luxury trades almost to a standstill in the 1580s.

Plantin's business records and letters referring to his commercial activities in lace and linen, which are by no means complete, offer valuable insight into the daily workings of the early lace trade. The archives also provide some clues as to the early development of bobbin and needle lace. The records from the 1550s mainly deal with embroidered linen and embroidered net, and some include the names of Plantin's suppliers and the items that they produced.[17] The Plantins traded in collars, cuffs, handkerchiefs, and coifs—often in large quantities. The simpler items were made of plain linen, but most were partly decorated. Other items are "gestipt" (stippled) or "gepaireld." "Stippen" is defined in a contemporary dictionary as embroidering with fine stitches.[18] It is tempting to interpret this as meaning the embroideries used to embellish shirts, collars, and cuffs (which did not yet include openwork), but early forms of openwork hems, also worked with tiny stitches, could match this description. "Gepaireld," which literally means "pearled," undoubtedly refers to the needle-made picots that were used as edgings on linen from at least the second quarter of the sixteenth century.[19] Initially widely spaced, they seem to have become more closely set over time and can be considered as an immediate antecedent of needle lace.[20] There is an absence of references to linens for use in the home (including napkins and tablecloths) and for the church (including albs, altar cloths, and the like) in the Plantin archives. What the Plantins did sell were fine linen fabrics and threads; these items were sometimes called "klooster draad" (convent threads), which no doubt refers to flax yarns suitable for fine embroidery and lacemaking.[21]

In the 1560s new terms appear in the Plantin records. In addition to the products sold previously, increasing amounts of "passementen" trimmings (no doubt early forms of bobbin lace) and "breynaet" were available. These items were always sold as lengths, and one consignment might consist of five hundred to six hundred ells. Like "stippen" and "pearlen," the word "breynaet" has completely disappeared from the Dutch language.

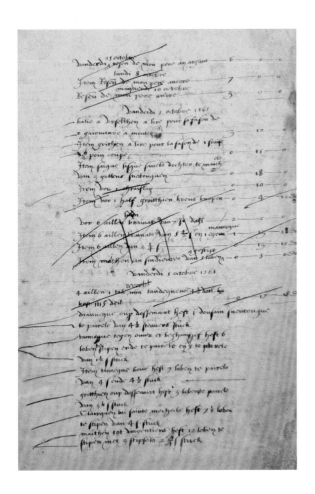

Today the verb "Breien" refers to knitting, but in the six-teenth century and in some contemporary Flemish dia-lects, it had a much broader meaning, including diverse techniques used to braid, knot, and interlace threads. Because some documents specify that breynaet was made on a pillow using bobbins, it is very likely that this term means "bobbin lace" in the Plantin business records. These mentions of tools indicate that the production of bobbin lace was a recent innovation in the early 1560s. What remains unclear, however, is whether passement and breynaet were always made with flax threads. In the seventeenth century, large quantities of mainly black silk bobbin lace were made in Antwerp.[22] Some of the passe-ments were sold by weight, which was the normal practice for bobbin lace when the cost of raw materials exceeded the cost of labor. Can one conclude, then, that some of the bobbin lace the Plantins sold was made of silver and gold thread? Both would have been readily available in Antwerp for use by silk and tapestry weavers and gold embroiderers, but because the Plantin archives do not include samples of the actual products sold, and because linen lace was sometimes sold by weight as well as length, it is difficult to know with certainty.[23]

However, the Plantin archives do provide detailed information on where the traded items were produced. The Plantin family members would supervise the execution of special commissions as well as the production of multi-ple items made according to the requirements and tastes of the buyer, sometimes in lots of over two hundred pieces. While still in their early teens, Martine and Catherine routinely traveled from Antwerp to Mechlin to supervise lacemakers in the town's *beguinage*, a community of lay religious women active in the Netherlands from the twelfth to the nineteenth century. In the 1560s the beguinage was well known for the quality of its embroidered nets, and price negotiations likely occupied at least some of the girls' time in Mechlin. The bulk of the Plantins' goods were traded through intermediaries, who were often enterprising women who had the products made by local workers. Antwerp and the surrounding villages, as well as Mechlin and Brussels, provided most of the labor. Martine oversaw more than thirty-five workers in Antwerp between 1565 and 1566, all of whom worked on contract. She recorded information about their dealings in her diaries (FIG. 4.3).[24] Embroidery and lace were also produced in the Netherlands in a town not very far from Antwerp called Breda, where the Plantins had family connections.

The Plantin archives include the names of middlemen as well as names of some of the lacemakers themselves, which is highly unusual for the period. Ledger books dating between 1563 and 1568 include approximately twenty names, among them Anna

FIG. 4.3
Martine Plantin's journal detailing commercial trade in cloth and lace, cords, etc., 1565–69. Ink on paper in leather-bound journal. Plantin Archives, Collectie Stad Antwerpen, Museum Plantin-Moretus, Arch, no. 440, fo. 2, recto.

Jourdains, Isabel Reyniers, Janneken van Dievelt, and Mayken Brawers.[25] Other names include Dinghen Verriet, who, like Tanneken Vertanghen, a *beguine* who served as an intermediary for the Plantins, lived in Mechlin and also supplied the family with thread.[26] Only one other official document includes details of this type: an ordinance issued in March of 1590 by the City of Ghent. The document argues against lacemaking as an occupation; citizens of the city could no longer find housemaids because lacemaking offered better pay.[27] As the ordinance stipulates, no one except young girls under the age of twelve living with their parents could continue any "travail aux fuseaux" (bobbin work). The girls and young women of Ghent were ordered to report their names, their place of residence, and the nature of their work to the town hall within eight days so that the city could determine whether it was acceptable.[28] The name of one middleman cited in the ordinance is "Pierre de Bruges alias Van Der Beke," but whether that means he resided in Bruges or not remains unclear; "de Bruges" may have been a surname. In summary, the connections revealed in the Plantin archive prove that from the outset, the early Flemish lace business was truly international. Thanks to this wide network of customers and manufacturers, knowledge of new techniques and designs must have spread rapidly to many parts of Europe.

Margaretha von der Marck, Fashion Purveyor and Businesswoman

As it did for Martine and Catherine Plantin, Antwerp figured prominently in the commercial dealings of Margaretha von der Marck (1527–1599), a member of the German nobility who acted as a purveyor of fashion to elite clients at several European courts.[29] Born in the Rhineland, Margaretha spent her long life there, as well as at her family's properties in the Ardennes and the Southern and Northern Netherlands (FIG. 4.4). In her early youth she spent a year at the court of the duc de Lorraine in Nancy, and at age seventeen, following her brother's death, she inherited much of her family's considerable fortune as well as the noble Arenberg title.[30] In 1547 Margaretha married Jean de Ligne, Baron von Barbançon (ca. 1525–1568); she was widowed when he died in his forties at the Battle of Heiligerlee. She would spend the next thirty years preserving the family estates. Margaretha's considerable talents enabled her to move in the highest social circles, to acquire noble titles, and to preserve the family patrimony during periods of political turmoil. In 1570 as "grande maîtresse de la Cour," she accompanied Elisabeth of Austria (1554–1592) on her bridal voyage to France for her marriage to Charles IX (1550–1574), and in 1576 Holy Roman emperor Maximilian II (1527–1576) bestowed upon Margaretha the title of "Gefürstete Gräfin" (imperial countess), which allowed the Arenberg family the right to vote in the Reichstag. She enjoyed the esteem of governors of the Spanish Netherlands, including Margaret of Parma (1522–1586; governor from 1559 to 1567), with whom she corresponded frequently between the years 1574 and 1585, as well as Alexander Farnese (1545–1592; governor from 1578 to 1592).[31] Many contemporaries wrote about Margaretha, among them the Dutch Calvinist historian Emmanuel van Meteren (1535–1612): "She was a wise and skillful lady."[32]

After her husband's death, Margaretha was faced with heavy taxes: over 120,000 florins was levied on her properties in the Northern Netherlands, and her estates in the

Frieda Sorber

FIG. 4.4

Margaretha von der Marck, from an album with eighteen portraits of the Croÿ and Arenberg families, ca. 1600. Leather binding, ink, gouache, and watercolor on parchment. Private collection.

Ardennes, the Spanish Netherlands, and the Eifel were plundered by Dutch looters. She was obligated to take on an additional debt of 12,000 florins when her eldest son, Charles (1550–1616), returned from a lavish three-year stay at the Spanish court. Widowed and deeply in debt, Margaretha had to be resourceful in raising money to satisfy her creditors.[33]

Although Margaretha's aristocratic status made her an unlikely businesswoman, she used her knowledge of textiles and her connections to European nobility to become a successful purveyor of fashion. Even before her husband's death, Margaretha had supplied ladies of the high nobility with fashionable fabrics and accessories. Letters between Margaretha and her sister Mechthild (1530–1603), who married Landgrave Ludwig Heinrich von Leuchtenberg (1529–1567) in 1550, about fashion-related matters occasionally resulted in Margaretha's sending merchandise to her sister for distribution beginning in the early 1560s.[34] Although this was not unusual at the time, Margaretha's commercial activities would expand considerably in later years, and she would eventually forge connections with clients across Europe.

Margaretha's surviving letters provide only a partial sense of her life and trading activity, but it is clear that she was involved in numerous lace-related transactions with affluent clients throughout Europe between 1565 and 1580. Her network stretched from the Southern Netherlands to France, Germany, Austria, and Italy. Margaretha dressed richly and fashionably, and women at various European courts were eager for her help to procure similar items. Linen fabrics intended for household use seem to have been Margaretha's most important merchandise, but shirts, collars, and hoods, as well as a variety of products ranging from sugar work, jewelry, and a dress made of gold cloth, were also important commodities.

In 1562 Margaretha sent her sister "quoiffes de Lassey," perhaps reminiscent of the lacis-work coiffes the Plantin family ordered from the Mechlin beguinage at the same time. In 1565 Hedwig, Duchess of Brunswick-Lüneburg-Harburg (1535–1616), asked Margaretha for samples of the "Huffen und Tuechen" (hoods and cloths) she was wearing.[35] While traveling in Italy in 1575, Margaretha met Eleanor of Austria, Duchess of Mantua (1534–1594), and Johanna of Austria, Grand Duchess of Tuscany (1547–1578). The sisters, daughters of Holy Roman emperor Ferdinand I, purchased textiles and trimmings from Margaretha over the next few years and may have been among her lace clients.[36] In 1577, Elisabeth, the dowager queen of France, having returned to Vienna after the 1574 death of her husband, King Charles IX of France (1550–1574), ordered rolls of patterned linen from Margaretha, probably for use in her household.[37] In 1579 Margaretha sent William, Duke of Jülich-Cleves-Berg (1516–1592), a selection of goods, including decorations for shirts, so that he could choose what to order.[38] Margaretha enjoyed a close relationship with William's four daughters and regularly supplied them with fashion-related items. She helped with preparations for their wedding garments; for example, she selected and instructed the tailors who would make a bridal skirt trimmed with "cantillia" (narrow bobbin lace often made of silver and gold) for the 1574 wedding of the second daughter, Anna.[39] Margaretha and her son Count Charles of Arenberg maintained an active correspondence with the Munich court about precious goods. Around 1570 or 1580, Margaretha sent lace from the Netherlands, and Charles sent horses and hunting gear.[40] Mechthild's son Landgrave Georg Ludwig (1563–1613) reminded his aunt Margaretha in 1582 that she should not forget to send him shirts, which may well have been adorned with fashionable embroidery and lace.[41]

During her lifetime, Margaretha corresponded with clients and dealers across Europe. She procured a portion of her goods from individuals in Cologne and also purchased items that were sent directly to the family seat of Arenberg (near Cologne). These items originated in the Spanish Netherlands, France, Italy, Spain, the Northern Netherlands, and Germany. In Antwerp she dealt with several merchants to purchase sugar, silk fabrics, gauzes, perfumes, *Ledertapete* (leather wall coverings), tapestries, linens, jewelry, and precious vases. Between 1578 and 1580, while in Antwerp, Margaretha ordered "passements de Milan," which might have been bobbin lace produced either in Milan or in Antwerp in the Milanese style. She may have met with some of these merchants again when she visited Antwerp in 1591.[42] An inventory taken following Margaretha's death in 1599 details numerous pieces of fine lace, hoods, collars, fine linens, and garments made from luxuriant textiles. The abundance and variety of goods suggest that Margaretha maintained a "stock" of items with which to supply her many clients.[43]

Margaretha's successful leveraging of her elite European connections to ensure a profitable business not only enabled her to retain her family's possessions and repay her debts but also made her a catalyst for the spread of fashion and luxury goods throughout the powerful European courts of Germany, Austria, Italy, France, and the Netherlands.

Royal Lace Commissions

While Antwerp remained a prominent center of lacemaking and dealing in the seventeenth and eighteenth centuries, lace made in Brussels was similarly known for its high quality. Brussels bobbin lace in particular was highly sought after by the Spanish and French courts and by elites elsewhere in Europe. In the early seventeenth century, the Spanish Netherlands were governed by Phillip II's daughter Isabella Clara Eugenia (1566–1633) and her husband, Archduke Albert of Austria (1559–1621; FIG. 4.5).[44]

ALBERTVS ET ISABELLA CLARA EVGENIA
AVSTRIACI BRABANTIAE DVCES.

FIG. 4.5

Jan Collaert II after Otto van Veen, *Portrait of Albrecht and Isabella Clara Eugenia*, 1600. Engraving, published by Hans Woutneel. Rijksmuseum, Amsterdam, RP-P-1908-2016.

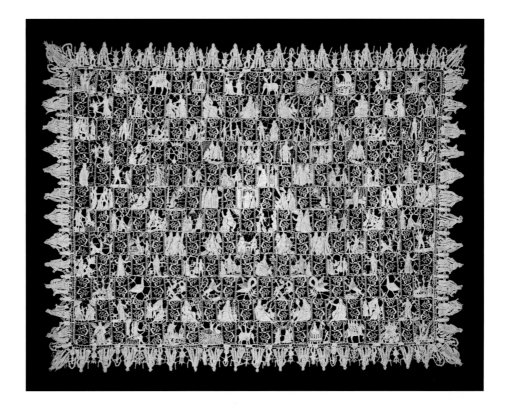

The couple were prominent supporters of the Counter-Reformation and made generous donations, which included valuable textiles, to churches in the Spanish Netherlands, Cologne, and Spain. Two unusual surviving lace coverlets in the Musées Royaux d'Art et d'Histoire (Royal Museum of Art and History) in Brussels and the Museum of Art and History in Geneva are associated with the ruling couple. Unfortunately, the provenance of these extraordinary objects is not confirmed, as only the record of their acquisition at the end of the nineteenth century is certain.[45]

The coverlet in Brussels is executed entirely in bobbin lace. Scholars and curators in the past have assumed it was made in 1599, when Albert and Isabella were married and gained control of the government of the Southern Netherlands (FIG. 4.6). However, a recent study by Ria Cooreman, curator of lace at the Royal Museum of Art and History in Brussels, has built on earlier attempts to determine the origin and precise date of the coverlet, revealing that this date is likely too early.[46] The coverlet's complex composition features coats of arms, portraits of Albert and Isabella and other European royalty to whom they were related, religious depictions, and scenes from an *Ommegang*—the ceremonial procession that welcomed the couple to Brussels, the most important city in the Southern Netherlands, in 1615.[47] Cooreman posits that the lacemakers who created this piece, which includes depictions of more than three hundred figures, were likely referencing printed images, including a series of twelve portraits published in 1593 by Flemish engraver Aegidius Sadeler (1570–1629). One section in particular supports a later date:

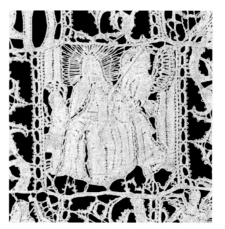

a depiction of Theresa of Avila based on a 1614 engraving by Flemish artist Antonius Wierix III (1555–1604; **FIGS. 4.7 AND 4.8**).[48] Other scenes and motifs are drawn from painted representations of the Ommegang that took place in Antwerp in 1615, meaning the coverlet must have been created in the early seventeenth century, likely between 1615 and 1621, and possibly as a gift to Isabella in commemoration of the 1615 event.[49]

The coverlet in Geneva, which is technically similar to the piece in Brussels, comprises bobbin-lace squares and sections of embroidered linen depicting coats of arms of the Spanish royal family and religious scenes (**FIG. 4.9**). It has not yet been the subject of a comparable in-depth analysis, but both coverlets are extraordinary masterpieces of lacemaking. Bobbin lace around 1600 consisted mainly of narrow bands with geometric patterns; the depiction of flowers and human figures was rare (**FIG. 4.10; SEE FIG. 3.14**). For example, what are probably the only Netherlandish lace samples from the early seventeenth century can be found in a small sample book in the Royal Museum of Art and History in Brussels that contains no identifying information (**FIG. 4.11**). These samples are perfectly preserved borders of bobbin lace with geometric designs, many created using finer flax threads than usual at the time.

The designers of the two sizable coverlets created large, bold compositions comprising dozens of scenes that each measure nearly eight inches square. Both coverlets are more than four and a half feet in length and width; such a surface area had likely

FIG. 4.7 (LEFT)
Antonius Wierix III, *St. Theresa*, ca. 1614–22. Engraving. The Metropolitan Museum of Art, New York, Harris Brisbane Dick Fund, 1953, 53.601.19 (143).

FIG. 4.8 (RIGHT)
Detail of a bobbin-lace coverlet depicting Archduke Albert and Isabella Clara Eugenia, Brussels, Southern Netherlands, ca. 1616–21. Musées Royaux d'Art et d'Histoire, Brussels, D.2543.00.

FIG. 4.9
Coverlet of thirty-two squares
(bobbin-lace squares alternating with
embroidered squares of openwork
and whitework), Southern
Netherlands, ca. 1599. Linen.
MAH Museum of Art and History,
City of Geneva, AD 6297.

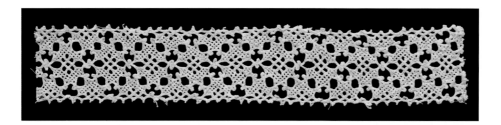

never before been produced in bobbin lace. As no archival documents relating to the coverlets have been found thus far, close analysis of the techniques can aid in revealing clues about the lacemakers involved in their creation. Because the lacemakers may have worked from line drawings inspired by engravings rather than from traditional bobbin-lace patterns, they were likely constantly developing new techniques and structures as they worked. If this assumption is correct, the coverlets are key pieces of technological innovation that must have been enormously beneficial for bobbin-lace-making skills in the Spanish Netherlands.[50]

While these two coverlets are unusual in their size as well as in their depiction of identifiable figures, three specially commissioned fragments of bobbin lace from the third quarter of the seventeenth century depict medallions with saints or monks (FIG. 4.12).[51] Another similar example—possibly a royal commission—is a border from the 1660s with the image of the Infante Charles (later Charles II), Crown Prince of Spain (1661–1700), pieces of which can be found in several collections (FIG. 4.13).[52]

FIG. 4.10 (TOP)
Bobbin-lace insert, Italy, 16th century. Linen. Textilmuseum St. Gallen, Acquired from the Estate of John Jacoby, 1954, 00969. Cat. 18.

FIG. 4.11 (BOTTOM)
Sample book, 1601–10. Lace and paper. Musées Royaux d'Art et d'Histoire, Brussels, D.0897.00.

FIG. 4.12 (OPPOSITE, LEFT)
Border with bobbin-lace representations of monks or saints and needle lace at edges of the mesh ground, second half of the 17th century. Linen. Collection MoMu Fashion Museum Antwerp, S76/8AB.

FIG. 4.13 (OPPOSITE, RIGHT)
Bobbin-lace border fragment depicting Charles II of Spain, Flanders, Southern Netherlands, probably Antwerp, 1665. Linen. Textilmuseum St. Gallen, Acquired from the Estate of John Jacoby, 1954, 00696. Cat. 56.

A number of other large-scale prestigious lace objects commissioned by the state were also produced by Flemish lacemakers in the eighteenth century. Among the most famous is the dress ordered in 1744 for Empress Maria Theresa of Austria (1717–1780).[53] Composed entirely of Brussels bobbin lace, the gown was unique and remarkable even compared to the high-quality, luxurious lace for which Flanders was known at that time. The gown's pattern pieces and matching palatine (cape) were made to shape and are an example of part lace. Over five months, multiple lacemakers created sections of the dress, which were then joined. The final garment, according to surviving records, was worth 25,000 guilders.[54] The resulting dress pleased the empress so much that she wore it for at least two full-length portraits, which depict it from slightly different angles (FIGS. 4.14 AND 4.15). Although the dress has not survived, a fragment in the Metropolitan Museum of Art shares motifs similar to those depicted in the portraits (FIG. 4.16).[55] Even more expensive was a dress made in 1760 for Isabella of Parma (1741–1763), the future wife of Maria Theresa's eldest son, Jozef, which was also commissioned by the state of Flanders for the couple's wedding in October that year. The existence of this dress is known only through archival records, including documents in the State Archives of Belgium. It was made with Brussels needle lace that alone cost more than 120,000 guilders, and as many as 1,800 lacemakers are said to have participated in its production.[56] Imperial commissions of this type likely sparked interest in large-scale, high-quality Brussels bobbin- and needle-lace objects in other countries. Large coverlets from the

mid-eighteenth century, often used at weddings and given as wedding gifts or to young mothers after the birth of a child, are preserved in many collections. A coverlet sold at auction in 2014 that is now on long-term loan to the Antwerp Fashion Museum incorporates motifs related to those on Maria Theresa's lace dress, including flowers, palm trees, and butterflies (FIG. 4.17).[57] Although there are no surviving archival documents relating to its commission and production, the coverlet is said to have been the property of the Bavarian ducal family before it came to the Spanish court in the early twentieth century.[58]

Archival Sources in Antwerp

Apart from the Plantin materials, most of the archival sources relating to lace production and trade in Antwerp date from the seventeenth and eighteenth centuries. The Antwerp city records office constitutes an important resource for information about the marketing of lace during this period. The "Insolvente Boedelskamer" (the Chamber of Insolvent Estates), as the name suggests, is the archive where the business records of insolvent companies and occasionally those that had ceased trading were deposited.[59] This repository houses a huge collection that includes parts of company archives, letters, and books from the seventeenth and eighteenth centuries. However, uncovering a full picture of the lace industry at this time is still challenging; firms dealing exclusively with lacemaking or selling were rare, despite the fact that it was an important commodity that was traded internationally by merchants dealing in luxury goods. As was the case for the Plantins, the sale of lace often went hand in hand with the sale of

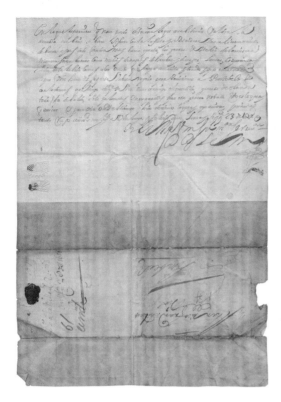

food and spices, gold and silver, jewelry, tapestries, gilt leather (*gouldleer*), woolen fabrics, and silks, as well as fashionable purses and gloves. Antwerp traders acquired this wide variety of wares locally or from other parts of Flanders and Brabant, notably Brussels.

Knowledge of how the Antwerp lace trade functioned can be derived primarily from business correspondence. Letters in the Antwerp city records office are supplemented by unstudied letters in the Moretus family archives and the Melijn family's late seventeenth-century letter books now in the Antwerp Fashion Museum.[60] These sources are complex, however, and they often provide only a partial picture of the industry. The Antwerp archives include letters written in many different languages (French, Dutch, German, English, Spanish, and Italian) and often also incorporate local dialects. Although the letters do not convey quantitative information about the extent of the lace trade, they do offer documentation of the numerous trade practices that were employed repeatedly throughout the seventeenth and eighteenth centuries, in particular related to terminology. Relatively small amounts of foreign lace, notably needle lace from Venice, were imported into Antwerp. Bobbin lace that was exported from Antwerp was referred to by various names. Brussels and Mechlin are the only cities represented in these names; other types were sold using trade titles that would suit the various foreign markets. For example, *point de la Reine* was both consumed locally and sent to France; *puntas*, *presillas*, and *filigranas* were sent to Spain and the Spanish colonies, to locations that are sometimes mentioned specifically, among them Mexico, Havana, and Lima (FIG. 4.18).[61] Lace made for export to Central and South America would travel from Antwerp to the Flemish port of Ostend on the North Sea and then sail to the port of Cadiz in Spain. Some of the lace was used locally in Spain, but most would continue across the ocean to be purchased and used in churches or worn by local residents in the Americas (SEE CHAPS. 6–8).

An Expanding Market for Flemish Lace

As the seventeenth century progressed, the fame of lace from Antwerp and the surrounding region (including Brussels and Mechlin) spread, and designs were adapted to specific markets. This was particularly true for bobbin lace made with continuous threads, known as straight lace. The flax threads used to create the highest-quality laces became increasingly finer and, by the early eighteenth century, their diameter approximated that of a human hair.[62] Geometric designs of early plaited lace evolved between 1600 and 1620 into recognizable floral patterns featuring roses, peonies, swirling stems with leaves, and the occasional tulip, all connected by brides (bars linking parts of the design) or a mesh ground (FIGS. 4.19 AND 4.20). Antwerp seems to have led the way in these

FIG. 4.17 (OPPOSITE)
Bobbin-lace coverlet, Brussels, Southern Netherlands, 1750–60. Linen. Collection MoMu Fashion Museum Antwerp, loan Koning Boudewijnstichting België, B15/16.

FIG. 4.18 (ABOVE)
Domingo de la Milla, letter from Lima to Henri François Schilders, enclosing two bobbin-lace samples, Old Flemish type, ground with square meshes and without ground, September 23, 1679. Ink on paper with lace. Collectie Stad Antwerpen, Museum Plantin-Moretus, SCH-HF. BA.112_23-09-1679.

developments, and it is therefore not surprising that foreign lacemakers were eager to acquire Flemish knowledge and lacemaking techniques.

Women from various regions of Europe traveled to the Southern Netherlands and to Antwerp in particular to learn Flemish textile techniques. As early as the mid-sixteenth century, the Plantin family brought several women from Paris to pursue embroidery. Approximately one hundred years later, Françoise Badar (1624–1677) came to Antwerp from Valenciennes to learn Flemish techniques that she would take back to France. She was instrumental in founding the important lace industry that flourished in Valenciennes in the eighteenth century and was the founder and director of the convent of the Ursulines in that city.[63] Nuns and other religious women like Badar would become major forces in the teaching and dissemination of lace techniques in Europe.

Although luxury trades and arts prospered in seventeenth-century Antwerp, there was also considerable poverty in the city. When the poor flocked to cities in times of famine, hoping to find work or sustenance, city authorities often regarded them as a threat to an orderly community, and the task of finding useful ways of employing them frequently fell to charitable institutions and individuals.[64] Because lacemaking was regarded as a respectable way for women to earn a living, several religious orders, like the Ursulines, established schools for girls in the seventeenth century, where pupils learned the rudiments of reading, writing, religion, and useful crafts such as sewing, spinning, and lacemaking.[65] The Maagdenhuis (Maidens' House) orphanage in Antwerp, originally founded in 1552 and then expanded between 1634 and 1636, was a similar organization; there young girls learned to sew and make lace, which was then sold for profit (FIG. 4.21). The orphanage's

FIG. 4.19 (TOP)
Bobbin-lace border, Antwerp, Southern Netherlands, ca. 1650. Linen. Textilmuseum St. Gallen, Acquired from the Estate of John Jacoby, 1954, 00587.

FIG. 4.20 (BOTTOM)
Bobbin-lace border, Antwerp, Southern Netherlands, 1640–60. Linen. Textilmuseum St. Gallen, Acquired from the Estate of John Jacoby, 1954, 00185.1-2.

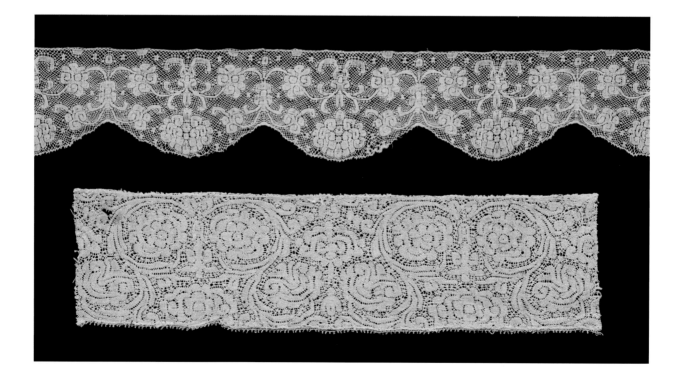

Frieda Sorber

order books from the second half of the seventeenth century are preserved in its archives.[66] Although no clear archival evidence indicates to whom they were selling, the Maagdenhuis's lace clients were likely primarily local (both resident laypeople and members of the clergy), and some of the goods may have been purchased by merchants for resale.

From the sixteenth through the nineteenth century, fashionable lace was sold in shops specializing in accessories including bonnets, lappets, and cuffs. Occasionally, such items were also made to specific customer requirements and might include a coat of arms or unusual motifs by request. In Antwerp during the eighteenth century, the Hoffinger sisters provided an international clientele with fashionable items from several countries, including local lace.[67] Whether they catered to specific preferences can no longer be determined, but by the early eighteenth century, regional preferences for lace seem to have developed. A large amount of the lace exported to the Northern Netherlands after 1750 appealed to locally prevailing tastes.[68]

From the middle of the seventeenth century, a style with densely worked, peony-like flowers came into fashion in the Netherlands and was popular throughout Europe for a short time (FIGS. 4.22–24). Unlike more open types of lace, densely worked bobbin and needle laces were relatively easy to wash and maintained their shape well; this fact may have played an important role in their popularity and subsequent spread. The Antwerp region continued to produce borders with peony-like flowers for the Dutch market, where the lace became an established component of regional costumes in the eighteenth and nineteenth centuries.

Eighteenth-Century Lace Industries in Flanders

The War of the Spanish Succession (1701–14) was significant for the Spanish Netherlands; the region became a part of the Austrian empire and remained so until French Revolutionary troops drove the Austrians out in 1793. Although international trade suffered throughout the eighteenth century, the Spanish market for lace was not entirely lost. Bobbin lace from the Austrian Netherlands remained an important international commodity and adapted readily to rapidly changing fashions. Various editions of Jacques Savary des Bruslons's 1793 *Dictionnaire portatif du commerce* mention lace from the Austrian Netherlands, notably Mechlin and Brussels.[69] In addition to bobbin lace, Brussels was also known for its refined needle lace. The city, which was a hub for the production of large pieces of bobbin lace made in separate parts, successfully made the transition from small borders to complete lace accessories with designs adapted to their shape. Cravat ends for men and cap backs and lappets for women provided ideal surfaces on which to display elaborate patterns executed in the finest threads (FIGS. 4.25 AND 4.26; SEE FIG. 10.11B).

FIG. 4.21
Joannes de Maré, *Orphans in the Maidens' House*, 1676. Oil on canvas. MAAGDENHUIS/Stad Antwerp, A178.

As Flemish lace borders for clothing, household goods, and ecclesiastical use became wider throughout the eighteenth century, new motifs were incorporated into their design.[70] Flowerpots or urns appeared alongside individual flowers, resulting in a composition that nineteenth-century lace historians, likely starting with Mrs. Fanny Bury Palliser (1805–1878), called *potten kant* (flowerpot).[71] Styles related to potten kant were produced in the Antwerp region throughout the nineteenth century and ranged from broad braids for the headdresses of the regional costumes of Friesland (a province in the Northern Netherlands) to seventeenth-century-style braids for women's bonnets on the Dutch islands of Marken and Urk.

Although eighteenth-century Antwerp was still a hub of international lacemaking and dealing, the city's merchants began to turn their attention to other commodities. The mass production of sugar and printed cottons, which involved large numbers of workers, may have dissuaded women from becoming lacemakers; there was at least a clear decline in lace production that coincided with the ascendancy of these industries. The Moretus family, still involved in the international lace trade, was one of the founding

FIG. 4.22 (TOP)

Bobbin-lace border, Antwerp, Southern Netherlands, mid-17th century. Linen. Collection MoMu Fashion Museum Antwerp, T80/130.

FIG. 4.23 (BOTTOM)

Bobbin-lace border, Antwerp, Southern Netherlands, second half of the 17th century. Linen. Collection MoMu Fashion Museum Antwerp, T80/135.

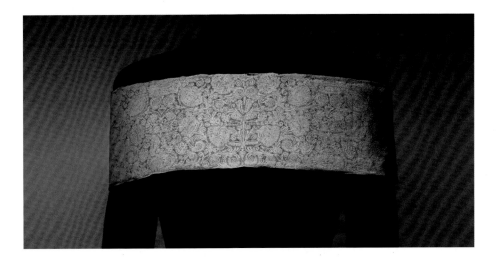

investors of a cotton-printing factory (*Cattoen-druckerije* or *katoendrukkerij*) established by the Compagnie de Beerenbrouck in 1753. At its height in 1769 the factory employed 576 workers, a number of whom were women.[72]

The Plantin-Moretus archives contain no references to the lace trade in the second half of the eighteenth century. As the importance of lace as a fashionable accessory declined at the end of the century, so, too, did its production in Antwerp.[73] While Brussels and Bruges continued to play an international role in the production and further development of lace in the nineteenth century, in Antwerp only a small number of merchants specialized in the regional Dutch market in which their ancestors had invested in the eighteenth century.

Archives and museum collections in Antwerp hold many keys to understanding the role of the city and surrounding region in the evolution of the early modern lace industry in the Southern Netherlands. From surviving sixteenth- and seventeenth-century merchant records, including those of the Plantin family and Margaretha von der Marck, it is possible to establish and trace the widespread influence and popularity of Flemish lace products, styles, and techniques. Alongside these documents, a number of significant large-scale Flemish lace commissions in the seventeenth and eighteenth centuries offer insight into this highly developed industry and help to uncover those individuals who designed, created, purchased, and wore Flemish lace during this period.

FIG. 4.24
Bobbin-lace border or bertha collar, Flanders, Southern Netherlands, probably Antwerp, ca. 1660. Linen. Textilmuseum St. Gallen, Acquired from the Estate of John Jacoby, 1954, 00691. Cat. 63.

1   Much of the published research about Martine and Catherine Plantin and their lace-trading activities can be found in three articles by Marie Risselin-Steenebrugen, former curator of the lace collection at the Musées Royaux d'Art et d'Histoire (Royal Museums of Art and History) in Brussels: "Martine et Catherine Plantin: Leur rôle dans la fabrication et le commerce de la lingerie et des dentelles au XVIe siècle," *Revue belge d'archéologie et d'histoire de l'art* 26, nos. 3–4 (1957): 169–88; which was republished in expanded form as "Les débuts de l'industrie dentellière—Martine et Catherine Plantin," *De Gulden Passer* 39 (1961): 77–124; and "Christophe Plantin, facteur de lingerie fine et en dentelles," *De Gulden Passer* 37 (1959): 74–111. For Martine's first day at the Plantin shop, see Risselin-Steenebrugen, "Les débuts de l'industrie dentellerie," 95.
2   Although ells had different measurements in different cities, 1 ell was approximately 27½ inches (70 centimeters) everywhere in Flanders.

3 Plantin was registered as a citizen of Antwerp on March 21, 1550. Leon Voet, *The Golden Compasses: The History of the House of Plantin-Moretus*, vol. 1 (Amsterdam: Vangendt; London: Routledge & Kegan Paul; New York: Abner Schram, 1969), 12.

4 Plantin, however, never published a pattern book for lace or embroidery. The only Belgian printer to do so, Jean Baptiste de Glen of Liège, issued *Dv debvoir des filles* in 1597, which cribbed from earlier Italian books. Jean Baptiste de Glen, *Dv debvoir des filles: Traicte brief, et fort vtile, divise en devx parties; La premiere est, de la dignite de la femme [. . .] L'autre traicte de la virginité* (Liege, Belgium: Chez Jean de Glen, 1597).

5 The *Biblia Regia* or *Biblia Polyglotta* was published by Plantin between 1566 and 1572 in Latin, Greek, Hebrew, Chaldean, and ancient Syrian. For details, see "La bible royale en cinq langues—Arias Montanus," Museum Plantin Moretus, https://www.museumplantinmoretus.be/fr/page/la-bible-royale-en-cinq-langues-arias-montanus.

6 Iris Cockelberghs, current director of Museum Plantin-Moretus, told the author in an interview that the linen and lace business sometimes kept the more famous book-printing business afloat.

7 Risselin-Steenebrugen, "Christophe Plantin," 75.

8 The Plantin family and their descendants the Moretus family occupied the house called de Gulden Passer (the Golden Compass) on the Vrijdagmarkt in Antwerp from the mid-16th to the end of the 19th century, when the house and its contents became the Museum Plantin-Moretus. The family preserved not only the majority of the 16th-century book-printing materials but also an extensive library and archive, which contains correspondence, household books, family papers, and business records from the 16th to the 19th century. For a history of the Plantin-Moretus family, see Voet, *Golden Compasses*.

9 Digitization is central to the mission of the Museum Plantin-Moretus, and a portion of the archives are available online: https://www.museumplantinmoretus.be/en/page/plantin-moretus-archive.

10 In a letter to Pope Gregory XIII on October 9, 1574, Plantin explains his reasoning: "What chiefly inspired this choice is that in my judgment no other place in the world could furnish more convenience for the trade I wished to practise. This city is easy of access; one sees the various nations congregating in the market-place, and here all the materials necessary for the practice of my craft are to be obtained; workers for all trades, who can be taught in a short time, are easily found." Quoted in Voet, *Golden Compasses*, 13.

11 Plantin refers to Gassen using this phrase in a 1570 letter to Çayas, reproduced in Max Rooses, *Christophe Plantin, Imprimeur Anversois* (Antwerp: Jos. Maes, 1896), 390.

12 Gassen's nephew, Jean, who assisted his uncle in the linen trade, would later marry Catherine. He died young after being attacked by thieves during a business trip in the Northern Netherlands. Voet, *Golden Compasses*, 154–55; and Rooses, *Christophe Plantin*, 220.

13 Rooses, *Christophe Plantin*, 390. Although it is difficult to estimate a comparable sum of money in 2022, the volume at which Plantin and Gassen were trading was very large. People during this period lived with multiple currencies, and lacemakers were often paid per item they produced. Even with surviving business records like those at the Museum Plantin-Moretus, it is often unclear how long it might have taken lacemakers to produce an item.

14 P. Gassen, journal detailing commercial trade of cloth and lace, cords, etc., 1565–69, MPM Ar. No. 440, fo 13, Plantin Archives, Museum Plantin-Moretus.

15 Risselin-Steenebrugen, "Christophe Plantin," 77–78, 100–101; and Voet, *Golden Compasses*, 244.

16 For a discussion of the Spanish Fury's impact on Plantin's press, see ibid., 84–94.

17 For example, Tanneken Vertanghen, lived in Mechlin and provided them with "lassis couvers de roses" (lacis covered in roses)

and "rézeaux" (network) as early as 1558. Book of sales including purchases of linen and fabrics, 1556–59, MPM Ar. no 34, F° 40, Plantin Archives, Museum Plantin-Moretus.

18 Cornelis Kiliaan, *Dictionarium Teutonic-Latinum* (Antwerp: Plantin, 1574), s.v. "Stippen."

19 In certain Dutch regional costumes, the picots were made as late as the early 20th century. The island of Marken is well known for its fine needlework on linen, related to 16th-century techniques and aesthetics. Working practices were documented there in the 1960s. Maria van Hemert, *De handwerken van het eiland Marken* (Arnhem, Netherlands: Openluchtmuseum, 1960).

20 An early example from the Southern Netherlands is an embroidered swaddling band that includes a depiction of the Holy Lamb and the Catholic declaration of faith in Latin in long-armed cross-stitch, openwork hems, and needle-made "pearls" measuring just over half an inch. The band is still in use to wrap a miraculous statuette of the Virgin Mary (dating to the early 16th century) in the Saint Waldetrudis Church in Herentals, near Antwerp. Frieda Sorber, "Het Windesel van het miraculeuze Beeld van Onze-Lieve-Vrouw in Zand in de Sint-Waldetrudiskerk te Herentals," *Historische Jaarboek van Herentals* 24 (2017): 72–81.

21 Book of sales including purchases of linen and fabrics, 1556–59, MPM Ar. no 34, F° 40. Plantin Archives, Museum Plantin-Moretus.

22 Although it is likely they were using flax in addition to silk, there is a lack of documented examples from the 16th century and no mention in the Plantin archives of the type of thread used for bobbin lace.

23 The Plantins and their Moretus descendants meticulously saved any piece of paper, no matter how small, with written information, a practice that continues to provide historians and art historians with a gold mine of information on a variety of subjects, linked not only to the family itself but also to those who intermarried with the Moretuses. Unfortunately, for dress and textile historians, the only textiles the family thought worth preserving were the samples attached to some 17th- and 18th-century documents. Business stock, personal clothing, and household linens were dispersed in the usual ways: through inheritance, through sale (often on the used clothes market, which was located on the family's doorstep on Antwerp's Vrijdagmarkt), and occasionally through gifts to Roman Catholic churches.

24 Risselin-Steenebrugen, "Les débuts de l'industrie dentellière," 81.

25 P. Gassen, journal detailing commercial trade in cloth, lace, etc., 1564–68, MPM Ar. no 439, Plantin Archives, Museum Plantin-Moretus.

26 Book detailing trade of leather and cloth works, etc., 1568–73, MPM Ar. no 442, fo 20, Plantin Archives, Museum Plantin-Moretus, cited in Risselin-Steenebrugen, "Christophe Plantin," 87.

27 Pierre Verhaegen, *Les industries à domiciles en Belgique*, vol. 4 (Brussels: Société Belge de librairie and J. Lebègue & Cie., 1902), 32–33.

28 Verhaegen, *La dentelle et la broderie*, 33.

29 For Margaretha's relation to Antwerp, see Peter Neu, *Margaretha von der Marck (1527–1599): Landesmutter, Geschäftsfrau und Händlerin, Katholikin* (Enghien, Belgium: Arenberg Stiftung, 2013), 69–74, 94–95, 104–6, 120–22.

30 Although her brother's death and that of her father made Margaretha the Countess of Arenberg, she continued to go by the name "von der Marck," only rarely adding "Arenberg" to her signature in letters. Neu, *Margaretha von der Marck*, 17–19, 25.

31 Ibid., 9, 11. The term "Southern Netherlands" refers to a region that was under the rule of various European powers from the 16th to the early 19th century. These included the Spanish Habsburgs from 1556 to 1714 (during this period it is often referred to as the "Spanish Netherlands"), the Austrian Habsburgs from 1714 to 1794, and France from 1794 to 1815.

32 "C'était une sage et habile dame." Quoted in L. P. Gachard, "Arenberg (Jean de Ligne, comte d')," in *Biographie nationale publiée* *par l'Académie royale des sciences, des lettres et des beaux-arts de Belgique*, vol. 1 (Brussels: H. Thiry-Van Buggenhoudt, 1866), 380.

33 Neu, *Margaretha von der Marck*, 64.

34 Ibid., 65–66.

35 Ibid.

36 Ibid., 69–72.

37 Ibid., 67. Elisabeth continued to order cloth from Margaretha until at least 1589.

38 Ibid., 86. Margaretha also supplied William with ribbons, accessories, and belts.

39 Ibid., 83.

40 Ibid., 76.

41 Ibid., 66.

42 On Margaretha's relations with Cologne and Antwerp, see ibid., 88–98, 104–6.

43 Ibid., 118.

44 The couple remained childless, and the Spanish Netherlands reverted to the Spanish Crown after the widowed Isabella retired to the Poor Clares convent in Tervuren. Ria Cooreman, "Albrecht and Isabella's Coverlet: A Story in Lace," in *P.LACE.S: Looking through Flemish Lace*, ed. Frieda Sorber et al. (Tielt, Belgium: Lannoo, 2021), 68.

45 The coverlet in Brussels (inv. 2543) was the subject of two publications in the first half of the 20th century: Eugène Van Overloop, *Matériaux pour servir à l'histoire de la dentelle en Belgique, 1ère série: Une dentelle de Bruxelles de 1599* (Brussels: Lamertin, 1908); and C. L. Truyens-Bredael, *Het Kantwerk van de Ommegang* (Antwerp: De Standaard Boekhandel, 1941).

46 Cooreman, "Albrecht and Isabella's Coverlet." Cooreman graciously shared her discoveries related to the iconographic sources of the scene depicted. For more information about the two coverlets, see the essays in "Key Pieces: The Brussels and Geneva Archdukes' Coverlets," in Sorber et al., *P.LACE.S*, 62–91.

47 Cooreman, "Albrecht and Isabella's Coverlet," 69–70.

48 Ibid., 67. See also Jean De La Croix, "Les images de Thérèse d'Avile et d'Anne de Jésus dans le couvre-pied de archiducs," *Bulletin van de Koninklijke Musea voor Kunst en Geschiedenis* 43–44 (1971–72): 89–98.

49 Ibid., 65–66, 74, 89.

50 Frieda Sorber, "The Archdukes' Coverlets: A Few Afterthoughts," in Sorber et al., *P.LACE.S*, 88–91.

51 Two fragments are preserved in the Antwerp Fashion Museum (inv. S76/8AB). Another, contained in a book of various lace pieces (inv. 3270), is kept in the Royal Museum of Art and History in Brussels.

52 Among the remaining fragments are examples in the Royal Museum of Art and History in Brussels (inv. 3269) and the Textilmuseum St. Gallen (inv. 00696). Marie Risselin-Steenebrugen, "Une dentelle à l'effigie de Charles II d'Espagne," *Bulletin des Musées Royaux d'Art et d'Histoire* 23 (1951): 65–68. Risselin-Steenebrugen mentions other pieces in the Jacoby Collection and the Victoria and Albert Museum, London.

53 The dress was commissioned as payment for back taxes owed to the court by the City of Ghent and was therefore an "obligatory gift." Michael Yonan, "Materializing Empire in an Eighteenth-Century Lace Gown," *Textile: The Journal of Cloth & Culture* 14, no. 3 (2016): 380–81.

54 Ibid., 381.

55 At the end of the 19th century, a large fragment of the dress, made into a cradle cover, was owned by the Kinsky family in Austria. Moriz Dreger, *Die Wiener Spitzenausstellung* (Leipzig, Germany: K. W. Hiersemann, 1906). Attempts by the author to trace the cover were unsuccessful.

56 Dirk Leyder and Frédérique Johan, "Isabella's canten cleedt (1760): Meer dan een banaal huwelijksgeschenk uit Vlaanderen," *Archieflink: Driemaandelijkse nieuwsbrief van't Archief* 9, no. 2 (April 2009): 4–5.

57 The coverlet was acquired in 2015 by the Brussels King Baudouin Foundation in London and is on long-term loan to the Antwerp

Fashion Museum (Inv. B15/2). A comparable coverlet is in the collection of the Royal Museum of Art and History in Brussels (inv. 3136). Risselin-Steenebrugen, "Une dentelle à l'effigie de Charles II d'Espagne," 43–49.

58 "Brabant Lace Bedspread," Cultural Heritage!, King Baudouin Foundation, https://www.heritage-kbf.be/collection/brabant-lace-bedspread.

59 For an overview of these papers, see the City of Antwerp's FelixArchives, https://felixarchief.antwerpen.be/archievenoverzicht/669303.

60 The Plantin-Moretus archives contain hundreds of letters to and from many European business contacts. The Melijn family were textile merchants in Antwerp. The archive of their commercial correspondence includes over 20,000 letters from the 17th and 18th centuries. Acc. T94/183-186, Antwerp Fashion Museum.

61 Information about Flemish lace trade with the Spanish colonies is particularly abundant. As Marguerite Coppens explains, "As trade with Spain and its colonies involved large quantities of goods, considerable financial risk and often several partners, every detail had to be set down on paper." Marguerite Coppens, "The Seventeenth and Eighteenth Centuries: The Large-Scale Merchants and Exports to the New World," in Sorber et al., *P.LACE.S*, 99.

62 For a technical study of several examples of Flemish lace in the Antwerp Fashion Museum's collection as well as an example of a package of 18th-century flax fibers, see Ina Vanden Berghe, "Technical Aspects of Materials Used in Seventeenth- and Eighteenth-Century Flemish Lace from the MoMu Collection, Antwerp," in Sorber et al., *P.LACE.S*, 156–79.

63 *Histoire de la vie de Mademoiselle Françoise Badar* (Liège, Belgium: Jean-François Broncart, 1726). Valenciennes was at that time part of the Southern Netherlands; from 1678 it would be part of France.

64 Anne-Marie Gering, "De Fundatie Terninck te Antwerpen (1697–1750)" (MA thesis, Katholieke Universteit Leuven, 1990).

65 The Ursulines were still active in the Southern Netherlands well into the 20th century; they founded the lace school in Bruges in 1911. Flemish Ursulines may also have influenced lacemaking at the Ursuline convent of Gorizia near Trieste in Italy, where designs made in Flanders under direct Flemish influence are preserved to this day. Thessy Schoenholzer Nichols and Raffaella Sgubin, eds., *I merletti del monastero di Sant'Orsola nelle collezioni dei Musei provinciali di Gorizia* (Gorizia, Italy: Musei provinciali, 2011).

66 Today the orphanage is the location of the Maagdenhuis Museum, which has three large paintings (inv. A176–A178) by Joannes de Maré (ca. 1640–after 1676) depicting orphans busy sewing and making bobbin lace.

67 Marguerite Coppens, "'Au Magasin de Paris': Une boutique de modes à Anvers dans la première moitié du XVIIIe siècle," *Revue belge d'archéologie et d'histoire de l'art* 52 (1983): 81–107.

68 Frieda Sorber, "After 1750: The Dutch Niche Market," in Sorber et al., *P.LACE.S*, 195.

69 Jacques Savary des Bruslons and Philémon-Louis Savary, *Dictionnaire universel de commerce* [. . .] (Paris: Chez la veuve Estienne, 1762), 46.

70 Wim Mertens, "Style Evolutions in Flemish Lace from the Late Sixteenth to the Mid-Eighteenth Centuries: An Overview," in Sorber et al., *P.LACE.S*, 214–15.

71 Fanny Bury Palliser, *History of Lace* (London: S. Low, Son & Marston, 1865), 154.

72 These "schieldermeiden" were responsible for adding color to the block-printed cotton with brushes. A. K. L. Thijs, "Aspecten van de opkomst der textieldrukkerij als grootbedrijf te Antwerpen in de achttiende eeuw," *Bijdragen en Mededelingen betreffende de Geschiedenis der Nederlanden* 86, no. 2 (1971): 202, 212.

73 Anne Winter, *Migrants and Urban Change: Newcomers to Antwerp, 1760–1860* (London: Taylor & Francis, 2015), 57.

FASHION AND LACE IN SPAIN
AND THE AMERICAS, 1500–1800

5 The Triumph of Lace: Spanish Portraiture in the Sixteenth and Seventeenth Centuries

Amalia Descalzo Lorenzo

COUPLED WITH FASHION, dress proves compellingly impactful.[1] Through intimate links with human beings, clothes convey meanings and communicate myriad messages regarding a person's life, social milieu, and epoch. Acknowledged since antiquity, this close relationship between dress and people is paramount to the construction of persona, hence the interest evinced by kings, nobles, aristocrats, and high-profile figures in presenting themselves arrayed in their choicest attire. Thanks to artistic depictions of people—particularly portraiture—we have been able to recognize the ability of costumes and styles to epitomize a court, a family, a society, or a country.

This signifying power of dress is apparent in the culture of Habsburg Spain (1516–1700). One of the most fascinating stages in the history of Spanish dress, it is defined not only by the contrivance of a uniquely national attire, but equally by the creation of garments distinctive to Western dress and fashion.[2] Starting with the establishment of the Spanish empire under the rule of the Catholic Monarchs, Ferdinand II of Aragon (1452–1516) and Isabella I of Castile (1469–1504), Spanish fashions that developed throughout the sixteenth century significantly influenced those worn in most of Europe. These fashions remained dominant well into the seventeenth century, when Spain's sartorial ascendancy was eclipsed by France under the reign of the Sun King, Louis XIV (1638–1715), wielding authority from the Palace of Versailles.[3] Contingent on political and economic sovereignty, ancien régime courts became creative fashion hubs, setting benchmarks for those espousing the latest trends.[4] However, we must bear in mind the rigid stratification of ancien régime society, governed by a dress code of sumptuary laws issued as pragmatic sanctions (a solemn royal decree known as *pragmática sanción*) since the thirteenth century. Consequently, dress became the most obvious sign of membership within a specific social class, and—though the styles, garments, and patterns were the same throughout society—differences were visibly manifest in the quality, colors, and trimmings of fabrics. During these centuries, dressing was a costly affair since certain textiles, dyes, and embellishments were classified as luxury items and as such were reserved exclusively for consumption by the affluent governing elite. Aimed at curbing exorbitant and ostentatious clothing, the law dictated by King Charles I (1500–1558) in 1534 in Toledo was very significant:

> We forbid and order that henceforth no one within or without our kingdoms and dominions, regardless of condition, quality, distinction, or rank, with the exception of Our Royal Highnesses and our children, dare either carry or wear brocade, gold and silver embossed cloth, cloth of gold or silver [woven from gold or silver threads], or any silk, braid, top stitching, galloons or any other trimming, embroidery, raised work or glitter made of gold or silver, whether real or fake, or pearls or seed pearls or stones, or any borders made of beadwork, silk or anything made on a frame.[5]

Trims, or *guarniciones*, played a significant role in Spanish fashion, given their overly elaborate splendor, thus contributing to the singularity of clothing observed in the portraits of this era.[6] The value of garments might have increased dramatically with the addition of labor-intensive finery such as embroidery, applied decoration, or lace. In referring to pragmatic sanctions seeking to rein in the use of trimmings, the costume historian Carmen Bernis (1919–2001) ascertained the variety and lavishness of ornaments, among which *puntas* and *randas* stood out as being the most sumptuous.[7] In 1537 Charles I reiterated the ban on gold and silver embroidery.[8] Despite having restrained the extravagance represented by this type of sumptuousness, restrictive measures backfired since the aforesaid decorative devices were replaced by yet costlier trimmings made in a variety of techniques, as "embroiderers gave their patterns to tailors and they, with their wives, made of *punto* [needle lace] what used to be made of embroidery, at double the cost"; therefore, what was crafted with galloons and trimmings was often worth more than silk itself.[9]

Historians agree on the difficulty of determining with certainty when and where lace first appeared.[10] Notwithstanding the ancient origins of this openwork form, lace acquired its definitive shapes and configurations in the sixteenth century. Treatises on lacemaking and lace pattern books hark back to this earlier period, confirming the importance and dissemination of this luxury item (SEE CHAP. 2).[11]

The emergence of lace also coincided with the preeminence of Spanish fashions on the European continent. At the end of the fifteenth century in the court of Castile, the *verdugo* (literally "green wood") made its appearance: reed or wood hoops were covered in rich fabric and sewn directly onto a woman's skirt. The resulting stiff armature or *verdugado* (the Spanish farthingale) created a conical form below the waist and was the first example of shaped skirts in Western fashion.[12] In addition to the original verdugo, shifts or chemises enhanced by Moorish motifs became major components in the formulation of a Spanish vestiary style for women.

The first references regarding the decorative use of lace relate to the making of undergarments. Since it emerged in the sixteenth century, lace has always been associated with personal linen goods. Worn under low-cut dresses, lace-tipped shifts gained exposure during the Renaissance. The aforementioned Moorish-style shifts (*camisas moriscas*) are considered noteworthy garments featuring fanciful necklines and sleeves. Impressive visual effects resulted from affixing rich garnishings to these Moorish-style shifts in the form of applied ribbons called *listas*, embroidery, and drawn-thread work employing silk and gold threads.[13] It is precisely on such shifts that drawn-thread work appeared as a forerunner of lace. The inventories of Queen Isabella the Catholic listed shifts with such work made of gold threads.[14] Moreover, ruff collars, or *gorgueras*—gracing chests and necks—displayed drawn-thread work, especially white ones made of linen. In 1477, Friar Hernando de Talavera (1428–1507), confessor and counselor to Queen Isabella, described the gorgueras worn at this time. Adopting a moralizing tone, Talavera stated that these specific ruff collars, which were lavishly "crafted and adorned with drawn thread work," covered backs while allowing breasts to show through.[15] Men's shirts were just as fancy. The vogue for these embellishments may account for the dissemination of the Italian trend of slashed sleeves that revealed the ornate fabric of the shirt worn underneath (FIG. 5.1).

A distinctive Spanish look originated prior to the mid-sixteenth century. Spanish fashion notably attained universality by exporting and imposing a preference for the

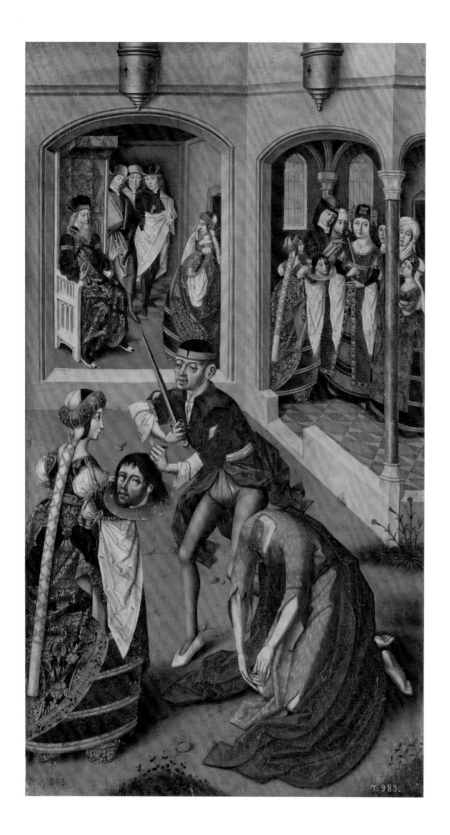

Amalia Descalzo Lorenzo

color black.[16] Foremost among the clothing items comprising the wardrobes of Spanish men and women alike, the *lechuguilla*—a wide ruff collar, pleated and stiffened with starch, and made of white linen or lace—took center stage.[17] Albeit not a Spanish invention, this accessory was well suited to the ideals that influenced Spanish fashion. This type of collar originated from a narrow frill adorning the neckline of shirts in the mid-sixteenth century that grew to extravagant proportions by the end of this time period (FIG. 5.2).

In effect, lace was eagerly adopted by elite men and women throughout Europe, and in Spain, it became the most luxurious trimming on lechuguilla collars in the second half of the sixteenth century. This fact is substantiated by contemporaneous portraits of kings and nobles underscoring their status by virtue of the elaborate lace enhancing their fine linen collars. Men and women shared similar types of collars, especially during this era, though certain feminine models appear more elaborate, such as the one worn by Queen Elisabeth of Valois (1545–1568; FIG. 5.3) in a portrait executed by her lady-in-waiting, the Italian painter Sofonisba Anguissola (1535–1625). Given its size, this lechuguilla collar corresponds to those still attached to shifts made of fine linen termed "Holland cloth." Complemented by exquisite hemstitches and trimmed with lace ruffles (*abanillos*) further enriched with gold spangles, this lechuguilla contrasts dramatically against the finely adorned black-velvet ceremonial garment (*saya*) worn by the queen.[18] Reinforced by a *cartón de pecho* (cardboard busk) and a *verdugado* shaping the queen's silhouette, this saya features sumptuous seed-pearl frogging and ruby buttons, a large train, sleeve cuffs trimmed with pointed-edge lace, and white satin detachable sleevelets appliquéd with gold galloon.[19]

At the beginning of the seventeenth century, lechuguilla collars increased in size, eventually becoming detachable, as was the case for matching cuffs. By that time, lechuguillas emerged as one of the quintessential Spanish accoutrements. Demanding painstaking care, these collars were starched, further whitened by using extremely expensive indigo powders imported from overseas colonies, and shaped by means of heated, goffering iron tongs.[20] As the diameter of such collars grew, so did their luxuriousness, including the prevailing use of lace, thereby leading in 1593 to a pragmatic sanction not only limiting their width but also forbidding lavish trimmings with the exception of one or two narrow rows of hemstitches on Holland cloth or linen. This ban proved ineffectual, as the collars remained voluminous. The lechuguilla flaunted by the Archduchess Isabella Clara Eugenia, Infanta of Spain (1566–1633), as portrayed by Frans Pourbus the Younger (1569–1622) around 1599, incorporates one of the most splendid lacework

FIG. 5.2

Antonio Moro, *Philip II*, ca. 1555. Oil on panel. Museo Nacional del Prado, Madrid, P002118.

patterns of the time (FIG. 5.4). Decorated with cutwork and detached needle-lace points, her collar rests on a circular metal underpropper hung along its perimeter with what appear to be tear-shaped metal pendants. In keeping with the size of the collar, the large cuffs are made of the same lace. The dress is spectacular: all its parts, including the *galerilla* (overgown), *jubón* (doublet), and *basquiña* (overskirt) are made of silk satin embroidered with interlocking rings, fleur-de-lis, anemones, and violets. Another linen item then deemed a luxury good, a handkerchief held in the infanta's left hand, features typical late sixteenth-century lace along its entire perimeter. The female figure standing beside the queen is elegantly turned out as befitting someone in attendance at court. Her dress consists of a black doublet and basquiña; yet here the basquiña, unlike the queen's, is shaped by a single cotton hoop.[21] Her lechuguilla and simple turned-back cuffs are trimmed with pointed bobbin-lace edgings.

Spanish dress barely changed in the first decades of the seventeenth century, and, though Spanish styles remained influential throughout the rest of Europe, French fashions steadily gained ground.[22] Spain, however, chose not to emulate French modes, instead clinging more than ever to its singular dress until the early eighteenth century, when it changed course following the enthronement of the first Bourbon king, Philip V (1683–1746).[23] Despite incessant pragmatic sanctions restricting the use of luxury trimmings such as lace, these continued to embellish enormous lechuguilla collars, particularly those worn by women, as men opted for plainer, considerably less ornate versions that were, admittedly, equally large.

FIG. 5.3
Sofonisba Anguissola, *Isabel de Valois holding a Portrait of Philip II*, 1561–65. Oil on canvas. Museo Nacional del Prado, Madrid, P001031.

Philip IV (1605–1665; FIG. 5.5) acceded to the throne of Spain in 1621, and in 1623 he decreed a pragmatic sanction that spurred a radical change in men's fashion but had no effect on that worn by women (FIG. 5.6). This royal decree limited the size and ornamentation of lechuguillas, which resulted in their replacement by smaller collars called *golillas*. The king's own prompt compliance ensured the effectiveness of this decree, and he has been credited with the invention of this collar type.[24] In seventeenth-century documents, the term "golilla" originally referred to the cardboard undercollar supporting the *valona* (Walloon collar), a white starched linen collar. The ancestor of the golilla is the *rotonde* collar worn in France; nevertheless, the Spanish golilla, unlike its French counterpart,

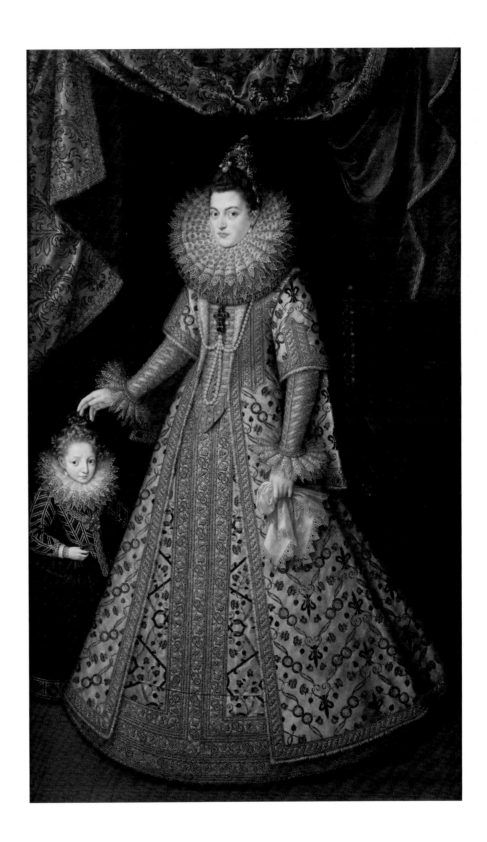

FIG. 5.4

Frans Pourbus the Younger, *Infanta
Isabel Clara Eugenia*, ca. 1599. Oil
on canvas. Patrimonio Nacional,
Monasterio de las Descalzas Reales,
Madrid, 00612215.

was characterized by its austere appearance devoid of trimmings (FIG. 5.7).

In addition to being paired with golillas, *valonas llanas* resting flat on the shoulders were equally fashion-able. In the seventeenth century, "valonas" denoted linen collars, having replaced lechuguillas for both men's and women's dress. These valonas were part of shifts and shirts usually trimmed with lace. The wardrobe accounts kept at the General Archive of the Royal Palace of Madrid reveal that shirts made for the king arrived by the dozens from Flanders, along with valonas and *vueltas* (cuff trimmings).[25] In the course of this century, the production of lace increased exponentially in Italy, Flanders, and from the mid-1660s, France, as both men's and women's wardrobes required excessive supplies of this commodity for clothing and undergarments (SEE CHAP. 9). A wide variety of lacemaking techniques caught on and flourished in many countries; nonetheless, lace

FIG. 5.5 (LEFT)
Rodrigo de Villandrando, *Prince Philip and the Dwarf, Miguel Soplillo*, ca. 1620. Oil on canvas. Museo Nacional del Prado, Madrid, P001234.

FIG. 5.6 (RIGHT)
Artist unknown, *Isabel de Bourbon, Queen of Spain, First Wife of Philip IV*, ca. 1620. Oil on canvas. Museo Nacional del Prado, Madrid, P001037.

made in the Netherlands remained unrivaled because of its fine linen and beautiful coloring. In 1692 don Diego de Ángulo, master of the royal wardrobe under King Charles II (1665–1700), commented on how the difficulty of finding high-quality lace in Spain had compelled him to import it from Flanders.[26] "The forty-four *varas* [a unit of length measuring around 32⅞ inches] of fine white lace with partridge-eye ground [a bobbin-lace stitch resembling perforated spots or eyes] from Brussels, in varying widths needed to trim two of the queen's bodices" referenced this precious import destined for members of the royal household.[27]

The first valonas intended for women's wear in Spain came from Italy; worn raised, these collars were pinned to a silver wire underpropper. Valonas were starched, whitened using indigo dye, and decorated with lace. This collar type is worn by the subject in the portrait by Diego Velázquez (1599–1660) titled *Doña Antonia de Ipeñarrieta y Galdós and Her Son, Luis* (**FIG. 5.8**). She sports a double valona, specific to Spanish fashion, trimmed along its border with hand-knotted fringing. This type of valona was worn in conjunction with the last Spanish farthingales or verdugados before they went out of fashion; in fact, the subject's saya with round sleeves is typical of the sixteenth century. Her son, don Luis, is decked out in a *vaquero* decorated with gold passementerie and featuring long and wide casaque sleeves hanging from the shoulders.[28] The collar and cuffs are trimmed with delicate, transparent lace points while the entire perimeter of the linen apron is bordered by deeply scalloped reticella lace with large, long-petaled rosette motifs culminating in picot edging. A bell hangs from his belt, serving to ward off the evil eye.

With the arrival of the first dresses shaped by a foundation garment termed *guardainfante*, valonas worn with underproppers fell out of favor and were replaced by flat valonas, such as the one worn by María of Austria, queen of Hungary (1606–1646), as painted by Frans Luycx (1604–1668) around 1635 (**FIG. 5.9**).[29] Here the valona frames a French-style neckline. Possibly Flemish, the wide lace collar with floral motifs and gently scalloped edges contrasts with the narrow black lace on the upper border of the neckline. The cuffs match the valona. This type of valona became known as a *cariñana* since it was introduced by María of Bourbon (1606–1692), the spouse of the French Prince of Carignano (in Spanish, Cariñan), who upon entering Madrid was elegantly attired in the French fashion.[30] Hairstyles also changed with the advent of the first guardainfantes: in tandem with skirts, the former gained width. These coiffures were adorned with luxurious lace along the lower contours. A portrait of doña Luisa Francisca de Guzmán y Medina Sidonia is an interesting depiction of early cariñanas (**FIG. 5.10**). The neckline of her dress is much wider than that of María of Austria and reveals the top edge of her white linen

shift embroidered in black silk. As in the previous portraits, the white scalloped lace with long-petaled rosettes and stylized floral patterns—located on both the neckline and the cuffs—stands out against the black fabric of the dress. Slashed doublets and sleeves revealing the white fabric of the shift were the height of fashion in the 1640s. In perfect harmony with her spectacular hairstyle, the sitter wears an impressive guardainfante consistent with styles from the end of this decade.

Artistic representations of extremely decorative valona collars resting on the shoulders of wearers include the portrait *María Teresa, Infanta of Spain* by Juan Bautista

FIG. 5.8 (LEFT)
Diego Rodriguez de Silva Velázquez, *Doña Antonia de Ipeñarrieta y Galdós and Her Son, Luis*, ca. 1632. Oil on canvas. Museo Nacional del Prado, Madrid, P001196.

FIG. 5.9 (RIGHT)
Frans Luycx, *Maria of Austria, Queen of Hungary*, ca. 1635. Oil on canvas. Museo Nacional del Prado, Madrid, P001272.

Martínez del Mazo (1612–1667), painted around 1645 (FIG. 5.11). The six-year-old infanta (1638–1683) is attired in a skirted doublet and basquiña, the latter supported by a guardainfante. In accordance with her young age, her arms are encased in long, wide casaque sleeves. Based on the accounts recorded by lacemakers, the valona and the cuffs could be made of cambric embellished with cutwork and scalloped lace of fine Flemish linen.[31] A similar valona is worn by the subject in *Portrait of a Young Lady* (FIG. 5.12), attributed to Velázquez. This superb painting attests to the use of lace among commoners: the social status of the model is conveyed by the subdued, neutral color

of her dress fabric (bright jewel-tone colors and black required prohibitively expensive dyes). The volume of her basquiña and the presence of a skirted doublet indicate that the sitter is wearing a guardainfante. Her doublet is trimmed with black passementerie along its hem as well as on its sleeves. The impressive white valona is edged with large scalloped lacework, probably bobbin lace. An oversimplified depiction of lace patterns resulted from Velázquez's swiftly sketched brushstrokes; the actual item would have plausibly featured more complex floral motifs befitting the Baroque aesthetic. The young woman's head is covered by a *manto* (a mantle or whole shawl), which was considered a requisite feminine accessory when stepping out into the street. Among the wide variety of manto styles available at the time, the most coveted were the "*mantos* of Seville, in deep black and trimmed with scalloped-edge lace and Flemish lace."[32]

In menswear, flat, shoulder-covering valonas garnered greater acceptance in the military sector than in civil society. The portrait *Don Tiburcio de Redín y Cruzat* (FIG. 5.13)

Amalia Descalzo Lorenzo

provides a striking example of this particular look: the sitter is handsomely dressed in military garb consisting of a coat richly trimmed with silver frogging. Underneath, he wears a leather jerkin (*coleto*), his waist girded by a wide crimson-red sash distinctive of the Spanish military. He also wears red breeches ending in lace-trimmed cuffs and brown leather boots. Probably made of cambric, his valona is outlined with scalloped lace and double hemstitches. In Velázquez's portrait *King Philip IV of Spain* (1644; **FIG. 5.14**), the monarch flaunts his military regalia comprising a crimson-colored plush outfit, a leather jerkin, and a doublet of silver cloth as evidenced by the sleeves, accessorized with an understated valona. At the opposite end of the social spectrum, the subject portrayed in the masterful work titled *Juan de Pareja* (**FIG. 5.15**) was Velázquez's enslaved assistant, in charge of mixing colors for the painter. A white valona with pointed-edge lace stands out against his dark, earthy-toned *ropilla*, black doublet sleeves, and shoulder belt.[33]

The reign of the last Habsburg king, Charles II (1661–1700), ushered in substantial changes in women's fashion compared to the preceding period under Philip IV.[34] The guardainfante became exclusively relegated to formal ceremonies, and novel foundation garments such as the *sacristán* and the *tontillo* made their appearance at court.[35] At this juncture, feminine attire included a doublet and a basquiña. These doublets had wide inverted U-shaped necklines both front and back that revealed women's shoulders. Arms and forearms were tightly encased in sleeves and further covered by globe-shaped

FIG. 5.14 (LEFT)
Diego Rodriguez de Silva Velázquez, *King Philip IV of Spain*, 1644. Oil on canvas. © The Frick Collection, New York, Henry Clay Frick Bequest, 1911.1.123.

FIG. 5.15 (RIGHT)
Diego Rodriguez de Silva Velázquez, *Juan de Pareja*, ca. 1650. Oil on canvas. The Metropolitan Museum of Art, New York, Purchase, Fletcher and Rogers Funds, and Bequest of Miss Adelaide Milton de Groot (1876–1967), by exchange, supplemented by gifts from friends of the Museum, 1971, 1971.86.

oversleeves, undoubtedly one of the most eye-catching details of this style. These doublets were worn over baleen-boned stays termed *cotilla* and embellished with lace. During this period, lace used to garnish men's and women's fashions was not necessarily linked to linen undergarments; however, lace prevailed as the most common trimming for these items. In 1679 the Countess d'Aulnoy (1652–1705) recorded that underneath their basquiñas, Spanish women wore about a dozen luxurious fabrics—each more beautiful than the next—trimmed with galloons, as well as gold and silver lace, all the way up to the waist, and white underskirts requiring many varas of cloth also adorned with lace.[36] The portrait of the second spouse of King Charles II, Queen Maria Anna of Neuburg (1667–1740), painted around 1690, is emblematic of fashions of the second half of the seventeenth century (FIG. 5.16).

The portrait *Doña Inés de Zúñiga, Countess of Monterrey* (ca. 1674; FIG. 5.17) is a stunning example of the extraordinarily ample width attained by the last guardainfante models. Despite the eccentric combination of silver, white, red, and black fabrics, this dress comes across as a harmonious whole. The doublet's neckline is edged with black lace and a strip of *point de Venise* lace (*puntos de España* in Spanish) that incorporated metallic

FIG. 5.16 (LEFT)
Claudio Coello, *Portrait of Queen Maria Anna of Neuberg*, ca. 1690–92. Oil on canvas. Museo de Bellas Artes de Bilbao, 69/62.

FIG. 5.17 (RIGHT)
Juan Carreño de Miranda, *Doña Inés de Zúñiga, Countess of Monterrey*, ca. 1674. Oil on canvas. Museo Lázaro Galdiano, Madrid, 01518.

threads. The rest of the doublet boasts an expertly wrought embellishment known in English by the French appellation *point d'Espagne* lace. The lower section of the basquiña is decorated with four bands of either Venetian coraline lace or point d'Espagne lace using silver threads.

One of the most striking portraits of this period, *Doña Nicolasa Manrique de Mendoza* (FIG. 5.18), was painted by Claudio Coello (1642–1693). Her dress is a veritable homage to lace. The entire neckline contour is bordered by *point de Milan* lace. The trimmings on the sleeves, the front section of the doublet, and the flounces are apparently Venetian lace. Finally, her hair is accessorized with lace as well as red ribbon bows.[37]

Men continued wearing Spanish or national attire under the reign of Charles II; even though golilla collars did not allow for decorative frills, ropilla sleeves greatly increased in volume, whereas the actual ropillas, alongside breeches, became scandalously tight-fitting. The subject of the portrait *Don Fernando de Valenzuela, Marquis of Villasierra* (FIG. 5.19)—popularly dubbed "the palace elf" given his easy access to the queen mother, Mariana of Austria (1634–1696)—wears a ropilla and a doublet with sleeves displaying an elegant, lobe-shaped, black lace trim running along its longitudinal opening. Similarly, *Portrait of a Nobleman* (FIG. 5.20), attributed to Bartolomé Esteban Murillo (1617–1682), represents the sitter wearing magnificent ropilla sleeves covered with undulating lace

FIG. 5.18 (LEFT)

Claudio Coello, *Doña Nicolasa Manrique de Mendoza*, ca. 1690–92. Oil on canvas. Instituto de Valencia de Don Juan Collection, Madrid, 6005.

FIG. 5.19 (RIGHT)

Juan Carreño de Miranda, *Don Fernando de Valenzuela, Marquis of Villasierra*, ca. 1660. Oil on canvas. Museo Lazaro Galdiano-Coleccion, Madrid, 05115.

FIG. 5.20
Attributed to Bartolomé Esteban
Murillo, *Portrait of a Nobleman*, 1677.
Oil on canvas. Private collection.

Amalia Descalzo Lorenzo

bands containing floral motifs, which are tied at the wrist with black silk bows. Lengthwise slits expose the white sleeves of a shirt worn underneath, whose cuffs are trimmed with white lace. This exquisite attire made of black silk with swirling floral motifs is a superb example of men's fashion at this historical moment.

Without effectively taking over, French styles nevertheless coexisted alongside idiosyncratic Spanish clothing items such as the golilla collar, especially during the 1679 marriage of Charles II and his first consort, Marie Louise of Orléans (1662–1689), the niece of Louis XIV. Men's dress included a coat (*casaca*), a sleeved waistcoat (*chupa*), and breeches (*calzones*), and a thigh-length shirt was accessorized by the cravat that was knotted around the neck with its two large ends hanging over the upper chest. Cravats, as well as shirt cuffs and flounces, were usually made of lace. They were further embellished with bows of red silk ribbon such as the one depicted in a portrait by Juan Carreño de Miranda (1614–1685) titled *Carlos II in Armour* (FIG. 5.21), destined to be sent to France on the occasion of the king's impending nuptials. This lace cravat was a wedding gift from his bride-to-be, Marie Louise of Orléans.

Throughout the reigns of the Habsburg monarchs, the sartorial splendor of Spain's Golden Age manifested itself in the rich garments and accessories worn by the royal family and the nobility. Sixteenth- and seventeenth-century portraits of elite men and women arrayed in silks, velvets, embroidery, and lace demonstrated the country's cultural predominance derived from its political, economic, and territorial hegemony not only in Europe but also in the Americas. Although fashionable Spanish dress developed independently from that of northern Europe during the seventeenth century, the images discussed in this chapter attest to the continuous extensive consumption of up-to-date Flemish and Italian laces during the period and reflect the high status associated with this recently introduced, increasingly sought-after, and costly textile. In these overtly self-serving representations, elaborate needle and bobbin laces stand out against the luxurious black garments characteristic of members of the Spanish court, serving as material signifiers of the sitters' political, social, and economic power. The presence of these prestigious and prominent embellishments alternatively evinces a trickle-down effect, as their cachet proved irresistible to markedly less privileged members of lower social strata, such as those subjects depicted by Velázquez in *Portrait of a Young Woman* and *Juan de Pareja*.

FIG. 5.21
Juan Carreño de Miranda, *Carlos II in Armour*, 1681. Oil on canvas. Museo Nacional del Prado, Madrid, P007101.

This chapter (including quotations unless otherwise noted) was translated from the Spanish by Patricia Cabral.

1   In the context of this chapter, the word "fashion" is used to define rapid changes of clothing styles that, in European history since the late medieval period, have been associated with royal and ducal courts and major urban centers. "Dress" is a more inclusive term that refers to all types of clothing worn by men and women across the socioeconomic spectrum. See, for example, Elizabeth Wilson, *Adorned in Dreams: Fashion and Modernity* (New Brunswick, NJ: Rutgers University Press, 2003), introduction and chap. 1.

2   This text is based on research carried out by its author, Amalia Descalzo Lorenzo, and her professor Carmen Bernis, and published in Carmen Bernis and Amalia Descalzo, "El vestido femenino español en la época de los Austrias," in *Vestir a la española en las cortes europeas (siglos XVI y XVII)*, vol. 1, ed. José Luis Colomer and Amalia Descalzo (Madrid: Centro de Estudios Europa Hispánica, 2014), 39–75; and Amalia Descalzo Lorenzo, "Vestirse a la moda en la España moderna," *Vínculos de historia*, no. 6 (2017): 105–346.

3   In Western fashion, structured undergarments were worn by women from the 16th century to the late 19th century. The earliest examples appeared in Spain, including the *verdugado*, which led to the *guardainfante*. These were followed by the pannier and side hoops worn throughout Europe in the 18th century. The cage crinoline that was prevalent in the mid-19th century was superseded by the bustle in the 1870s and 1880s.

4   Pedro Álvarez de Miranda, *Palabras e ideas: El léxico de la ilustración temprana en España (1680–1760)* (Madrid: Real Academia Española, 1992), 655. Álvarez de Miranda affirms that the first appearance of the term *moda* (fashion) in Castilian Spanish is found in the 1641 novel titled *El diablo cojuelo*: "two Knights dressed according to fashion." Remaining unfamiliar in the 17th century, this term became popular in the 18th century. Denoting "habits and customs," as well as "mode and manner," this term underwent semantic variations starting in the 14th century, as attested by documents dating from this period. Accordingly—and despite the reticence of certain fashion scholars who judge the use of the term "moda" as either incorrect or anachronistic in historic contexts predating the 17th century—here it is employed as an apposite signifier of sartorial phenomena and trends.

5   "Defendemos y mandamos, que agora ni de aquí adelante ninguna persona de nuestros Reinos y Señoríos ni fuera de ellos, de cualquier condición, calidad, preeminencia o dignidad que sea, excepto nuestras Personas Reales y nuestros hijos, sean osados de traer ni vestir brocado, ni tela de oro ni plata tirada, ni de hilo de oro ni plata, ni seda alguna que lleve oro ni plata, ni cordón ni pespunte, ni pasamano ni otra cosa alguna de ellos, ni bordado ni recamado, ni escarchado de oro o plata fino o falso, o de perlas o aljófar o piedras, ni guarnición alguna de abalorio, de seda, ni cosa hecha en bastidor." "Novísima recopilación de las leyes de España," in *Los códigos españoles concordados y anotados*, tomo III, libro VI, título XIII, ley I (1847–51), 267–68, Biblioteca Jurídica Digital, https://www.boe.es.

6   "The term *guarnición* [which may translate as "trim," or more literally as "garnish"] comes from the verb *guarnir*, an old Castilian word taken from French meaning to adorn . . . and from the verb *guarnecer* [coined at a later date] came the word *guarnición* meaning adornment, an embellishment that jointly enhances and ennobles the thing it garnishes." Sebastián de Covarrubias Orozco, *Tesoro de la lengua castellana o española*, ed. Felipe C. R. Maldonado (1611; Madrid: Editorial Castalia, 1995), 612.

7   Carmen Bernis, "Tejidos y guarniciones," in *El traje y los tipos sociales en El Quijote* (Madrid: Ediciones El Viso, 2001), 281–92. The term *puntas* refers to any openwork with pointed or otherwise undulate or scalloped borders, also denominated "lace points." The term *puntas en las randas* (drawn-thread lace trims) appears in

Covarrubias Orozco, *Tesoro de la lengua castellana*, 841. "Puntas" also designates lace made of linen, silk, or any other material with a scalloped edge on one of its borders, according to the *Diccionario de autoridades*, vol. 5 (Madrid: Real Academia Española, 1990), 432. "*Randa*: openwork done with needles or bobbins on a loom," in Covarrubias Orozco, *Tesoro de la lengua castellana*, 849.

8   *Las pregmáticas y capítulos que su magestad del Emperador y Rey nuestro señor hizo en las Cortes de Valladolid, el año de mil e quinientos e treinta y siete; con la Declaración que sobre los trajes y sedas hizo* (Medina del Campo: Pedro de Castro, 1545), Biblioteca del Banco de España 2017, Signatura: FEV-SV-M-00295.

9   Florence Lewis May, *Hispanic Lace and Lace Making* (New York: Hispanic Society of America, 1939), 110.

10   Santina M. Levey, *Lace: A History* (Leeds: W. S. Maney & Son; London: Victoria and Albert Museum, 1983), 1–3.

11   In the 16th century, dress and its attendant paraphernalia became of paramount interest, triggering the appearance of the first works dedicated to this subject such as one written by Cristoph Weiditz, published in 1529; in addition, writings devoted to lace entered the scene, including an outstanding example by Cesare Vecellio titled *Corona delle Nobili et Virtuose Donne*, since its first publication in 1591 to the late 20th century.

12   Amalia Descalzo Lorenzo, "Spanish Foundation Garments in the Habsburg Period," in *Structuring Fashion: Foundation Garments through History* (Munich, Germany: Bayerisches Nationalmuseum, 2019), 39–49.

13   Shifts with gold-thread lace were among the assets seized from the Moors of Granada upon their expulsion from Spain. Carmen Bernis, "Las mujeres," in *Trajes y modas en la España de los Reyes Católicos*, vol. 1 (Madrid: Instituto Diego Velázquez, Consejo Superior de Investigaciones Científicas, 1978), 50.

14   María del Cristo González Marrero, *La casa de Isabel la Católica: Espacios domésticos y vida cotidiana* (Ávila, Spain: Diputación Provincial de Ávila; Ávila, Spain: Institución Gran Duque de Alba, 2005), 265–82.

15   Carmen Bernis, *Indumentaria española en tiempos de Carlos V* (Madrid: Instituto Diego Velázquez, Consejo Superior de Investigaciones Científicas, 1962), 92.

16   Dyeing fabrics in certain colors during the 16th and 17th centuries represented a veritable challenge. The introduction of natural wood dyes imported from the Americas, such as *palo de Campeche* (logwood dye), solved longstanding technical difficulties. Logwood dye supplied a high concentration of deep black colorant, making it an indispensable product. Dyeing silks black proved a lengthy and onerous process, leading to rather extravagant methods. The entire undertaking entailed nine stages—including cold water baths, acid dilutions, and successive decoctions—in order to obtain the desired shade of black. Once dyed, silk acquired an undesirable coarse texture; consequently, the last step consisted of sprucing up the appearance and softening the hand of the fabric. A softener was prepared by dissolving soap in boiling water and adding a handful of aniseed or any other aromatic plant. When the aforesaid mixture cooled down, it was used in washing the silk. For more information on this topic, see Ana Roquero, *Tintes y tintoreros de América: Catálogo de materias primas y registro etnográfico de México, Centro América, Andes Centrales y Selva Amazónica* (Madrid: Instituto del Patrimonio Histórico Español, 2006), 122–27. The following publications offer interesting facts relating to the color black and its presence in menswear throughout history: John Harvey, *Des hommes en noir: Du costume masculin à travers les siècles* (Paris: Éditions Abbeville, 1998), 83–116; and José Luis Colomer, "El negro y la image real," in Colomer and Descalzo, eds., *Vestir a la española en las cortes europeas (siglos XVI y XVII)*, 77–111.

17   "*Lechuguillas*: collars or collar bands of varied widths, made of

Holland cloth or linen, and gathered to create wave shapes similar to the ruffled look of lettuce leaves." Covarrubias Orozco, *Tesoro de la lengua castellana*, 705.

18 "*Abanillo*: also meaning inverted pleats, or the hollowed portion of frilled collars worn of yore." *Diccionario de autoridades*, 5:5. The terms *abanino* or *abanico* also refer to the crimping of linen collars. Among the upper classes of the 16th and 17th centuries, the term *saya* denoted a formal bodice-and-overskirt ensemble.

19 The cardboard busk or *cartón de pecho* appears in the second half of the 16th century in Spain. This foundation garment may be considered the ancestor of later corsets. Cardboard stays flattened female breasts, initially using wooden or cardboard boning and later replaced with baleen boning. Of particular interest is the description on this subject provided by the Countess D'Aulnoy in her travel memoir *Relación del viaje de España* (Madrid: Akal, 1986), 234.

20 For more on lechuguilla collars, see Bernis, *El traje y los tipos sociales*.

21 Toward the end of the 16th century, following the invention of the verdugado, other models of foundation garments emerged in Europe, shaping and expanding skirts in alternate manners. These European models were either Flemish—a thick cotton hoop placed at the level of the hips—or French—a sort of platform, possibly made of wicker, placed at the level of the waist.

Based on Pourbus's depiction of the Infanta's attendant, it seems that she may have a developmental disability, perhaps as a result of rickets. For further research on attendants at the Habsburg court, see Alfonso E. Pérez Sánchez, Julián Gállego, and Manuela B. Mena Marqués, *Monstruos, enanos y bufones en la Corte de los Austrias*, exh. cat. (Madrid: Amigos del Museo del Prado, D.L., 1986).

22 At the end of the 15th century, it became customary for the Spanish court to impose its own fashions, thereby pushing back against the introduction of French sartorial trends. Spanish men's dress comprised a doublet worn over a shirt, a *ropilla* worn over the doublet, breeches (*calzones*) worn over underpants (*calzoncillos*), stockings, and leather shoes. A cloak, or *ferreruelo*, became an essential item of clothing. Distinctive elements of Spanish dress included the prevalent use of black, the *golilla* collar, as well as a tendency toward austerity. Spanish dress was required of those attending formal ceremonies or events. Starting with the reign of Philip IV, de rigueur Spanish fashions reached other spheres despite not being mandatory. The only surviving Spanish outfit (*traje a la española*) from the mid-17th century belonged to Ambassador-at-Large Nils Nilsson Brahe (1633–99), a young Swedish count chosen to notify the monarchs of Spain of the abdication of Queen Christina of Sweden (1626–89) and the ascension to the throne of Charles X (1622–60) Gustav. Upon arriving in Madrid in January of 1655, he had to commission a traje a la española from a tailor. Fortunately, when Brahe returned to his native Sweden, he brought back with him this set of garments, which are currently preserved as part of the museum collection of Skokloster Castle. Lena Rangström, ed., "Fashion in Spanish and Nils Nilsson Brahe's Costume of 1655," in *Lions of Fashion: Male Fashion of the 16th, 17th, 18th Centuries* (Stockholm: Livrustkammeren, 2002), 365–66.

23 Amalia Descalzo Lorenzo and Carlos Gómez Centurión Jiménez, "El Real Guardarropa y la introducción de la moda francesa en la corte de Felipe V," in *La herencia de Borgoña: La hacienda de la Reales Casas durante el reinado de Felipe V*, ed. Carlos Gómez-Centurión Jiménez and Juan A. Sánchez Belén (Madrid: Centro de Estudios Políticos y Constitucionales, 1998), 159–87.

24 Manuel José Ayala, "Noticia del origen y principio del uso de las Golillas en España. Providencia que tomó el Consejo de Castilla contra un Golillero mandando quemar las que tenía hechas para la Personas Reales con sus moldes e instrumentos, por opuestas a la reforma que se intentaba hacer de trages" [News of the origin and initial use of golillas in Spain. Ordinance issued by the Council of Castile against a *golillero* (a golilla maker) ordering him to burn those golillas intended for Royal Persons made with his molds and instruments since the said golillas contravene the dress reform efforts being implemented], *Miscelánea*, tomo XXXVII (1767–97), 240, II/2850al, Real Biblioteca del Palacio Real de Madrid.

25 Amalia Descalzo Lorenzo, "El retrato y la moda en España (1661–1746)," 3 vols. (PhD diss., Universidad Autónoma de Madrid, Facultad de Filosofía y Letras, 2003).

26 "Guardarropa," in *Cuentas del Rey Carlos II*, leg. 911, 1690, Sección Administrativa, Archivo General de Palacio de Madrid.

27 "Mercaderes de sedas, lienzos y telas," in *Cuentas de particulares*, leg. 5256, 1679–99, Archivo General de Palacio de Madrid.

28 The vaquero is a garment of Turkish origin. Although it was worn by both men and women in specific instances requiring greater ease of movement, it was mainly destined for children—boys and girls—from the second half of the 16th century into the 17th century. According to original patterns dating from this time period, this type of dress had a fitted torso, an ample skirt, and two pairs of sleeves: a first pair covered the arms, whereas a second pair consisted of long, flat, shoulder-hanging sleeves. The latter were also termed "casaque sleeves."

29 The guardainfante was a 17th-century Spanish foundation garment, detached from underskirts, which expanded skirts into large bell shapes. Velázquez depicted garments supported by this contraption in his portraits of courtiers and members of the royal family; nevertheless, it was worn by women of all social classes. Amalia Descalzo Lorenzo, "Velázquez y la moda: Aproximación a la identidad de la dama del abanico," in *In sapientia libertas: Escritos en homenaje al profesor Alfonso Emilio Pérez Sánchez* (Madrid: Museo Nacional del Prado; Seville, Spain: Fundación Focus-Abengoa, 2007), 435–40.

30 Rodrigo Méndez Silva, *Diálogo compendioso de la antigüedad y cosas memorables de la noble y coronada villa de Madrid y recibimiento que en ella hizo su Magestad católica, con la grandeza de su Corte a la princesa de Cariñán, clarísima consorte del serenísimo príncipe Tomas, con sus genealogías: Al señor don Alonso Pérez de Guzmán, patriarca de las Indias* (Madrid: Viuda de Alonso Martín, 1637).

31 *Cuentas de costureras, modistas y encajeras*, leg. 5278-1, exp. 1, 1586–1672, Administración General, Archivo General de Palacio de Madrid.

32 "Mantos de Sevilla, de un negro intenso guarnecidos con puntas y encajes de Flandes." "Carta de Dote de Ana Moreno," 1643, protocolo nº 6794, fol. 338, Archivo Histórico de Protocolos, Madrid. Seville mantles are repeatedly mentioned and described in inventories and dowry letters consulted at the Protocol Historical Archive of Madrid. The source cited above provides the following information: "Vestidos: un manto de Sevilla de los buenos nuevo con puntas y encajes de Flandes tasado en trecientos reales" (Dresses: a Seville mantle of good quality, new, and with pointed-edge lace trims and lacework appraised at 300 reales).

33 Typically Spanish, the ropilla was a short overgarment with sleeve caps surrounded by a fold (*brahón*) and hanging sleeves; it could be tightened at the waist and was placed over a doublet.

34 Descalzo Lorenzo, "El retrato y la moda en España (1661–1746)."

35 The sacristán consisted of a series of five or six circular hoops made of thick metal wires—the top one surrounding the waist—attached by ribbons and widening in diameter from top to bottom. The tontillo was configured by sewing hoops directly onto an underskirt, an assemblage system replicating that of the preceding verdugado, and possibly heralding French side hoops called panniers.

36 D'Aulnoy, *Relación del viaje de España*, 233.

37 The details relative to the lace featured in this portrait of Nicolasa Manrique de Mendoza are based on González Mena, *Catálogo de encajes*, 127.

6 "A Desire of Being Distinguished by an Elegant Dress Is Universal": Clothing, Status, and Convenience in Eighteenth-Century Spanish America

Mariselle Meléndez

I N THEIR MONUMENTAL WORK *Relación histórica del viage a la América Meridional* (*A Voyage to South America*; 1748), Jorge Juan (1713–1773) and Antonio de Ulloa (1716–1795) discuss the fashion styles and preferences of the inhabitants of the Viceroyalty of Peru.[1] In the case of women in particular, they state that in Peru, no matter their social status or race, "a desire of being distinguished by an elegant dress is universal."[2] In fact, they underscore that "the lower classes of women, even to the very negroes, affect, according to their abilities, to imitate their betters, not only in the fashion of their dress, but also in the richness of it."[3] For the authors, the desire to dress fashionably was so ingrained in colonial Spanish American women that the incorporation of expensive textiles from abroad as well as those produced regionally gave way to original fashion styles. In eighteenth-century Spanish America, to dress well became a way of life and a form of self-expression. This essay focuses on two important topics through which we can read fashion in this period: first, the love for ostentatious fashion and, second, the innovation in fashionable styles guided by local taste.

Dressing in Excess

In a letter written in 1791 to the editors of the Peruvian newspaper *Mercurio peruano* (1790–95), a distraught husband vented his frustration about the excessive expenses that his beautiful wife had incurred. This letter serves as an example of the love for extravagant fashion that Juan and Ulloa witnessed in Peruvian women when they visited South America. In it, the husband recounts how his wife spends prodigally on household items, care from doctors, and gastronomic preferences, but his greatest complaint is her spending on fashion. The husband titles his missive "Letter written to the Society about the excessive expenses of a *tapada*" (for an example of a woman dressed in tapada fashion, SEE FIG. 6.1).[4] The account offers pertinent information about how the consumption of luxurious fashion among upper-class women in Spanish America was perceived as a visible marker and reminder of social status and prestige. It offers a glimpse of the active role that women

FIG. 6.1
"Spanish woman with mantelet" ("Española con manto"), from Baltasar Martínez Compañón, *Trujillo del Perú*, vol. 2, plate 5, 1779–89. Ink on paper. Patrimonio Nacional. Real Biblioteca II/344, plate 5.

had in the production and consumption of clothes. In his letter, the husband complains that his wife thinks it necessary to wear different outfits for every social occasion. He states that in the summer she wears four different upper petticoats (known as *faldellines*) while in the winter she opts for two. All this is in addition to the exorbitant amount that she spends on expensive shoes and on her hairdresser.

For the husband, the existence of a whole human enterprise fostering consumption by women like his wife is a problem. To this effect, he adds that his wife's passion for new luxurious fashion is due to the fact that the silversmith constantly "renews all fashion styles" while the dressmaker "invents them, changes them, and changes them again."[5] To add to this problem, "the merchant sells his wife lace, satin, brocade, and lamé on credit."[6] This passage elucidates the impact that the global enterprise of fashion had on Spanish America in the eighteenth century. The luxurious textiles used to make upper petticoats underscore the accessibility of global items through an active transoceanic commerce that benefited many. Lace, satin, brocade, and fabrics with gold and silver threads were highly valued and sought after to make the famous faldellines that were so popular in the Spanish American colonies, particularly in Peru.[7]

Visual sources of the period demonstrate that the husband in the *Mercurio peruano* was not exaggerating when he pointed out the accessibility of luxury fabrics in Peru. Baltasar Jaime Martínez Compañón (1737–1797), in *Trujillo del Perú* (1779–89), depicts an "Española con mantilla y bolador" (Spanish woman with mantilla and sash) wearing a white lace mantilla with a red sash on top (FIG. 6.2).[8] Her calf-length faldellín, seemingly embroidered with a floral vine pattern, displays her embroidered silk stockings. The skirt is adorned with a fine lace apron and underskirt. In one of the *casta* paintings ordered by Manuel Amat y Junyent (1707–1782), the viceroy of Peru from 1761 to 1776, the Spanish woman is also dressed in a gold-brocaded silk and lace (FIG. 6.3).[9] More importantly, the love for luxury fabrics was not the sole purview of Spanish women; women of mixed backgrounds were also able to integrate them into their fashion, as pictured in Vicente Albán's oil painting of the mestiza prostitute from Quito known by the term *yapanga* (SEE FIG. 8.2).[10]

In the case of the husband who sent the letter to the *Mercurio peruano*, he was fully aware that fashion in the Peruvian capital had become a profitable enterprise in which tailors, silversmiths, and merchants were active participants. He even complained that the merchant kept selling to his wife on credit when she could not pay up front. It is clear that fashion allowed many women to express their identity through the act of choosing independently and disregarding their husbands' consent. In fact, in another letter published in the same newspaper a month later, a woman using the pseudonym M. Antispásia responds to the first letter, criticizing the husband's impulse to monitor and manage his wife's desire to dress differently according to the social occasion. She

FIG. 6.2
"Spanish woman with mantilla and sash" ("Española con mantilla y bolador"), from Baltasar Martínez Compañón, *Trujillo del Perú*, vol. 2, plate 2, 1779–89. Ink on paper. Patrimonio Nacional. Real Biblioteca II/344, plate 2.

states that there is no reason to follow men's wishes and "slovenly taste" (*gusto estra-falario*) and that men should allow women "to live in peace" (*vivir en paz*).[11] Fashion in the eighteenth century became, for women, a matter of taste and independence. As Beverly Lemire and Giorgio Riello argue, fashion artifacts act as "active agents in history" in the sense that they have "communicative, performative, emotive, and expressive capacities."[12] This, in fact, is the case of the expensive faldellines that the wife insisted on owning and wearing. In Spain Rebecca Haidt observes that "women were active participants in the clothing and textile circulations crucial to eighteenth-century urban economic life."[13] I would argue that the same can be said about Spanish America. If fashion, as Haidt adds, "was impossible to divide neatly from raw materials, labor, commerce, or ideas about productivity and economic growth," then it is important to note how women in Spanish America aimed to create their own sense of style through their fascination with and consumption of sumptuous textiles.[14]

Observations made by Juan and Ulloa years before coincide with the information offered in the *Mercurio peruano*. The authors reserved the most detailed descriptions in their account for the clothing preferences of the inhabitants of Lima. They first state that men from all castas basically dress the same as the Spaniards do and that it was difficult to distinguish a man's social status because all his garments were constructed using the same textiles. They commented that *mulatos* and other lower-class individuals "dressed in a tissue equal to anything that can be worn by a more opulent person. They

FIG. 6.3

Spaniard. White People. Almost of pure lineage (Español Gente blanca Quasi limpio de su Origen), 1751–1800. Oil on canvas. Museo Nacional de Antropología, Madrid, CE5256.

all greatly affect fine cloths."[15] They add that there is no place in the Americas where the fabric imported from other countries is used more creatively to display opulence. They also state that Lima's inhabitants are great consumers of foreign textiles, despite the fact that such fabrics are much more costly than they would be in Europe. Furthermore, they emphasize that in Lima, the fact that "vanity and ostentation [were not] restrained by custom or law" contributed to the blurring of social classifications based on what clothes people were allowed to wear.[16] And if this was generally the case for men, the authors underline that the same issues for women were far worse. For this reason, they found it of great relevance to devote a lengthy discussion to women's obsession with expensive fabrics.

To begin this discussion, Juan and Ulloa note that women's enthusiasm for wearing lace in Lima was shared even among those of lesser status. As they observe, "In the choice of laces their women carried their taste to a prodigious excess."[17] This fact is evident in the casta paintings commissioned by Viceroy Amat y Junyent in 1770, one of which depicts a sumptuously dressed Indigenous woman (FIG. 6.4) and another a woman of African descent (FIG. 6.5). Some Black women even incorporated lace in their attire but not as frequently as noblewomen.[18] According to the authors, "The laces are sewed to their linen, which is of the finest sort, though very little of it is seen, the greatest part of it, especially in some addresses, being always covered with lace, so that the little which appears seems rather for ornament than use."[19] This use of lace is clear in the casta paintings commissioned by the viceroy. The authors add that the lace worn by women in Lima in their lower skirt was so fine that the garters were visible underneath.[20] These garters were made of gold and silver embroidery and, on occasion, decorated with pearls. Women even purposely wore their faldellín short, with a calf-length hemline exposing the white lace underskirt known as *fustan*, which was visible from the floor to the ankles.

The woman labeled *A* in an illustration included in the section devoted to the description of the inhabitants of Peru wears this style (FIG. 6.6). On the use of lace, the authors conclude, "These laces too must be all of Flanders manufacture, no woman of rank condescending to look on any other."[21] Women in Lima were fully aware of the value of expensive imported fabrics when it came to exhibiting social status but opted to incorporate it according to their own individual preferences.

Finally, the attention women paid to their hairstyles is also worth noting. Juan and Ulloa describe how women styled their long hair by tying it up in the back in six braided locks, balancing them atop the head with a golden

bodkin called a *polizon*. The braids were folded to fall above their shoulders and decorated with diamond aigrettes, or *trembleques de diamantes*, as the women called them. They added curls over the forehead and down the sides of their ears, affixing a large black patch of velvet on each temple, as depicted in the Peruvian casta painting *Spaniard and Mestiza Produce Mestizo Quadroon* (FIG. 6.7).[22] Women also wore bright earrings with pearls, from which they sometimes hung their braids. This style is evident in Vicente Albán's *Noblewoman with Her Black Slave* (FIG. 6.8). Over their neck they wore rosaries made of large pearls as depicted in Albán's painting. For special social events, they wore embroidery inlaid with jewels known as *intillos*, diamond rings, and pearl and diamond bracelets set in gold or an imitation of gold known as *tumbaga*.[23] Juan and Ulloa concluded that the cost of a noblewoman's outfit for social events "covered with the most expensive lace instead of linen, and glittering from head to toe with jewels," could exceed 30,000 or 40,000 pesos because of all the lace, diamonds, gold, silver, and pearls used.[24]

One can understand, within this context, why the husband of the tapada woman in the *Mercurio peruano* was so alarmed at the excessive expenses that his wife incurred. In Peru's capital, fashion and luxury went hand in hand, allowing women to display and express their taste in various ways, with sole knowledge of what dressing well entailed at the time and how to creatively play with fabrics and style. This desire to innovate did not escape the authors, who affirmed that "their dress is very different from the European, which the custom of the country alone can render excusable; indeed to Spaniards at

FIG. 6.5

Mulatta and Spaniard Produce Mulatto Quadroon (*Mulata. con Español. Produsen. Quarteron de. Mulato*), 1751–1800. Oil on canvas. Museo Nacional de Antropología, Madrid, CE5252.

FIG. 6.6

Jorge Juan and Antonio de Ulloa, *Relación histórica del viage a la América Meridional hecho de orden de S. Mag. para medir algunos grados de meridiano terrestre y venir por ellos en conocimiento de la verdadera figura y magnitud de la Tierra con otras varias observaciones astronomicas y phisicas*, fig. 8.2. Madrid: Por Antonio Marin, 1748. Engraving. Archive.org, John Carter Brown Library.

the first coming over it appears extremely indecent."[25] For Europeans it was difficult to comprehend how local needs and taste made this exceptionally ostentatious dress acceptable to the inhabitants of Lima.

Fashion Tastes and Needs: The Transoceanic Meets the Local

News in the *Mercurio* offers a picture of the textiles and fashionable garments that were exported from and imported to the Viceroyalty of Peru, and, in particular, its capital city of Lima. For example, cotton was a popular export item shipped from Lima to Buenos Aires, as was *Paño de Quito*, a type of wool that at the time was facing fierce competition due to the cheaper wool coming from Europe.[26] With Chile, merchants in Lima primarily exported wool from Quito, as well as textiles of Spanish American origin known as *ropa de la tierra*.[27] From the port of Guayaquil, Lima received wool of ordinary quality referred to as *paños ordinarios*, hats made of straw, stitched wool of poor quality described as *piezas de sayales*, satin, and white linen.[28] The port of Callao in Peru exported to the port of Cadiz in Spain vicuña wool, linen, sailcoth (*lona*), and feathered hats (*sombreros de pluma*).[29] Finally, from the Philippines and Cadiz, the port of Callao received wool. These shipment records of transoceanic exchanges underline the global impact that all

types of textiles had in Spanish America. They also demonstrate how Spanish America participated as an active producer of certain textiles. Juan and Ulloa had already noted that in the Cajamarca and Chachapoyas mountains in the Peruvian Andes different types of cotton were produced and exported, while Potosí and Cuzco produced and exported vicuña wool. The importance of the vicuña is reflected in the inclusion of the animal in Juan and Ulloa's illustration of Andean camelids (labeled *H* in FIG. 6.6). They also mention that the same area produced "fine textiles," referred to as *Texidos finos*, that were sent to Lima and then exported to Quito and Panama.[30]

One must remember that since the early sixteenth century, a global trade between Asia and the Americas via the Mexican port city of Acapulco facilitated the exchange of goods between the two continents.[31] With regard to fashion, textiles including colorful silks and fine linens were exported from Asia to the Americas, which brought great quantities of silver to Asia in return. The commercial trade was so successful that riches from Asia and the Americas served to dress Spain's empire, as Timothy Brook argues when discussing the 1761 illustration map "Aspecto symbólico del mundo hispánico" (Symbolic aspect of the Hispanic world; FIG. 6.9). The illustration captures "the robust global empire" and "Spain's world dominance," with the "Philippines as the base of Hispania," where Spain's success stands.[32] In this map, the allegorical figure of Hispania is richly dressed, with the Americas serving as her mantle. As Brook notes, "the creases of her dress chart the routes of the galleons to Acapulco, Mexico, from the Philippine

FIG. 6.7
Spaniard and Mestiza Produce Mestizo Quadroon (Español. Mestiza. Producen Quarterona de mestizo), 1751–1800. Oil on canvas. Museo Nacional de Antropología, Madrid, CE5246.

archipelago at her feet."[33] Although Brook's brief discussion of this map stresses the importance that the Philippines' trade with the Americas (and vice versa) had as part "of a growing network of goods and people circulating the globe," I would like to emphasize the figurative role that fashion plays in this map as a marker of distinction.[34] Important to notice is how the mantle "dresses" the empire, underlining that Spanish America was not a mere recipient of goods. The variety of textiles acquired through trade, along with those produced in the American territories, contributed to a desire to adapt Asian and European fabrics to Spanish American needs and tastes.

Notable also is the fact that women were heavily involved in the production of textiles, as shown in a series of illustrations by Martínez Compañón (FIGS. 6.10 AND 6.11; SEE ALSO FIGS. 7.20 AND 8.15). In one illustration, Compañón depicts an Indigenous woman making silk trim in what appears to be a beautiful Andean pattern (SEE FIG. 7.20). Another illustration shows two Indigenous women in the process of spinning yarn or thread with the use of a spinning wheel, and a third portrays a group of mestiza women from Chachapoyas embroidering *rengos*.[35] The women are hand-embroidering patterns of local flora and fauna onto a length of *piña* cloth, a fabric of Philippine origin made from pineapple fiber. It had been produced since the sixteenth century, and according to Marlene Flores Ramos, "the cloth is very sheer; it is as lustrous as silk and has the strength of linen. It lends itself exquisitely to hand embroidery producing a very delicate and intricate lace."[36] In this fascinating image, the transpacific textile is transformed by the native women into a regionally specific artifact and showcases the artistry and skills necessary to produce a textile that looks like lace. Men were also involved in the

FIG. 6.8
Vicente Albán, *Noblewoman with Her Black Slave (Sra. principal con su negra esclava)*, 1783. Oil on canvas. Los Angeles County Museum of Art, Purchased with funds provided by the Bernard and Edith Lewin Collection of Mexican Art Deaccession Fund, M.2014.89.1.

"A Desire of Being Distinguished by an Elegant Dress Is Universal"

FIG. 6.9

"Symbolic Aspect of the Hispanic World" ("Aspecto symbólico del mundo Hispánico") from Vicente Memije, *Theses Matemáticas de Cosmographia, Geographia y Hydrographía*. Manilia: Vicente de Memije, 1761. Engraving. © British Library Board, Maps K.Top.118.19.

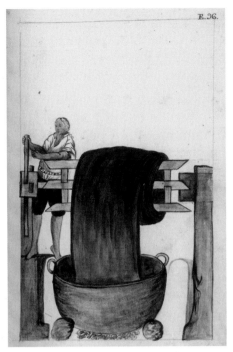

production of local textiles, as illustrated in the watercolor of an Indigenous man dyeing what is likely cotton fabric (FIG. 6.11). One can argue that the transatlantic and transpacific commerce of textiles united global imaginaries that, in the case of the inhabitants of the Spanish colonies, served as instruments to construct their own identities and to claim a sense of belonging to a certain social class. Through fashion, women and men in the colonies acquired prestige, status, and employment. More importantly, textiles were transformed and modified to fit local taste and did not function simply as a copy of European norms.

Alonso Carrió de la Vandera (ca. 1714–1783), author of *El lazarillo de ciegos caminantes* (1775), offers an example of how elite women integrated local styles into European trends through a comparative discussion of the fashion preferences among women in the viceregal capitals of Mexico and Lima during this period.[37] Through the voice of the Indigenous narrator Concolorcorvo, the author briefly describes the differences between the dress styles of upper-class women in Mexico and those in Lima, stating that Mexican women tend to follow European fashions much more closely, including the types of shoes they wear. However, he emphasizes that these women also integrated certain Indigenous stylistic elements, as they wore a "*mestizo* dress" that, according to him, "from the waist up imitated something of the indigenous garb, in the use of huipiles and *quesquémeles*, summer ankle-length tunics and winter shawls." The author adds that this style, called *cotones*, became "a new invention among young courtesan women."[38] As previously stated, fashion at the time was not a one-way adaptation in which all the influences came from Europe. In this case, the huipil is a type of tunic

FIG. 6.10 (LEFT)

"Indigenous women spinning on a spinning wheel" ("Yndias hilando al torno") from Baltasar Martínez Compañón, *Trujillo del Perú*, vol. 2, plate 101, 1779–89. Ink on paper. Patrimonio Nacional. Real Biblioteca II/344, plate 101.

FIG. 6.11 (RIGHT)

"Indigenous man dyeing fabric" ("Yndio tiñendo ropa") from Baltasar Martínez Compañón, *Trujillo del Perú*, vol. 2, plate 96, 1779–89. Ink on paper. Patrimonio Nacional. Real Biblioteca II/344, plate 96.

sewn from two to five rectangular pieces of fabric that was worn by Indigenous women of any social rank in Mesoamerica prior to the arrival of the Spanish in the Americas (FIG. 6.12).[39] Woven in cotton, silk, or wool, depending on the local climate, the traditional huipil was subsequently embroidered with mostly geometric motifs but also Indigenous religious symbology.[40] On the other hand, the *qu(e)squémel* (also spelled *quesquémetl, quezquemitl,* or *quechquémitl*) is described as an Indigenous Mexican garment worn by the Nahuatl elite in pre-Hispanic times. The triangular form consists of "a cloth with a neck hole cut in the center; it is pulled on over the head and usually falls to a point in front and back."[41] It was used only by noblewomen and priestesses in ceremonies and worn over a huipil (FIG. 6.13). However, after Spanish colonization of Mexico, all Indigenous women, no matter their social rank, began to wear it.[42] Pre-Hispanic quesquémeles were made of wool for warmth, but later cotton was used as well. Because of its triangular form, it was easy to put on and also very practical, as it allowed for freedom of movement. These two garments that Carrió de la Vandera describes as very popular among women in eighteenth-century Mexico draw attention to how fashion in the Spanish colonies was the result of a mixed set of influences ranging from local Indigenous traditional dress to contemporary European and Asian influences. In the eighteenth century, fashion was a "glocal" commodity, where the global and the local converged to create something different.

FIG. 6.12

Malinztin (or "La Malinche") and a group of Aztec women represented wearing huipiles in a detail from *Lienzo de Tlaxcala*, Texas Fragment, ca. 1530–40. Painted cotton. Benson Latin American Collection, LLILAS Benson Latin American Studies and Collections, University of Texas at Austin, Ex-Stendahl Collection, 1993–24.

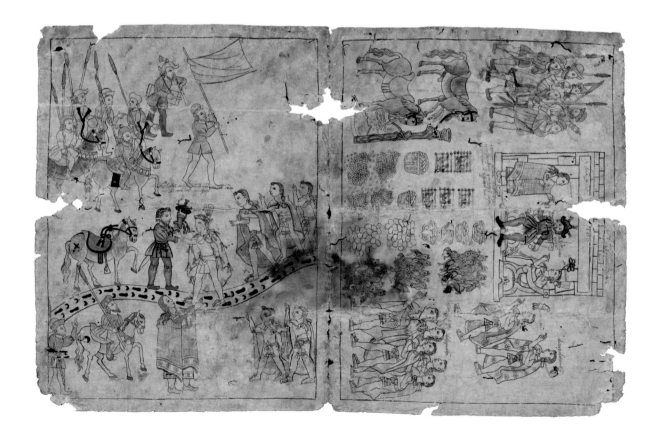

This adaptation of Indigenous garb by upper-class women in Spanish America is also noted by Juan and Ulloa in their travels through Cartagena de Indias. They remark that Spanish women living in the port city wore a style of clothing called a *pollera* that they describe as "a kind of petticoat . . . made of thin silk, without any lining and on their body, a very thin white waistcoat" that they can only wear in the winter, "it being insupportable in summer."[43] The waistcoat, referred to as *jubón* or *Almilla blanca*, protected them from the cold weather. When women attended public events, they added a mantelet (*manto*). The authors also note that those women who were not legitimately white wore a "taffeta petticoat" (*basquiña de tafetan*) over their pollera in a variety of colors except black.[44] They covered their heads with a cap of "fine white lining covered with lace," adding adornments in order to look elegant.[45] Taking into consideration, as James Middleton suggests, that "the pollera ensemble" is "the product of a collision between the informal, at home-dress of elite seventeenth-century Peruvian women and the dress of the elite of pre-Hispanic women," one can argue that this fashion style crossed borders as it was witnessed in Cartagena de Indias.[46] It is another example of how the local transformed the global as a result of environmental circumstances. Matters of practicality also added to the preference for the pollera as, according to Juan and Ulloa, it allowed women to move more freely.

Clothing as a practical artifact was also key for Indigenous women at the time. Juan and Ulloa comment that Indigenous women from the lower classes wore a special garment that they referred to as *tupu*, which was a one-piece dress made of locally produced cotton.[47] The dress was pinned at the shoulders and extended to the calves and was similar in length to the garment worn by the "India ordinaria" (Ordinary Indigenous woman) that the authors include in their illustration showing the categorization of Indigenous women based on their clothing (FIG. 6.14).[48] In depictions of women from the lower classes, it is interesting to note that the versatility of their garments allows them to perform a variety of tasks. In this particular image, the Indigenous woman is able to carry a baby while her hands remain free. A similar example is captured in Martínez Compañón's *Trujillo del Perú* (FIG. 6.15), where he depicts an Indigenous woman from the valleys wearing a similar style of clothing that allows her to weave a colorful textile while taking care of her child.

Even for noble Indigenous women, fashion served a function beyond a mark of distinction. Juan and Ulloa make a point to emphasize how differently *cacica* Indians dressed from other Indigenous women.[49] They wore wool polleras decorated with silk

FIG. 6.13

Quechquémitl from *Códice Vaticano Ríos*, 61r, ca. 1566. Ink on paper. © 2022 Biblioteca Apostolica Vaticana, Vat.lat.3738.

ribbons and, on other occasions, a type of black skirt tied with a ribbon at the waist, which did not wrap around like the faldellín did.[50] They also preferred a *lliclla* that went all the way down to the pollera; they pinned this longer lliclla at the chest with a large silver pin, as depicted in the image that the authors include of the noble Indigenous woman ("India palla"; SEE FIG. 6.14).[51] This image illustrates well how Indigenous women from the upper classes still preserved their pre-Hispanic garments, which, as Elena Phipps reminds us, "are basically rectangular pieces of cloth," although endowed with "subtle and abstract traits" that indicated social status or region of origin, among other things.[52] The authors also pay particular attention to the hair decorations of these Indigenous noblewomen, indicating that they wore what was referred to as a *colla*, or a white cloth (*paño*) folded several times with a piece hanging down the back (see the "Yndia Palla"). The colla not only served as a marker of distinction but also protected the wearer from the sun.

Finally, adaptations of Indigenous attire by the Spanish elites are another example of how the natural environment dictated fashion. The image "Spaniards in Chilean dress" (*Españoles en el traje de Chile*) that Juan and Ulloa included helps underscore how geography also influenced what people wore (FIG. 6.16). The authors observe that

FIG. 6.14

Jorge Juan and Antonio de Ulloa, *Relación histórica del viage a la América Meridional hecho de orden de S. Mag. para medir algunos grados de meridiano terrestre y venir por ellos en conocimiento de la verdadera figura y magnitud de la Tierra con otras varias observaciones astronomicas y phisicas*, page 378. Madrid: Por Antonio Marin, 1748. Engraving. Archive.org, John Carter Brown Library.

women and men in Chile did not wear clothing as ostentatious as that of the people in Lima or Quito. According to their observations, all men, no matter their racial or social background, wore the "Poncho garb" (*Trage de los Ponchos*). The authors explain that due to weather and environmental conditions Indigenous men and women in Chile all dressed with ponchos and mantas woven from wool.[53] In fact, in the lexical appendix ("Índice general") added to the last volume of their book, Juan and Ulloa offer a description of the word "Poncho," describing it as a "type of clothing style used in Chile" (*ropage que se usa en Chile*).[54] They add that the ponchos were exported to Buenos Aires, among other places in South America. For the Spaniards who arrived in these new environments, Chilean dress became part of their wardrobes. These Indigenous garments offered more mobility in addition to warmth in these harsh environments. A similar adaptation can be found in Martínez Compañón's description of a Spanish man on horseback who is wearing a poncho-style garment woven with identifiable Andean designs (FIG. 6.17). In this sense, as Stephanie Saunders suggests, under the "politics of colonialism and empire," clothing that had been used "for corporeal covering and protection" turned into fashion for others, as is the case with the Spanish men in these last two images.[55] All the cases discussed in this essay underline the fact that fashion "as a cultural process is a profoundly social experience that invites individual and collective bodies to assume certain identities, and at times also to transgress limits and create new ones."[56] In eighteenth-century Spanish America, government impositions were challenged repeatedly by citizens with a desire to express their cultural and social identities through clothing and to foster a sense of belonging. As I have demonstrated elsewhere, the colonial decrees pronounced in the eighteenth century against the abuse of superfluous clothing and expenses by women offer "solid evidence of the anxiety that colonial authorities felt towards women's control over their own bodies when deciding what to wear and how much to spend for it."[57] However, as Tamara Walker has expressed more recently in relation to the Black female population in Lima, colonial officials in the eighteenth century continued "to struggle to regulate access to clothing." As Walker adds, the reason behind this is that "beyond the Spaniards who used their slaves as indices of their own status, and the slaves who stole clothing to outfit themselves and their social intimates in finery, were slaveholders who facilitated slaves' ability to dress in ways that

FIG. 6.15
"Indigenous woman from Valles spinning" ("Yndia de Valles texiendo"), from Baltasar Martínez Compañón, *Trujillo del Perú*, vol. 2, plate 100, 1779–89. Ink on paper. Patrimonio Nacional. Real Biblioteca II/344, plate 100.

reflected their own sense of self (particularly as they gained access to freedom)."[58] A sense of belonging to society was the main impulse behind the desire to dress beyond the limits associated with their social class.

Conclusion

The use of textiles as a sign of social status was not new to the native populations of the viceroyalties. It is important to understand that, since pre-Hispanic times, textiles represented symbols of power, markers of social status and cultural prestige, artifacts of decoration, tribute to emperors, and crucial protection against the elements for Indigenous societies in the Americas.[59] Eighteenth-century written sources, along with visual depictions from the period, offer a glimpse of the role that fashion incorporating lace, silk, cotton, wool, linen, and gold and silver fabrics occupied in the daily lives of all sectors of Spanish American colonial society. These records also demonstrate that fashion in the colonies was not a pure imitation of European tendencies, but rather the result of regional and global influences. As James Middleton observes in his study of the pollera in the eighteenth century, "It is curious, and indeed unique in the

FIG. 6.16 (ABOVE)

Jorge Juan and Antonio de Ulloa, "Spaniards in Chilean dress" ("Españoles en el trage de Chile"), from *Relación histórica del viage a la América Meridional hecho de orden de S. Mag. para medir algunos grados de meridiano terrestre y venir por ellos en conocimiento de la verdadera figura y magnitud de la Tierra con otras varias observaciones astronomicas y phisicas*, page 328. Madrid: Por Antonio Marin, 1748. Engraving. Archive.org, John Carter Brown Library.

FIG. 6.17 (OPPOSITE)

"Spanish man on horseback" ("Español a cavallo"), from Baltasar Martínez Compañón, *Trujillo del Perú*, vol. 2, plate 8, 1779–89. Ink on paper. Patrimonio Nacional. Real Biblioteca II/344, plate 8.

eighteenth-century Atlantic World, that the women of viceregal Peru chose to reject hegemonic international style, and to spend their money instead on the home-grown alternative."[60] In my view, geography and natural environment contributed to the decision not to totally reject but rather to incorporate and transform the transpacific and transatlantic luxurious fashion trends to local traditional styles. In the eighteenth century, taste in fashion was the result of experimentation with foreign and regional textiles; such is the case of the pollera, in which silk and lace were incorporated into traditional Indigenous patterns dating back to the pre-Hispanic period. For both men and women, social distinction played an important role in what they wore as well as when and how, and what textiles they selected for their garments. In eighteenth-century Spanish America, fashion was the result of many cultural influences that combined with local needs and preferences to give birth to innovation.

1   Jorge Juan and Antonio de Ulloa, *Relación histórica del viage a la América Meridional hecho de orden de S. Mag. para medir algunos grados de meridiano terrestre y venir por ellos en conocimiento de la verdadera figura y magnitud de la Tierra con otras varias observaciones astronomicas y phisicas* (Madrid: Antonio Marín, 1748). Quotations in English are from Jorge Juan and Antonio de Ulloa, *A Voyage to South America, Describing at Large the Spanish Cities, Towns, Provinces, &c. on That Extensive Continent: Undertaken by Command of the King of Spain*, trans. John Adams (1748; London: J. Brookdale, 1806) and are accompanied by the original Spanish text in the footnotes. Please note that the division of chapters in the English edition does not coincide with the Spanish original, so when quoting in English only the volume and the page number are indicated.
2   Juan and Ulloa, *A Voyage to South America*, 2:68; Juan and Ulloa, *Relación*, vol. 2, book 6, chap. 5, 81: "El aseo y primor es tan general en todas."
3   Juan and Ulloa, *A Voyage to South America*, 2:68; Juan and Ulloa, *Relación*, vol. 2, book 6, chap. 5, 81: "Las demas clases de Mugeres siguen el exemplo de las Señora, assi en la moda de su Vestuario, como en la pompa de èl, llegando la suntuosidad de las Galas hasta las Negras."
4   P. Fixiogamio, "Carta escrita a la Sociedad sobre los gastos excesivos de una Tapada," *Mercurio peruano*, February 10, 1791, 111–14. The *Mercurio peruano* was founded by the Sociedad Académica de Amantes del País (Academic Society of Lovers of the Country), a group of young intellectual Creoles mainly from Lima. The word "Society" refers to the founders of this group and editors of the newspaper. The term *tapada* refers to a woman who dressed in a style that originated in Spain and was adapted in Spanish America. This style was composed of a mantelet (*manto*) used to cover the entire face, with the exception of one eye. The rest of the mantelet was wrapped around the shoulders to the waist. Women in Spain incorporated this Moorish style and made it a popular fashion. Enrique Rodríguez-Solís, *Historia de la prostitución en España y en América* (Madrid: Biblioteca Nueva, 1921), 126. All translations from

18th-century primary sources are by the author unless otherwise specified.
5   Fixiogamio, "Carta escrita a la Sociedad," 113–14: "renueva todas las modas"; "las inventa, las muda, y las remuda." All quotations from the *Mercurio peruano* and other primary sources discussed in this chapter follow the orthography of that time.
6   Ibid.: "le fia a mi Muger los encajes, los rasos, y los espolines, y las lamas." According to the 18th-century *Diccionario de autoridades*, *espolín* is a "certain type of silk strewn and woven with flower patterns, known today as gold or silk brocade" (cierto género de tela de seda, fabricada con flores esparcidas, y en cierta manera sobretexidas como el que hoy se dice Brocado de oro, ù seda). *Diccionario de autoridades*, 3 vols. (1732; Madrid: Editorial Gredos, 1990), 2:611.
7   *Faldellín* refers to an upper petticoat that functioned as a skirt. In early modern Spain the faldellín was considered an undergarment (*ropa interior*) that women wore from the waist down. *Diccionario de autoridades*, 2:710. However, as James Middleton explains, "the *faldellín* was worn as an outer garment by some early-seventeenth century Spanish workers, and this origin has been proposed for the Andean faldellín." "Their Dress Is Very Different: The Development of the Peruvian Pollera and the Genesis of the Andean Chola," in "Interwoven: Dress that Crosses Borders and Challenges Boundaries," ed. Jennifer Daley and Alison Fairhurst, special issue, *Journal of Dress History* 2, no. 1 (2018): 95.
8   Martínez Compañón decided to record a complete history of the province of Trujillo, Peru, based upon six years of observations of the inhabitants; their cultural practices, customs, and architecture; Indigenous antiquities; and the natural history of the province. The result was a nine-volume series of watercolor illustrations. An index listing the title and number of each illustration accompanied each of the nine volumes.
9   This is one of a group of twenty paintings that the viceroy sent to King Charles III in 1770 to be part of the Gabinete de Historia Natural. For more information about these casta paintings, see Pilar Romero de Tejada, "Los cuadros de mestizaje del Virrey Amat,"

in *Los cuadros de mestizaje del Virrey Amat: La representación etnográfica en el Perú colonial*, ed. Natalia Majluf (Lima: Museo de Arte de Lima, 2000), 17–47. See also Tamara Walker, *Exquisite Slaves: Race, Clothing, and Status in Colonial Lima* (Cambridge: Cambridge University Press, 2017).

10 General information about Vicente Albán's series of six canvases painted in Quito can be found in Daniela Bleichmar, *Visual Voyages: Images of Latin American Nature from Columbus to Darwin* (New Haven, CT: Yale University Press, 2017), 150–53.

11 M. Antispásia, "Carta escrita a la Sociedad en contraposicion de la de Fixiogamio inserta en el Mercurio numero 12," *Mercurio peruano*, March 3, 1791, 161–64.

12 Beverly Lemire and Giorgio Riello, "Fashion in the Four Parts of the World: Time, Space and Early Modern Global Change," in *Dressing Global Bodies: The Political Power of Dress in World History* (New York: Routledge, 2020), 41–64.

13 Rebecca Haidt, *Women, Work and Clothing in Eighteenth-Century Spain* (Oxford: Voltaire Foundation, University of Oxford, 2011), 1. Haidt argues that women's agency in 18th-century Spain could be seen in urban clothing and cloth circulations. She notes that "the clothing, ribbons and other accoutrements of 'fashion' had every connection to questions of labor, productivity and economic development" (ibid., 2).

14 Ibid., 9.

15 Juan and Ulloa, *A Voyage to South America*, 2:56; Juan and Ulloa, *Relación*, vol. 2, book 1, chap. 5, 71: "y assi no es reparable vèr un *Mulato* u otro Hombre de Oficio con un rico tisu . . . Todos visten con mucha ostentación." *Mulato* at the time referred to the offspring of Africans and Spaniards. However, as Ilona Katzew points out, in the late 18th century "as the participation of Africans in the military acquired more urgency, mulatto was changed to *moreno* and *pardo*, euphemistic terms that referred to this group's darker complexion and that were devoid of the pejorative connotation of the former term mulatto." Ilona Katzew, *Casta Painting: Images of Race in Eighteenth-Century Mexico* (New Haven, CT: Yale University Press, 2004), 44.

16 Sumptuary laws enacted since 1571 already prohibited Black women and free Mulatto women from wearing gold, silk, shawls, velvet, or pearls. This regulation, titled "That Blacks and free Mulattas should not wear gold, silk, shawls, or pearls" (Que las Negras y las Mulatas horras, no traygan oro, seda, mantos ni perlas), was included in the *Recopilación de las leyes de Indias*, 3rd ed. (Madrid: Imprenta de Don Bartholome Ulloa, 1774), book 7, title 5, law 28. In the 18th century more sumptuary laws were decreed by the Crown to control the propensity of non-elite women to wear clothes and adornments that were viewed as the exclusive property of white Spanish and Creole women. The *Real Pragmática*, enacted in 1716, passed a law titled "Pragmatic against the abuse of garments and other superfluous expenses" (Pragmática contra el abuso de trajes y otros gastos superfluos), which prohibited men and women from wearing "any clothes that had gold and silver" (ropas algunas que tuviesen oro y plata) or any dress with pearls and precious jewels. Richard Konetzke, *Colección de documentos para la historia de la formación social de Hispanoamérica, 1493–1810*, vol. 3 (Madrid: Consejo Superior de Investigaciones Científicas, 1962), 124–26. Black or white lace made of silk was prohibited, too, and no lace from Geneva was to be used in any women's dresses, gloves, hats, or stockings (ibid., 126). Only if the lace was of Spanish origin were women allowed to use it in their attire. For more on these sumptuary laws, see Mariselle Meléndez, "Visualizing Difference: The Rhetoric of Clothing in Colonial Spanish America," in *The Latin American Fashion Reader*, ed. Regina Root (New York: Berg, 2005), 17–30.

17 Juan and Ulloa, *A Voyage to South America*, 2:56; Juan and Ulloa, *Relación*, vol. 3, book 1, chap. 5, 72: "En la elección y gusto de los *Encages*, de que se ha de componer el Vestuario, se pone el mayor cuidado."

18 The incorporation of elegant fabrics in Black women's attire had been a major concern since the 17th century. As Tamara Walker observes, in 1631 Lima's city council "renewed a years-old ban prohibiting enslaved and free women of African descent from wearing silk, gold, silver, and slippers adorned with silver bells." *Exquisite Slaves*, 33.

19 Juan and Ulloa, *A Voyage to South America*, 2:56; Juan and Ulloa, *Relación*, vol. 3, book 1, chap. 5, 72: "Los Encages pues se transforman en la Tela, y la parte, que entra en ellos de aquellos Lienzos mas finos, y delicados, solo queda en aprehension."

20 Juan and Ulloa, *A Voyage to South America*, 2:56.

21 Ibid.; Juan and Ulloa, *Relación*, vol. 3, book 1, chap. 5, 72: "y estos [Encages] han de ser de la superior calidad de Flandes, porque todos otros se reputan por communes."

22 These black patches of velvet were also pictured in portraits of women in Mexico. On some of these portraits, see Michael A. Brown, "Portraits and Patrons in the Colonial Americas," in *Behind Closed Doors: Art in the Spanish American Home, 1492–1898*, ed. Richard Aste (New York: Brooklyn Museum; New York: Monacelli Press, 2013), 131–60.

23 *Tumbaga* was a metal alloy from Asia, composed primarily of copper that was mixed with gold so as to give it the appearance of gold. *Diccionario de autoridades*, 3:374. The word is of Malay origin. In English this material is known as "tombac" or "tombak." *Webster's Universal Dictionary of the English Language*, 2 vols. (Cleveland, OH: World Syndicate, 1939), 2:1756.

24 Juan and Ulloa, *A Voyage to South America*, 2:60; Juan and Ulloa, *Relación*, vol. 3, book 1, chap. 5, 77: "con que vestida una de aquellas Señoras toda ella de Encages en lugar de Lienzos, quedando las Telas mas ricas confusas con la variedad."

25 Juan and Ulloa, *A Voyage to South America*, 2:56; Juan and Ulloa, *Relación*, vol. 3, book 1, chap. 5, 72: "La moda del Trage, bien diferente del de *Europa*, y que le hace tolerable el uso de aquel Pais, por mas que à los Españoles les parezca poco decoroso."

26 Statistics documenting the commercial exchanges between the Viceroyalty of Peru and other viceroyalties were published in the *Mercurio* several times a year. Regarding the decrease in wool revenue, the newspaper added a table illustrating that, because of the free trade policies imposed by Spain in the 1770s, "it has decreased significantly given the abundance of cheap European wools" (se ha minorado mucho por lo barato, y abundante de las Lanas de Europa); *Mercurio peruano*, March 24, 1791, 229.

27 The term *ropa de la tierra* (literally "clothing of the earth") was used to refer to clothing of lesser quality made in the New World in order to distinguish it from the clothing made in Castilla. *Diccionario panhispánico del español jurídico* (Madrid: Real Academia Española, 2020), https://dpej.rae.es.

28 For a definition of *sayal*, see *Diccionario de autoridades*, 3:493.

29 It is important to note that *vicuña* was considered by the Incas as "the most precious of the camelids" on account of its very fine, soft, and valuable fleece. Elena Phipps and Johanna Hecht, "Andean Christianity and Its Cults," in *The Colonial Andes: Tapestries and Silverwork, 1530–1830*, ed. Elena Phipps, Johanna Hecht, and Cristina Esteras Martín, exh. cat. (New York: Metropolitan Museum of Art; New Haven, CT: Yale University Press, 2004), 276.

30 Juan and Ulloa, *Relación*, vol. 2, book 1, chap. 15, 229. They also commented that in the missions of Paraguay, production of cotton was abundant.

31 According to Timothy Brook, regular trade between Asia and the Americas emerged around 1573 and lasted until 1815. Spanish commercial fleets carried valuable goods from Asia, such as "porcelain, silks, and spices." Timothy Brook, "Prologue: Coming onto the Map,"

in *Made in the Americas: The New World Discovers Asia*, ed. Dennis Carr (Boston: MFA Publications, 2015), 15.

32 Ibid., 16.

33 Ibid.

34 Ibid.

35 The author uses the word *rengos*, but that word does not appear in any of the Spanish dictionaries including Sebastián de Covarrubias Orozco's *Tesoro de la lengua castellana o española* or *Diccionario de autoridades*. However, the Real Academia Española's *Corpus diacrónico del español*, https://corpus.rae.es/cordenet.html, lists the word *rengues* as appearing in Carlos Sigüenza y Góngora's *Triunfo parténico* (1683) when referring to the fabric upon which beautiful embroideries were made. Within this context, rengue refers to *piña* cloth, which in Asia was used to make sheer shawls, scarfs, and hand-kerchiefs. Mary Brooks Picken, *A Dictionary of Costume and Fashion: Historic and Modern* (Mineola, NY: Dover, 1999), 252.

36 Marlene Flores Ramos, "The Filipina Bordadoras and the Emergence of Fine European-Style Embroidery Tradition in Colonial Philippines, 19th to Early-20th Centuries" (MA diss., Mount Saint Vincent University, Nova Scotia, 2016), 2, Wayback Machine, https://web.archive.org/web/20200212094914/https://pdfs.semanticscholar.org/4fda/da033e330b2bafcbe40f40dae90084c2d512.pdf.

37 For an earlier discussion of the role of clothing as a tool of management and surveillance, see Mariselle Meléndez, *Raza, género e hibridez en* El lazarillo de ciegos caminantes, Studies in the Romance Languages and Literatures (Chapel Hill, NC: University of North Carolina Press, 1999), chap. 5, 166–75.

38 Alonso Carrió de la Vandera, *Lazarillo de ciegos caminantes* (1775; Caracas: Biblioteca Ayacucho, 1985), 216: "de medio cuerpo arriba imitaba en algo al de las indias, en los [h]uipiles y qu(e)squémeles, tobajillas de verano y mantones de (hin)vierno"; "de nueva invención entre las señoritas." In the 18th century, *cotón* referred to a cotton fabric that was painted in different colors, imitating Chinese brocade, and it was used, among other things, to make curtains, bedspreads, and children's clothes. *Diccionario de autoridades*, 1:646. Donna Pierce mentions that, in colonial Latin America, painted or printed cotton with large floral motifs imitating the imported fabrics from India were made in local workshops and were known as *indianilla*. Donna Pierce, "By the Boatload: Receiving and Recreating the Arts of Asia," in Carr, *Made in the Americas*, 70. In the case of *El lazarillo*, no floral design is mentioned.

39 There is ample evidence for the relevance of textiles in Mesoamerican societies. As Kathryn Klein points out, "the universal Mesoamerican use of the word *flower* in association with textiles—albeit in different Mesoamerican languages—symbolically refers to fertility, beauty and divinity, life, and the regenerative properties of death. The fact that most of the physical components of pre-Columbian Mesoamerican textiles (i.e., fibers and dyestuffs) were made of plant materials also indicates their natural connection to flowers." Kathryn Klein, "Conservation and Cultural Identity," in *The Unbroken Thread: Conserving Textile Traditions of Oaxaca* (Los Angeles: Getty Conservation Institute, 1997), 14.

40 The huipil has, since pre-Hispanic times, been charged with Indigenous symbolism relating to religious views interconnected with the understanding of the universe. Color, geometric forms, and woven images of flora and fauna were added as a reflection of such views. Regina A. Root, "Introduction," in *The Latin American Fashion Reader*, 1–13. More significantly, huipiles are still worn by Mesoamerican women of Indigenous descent today. Elyse Demaray, Melody Keim-Shenk, and Mary A. Littrell, "Representations of Tradition in Latin American Boundary Textile Art," in Root, *The Latin American Fashion Reader*, 142–59.

41 *Nahuatl Dictionary*, s.v. "Quechquemitl," https://nahuatl.uoregon.edu.

42 Root, "Introduction," in *The Latin American Fashion Reader*, 3.

43 Juan and Ulloa, *A Voyage to South America*, 1:32; Juan and Ulloa, *Relación*, vol. 1, book 1, chap. 4, 44–45: "esta es hecha de Tafetan Sencillo y sin aforro porque los Calores no les permiten otra cosa y de medio Cuerpo arriba un Jubon, o Almilla blanca muy ligera." According to Middleton, the pollera was a type of skirt "created by South American women as an alternative to the French-inspired fashions." *Pollera* means "chicken keeper," and the name was given to the skirt "because it resembled the baskets in which chickens were kept in the early-modern Atlantic world." Middleton, "Their Dress Is Very Different," 101.

44 In colonial times whiteness was seen as related to Spanish origin, and it was also associated with purity of blood. As Ann Twinam states, since the 15th century, "The purity of blood ordinances provided guidelines by which Spaniards could identify each other through a shared obsession with Catholic orthodoxy." Ann Twinam, *Public Lives, Private Secrets: Gender, Honor, Sexuality and Illegitimacy in Colonial Spanish America* (Stanford, CA: Stanford University Press, 1999), 42. In the 18th century, as Twinam adds, "if the percentage of mixed blood over time descended to less than one-eighth, the individual was technically white and met the requirements for *limpieza de sangre*" (ibid., 44). Clothing served as another cultural apparatus for further passing as white. The basquine dress is Spanish in origin, as it was considered at the time an "ornamental outer petticoat worn by Basque and Spanish peasant women." Picken, *A Dictionary of Costume and Fashion*, 16.

45 Juan and Ulloa, *A Voyage to South America*, 1:33; Juan and Ulloa, *Relación*, vol. 1, book 1, chap. 4, 45: "de un Lienzo blanco, fino, y muy lleno de Encages."

46 Middleton, "Their Dress Is Very Different," 93.

47 The *tupu* dress dated from pre-Hispanic times and, according to Elena Phipps, was called *anacus* by some early Spanish chroniclers. It was the typical dress for Andean women, and it is still worn in Highland communities in the Andes today. Elena Phipps, "Garments and Identity in the Colonial Andes," in Phipps, Hecht, and Esteras Martín, eds., *The Colonial Andes*, 20–21. For visual images of Andean garments including the *tupu* and *llicila*, see Phipps's chapter.

48 Juan and Ulloa, *Relación*, vol. 1, book 5, chap. 5, 369.

49 They describe *cacicas* as the wives of governors, local chief officers, and magistrates; cacicas were considered noblewomen. For an extensive study on cacicas in Spanish America, see Margarita Ochoa and Sara Vicuña Guengerich, eds., *Cacicas: The Indigenous Leaders of Spanish America, 1492–1825* (Norman, OK: University of Oklahoma Press, 2021).

50 Juan and Ulloa, *Relación*, vol. 1, book 5, chap. 5, 369.

51 The *Ilicla* also dates from pre-Hispanic times and was designed following "traditional systems of symmetry and order." Phipps, "Garments and Identity," 21.

52 Phipps, "Garments and Identity," 19.

53 Juan and Ulloa, *A Voyage to South America*, 2:281.

54 Juan and Ulloa, *Relación*, 4:589. The appendix was not included in the English edition.

55 Stephanie Saunders, *Fashion, Gender and Agency in Latin American and Spanish Literature* (Woodbridge, UK: Tamesis, 2021), 18.

56 Root, "Introduction," in *The Latin American Fashion Reader*, 1.

57 Meléndez, "Visualizing Difference," 27.

58 Walker, *Exquisite Slaves*, 93.

59 Eduardo Matos Moctezuma, *Textiles indígenas: Patrimonio cultural de México* (Mexico, DF: Fundación Cultural Serafín, 1996), 17.

60 Middleton, "Their Dress Is Very Different," 89.

7   "A Prodigious Excess": Lace in New Spain and Peru, ca. 1600–1800

James Middleton

In the choice of laces, the women carry their taste to a prodigious excess; nor is this an emulation confined to persons of quality, but has spread through all ranks, except the lowest class. . . . The laces are sewn to their linen which is of the finest sort, though very little of it is seen, the greatest part of it, especially in some dresses, being always covered with lace, so that the little which appears seems rather for ornament than use. These laces too must be all of Flanders manufacture, no woman of rank condescending to look on any other.

— Jorge Juan (1713–1773) and Antonio de Ulloa (1716–1795), *A Voyage to South America*, 1748[1]

A S THE ABOVE EPIGRAPH ATTESTS, few world cultures have been as profoundly enamored with luxurious textiles as that of Spanish Colonial America. The spectacular mineral wealth—derived principally from silver—of New Spain (Mexico) and Peru, combined with the colonies' position at the nexus of the early modern world's most lucrative trade routes, enabled wealthy Americans to choose the best (or most expensive) goods that both Europe and Asia could provide.[2] It is also worth noting that fine textiles occupied a privileged place in the pre-Hispanic cultures of both Mexico and Peru and that this aspect of Indigenous culture persisted after the Spanish conquest.[3]

Lace, among the most sought-after textiles of an acquisitive era, probably arrived in the Viceroyalties of New Spain and Peru around 1580, shortly after its appearance in Spain.[4] A flourishing American market for luxury textiles existed well before lace's appearance on the European scene, and it seems safe to assume that lace became available in Mexico City and Lima within months of its appearance in Madrid and Seville. Strong trade links existed between Flanders, Seville, and the New World, and most—if not all—of the newly available material would have been of Flemish origin.[5]

Because relatively few New Spanish or Peruvian portraits that date before about 1670 exist, it is difficult to gauge lace's immediate effect on New World dress. The reason for this is that—according to Spanish rules of appropriateness—it was necessary to be eminent in order to have one's portrait painted.[6] To be merely rich was not enough, and it would have been the height of presumption for a Spanish merchant to have his likeness painted, unlike his French, English, and German colleagues, for whom this practice was acceptable. For the Spanish New World these rules would change only in the eighteenth century. Thus, lace appears in a small number of pre-1670 portraits of viceroys, bishops, and very few women. Beyond portraiture, lace appears frequently in Peruvian sacred painting, but seldom in New Spanish sacred painting. Lace-derived patterns also became part of the visual lexicon of Andean muralists and tapestry weavers, though not in New Spain (FIG. 7.1).[7]

The first known Mexican portrait of a woman, probably painted about 1600 (seen here in an seventeenth-century copy; FIG. 7.2), illustrates the way lace was used in the late sixteenth and early seventeenth centuries: worn at the neck and wrists or as trimming for soft accessories like veils or kerchiefs.[8] At this early date, lace was always associated with the wearer's personal linen, principally the collar and cuffs of the launderable shirts

FIG. 7.1

Woman's manta (*lliclla*), Lake Titicaca area, probably Inca, ca. 1500–1700. Cotton yarn, camelid hair yarn, silk yarn, vicuña hair yarn, viscacha hair yarn, dye, and metallic thread. National Museum of the American Indian, Smithsonian Institution, Washington, DC, 05/3773.

and chemises that were worn under the era's outer garments, which were generally made of difficult-to-clean materials like silk and fine wool.

In this painting, doña Inés de Velasco (who achieved her eminence by founding a convent) wears a black gown in the international Spanish mode, with ruff and cuffs of lace-edged linen, and a black silk veil trimmed with a finer, sawtooth-edged lace.[9] Her dress might have been worn anywhere in Catholic Europe between about 1570 and 1620; the international mode for Spanish-style clothing coincided with Spain's era of geopolitical preeminence and was helped along by the first published tailors' manuals, all of Spanish origin.[10]

However, a real rupture occurred in Spanish dress when the use of lace, among other luxury textiles, was severely restricted by Philip IV in a 1623 edict (SEE CHAP. 6) that had the effect of fossilizing elite dress in sixteenth-century forms. As the rest of Europe moved sartorially on, Spain—largely because of the abstemious tastes of Philip IV—continued to ring changes on a repertoire of forms developed by sixteenth-century tailors.[11] For women's dress this resulted in the *guardinfante* gowns made famous by Diego Velázquez. Men's dress, however, remained stagnant for most of Philip's reign, as sixteenth-century forms became ever simpler and ornament was reduced.

The most onerous result of the edict was the replacement of the neck ruff—which might use as much as forty yards of expensive, imported lace—with a stiff collar of starched linen, wire, and cardboard known as a *golilla* (technically the golilla was the wire and cardboard support of a starched *valona* [i.e., Walloon] collar, but for practical purposes the collar is known by the name of the support).[12] Although it is clear that the severest aspects of the 1623 edict had been relaxed well before the king's 1664 death, it is also clear

FIG. 7.2
Copy after Baltasar de Echave Orio, *Doña Inés de Velasco*, 17th century. Oil on canvas. Isabella Stewart Gardner Museum, Boston, P33e13.

that no one in Spain was taking significant sartorial chances.[13] In the later seventeenth century, the valona collar—now without starch—would acquire more and more lace, gradually transforming into an accessory that resembled the lacy ends of the Louis XIV–era cravat (FIG. 7.3), although it was in fact a vestigial collar.[14]

The End of an Edict

Although eighteenth-century chroniclers were ever eager to point out Hispanic women's profligate use of lace, the first Americans to use lace extravagantly were men. As noted above, following the demise of the international Spanish mode, seventeenth-century Spanish dress became unmoored from European fashion. The approximately forty years between the death of Philip IV and the general acceptance of international-style garments in the eighteenth century saw a multitude of influences. Tailors continued to create garments using long-established construction techniques that incorporated some international influences but rejected others, for example, adopting an international Anglo-French silhouette while retaining an earlier seventeenth-century Spanish-style sleeve (SEE FIG. 7.5). The new king, Carlos II, four years old at the death of Philip IV, was in no position to lead fashion. He would—because he hated the uncomfortable *golilla*—eventually champion the introduction of the international Anglo-French suit.[15]

Portraits from the late seventeenth and early eighteenth centuries illustrate some of these compromises between older tailoring techniques and a selective application of certain international trends. A 1672 portrait of the Count of Lemos (viceroy of Peru, 1667–72; FIG. 7.4) shows the flamboyant use of lace by late seventeenth-century men. It appears here both in its conventional associations with personal linen (at his cuffs and the collar of his voluminous shirt) and in more unexpected places, such as at His Excellency's boot tops and outer garments—liberally applied flat and used in the same way as trim or braid. Some of the lace used on his outer garments appears to be metallic.

Indeed, lace has been used so profusely here that it is difficult to understand the cut of His Excellency's garments. These can be partially explained by a variant of the well-known Peruvian genre of angel musketeers (FIG. 7.5). The Archangel Raphael, who here carries a sword rather than a musket, was painted in the early eighteenth century by a once-known Andean artist. His dress consists of a loose outer jacket (*ropilla*, or jerkin) whose ample sleeves open at the front seam (*mangas redondas*) to reveal a fine linen shirt, embellished with deep lace cuffs and a soft valona collar.

The Mexican gentleman who appears in a donor portrait from a larger composition dated 1702 (FIG. 7.6) shows New Spain's selective adoption of the Anglo-French silhouette,

FIG. 7.3
Coraline needle-lace cravat ends, Venice or France, ca. 1700. Linen. Textilmuseum St. Gallen, Gift of Leopold Iklé, 1905, 01214 and 01213. Cats. 81 and 83.

FIG. 7.4 (LEFT)
Artist unknown, *Don Pedro Antonio
Fernández de Castro, X Conde de
Lemos, Viceroy of Perú*, 1672. Oil
on canvas. Museo de Arte Español
Enrique Larreta, Buenos Aires.

FIG. 7.5 (RIGHT)
Artist unknown, *Archangel Raphael*,
1700–30. Oil on canvas. Museo Pedro
de Osma, Lima.

in which international details mix with older Spanish construction ideas. He wears a jacket very similar in cut to that worn by the Peruvian Archangel Raphael (SEE FIG. 7.5), but the ensemble has been tweaked to superficially resemble the contemporary Anglo-French suit. The archangel's voluminous sleeves have been replaced by the fitted, cuffed sleeves that would persist through the eighteenth century, and the soft valona collar—worn over a butterfly bow—has assumed the appearance of an eighteenth-century jabot.

By about 1715 the international style of an Anglo-French men's suit had largely replaced the hybridized men's clothing of the previous decades. From that point on, upper-class men's dress became entirely European. Close examination of portraits made after 1720 reveals that lace was no longer an essential element of a well-dressed man's wardrobe: in later eighteenth-century portraits, collars and cuffs are as likely to be furnished with ruffled fabric as with lace.[16]

The Duke of Linares (FIG. 7.7), who served as viceroy of New Spain from 1711 to 1716, exemplifies the brief period during which fully Europeanized New World men's dress coincided with the post-edict fashion for excessive lace. It might be said that the viceroy-duke's portrait represents the last hurrah of the extravagant use of lace by American men. His Excellency wears a luxuriant, loosely painted cravat (now completely divorced from the valona collar) of fine bobbin lace that seems to match his cuffs. Interestingly, both the jacket and lace are different in the two versions of this half-length portrait, as they are in the two further extant versions of a related full-length portrait.[17] The depicted laces may or may not be "portraits" of actual textiles belonging to His Excellency. It seems likely that the artist (Juan Rodriguez Juárez, 1625–1728), following standard contemporary practice, had access to different examples of high-quality textiles, and the Duke of Linares would certainly have had the means to acquire such fine lace.[18]

A final example of a Peruvian gentleman shows the conservative style persisting into the second half of the eighteenth century. Painted about 1760, Simón de la Valle y Cuadra was a resident of Trujillo but likely sat for his portrait in Lima (FIG. 7.8). His shoulder-length wig is approximately three decades out of date, which may reflect his provincial status or personal preference due to age. His lace ruffles, however, are consistent with his formal gray suit.

FIG. 7.6
Juan Correa, *Immaculate Conception with Donor*, 1701. Oil on canvas. Convento Dominicas de Clausura de Tudeja, Tudela Spain.

El Ex.^{MO} S.^{OR} D.^{DO} FERN. L ENCASTRE Y NOROÑA D.^V D LINARES. VIRREY. AÑO DE 17..

Lace and High-Status Women

The New Spanish and Peruvian women who were most apt to have their portraits painted were aristocrats connected to the viceregal courts. In a recently rediscovered portrait of a Mexican viceroy's daughter painted circa 1670 (FIG. 7.9), doña María Luisa de Toledo wears the successor style to Velázquez's *infanta* dresses, whose cut is essentially the same but is no longer inflated by a vast guardinfante hoop.[19] Approximately

FIG. 7.7

Attributed to Juan Rodríguez Juárez, *Fernando de Alencastre Noroña y Silva, Duke of Linares*, ca. 1711–16. Oil on canvas. Gobierno de la Ciudad de México, Secretaría de Cultura de la Ciudad de México y Salón de Cabildos.

contemporaneous with the Count of Lemos (SEE FIG. 7.4), her portrait shows a similar manner of using lace, not only as an accessory to her personal linen (collar and cuffs) but also applied flat to her gown. Lace also appears at the cuffs of her Indigenous attendant.

As with men's styles, late seventeenth- and early eighteenth-century Hispanic women's fashion also applied superficially up-to-date features to garments made according to older tailoring techniques. A case in point is the eighteenth century's most popular female garment, the *casaquín* bodice, which combined old-fashioned *à la española* tailoring with a more modern *à la francesa* silhouette.[20] However, it is important to note here that the "à la francesa style" was meant as a catchall term for clothing in the international eighteenth-century mode and should not be confused with the *robe à la française*, a specific garment with a distinctive shoulders-to-ankles pleat of loose fabric.[21] The casaquín bodice was essentially a seventeenth-century garment brought cosmetically into the eighteenth century with elbow-length sleeves and a more fashionably up-to-date neckline. It was characterized by its peplum, a possible relic of the guardinfante mode. Although it generally had a square neckline, María Juliana Rita de Nuñez Villavicencio, painted in 1733, wears hers with a décolleté V-neckline (FIG. 7.10). Lace appears conventionally at her collar and cuffs as well as on the sheer apron she wears over her skirt, a further nod to eighteenth-century style.

The casaquín mode was impressively long-lived. In a portrait dated around 1771 to 1772 (FIG. 7.11), Micaela Esquibel wears a bodice that might have been made fifty years earlier and whose square neckline shows lace in one of its most typical eighteenth-century uses.[22] Looking at the larger painted record, that is, at paintings that represent scenes of daily life such as *casta* paintings, ex-votos, and *biombos* (decorative folding screens), it seems clear that the casaquín was the dominant eighteenth-century style for women. The more specific record of elite portraiture gives ample evidence that international-style gowns were known in New Spain, especially after about 1750. I believe, however, that the portraits, recording a very specific class of people, make the Anglo-French "robe-à-la" seem more important than it really was, and that the style-scene recorded in casta paintings, ex votos, and biombos likely offers a truer picture of what women really wore.

Post-1750 examples of the *robe à la française* and *à l'anglaise* are found not only in painted portraits but in the form of extant garments as well, attesting that Mexican tailors were able to produce French-style gowns that would not have been out of place in London or Paris. These still exist in some numbers, especially in the collections of the Museo Nacional de Historia (Chapultepec) and Museo Nacional del Virreinato (Tepotzotlán). It does seem likely, however, that although international-style gowns were known and made, the various *robes-à-la* (known under the collective title of gowns "à la francesa")

FIG. 7.8
Artist unknown, *Portrait of Simón de la Valle y Cuadra*, ca. 1760. Oil on canvas. Denver Art Museum, Funds from Jan & Frederick R. Mayer, Carl & Marilynn Thoma, Jim & Marybeth Vogelzang, Lorraine & Harley Higbie, 2000.250.1. Cat. 66.

James Middleton

FIG. 7.9

Attributed to Antonio Rodríguez
Beltrán, *María Luísa de Toledo with
Indigenous Companion*, ca. 1670.
Oil on canvas. Museo del Prado,
Madrid, P003608.

R.^{to} de la S.^{ra} D.ª Micaela Esquibel. M.^e que fue de N.^{tra}. M.R.M. Ab.^t Sor Maria Ana Fundadora del Convento de Sta Coleta, y pobres Capuchinas de N.^{tra}. S.^{ra} de Guada lupe.

FIG. 7.10 (LEFT)

Artist unknown, *María Juliana Rita Nuñez de Villavicencio y Peredo,* ca. 1735. Oil on canvas. Private collection, Mexico City.

FIG. 7.11 (RIGHT)

Artist unknown, *Portrait of Doña Micaela Esquibel,* late 1700s. Oil on canvas. Denver Art Museum, Gift of Robert J. Stroessner, 1991.1166.

were never widely fashionable. The very fact of their survival suggests that they were not much worn and may have been primarily reserved for court functions and other events of extreme formality. It is probable that very few people beyond central Mexico City ever saw such a dress.

The earliest à la francesa gowns seen in Mexico were noted by chroniclers in the 1750s and tended to vary somewhat from the international model, just as the earliest international-style men's suits varied from the European model.[23] They are thus of greater interest to the researcher looking for more local and individuated interpretations of the mode. In a donor portrait dated to about 1760, a sitter who is possibly María Bárbara Guadalupe de Ovando, Countess of Santiago de Calimaya (**FIG. 7.12**), wears what appears to be a robe à la française in salmon-colored silk moiré extensively trimmed with silver bobbin lace and further embellished with silver cord lacing secured with silver buttons over the lower part of the stomacher.[24] Although her *engageantes* (sleeve cuffs) are whitework, her jabot-like palatine is of black bobbin lace and is—from a European point of view—unexpected.

The unknown subject of the only known Mexican portrait miniature painted on silver (recently acquired by the Denver Art Museum; FIG. 7.13) may well be the daughter or wife of one of Mexico's great silver magnates, who were among the wealthiest people in the eighteenth-century world.[25] The sitter's spectacular ensemble reflects this connection. She wears a court gown, the most formal clothing available to New Spanish women. It is identifiable by its three component pieces: a bodice (clearly separate from the skirt because of the tabs visible at the waist), a skirt worn over pannier hoops, and a separate train (the swags of fabric evident near the sitter's wrists), which match the three component parts of the French *grand habit de cour* ordained for court usage in the 1680s by Louis XIV. Like the Countess of Santiago (SEE FIG. 7.12), she wears three different kinds of lace and in the same places. Her gold metallic lace fichu is remarkably similar to the one worn by the countess, and she wears similar bobbin-lace engageantes, as well as black bobbin lace in her hair ornament. It is doubtful that three-piece court gowns were obligatory (as they were in Spain) for events at the viceregal palace. There are too few portraits featuring these elaborate garments for the practice to have been very widespread, and it seems more likely that a *traje de corte* was an aspirational gesture on the part of nouveau-riche miners and merchants who avidly purchased titles from the Spanish Crown.[26]

An unknown lady, painted around 1785 (FIG. 7.14), makes abundant use of lace in her tucked-in fichu and her deep engageantes and as applied trim on her robe à l'anglaise. Her extravagant hairstyle, out of style in Europe by the time the picture was painted, helps to establish a date for the picture. Hair fashions in Madrid lagged about ten years behind the rest of Europe, but Mexico City was only months behind Madrid.[27] The fashion for gigantic coiffures in Mexico can be dated fairly precisely by their abrupt appearance in the portrait record around 1785. Prior to that date, women's hairstyles were generally simple enough to be arranged by a ladies' maid, but styles clearly needing the skill of a professional hairdresser began to appear in portraits after about 1785. Is it possible that a boatload of hairdressers arrived in that year?[28]

The Peruvian woman, María del Carmen Cortés Santelizes y Cartavio (FIG. 7.15), the wife of Simón de la Valle y Cuadra (SEE FIG. 7.8), wears a typical mid-eighteenth-century robe à l'anglaise or à la française. Although her simple, pulled-back hairstyle and her immense bow (matching her gown) are strongly local, her gown is actually rather

FIG. 7.12 (ABOVE, LEFT)
Artist unknown, *Woman of the Sánchez Navarro Family (possibly María Bárbara de Ovando y Rivadeneyra, Countess of Santiago de Calimaya)*, mid-18th century. Oil on canvas. Private collection.

FIG. 7.13
Artist unknown, *Portrait of a Lady*, ca. 1770. Oil on silver sheet. Denver Art Museum, Funds from Carl Patterson in honor of Julie Wilson Frick, 2018.305.

atypical for Peru. Eighteenth-century Peruvian women largely rejected the era's international modes in favor of an intensely local style, examples of which are included in the following section.²⁹

Colonial Casual

The chroniclers Juan and Ulloa noted of women's dress in Lima in 1748 that "the laces are sewn to their linen which is of the finest sort, though very little of it is seen, the greatest part of it, especially in some dresses, being always covered with lace, so that the little which appears seems rather for ornament than use. These laces too must be all of Flanders manufacture, no woman of rank condescending to look on any other."³⁰

Although this discussion has relied on depictions of extremely formal clothing that was worn only occasionally by those high-status people who were most likely to have their portraits painted, lace was also used—and its wearers took their greatest sartorial risks in using it—beyond the ambit of the viceregal courts. In this regard, Spanish Colonial Americans were either very much au courant with—or possibly even somewhat in advance of—those fashionable eighteenth-century Europeans who had begun to make working-class and informal garments in luxurious materials, like the French *caraco* jacket, itself adapted from Caribbean garments.

FIG. 7.14 (LEFT)

Miguel de Herrera, *Possible Portrait of María Manuela Josefa de Loreto Rita Modesta Gómez de Cervantes y Padilla, heredera de los marqueses de Santa Fe de Guardiola*, ca. 1782. Oil on canvas. Colección Museo Franz Mayer, Mexico City, 07437.

FIG. 7.15 (RIGHT)

Artist unknown, *Portrait of María del Carmen Cortés Santelizes y Cartavio*, ca. 1760. Oil on canvas. Denver Art Museum, Funds from Jan & Frederick R. Mayer, Carl & Marilynn Thoma, Jim & Marybeth Vogelzang, Lorraine & Harley Higbie, 2000.250.2. Cat. 67.

A perfect example of this sort of radically luxurious informality is evident in the donor figure from a larger composition featuring Saint Rose of Lima, painted in New Spain between 1710 and 1720 (FIG. 7.16). Unlike the fitted and corseted styles previously mentioned, the sitter wears a loose jacket of the sort worn by middle-class women in seventeenth-century Dutch paintings but here rendered in a silk, possibly of Asian origin, that has been elaborately decorated with applied braid and accessorized with a stupendous emerald brooch and matching earrings.[31] Recalling the early use of lace as a trimming on personal linen, it is worth noting that the base fabric—surely linen—of her chemise (the T-shaped universal women's undergarment) is entirely obscured by lace.

The lace-trimmed chemise of a New Spanish woman at the other end of the social spectrum can be seen in Manuel de Arrellano's *Diceño de Mulata*, securely dated to 1711 (FIG. 7.17). She wears a similar, though unrelated, garment known as a *manga*, which—because of sumptuary law—was worn only by women of African descent.[32] The manga was essentially a petticoat worn over the shoulders as a mantle. The garment is described in an account by the English traveler Thomas Gage, written in 1648:

FIG. 7.16 (LEFT)
Juan Rodríguez Juárez, *St. Rose of Lima with Christ Child and Donor*, ca. 1700. Oil on canvas. Denver Art Museum, Gift of the Collection of Frederick and Jan Meyer, 2014.216.

FIG. 7.17 (RIGHT)
Attributed to Manuel de Arellano, *Rendering of a Mulatta (Diceño de Mulata)*, 1711. Oil on canvas. Collection of Jan and Frederick Mayer, on loan to the Denver Art Museum, TL-43374.

And when they goe abroad, they use a white mantle of lawne or cambricke rounded with a broad lace, which some put over their heads, the breadth reaching only to their middle be-hind, that their girdle and ribbands may be seen, and the two ends before reaching to the ground almost; others cast their mantles only upon their shoulders, and swaggerers like [*sic*], cast the one and over the left shoulder, that they may the better jog the right arme, and shew their broad sleeve as they walke along; others instead of this mantle use some rich silke petticoat, to hang upon their left shoulder, while with their right arm they support the lower part of it, more like roaring boyes then honest civil maids.[33]

Another ensemble that emphasized an embellished chemise was the eighteenth-century *pollera* ensemble worn in western South America. As noted above, and for reasons that are far from clear, eighteenth-century South Americans were the only women in the European sphere to seriously challenge the hegemony of international eighteenth-century style. They developed in its stead the pollera ensemble (named for its full skirt thought to resemble a chicken cage).[34] The ancestor of the dress of the stereotypical full-skirted, bowler-hatted Andean peasant woman, the eighteenth-century pollera, seen in a watercolor drawing of about 1780 (**FIG. 7.18**), was a high-style garment.[35]

While it was made of the same luxurious materials as the internationalized fashions worn in New Spain, the pollera mode firmly rejected international influence.

The pollera ensemble consisted of a very full, short skirt that revealed the lacy flounce of an underskirt, a chemise lavishly decorated with lace, and a short lace-trimmed waistcoat and shawl. The French traveler Amédée-Francois Frézier condescendingly described the ensemble in 1717:

> They love to be richly dress'd, whatsoever the costs, even in the most private Places: Even their very Smocks, and Fustian-Wastecoats they wear over them, are full of Lace; and their prodigality extends to put it upon Socks and Sheets. The upper petticoat they most commonly wear, call'd *Faldellín*, is open before and has three rows of lace, the Middlemost of Gold and Silver, extraordinary wide [*sic*], sew'd on Silk Galloons, which terminate at the Edges. . . . Their upper Wastecoat, which they call *Jubón* is either rich Cloth of Gold, or, in hot weather, of fine Linnen, covered with an abundance of Lace, confusedly put on; The Sleeves are large and have a Pouch hanging down to the knees.[36]

The pollera ensemble startled European travelers, to whom it looked like underwear, unconfined as it was by the corsets and hoops that were so vital to contemporary European women's dress. In 1748 Juan and Ulloa noted that "their dress is very different from the European, which the custom of the country alone can render excusable; indeed, to Spaniards at their first coming over it appears extremely indecent."[37]

We can see this shocking state of affairs firsthand in an image from a Peruvian series of casta paintings commissioned by a departing viceroy (FIG. 7.19). Casta (literally, "caste") paintings typically showed an interracial couple with their offspring, giving the racial identity of each of the sitters—here a Spanish man and a woman whose racial identity is given as *quarterona de mestizo* (i.e., with a single Indigenous grandparent) and her child, both dressed in the most extravagant version of the pollera mode.[38] Notwithstanding Frézier's harsh, gallic judgment, the lace used in the pollera style—while certainly abundant—doesn't seem too terribly confused.

The picture underlines the paradox that while Peruvian gentlemen wore European clothing in the latest style (here with plenty of lace, fashionably used), Peruvian women tended not to. Clearly, if men had access to the latest European styles, women must have had the same; the reasons that they chose not to use it are not yet known. What concerns us is the stupendous amount of lace the woman is wearing, especially in her rolled sleeves—so unlike anything known in contemporary Europe.

FIG. 7.19

Mestizo Quadroon and Spaniard produce Mestizo Quinterona (Quarterona de Mestizo. Español. Producen Quinterona de Mestizo), ca. 1771–76. Oil on canvas. Museo Nacional de Antropología, Madrid, CE5247.

Another Peruvian watercolor drawing from the same manuscript as the previously mentioned drawing (SEE FIG. 7.18) may be the single extant depiction of lacemaking to survive from the colonial Americas (FIG. 7.20). It shows a *mestiza* woman (of mixed Spanish and Indigenous blood) making a large panel of bobbin lace, possibly destined for use as a pollera petticoat (or perhaps for an ecclesiastical garment or altar frontal).[39]

Both in New Spain and in Peru, Indigenous people used lace in individual and inventive ways. Returning to New Spain, we see a high-status Indigenous woman (FIG. 7.21) wearing a luxurious version of the pre-Hispanic *huipil* (the Nahuatl word for "women's shirt"). In its classic form, the huipil was a large square of cotton with a center aperture for the head, worn over the shoulders and seamed on the sides with arm holes at the fold. This version of the huipil is still worn and has been worn continuously since before Spanish colonization. In the eighteenth century, however, a version of the garment was developed by elite Indigenous women of the old noble caste. The high-style huipil was made entirely of imported lace and cut like an ecclesiastical surplice. Sharing only its name with the pre-Hispanic garment, the new-style huipil was nevertheless construed as a native garment.[40]

Lace came to be particularly identified with Indigenous festival clothing. The Spanish invasion of South America marked a decisive rupture with the area's precolonial past. Immediately following the Spanish conquest, missionaries made a largely successful effort to replace "indecent" Indigenous garments with European shirts and trousers.[41] Many Indigenous garments were prohibited. In place of the old, Indigenous people wore increasingly fanciful garments for festival purposes that were based on the missionary-imposed shirt-and-trouser styles. The lace-covered dance costumes featured in a 1763 manuscript (FIG. 7.22) are perfect examples of such embellished garments: completely Indigenous-identified yet of foreign imposition and made with European materials.

Epilogue

I was told by a lady here, that on the death of her grandchild, he was not only enveloped in rich lace, but the diamonds of three condesas and four marquesas were collected together and put on him, necklaces, bracelets, rings, brooches and tiaras, to the value of several hundred thousand dollars. The street was hung with draperies, and a band of music played, whilst he was visited by all the titled relatives of the family in his dead splendor.

—Frances Erskine Calderón de la Barca (1804–1882), *Life in Mexico*, 1843[42]

FIG. 7.20
"A Mestiza of Valles weaving trensilla" ("Mestiza de Valles texiendo trencilla"), from Baltasar Martínez Compañón, *Trujillo del Perú*, vol. 2, plate 103, 1779–89. Ink on paper. Patrimonio Nacional, Real Biblioteca II/344, plate 103.

El Niño D. José Manuel. de Cervantes y Velasco, Naciò en 22. de ... Mayo de 1804. y Murio à 12. de febrero. de 1805. de edad de 8. meses. 21 dias.

An early nineteenth-century funerary portrait of a privileged child named Manuel de Cervantes y Velasco (FIG. 7.23) shows him dressed in the conventionalized Roman armor thought suitable to New World representations of angels.[43] Indeed, nineteenth-century *norteamericanos* also put their dead on display, but always in conservative clothing. The idea of putting the body of a deceased child on display in an ornate costume is deeply foreign—even offensive—to the northern European and Protestant sensibilities that have shaped North American mortuary culture. This was certainly the case in the early 1840s, when the Scottish American wife of Spain's first minister to independent Mexico wrote the above account, further noting that when grief "seeks consolation in display, it must be less profound than when it shuns it."[44]

But this is to miss the essential Latin-Catholic attitude that gives spiritual and moral value to ostentation and display, an attitude that continues to cause Anglos deep discomfort when confronted with Latin sacred spaces (experience has taught me that a certain type of *norteamericano* touring a Mexican or Peruvian church will invariably point out that the gold leaf of its altars would be better used to aid the poor, something he would not dream of suggesting in his own country). To cover a deceased child, "the last scion of a noble house" who, had he lived, would have been the count of Santiago de Calimaya, in jewels and costly laces was to honor him and to sanctify his family's grief.[45] The image also clearly records one of lace's principal uses beyond the sartorial: bedclothes were routinely trimmed in lace, as can be seen in numerous paintings of sickrooms depicted in the corpus of Mexican votive painting.[46]

FIG. 7.23
El Niño José Manuel de Cervantes y Velasco, 1805. Oil on canvas. Eduardo R. Bezaury Creel.

Finally, it may be surprising to some readers that those iconic elements of traditional "Latin" women's dress—the lacy *mantilla* and lace-flounced skirt—have been absent from this study, but these garments were introduced from Spain after independence and had no place in the colonial style-scenes.[47] Indeed, in the nineteenth century some spectacular laces (particularly mantillas) were manufactured in Europe for the Spanish American market, but lace only assumed its stereotypical mantilla-and-flounce character after the nineteenth century's wars of independence.[48]

I would like to thank Noel Gieleghem, Linda McAllister, James Oles, and Jorge Rivas for their help with this project.

1 Jorge Juan and Antonio Ulloa, *A Voyage to South America, Describing at Large the Spanish Cities, Towns, Provinces, &c. on That Extensive Continent: Undertaken by Command of the King of Spain*, trans. John Adams (1748; London: J. Brookdale, 1806), 2:56.
2 Latin America produced about 150,000 tons of silver between 1500 and 1800, accounting for more than 80 percent of world production during that time. Although mining revenues had actually begun to decline around 1590, at the end of the 16th century, Peru was producing around 10 million silver pesos per annum. Mexico in the same era produced 4 million pesos per annum. Mexican production outstripped Peruvian by the 18th century, and Mexico remains the world's largest silver producer, followed by China and Peru. M. Garside, "Silver Production in Major Countries 2010–2020," Statista, February 16, 2021, https://www.statista.com/statistics /264640/silver-production-by-country/; Alejandra B. Osorio, *Inventing Lima: Baroque Modernity in Peru's South Sea Metropolis* (New York: Palgrave MacMillan, 2008), 25–26; and Peter Bakewell, *A History of Latin America to 1825*, 3rd ed. (Oxford: Blackwell, 2010), 353–54. New Spain comprised (at its height) today's Mexico, the Antilles, the US Southwest, Central America to the northern boundary of today's Panama, and the Philippines. Its capital was Mexico City, which gave its name colloquially to the entire territory, as it did to today's nation-state. The Viceroyalty of Peru comprised today's Peru and southern Ecuador, Chile, and Bolivia. Both were governed by viceroys, officials of noble rank who were appointed for a (generally) six-year term. See also ibid., 250–54.
3 Jorge F. Rivas Pérez, "Domestic Display in the Spanish Overseas Territories," in *Behind Closed Doors: Art in the Spanish American Home, 1492–1892*, ed. Richard Aste, exh. cat. (New York: Brooklyn Museum, 2014), 55–57. See also Elena Phipps, Johanna Hecht, and Christina Esteras Martín, eds., *The Colonial Andes: Tapestries and Silverwork, 1530–1830*, exh. cat. (New York: Metropolitan Museum of Art; New Haven, CT: Yale University Press, 2004).
4 Peter Boyd-Bowman, "Spanish and European Textiles in Sixteenth Century Mexico," *Americas* 29, no. 3 (January 1973): 334–58.
5 Ibid.
6 Especially learned or particularly saintly figures might also qualify. For portrait theory, see Michael Brown, "Image of an Empire: Portraiture in Spain, New Spain and the Viceroyalties of New Spain and Peru," in *Painting of the Kingdoms: Shared Identities; Territories of the Spanish Monarchy, 16th–18th Centuries*, ed. Juana Gutiérrez Haces (México, DF: Fomento Cultural Banamex, 2009), 1: 446–503; and Laura R. Bass, *The Drama of the Portrait: Theater and Visual Culture in Early Modern Spain* (University Park, PA: Pennsylvania State University Press, 2008).
7 See Maya Stanfield-Mazzi, *Clothing the New World Church:*

Liturgical Textiles of Spanish America, 1520–1820 (Notre Dame, IN: Notre Dame University Press, 2021); and Phipps, *The Colonial Andes*.
8 The earliest-known woman's portrait from Peru, of doña Usenda de Loayza y Bazán, a patroness of Cuzco's Mercedarian convent, dates to about 1624. Teófilo Benavente Velarde, *Pintores cusqueños de la colonia* (Lima: Municipalidad del Qosqo, 1995), 24–25, gives the date of this portrait as 1600, but Manuel de Mendiburu, *Diccionario historico-biografico del Peru* (Lima, 1885), 52–53, gives the date of the first of doña Usenda's three weddings as 1624 (the others occurred in 1626 and 1628) and gives the date of her last will and testament as 1646.
9 The portrait was identified by Michael Brown of the San Diego Art Museum. Michael Brown, "Spanish Presence in a Fledgling Republic," in *New England/New Spain: Portraiture in the Colonial Americas*, ed. Donna Pierce (Denver: Mayer Center, Denver Art Museum, 2016), 208–10.
10 The Spanish mode was also disseminated by the world's first published books of tailors' patterns. The two earliest, Juan de Alcega's *Libro de geometria, pratica, y traça* (Álava, Spain, 1580; repr. Madrid, 1589) and Diego de Freyle's *Geometría y traça para el oficio de los sastres* (Seville, 1588) were followed by *Geometría y traças* by Baltasar Segovia (Barcelona, 1617), the *Libro de geometria y traça* of Juan Berguén (1618), and the *Tratado de geometría y traça*, of Francisco de la Rocha (Valencia, 1618). Beginning with—and largely based upon—the work of Alcega, all these sought to elevate tailoring to a status among the liberal arts via its associations with geometry. Brian Reade, *The Dominance of Spain* (London: Harrap, 1951), 14. See also Ruth de la Puerta Escribano, "Los tratados del arte del vestido en la España moderna," *Archivo español de arte* 74, no. 293 (2001): 45–65.
11 Amalia Descalzo, "El traje masculino en la época de los Austrias," in *Vestir a la española en las cortes europeas*, ed. José Luis Colomer and Amalia Descalzo (Madrid: Centro de Estudios Europa Hispánica, 2014), 28–29.
12 Noel Gieleghem, who kindly shared this information, is among the growing group of scholar-artisans who are doing the important work of the hands-on historical re-creation of early modern clothing. Descalzo, "El traje masculino," 29.
13 Portraits of the king from the 1640s onward show him in violation of the edict, such as the 1644 portrait of Philip IV by Diego Velázquez at the Frick Collection in New York (SEE FIG. 5.14). See Jonathan Brown, *Velázquez: Painter and Courtier* (New Haven, CT: Yale University Press, 1986), 171.
14 James Middleton, "Reading Dress in New Spanish Portraiture," in Pierce, *New England/New Spain*, 107.
15 Descalzo, "El traje masculino," 29.
16 This observation is the anecdotal result of looking with new eyes on a corpus of paintings (colonial portraits) with which I have been intimate for a long time.
17 Inmaculada Rodríguez Moya, *La mirada del virrey: Iconografía del*

poder en la Nueva España (Castellón de la Plana, Spain: Universitat Jaume I, 2003).

18   To name but two examples, Rembrandt is known to have had a collection of costume pieces that he used in his portraits, as did John Singleton Copley, who painted numerous sitters in costumes that belonged to him. Arthur K. Wheelock Jr., "Rembrandt van Rijn and Workshop (Probably Govaert Flinck), *Man in Oriental Costume*, c. 1635," National Gallery of Art (online collection), https://www.nga.gov/content/dam/ngaweb/collection/artobject/572/versions/2014-04-24_artobject_572.pdf; and Isabel Breskin, "'On the Periphery of a Greater World': John Singleton Copley's 'Turquerie' Portraits," *Winterthur Portfolio* 36, no. 2/3 (Summer–Autumn, 2001): 97–123.

19   Andrés Gutierrez Usillos, *La hija del virrey: El mundo femenino novohispano en el siglo XVII* (Madrid: Ministerio de Cultura y Deporte, 2019).

20   The term *casaquín* was not used in the 18th century but applied later. Its contemporary designation would simply have been *cuerpo*, meaning "bodice." It is not quite clear whether the French casaquin, a bodice-with-peplum descended from working-class clothing that gave this bodice its name, is in fact related to the Hispanic casaquín, which is not working-class descended and seems to predate the French/international fashion for the casaquin. I thank Michele Majer for calling this issue to my attention.

21   Middleton, "Reading Dress in New Spanish Portraiture," 125–28.

22   This portrait was incorrectly dated to "circa 1750" in ibid.

23   José Manuel Castro Santa Ana noted such a garment worn by the vicereine marquesa de las Amarillas in October of 1756, quoted in Manuel Romero de Terreros, *Bocetos de la vida social en la Nueva España* (Guadalajara, Mexico: Impenta de F. Jaime, 1919), 47.

24   I wrote extensively about this portrait in "Reading Dress in New Spanish Portraiture," 125–27. A related portrait of the same subject also exists, which features a salmon-colored silk damask with a button-laced front closure and appliquéd lace. That second ensemble features several different sorts of lace: the lace applied to her gown, her *engageantes* (sleeve cuffs), the (nearly invisible) lace inside her neckline (which may be embroidered whitework rather than lace), and her jabot-like fichu and tiny cap, both of black bobbin lace.

25   For New World wealth and aristocratic status, see D. A. Brading, *Miners and Merchants in Bourbon Mexico, 1763–1810* (Cambridge: Cambridge University Press, 1971); Doris M. Ladd, *The Mexican Nobility at Independence* (Austin: Institute of Latin American Studies, 1976); and Paul Rizo-Patrón Boylan, *Linaje, dote y poder: La nobleza de Lima de 1700 a 1850* (Lima: Pontifica Universidad Católica del Perú Fondo Editorial, 2000).

26   On court costume see Middleton, "Reading Dress in New Spanish Portraiture," 128–31; and Pierre Arizzoli-Clémentel and Pascal Gorguet Ballesteros, *Fastes de cour et cérémonies royales: Le costume de cour en Europe, 1650–1800*, exh. cat. (Paris: Éditions de la Réunion des musées nationaux, 2009).

27   Unfortunately, on the topic of the transmission of styles to the New World, all there is to rely on is the painted record. There is not sufficient textual evidence to understand how this transfer happened, and when the chroniclers *do* speak of a new style, they too often give it a name that is difficult for us to interpret. As previously noted, Castro Santa Ana put the vicereine marquesa de las Amarillas in an otherwise unknown garment he calls a *gudriel*. Romero de Terreros, *Bocetos de la vida social*, 47. This has been presumed by historians to be the first appearance of an à la francesa gown in Mexico, but the specifics are still uncertain.

28   The Spanish artists sent by Carlos III to establish a fine arts academy in Mexico City, the Academia de San Carlos, also arrived in 1785, and it is intriguing to imagine that professional hairdressers shared the voyage with the academicians. Jean Charlot, *Mexican Art and the Academy of San Carlos, 1785–1915* (Austin: University of Texas Press, 1962).

29   James Middleton, "Their Dress Is Very Different: The Development of the Peruvian Pollera and the Genesis of the Andean Chola," in "Interwoven: Dress that Crosses Borders and Challenges Boundaries," ed. Jennifer Daley and Alison Fairhurst, special issue, *Journal of Dress History* 2, no. 1 (Spring 2018): 87–105.

30   Juan and Ulloa, *A Voyage to South America*, 2:56.

31   For a more in-depth discussion of this garment, see Middleton, "Reading Dress in New Spanish Portraiture," 101–46.

32   The manga was ordained for women of African descent by Felipe II in a 1571 edict. *Recopilación de las leyes de los reynos de Indias mandadas a imprimir y publicar por la Magestad Católica del rey don Cárlos II (Madrid, 1791)*, 369–70: "D. Felipe II en Madrid, 11 Febrero de 1571. salvo mantellinas, que lleguen poco mas abaxo de la cintura."

33   Thomas Gage, *The English American, His Travails by Sea and Land* [. . .] (London, 1677), 124–25.

34   Middleton, "Their Dress Is Very Different."

35   Curiously, while the costume is accurate, the drawing itself is based on a French engraving of 1777, itself based on a lost Peruvian original. Ibid.

36   Amédée-François Frézier, *A Voyage to the South-Sea and along the Coasts of Chili and Peru, in the Years 1712, 1713, and 1714* [. . .] (London: Bowyer, 1717), 259.

37   Juan and Ulloa, *A Voyage to South America*, 2:72.

38   For further reading on casta paintings, see Ilona Katzew, *Casta Painting: Images of Race in Eighteenth-Century Mexico* (New Haven, CT: Yale University Press, 2004).

39   Stanfield-Mazzi, *Clothing the New World Church*, 293–95.

40   Martha Sandoval Villegas, "El huipil precortesiano y novohispano: Transmutaciones simbólicas y estilísticas de una prenda indígena," in *Congreso Internacional Imagen y Apariencia: Universidad de Murcia, 19–21 noviembre 2008*, ed. María Concepción de la Peña Velasco and Manuel Pérez Sánchez (Murcia, Spain: Universidad de Murcia, Servicio de Publicaciones, 2009), n.p., https://www.academia.edu/9537806/EL_HUIPIL_PRECORTESIANO_Y_NOVOHISPANO_TRANSMUTACIONES_SIMB%C3%93LICAS_Y_ESTIL%C3%8DSTICAS_DE_UNA_PRENDA_IND%C3%8DGENA.

41   Patricia Reiff Anawalt, *The Worldwide History of Dress* (London: Thames and Hudson, 2007), 428; Phipps, *The Colonial Andes*, 17, 20; and Neil de Marchi and Hans J. Van Migroet, "The Flemish Textiles Trade and New Imagery in Colonial Mexico (1524–1646)," in Gutiérrez Haces, *Painting of the Kingdoms*, 3:878–924.

42   Frances Erskine Calderón de la Barca, *Life in Mexico during a Residence of Two Years in That Country* (Boston: Little and Brown, 1843), 89.

43   Gutierre Aceves, "Imagenes de la Inocencia eterna," in "El arte ritual de la muerte niña," special issue, *Artes de México*, no. 15 (1992): 26–49.

44   Calderón de la Barca, *Life in Mexico*, 89.

45   Ibid.

46   Pilar Gonzalbo Aizpuru, "Lo prodigioso cotidiano en los exvotos novohispanos," in *Dones y promesas: 500 años de arte ofrenda (exvotos mexicanos)* (México, DF: Centro Cultural/Arte Contemporáneo, Fundación Cultural Televisa, 1996), 47–63.

47   Virginia Armella de Aspe, Teresa Castelló Yturbide, and Ignacio Borja Martínez, *La historia de México a través de la indumentaria* (México, DF: Inbursa, 1988), 99–123; and Chloe Sayer, *Costumes of Mexico* (Austin: University of Texas Press, 1985), 96–117.

48   Armella de Aspe, *La historia de México*, 115, shows a French mantilla made about 1870 for the Mexican market and featuring the Mexican national crest, an eagle perched on a cactus with a serpent in its mouth.

8   "Covered in Much Fine Lace": Dress in the Viceroyalty of New Granada

Laura Beltrán-Rubio

I N A LATE EIGHTEENTH-CENTURY PORTRAIT of a young *yapanga*, lace is a prominent
feature. She wears a beautiful ensemble of a white chemise, an apronlike garment
over her abdomen, and a red *faldellín* with sumptuous jewels and ribbon bows
(FIG. 8.1).[1] The painting details her fine needle-lace collar and cuffs as well as the
trimmings that extend down the sleeves. The apronlike garment is also needle lace, with
alternating floral motifs framed by lozenges, and additional floral and scrolling motifs on
the ruffled border are meticulously depicted. A curtain in the background is also made
with white lace. The yapanga's outfit recalls the styles worn by the three women depicted
in a series of socioracial categories signed by Vicente Albán (active 1769–1796) in 1783,
likely one of the most famous secular works of art from colonial Quito (FIG. 8.2; SEE ALSO
FIG. 6.8). Such detailed depictions of lace adorn—and elevate and complete—the elegant
attire of sitters for portraits and function as symbols of wealth and status in the different cities of the Viceroyalty of New Granada (the present-day territories of Colombia,
Ecuador, Venezuela, and Guyana) in what is now called South America.

FIG. 8.1
Artist unknown, *Yapanga*, 18th or 19th
century. Oil on canvas (?). Colección
Casa de la Cultura Ecuatoriana, Quito.

Through their painted portraits, colonial sitters were able to fashion their personal identities and perform their elite personae.
Fashionable dress and luxurious textiles, including
lace, became indispensable tools of representation
in portraits. With its delicate, time-consuming
construction, lace served as a symbol of the power
and sophistication of both religious and secular
elites, especially as accessories of lace constituted
some of the most expensive elements of fashionable dress. In New Granada lace appears frequently
as a prized possession in archival documents from
the colonial period. Both needle and bobbin laces
were imported from European centers of production in Flanders, Barcelona, and Milan, and knitted
lace was produced locally, building from openwork
textile techniques inherited from the textile traditions of Indigenous cultures. Wearing lace thus
symbolized access to the global trade networks
that connected the far reaches of the Spanish
empire. Through a multimethodological approach
that combines the visual analysis of portraits with
archival study into inventories, dowries, and wills,
this essay demonstrates the importance of lace
as a luxury commodity in the Viceroyalty of New
Granada, which resulted from the fusion of Andean
and European systems of value.

The Viceroyalty of New Granada was created
on April 29, 1717, in a *real cédula* (royal decree) that
unified the provinces of Nuevo Reino de Granada,
Cartagena, Santa Marta, Maracaibo, Caracas,

Guayana, Antioquia, Popayán, and San Francisco de Quito.[2] While these territories housed some of the first cities founded by the Spanish invaders in the sixteenth century, they received little attention from the Spanish Crown through most of the colonial period. Emphasis was initially given to the Viceroyalties of New Spain (founded in 1535) and Peru (founded in 1543), which quickly became the main sources of wealth for the Spanish empire. It was not until the eighteenth century that New Granada was declared a viceroyalty in its own right. This coincided with a decline in the extraction of precious metal and the seeming loss of control over the Spanish territories overseas that brought about a series of administrative and political changes known as the "Bourbon Reforms."[3] Although the Viceroyalty of New Granada was created with the hopes of bringing new wealth to the Spanish Crown, its functioning and the installation of a viceroy and his court increased the administrative costs of maintaining the empire overseas without providing the expected returns. The viceroyalty was thus dissolved in 1723, only to be restored definitively in 1739 with the addition of the provinces of Panama (FIG. 8.3).[4]

Santa Fe (present-day Bogotá, Colombia) became the capital city of the Viceroyalty of New Granada, which also incorporated the important port city of Cartagena de Indias, wealthy Popayán, the large historic city of Tunja, and a rich artistic center in Quito. Situated between New Granada's main maritime port in Cartagena de Indias and the Viceroyalty of Peru, Santa Fe frequently housed migrant Spaniards for relatively short stays and had acquired a cosmopolitan character by the eighteenth century.[5] A census from 1779 lists 16,419 inhabitants of this city, most of whom were free and of Spanish descent.[6] By 1800 the population of Santa Fe had risen to 21,463.[7]

With its establishment as the administrative center of the Viceroyalty of New Granada in 1739, Santa Fe became home to the viceroy and his court. The Spanish nobility brought with them a number of courtly practices of display that included, for example, the series of festivities that welcomed the viceroys into the city and reflected the internal mechanisms of power and distinction in the colonial Americas.[8] Promenades, processions, sermons, bullfights, and monarchical pledges and obsequies formed the repertoire of festive rituals and public ceremonies in Santa Fe and other viceregal cities. All these events were charged with symbolism through which participants attempted to demonstrate, and perhaps even perform, their status as members of both colonial cities

FIG. 8.2
Vicente Albán, *Yapanga Woman from Quito in the Dress Used by the Class of Women Who Try to Please (Yapanga de Quito con el trage que usan esta clase de Mugeres que tratan de agradar)*, 1783. Oil on canvas. Museo de América, Madrid, 00074.

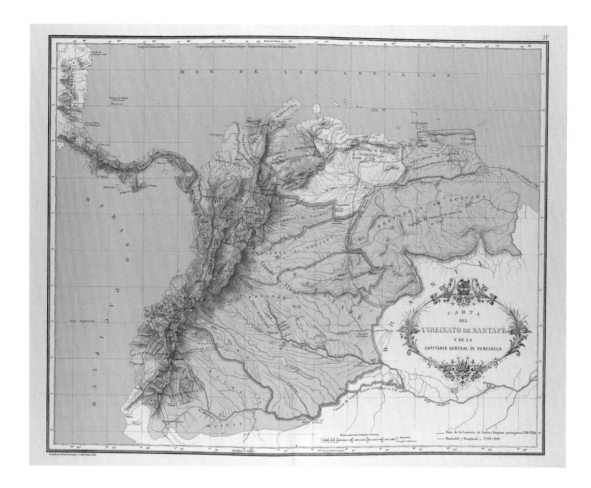

and the viceregal courts.[9] The establishment of a viceregal court in Santa Fe and the events in which the members of this court participated also fostered the development of fashionable consumption and self-fashioning practices among the elites. At the same time, and perhaps not coincidentally, elite portraits became increasingly prominent, following a trend that has been identified throughout the Spanish American colonies in the eighteenth century.[10]

Portraits of the viceroys of New Granada, most of which have been attributed to the local artist Joaquín Gutiérrez (active ca. 1750s–ca. 1780s) and were likely created as a series, constitute the most thoroughly studied portraits of the viceroyalty (for two such examples, see FIGS. 8.4 AND 8.5). Most of them represent the different viceroys of New Granada in three-quarter views inside their offices, surrounded by the objects that speak to both their power and their status as representatives of the king of Spain in the colonies: the letters, swords, and *vara de justicia* (rod of justice) that symbolize their role in public office, for example. Most importantly, the viceroys are depicted wearing a uniform inspired by French fashions of the period: dark greenish-blue breeches and coats with red cuffs and red waistcoats, de riguer wig and cravat accessories, as well as

FIG. 8.3 (ABOVE)
Agustín Codazzi, "Virreinato de Santa Fé y Capitanía General de Venezuela en 1742," from *Atlas geográfico e histórico de la República de Colombia*, plate 4, 1890. General Collection, Beinecke Rare Book and Manuscript Library, Yale University, New Haven, Connecticut, Atlas Coll. Colombia EEhe 889C.

FIG. 8.4 (OPPOSITE, TOP)
Attributed to Joaquín Gutiérrez, *José Alfonso Pizarro, Viceroy from 1749 to 1753*, 18th century. Oil on canvas. Colección Museo Colonial, Bogotá, 03.1.102.

FIG. 8.5 (OPPOSITE, BOTTOM)
Attributed to Joaquín Gutiérrez, *Manuel Antonio Flores Maldonado, Viceroy from 1776 to 1782*, 18th century. Oil on canvas. Colección Museo Colonial, Bogotá, 03.1.107.

crosses, pendants, and other symbols of religion and power. Both the coat and waistcoat are heavily embroidered with gold scrolling motifs, and the sleeves and cravats often feature luxuriant pieces of lace. This uniform is most commonly seen in portraits from the second half of the eighteenth century, although it seems to have developed from the 1720s onward and coincided with a militarization of the Spanish colonies as a strategic response to both internal rebellions and foreign threats.[11] Curiously, the unique details of lace seem to reflect the individual tastes of each of the viceroys in the series.

Among the portraits of the viceroys, that of don Jorge de Villalonga, the first official viceroy of New Granada (r. 1719–24) stands out (FIG. 8.6). Likely completed before 1740 by an unidentified local artist, the portrait depicts the viceroy elegantly dressed in the French styles that were fashionable at the time of his reign, but without the uniform established in the later portrait series. Viceroy Villalonga wears a mauve coat embroidered with brown vegetal and scrolling motifs, buttoned over a brown waistcoat and gray breeches. His cravat is made entirely of exquisite needle lace with scrolling motifs, which is covering the opening of the coat at his chest. Matching needle-lace sleeves framing his hands extend from below the large coat cuffs.

Dress is an essential visual aspect in the portraits of viceroys. In fact, Emily Engel has suggested that "the uniform of the viceroy's office becomes a secondary subject of the portrait with its precisely rendered, undulating embroidery patterning and luxurious fabrics."[12] The rich lace accessories symbolize the viceroys' power and status in the colonial society of New Granada and position them as important consumers in a global luxury market. The ubiquity of lace in these portraits also reflects a larger trend in the Spanish world, in which this imported textile had become an indispensable and highly valued accessory of those in power since Habsburg times.

Not unique to the portraits of viceroys, fashionable dress and lace also appear in a number of portraits of New Grenadine elites. For example, in a double portrait dedicated to Saint Joseph, don Antonio Flores y de Vergara, marqués de Miraflores (1667–1764), and his wife, doña María Margarita Carrión y Vaca (1718–1782), are depicted in three-quarter view facing each other and dressed in the typical attire worn by fashionable *quiteños* of the time (FIG. 8.7). On the left, the marqués wears a navy coat with silver buttons and galloon on the red revers, and on the right, the marquesa wears a red bodice and faldellín. In

FIG. 8.6

Artist unknown, *Jorge de Villalonga, Viceroy from 1719 to 1724*, ca. 1740. Oil on canvas. Colección Museo Colonial, Bogotá, 03.1.152.

both cases, delicate, semitransparent pieces of lace adorn the outfits: on the marqués's cuffs and the frontal closure of the coat and around the marquesa's neck and on her *engageantes*. In a second double portrait of the tax collector don Fernando de Merizalde and his wife, doña María Josefa Aguada, dedicated to Nuestra Señora de El Quinche, the donors wear luxuriant fashions with fine lace at the collar and sleeves (FIG. 8.8). A third portrait with an image of *La Piedad* attributed to Baltasar Vargas de Figueroa (1629–ca. 1667) from Santa Fe evidences that the genre of portraits of fashionably dressed donors had begun appearing as early as the seventeenth century in the northern Andes (FIG. 8.9). The couple depicted in this portrait are possibly María Arias de Ugarte (d. 1647) and her husband, Juan de Zapiaín, of Santa Fe, benefactors of the local convent of Santa Clara.[13] Like the examples from the Province of Quito, they are sumptuously dressed. Ugarte wears a scallop-edged lace collar, and both have deep lace cuffs that are shown to advantage by the donors' clasped hands at the lower edge of the painting.

Stand-alone secular portraits of women are relatively rare in New Granada.[14] In most cases, portraits of women were paired with those of their husbands. Such is the case of a portrait pair of the marqueses de San Jorge from Santa Fe, painted by Joaquín Gutiérrez in 1775. The marqués, Jorge Miguel Lozano de Peralta (1731–1793), is dressed in a gray ensemble of coat, waistcoat, and breeches decorated with gold-colored vegetal scrolls paired with a lace cravat and sleeve cuffs (FIG. 8.10). The marquesa, Maria Thadea González (1736–ca. 1777), wears what seems to be either a *robe à l'anglaise* (with

a fitted back) or a *robe à la française* (with loose pleats at the back) and lace engageantes. Importantly, the golden trimmings that adorn the cuffs, bodice, and stomacher seem to be made of gold metallic bobbin lace (FIG. 8.11).

Lace made with gold and silver thread was particularly luxurious, since it combined the use of precious metals and the creation of time-consuming lace (FIG. 8.12). Weaving

FIG. 8.9

Attributed to Baltasar Vargas de Figueroa, *La Piedad*, 17th century. Oil on canvas. Colección Museo Santa Clara, Bogotá, 03.1.102.

of silver and gold was unknown in the Andes before the Spanish invasion, but, as Elena Phipps has demonstrated, Andean weavers began incorporating metallic yarns into their textiles during the colonial period.[15] The origin of such yarns is still unknown, and a

thorough study of metallic lace in the Andes has yet to be undertaken. Lacelike cloths made with metallic thread could have come from Castilla, Spain, as demonstrated by listings of "Redecillas de Seda, y plata" (silk and silver nets) imported to Quito in 1799.[16] Garments such as capes and dresses made in velvet or brocaded fabrics and trimmed with silver "gauze" are also listed in inventories from Santa Fe.[17]

FIG. 8.10 (ABOVE, LEFT)

Joaquín Gutiérrez, *Portrait of Don José Miguel Lozano de Peralta, 1r Marqués de San Jorge de Bogota*, 1775. Oil on canvas. Colección Museo Colonial, Bogotá, 03.1.099.

FIG. 8.11 (ABOVE, RIGHT)

Joaquín Gutiérrez, *Portrait of Doña María Tadea González Manrique del Frago y Bonís, Marquesa de San Jorge*, 1775. Oil on canvas. Colección Museo Colonial, Bogotá, 03.1.100.

FIG. 8.12 (RIGHT)

Detail of lace made with silver and gold threads in the "Spanish style." Collection of Iván Cruz Cevallos, Quito.

The portraits introduced in this chapter can be understood in a variety of ways. They constitute prime examples of what Emily Engel has termed "official portraits." These include portraits of viceroys, elite and ecclesiastical portraits, self-portraits of artists, and portraits of Inka rulers, and they collectively embody an important narrative in the history of colonial power in the Spanish Americas.[18] However, with their emphasis on dress and the fashionability of the sitters, these portraits are also exquisite expressions of what Mexican historian Marita Martínez del Río de Redo has called "retratos de ostentación" (portraits of ostentation). In these portraits, sitters are often depicted to showcase fashionably dressed bodies, usually in a three-quarter or full-length view, in the interior of their houses, and, occasionally, surrounded by objects and sumptuous pieces of furniture that speak to their status.[19] As a highly valued luxury item, lace is an essential element in the performance of wealth, power, and elite identities in New Grenadine official portraits and portraits of ostentation.

Most of the lace in the portraits discussed above was likely imported into the Americas from Spain and its European territories, including Flanders. In fact, lace features prominently among the *efectos de Castilla* imported from Spain in the archival documents that survive from the period.[20] For example, the 1799 testament of doña Juana de Argandoña from Quito includes a mantle and a pink brocade faldellín, both with lace from Castilla.[21] A legal document from 1799 contesting the taxes charged for a large import of *géneros y ropas de Castilla* (merchandise and cloths from Castilla) includes dozens of *puntas flandinas* (lace from Flanders), *redecillas de seda* (silk nets), *puntas finas* (fine lace), and "gazas de Milán . . . con puntas" (gauze from Milan with lace).[22] Finally, an inventory from Popayán lists some "encajes de Barz[elo]na" (lace from Barcelona) among doña Javiera de Valencia y Castillo's (d. 1793) belongings.[23]

In addition to imported lace, a variety of lacelike cloths were also created in South America as a result of the conjunction of Andean and European openwork textile

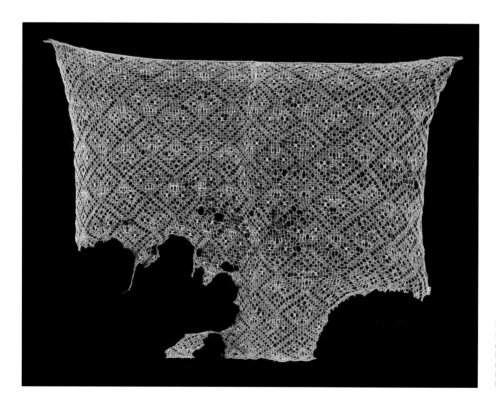

FIG. 8.13
Unidentified Chancay artist, embroidered square-mesh-openwork headcloth with diamond feline-snake motifs, ca. 1000–1476. Cotton. Museum of Fine Arts Boston, Gift of Mrs. Samuel Cabot, 60.1134.

Laura Beltrán-Rubio

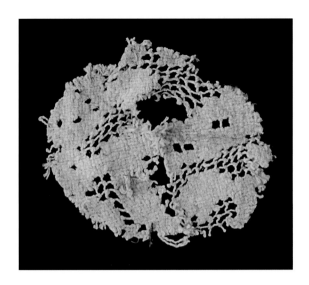

techniques. Gauzelike openwork textiles were made in the Andes well before the Spanish invasion, using the cotton fibers native to South America (*Gossypium barbadense*). The best-preserved examples of pre-Hispanic openwork cottons are from the coastal Andes, such as a Chancay headcloth now at the Museum of Fine Arts, Boston (FIG. 8.13). However, it is likely that several Indigenous cultures throughout the Americas also created openwork cotton textiles. During the colonial period, these pre-Hispanic techniques were adapted to imitate European lace, as evidenced in a white cotton cloth with an openwork pattern on one end and fringes, which was excavated from the archaeological site of Magdalena del Cao Viejo in present-day Peru (FIG. 8.14).[24]

Lacemaking in South America frequently used the cotton fibers native to the region. Before the Spanish invasion, lacelike cloths could be made by using embroidery techniques or by manipulating woven structures. The latter could be achieved by crossing adjacent warp threads of a loose plain weave or by adding discontinuous or meandering weft threads to create openings in woven cloths.[25] After the arrival of the Spaniards, lacemaking in the Andes borrowed from both ancestral Indigenous openwork cotton techniques and European needle and bobbin lacemaking techniques.[26] Lacelike textiles such as *randas* and *rengos* were produced in South America using needle-lace techniques, and *trencillas* were created using straight bobbin-lace techniques. Art historian Maya Stanfield-Mazzi has found evidence of bobbin-lace production in Chachapoyas (in present-day Peru) in 1713, which had been made with cotton thread likely produced in Pasto (in present-day Colombia).[27] Technologies for creating filet, needle, and bobbin lace were also introduced by Spanish missionaries and conquistadors, and it is very likely that women were in charge of creating most of these pieces in South America, as is suggested in a number of illustrations from Baltasar Jaime Martínez Compañón's (1737–1797) manuscript *Trujillo del Peru* (FIG. 8.15; SEE FIGS. 6.10, 6.11, AND 7.20).[28]

Regardless of their origin, lace and lacelike cloths became highly valued throughout the colonial Andes and were used extensively in New Grenadine fashions. Carolyn Dean has argued that the introduction of lace into the Andean dress system "should be understood as a product of the traditional Andean appreciation of fine fabric" in which "lace has been adapted to an Andean system of costuming, rather than serving as a means of Hispanicizing" Indigenous dress.[29] In this way, lace can be understood as an expression or perhaps an adaptation of *cumbi* in the colonial Andes. "Cumbi" is a word in Quechua that refers to "a finely woven textile made from the highest quality alpaca fibers."[30] Cumbi represented the finest and most luxuriant textiles in the Tawantinsuyu, and their use, design, and production were strictly controlled by the Inka.[31] Labor intensity was one of the most notable qualities of cumbi, and the value of these fine textiles stemmed precisely from the time and effort taken to produce them.[32] The appreciation of labor intensity in the creation of textiles might have been a reason for the adoption of lace

FIG. 8.14
Fragment of filet lace, Magdalena del Cao Viejo, Trujillo, Peru, before 1712. Cotton. Museo Cao, Complejo Arqueológico el Brujo.

among Indigenous and mestizo elites in the colonial Andes, for, as Dean has argued, both cumbi and lace are "intricately decorated, labor-intensive, and costly."[33]

However, neither the apparently close relationship between lace and cumbi nor the value attached to lace as a luxury commodity by Europeans fully explains the sustained preference for lace among the New Grenadine elites, since the Tawantinsuyu only extended to the southern regions of the viceroyalty. Fine textiles with intricate patterns were highly valued among the Muisca and Guane cultures of the Andean highlands farther north. Both the Muisca and the Guane produced dye-painted *mantas* (blankets or cotton cloths) with a variety of patterns made up of interlocking geometric designs and featuring, at times, angular human figures (**FIGS. 8.16 AND 8.17**). These other Indigenous systems of value might have influenced local conceptions about lace and the value attached to it in the different cities of New Granada. Because the Muisca and Guane inhabited the highlands, where cotton did not grow, they acquired the fibers necessary for the creation of their mantas through trade with peoples from the lowlands. The exchange of local products to acquire cotton reflects wider Andean principles of reciprocity, through which fine cumbi from the lowlands could have also been acquired.

This exchange continued through the colonial period, during which mantas were collected from Indigenous peoples and their descendants as tribute to the Spanish Crown. Cotton cloths could have been used to create everyday clothing and as support for a variety of works of art.[34] Fine textiles, such as cumbi and lace, were highly valuable and might have functioned as a means of exchange in the absence of bullion. For example, doña Juana de Argandoña demands in her 1799 testament that a chemise with fine lace and a matching doublet be sold to cover the cost of her funeral.[35] Textile goods were also often-cited commodities pawned by the colonial inhabitants of New Granada, reflecting a trend that became popular throughout the early modern Atlantic where people would exchange textiles for bullion or other goods in times of economic hardship.[36] A 1776 inventory of don Juan Tenorio (d. ca. 1776) lists *sayas* (skirts), *polleras* (petticoats), a *chupa* (waistcoat), and a faldellín, some of them with fine lace trimmings, that were among his belongings at the time of his death, having been pawned by women of Quito.[37] Other archival documents of the time also evidence the high value of lace in New Granada: fine lace could be sold for twelve to sixteen reales per length (*vara*), while "ordinary" lace could cost eight reales per vara.[38] In the same document, a cigar case made with fine silver is valued at twelve reales.[39]

The high value attached to lace in this particular context might have been the result of its appreciation by the Andean and European cultures that intermixed during

FIG. 8.15

"Mestizas of Chachapoyas Sewing Rengo" ("Mestizas de Chachapoyas cosiendo rengos"), from Baltasar Martínez Compañón, *Trujillo del Perú*, vol. 2, plate 104, 1779–89. Ink on paper. Patrimonio Nacional, Real Biblioteca II/344, plate 104.

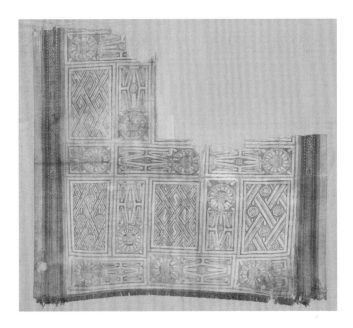

the colonial period. It is thus not surprising that lace features so prominently in the portraits representing the wealthy upper classes from the Viceroyalty of New Granada. In the Spanish American colonies, these paintings were displayed in elite homes and civic spaces such as public buildings and religious or secular offices, where a range of viewers including important guests, servants, and enslaved people could see them.[40] Even when displayed inside private residences, portraits were essential to the formation of the public personae and identities of individuals. This is particularly significant when considering the semipublic nature of colonial homes, which were commonly frequented by members of the extended family and family associates.[41] Lace in portraits, therefore, functioned as a statement of the wealth, power, and fashionability of the sitters—as it did when actually worn on the body to parade in the streets of the viceroyalty's urban centers.

1   The term *yapanga* is thought to refer to a woman of mixed Indigenous and European ethnicities, although it is believed to denote women of "loose morals" as well. The apronlike garment is likely a *bolsicón*, a sort of pocket or bag that women would use to carry their belongings. The *faldellín* was a type of A-shaped, possibly pleated skirt that became fashionable among the women of the Viceroyalties of New Granada and Peru in the 18th century. Its origin as a sort of petticoat traces back to the beginning of the century in Spain, but its use as an outer skirt seems to have been quite unique to the Spanish colonies in South America. All three terms are

interconnected, and I discuss them further in Laura Beltrán-Rubio, "Cuerpos, moda y género en el Virreinato de la Nueva Granada: Un estudio a partir de la pollera y el faldellín," *Miradas* 5 (2022).

2 Gonzalo Hernández de Alba, "El virreinato de la Nueva Granada," *Credencial historia* 20 (1991), https://www.banrepcultural.org /biblioteca-virtual/credencial-historia/numero-20/el-virreinato -de-la-nueva-granada.

3 For an overview of the Bourbon Reforms, see Ann Twinam, *Public Lives, Private Secrets: Gender, Honor, Sexuality, and Illegitimacy in Colonial Spanish America* (Stanford, CA: Stanford University Press, 1999).

4 Hernández de Alba, "El virreinato de la Nueva Granada."

5 Emily Engel, *Pictured Politics: Visualizing Colonial History in South American Portrait Collections* (Austin: University of Texas Press, 2020), 7.

6 Pilar López-Bejarano, "Maneras de trabajar Santafé de Bogotá (siglo XVIII)," *Illes i Imperis* 21 (2019): 18.

7 José María Salazar, "Memoria descriptiva del reino de Santafé de Bogotá," *Semanario del Nuevo Reyno de Granada*, ed. Francisco José de Caldas (Bogotá: Editorial Kelly, 1942), 216–17.

8 Diana Marcela Aristizábal García, *Poder y distinción colonial: Las fiestas del virrey presente y el rey ausente (Nueva Granada 1770–1800)* (Bogotá: Universidad del Rosario, 2011).

9 Héctor Lara Romero, *Fiestas y juegos en el Reino de la Nueva Granada: Siglos XVI–XVIII* (Bogotá: Universidad Distrital Francisco José de Caldas, 2015).

10 See, for example, Elizabeth P. Benson et al., *Retratos: 2,000 Years of Latin American Portraits* (New Haven, CT: Yale University Press, 2009).

11 Engel, *Pictured Politics*, 70.

12 Ibid., 84.

13 Museo Iglesia Santa Clara, *Catálogo Museo Santa Clara* (Bogotá: Ministerio de Cultura, 2014), 107.

14 Most 18th-century portraits from the Spanish Americas depict male sitters, with a much smaller number of known female portraits. In the Viceroyalty of New Granada, portraits of *monjas muertas* (dead nuns), dressed in their habits and, at times, crowned with flowers, flourished above any other forms of female portraiture. Jaime Humberto Borja Gómez, "Un panorama del retrato en América," in *Los ingenios del pincel: Geografía de la pintura y la cultura visual en la América colonial* (Bogotá: Universidad de Los Andes, 2021), https://losingeniosdelpincel.uniandes.edu.co/un-panorama-del-re-trato-en-america/; and Jaime Humberto Borja Gómez, "Las mujeres en el retrato americano," in *El ingenio del pincel*, https://losingenios-delpincel.uniandes.edu.co/las-mujeres-en-el-retrato-americano/.

15 Elena Phipps, "Woven Silver and Gold: Metallic Yarns in Colonial Andean Textiles," in "Paradoxes and Parallels in the New World," ed. Georgia de Havenon, special issue, *Source: Notes in the History of Art* 29, no. 3 (2010): 4–11.

16 Juan Francisco de Saabedra and Carlos de Araujo, "Expediente sobre Dxos de Tassador de ropas que sigue Dn. Juan Francisco de Saabedra, contra Dn. Carlos de Araujo," 1779, caja 8, exp. 2, fol. 15r, Ropas, Archivo Nacional Histórico de Quito, Quito (hereafter abbreviated ANHQ). Unless otherwise noted, all translations are my own.

17 See, for example, "Cuenta de los bienes repartidos entre los herederos de don Luis Azuola y Micaela de la Rocha," 1791, tomo 3, fol. 340r, Testamentarias, Cundinamarca, Archivo General de la Nación, Bogotá DC.

18 Engel, *Pictured Politics*, 2.

19 Marita Martínez del Río de Redo, "Teatro de maravillas: Magnificencia barroca," *Artes de México: Retrato novohispano* 25 (July–August 1994): 53–63.

20 For a general study of the circulation and commerce of goods imported from Castilla, see Nathalie Moreno Rivera, "Circulación de efectos de Castilla en el Virreinato de la Nueva Granada a finales del siglo XVIII," *Fronteras de la historia* 18, no. 1 (2013): 211–49.

21 "Una Mantilla de Bayeta blanca de Castilla con su . . . encaje fino" and "un Faldellin de Brocado rosado, con Puntas de hilo de Castilla." Juana de Argandoña, "Testamento," 1799, Notaria 6, vol. 99, fols. 481r, 480r, ANHQ.

22 Saabedra and Araujo, "Expediente sobre Dxos de Tassador de ropas," fol. 15r, ANHQ.

23 Andrés José Pérez de Arroyo, María Josefa Valencia, and Melchor de Valencia, "Inventario extrajudicial de doña Javiera de Valencia y Castillo," 1793, caja 13, carpeta 2, fol. 109v, Archivo Histórico Cipriano Rodríguez Santa María, Universidad de la Sabana, Chia, Colombia (hereafter abbreviated AHCRS).

24 Maya Stanfield-Mazzi, *Clothing the New World Church: Liturgical Textiles of Spanish America, 1520–1820* (Notre Dame, IN: University of Notre Dame Press, 2021), 288–89.

25 Ibid., 286.

26 Ibid., 230.

27 Ibid., 295n197.

28 Ibid., 290–97. For evidence on women's involvement in the manufacture of Chachapoyas hangings and lace-type fabrics, see ibid., 230.

29 Carolyn Dean, *Inka Bodies and the Body of Christ: Corpus Christi in Colonial Cuzco, Peru* (Durham, NC: Duke University Press, 1999), 125–26.

30 Julia McHugh, "Andean Textiles," Heilbrunn Timeline of Art History, Metropolitan Museum of Art, http://www.metmuseum .org/toah/hd/antx/hd_antx.htm.

31 *Tawantinsuyu* is the term in Quechua (the language of the Inka) for what has been otherwise called the "Inka Empire."

32 Rebecca Stone-Miller, "To Weave for the Sun: An Introduction to the Fiber Arts of the Ancient Andes," in *To Weave for the Sun: Andean Textiles in the Museum of Fine Arts, Boston*, ed. Rebecca Stone-Miller (Boston: Museum of Fine Arts, 1992), 20.

33 Dean, *Inka Bodies*, 125.

34 Laura Liliana Vargas Murcia, "De Nencatacoa a San Lucas: Mantas muiscas de algodón como soporte pictórico en el Nuevo Reino de Granada," *UCOARTE* 4 (2015): 25–43.

35 Argandoña, "Testamento," fols. 481r, 480r: "Dejo una camisa de Clarin, quarzeada con encajes nebados con su Jubon delo mismo, quiero, y es mi voluntad, sevenda para ayuda demi funeral, y entierro."

36 See, for example, Jane E. Mangan, *Trading Roles: Gender, Ethnicity, and the Urban Economy in Colonial Potosí* (Durham, NC: Duke University Press, 2005). Other examples outside the Spanish Americas include Alice Dolan, "The Fabric of Life: Linen and Life Cycle in England, 1878–1810" (PhD diss., University of Hertfordshire, 2015); William Farrell, "Silk and Globalisation in Eighteenth-Century London: Commodities, People and Connections c.1720–1800" (PhD diss., University of London, 2014); and Beverly Lemire, "Transforming Consumer Custom: Linens, Cottons, and the English Market, 1660–1800," in *The European Linen Industry in Historical Perspective*, ed. Brenda Collins and Philip Ollerenshaw (Oxford: Oxford University Press, 2003).

37 José de Caldas, "Inventario de la testamentaria de Juan Tenorio," 1776, caja 30, carpeta 4, fol. 9r, AHCRS.

38 Saabedra and Araujo, "Expediente sobre Dxos de Tassador de ropas," fol. 11v.

39 Ibid., fol. 12r.

40 Leslie E. Todd, "Intertextual Intimacy: An Investigation of the Relationship between Word and Image in Eighteenth-Century Quito," *Hemisphere: Visual Culture of the Americas* 10 (2017): 6–31.

41 Maya Stanfield-Mazzi, "The Possessor's Agency: Private Art Collecting in the Colonial Andes," *Colonial Latin American Review* 18, no. 3 (2009): 342.

THE DOMINANCE OF FRANCE, 1660–1790

9 Lace, an Economic Factor in France during the Reign of Louis XIV

Denis Bruna

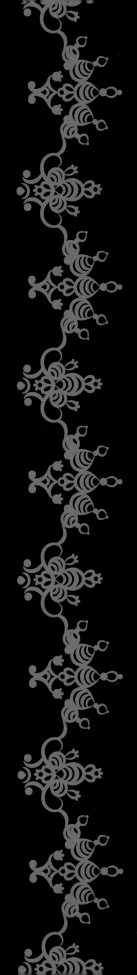

A SMALL, BRIGHTLY COLORED COLLECTIBLE CARD from the end of the nineteenth century titled *History of Lace* shows Jean-Baptiste Colbert (1619–1683) presenting a long piece of lace on a tray to Louis XIV (1638–1715; FIG. 9.1). Two inserts on the card's right edge show details of *point d'Alençon* and *point Colbert* lace. Merchants distributed this type of pedagogical advertising image to nineteenth-century customers who bought Liebig meat extract. Children and collectors would try to gather all six cards in the series, each of which provided them with some historical information. Indeed, on the back, a text of some ten lines specifies that "Venice had monopolized the production of fine needle lace, and its sales to the court of France, the center of all that was elegant, were immense." It also notes that "Colbert, Louis XIV's intelligent minister, the great protector of French industry and commerce, decided to make his country independent in this regard." This description, which comes out of a patriotic tradition in French historiography, is astonishingly dated, given that Colbert—whose statue in front of the National Assembly was recently tagged—is remembered today less as the "builder" of France than as the initiator of the *Code noir*, the 1685 text regulating the status of Black slaves in the French islands in the Americas.[1] The aim of this chapter, however, is to try to understand how lace—sometimes regarded as an outmoded craft—could be at the center of a tough commercial conflict marked by royal decrees, secret agents, coded letters, condemnations, and the poaching of workers.

FIG. 9.1

"Histoire de la dentelle: Louis XIV et Colbert," advertising card for Liebig Company, late 19th century. Chromolithograph. Private collection.

Denis Bruna

Archival documents and portraits of aristocrats, nobles, and the rich merchant bourgeoisie show that some fifty years before Colbert set out to solve the economic problem of lace in France, lace production for dress and furnishings was well established in Europe, including in France.[2] The fashion for large white collars turned down on the shoulders, ample shirts with showy cuffs, scarves, handkerchiefs, boot tops, bonnets, aprons, tablecloths, and liturgical vestments for high clergy all required large amounts of lace (FIG. 9.2). Venice, Genoa, and many northern European towns manufactured lace and sold it everywhere. France produced lace as well; archival documents mention lace fabrication in Lille, Calais, Sedan, and Arras, as well as in Normandy, Le Havre, Dieppe, Rouen, and Honfleur. Small family workshops in towns, townships, and the countryside, not forgetting the cheap labor available in convents and orphanages, produced lace thanks to the circulation of model books (SEE CHAP. 2). Yet French production was scattered and artisanal, and the lace gathered by notions sellers for their shops in the cities was insufficient in quantity and not to the taste of the rich consumers who preferred beautiful lace from abroad. Around 1640 demand intensified because fashion called for the greater display of lace. For proud customers, elegance and the affirmation of rank were inconceivable without exhibiting the delicate and costly trimmings of white thread. A half-length portrait of Louis XIV as a child depicts him wearing a collar, cuffs, and apron with heavily scalloped lace (FIG. 9.3). In fact, not only was lace a high-quality sartorial ornament, but it also played a decisive role as a marker of social status, more so than jewelry, as seen in an engraving of shop interiors within the Galerie du Palais in Paris around 1638 (SEE FIG. 2.11).

In the first half of the seventeenth century, the lace industry reached its apex in the rich United Provinces (the Netherlands) and the southern part of the Low Countries, in regions where the raw material (linen) abounded and where workers' skills in bleaching and spinning were unmatched. The towns of Mechlin, Binche, Bruges, and Brussels set about producing lace and selling it all across Europe, all the way to Italy, despite

FIG. 9.2
Ferdinand Elle, *Henry de Lorraine, Marquis de Mouy*, 1631. Oil on canvas. Musée des Beaux-Arts, Reims, 828.1.2.

the well-established lace industry traditions in Venice and Genoa. Made using bobbins, these soft white pieces of linen provided the sought-after contrast to the fashionable ensembles tailored from dark cloth (FIG. 9.4).[3]

Around 1650 the large-scale Italian industry reached a turning point with the appearance of *gros point de Venise*. This lace was new: practically sculptural with large, lively rinceaux and highlighted by thick threads in relief (FIG. 9.5). The slightly raised Baroque lines contrasted with the flat parts of the design worked in all kinds of small, fanciful stitches. Gros point de Venise was inimitable: it could not be produced using the northern bobbin technique, which is why it became all the rage in women's as well as men's fashion.[4] One of the characters in Raymond Poisson's 1662 comedy, *Le baron de la Crasse*, complains about the cost of a collar worked in point de Venise:

> But the cursed flap costs me more than all the rest?
> I wanted one of those points de Venise;
> A pest 'on it! this mean, and dear merchandise!
> It's crazy: when I wear this flap, I'm putting
> Thirty-two good acres of vineyards on my neck.[5]

FIG. 9.3 (ABOVE)
Attributed to Claude Deruet, *Louis XIV as a Child*, ca. 1642–43. Oil on canvas. Musée des Beaux-Arts, Orléans, 916.

FIG. 9.4 (LEFT)
Mathieu Le Nain, *The Academy* (also *The Meeting of the Amateurs*), ca. 1640. Oil on canvas. Musée du Louvre, Paris, RF701.

FIG. 9.5 (OPPOSITE)
Point de Venise needle-lace border, Venice; Orne, France; or Great Britain, 1675–1715, with late 19th-century edgings. Linen. Textilmuseum St. Gallen, Acquired from the Estate of John Jacoby, 1954, 01141. Cat. 32.

Denis Bruna

A decree signed by Louis XIV, dated November 17, 1660, and titled "Declaration against the Luxury of Outfits, Coaches, and Ornaments," sought to "prevent excessive spending on trimmings, lace, and other threadwork, most of which come from foreign countries." To this end, "all merchants and other persons" were explicitly prohibited from "either selling or retailing any trimmings, lace, *entretoile*, *points de Gênes* . . . or any other trimmings or lace of France" under "penalty of confiscation and a fine of fifteen hundred *livres*." The text then alludes to the point de Venise used to decorate the canons (a kind of stocking embellished with ample flounces of lace) that delighted elegant men and whose cost was judged "excessive" and "intolerable" (FIG. 9.6).[6] The rapid succession of royal decrees prohibiting lace in 1661, 1662, and 1664 underscores their inefficacy. In fact, despite these prohibitions and sanctions, imports of point de Venise and point de Gênes ornamentation continued to rise.

As in the preceding centuries, sumptuary laws were economically motivated. They were meant to reduce capital flight by prohibiting the purchase of foreign luxury goods. Moral preoccupations, too, played a role in the promulgation of these texts, which intended to reform clothing deemed indecent for the luxury and sins it gave rise to. In response to a Christian tradition of modesty and virtue, the 1660 law described above prohibited decorating one's clothing even with lace produced in France—unless it sought to reserve these expensive ornaments for the kingdom's great, like Colbert himself, who in the portrait by Claude Lefèbvre (1632–1675) of 1665/66 is wearing a collar of Venetian lace (FIG. 9.7).

In the middle of the seventeenth century, lace was an outrageously expensive product. Making the most beautiful needlework was a slow process, yielding a few centimeters a day, and transport was slow and hazardous. Furthermore, the profit shares of merchants and intermediaries were excessive, not to mention the impact of import duties on the final price of lace. The flight of capital to Venice amounted to the colossal sum of several million livres.[7]

Such was the thorny economic context in which Jean-Baptiste Colbert intervened.[8] After the arrest of his predecessor and rival, Nicolas Fouquet (1615–1680), Colbert became intendant of finances in 1661 and controller-general of finances in 1665. Emboldened by the trust Louis XIV placed in him, he expanded his authority and oversaw numerous state departments including navy, waters and forests, mines, the King's Buildings, trade, manufactures, and so on. Given the inadequacy of the recurrent sumptuary laws

FIG. 9.6

Louis XIV, from *Généalogies des maisons royales et princières et de leurs ramifications, pièces originales, copies, dessins et aquarelles provenant de François Roger de Gaignières*, 1660. Ink on paper. Bibliothèque nationale de France, département des manuscrits, Paris, CLAIRAMBAULT 633, folio 313.

of the 1660s, Colbert chose a different path and instead promoted the local lace industry.

The minister's strategy is laid out in the "Declaration to Establish a Manufacture of All Kinds of Threadwork," scrupulously drawn up by Colbert and his collaborators, signed by Louis XIV, and published on August 5, 1665 (FIG. 9.8).[9] It begins by stating that a manufacture of any kind pursues two essential goals: to provide subjects with work and to prevent capital flight to foreign countries.

The text then names Jean Pluimers as well as Paul and Catherine de Marcq as "voluntaries" for establishing the "Manufacture of threadwork" with an exclusive right, granted for nine years, to produce French lace. Jean Pluimers (or Pluymers), who hailed from Tournai, is often referred to in other documents as a *bourgeois de Paris*; Paul and Catherine de Marcq were his niece and nephew. Studies have shown that administrators, high-level civil servants, businessmen, and all kinds of merchants were interested in setting up and running these manufactories, and even more so in their profits.[10] The intervention of these private persons in the creation of a royal manufacture might come as a surprise, but in 1665, the finances of the kingdom were still quite unstable. France was coming out of several years of warfare, and the Fronde had severely weakened the kingdom, so much so that although the lace manufactures were royal enterprises, they were set up with the money of rich investors.[11]

The particularity of the manufacture is specified three times in the declaration: it is defined as a manufacture of "threadwork in the manner of the lace made in Venice, Genoa, and foreign countries both with needles and on pillows."[12] The new creations—or these imitations, at least—were henceforth called *points de France*.

To produce lace as faithful to those made abroad, and of equal quality, Pluimers and his niece and nephew were charged with bringing thirty lace masters from Venice and two hundred lace workers from Flanders (FIG. 9.9). These female laborers

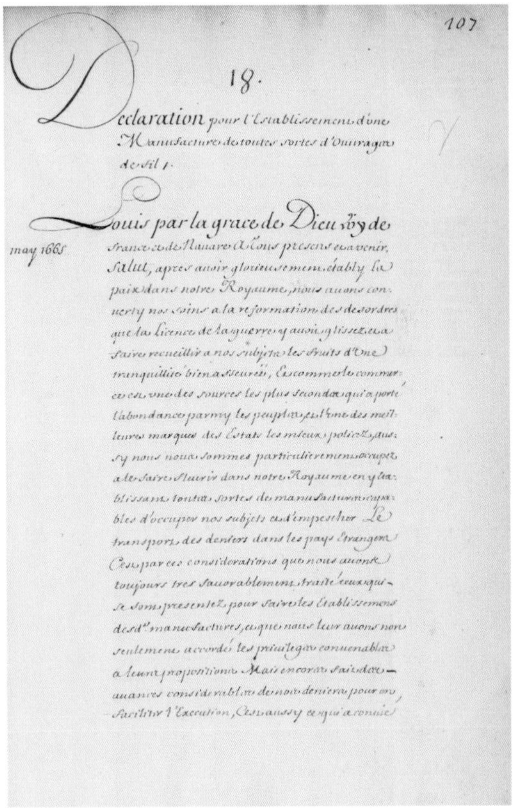

FIG. 9.7 (ABOVE)
Claude Lefèbvre, *Jean-Baptiste Colbert*, 1666. Oil on canvas. Musée national des châteaux de Versailles et de Trianon, Versailles, MV 2185.

FIG. 9.8 (RIGHT)
"Déclaration pour l'établissement d'une manufacture de toutes sortes de points de fil," from *Recueil d'arrêts du Conseil d'État, du Conseil du commerce et de privilèges royaux concernant les manufactures*, 1661–69. Ink on paper. Bibliothèque nationale de France, département des manuscrits, cote, Paris, Cinq cents de Colbert 207, fol. 107.

were sent to towns across the realm chosen for the establishment of manufactories, including Le Quesnoy, Arras, Reims, Sedan, Château-Thierry, Loudun, Alençon, and Aurillac. The declaration specifies that these women were to teach foreign styles to French workers who were already making lace in several cities but needed to perfect their techniques to be able to produce the gros point de Venise so much in demand at the time.[13] The foreign lacemakers who were brought to France at great expense were promised naturalization.[14] As one might expect, Italian authorities did not appreciate their workers departing for France. In Venice the senate tried to dissuade them by means of decrees. Those lacemakers who had already accepted the French offer were asked to return to Italy or risk being killed by an emissary. It is therefore understandable that

FIG. 9.9

Johannes Vermeer, *The Lacemaker*, ca. 1669–70. Oil on canvas on wood. Musée du Louvre, Paris, MI 1448.

many of the letters written by the French ambassador in Venice, Cardinal Pierre de Bonzy (or Piero de Bonzi), and addressed to Colbert were encoded. Those that were not reveal that the cardinal, who was loyal to Louis XIV, managed, thanks to some well-placed spies, to obtain a significant amount of information on the making of Venetian lace, the organization of its production, and the sale of the final product.[15]

The eight towns cited in the 1665 declaration were in no way accidental. Spread across the kingdom, several of them were known for a long and illustrious tradition of lacemaking. This was the case in Sedan, Alençon, and Aurillac, where there were skilled lacemakers who only needed to familiarize themselves with gros point de Venise. Other towns were chosen based on Colbert's personal interests. Such was the case for Reims, his hometown, to which he remained attached. Members of his family lived there—including his sister Claire, abbess of the Saint Claire monastery—and some of them took an interest in the lace manufactory. As a result, the minister was always well informed about the state of the industry. Colbert, who also had connections with Auxerre, acquired the neighboring barony of Seignelay in 1657 and received the permission of Louis XIV to appoint his brother Nicolas bishop of Auxerre in 1671.

Unlike private and family-run workshops—where women worked at their own rhythm and could be interrupted by the needs of the children and livestock in their care—the primary function of a manufactory was to bring together a large number of workers in one place under the direction of a supervisor to maintain discipline. In the new threadwork manufactories, workers had to familiarize themselves with the techniques taught by the Venetian lacemakers. They were also obliged to work specified hours on-site and not to divulge the designs that they were producing. In each of the towns, the managers made use of Italian and Flemish "mistresses" and women who ran the workshops and of French workers who had lived abroad and had thorough knowledge of the techniques. Such was the case of a certain Marie de Voullemin, who had learned the art of lacemaking in Venice and ran the manufacture in Auxerre.[16]

Nonetheless, in most towns, setting up the manufactories was not an easy task. French lacemakers were hostile to the foundation of new establishments likely to compete with their work. These women, who had previously worked in their homes, chafed at the supervision and control in shared spaces and at learning a new technique, which required time that they were not paid for. In parallel, the abundance of rules and taxes promoted fraud and trafficking. In Alençon, for instance, the Benedictine sisters traded their lace outside the manufacturing system. Thanks to the privileged status of convents and nuns, however, the sisters were not prosecuted.[17] In addition, foreign lace continued to circulate as much as ever.

At the beginning, the royal lace manufactures set out to copy gros point de Venise, no doubt a necessary step in competing against its popularity. But Colbert knew that imitations would not conquer new markets, and so point de France became an original style of lace with decorative and technical particularities that ensured its success.[18]

The designs that served as models for the lacemakers at the manufactories were the work of great French artists working in Paris for the king and a refined clientele. The decoration of flounces worked in point de France in the last third of the seventeenth century shows familiarity with models by Charles Le Brun (1619–1690), painter to

Louis XIV since 1662; Jacques Bailly (1629–1679), also *peintre du Roi*; François Bonnemer (1638–1689), painter and engraver; and the ornamental designer, decorator, and engraver Jean Bérain, père (1640–1711).[19] Point de France differed from its predecessors in that it abandoned the heavy Baroque volutes of the Venetian lace and adopted a lighter design. French lace was now characterized by a subdued floral pattern arranged along architectural vertical axes of symmetry referred to as *décor à la Bérain* (FIGS. 9.10–12).[20] The new lace exemplified the classical taste of French decorative arts of the period, which included the wood or metal marquetry of furniture by Jean-Philippe Boulle (ca. 1690–1744; FIG. 9.13), sculpted panels, wrought iron, and woven and embroidered silks. From a technical point of view, point de France of the 1670s is delicate lace without relief, unlike gros point de Venise, which is instantly recognizable by the *fleuron* highlighted by raised stitches. Moreover, Venetian lace, because of its relief and rigidity, was generally worn flat, whereas lace in point de France could be ruffled and was therefore easily adaptable to the new fashionable cravats (FIG. 9.14) and frelange headdresses, whose lace had to be carefully pleated (FIG. 9.15; SEE FIG. 10.3). The *lingère* in a 1695 engraving by Nicolas de Larmessin (1638–1695) wears pleated frelanges on her

FIG. 9.10 (OPPOSITE)

Point de France needle-lace border, France, 1695–1710. Linen. Textilmuseum St. Gallen, Acquired from the Estate of John Jacoby, 1954, 01231. Cat. 86.

FIG. 9.11 (ABOVE)

Point de France needle-lace border or flounce, Orne, France, ca. 1700, with 19th-century additions. Linen. Textilmuseum St. Gallen, Acquired from the Estate of John Jacoby, 1954, 01232.

FIG. 9.12 (RIGHT)

Jean Bérain, "Composition décorative, recueil d'arabesques," from *Ornament Designs Invented by J. Bérain*, plate 65, published by Jacques III Thuret, 1711 or after. Engraving. The Metropolitan Museum of Art, New York, Rogers Fund, 1915, transferred from the Library, 21.36.141.

head and over her shoulders and holds a cravat with ruffled lace ends in her right hand (FIG. 9.16).

The success of French lace was due to the fact that these products were sold in Paris, where the monied clientele for such articles lived, and generally in select stores: only four shops, which were granted the inscription "Royal Manufacture of lace, trimmings, and threadwork of France," were authorized to sell this lace.[21]

Thanks to its novelty, point de France quickly imposed itself in France, across Europe, and even in Venice, as the inventory of a Venetian merchant suggests. Dated 1671—a mere six years after the declaration establishing the French manufactures—the document lists "'Merli alla Colberta,' or laces à la Colbert" as among the shop's most expensive items.[22] Now, as early as 1670, it was the Venetian authorities who were up in arms against the importation of foreign lace. Weakened, the Venice lace industry began to copy point de France.[23]

The wardrobe inventories of the French kingdom's wealthy and powerful and those of the churches to which rich ladies donated altar frontals, and above all the large number of portraits depicting sitters covered in delicate lace cravats, cuffs, collars,

FIG. 9.13 (ABOVE)

Jean-Philippe Boulle, one of three plates from a suite of four grotesque designs for marquetry panels, published by Nicholas Gautrot, ca. 1720–39. Engraving. Bibliothèque nationale de France, département Arsenal, Paris, EST-184 (224).

FIG. 9.14 (BELOW)

Point de France needle-lace cravat end, France, late 17th century. Linen. The Metropolitan Museum of Art, New York, Gift of Mrs. Edward S. Harkness, 1930, 30.135.143.

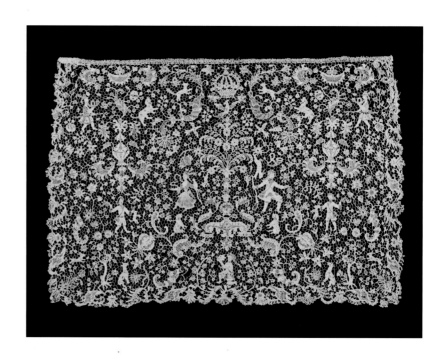

bonnets, and the like are eloquent testimonies to the success of point de France (FIG. 9.17). In a letter dated January 12, 1674, Madame de Sévigné (1626–1696) compares Mademoiselle de Blois to an angel, "dressed in black velvet with diamonds, an apron and bib in *point de France*."[24]

The nine-year right described in the 1665 declaration was not renewed in the manufactories founded by Colbert. Point de France disappeared when the company's monopoly was lifted in 1675. The products of French lacemakers that continued to work the white threads often took the name of the towns where they were employed, hence the designations "Alençon lace" or "Sedan lace." The revocation of the Edict of Nantes in 1685 severely weakened the French industry, particularly in Normandy, where many Protestants working in lace manufacturing were forced to emigrate. The lacemaking population in this region was reduced by half.[25] This situation benefited several towns in the north, such as Valenciennes, Mechlin, and Brussels. The Brussels merchants who, in 1665, had lamented the poaching of their best workers thanks to Colbert's decree prospered once more. At the end of the seventeenth century, fine and light Brussels lace reached new heights of perfection and imposed itself in European fashion. The text on the Liebig collector's card celebrating Colbert does not mention this reversal of fortune.

FIG. 9.17
Point de France needle-lace scarf or trimming for an alb hem, Alençon, France, ca. 1690. Linen. Musée des Arts decoratifs, Paris, 24067.

This chapter (including quotations unless otherwise noted) was translated from the French by Nils Schott.

1 *Le code noir ou Edit du roy* [. . .] (Paris, 1718). Unless otherwise noted, all translations are by Nils Schott. It is beyond the scope of this chapter to examine Colbert's role in France's racist history.
2 The literature on the history of lace is very rich. In particular, see Fanny Bury Palliser, *A History of Lace*, 3rd ed. (London: Sampson Low, Marston, Low, & Searle, 1875), Internet Archive, https://archive.org/details/historyoflace1875pall/; Santina M. Levey, *Lace: A History* (Leeds, UK: W. S. Maney & Son; London: Victoria and Albert Museum, 1983); and Anne Kraatz, *Dentelles* (Paris: Adam Biro, 1988).
3 Palliser, *A History of Lace*, 62–70; Kraatz, *Dentelles*, 90–92.
4 Ibid., 42.
5 Raymond Poisson, *Le baron de la Crasse* (Paris: de Luyne, 1662), scène II, 10, BnF Gallica, https://gallica.bnf.fr/ark:/12148/bpt6k83245v?rk=21459;2:

   Mais le maudis rabat me cousta plus que tout ?
   J'en voulus avoir un de ces points de Venise ;
   La peste ! La mechante, et chere marchandise !
   En mettant ce rabat, je mis, c'est estre fou,
   Trente-deux bons arpens de vignoble à mon cou.

6 "Déclaration contre le luxe des habits, carrosses et ornemens," no. 357 in *Recueil général des anciennes lois françaises depuis l'an 420 jusqu'à la Révolution de 1789* [. . .], vol. 17 (Paris: Belin-Leprieur, 1829), 384–85, BnF Gallica, https://gallica.bnf.fr/ark:/12148/bpt-6k517036?rk=557942.
7 Nicole Ovaere-Raudet, *Les manufactures de dentelle de Colbert* (Bourges, France: Cercle généalogique du Haut-Berry, 2018), 20.
8 On Colbert and the establishment of lace manufactures in France, see ibid.

9 "Déclaration pour l'établissement d'une manufacture de toutes sortes de points de fil," transcribed in ibid., 65.
10 Paul-Martin Bondois, "Colbert et l'industrie de la dentelle: Le 'Point de France' à Reims et à Sedan d'après des documents inédits," *Revue d'histoire économique et sociale* 13, no. 4 (1925): 370.
11 The Fronde (1648–53) was a period of political conflict that impacted the French realm before Louis XIV ascended the throne in 1661.
12 "Déclaration," transcribed in Ovaere-Raudet, *Les manufactures de dentelle*, 65.
13 Ovaere-Raudet, *Les manufactures de dentelle*, 32.
14 Ibid., 27.
15 Kraatz, *Dentelles*, 46; and Ovaere-Raudet, *Les manufactures de dentelle*, 27.
16 Bondois, "Colbert et l'industrie," 371.
17 Ovaere-Raudet, *Les manufactures de dentelle*, 33, 35.
18 Kraatz, *Dentelles*, 48.
19 Anne Kraatz, "Lace at the Court of Louis XIV," *Magazine Antiques* (June 1981): 1372.
20 Kraatz, "Lace at the Court of Louis XIV," 1371.
21 Hôtel de la Monnaie, *Colbert 1619–1683*, exh. cat. (Paris: Archives nationales, 1983), 163.
22 Anne Kraatz, "The Inventory of a Venetian Lace Merchant in the Year 1671," *Bulletin de liaison du Centre international d'étude des textiles anciens*, nos. 55–56 (1982): 129.
23 Kraatz, *Dentelles*, 50.
24 *Lettres de Madame de Sévigné avec les notes de tous les commentateurs*, vol. 2 (Paris: Firmin-Didot frères, 1853), 201, BnF Gallica, https://gallica.bnf.fr/ark:/12148/bpt6k6101781m/f208.item.
25 Kraatz, *Dentelles*, 50.

10 Lace *à la Mode* in France, ca. 1690–1790

Lesley Ellis Miller

BOUT ONE HUNDRED YEARS AFTER Jean-Baptiste Colbert's short-lived promotion of lace production in France, the court painter François-Hubert Drouais (1727–1775) completed his magnificent portrait of Jeanne-Antoinette Poisson, marquise de Pompadour (1721–1764), resplendent in a painted silk gown and dripping with lace from head to toe (FIG. 10.1). Genteelly employed at her embroidery frame in her apartment at Versailles, the former *maîtresse-en-titre* and faithful confidante of Louis XV (1710–1774) wears fashionable attire expressive of her status, taste, and wealth.[1] The deep flounce adorning her petticoat, the elaborate sleeve ruffles falling gracefully over her elbows, the border around the décolletage of her chemise, and the cap decently covering her powdered hair constituted a small proportion of the lace she then owned. Indeed, after her death, her lace accessories took a whole afternoon to list and accounted for about 44 percent of the value of her entire wardrobe (some 22,800 livres).[2] Many were associated with the French centers of Alençon, Argentan, and Valenciennes and the (now) Belgian cities of Mechlin and Brussels, from which point d'Angleterre probably came.[3] There were also examples of lace not specifically associated with a place: some *blondes* (blonde or silk lace), some *petites dentelles* (literally little lace, sometimes called *mignonette*), and some *dentelles à la paysanne* (peasant-style lace).[4] The more expensive categories comprised sets of matching accessories or trimmed formal and fashionable gowns; the lower-value lace was attached to linen chemises or nightcaps.[5] The marquise's possessions probably represented many years of accumulation, to go by the annual purchases of her successor as official mistress.[6]

Many other portraits of elite society act as snapshots of lace in ceremonial and fashionable dress in France between 1690 and 1790, though documentary evidence has not necessarily survived to tie the lace directly to the subjects' possessions. They intimate that the quantity and quality of accessories and trimmings in men's, women's, and children's wardrobes changed over time. At the beginning of the period, men's cravats and women's *frelange* headdresses were focal points (FIGS. 10.2 AND 10.3); by the mid-eighteenth century, the cravat had been abandoned in favor of shirt ruffles, the frelange replaced by a smaller cap that fitted the head more closely (FIGS. 10.4 AND

FIG. 10.1 (PREVIOUS)
François-Hubert Drouais, *Madame de Pompadour at Her Embroidery Frame*, 1763–64. Oil on canvas. The National Gallery, London, NG6440.

FIG. 10.2 (BELOW)
Nicolas de Largillière, *James Francis Edward Stuart and Louisa Marie Theresa Stuart*, 1695. Oil on canvas. National Portrait Gallery, London, Bequeathed by Horatio William Walpole, 4th Earl of Oxford, 1895, NPG 976.

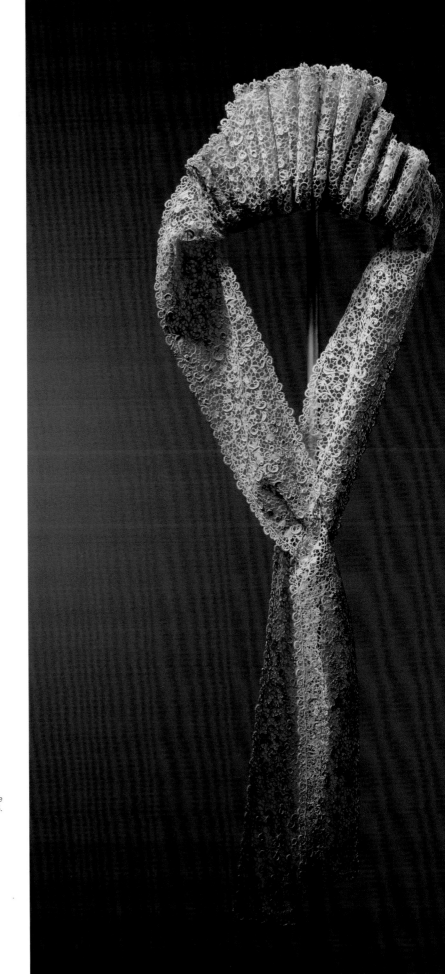

FIG. 10.3

Point de France needle-lace *frelange*
with lappets, Orne, France, ca. 1695.
Linen. Textilmuseum St. Gallen,
Acquired from the Estate of John
Jacoby, 1954, 01246. Cat. 87.

10.5); and by the end of the century, much less heavily patterned lace bedecked neck, wrist, or elbow and extravagant coiffures (FIGS. 10.6 AND 10.7).[7] Throughout the period women's fashions boasted a wider range of lace accessories than men's, in the form of aprons, caps, fichus, headdresses, palatines, and petticoat flounces. Over the decades the design of the lace itself changed broadly in line with fashionable silk patterns.[8]

This essay contextualizes these snapshots by considering the making, acquisition, and use of lace. It moves from workshop to shop to salon, introducing some of the people whose livelihoods and aspirations revolved around this expensive commodity. The focus is on fashion, although lace was also used liberally for furnishings by the upper echelons of society and for liturgical vestments and cloths. The action takes place in France, although not all the lace was made there.

Materials and Manufacture

The marquise's inventory introduces the prestige lacemaking centers, whose names were increasingly attached to a particular style or technique. Alençon and Argentan were in northwest France, Valenciennes in the northeast. The latter had been under French rule only since 1678 and, in the longer term, maintained its strong connections with Brussels and Mechlin on the other side of the (now) Belgian border. All were located in

FIG. 10.4 (LEFT)

Charles Antoine Coypel, *François de Jullienne and Marie Élisabeth de Jullienne*, 1743. Pastel, black chalk, and watercolor, with traces of black-chalk underdrawing. The Metropolitan Museum of Art, New York, Purchase, Mrs. Charles Wrightsman Gift, in honor of Annette de la Renta, 2011, 2011.84.

FIG. 10.5 (RIGHT)

Brussels or point d'Angleterre bobbin-lace cap back, Brussels, Southern Netherlands, ca. 1750. Linen. Textilmuseum St. Gallen, Acquired from the Estate of John Jacoby, 1954, 00731. Cat. 120.

areas of linen production and had ready access to finely spun thread. They were actively making lace by the early seventeenth century, grew in the third quarter of the century, weathered the detrimental economic and political upheavals of the end of the century, and flourished again from the second till the final decade of the eighteenth century, after which lace fell from fashion until the early nineteenth century.[9] Broadly speaking, their distinctive styles had evolved from two different traditions: in Normandy from Italian needle lace (SEE CHAP. 9) and in Valenciennes from Flemish bobbin lace (SEE CHAP. 4).[10] In the south of France, the towns of Aurillac and Le Puy in the Auvergne were the main centers of silk and metal lace production until the end of the seventeenth century. Trade with Spain facilitated the supply of both raw silk and precious metals and ensured export markets for finished goods (SEE CHAP. 5). In the eighteenth century, such lace tended to be made in the environs of Paris, Lyon, and other large cities, with some production of both silk and thread (linen) lace continuing in the Languedoc.[11]

Foregrounding urban centers obscures the extent to which lace was made in their hinterland, in the surrounding villages and countryside, as well as elsewhere in France. The tools of the trade—including pins, bobbins, and cushions—were relatively inexpensive,

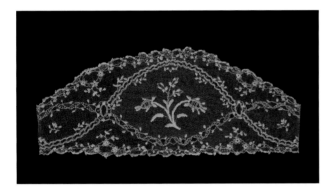

FIG. 10.6 (LEFT)
Needle-lace sleeve ruffles (*engageantes*), Alençon or Argentan, France, 1780–90, reworked in the 19th century. Linen. Textilmuseum St. Gallen, Acquired from the Estate of John Jacoby, 1954, 02143.1-2. Cat. 116.

FIG. 10.7 (RIGHT)
Adolf-Ulrik Wertmüller, *Marie-Antoinette with Marie Thérèse or Madame Royale and the First Dauphin Louis Joseph Xavier François Walking in the Park of Trianon*, 1785. Oil on canvas. Nationalmuseum, Stockholm, NM 1032.

simple to acquire or make, and highly portable (FIG. 10.8). A maker needed only a clean space and table, a supply of materials, and a design before setting up her equipment and twisting her threads in appropriate configurations (FIGS. 10.9 AND 10.10). Materials and techniques were not restricted to a particular area in the eighteenth century. Blonde, in vogue from the late 1720s, was being made in Alençon by 1754, while in 1772 an advertisement in the Lyonnais commercial press revealed, "Madame de Bellemarre continues to teach Alençon and Argentan lace, with success, as proven by the works made by different ladies she has had the honor of teaching."[12] Her address in the city suggests she may have taught both genteel ladies and future wage earners.

Lacemaking was largely a female occupation: widows, wives, and spinsters were involved. It was not governed by a guild, nor by official regulations about the quality of products, the training and conduct of apprentices, or workshop practices. Religious and charitable institutions were key players in providing training and employment; both had their own demanding rules and codes of behavior. They interacted with lace merchants who invested in materials and designs, put out work to lacemakers, and negotiated sales beyond the locality. Skills were passed from mother to daughter, gained in convents or poorhouses or through indenture to an experienced "mistress." Learning such intricate work usually began around the age of ten and was expected to take between five and eight years.[13] This length of time was comparable with the six years served to become a master embroiderer in Paris, but long in comparison with the three years required to become a *couturière* (seamstress).[14] Subsequent wages did not reflect the long training and laborious application of this savoir faire, with two to thirteen sols per day paid across France between the 1720s and 1770s.[15] At the bottom end of the spectrum, these sums were similar to spinners' earnings in the Valenciennes area (three to four sols) and embroideresses' in Lyon (five to six sols), but lower than those of the *marchandes de modes* (milliners) who were earning twenty sols per day by the 1780s.[16] A skilled male artisan in Paris, however,

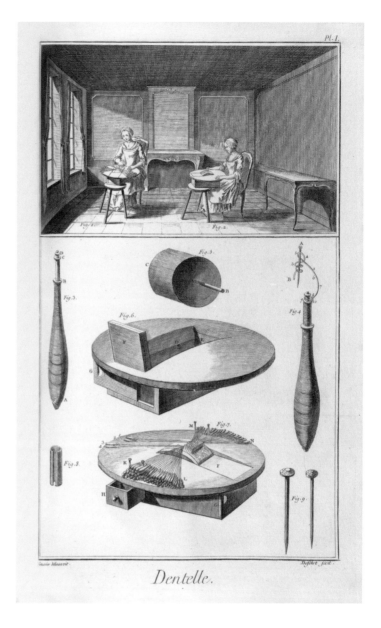

FIG. 10.8
Two lacemakers, the first making lace and the second pricking a pattern on green vellum, "Dentelle et façon du point," from Denis Diderot and Jean le Rond d'Alembert, eds., *Recueil de Planches, sur les Sciences, Les Arts Libéraux, et Les Arts Méchaniques, avec leur explication: Troisième Livraison*, Briasson, Paris, 1765, vol. 3, plate 1. Engraving. The Metropolitan Museum of Art, New York, Harris Brisbane Dick Fund, 1933, 33.23(3). Cat. 4.

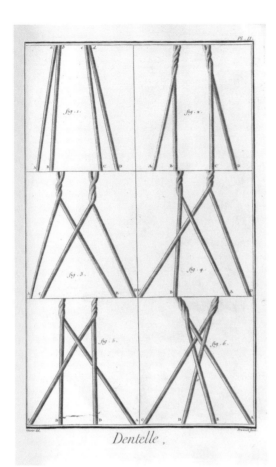

expected to earn about double this last amount.[17] Not surprisingly, as the cost of living rose in the late 1780s, some lacemakers turned to different ways of earning income, often free from occupational hazards such as loss of sight.[18]

Work took place in town or country, in communal workshops or in the maker's home. Women could, therefore, juggle this income generation with domestic and seasonal activities, such as raising a family or helping with agricultural tasks.[19] They used their own bobbins and cushions, and their commissioning merchants recorded the materials the lacemaker had received in a ledger, which the lacemaker kept as evidence of their arrangement.[20] Payment followed the completion of the piece, which could take months to make: half an ell of the finest Valenciennes took a year; a pair of ruffles—no doubt similar to those worn by the marquise de Pompadour—ten to twelve months. In contrast, makers might produce three to four ells per annum of the finest Lille lace and as much as fifty ells of coarser work.[21] The fineness of thread and the width, shape, and design of the piece dictated the speed of execution and consequent value. Prices varied: from 1 livre 5 sols to 6 livres 12 sols for narrow Perpignan lace in 1737; 1 livre 10 sols to 80 livres per ell for true Valenciennes; 24 to 34 livres for Angleterre in 1760; 3 to 6 livres for Lille;

1 sol to 5 livres for blondes, and 9 sols to 4 livres for metal lace in the 1780s (FIGS. 10.11A-E).[22] Many lacemakers needed advances in order to survive, and such advances were evidently calculated on the basis of the value of the end product.[23]

Merchants (men and women) sat between makers (women) and consumers (men and women). They were numerous in major centers, but their numbers fluctuated with demand and circumstance. In Alençon there were eighty in 1757, but only twenty-four in 1800; in Valenciennes, twenty-two at midcentury, and four in 1788.[24] Their enterprises varied in size and longevity. The correspondence and account books of the Tribout family of Valenciennes, active between 1748 and 1795, reveal that they employed 200 lacemakers between 1753 and 1755, including girls from the local convents, and 394 in 1779.[25] François-Joseph Tribout (1723–1786) was highly regarded midcentury for encouraging "his workers to excel" and for having "continually new products" in his premises.[26] By contrast, in 1778 in Lyon the little-known Catherine Bonnard, widow of Antoine Baisse, was supplying just ten women with metal and silk threads and patterns.[27]

The acquisition of designs fit for purpose was one of the most significant aspects of the merchants' role. There were different types of designs, as a midcentury article on silk lace in the *Encyclopédie* explained: *blondes de fantaisie* (fancy blondes) and *blondes travaillées* (worked blondes). The first were those "which are subject to the caprice of fashion and taste"; they always had solidly worked patterns or flowers. The second were rather different: "the design correct and well chosen, combined with a delicate execution, makes a piece whose permanent beauty is assured, independent of caprice, fashion and circumstance." These blondes often imitated expensive thread lace and were evidently as costly as they were desirable.[28] This same article underlined how much milliners liked the fancy variety for trimming gowns, headdresses, palatines, and ruffles.

The patterns were drawn by painters or draftsmen locally or brought from Paris or Brussels. In some centers, there was already a strong artistic community, and by midcentury schools of drawing were being founded to serve local industries as well as train artists: those in Lille (1755), Lyon (1757), Amiens (1758), and Valenciennes (1785) may well have served, directly or indirectly, lacemaking as well as other textile trades.[29] Brussels patterns were appreciated to such an extent in Valenciennes that Tribout sent his daughter Claire (b. 1753) to take drawing lessons there in 1770. Subsequently, she spent time in Paris, where she copied old designs, a tried and tested method of developing novel textile patterns.[30] When Claire took over her parents' business in 1779, she continued to make designs and receive them from elsewhere.[31] Her instructions to her correspondents related both to the forms needed for fashionable accessories and to the motifs on the lace. She was also very clear about the ownership of such creative work, informing a client in 1791 that "each merchant has designs that are particular to him and which he does not share . . . I make all my designs myself; but they are for my business and I sell none."[32] Already, a century earlier, merchants in Alençon had bewailed the theft of designs they had made over three or four years, calling for protection of what was an important commercial asset.[33]

(OPPOSITE, LEFT TO RIGHT)

FIG. 10.11A
Point de France needle-lace lappet, Orne, France; or Venice, ca. 1700. Linen. Textilmuseum St. Gallen, Acquired from the Estate of John Jacoby, 1954, 01203. Cat. 115.

FIG. 10.11B
Brussels needle-lace lappet, Brussels, Southern Netherlands, first half of the 18th century. Linen. Textilmuseum St. Gallen, Acquired from the Estate of John Jacoby, 1954, 00721. Cat. 114.

FIG. 10.11C
Bobbin-lace lappet, Mechlin, Southern Netherlands, ca. 1740. Linen. Textilmuseum St. Gallen, Acquired from the Estate of John Jacoby, 1954, 03047. Cat. 110.

FIG. 10.11D
Point d'Alençon needle-lace lappet, Alençon or Argentan, France, ca. 1750. Linen. Textilmuseum St. Gallen, Acquired from the Estate of John Jacoby, 1954, 00729.1-2. Cat. 107.

FIG. 10.11E
Point d'Alençon needle-lace lappet, Alençon or Argentan, France, 1750–60. Linen. Textilmuseum St. Gallen, Acquired from the Estate of John Jacoby, 1954, 02133.1-2. Cat. 92.

Purchase and Persuasion

The Tribouts, like other merchants, were also active in making sales nationally and internationally, contacting prestigious private clients directly, and supplying middlemen in other cities. Most of their trade was with Paris, lace being one of the twenty categories of luxury goods sold by the *marchands merciers* (luxury retailers) of the faubourg Saint-Honoré. These merchants, "who made nothing, yet sold everything," were at the apex of the trade, in possession of the capital and credit necessary to invest speculatively in a wide range of luxury stock for their well-appointed shops.[34] As early as 1678 *Le Mercure galant* captured one such luxury emporium in print (FIG. 10.12), devoting some commentary in the accompanying text to the latest fashions in lace.[35] An elegant couple, surrounded by a range of fabrics and accoutrements, peruse *point d'Espagne* (metal lace) for gentlemen's hose and sashes and *point de France* (needle lace) for their cravats (for an example of point de France, SEE FIG. 10.3), the former to adorn women's skirts and aprons and the latter for their palatines. There was also lace embroidered in colors.

FIG. 10.12
Jean Bérain, "Garde-robes pour dames et pour hommes," from *Le Mercure galant*, engraved by Jean Lepautre, January 1678. Engraving. Bibliothèque nationale de France, 8-H-26484.

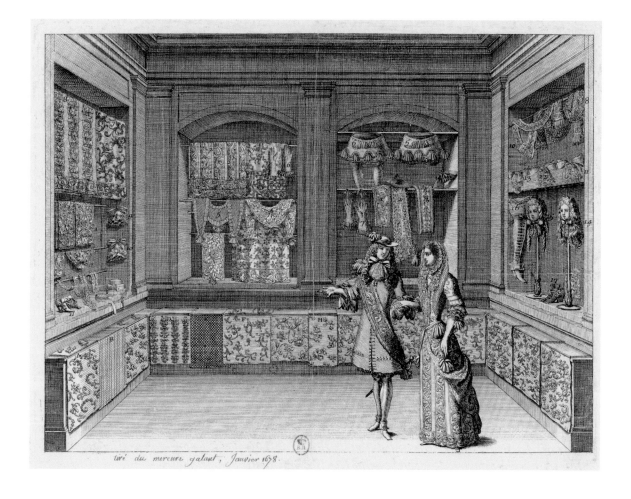

tiré du mercure galant, Janvier 1678.

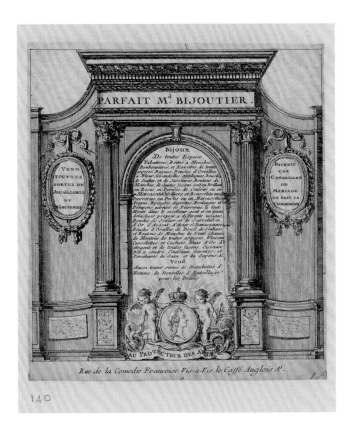

Such shops, "where luxury was only surpassed by the flow of witty words and civilities around prices," benefited from networks across France and beyond, including family connections in centers of lace production.[36] For example, Thomas Mercier from Alençon made his fortune in Paris as a marchand mercier between 1762 and his brother Jacques's death in 1790, relying on a ready supply of lace from the family *fabrique* (manufacture/business) in their hometown.[37] Lace was presumably only one of the goods he sold, as other mercers bought a variety to combine into customized packages for their clients. Indeed, the jeweler Parfait stated on his trade card in the 1730s, "Also sells all sorts of men's ruffles, in lace and stiffened with canvas for mourning. Supplies marriage lists and undertakes commissions" (FIG. 10.13). Diamonds and lace were happy companions in the marriage "basket" given by a well-heeled husband to his new wife.[38] Items like the magnificent fan leaf with the conjoined coat of arms of King Ferdinand VI of Spain and his wife, Maria Magdalena Barbara, Infanta of Portugal (FIG. 10.14), were made to commission, the lace probably ordered from Brussels, mounted by a specialist fanmaker in Paris to be sold by a marchand mercier. In contrast, on a more modest level, in Dufour's 1770s pitch, handkerchiefs, blonde, and gauze mingled with stationery, paper, and implements for drawing, writing, and music, haberdashery, and trinkets (FIG. 10.15).

Lace was also sold in simpler fixed premises, at fairs, in the streets, and on the road, by specialist *marchands de dentelles* (lace merchants) or *marchands de blondes* (blonde merchants), as well as by *crieurs* (hawkers) and *colporteurs* (itinerant peddlers), and through auctions of the possessions of the recently deceased.[39] It was kept by *marchandes lingères* (female linen merchants) and milliners (FIG. 10.16). In the stock of a recently deceased lingère in Paris in 1752, lace sat alongside the types of textiles to which it was often attached: "Linens of all qualities: muslin, lace, dimity, fustian, shirts for men and women, in every size, layettes, etc., women's powdering cloaks, furnishings, etc."[40] In Lyon the Demoiselles Caminet, milliners, advertised decorative textiles in 1762—printed cottons of all types, as well as linens, muslins, embroideries, ribbons, black-and-white thread, and silk lace, and nine years later a similar shop nearby sold printed cottons, muslins, silks and half silks, wool, ticking, and *cirsaka* for men's waistcoats, as well as white and black blonde and lace from Le Puy.[41]

On the eve of the French Revolution (1789–1799), nine lace and four blonde merchants resided in the commercial quarter between the church of Saint-Nizier and the river Saône, the understated Lyonnais equivalent of the faubourg Saint-Honoré; three were widows

FIG. 10.13

Trade Card and Possible Invoice of Parfait, Jeweller, Au Protecteur des Arts, Paris, 1735. Engraving. Waddesdon (National Trust) Bequest of James de Rothschild, 1957, 3686.1.73.140.

who ran their deceased husband's business.[42] Their premises no doubt resembled those of seventy-year-old Demoiselle Villion or fifty-six-year-old Pierre Seguin. In 1760 the former managed a ground-floor shop that had not only glass frontage but also a glass partition between the front and back shop. The front was furnished with two benches, four stools, a *banque* (counter/cash desk), and twelve shelves on which sat twenty-three boxes. The shelves were covered with green fabric, and there were four *tapis de boutique* (shop covers) trimmed with lace and muslin to show off wares, most of which were locked away in a cupboard in the back shop. All fittings were well worn, but a mirror in a gilded frame suggested better times. In contrast Seguin rented a flat in Lyon and owned a property in the country north of Lyon in 1786. In town his *magasin* on the first floor was both storeroom and salesroom, furnished with four pine chairs, three pine stools, two walnut stools, and a walnut counter, a painted wall hanging, a large mirror in an ornate gilded frame above the fireplace with copper candle holders, appropriate equipment in the hearth, and a metal birdcage. Here, too, the lace was kept in a cupboard.[43] These spaces were certainly not as sumptuous as those of some Parisian mercers, but they were respectable, with touches of comfort.

Seguin specialized in blonde lace, which he mainly sold by the ell, but he also had in stock twenty-eight caps with lappets and twenty-four samples of different qualities of lace—presumably cards from which customers could choose patterns and make orders, a similar filing system to Demoiselle Villion's. In her case the numbers were attached to different lace (designs) from Flanders, Lille, and Valenciennes, as well as Angleterre and mignonette.[44] Villion's merchandise was valued at 8,540 livres, Paul Rocherol's at 17,847 livres in 1783, and Seguin's at 4,848 livres just three years later.[45] A much lower value of 1,220 livres was assigned to that of Femme Bariot, a *crieuse de blondes* (female hawker of blondes) who had plied her trade on the streets of Lyon.[46] The description of her lace was much more in keeping with the narrow laces collected from Perpignan on behalf of the secretary of state for the navy in 1737 (FIG. 10.17) or the wares of the lace seller in Gabriel

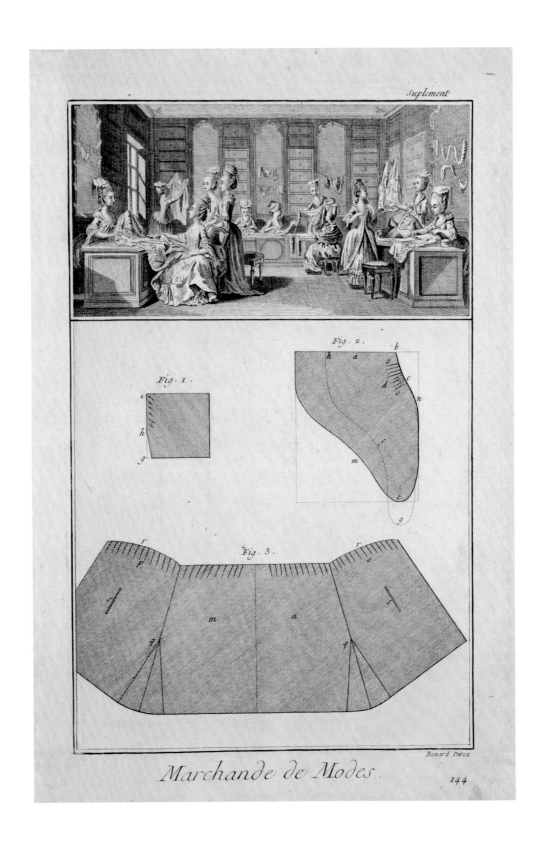

Gresly's painting of 1751 (FIG. 10.18), although she was dealing in silk, not thread, lace.[47] Some lengths had zigzag patterns, some a little chenille for texture (a simpler version of the effects visible in the earlier sleeve ruffle in FIG. 10.19). Certain lengths were kept in little packets, and the whole bundle was easy to wrap and transport after her death in a piece of printed cotton, tied with string, the knots sealed with red Spanish wax stamped with the king's coat of arms.[48]

This Lyonnaise crieuse had walked the streets wearing printed cotton and coarse linen in marked contrast to the garb of François Boucher's charming silk-clad milliner who presents her wares to a lady in her Parisian bedchamber (FIG. 10.20). The latter recalls the seductive descriptions that permeated the literature of the period, in which such working girls or *grisettes* acted as shopkeepers' emissaries, taking their wares to clients' homes or lodgings. In *A Sentimental Journey* (1768), Laurence Sterne's hero assumed "a stranger in Paris should have the opportunities presented to him of buying lace and silk stockings and ruffles, *et tout cela*—and 'tis nothing if a woman comes [to his lodgings] with a band box." Obligingly, his *maître d'hôtel* found just such a "Grisset," who "open'd her little magazine, laid all her laces one after another before me—unfolded and folded them up again one by one with the most patient sweetness . . . the poor creature seem'd anxious to get a penny; and laid herself out to win me, and not so much in a manner which seem'd artful, as in one I felt simple and caressing . . . my heart relented . . . and I laid three [louis] out on a pair of ruffles."[49]

Rules and Respectability

Sterne signals the importance not only of domestic but also of foreign consumers to French merchants and shopkeepers, whether in lace or other fashionable commodities. Visitors could take advantage of shops and services when in France, whether they were there in an official or business capacity or as tourists intent on

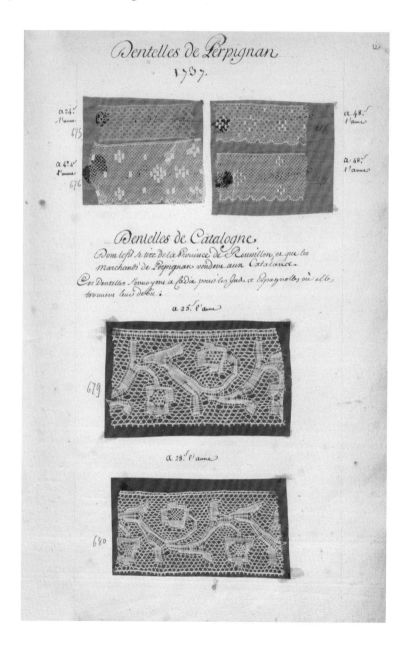

FIG. 10.17

Lace from Perpignan and Catalonia, from *Échantillons d'étoffes et de toiles des manufactures de France, receuillis par le Maréchal de Richelieu*, 1737, vol. 2, samples 675–81. Album in folio. Bibliothèque nationale de France, département Estampes et photographie, RESERVE LH-45 (A)-BOITE FOL.

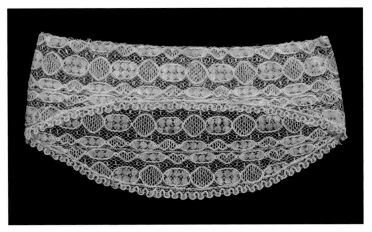

sampling French sights and experiences. They were not, however, simply responding to the beauty and accessibility of the textiles or the blandishments of salesmen and saleswomen, but also to the requirements of the society in which they were residing. Louis XIV (r. 1643–1715) had established an economic policy that encouraged the consumption of French luxury goods and set rules about the splendid clothing that permitted access to the court at Versailles.[50] By the time of his death in 1715, much court ritual seemed antiquated, but it, nonetheless, lingered on until the Revolution. Concurrently, Paris, with its cosmopolitan mix of nobles, wealthy financiers and merchants, ambassadors, and

FIG. 10.21
Nicolas de Largillière, *Konrad Detlef, Count von Dehn*, 1724. Oil on canvas. Herzog Anton Ulrich Museum, Braunschweig, Germany, GG 521.

FIG. 10.22
Bobbin-lace cravat end, Brussels,
Southern Netherlands, 1720s. Linen.
© Victoria and Albert Museum,
London, 154-1893.

Lace *à la Mode* in France, ca. 1690–1790

grand tourists, adopted a more informal lifestyle that championed fashion. Seasonal change was de rigueur in luxury textiles—woven, embroidered, and painted silks, printed and painted cottons and linens, and, of course, lace, which continued to act as a mark of distinction.[51]

In this privileged environment, the king's painters mastered the depiction of their patrons' and peers' lace. Consider the attire of the ambassador Konrad Detlef (1688–1753), Count von Dehn (FIG. 10.21). Sent to Paris in 1723 by the Duke of Braunschweig-Wolfenbüttel to congratulate Louis XV on his ascension to the throne, he was subsequently painted in full court dress by Nicolas de Largillière (1656–1746): his brocaded silk coat boasts a lacelike pattern, similar to the fashionable lace of which his cravat and ruffles were made. Soft and densely patterned in the fashionable style of the 1720s, their needle lace echoes that of bobbin lace (see the cravat end in FIG. 10.22). Forty years later, Isabella Fitzroy (1726–1782), Countess of Hertford, wife of the British ambassador, was presented at court in the French *grand habit* (FIG. 10.23), having followed the

duchesse de Nivernois's sartorial advice. Alexandre Roslin (1718–1793) celebrated the layering of luxury in color, sheen, and texture: around the sitter's neck, a sparkling diamond parure complements her palatine's delicate white lace, with its intertwined tufts of colored silks; the polychrome silk and gold of the gown appear unveiled and also veiled by a black gauze *mantelet* (cape) with a small geometric pattern and ruched border; triple white sleeve ruffles and black lace lappets complete the lace requirements for court dress.[52] Just over twenty years later, such lappets were the concern of Abigail Adams (1744–1818), wife of the first United States minister plenipotentiary to Great Britain—to wear at the court in London. She asked Thomas Jefferson (1743–1826), her husband's counterpart in Paris, to send her the necessary "twelve ells of black lace at six or seven livres per ell," even suggesting that "some gentleman coming this way will be so kind as to put them in his pocket."[53] Such lace was available from London mercers' shops, so Abigail's intentions may have been both patriotic and economic: she knew French

FIG. 10.23
Alexander Roslin, *Isabella, Countess of Hertford*, 1765. Oil on canvas. © The Hunterian, University of Glasgow, GLAHA 43803.

products and prices from her time in France and avoided buying British while taking advantage of "the diplomatic bag" to bypass both import duty and transportation costs.[54]

The very painters who captured lace so magnificently on canvas dressed appropriately in their studios, at court, or in Parisian salons. Their wardrobes contained ample supplies of plain linen and a modicum of lace. Hyacinthe Rigaud (1659–1743), famed for his virtuoso representation of Louis XIV, usually chose plain linen and certainly no more than a touch of lace for his self-portraits.[55] When he died, however, his wardrobe contained twenty shirts, of which eight were trimmed with "different old lace," while "different lace with bars and mesh" adorned twelve very old cravats and four pairs of ruffles.[56] Thirty years later, the much younger Louis Michel Van Loo (1707–1771) was better endowed with sixty-three shirts, but a smaller proportion, though not dissimilar number (six), were of "Holland [the finest linen] trimmed with different ruffles of Angleterre, needlelace and others," and a seventh was described as "Holland with a lace trimming and cravat for the ceremonies of the Order of St Michael." All lace-embellished items were valued together at an eye-watering 800 livres.[57] Van Loo did not present himself in the fossilized ceremonial garb of his order in the 1762 and 1763 portraits of himself. Instead he boldly draped his splendid shot silk nightgown over its matching waistcoat and breeches, offering a tantalizing glimpse of fashionable lace at wrist and chest, his shirt left nonchalantly open at the neck (FIG. 10.24).[58] He thus eloquently combined grandeur with informality.

These court artists mixed with members of the social and intellectual elite, such as the veterinary surgeon, encyclopedist, author, and noble Claude Bourgelat (1712–1779). Active in Lyon till 1765 and then resident in Paris till his death in 1779, Bourgelat had a plentiful supply of linen and surely "needed" more lace than the artists. Accordingly, at the time of his death, he owned twenty-five pairs of lace ruffles, including one pair of Angleterre and fifteen of Valenciennes. He had double that number in other sets of linen ruffles, which were valued at 400 livres, some 200 livres less than the lace ones.[59] He was certainly equipped for gatherings where, according to Louis-Sébastien Mercier (1740–1814), an astute and acerbic commentator on the mores of the French capital, "one seems to be affrontingly naked, if one does not wear velvet, lace and metal trimmings." Indeed, lace was a prerequisite for entry to some townhouses:

> Do you know the story of that gentleman who only having one lace ruffle, showed it to the servant at the door of a townhouse as a certain passport to entry, hiding carefully under the skirt of his waistcoat the other ruffle which was, alas, made of muslin? . . . In the heat of conversation . . . he was foolish enough to reveal the scandalous ruffle. . . . This revelation offended the mistress of the house so much that she summoned her doorkeeper immediately to reprimand him. He did not understand because in the meantime the man had hidden again his humble muslin and was gesticulating with the hand with the lace ruffle.[60]

This vignette captures lace in action, the expressive gestures suited to its fluid movement as the hand rose and fell with more or less grace, a characteristic that Mercier again referenced in his amused observation of dentists in the faubourg Saint-Honoré at a time when their trade's reputation and fortunes were rising.[61] Having adopted the sales

methods and fashionable attire favored by the neighborhood's wealthy shopkeepers, such men performed extractions deftly: "The dentist makes you sit down, lifts his lace ruffle, pulls your tooth with a well-dressed hand, and then offers you a gargle."[62] The humor undoubtedly rests in the contrast between aspirational clothing and the actual manual realities of the job. Whether dealing with old, dirty, or damaged lace, the services of the specialist *blanchisseuses de dentelles* (lace washerwomen) and *raccommodeuses de*

FIG. 10.24

Louis Michel Van Loo, *Self-Portrait Painting His Father*, 1762. Oil on canvas. Musée national des châteaux de Versailles et de Trianon, MV5827.

dentelles (lace menders) were surely in much demand. These women plied their trade independently in big cities, after about two years of training.[63] Similar "professional" skills in washing or bleaching and mending were cited by servants in search of employment. One prospective maid or governess in Lyon specified that she could "dress hair, wash, sew, mend lace, and [do] other useful things."[64]

This offer of services to a good home in the provinces suggests that there were sufficient lace wearers outside Paris to merit foregrounding these skills. Large cities enriched by trade, such as Bordeaux, Lyon, and Marseilles, certainly had wealthy inhabitants who had both the opportunity to display lace and the wealth to buy it. These consumers included the intendants, governors, and inspectors sent from Paris, as well as members of the local nobility, bourgeoisie, and mercantile classes, many of whom frequented the capital. Such goods had even reached the remote mountainous areas by the end of the seventeenth century.

The impoverished noble Jean-Marie Roland de la Platière (1734–1793) and his wife, Marie-Jeanne Philipon (1754–1793), the daughter of a Parisian printer, pondered their clothing needs when he was appointed inspector of manufactures in Amiens in 1779. Having lived frugally in the Beaujolais for some years, their main concern was to fit in with people of the same rank in their new city. Madame Roland, brought up to do her own sewing, believed she could survive without buying any linen for two years, by replenishing her wardrobe with three gowns, and with relatively little outlay on lace: "As for the sleeves, fichus and caps, which it's normal to have made of lace, that will mean another 12 to 14 *louis* [288–336 livres], keeping to what is respectable without trying to be elegant, but without overdoing an affected simplicity. I have some of my mother's lace, which I should like to use, but since there are no complete sets and the design is old fashioned, it may be difficult to adapt, or to avoid looking rather thrown together."[65]

Balancing economy, fashion, and respectability surely served them well when they moved to Lyon in the early 1780s, as that city was not renowned for ostentatious display despite its dominant trade in fashionable silks.[66] There, in academic circles, Roland met the municipal elite, including, no doubt, the elderly royal academician Donat Nonnotte (1708–1785), who had been the city's official painter since 1762. Patronized by aristocratic governors, prelates, magistrates, and wealthy bourgeois, Nonnotte painted his fair share of lace in Lyon.[67] His own and his clients' preferences tended, however, to be more modest than those of his Parisian contemporary Van Loo. The pendants of himself and his wife, Elisabeth Bastard de la Gravière (1699–1774), painted around the time they settled in Lyon, suggest decent and unpretentious domesticity and decorum, the artist's ruffles being similar to his wife's cap but simple in comparison with her ruffles (FIGS. 10.25-27). By the time Nonnotte died thirty years later, he owned no lace.[68]

Conclusion

The marquise de Pompadour's display and consumption of fashionable lace prompted the journey in this essay from workshop to salon, from the court of Louis XIV to the French Revolution. Along the way, women have proved skilled, ill-remunerated makers; shrewd, capable merchants; and conspicuous, thoughtful consumers. Wages and prices

have offered insights into the range of different laces available, from modest mignonette within the means of well-off artisans to virtuoso pieces of Argentan, which were only within the reach of the upper echelons of society. In the latter case, a complete set of lappets, cap, ruffles, and stomacher for court might cost about ten times the amount a well-paid lacemaker earned in a year and was likely the work of more than one maker.[69]

Lace survived the fall of the Bastille in 1789, but the quantity and type in use differed markedly from those of the marquise's heyday. The educator and novelist Stéphanie-Félicité, comtesse de Genlis (1747–1830), epitomized a trend she was to describe in her treatise on luxury and hospitality: for her 1790 portrait she wore deliciously simple luxury (FIG. 10.28), a plain silk gown and ribbons, much fine, plain snowy white linen, complemented by the lightest of lace (similar to that in FIG. 10.29). "It is certain," she claimed a year later, "that the upkeep of women is much more expensive since they dress only in linen and cloth, when before they wore lace and the most beautiful silks from our manufactures."[70] Two years later she and many of her compatriots fled into exile, including the redoubtable Valenciennes lace merchant Claire Tribout, who confirmed the impact of this shift in fashion and the political situation for her business: "The aristocracy have departed; the rich are suffering because of this Revolution and are making economies, they are settling for other types of lace of less value."[71] The Nation seized her goods and sold them on February 25, 1795. This was a temporary setback, as Claire Tribout-Beauvallon et comp., manufacturer from Valenciennes, was again present in Leipzig in 1797 and 1802, selling an assortment of French linen, baptiste, and all sorts of white goods.[72]

FIG. 10.28 (BOTTOM)

Adélaïde Labille-Guiard, *Portrait of Madame de Genlis*, 1790. Oil on canvas laid down on board. Los Angeles County Museum of Art, Purchased with funds provided by the William Randolph Hearst Collection, Arnold S. Kirkeby, and other donors by exchange, 91.2.

FIG. 10.29 (TOP)

Point d'Argentan needle-lace border, Argentan or Alençon, France, 1780–90. Linen. Textilmuseum St. Gallen, 40158. Cat. 95.

I am grateful to Tabitha Baker, Anne-Marie Benson, Moïra Dato, and Susan North, who have kindly responded to queries on a range of subjects from French wages, fans, and account books to English dress terminology. Clare Browne, with her usual friendship, generosity, and expertise, has encouraged my first forays into writing about French lace production and consumption, while Michele Majer and Emma Cormack have meticulously and kindly guided me into their exhibition and the St. Gallen collections on loan. Staff at the Archives départementales du Rhône have been unfailingly courteous and efficient in processing long-distance requests for documents. In English, the pioneering history of European lace is Santina Levey, *Lace: A History* (Leeds, UK: W. S. Maney & Son; London: Victoria and Albert Museum, 1983), to which I owe an enormous debt.

Translations from French are the author's own, unless taken from an English-language publication.

1   On the marquise as patron of the arts, see Xavier Salmon, ed., *Madame de Pompadour et les arts*, exh. cat. (Paris: Réunion des musées nationaux, 2002).

2   The lace accessories were inventoried on July 21, 1764. "Succession de Madame de Pompadour," vol. 2, 1764 (Collections numérisées de la bibliothèque de l'INHA, https://bibliotheque -numerique.inha.fr/collection/item/32485-succession-de-madame -de-pompadour-1764-tome-2?offset=1); transcribed in Jean Cordey, ed., *Inventaire des biens de Madame de Pompadour, rédigé après son décès* (Paris: Francisque Lefrançois pour La société des biblio-philes françois, 1939). This calculation is based on Cordey, 77–82. Total value of wardrobe: 52,536 livres. The amount is approximate because some household furnishings trimmed in or made of lace are listed among the dress items.

A note on currency and measurements: The livre tournois is the basic currency used here: 1 livre was worth 20 sols/sous; 1 louis d'or was worth 24 livres. The *aune* (ell) was the standard measurement and was equivalent to about 45 inches (114 cm).

3   The name may well come from the major market for these goods. Levey, *Lace*, 45.

4   *Blonde*: name applied to a large group of bobbin laces made originally of undyed cream silk from Nanking but also of white and black silk, and copied in linen thread. *Mignonette*: inexpensive light thread lace, with a fancy mesh ground; also known as *blonde de fil*. Ibid., 56, 122.

5   For the head, *barbes* (lappets), *bonnets* (caps), and *coeffes* (head-dresses or hair styles); for the neck, *palatine* (tippet; a long scarflike item in fur or lace); for sleeves, *manchettes* and *engageantes* (sleeve ruffles); for the body, *devant-gorge* (stomacher), *fichu* (kerchief or fichu); for skirt, *falbala* (furbelow). Most are defined in contemporary dictionaries. *Dictionnaires d'autrefois: French Dictionaries of the 17th, 18th, 19th and 20th Centuries* (online database), ARTFL Project, University of Chicago, https://artfl-project.uchicago.edu/content /dictionnaires-dautrefois.

6   Comptes de Madame la comtesse de Dubarry, Département des manuscrits, Français, ms. 8157, Bibliothèque nationale de France (hereafter BnF), Paris, Corpus électroniques, Centre de recherche du château de Versailles, https://chateauversailles-recherche.fr/francais /ressources-documentaires/corpus-electroniques/sources-manuscrites /comptes-de-la-comtesse-du-barry. The same applied to their royal lover. Marie Chiozzotto, "Les apparences vestimentaires de Louis XV: La composition de la garde-robe du souverain pour l'année 1772," *Apparences* 4 (2012): pars. 27, 32, OpenEdition Journals, https://doi .org/10.4000/apparences.1179.

7   *Fontange* has been used in some recent publications to describe this item of headdress and conforms to the definition in

Denis Diderot and Jean le Rond d'Alembert, eds., *Encyclopédie, ou Dictionnaire raisonné des sciences et métiers* (Paris: Briasson, 1751–59) 7:105–6. Strictly speaking, the *fontange* (called after Madame de Fontanges) comprised the ribbons that tied up the hair, while the wire over which the cap was draped was called the *commode*. This term came to be applied to the cap itself. When a cap was draped in lace it was called a *frelange*. Levey, *Lace*, 41n21; and Diana De Marly, *Louis XIV & Versailles* (London: B. T. Batsford, 1987), 92–93.

8   See the clever juxtapositions in Textilmuseum St. Gallen and Iklé-Frischknecht-Stiftung, *Historische Spitzen: Die Leopold-Iklé Sammlung im Textilmuseum St. Gallen*, exh. cat. (Stuttgart, Germany: Arnoldsche, 2018), 231, 238; Joanna Hashagen and Santina M. Levey, *Fine & Fashionable: Lace from the Blackborne Collection*, exh. cat. (Barnard Castle, UK: Bowes Museum, 2006), 43–56. No evidence has been found to date to suggest that lace patterns were changing either seasonally or annually.

9   Arthur Malotet, *La dentelle à Valenciennes* (Paris: Jean Schemit, 1927), chaps. 1–6; and Philippe Guignet, "The Lacemakers of Valenciennes in the Eighteenth Century: An Economic and Social Study of a Group of Female Workers under the Ancien Regime," *Textile History* 10 (1979): 96–113.

10   Though Sedan also specialized in needle lace. Levey provides a thorough discussion of the French and Flemish laces and their tech-niques in *Lace*, 43–57; and Anne Kraatz provides a useful overview in "The Eighteenth Century: Femininity," in *Lace: History and Fashion* (New York: Rizzoli, 1989), 71–104.

11   Olwen Hufton, "Women and the Family Economy in Eighteenth-Century France," *French Historical Studies* 9, no. 1 (Spring 1975): 14–17; Levey, *Lace*, 54; and Olivier Le Gouic, *Lyon et la mer au XVIIIe siècle: Connexions atlantiques et commerce colonial* (Rennes, France: Presses universitaires de Rennes, 2011), esp. chap. 9.

12   Levey, *Lace*, 56, 45, citing *Le Mercure* (1726, 1730) and Philémon Louis Savary, *Supplément au Dictionnaire universel de commerce* (1730). *Affiches, annonces et avis divers de la ville de Lyon* (Lyon, France: Aimé Delaroche, January 9, 1772), 8.

13   Examples from a project in Valenciennes (1720s), cited in Malotet, *La dentelle*, 19; contracts in Argentan (1763) and Alençon (1770) cited in Gérasime Bonnaire Despierres, *Histoire du point d'Alençon, depuis son origine jusqu'à nos jours* (Paris: Librairie Renouard, 1886), 96, 85.

14   Women were excluded from most guilds. Tabitha Baker, "The Embroidery Trade in Eighteenth-Century Paris and Lyon" (PhD thesis, University of Warwick, 2019), 230ff; Clare Haru Crowston, *Fabricating Women: The Seamstresses of Old Régime France, 1675–1791* (Durham, NC: Duke University Press, 2001), 309–12. It took only two years to train as a *lingère*. Diderot, *Encyclopédie*, vol. 9 (1765), 555.

15   Annual amount of 56 to 182 livres is based on a 280-day working year. Despierres, *Histoire du point d'Alençon*, 112; Guignet, "The Lacemakers," 103 (based on records for the period 1748–75); and Hufton, "Women and the Family," 15–16. On general levels of income, see Jean Sgard, "L'échelle des revenus," *Dix-huitième siècle* 14 (1982): 425–33, Persée portal online, https://doi.org/10.3406/dhs.1982.1412; and on disparity between women's skill and wages, Geraldine Sheridan, *Louder Than Words: Ways of Seeing Women Workers in Eighteenth-Century France* (Lubbock: Texas Tech University Press, 2009), 111–12.

16   Malotet, *La dentelle*, 40; and Guignet, "The Lacemakers," 104. With regard to embroiderers, the Parisian *marchand brodeur* St. Aubin indicated a daily rate of 25 sols in 1770, but in the 1780s in Lyon, some were receiving about 5.5 sols. Baker, "The Embroidery Trade," 289–90. I use the term "milliner" as the nearest 18th-century translation for the French term *marchande de modes* (which trans-lates literally as "fashion merchant").

17   Five hundred livres a year. Daniel Roche, *The People of Paris*

(Leamington Spa, UK: Berg, 1987), 87; and Sgard, "L'échelle des revenus," 426.

18 Malotet, *La dentelle*, 21.

19 Ibid., 41, 52.

20 The return of materials and requests for payment are recorded in postmortem inventories. See, for example, Inventaire-après-décès Veuve Baisse/Besse, December 9, 1778, fols. 11–11v, 14v–16, Série BP2270, Archives départementales du Rhône, Lyon (hereafter ADR).

21 Levey, *Lace*, 26, 35–37, 39ff; Hufton, "Women and the Family," 14–17.

22 Lace from Perpignan and Catalonia, "Echantillons d'etoffes et toiles des manufactures de France recueillis par le Maréchal de Richelieu," vol. 2, fols. 664–74, Cabinet des Estampes, Lh45 (A), BnF, and digitized, BnF Catalogue général (online), https://catalogue.bnf .fr/ark:/12148/cb40505272z. The material (linen thread) accounted for 7–9 percent of the cost of the end product in Valenciennes, according to Guignet, "The Lacemakers," 102; and Malotet, *La dentelle*, 52; Levey, *Lace*, 50. Evidence for Lyon comes from inventories of stock taken there between 1760 and 1786, with the caveat that these values may merely have encompassed materials and labor and excluded the merchant's anticipated profit: Inventaire-après-décès Thérèse Villion, *marchande de dentelles*, August 30, 1760, Série BP2218, ADR; Inventaire-après-décès Veuve Antoine Baisse/Besse, *maître et marchand de dentelles*, November 30, 1778, Série BP2270, ADR; Inventaire-après-décès Pierre Rocherol, *marchand détaillant en blondes*, August 3, 1783, Série BP2282, ADR; Inventaire-après-décès Pierre Seguin, *marchand de blondes*, March 20, 1786, Série BP2293, ADR.

23 Guignet, "The Lacemakers," 105.

24 Despierres, *Histoire du point d'Alençon*, 134, 138. Malotet, *La dentelle*, 23, 42.

25 Ibid., 35; and Guignet, "The Lacemakers," 105.

26 Ibid., 99. Admittedly, it was his wife's nephew, a local thread manufacturer, who made this claim in 1761. Tribout's wife, Anne-Cécile Dannezan (1724–1776), was the daughter of another *marchand de dentelles*.

27 Inventaire-après-décès Veuve Baisse, December 9, 1778.

28 Diderot, *Encyclopédie*, vol. 2 (1752), 287.

29 On schools, see Reed Benhamou, *Public and Private Art Education in France, 1648–1793* (Oxford: Voltaire Foundation, 1993); and Agnès Lahalle, *Les écoles de dessin au XVIIIe siècle: Entre arts libéraux et arts mécaniques* (Rennes, France: Presses universitaires de Rennes, 2006).

30 In the case of silk design, see Nicolas Joubert de l'Hiberderie, *Le dessinateur pour les étoffes d'or, d'argent et de soie* (Paris: Jorry, 1765).

31 Malotet, *La dentelle*, 48–49.

32 Ibid., 50.

33 Despierres, *Histoire du point d'Alençon*, 64; and Levey, *Lace*, 37.

34 Malotet, *La dentelle*, 24–25. Private clients included the daughter of Louis XV, his mistress Madame du Barry, successor of the marquise de Pompadour, and the prince de Conti, as well as many dukes and duchesses, earls and countesses, and marquises and marchionesses. Additionally, 45.6 percent of their correspondence was with Paris and 19.45 with the Austrian Low Countries, especially Brussels. They also had contacts in Koblenz, Genoa, Naples, Rome, and Vienna and attended major fairs such as that in Leipzig. Guignet, "The Lacemakers," 100. Diderot, *Encylopdie*, vol. 10 (1765), 369. Carolyn Sargentson, *Merchants and Luxury Markets: The Marchands Merciers of Eighteenth-Century Paris* (London: Victoria and Albert Museum; Los Angeles: J. Paul Getty Museum, 1996), chap. 1, 7–16; Laurence Croq, "Les chemins de la mercerie, le renouvellement de la marchandise parisienne (années 1660–1760)," in *Mobilité et transmission dans les sociétés de l'Europe moderne*, online ed. (Rennes, France: Presses universitaires de Rennes, 2009), 87–122, https://doi .org/10.4000/books.pur.98810.

35 Corinne Thépaut-Cabasset, ed., *L'esprit des modes au Grand Siècle* (Paris: CTHS, 2010), 86–93.

36 Liger, *Le voyageur fidèle* (1715), quoted in Sargentson, *Merchants and Luxury Markets*, 2.

37 Despierres, *Histoire du point d'Alençon*, 140–42.

38 On the contents of the *corbeilles* of Madame La Tour du Pin and Marie-Antoinette, see Kimberly Chrisman-Campbell, *Fashion Victims: Dress at the Court of Louis XVI and Marie-Antoinette* (New Haven, CT: Yale University Press, 2015), 89.

39 Jennifer M. Jones, *Sexing la Mode: Gender, Fashion and Commercial Culture in Old Regime France* (New York: Berg, 2004), in particular chap. 6, "Selling Fashion," 179–210; and Laurence Fontaine, *History of Pedlars in Europe* (Cambridge: Polity Press, 1996). For an example of an auction, see *Affiches* (Lyon, June 3, 1764), 94.

40 In this context, *linge* (linens) applied to most lightweight vegetable fibers. *Annonces, affiches et avis divers* (Paris: Imprimerie Jacques Guérin, February 24, 1752), 125.

41 *Affiches* (Lyon, France, October 10, 1762), 168–69; and *Affiches* (September 25, 1771), 182.

42 Veuves Gallet, Rocherolles/Rocherol (d. 1807), and Seguin, *Indicateur alphabétique de Lyon* (Lyon, France: Aimé Delaroche, 1788).

43 Inventaire-après-décès Seguin, March 20, 1786, fols. 3–4.

44 Inventaire-après-décès Villion, August 30, 1760, fols. 3–7.

45 Ibid.; Inventaire-après-décès Rocherol, March 20, 1786; Inventaire-après-décès Seguin, July 3, 1783. Villion also stocked 2,671 livres worth of linens. No actual description of Rocherol's merchandise is given, just an "Inventaire des marchandises et blondes et dentelles" of seventeen unnumbered pages comprising lists of figures signed off by the lace-merchant experts Tavernier and Yssartel.

46 Inventaire-après-décès Femme Bariot, October 2, 1783, Série BP2283, ADR.

47 A recently discovered document in the archives of the Cabinet des Estampes at the Bibliothèque nationale de France reveals that the Maréchal de Richelieu acquired this collection of eight volumes of textile samples dating from 1715 to 1737 from the collection of Jean-Philippe Phélypeaux, comte de Maurepas (1701–1781), who, in his role as secretary of state for the navy, was particularly interested in showing the excellence of French manufacturing and the country's ability to compete with England. Corinne Le Bitouzé, curator of prints and drawings, online presentation, Facebook, July 15, 2020, https:// www.facebook.com/watch/live/?v=2671685139824998&ref=watch _permalink.

48 Inventaire-après-décès femme Bario, *crieuse de blondes*, October 2, 1783, fol. 2v, Série BP2283, ADR. Her basic household goods and clothing were worth less than her merchandise at a mere 835 livres. The bailiffs moved the goods in this way.

49 Laurence Sterne, *A Sentimental Journey* (1768; London: Penguin Classics, 2005), 93. The value of 3 louis was 72 livres. On the broader subject, see Jones, *Sexing la Mode*, in particular chap. 5, "Coquettes and Grisettes," 145–78.

50 Philip Mansell, *Dressed to Rule: Royal and Court Costume from Louis XIV to Elizabeth II* (New Haven, CT: Yale University Press, 2005), 1–17; Joan DeJean, *The Essence of Style: How the French Invented High Fashion, Fine Food, Chic Cafés, Style, Sophistication and Glamour* (New York: Free Press, 2006); Pierre Arizzoli-Clémentel and Pascal Gorguet Ballesteros, eds., *Fastes de cour et cérémonies royales: Le costume de cour en Europe 1650–1800*, exh. cat. (Paris: Éditions de la Réunion des musées nationaux, 2009); and Daniëlle Kisluk-Grosheide and Bertrand Rondot, eds., *Visiteurs de Versailles: Voyageurs, princes, ambassadeurs 1682–1789*, exh. cat. (Paris: Gallimard, 2017).

51 Joan DeJean, *The Age of Comfort: When Paris Discovered Casual*

and the Modern Home Began (New York: Bloomsbury, 2010); and Joan DeJean, How Paris Became Paris: The Invention of the Modern City (New York: Bloomsbury, 2015).

52 For many examples of Roslin's mastery of lace, see Magnus Olausson and Xavier Salmon, Alexandre Roslin: Un portraitiste pour l'Europe (Paris: Éditions de la Réunion des musées nationaux, 2008).

53 Abigail Adams to Thomas Jefferson, February 11, 1786, Grosvenor Square, London, Gilder Lehrman Institute of American History, New York. A later response from Jefferson suggested that this first request had not gone well, as in February 1787 he wrote of a different batch of lace, "Mr. Cairnes has taken charge of 15. aunes [ells] of black lace for you at 9 livres the aune, purchased by Petit [Jefferson's manservant] and therefore I hope better purchased than some things have been for you." Thomas Jefferson to Abigail Adams, February 22, 1787, Paris, in The Papers of Thomas Jefferson, Volume 11: 1 January to 6 August 1787, online ed. (Princeton, NJ: Princeton University Press, 1955), 174–75, https://jeffersonpapers.princeton.edu/selected-documents/abigail-adams.

54 She had done so previously in her capacity as a merchant importing European textiles between 1778 and 1783, when her husband was in Europe. She continued to wear fashionable lace into the 1790s, likely imported from France, as American lacemaking was still in its infancy. Woody Holton, Abigail Adams (New York: Free Press, 2010), chaps. 12–16. On US lace, see Marta Cotterell Raffel, The Laces of Ipswich: The Art and Economics of an Early American Industry, 1750–1840 (Hanover, NH: University Press of New England, 2003).

55 For example, Hyacinthe Rigaud, Louis XIV of France, 1701. Oil on canvas, 109⅛ × 76⅜ in. (277 × 194 cm). Paris, Musée du Louvre, INV 7492; Hyacinthe Rigaud, Self-Portrait, 1698. Oil on canvas, 32¾ × 26⅜ in. (83 × 67 cm). Musée Hyacinthe Rigaud, D53.1.1; and Hyacinthe Rigaud, Self-Portrait, 1700–10. Oil on canvas, 25⅞ × 21⅛ in. (65.5 × 53.5 cm). Museu Nacional d'Art de Catalunya, 024233-000.

56 "6 mars 1744 Inventaire-après-décès Hyacinthe Rigaud, transcription," transcribed by Ariane James-Sarazin, 2nd ed. (Paris, 2003), Mediterranées, managed by Agnès and Robert Viñas, https://mediterranees.net/art_roussillon/rigaud/inventaire.html.

57 Christine Rolland, ed., Autour des Van Loo: Peinture, commerce des tissus et espionnage en Europe (1250–1830) (Mont-Saint-Aignan: Publications des universités de Rouen et du Havre, 2012), 56–57, transcription from Inventaire-après-décès, April 22, 1771, Minutier central LVI: 166 (Picquais), Archives nationales de France.

58 See, too, Louis Michel Van Loo, with his sister Marie-Anne, working on the portrait of his father Jean-Baptiste Van Loo, 1763. Oil on canvas, 90⅝ × 63¾ in. (230 × 162 cm). Musée national des châteaux de Versailles et de Trianon, Versailles, MV6774, Gift of Madame Wallerstein.

59 His other linen was valued at 680 livres; his redingote and his robes de chambre at 48; his suits at 800; and his three wigs and two pairs of shoes together at 3 livres. He also owned valuable jewelry in the form of snuff boxes, watch, cane, buckles, buttons, and rings. Hugues Plaideux, "L'inventaire après décès de Claude Bourgelat," Bulletin de la Société français de l'histoire de la médecine et des sciences vétérinaires 10 (2010): 136, 138.

60 Louis-Sébastien Mercier, Le tableau de Paris, vol. 1 (Hamburg, Germany: Virchaux et Compagnie; Neuchâtel, Switzerland: Samuel Fauche, 1781), 269–71.

61 Colin Jones, "The Making of a Revolution," in The Smile Revolution in Eighteenth-Century Paris (Oxford: Oxford University Press, 2014), 98–127.

62 Louis-Sébastien Mercier, Le tableau de Paris, vol. 8 (Amsterdam, 1783), 75.

63 Contracts with Veuve Auclerc, July 4, 1754, and July 12, 1755, Série 8B4028, Fonds Auclerc, ADR.

64 Affiches (Lyon, France, July 7, 1771), 136.

65 Siân Reynolds, Marriage and Revolution: Monsieur & Madame Roland (Oxford: Oxford University Press, 2012), 97–98, quoting a letter of May 23, 1779. I have adjusted this translation slightly by substituting the word "cap" for "bonnet," as it seems a more appropriate translation of the French bonnet in this particular context.

66 Françoise Bayard, Vivre à Lyon sous l'Ancien Régime (Paris: Perrin, 1997), 260.

67 Lesley Ellis Miller, "Dressing Down in Eighteenth-Century Lyon: The Clothing of Silk Designers from Their Inventaires-après-décès," Costume 29, no. 1 (1995): 25–39; Lesley Ellis Miller, "A Portrait of the 'Raphael of Silk Design,'" V&A Online Journal, no. 4 (Summer 2012): http://www.vam.ac.uk/content/journals/research-journal/issue-no.-4-summer-2012/a-portrait-of-the-raphael-of-silk-design/.

68 Inventaire-après-décès Donat Nonnotte, March 17, 1785, fols. 13–14v, Série BP2289, ADR.

69 1,500 livres. Comptes de Madame la comtesse de Dubarry, loc. 223–28, ms. 8157, BnF.

70 Madame de Brulart [pseud.], Discours sur le luxe et l'hospitalité: Considérés sous leurs rapports avec les mœurs et l'éducation nationale (Paris: Onfroy, 1791), 6. An interesting and indirect observation on the demands of keeping plain fabrics clean.

71 Quoted in Guignet, "The Lacemakers," 99.

72 Allgemeine merkantilische Erdbeschreibung auch Handlungs- und Fabriken Addressbuch (Liepzig, Germany: August Schumann, 1802), 228. On the significance of Leipzig, see Gérard Gayot, "La main invisible qui guidait les marchands aux foires de Leipzig: Enquête sur un haut lieu de la réalisation des bénéfices, 1750–1830," Revue d'histoire moderne & contemporaine 48, no. 2 (2001): 72–103.

MECHANIZATION AND REVIVALISM IN THE LACE INDUSTRIES, 1800–1925

11 Fashion and the Lace Industries in France, Belgium, and England, 1800–1900

Emma Cormack and Michele Majer

THE STORY OF THE NINETEENTH-CENTURY LACE INDUSTRIES in France, Belgium, and England is one of a slow revival that marked the first three decades, a midcentury boom, a gradual, erratic decline from the 1870s, and a resurgence at the turn of the twentieth century before the final collapse brought on by World War I.[1] Throughout the period, the vicissitudes of these industries depended on the rapidly changing female silhouette, manufacturers' abilities to adapt their goods in response to these shifts, and political events including the fall of the First Empire in 1815 and that of the Second Empire in 1870 in France.[2] Both hand- and machine-made laces vied for a burgeoning market, a reflection of the expanding middle classes eager to adopt the finery of their social superiors that had long been associated with great wealth and status (SEE CHAP. 1). While elite consumers continued to purchase "real" (handmade) lace, those less affluent had access to well-made, well-designed, and less expensive copies. Due to the ongoing competition from machine lace and the resulting blurring of social hierarchies, the handmade lace industry began to create pieces that were technically, if not stylistically, challenging to replicate. In addition to a fast-growing fashion press that charted the latest modes in dress and accessories, world's fairs, their accompanying reports, and department stores devoted significant space and coverage to lace of all types, particularly in the second half of the century. Through such documentation and consumption, the diligent lacemaker became a cultural icon. By about 1900, however, despite efforts to sustain the handmade lace industry, machine lace took over, becoming the primary method of twentieth-century production.[3]

Fashion and Lace, 1800–1900

At the start of the nineteenth century, lace—an essential component of a stylish toilette throughout the previous century—was almost nowhere in sight. The French Revolution (1789–99) had dealt a destructive blow to that country's industry and impacted the European manufacture and consumption of lace more broadly (SEE CHAP. 10). The columnar white cotton chemise gown inspired by classical antiquity that dominated women's wardrobes until well into the 1810s was often unadorned, and its pared-down appearance eschewed all but the plainest lace in the form of narrow edgings around the low neckline and on the short sleeves (FIG. 11.1).[4] In addition to these understated trimmings, minimally patterned net-based lace that had gained popularity in the late eighteenth century was also used for bonnet veils, fichus, and mantelets (FIG. 11.2). In the first two decades of the century, the preferred laces chosen by elegant women to complement the simplicity

FIG. 11.1 (BELOW)
Jean Auguste Dominique Ingres, *Madame Rivière*, ca. 1805. Oil on canvas. Musée du Louvre, Paris, MI 1446.

FIG. 11.2 (OPPOSITE, TOP)
"Cheveux à la Titus, petit Fichu quadrillé, Mantelet de Gaze, garni en dentelle, Dessiné sur le Boulevart de la Magdeleine," from *Journal des Dames et des Modes, Costumes Parisiens*, May 25, 1798, An 6 (21). Hand-colored engraving on paper, published by Sellèque, Pierre de la Mésangère. Rijksmuseum, Amsterdam, Purchased with the support of the F.G. Waller-Fonds, 2009, RP-P-2009-2259.

FIG. 11.3 (OPPOSITE, BOTTOM)
Jacques-Louis David, *Coronation of Emperor Napoleon and Josephine at Notre-Dame, December 2, 1804*, ca. 1806–7. Oil on canvas. Musée du Louvre, Paris, 3699.

An 6. Costume Parisien. (21)

Cheveux à la Titus, poté Fichu quadrille. Mantelet
de Gaze, garni en Dentelle.
Dessiné par le Boulevart de la Magdeleine.

of their chemise gowns were Brussels as well as both natural-colored and black silk blonde.[5] Although machine-made silk net was an invention of the eighteenth century, it was John Heathcoat's bobbinet machine, patented in 1808 and again in 1809, that created a fabric that most closely resembled handmade bobbin mesh and led the way to further improvements in lacemaking machines.[6] Across the Channel in France, machine net, or tulle, was produced in large quantities in the cities of Lyon and Nîmes.[7] In order to better imitate delicately patterned handmade laces, early European-made machine nets were often embroidered with floral-and-foliate sprigs and other motifs by women and children.[8]

In France, especially, women's daywear was in marked contrast to the lavishness of court attire, formalized by Napoleon at the time of his coronation as emperor in December 1804 (FIG. 11.3). The artist Jean-Baptiste Isabey designed the heavily embroidered silk velvet and satin ensembles for the imperial couple as well as the gowns, trains, and highly regulated uniforms worn by Napoleon's immediate family and members of his household. Lace featured prominently in these spectacular costumes, particularly the sixteenth-century-inspired standing collars, or *chérusques*, that accessorized women's dresses.[9] However, despite Napoleon's insistence that French lace should be adopted at court and his active support of the Alençon needle-lace industry, wealthy men and women, including those in his circle, favored Brussels bobbin lace, and the emperor's efforts were not sufficient to fully revive the domestic industry before his fall from power in 1815.[10]

By 1820 fashion had moved away from the slender Grecian shape of the turn of the century and reflected instead the more recent historicizing influence of the sixteenth and seventeenth centuries. Exuberant Romantic modes were at their most extreme from the mid-1820s to the mid-1830s. Wide, off-the-shoulder necklines, sleeves that ballooned to outsize proportions, and full, ankle-revealing skirts held out

by multiple petticoats provided greater opportunity for the display of lace. Deep berthas and flounces floated over bodices and around the hems of evening gowns, respectively, while lace accessories including caps, collars, shawls, pelerines, and bonnet veils completed the daytime toilettes (FIG. 11.4). Entire lace dresses, worn over matching or contrasting silk underdresses, were also in vogue, including for wedding gowns (FIG. 11.5). While the delicately sprigged lace of the two previous decades remained popular into the early 1820s, larger patterns better suited to the expansive silhouette gained favor. Stylized floral sprays with scrolling

 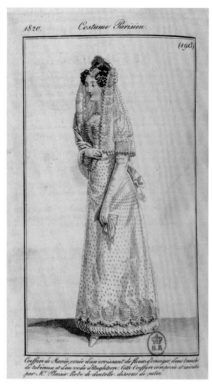

foliage decorated the scalloped edges of bobbin lace, especially natural-colored silk blonde, which was the most fashionable (FIG. 11.6).[11] Although the trend toward more complex patterns primarily benefited handmade lace, application laces including those manufactured in Brussels and Honiton, England, in which separate, handmade motifs were applied to a machine-net ground, approximated the look of higher-end goods and "reduce[d] even further the gap between the cost of real and hand-embroidered lace."[12] This development accelerated in the second half of the century.

The 1840s fashionable silhouette in conjunction with stylistic and technical innovations in hand- and machine-made laces secured the increasing prosperity of both industries. The overblown hourglass shape of the 1830s contracted, especially in the upper body, limiting the use of lace for daywear to small collars and cuffs at the high neckline and at the end of long, tight-fitting sleeves (FIG. 11.7). However, lace accessories from small caps to large shawls were extensively reported on and illustrated in fashion periodicals, affirming their importance for the well-turned-out woman and reflecting the elaborately codified dress etiquette that governed female attire. Fashion plates and portraits of elite sitters in evening dress convey the continued vogue for lace berthas and tiered flounces as well as the shift away from natural-colored blonde to black, a trend that would persist through the 1860s (FIGS. 11.8 AND 11.9). Voluminous bell-shaped skirts advantageously displayed the rich texture and large floral patterns of black lace, especially when worn over solid-colored silks and satins. The town of Chantilly gave its

FIG. 11.4 (ABOVE, LEFT)
Journal des Dames et des Modes, Costumes Parisiens, March 20, 1829. Engraving on paper. Bibliothèque Nationale de France. RES 8-LC14-4.

FIG. 11.5 (ABOVE, RIGHT)
Journal des Dames et des Modes, Costumes Parisiens, July 15, 1820. Engraving on paper. Bibliothèque Nationale de France. RES 8-LC14-4.

FIG. 11.6 (OPPOSITE, TOP)
Handmade blonde bobbin-lace border, probably Neuchâtel, France, ca. 1830. Silk. Textilmuseum St. Gallen, 03639. Cat. 125.

FIG. 11.7 (OPPOSITE, BOTTOM)
Fashions for May 1842, plate 003, 1842. Engraving on paper. The Metropolitan Museum of Art, New York, Gift of Woodman Thompson, b17509853.

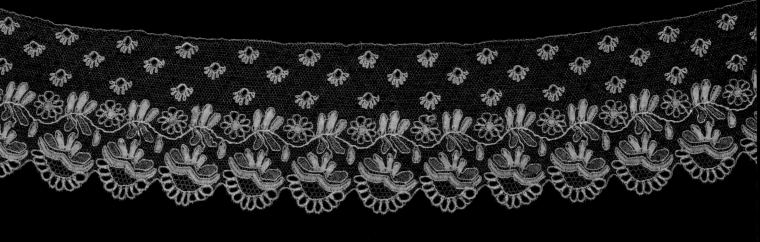

name to the black bobbin lace made "with a non-shiny silk thread called *grenadine*" that was enormously popular in the mid-nineteenth century.[13]

The cachet associated with "real" lace as a signifier of status, which was already acknowledged at the beginning of the century, became more pronounced by the 1840s, when advances in machine technology enabled close copying of lace made by hand. In July 1847, reporting on the "fine ground and rich pattern" of black lace shawls that were "coming very much into request," the London *Ladies Cabinet* declared, "if real they are

very expensive, but in truth our imitation lace is now carried to such a degree of perfection that it is only a connoisseur of lace, that can distinguish the imitation from the real."[14] The richest consumers—royalty and members of the aristocracy—vaunted their purchasing power by wearing expensive handmade laces including *point d'Alençon*, known as "la reine des aiguilles" (the queen of the needles), Valenciennes, Brussels, and Honiton.[15] For her wedding to Prince Albert of Saxe-Coburg (1819–1861) on February 10, 1840, Queen Victoria (r. 1837–1901) wore a gown of white silk satin trimmed with a deep bertha, sleeve frills, and flounce of specially commissioned Honiton bobbin lace with an eighteenth-century-inspired design that marked an important example of royal patronage (FIG. 11.10).[16] At the same time, lace of the seventeenth and eighteenth centuries whose patterns were adapted by contemporary designers reappeared as trimmings on gowns, communicating both wealth and lineage as well as anticipating a growing interest in the wearing and collecting of this historical material.[17]

Fashions in the 1850s and 1860s were dominated by the impressive dimensions of the crinoline skirt and designers' ability to produce large-scale, sophisticated patterns that could be translated well into the delicate medium of lace. These spreading skirts provided the perfect foil not only for lace flounces that often appeared on evening gowns, but also for the oversized triangular shawls that became de rigueur for elegant women (FIGS. 11.11 AND 11.12). Lace designs of these

decades are notable for their luxuriance that incorporates strapwork and undulating ribbon motifs and the naturalism of the ubiquitous florals and foliage; in handmade lace, these were produced by shaded effects that feature subtle differences in the density of the stitches and by layered three-dimensional elements.

Among the most desirable laces were Chantilly, Brussels application, and point d'Alençon. The finest demonstrate the virtuosity of midcentury lacemaking, and they were often featured at the world's fairs held in London and Paris between 1851 and 1867.[18] Judging by the many surviving examples, including those made by machine, as well as its frequent appearance in fashion periodicals, Chantilly was the clear favorite, followed by Brussels application, while only the wealthiest clients could afford the prestigious and costly point d'Alençon (FIGS. 11.13 AND 11.14).[19] The trendsetting Empress Eugénie (1826–1920), whose every fashion move was closely followed in France as well as in Britain and the United States, was a patron of the French lace industry. In April 1854, she commissioned designs for two sets of handmade dress trimmings, one in Chantilly and

FIG. 11.8 (ABOVE, LEFT)
Franz Xaver Winterhalter, *Marie-Caroline-Auguste de Bourbon-Salerne, duchesse d'Aumale*, ca. 1845. Oil on canvas. Musée national des châteaux de Versailles et de Trianon, Versailles, MV5103.

FIG. 11.9 (ABOVE, RIGHT)
Franz Xaver Winterhalter, *Marie-Amélie de Bourbon, Princess of the Two Sicilies, duchess of Orléans, Queen of France, 1830*, 1842. Oil on canvas. Musée national des châteaux de Versailles et de Trianon, Versailles, MV5111.

FIG. 11.10 (OPPOSITE)
Franz Xaver Winterhalter, *Queen Victoria*, ca. 1842. Oil on canvas. Royal Collection Trust/© Her Majesty Queen Elizabeth II 2022, RCIN 401413.

Fashion and the Lace Industries in France, Belgium, and England, 1800–1900

the other in point d'Alençon (FIG. 11.15).[20] In addition to handmade Chantilly, high-end machine imitations were hard to distinguish, even to the cognoscenti, and considerably more affordable.[21]

As had Napoleon's fall from power in 1815, the Franco-Prussian War (1870–71) and the exile of Napoleon III and Eugénie destabilized the closely allied French and Belgian lace industries. Further, over the last thirty years of the century, the increased tempo of changes in fashion and the widespread adoption of tailored wool day suits by women of all classes proved challenging for lace manufacturers. Nevertheless, lace was still in great demand for a variety of accessories and as trimming, especially for opulent evening wear (FIGS. 11.16-19). During the lace revival that occurred between 1885 and 1905, its consumption doubled, before falling off once again prior to World War I.[22] In order to keep up with frequent shifts in the silhouette, lace firms offered a range of conservative

FIG. 11.11 (ABOVE, LEFT)
Woman's dress, probably United States, North and Central America, ca. 1866–68. Silk satin and cotton. Philadelphia Museum of Art; Gift of Mr. and Mrs. W. W. Keen Butcher, 1997, 1997-80-1a–c.

FIG. 11.12 (ABOVE, RIGHT)
Albert Chereau, *Modes de Paris: Petit Courrier des Dames*, plate 26, ca. 1866. Engraving on paper, printed by Gilquin fils. The Metropolitan Museum of Art, New York, Gift of Lee Simonson, b17509853.

FIG. 11.13 (OPPOSITE)
Handmade Chantilly bobbin-lace shawl, France or Belgium, 1860–70. Silk. Textilmuseum St. Gallen, 00486. Cat. 129.

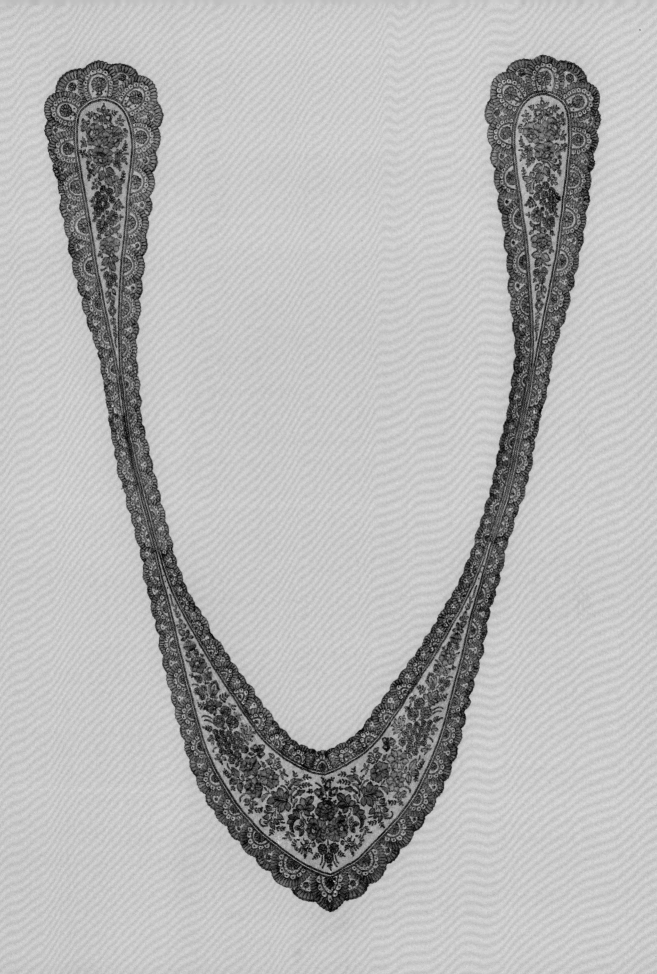

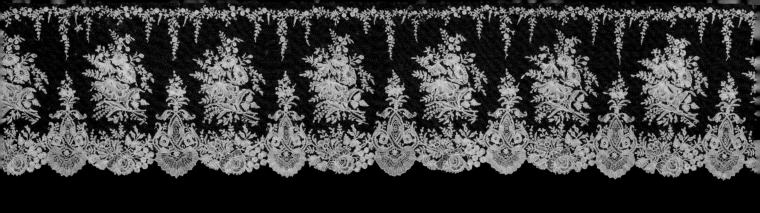

styles that corresponded to the historical eclecticism of women's dress. Along with the expanding desire for antique lace among affluent consumers, seventeenth- and eighteenth-century-inspired laces such as Maltese and the deliberately named *point Colbert* that emerged during the boom years became increasingly popular and constituted a safe sales choice.[23] Among the machine-made products that also imitated earlier models was the recently invented chemical lace, especially the types manufactured in Switzerland, which would come to dominate the market (SEE CHAP. 14). At the turn of the twentieth century, few of the major lace entrepreneurs in France, Belgium, and England were willing to fully embrace the radically different Art Nouveau aesthetic, unlike their counterparts in Switzerland and Austria. According to an article in *Art et décoration* on the 1900 Paris Exhibition, the best examples of modern lace were presented by the École des Arts Décoratifs in Vienna (FIG. 11.20).[24]

Lace Industries in France, Belgium, and England

Following the establishment of a tightly controlled industry in the seventeenth century (SEE CHAPS. 9 AND 10), France boasted the strongest and best organized of the European lace industries and in 1851 was home to 240,000 of Europe's 535,000 laceworkers.[25] In addition to royal patronage, the role of Paris as the center of fashion was integral to the industry's success; the country's handmade lace centers in Valenciennes, Argentan, and Alençon (among others) and those centers of machine-made lace in Calais and Caudry maintained close ties to the city's designers and manufacturers.[26] Though its lace industry was not as securely organized, and it relied heavily on France for designs, Belgium rivaled France for certain stretches of the century, and handmade lace produced by Belgian laceworkers was valued for its superiority of material and technique.[27] Britain's nineteenth-century handmade industry was small and disorganized in comparison with those of France and Belgium, as it relied on two geographical centers of lace production in the East Midlands and Devon, neither of which was in constant communication with London.[28] However, it was in the realm of machine-made lace that Britain flourished. British inventors and manufacturers led Europe in developing new technologies;

FIG. 11.14 (ABOVE)

Brussels application lace flounce (handmade needle and bobbin lace and machine lace), Brussels, mid-19th century. Cotton. Textilmuseum St. Gallen, Acquired from the Estate of John Jacoby, 1954, 58641. Cat. 130.

FIG. 11.15 (OPPOSITE)

Pierre Désiré Guillemet after Franz Xaver Winterhalter, *Empress Eugénie*, 1856. Oil on canvas. Musée d'Orsay, Paris, 20067.

Fashion and the Lace Industries in France, Belgium, and England, 1800–1900

throughout the century they would improve upon and adapt these, leading to the eventual deterioration of the handmade industry.

Handmade Industry

Although there were certainly regional differences, handmade lace industries in these three countries operated in much the same way, following traditions established in earlier centuries. This organization comprised lacemakers (women and girls) who worked in the home, in workshops, or in schools; local intermediaries referred to as "factors" (sometimes men, but usually women), who were responsible for transmitting patterns and materials to lacemakers, supervising their work, and passing it on to merchants; lace designers (usually men); and, at the top level, those merchants and dealers (also usually men) who sold the finished lace.

Laceworkers learned their craft very young, many long before age ten, in dedicated schools often operated by religious leaders. In certain areas of France, lace and design schools established throughout the century aimed to combat the decline of local industries and, from the 1850s onward, the increasing mechanization of the industry.[29] Many lace schools in Britain were operated by lace merchants themselves, who hoped long-term investment in training workers would be commercially beneficial in the future.[30] In Belgium a clear picture of the industry survives thanks to a study commissioned by the Belgian Ministry of Industry and Work, which was published in 1902 by Pierre Verhaegen (b. 1873). Verhaegen notes that there were 17,121 students attending 369 lace schools in Belgium by 1851.[31] These students were supervised in workrooms by mistresses responsible for the quality and speed of their pupils' lace production (FIG. 11.21).

FIG. 11.18

Dress, United States, 1880. Silk and lace. Brooklyn Museum Costume Collection at The Metropolitan Museum of Art, New York, Gift of the Brooklyn Museum, 2009; Gift of Helen Rice, 1946, 2009.300.678a,b.

The Belgian and British lace industries relied on factors to serve as liaisons between laceworkers and merchants. In Britain, for example, local lace factors in Devon could be the town's shopkeepers or other individuals whose involvement in the industry fluctuated depending on the demand for lace.[32] More often than not, factors were women with knowledge of the process (having at one point been laceworkers themselves) and had a direct hand in making the finished lace; they might prick pinholes to prepare the pattern or finish the lace themselves after receiving it from the laceworker (FIG. 11.22). Factors often relied on the "putting-out" or "truck" system, in which workers were compensated for their labor with materials necessary for making the lace ordered by the merchants.[33]

Among the leading handmade lace producers of the nineteenth century were French firms Videcoq & Simon, Auguste Lefébure, and the Compagnie des Indes, which would eventually become Verdé, Delisle & Cie.[34] Videcoq & Simon exhibited fine examples of lace (some of which would be acquired by Queen Victoria and Empress Eugénie) at several international exhibitions and was responsible for sustaining and reviving the Alençon industry in the 1840s.[35] Auguste Lefébure's commercial success relied on a combination of closely supervised labor and the sophisticated designs of Alcide Roussel, who was educated in French lace schools and became one of the best-known lace designers of the century. From 1856 on, Roussel won numerous awards at international exhibitions, and his designs were among those that Ernest Lefébure illustrated in *Broderie et dentelles*, first published in 1887 and revised in 1904.[36] Roussel also designed lace for the Compagnie des Indes. In the mid-1850s, Parisian customers could purchase lace and shawls from their shop on the corner of rue de Richelieu (FIG. 11.23). All three of these leading firms exhibited successfully at the Paris International Exhibition of 1867, the most impressive piece being a set of Lefébure point d'Alençon dress flounces "of most artistic and harmonious design" that were priced at 85,000 francs (it is likely that these point d'Alençon flounces are the same pieces now preserved in the Victoria and Albert Museum; FIG. 11.24).[37]

British lacemaker Mrs. Charlotte E. Treadwin (1820–1890) of Exeter also exhibited lace at the 1867 exhibition. She was one of the region's largest dealers and the century's best-known producer of Honiton lace (FIG. 11.25) as well as lace based on Venetian rose point, Valenciennes, and other popular historical styles.[38] A report on the 1874 International Exhibition written by Mrs. Fanny Bury Palliser (1805–1878) commends her, stating that

"the most meritorious works of the Devonshire lace-workers are the reproductions of old lace by Mrs. Treadwin, which leave nothing to desire in excellence, precision, and freshness."[39] Often referred to in period newspapers as "Lace-maker to the Queen," Mrs. Treadwin published a book around 1874 containing detailed instructions for creating both antique-style and contemporary laces, including Honiton.[40] Although this interest in antique lace sustained the industry for stretches of the late nineteenth century, makers of hand-made lace were unable to compete with machines that could rapidly adapt to imitate their techniques.

Machine Innovation

In the changing landscape of the lucrative machine-lace industry, Britain played a key role. It industrialized before France and produced a series of inventions that would revolutionize the machine production of lace.[41] The stocking frame, the first iteration of which was invented between 1586 and 1589 by Reverend William Lee (ca. 1556–1610) of Calverton, near Nottingham, laid the groundwork for machine tulle and net grounds.[42] Approximately two hundred years later, machines developed from his model were first used to create lacelike textiles, and the first decades of the nineteenth century saw numerous improvements on Lee's foundational design.[43] Among these were the warp frame, developed by British mechanic Josiah Crane in 1775, which in the early nineteenth century produced net that rivaled French silk point nets.[44]

The next development crucial to the evolution of the machine-lace industry was Heathcoat's aforementioned bobbinet machine. This machine was a departure from earlier inventions in that the movement of its parts imitated the twisting threads of a lacemaker's bobbins (FIG. 11.26).[45] In 1809 Heathcoat patented the second iteration of his design, called the Old Loughborough. In 1815 one of Heathcoat's former workers successfully smuggled

FIG. 11.21 (LEFT)
M. Joseph Casier, "École Dentellière des Sœurs Apostolines (couvent de Jérusalem), A Bruges," from Pierre Verhaegaen, *La Dentelle et la Broderie sur Tulle*, 1902, vol. 2, fig. 1. Printed by J. Lebègue et cie, Brussels. Archive.org, Getty Research Institute.

FIG. 11.22 (RIGHT)
Valenciennes bobbin-lace pattern and sample, Belgium, late 19th century. Cotton, ink, and paper. Division of Cultural and Community Life, National Museum of American History, Smithsonian Institution, Washington, DC, 2013.0121.29.

an Old Loughborough into France, where it was set up in Valenciennes and then moved to nearby Douay, thus introducing the valuable technology to continental Europe.[46] By 1820, following additional modifications, it could produce nets up to 54 inches (137 centimeters) wide that could be hand embroidered for a result almost indistinguishable from the fully handmade embroidered net made in the East Midlands at the time.[47] In his efforts to apply jacquard technology to his bobbinet machine, Heathcoat implemented numerous improvements to his original design, patenting more than ten modifications between 1809 and 1843.[48]

Both the Pusher and Leavers machines were developed from Heathcoat's Old Loughborough technology. First constructed by Samuel Clark and James Mart from Nottingham in 1812, the Pusher machine could produce plain net identical to Old Loughborough net.[49] Although the production process was slow, the machine enabled easy patterning and was therefore able, after the incorporation of the jacquard mechanism in 1839, to produce faithful imitations of the large Chantilly bobbin-lace shawls popular between 1850 and 1870 (FIGS. 11.27 AND 11.28).[50] The success of the Leavers machine, which was invented in 1813 or 1814 by framesmith John Levers of Sutton-in-Ashfield,

FIG. 11.23 (TOP)

"Magasin de cachemires et dentelles de la Compagnie des Indes, rue de Richelieu, nº 80," from *L'Illustration*, December 16, 1854, 412. Engraving on paper. Hathitrust.org, University of California.

FIG. 11.24 (BOTTOM)

Alcide Roussel, produced by Lefébure et Fils, set of needle-lace flounces, Bayeux, France, 1867. Linen. © Victoria and Albert Museum, London, T.59 to C-1949.

Fashion and the Lace Industries in France, Belgium, and England, 1800–1900

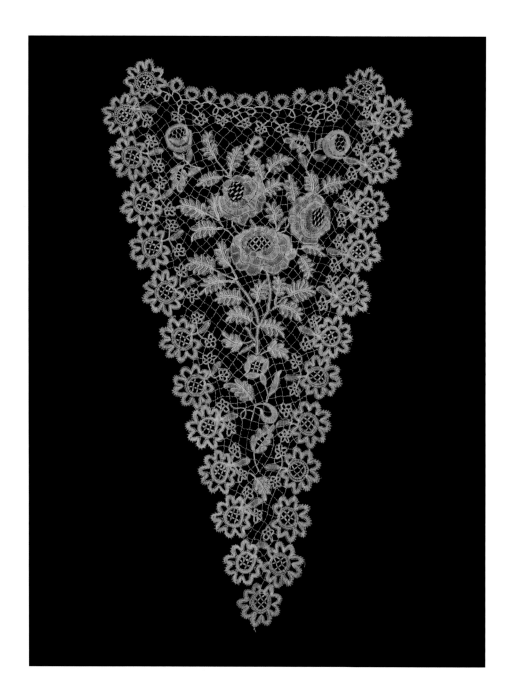

also lies in its 1841 incorporation of the jacquard attachment, which propelled the production of machine-made lace forward.[51] The two final important innovations of this period are the hand-embroidery machine and the Schiffli machine, developed in northeastern Switzerland in 1828 and 1863, respectively (SEE CHAP. 14).[52] Swiss lace made using these embroidery machines was exported to France and Britain, and by

FIG. 11.25

Handmade Honiton bobbin-lace stomacher or vestee, Honiton, England, ca. 1860. Cotton. Textilmuseum St. Gallen, Acquired from the Estate of John Jacoby, 1954, 03063. Cat. 131.

the mid-1880s, the popularity of this textile, often called "guipure" or "Swiss chemical lace," posed a strong threat to Leavers lace as well as machine lace made in Calais.[53]

Machine Industry

In Britain and France, production of machine-made lace was centered in the East Midlands and Calais, respectively. Like the handmade lace trade, this industry comprised workers at multiple levels: the machine owners, who might also work as machine operators (called "twist hands"), and the large number of women and children (or "lace runners") who prepared and finished the lace produced by those machines.[54] Women in this industry were largely relegated to low-paying, "low-skilled" positions, and along with the children the industry relied on until the implementation of child labor laws, they formed the mass of "invisible" labor supporting the highly lucrative lace trade.[55]

Between 1810 and 1860, the British machine-lace trade operated primarily in homes and small workshops.[56] Most of the lace produced in this area was destined for export: annual output in 1856 in Britain was an estimated £100,000, and exports of plain and fancy tulles and machine laces totaled £1.15 million.[57] Laceworkers and lace machine technology also left the East Midlands region throughout the nineteenth century, including to Ayrshire, Scotland, in the 1870s, where Nottingham lace machines are still in operation.[58] Historian Fabrice Bensimon's focused study of the migration of hundreds of East Midlands laceworkers to Calais between 1815 and 1870 reveals the deep connections between these two centers of production. In the 1820s, after the Napoleonic Wars and the expiration of Heathcoat's patent in 1823, wages for twist hands in Nottingham fell, and British workers made their way across the Channel. Although various export and trade regulations attempted to curb this flow of workers, machines, materials, and ideas from Britain to France, smuggling was prolific, and by 1832 there were already an estimated two thousand machines in Calais.[59]

Early machine-made nets were embellished using embroidery techniques or by applying woven motifs, a task undertaken by women and children working in the home (FIG. 11.29).[60] Like their counterparts making handmade lace, women and girls in this profession were vulnerable to exploitation, low wages, and poor working conditions. In 1843–44 British writer Charlotte Elizabeth Tonna (1790–1846) published *The Wrongs of Woman*, the fictional story of a young girl named Kate Clark who leaves her countryside home to work in the machine-lace industry.[61] The author's opinions of the trade come through clearly in her explanation of this skewed balance of power:

FIG. 11.26
Heathcoat's bobbinet machine from William Felkin, *History of the Machine-Wrought Hosiery and Lace Manufactures*, plate 5, 191. Published by Longmans, Green, and Company, London, 1867. Bard Graduate Center Library, New York.

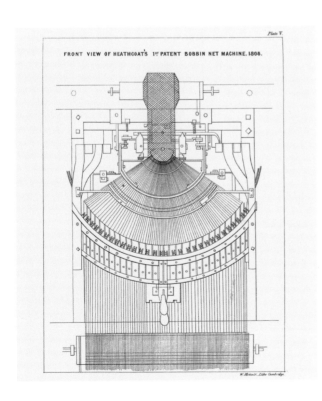

Plate V.

FRONT VIEW OF HEATHCOAT'S 1ST PATENT BOBBIN NET MACHINE. 1808.

550.—Nottingham Lace-running or Embroidering.

"the greater competition among the wretched, who *must* find employment or starve, the more free are those who employ them to impose hard terms."[62] Kate's inhospitable working conditions are in sharp contrast to the expensive lace that she produces, which was destined for sale to fashionable middle-class consumers.

Industry Expansion and Middle-Class Lace Consumption

Although affordable machine-made lace had been available before the 1850s, drastic developments in consumer culture and the evolution of department stores helped propel the fashion for lace and lace accessories forward.[63] In France so-called *magasins de nouveautés* of the 1830s and 1840s paved the way for the large department stores that would come to characterize Second Empire Paris and the last decades of the century. The magasins de nouveautés stocked drapery and dry goods including lace, accessories, lingerie, hosiery, fabric, and ready-to-wear garments.[64] In the 1840s among the largest of these establishments was La Ville de Paris, which opened in 1841 and three years later boasted 150 employees and annual sales between 10 and 12 million francs.[65] Le Bon Marché was the largest of the nineteenth-century Parisian department stores, which offered customers all the products listed above in addition to furniture, art, and home goods. Originally opened in 1838, Le Bon Marché was completely remodeled and revitalized in 1852 by Aristide Boucicaut (1810–1877), and in 1869 the store moved into its purpose-built structure, which still occupies an entire city block on the rue de Sèvres.[66] Eight years after this reopening, the store employed 1,788 men and women, and annual sales had tripled to reach a massive 73 million francs.[67] Here, customers could peruse a staggering variety of goods for sale, including lace of all different types in the form of the latest fashionable accessories.

Literature of the period offers a glimpse of how customers may have experienced shopping in stores such as Le Bon Marché. The most famous of these fictional accounts is Émile Zola's 1883 *Au bonheur des dames (The Ladies' Paradise)*.[68] The novel is replete with detailed descriptions of extravagant sales and sumptuous displays. Lace features prominently, giving a clear sense of the wide variety of styles that fashionable Parisian consumers could purchase both in the store and via catalogue (FIG. 11.30). Upon arriving in Paris, Denise—the novel's main character—is awestruck at the goods on display in the store windows:

[Denise] had never seen anything like this! She was rooted to the pavement in admiration. At the back, a long scarf worked in Bruges lace, and costing a

FIG. 11.27 (OPPOSITE, TOP)
Machine-made Chantilly shawl, Europe, 1850–75. Silk. Textilmuseum St. Gallen, 61937.

FIG. 11.28 (OPPOSITE, BOTTOM)
Handmade Chantilly bobbin-lace shawl, France or Belgium, ca. 1860. Silk. Textilmuseum St. Gallen, Acquired from the Estate of John Jacoby, 1954, 00480. Cat. 124.

FIG. 11.29 (ABOVE)
"Nottingham Lace-running or Embroidering," from Charles Knight, *Pictorial Gallery of Arts, Useful Arts*, vol. 1, 129. Published by C. Knight and Co., London, 1845. Printed by William Clowes and Sons, London. Archive.org, Wellcome Library.

considerable amount, was spread out like an altar cloth, its two reddish-white wings unfurled; flounces of Alençon lace were strewn like garlands; then there was a cascade of every kind of lace—Mechlin, Valenciennes, Brussels appliqué, Venetian rose-point—streaming down like a snowfall.[69]

Zola blends feelings of overstimulation with the tactile experience of shopping in the store and examining goods—often lace—for sale. In one scene, several women looking at a selection of lace "were becoming intoxicated with it. Pieces were being unwound, passed from one woman to another, drawing them even closer together, linking them with light strands."[70] In another scene, a character named Madame de Boves asks a salesman to pull various types of lace for her, and after half an hour, "she was plunging her hands into the growing cascade of pillow lace, Mechlin lace, Valenciennes, Chantilly, her fingers trembling with desire, her face gradually warming with sensual joy."[71] Zola's descriptions of the bustling commercial establishment help conjure the store's electric atmosphere (FIG. 11.31).

The ready availability of lace in department stores coincided with the prolific use of lace in fashion between 1850 and 1870.[72] As previously introduced, one result of this accessibility was an increasingly ambiguous distinction between the "real" (handmade) lace and the "faux" (machine-made) lace, which could blur those class hierarchies typically communicated through dress. As fashionable women of the middle classes could purchase and wear imitations of popular handmade lace, wealthy consumers redoubled their support of expensive, handmade laces such as those from Alençon and Brussels and antique lace in particular. Expensive antique lace resumed its status as a signifier of wealth and social standing, and wearing it necessitated a knowledge of those desirable laces produced in earlier centuries (SEE CHAP. 12). A proliferation of publications around the turn of the twentieth century aimed to instruct readers in identifying the differences between handmade and machine-made laces and usually extolled the virtues of handwork over machine production.[73] Gender is deeply entangled in this discourse. The handwork of female lacemakers was central to later nineteenth-century public opinions about the merits and drawbacks of industrialized lace production and the dire threat it posed to the handmade industries.

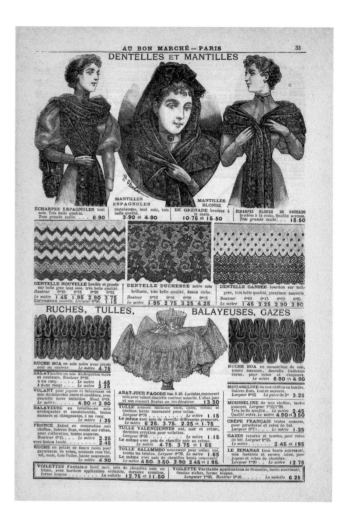

FIG. 11.30
Dentelles et Mantilles, *Au Bon Marché - Paris* catalogue, 1892, 33. Engraving on paper. Private collection.

"Art gracieux, travail bienfaisant": The Lacemaker and Female Labor

The increasing mechanization of the lace industry was applauded by many as a testament to industrial progress. At the same time, it also prompted a backlash against what were perceived as societal ills associated with factory production in which female workers suffered exposure to harsh conditions and—in the case of mothers—separation from their children. In this narrative, the lacemaker, ensconced in a rural, domestic setting, came to represent a model of acceptable feminine labor that maintained traditional gender roles. Lacemaking "allowed" a woman to attend to her primary responsibilities of child-rearing and to assist with agricultural tasks during the summer months.[74] Further, in contrast to the monotonous uniformity of machine-made lace, the presence of the lacemaker's "hand" signified the superiority of her artistic creation and manifested her sex-based suitability for this type of work (FIG. 11.32).[75] Although, as we have seen, women were involved in the handmade lace industry as successful manufacturers, workshop supervisors, and teachers, it was the lacemaker who symbolized the bulwark against the menace of the machine that threatened to destroy a centuries-old artisanal skill and upend the ideal family structure.[76]

Numerous male- and female-authored publications from the mid- to late nineteenth century on the history of lace frequently commended the benefits of domestic

FIG. 11.31

Charles Fichot, "Escalier conduisant aux comptoirs des trousseaux, lingerie, jupes et dentelles" (Stairs leading to the counters for trousseaus, lingerie, skirts and laces), Au Bon Marché, *L'Illustration*, ca. 1885, 127. Engraving on paper, engraved by Joseph Burn Smeeton. Private collection.

ESCALIER CONDUISANT AUX COMPTOIRS DES TROUSSEAUX, LINGERIE, JUPES ET DENTELLES

259 Fashion and the Lace Industries in France, Belgium, and England, 1800–1900

lacemaking in a country village and often referred to the salubrious nature of the work, its appropriateness for the delicacy and nimbleness of women's hands as well as their demure temperament and maternal role, and its promotion of morality and well-being.[77] Writing about the Belgian industry in 1843, François Fertiault (1814–1915) invoked "the beneficent influence," "the well-being and ease," and "the morality" that reigned in the rural areas of handmade lace production and contrasted these with "the disorder, the vices resulting from joint work, the misery and its awful procession" associated with factory work.[78] Not quite twenty years later, *L'indicateur de Bayeux* concurred with this view, noting that "our lace industry [is] so interesting, so hygienic, so moral, because it does not coop up the workers that it employs in unhealthy workshops where youth withers, where the heart wilts."[79] In commenting on what it described as the "small" sum of money earned by the "hands" (as they were called) who worked for the Exeter-based manufacturer Mrs. Treadwin, the author of an 1889 article on Honiton lace reminded readers that not only were food and housing cheaper in the countryside, but "the comparative healthfulness of work in a country cottage and a city factory should also be taken into account in considering the desirability of preserving such village industries as that of Honiton lace."[80] In 1904, as the handmade lace industry went into irreversible decline, Ernest Lefébure cited a contemporary elegiac description of the lacemaker and her idyllic life, from childhood to old age, that promoted it as "gracious art, beneficial work."[81]

FIG. 11.32
Bergeret & Cie, "Les Dentelles" postcard series, Nancy, France, ca. 1900. Private collection.

Although the well-known art critic and publisher Charles Blanc (1813–1882) also privileged handmade lace, he questioned the human cost:

> When one travels in Flanders, in the Brabant, in Normandy, in Auvergne, when one sees young girls at the windows of a first floor, bent over their cushion, manipulating countless bobbins around countless pins.... One asks oneself if the life of these creatures who are born to please and to be loved should be entirely absorbed by making other creatures more attractive and more lovable, and one wants to hope that these machines, which had first seemed an instrument of slavery, will one day become a means of comfort and freedom.[82]

In spite of his romanticized portrayal of young lacemakers in their bucolic sanctuary, Blanc acknowledged that machines might, in fact, offer an alternative—and more rewarding—life than that spent toiling in the service of other, more fortunate women.

Conclusion

Although the nineteenth-century lace industries of France, Belgium, and England experienced periods of hardship, lace regained and maintained the position as a marker of social status and affluence that it had lost at the end of the previous century. Both hand and machine industries responded to the demands of women's fashionable dress, introducing new techniques and designs. Manufacturers of handmade lace met the challenges to rebuild this sector of the luxury economy, establishing schools and workshops and seeking out talented designers. Machine lace entrepreneurs, determined to tap into the growing middle-class market, worked tirelessly to speed up production and more closely replicate handmade lace. The midcentury marked a high point in the two industries both technically and stylistically: lace of the 1850s and 1860s attests to designers' creativity, lacemakers' skills, and technological innovations. The tensions created by expanding mechanization reflected wider concerns about the impact of rapid industrialization on society in these three countries, pitting the soulless machine against the individual (male or female) artisan and endangering the role of women as guardians of the home. World War I dealt an irreversible blow to the handmade lace industry, and, from the 1920s, women's informal daywear relied significantly less on lace trimmings and accessories. However, the machine-made lace used by leading couturiers and couturieres for evening wear and, increasingly, by manufacturers of lingerie in the twentieth and twenty-first centuries depends on the innovations of, and often the same technology as, the nineteenth century.

1   It is beyond the scope of this chapter to address the well-established lacemaking industries in other parts of Europe that included Ireland, Italy, Spain, and Switzerland. In addition to other chapters in this publication, see, for example, Santina Levey, *Lace: A History* (Leeds, UK: W. S. Maney & Son; London: Victoria and Albert Museum, 1983); and Florence Lewis May, *Hispanic Lace and Lace Making* (New York: Hispanic Society of America, 1939).

2   Lace was worn by men at the Napoleonic and other European courts in the early 19th century, but the sobriety of their day dress favored linen or muslin shirt ruffles and cravats. By about 1820, lace became exclusively associated with women's dress. Although lace was used as trimming for undergarments, this chapter focuses on lace worn with day and evening wear.

3   Regarding the efforts to revitalize or sustain the lace industry in France, see, for example, Alice Gandin, "Un nom, une famille: Les Lefébure, industriels et artistes de la dentelle (1829–1932)," in *Dentelles: Quand la mode ne tient qu'à un fil*, ed. Alice Gandin and Julie Romain (Paris: Somogy; Caen, France: Musée de Normandie, 2012), 117–19; and Ernest Lefébure, *Broderie et dentelles* (Paris: Alcide Picard & Kaan, 1904), 320–24. In late 19th-century England, John Ruskin was involved in reviving the production of linen fabric that incorporated drawn- and cutwork and needlepoint lace in the Lake District. Elizabeth Pricket, *Ruskin Lace & Linen* (New York: Dover Publications, 1985). About lace revivals in Italy and the United States, SEE CHAP. 13.

4   Although women's dresses at this time were also made of linen, printed cotton, and silk (the latter especially for evening wear), white cotton was the most popular fabric for daywear, and for more formal occasions it might be embroidered with cotton, silk, wool, or metallic thread. This is evident in both French and English fashion plates and the large number of surviving garments in museum collections.

5   For an overview of lace and fashion during the period 1780–1815, see Levey, *Lace*, 77–78, 80–84.

6   Ibid., 80. Levey notes the importance of Heathcoat's machine on two other counts in addition to its suitability for current fashions: "it was easily adapted for power-driving and thus was soon established within a factory system . . . [and] it was able before long to work with cotton thread and so helped to spread the use of cotton [rather than linen or silk] to all branches of the lace industry, including hand-made lace" ibid. For the development of lacemaking machines prior to and including Heathcoat's invention, see ibid., 78–80; Patricia Wardle, *Victorian Lace* (New York: Frederick A. Praeger, 1969), 219–23; and Pat Earnshaw, *Lace Machines and Machine Laces* (London: B. T. Batsford, 1986), chaps. 2, 3.

7   A variant of the stocking frame was brought to Lyon from England sometime after 1774 to produce silk net, which was known as "Tulle simple et double." Over the following decades, improvements were made to these machines, and, by the end of the century, "there were 2,000 of these machines in use" in Lyon and Nîmes. Wardle, *Victorian Lace*, 244.

8   Levey, *Lace*, 79. Levey states that by 1810, "there were between fifteen and eighteen hundred point net frames in Nottingham . . . while a whole new branch of the industry had developed with the employment of 15,000 women and children engaged in 'spotting' the net and tens of thousands in the vicinity . . . decorating it with tambour work and needle-run embroidery" (ibid.). Lacemakers in the town of Coggeshall, in Essex, were also known for their tambour work on machine-made net. The technique was introduced in the area in 1812 by a French or Flemish man named Drago (or Draygo), who taught women to embroider in chain stitch using tambour hooks. Pat Earnshaw, *A Dictionary of Lace* (Princes Risborough, UK: Shire Publications, 1982), 33–34.

9   Alexandra Bosc, "Du triomphe au désamour," in Gandin and Romain, *Dentelles*, 69–70.

10   Levey, *Lace*, 82–83.

11   The finest quality was made in Chantilly in the Île-de-France and Caen and Bayeux in Normandy. Black silk blonde was also made in these centers, primarily for the Spanish market. Ibid., 89.

12   Ibid., 88. Although both the Pusher and Leavers machines, introduced in England in 1812 and 1813, respectively, were in wide use by the 1830s, they were not yet fully capable of imitating richly patterned handmade lace.

13   Ibid., 89. Manufacturers in Caen and Bayeux also switched to making black lace.

14   Quoted in ibid., 93.

15   Félix Aubry, "Classe XXIV: Dentelles, broderie, passementerie, tapisserie," in *Exposition universelle de Londres de 1862: Rapports des membres de la section française du jury international sur l'ensemble de l'Exposition*, vol. 5, ed. M. Michel Chevalier (Paris: Imprimerie et Librairie Centrales des Chemins de Fer, 1862), 216. A decade earlier in February 1851, the periodical *Conseiller des dames et des demoiselles* underscored the extensive use of lace and referred to point d'Alençon as "la plus noble, la plus rare des dentelles" (the noblest, the rarest of laces). Quoted in Bosc, "Du triomphe au désamour," 73. Unless otherwise noted, all translations are our own.

16   For a thorough discussion of this gown and its lace, see Kay Staniland, "Queen Victoria's Wedding Dress and Lace," *Costume* 17, no. 1 (1983): 1–32. This commission from Queen Victoria was especially important to the still-struggling Honiton lace industry.

17   Levey, *Lace*, 89. Levey indicates that, at this time, designers of both woven silks and lace had not been trained to create large-scale patterns, and they frequently looked to historical designs.

18   Levey notes that the Great Exhibition of 1851 in London "marked the close of the first stage in the expansion of the lace trade, and . . . it also marked the beginning of a period of critically-aware experimentation both in design and in lace technique." *Lace*, 98.

19   See the glossary in this volume for definitions of these three laces. In addition to Chantilly, Caen, and Bayeux, black "Chantilly" lace was also made in Enghien and Grammont in Belgium. Levey, *Lace*, 102. Brussels application was a major product of the Belgian industry and, from the 1850s, was generally made with a machine-net ground to which motifs of bobbin, needle, or a combination of the two were added (ibid., 103). Regarding the use of cotton thread that increasingly replaced linen for Chantilly produced in France, see Wardle, *Victorian Lace*, 65, and for the use of English machine-spun cotton for Brussels and Valenciennes, 88. In her article "Lace and Embroidery," published in conjunction with the 1867 London exhibition, lace expert Fanny Bury Palliser noted that the availability of inexpensive machine-made options did not reduce demand for handmade lace. Fanny Bury Palliser, "Lace and Embroidery," in *The Illustrated Catalogue of the Universal Exhibition, Published with the Art Journal* (New York: Virtue & Co., 1868), 117–18.

20   The winners of the commissions were selected from among twenty-five manufacturers. The point d'Alençon set, made by the well-known firm Videcoq & Simon, was written up in the *Journal d'Alençon* of 1855 and exhibited at the Paris Exposition that year. Wardle, *Victorian Lace*, 50–51. For Eugénie as a patron of lace, see Bosc, "Du triomphe au désamour," 73; and Alison McQueen, "Eugénie impératrice: La politique de la dentelle au Second Empire," in Gandin and Romain, *Dentelles*, 79–87.

21   Wardle, *Victorian Lace*, 30. In his report on the 1862 London exhibition, Félix Aubry referred to the increasing perfection and consumption of machine-made blonde lace, noting that improvements in manufacturing made it "almost impossible, even on close inspection, to distinguish real blonde from an imitation product, whose price is however four or five times lower" (Les perfectionnements dans la fabrication de cette sorte de dentelle sont si-complets

qu'il est en quelque sorte impossible, même en regardant de près, de distinguer une véritable blonde d'un produit en imitation, dont le prix est cependant quatre à cinq fois moins élevé). Aubry, "Classe XXIV," 218.

22 Levey cites sales at the London department store Peter Robinson's that "rose from £15,964 in 1885 to £25,958 in 1895 to reach a peak of £33,193 in 1906." *Lace*, 108.

23 Regarding the vogue for antique lace, see Levey, *Lace*, 110–11. As the name implies, Maltese lace was initially produced on the island of Malta. Introduced there in the 1830s, it was originally made with black silk and was based on what is referred to as peasant lace of northern Italy, which had evolved from 17th-century Genoese lace. By the late 1850s, cotton Maltese lace was also produced in the Le Puy region of France, Barcelona, Belgium, and the English Midlands. From the 1860s, Maltese lace became much denser, and this heavier style remained fashionable through the end of the century. Ibid., 105. Point Colbert was introduced by Auguste Lefébure, the leading lace manufacturer in Bayeux, in 1855. This needle lace, inspired by 18th-century Alençon, paid homage to the founder of the French lace industry (SEE CHAP. 9). Wardle, *Victorian Lace*, 62–64.

24 Gustave Soulier, "La broderie et la dentelle à l'Exposition," *Art et décoration: Revue mensuelle d'art moderne* 9 (1901): 13–20. Soulier illustrates several pieces from the École des Arts Décoratifs in Vienna and indicates that they were the most beautiful examples of lace at the exhibition. Prof. J. Hrdlička, who taught at the Viennese school, published a book of influential designs in 1902. Levey, *Lace*, 117; Anne Kraatz, *Lace: History and Fashion*, trans. Pat Earnshaw (New York: Rizzoli, 1989), 163. In France Félix Aubert was most closely associated with introducing lace designs in the Art Nouveau style. Rossella Froissart Pezone, "La dentelle moderne: Félix Aubert et la polychrome de Courseulles," in Gandin and Romain, *Dentelles*, 120–29.

25 Félix Aubry, *Rapport sur les dentelles, les blondes, les tulles et les broderies: Fait à la Commission française du jury international de l'Exposition universelle de Londres* (Paris: Imprimerie Impériale, 1854), 81–82. Since lacemaking was primarily a domestic industry practiced by women, it is difficult to track their numbers using resources such as census records. David Hopkin, "Working, Singing, and Telling in the 19th-Century Flemish Pillow-Lace Industry," *Textile* 18, no. 1 (2019): 53–68, 55.

26 Wardle, *Victorian Lace*, 43.

27 Levey, *Lace*, 89–90.

28 Wardle, *Victorian Lace*, 133.

29 Ibid., 44; Stéphane Lembré, "Les écoles de dentellières en France et en Belgique des années 1850 aux années 1930," *Histoire de l'éducation* 123 (2009): 46.

30 G. F. R. Spenceley, "The English Pillow Lace Industry, 1840–80: A Rural Industry in Competition with Machinery," *Business History* 19, no. 1 (1977): 68–87. Approximately 20 percent of the labor these merchants relied on was done by children, who were instructed from an early age so as to ensure that the lace they would eventually produce as adults was up to standard.

31 Pierre Verhaegen, *La dentelle et la broderie sur tulle*, vol. 4 of *Les industries à domiciles en Belgique* (Brussels: Société Belge de librairie and J. Lebègue, 1902), 203. More than 30 percent of these organizations were under religious direction. Verhaegen notes that convents in particular also provided basic instruction in reading, writing, and sewing. They often continued to operate as factors for former students and were generally more concerned about the well-being of their workers. Wardle, *Victorian Lace*, 91.

32 Spenceley, "English Pillow Lace Industry," 70.

33 Wardle, *Victorian Lace*, 90–91. Although handmade needle or bobbin lace was a relatively inexpensive craft that required a small number of tools, high-quality linen thread was expensive.

34 Levey, *Lace*, 98. The Compagnie des Indes was so named because it initially sold goods from Kashmir. Upon narrowing its focus to French- and Belgian-made laces, the company changed its name in 1865.

35 Levey, *Lace*, 98; and Édouard Gorges, *Revue de l'exposition universelle: Les merveilles de la civilisation* (Paris: Ferdinand Sartorius, 1856), 190.

36 Levey, *Lace*, 99; Lefébure, *Broderie et dentelles*, 248.

37 Fanny Bury Palliser, *A History of Lace*, 3rd ed. (London: Sampson Low, Marston, Low, & Searle, 1875), 172, quoted in Levey, *Lace*, 99.

38 Palliser, *History of Lace*, 367.

39 Fanny Bury Palliser, "The International Exhibition, 1874," *Art-Journal* 13 (1874): 173–74. Mrs. Treadwin's lacemakers were carefully trained; as Spenceley notes, she established schools where children were taught by skilled mistresses who could receive a wage two to three times larger than most workers at the time. Spenceley, "English Pillow Lace Industry," 75.

40 C. E. Treadwin, *Antique Point and Honiton Lace* (London: Ward, Lock and Tyler, 1873), 1.

41 A comprehensive discussion is beyond the scope of this chapter, but this overview of the most important innovations and technologies aims to contextualize the changing landscape of the lucrative 19th-century lace industry. Pat Earnshaw's *Lace Machines and Machine Laces* is an invaluable resource that includes mechanical diagrams and detailed explanations of new production processes. Likewise, lace manufacturer William Felkin (1795–1874) offers an exhaustive record of Britain's mechanical industry in his *History of the Machine-Wrought Hosiery and Lace Manufactures* (London: Longmans, Green, 1867).

42 Henri Hénon, *L'industrie des tulles & dentelles mécaniques dans Le Pas-de-Calais, 1815–1900* (Paris: Belin frères, 1900), 19.

43 Earnshaw, *Lace Machines and Machine Laces*, 16; and Felkin, *History of the Machine-Wrought Hosiery and Lace Manufactures*, 54.

44 Earnshaw, *Lace Machines and Machine Laces*, 37.

45 Felkin, *History of the Machine-Wrought Hosiery and Lace Manufactures*, 190–91, 194. Heathcoat explained to Felkin how he developed the design for his first machine after observing a Northamptonshire laceworker; its resulting fanlike structure clearly mimics the arrangement of bobbins on a lace pillow.

46 Earnshaw, *Lace Machines and Machine Laces*, 72. Valenciennes and Douay are in the north of France near the Belgian border. On the topic of smuggling lace, machinery, and materials between Europe and Britain, see Fabrice Bensimon, "The Emigration of British Lacemakers to Continental Europe (1816–1860s)," *Continuity and Change* 34, no. 1 (2019): 15–41. For Heathcoat's struggles with patent infringements, and with competition after the expiration of his patent in 1823, see Earnshaw, *Lace Machines and Machine Laces*, 71–74.

47 Levey, *Lace*, 80. Levey notes here that the first of these machines "was worked by an exceptionally hefty frame-hand called Simpson, who promptly earned £5 for three days' work."

48 Bennet Woodcroft, *Titles of Patents of Invention, Chronologically Arranged: From March 2, 1617 (14 James I.) to October 1, 1852 (16 Victoriae)* (London: G. E. Eyre & W. Spottiswoode, 1854); Bennet Woodcroft, *Titles of Patents of Invention: Chronologically Arranged from March 2, 1617 (14 James I.) to October 1, 1852 (16 Victoriae); Part 2, Issues 4801–14359* (London: G. E. Eyre and W. Spottiswoode, 1854); and Earnshaw, *Machine Lace and Lace Machines*, 72. In 1801 in Lyon, Joseph Marie Jacquard (1752–1834) developed a method for mechanizing the weaving process using a punch-card system attached to a loom. Compared to the earlier drawloom, the jacquard mechanism enabled the more efficient production of complicated weave structures. The jacquard loom would not be fully established in commercial production of woven textiles in Lyon until

1815. Stephen Wilson introduced the jacquard loom to Britain in the 1820s, and it would be used there extensively by the 1840s. Natalie Rothstein, "The Introduction of the Jacquard Loom to Great Britain," in *Studies in Textile History*, ed. V. Gervers (Toronto: Royal Ontario Museum, 1977), 282.

49 Felkin, *History of the Machine-Wrought Hosiery and Lace Manufactures*, 292. The Pusher machine was so named because it relied on a system of bobbins and carriages that were worked by separate prongs called "pushers." Wardle, *Victorian Lace*, 223.

50 Earnshaw, *Dictionary of Lace*, 100.

51 Felkin, *History of the Machine-Wrought Hosiery and Lace Manufactures*, 272; and Hénon, *L'industrie des tulles*, 29. Unlike the two-tiered system utilized by the Old Loughborough, the Leavers machine (like the Pusher) relied on a single tier of very thinly worked metal carriages. Earnshaw, *Dictionary of Lace*, 98–99.

52 Ibid., 166–67; and Levey, *Lace*, 116. The Textilmuseum St. Gallen houses one of the last remaining examples of a working hand-embroidery machine from around 1890. Visitors to the museum can watch periodically throughout the week as machine operator Maria Weber works.

53 Wardle, *Victorian Lace*, 252; and Earnshaw, *Lace Machines and Machine Laces*, 232. In addition to lace, the machines themselves were exported from Switzerland to Germany, Poland, and the United States, including to New York and New Jersey. Ibid., 231.

54 Gail Baxter, "Hidden Hands and Missing Persons," *Textile* 18, no. 1 (2020): 41.

55 Fabrice Bensimon, "Women and Children in the Machine-Made Lace Industry in Britain and France (1810–60)," *Textile* 18, no. 1 (2020): 71.

56 By 1829 almost half the machines in the East Midlands belonged to individuals who owned and operated between one and three machines. Ibid., 74–75. Male twist hands were usually assisted by boys who threaded the machines and wound and changed bobbins. Although early lace machines may have required some strength to operate, by the 1860s, when the industry was steam-powered, women were still largely excluded from working in machine operator positions that offered a higher wage and were instead typically employed as lace runners who were responsible for cleaning and finishing the lace after it was removed from the machines. Elaine Freedgood, "'Fine Fingers': Victorian Handmade Lace and Utopian Consumption," *Victorian Studies* 45, no. 4 (Summer 2003): 628. See also Maxine Berg, "What Difference Did Women's Work Make to the Industrial Revolution?," *History Workshop Journal* 35, no. 1 (Spring 1993): 22–44.

57 Samuel Ferguson Jr., *Histoire du tulle et des dentelles mécaniques en Angleterre et en France* (Paris: E. Lacroix, 1862), 157.

58 Originally founded in 1900 as Morton Young and Borland Ltd., today Scottish manufacturer MYB Textiles relies on original Nottingham machines to produce patterned lace.

59 Bensimon, "Emigration of British Lacemakers," 21, 24. Lace machines and factories were established in other French towns including Lille, Douai, Rouen, Paris, and Cambrai (as well as locations as far away as Switzerland, Belgium, and the United States), but Calais was the continental center of production.

60 Earnshaw, *Lace Machines and Machine Laces*, 90.

61 Charlotte Elizabeth Tonna, *The Wrongs of Woman* (New York: John S. Taylor, 1844).

62 Ibid., 24.

63 At the beginning of the 19th century, lace was available for purchase much in the same manner as in the previous century: in specialty shops in larger cities, from itinerant lace merchants who traveled from town to town selling their wares, or, for those consumers in smaller towns, from market stalls selling haberdashery. Many

of the larger retailers in London also supplied their goods wholesale, and merchants from all areas of the country might come into the city to buy goods to sell in their shops. Alison Adburgham, *Shops and Shopping, 1800–1914: Where, and in What Manner the Well-Dressed Englishwoman Bought Her Clothes* (London: George Allen & Unwin, 1964), 2–3, 37.

64 Michael B. Miller, *The Bon Marché: Bourgeois Culture and the Department Store, 1869–1920* (Princeton, NJ: Princeton University Press, 1981), 21–25.

65 Ibid., 25. La Ville de Paris offered its customers a new shopping experience that included fixed prices and the ability to return and exchange purchases, all of which would become defining characteristics of the department stores established in the following two decades.

66 Ibid., 27n15. Monumental architecture and sumptuous displays characterized Le Bon Marché's massive building and revolutionary marketing and publicity practices made it the epitome of the modern marketplace, with stores such as Le Printemps, Magasins du Louvre, and La Samaritaine following in its path over the course of the century.

67 Ibid., 43.

68 Zola conducted extensive research in Le Bon Marché and Magasins du Louvre so as to accurately convey what he referred to as "the poetry of modern activity." Émile Zola, notes for *Au bonheur des dames*, NAF10277, 2, Bibliothèque Nationale de France, Paris.

69 Émile Zola, *The Ladies' Paradise*, trans. Brian Nelson, 2nd ed. (Oxford: Oxford University Press, 2008), 6. An extensive body of scholarship on the consumer revolution in Europe during this period notes compelling connections between gender and these new sites of urban consumption. See, for example, H. Hazel Hahn, *Scenes of Parisian Modernity: Culture and Consumption in the Nineteenth Century* (New York: Palgrave Macmillan, 2009); Lisa Tiersten, *Marianne in the Marketplace: Envisioning Consumer Society in Fin-de-Siècle France* (Berkeley: University of California Press, 2001); Victoria E. Thompson, *The Virtuous Marketplace: Women and Men, Money and Politics in Paris, 1830–1870* (Baltimore: John Hopkins University Press, 2000); Rosalind H. Williams, *Dream Worlds: Mass Consumption in Late Nineteenth-Century France* (Berkeley: University of California Press, 1982); and Phillipe Perrot, *Fashioning the Bourgeoisie: A History of Clothing in the Nineteenth Century* (Princeton, NJ: Princeton University Press, 1994).

70 Zola, *Ladies' Paradise*, 83.

71 Ibid., 110. Zola reveals that Madame de Boves, who "in fact had nothing but her cab-fare in her purse," is driven to steal the lace in front of her. She is confronted by the store's inspector, and it is revealed that she has concealed a total of 14,000 francs' worth of lace, including twelve yards of Alençon point (at 1,000 francs per yard), a handkerchief, a fan, and a cravat (ibid., 110, 421–22).

72 Although too broad a topic to address in this essay, furnishing lace was used extensively in fashionable 19th-century interiors.

73 Among the numerous examples of practical guides published during this period are Ernest Lefébure's *Embroidery and Lace: Their Manufacture and History* (London: H. Grevel; Philadelphia: J. B. Lippincott Company, 1889); Mrs. F. Nevill Jackson's *A History of Hand-Made Lace* (London: L. Upcott Gill, 1900); Fanny Bury Palliser's *History of Lace*, 4th ed. (New York: C. Scribner's Sons, 1902); Samuel L. Goldberg's *Lace, Its Origin and History* (New York: Brentano's, 1904); and Margaret Jourdain's *Old Lace: A Handbook for Collectors* (London: B. T. Batsford; New York: Charles Scribner's Sons, 1909). These publications coincided with a revival in interest in antique lace, encouraged by the development of charitable lace societies. For further reading, see Geoff Spenceley, "The Lace Associations: Philanthropic Movements to Preserve the Production of Hand-Made

Lace in Late Victorian and Edwardian England," *Victorian Studies* 16, no. 4 (June 1973): 433–52.

74 This seasonal division of labor in France was commented upon throughout the century; see Pierre Coftier, "Ouvrières, 'L'oisiveté coupable et le labeur forcé,'" in Gandin and Romain, *Dentelles*, 55–56. Coftier cites the *Enquête sur la condition ouvrière* (1872), which also noted that lacemakers earned considerably higher wages when they worked in the fields. "Ouvrières," 56.

75 In his preface to *Broderie et dentelles*, Ernest Lefébure describes lace as "la plus poétique des tissus" (the most poetic of fabrics) and asks whether "si ce n'est pas par l'aiguille et le fuseau, plutôt que par le pinceau, le burin, le ciseau, etc. que l'influence de la femme doit s'affirmer dans les arts. Dans ce domaine elle règne en souveraine." (If it is not by the needle and the bobbin rather than the brush, the chisel, the scissor, etc., that the influence of woman must affirm itself in the arts. In this domain, she reigns as a sovereign.) *Broderie et dentelles*, 7. In *L'art dans la parure*, Charles Blanc describes the trace of the lacemaker's hand, even when faithfully following a design on parchment, that cannot be replicated by machine. *L'art dans la parure et dans le vêtement* (Paris: Librairie Renouard, 1875), 287, 306.

76 Literary historian Elaine Freedgood argues that while the lacemaker was obliged to produce a commodity for exchange, her labor ostensibly transcended the "vagaries" of this transaction, and "lace making [was] its own reward because it promote[d] such excellent qualities as individuality, artistry, cleanliness, and industriousness." In this process, "the hands of the workers [were] detached from their bodies . . . partially to rematerialize the alienating and sometimes terrifying abstractions that attend commodity exchange." Freedgood, "'Fine Fingers,'" 636, 628.

77 See, for example, François Fertiault, *Histoire de la dentelle* (Paris: Au Dépôt Belge, Maison Fragati, 1843); Blanc, *L'art dans la parure*; and Lefébure, *Broderie et dentelles*. In her article on lace books, Elaine Freedgood discusses Lefébure's book as well as Fanny Bury Palliser's *History of Lace* (the first edition was published by W. Clowes [London] in 1865), Mrs. F. Nevill Jackson's *History of Hand-Made Lace*, and Thomas Wright's *Romance of the Lace Pillow: Being the History of Lace-Making in Bucks, Beds, Northants and Neighbouring Counties, Together with Some Account of the Lace Industries of Devon and Ireland* (Olney, UK: H. H. Armstrong, 1919). Freedgood, "'Fine

Fingers.'" Freedgood further argues that the lace books themselves invent "a mode of apparently utopian commodity consumption" and offer "the promise that gender unity will resolve or replace class conflict" (Ibid., 625, 636).

78 "Heureusement l'industrie de la dentelle . . . n'a jamais exercé sur la condition des populations qu'y se livrent qu'une influence bienfaisante." Fertiault, *Histoire de la dentelle*, 82. "Le bien-être et l'aisance règnent d'ordinaire au sein des pays qui fabriquent la dentelle" (Ibid., 83); "le bien-être et la moralité se répandent grâce à elle [the lace industry] dans les contrées où elle se fixe" (Ibid., 85). "D'une part, l'ordre, l'aisance, la vie intérieure avec ses habitudes morales et regulières; d'autre part le désordre, les vices résultant du travail en commun, la misère et son affreux cortège" (Ibid., 86).

79 "Notre industrie dentellière, cette industrie si intéressante, si hygiénique, si morale, parce qu'elle ne parque pas les ouvrières qu'elle emploie dans des ateliers insalubres, où la jeunesse s'étiole, où le coeur se flétrit." *L'indicateur de Bayeux*, December 24, 1861, quoted in Coftier, "Ouvrières," 59.

80 "Honiton Lace," *Berrow's Worcester Journal* (April 20, 1889): 7.

81 "Art gracieux, travail bienfaisant." Quoted in Lefébure, *Broderie et dentelles*, 321. Lefébure cites Fernand Engerand, whom he identifies as a deputy from Calvados, on whose initiative the French parliament passed a law in 1903 that reorganized the teaching of handmade lace in primary and other schools in regions where lacemaking was established (Ibid., 323). In the rest of the extended quotation, Engerand maintains that lacemaking is compatible with the obligations of rural life and the ideal work for women since it is not physically taxing and allows old women to earn money until they die.

82 Blanc, *L'art dans la parure*, 307–8: "Quand on voyage les Flandres, dans le Brabant, en Normandie, en Auvergne, quand on voit aux fenêtres d'un rez de chaussée des jeunes filles, courbées sur leur coussin, manier d'innombrables fuseaux autour d'innombrables épingles. . . . On se demande si la vie de cés créatures qui sont nées pour plaire et pour être aimées doit être absorbée tout entière à rendre plus attrayantes et plus aimables d'autres créatures, et l'on veut espérer alors que ces machines, qui avaient paru d'abord d'un instrument d'esclavage, pourront devenir quelque jour un moyen de soulagement et de liberté."

35-A. BLACKBORNE &

35 SOUTH AUDLEY STREET LONDON. W.

12 Ahead of the Curve: A. Blackborne & Co. and the Late Nineteenth-Century British Lace Industry

Annabel Bonnin Talbot

B Y THE MID-NINETEENTH CENTURY, lace had fully recovered its cachet as an indicator of status and feminine elegance, and both the hand- and machine-made lace industries in Europe were thriving (SEE CHAP. 11). Wealthy consumers spent large sums of money on "real" lace to maintain their prestige and assert their spending power, while middle-class women, eager to emulate the fashionable accessories of their social superiors, purchased a variety of machine laces that closely resembled their handmade counterparts. At the same time, the trend in lace design that was influenced by laces of the seventeenth and eighteenth centuries encouraged the vogue for collecting and wearing antique lace among elite women. During the second half of the century, publications in English and French instructed the general public and a growing number of specialists on the complex history of lace and fueled the appreciation of early lace as a fine decorative art (SEE CHAP. 14).[1] In the marketplace, merchants of antique and new handmade lace supplied an affluent clientele and, increasingly, museums with this sought-after commodity. London trade directories of this period included listings for "lacemen" who were located throughout the city. Among these retailers was A. Blackborne & Co., established in 1850 by Anthony Blackborne (1824–1878).[2] This firm, which would be in operation until 1952, was particularly successful in acquiring, exhibiting, and selling outstanding examples of contemporary handmade and historical lace, as is evident from the Blackborne Collection at the Bowes Museum in England.

An examination of this collection and archival material related to the company's activities alongside contemporary sources offers a picture of A. Blackborne & Co.'s business and the forces that shaped it, including how the firm obtained and sold its historical pieces. The creation of A. Blackborne & Co. coincided with new patterns in retail; the boom in the hand- and machine-made lace industries; the vogue for historicizing and

FIG. 12.1 (LEFT)

Anthony Blackborne, ca. 1860s. The Bowes Museum, County Durham, the Blackborne Lace Collection Archive.

FIG. 12.2 (RIGHT)

William Goodfellow, photograph of Arthur Blackborne, London, ca. 1870s. The Bowes Museum, County Durham, the Blackborne Lace Collection Archive.

historical lace, which was part of a broader trend of selling and buying antiques; and the rise of international exhibitions. Throughout the second half of the nineteenth century and first decades of the twentieth century, A. Blackborne & Co. navigated the volatile lace market, which was susceptible to rapid changes in fashion. As prominent retailers, exhibitors, and judges at world's fairs, the Blackbornes were active participants in the trajectory of the lace market in Britain, both responding to and influencing its progression.

The Blackborne Lace Collection at the Bowes Museum

Carefully compiled by Anthony Blackborne and his son Arthur Blackborne (1856–1952), the Blackborne Collection at the Bowes Museum in Barnard Castle, England, is one of the world's finest collections of historic handmade lace (FIGS. 12.1–3). The collection charts the history of European lace from the 1600s to the early twentieth century. In 2007 Dr. and Mrs. Ellis Tinsley, direct descendants of the Blackbornes, donated the collection of over four thousand pieces of lace to the Bowes Museum. The gift was facilitated by Santina Levey (1938–2017), a curator in the Department of Costume and Textiles at the Victoria and Albert Museum, who had worked with the collection for many years.[3] To mark the bequest, the Bowes Museum held an extensive exhibition titled *Fine & Fashionable: Lace from the Blackborne Collection* in 2006 and published an accompanying catalogue.[4]

The Blackborne Collection comprises four areas: the main collection, the lappet collection, the cap back collection, and the study collection (FIGS. 12.4 AND 12.5). The quality and quantity of the lace in each section give the entire collection international significance, with objects illustrating the development of technique and skill, as well as changes in design in needle and bobbin laces over a period of four centuries. In addition to the Blackborne archive, which contains Arthur Blackborne's notebooks, collection

FIG. 12.3
The Bowes Museum, Barnard Castle, England. The Bowes Museum, County Durham.

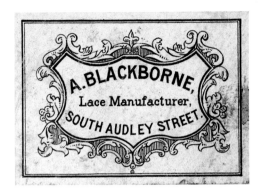

notes, a small selection of correspondence, and his unpublished book, as well as a number of news clippings, books, and photographs, the collection helps trace this story and underscores the Blackbornes' highly regarded position and influence between 1850 and 1920 (FIG. 12.6).

A. Blackborne & Co. and the London Lace Trade, 1850–1910

Born in 1824, Anthony Blackborne worked as a shopkeeper's apprentice in Essex until 1845. That year, at age twenty-one, he moved to London and worked for the Turpin family. Around 1850, his employer, Charles Turpin (1788–1864), financially supported the founding of a wholesale business called A. Blackborne & Co., and in 1852, Anthony married Ann Turpin (ca. 1830–1906), Charles's daughter.[5] By 1853, Blackborne, having moved from wholesale to retail, was operating at 56A South Audley Street in London's fashionable Mayfair neighborhood. Here he traded in contemporary handmade lace aimed at elite consumers during a period of economic growth that challenged the expanding machine-lace market (FIG. 12.7).[6] The firm would occupy five other locations on or near South Audley Street until its closure. Anthony's third son, Arthur, joined A. Blackborne & Co. in 1872 at the age of sixteen. In an interview more than thirty years later, Arthur emphasized his early connections to the trade, saying that he was "practically born in lace."[7] Through their entrepreneurial acumen, the father-and-son team worked their way to the top of their trade and developed mutually beneficial relationships with contemporary trendsetters, museum curators, and writers. In January 1902, Arthur Blackborne was granted a warrant as "lace merchant in ordinary" to Queen Alexandra, who was much admired for her sartorial elegance (FIG. 12.8). These associations further informed the Blackbornes' deep understanding of lace and its value as a retail commodity, ensuring the success of their lucrative commercial activities.

Through the *Court Journal* (1829–1925), a periodical in which A. Blackborne & Co. advertised and was featured, it is possible to trace how the business expanded and established its reputation between 1850 and 1870.[8] In April 1853, Anthony placed an advertisement in the *Journal*, whose readership included well-born and wealthy consumers, announcing that "A. Blackborne begs most respectfully to inform the Nobility and Gentry that he has just received a great Novelty in Brussells [*sic*] Lace for Bridal Costume, and begs to invite an inspection of his stock of Brussels goods, consisting of Flounces, Shawls, Scarfs, Veils . . . which he is enabled to offer considerably under their usual price." The advertisement also informed readers that the shop was the "Foreign and Irish Lace Depot."[9] In June 1853, another advertisement stated that A. Blackborne & Co. sold Spanish lace, which would become the company's main stock-in-trade. Black lace, often worn in combination with vivid colors, was particularly associated with Spanish fashion and remained popular through the end of the nineteenth century (FIG. 12.9).[10]

The *Court Journal* offers further insight into A. Blackborne & Co.'s commercial development in 1859, which was a significant year for the firm. Anthony positioned himself

FIG. 12.4 (OPPOSITE, TOP)
One of a pair of Brussels bobbin-lace cravat ends, Flanders, Southern Netherlands, ca. 1720s–30s. Linen. The Bowes Museum, County Durham, the Blackborne Lace Collection, 2007.1.1.264.

FIG. 12.5 (OPPOSITE, BOTTOM)
Mechlin bobbin-lace lappet, Flanders, Southern Netherlands, 1735–45. Linen. The Bowes Museum, County Durham, the Blackborne Lace Collection, 2007.1.2.335.

FIG. 12.6 (ABOVE)
Label from the lid of a Blackborne delivery box, London, 19th century. Ink on paper. The Bowes Museum, County Durham, the Blackborne Lace Collection Archive.

as "Master Lace Dealer," and the business attracted high-ranking customers.[11] In 1859 alone, there were six references to A. Blackborne & Co. having supplied lace trousseaux to elite brides and members of the aristocracy (FIG. 12.10). For example, on January 1, Blackborne was cited as supplying the trousseau for the wedding of the Hon. Miss Byng and Captain Hedworth Hylton Jolliffe, member of Parliament for Wells, Somerset.[12] On March 5 that year, the same column related that A. Blackborne & Co. provided the lace trousseau for the marriage of Lady Harriet De Burgh, daughter of the Marquis and Marchioness of Clanricarde, to T. V. Wentworth, Esq.[13] In an indication of their increasing success, this issue also informed readers that the company had moved to larger retail premises at 35 South Audley Street (FIG. 12.11).[14]

In a May 28, 1859 advertisement, Anthony Blackborne promoted himself as a "Connoisseur of lace" and shared that he had "an antique Bridal Veil with real Bruxelles Ground, that was the property of a lady" available for sale (FIG. 12.12).[15] This may signify the company's first entry into the antique lace market for which it would later become well known. A month later, Anthony announced his acquisition of Jane Clarke's (1794–1859) entire stock of lace, noting that "every article is marked in plain figures at prices that will enable purchasers to possess themselves of

antique and modern lace on such terms that can never occur again when this costly collection is distributed," and indicated it would be for sale early the following month.[16] Clarke, who was an important figure in nineteenth-century high-end fashion in England, operated shops on London's Regent Street as well as in Manchester and Liverpool and also exhibited at the Great Exhibition of 1851.[17] Blackborne's advertisement appeared two days after he submitted tender for the purchase of the collection.[18]

So significant was Jane Clarke's collection that on July 2 the *Court Journal* reported on the Blackborne purchase and highlighted that it was particularly rich in lace from the Louis XIV period, English and Irish point laces, and "all that is rare, elegant, and of the best taste." The article further notes that the sale was of great importance to "connoisseurs and manufacturers [who] will avail themselves of the first intimation given of its disposal to secure those specimens best suited to their taste."[19] Among the more noteworthy items was a lace dress purportedly having once belonged to Marie-Antoinette. Originally priced at 800 guineas, the dress was offered at 225 guineas, so the firm could sell it quickly and return to dealing in its "ordinary stock and trade."[20] On July 9, Anthony again advertised his acquisition of the entire Clarke collection, announcing to "the Nobility and the Public" that he had purchased the stock "at an

FIG. 12.7
A. Blackborne & Co. business card, ca. 1897–1901, and Arthur Blackborne business card listed with juries served, after 1912. Ink on paper. The Bowes Museum, County Durham, the Blackborne Lace Collection Archive.

immense sacrifice from the original cost ... [and] that the whole [was] now on Sale without reserve."[21] Blackborne's purchase of Clarke's collection and his expansion into the antique lace trade were noticed at the highest level of British society; in November 1859, the *Court Journal* reported that "Her Royal Highness the Princess Frederick William of Prussia" (Queen Victoria's oldest child, who was, before her marriage, Victoria, Princess Royal) and the Countess Lynar and Count Perponcher visited Blackborne's shop and were "pleased to inspect his antique lace."[22]

These advertisements and notices in the *Court Journal* underscore A. Blackborne & Co.'s reputation as self-described connoisseurs and how the business catered to the market for top-quality antique lace. The specific mention of both connoisseurs and manufacturers highlights the appeal of old lace to collectors for whom it was an acknowledged symbol of discernment and wealth and to those in the industry who might copy or adapt designs for mass production. The firm's growth increased dramatically with the acquisition of Clarke's lace collection, and by 1861, Anthony Blackborne was employing a business manager and nine live-in assistants.[23]

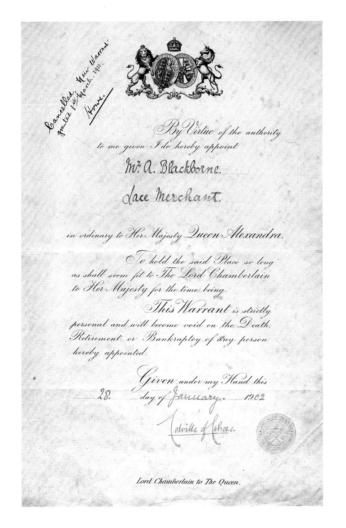

"Laid up in Lavender": Anthony Blackborne and the Antique Lace Trade

The 1852 establishment of A. Blackborne & Co. on South Audley Street followed a period of significant growth in London's antiques trade. Between approximately 1820 and 1840, the number of merchants specializing in the sale of antiques increased dramatically, a change indicative of broader shifting perceptions of historical objects.[24] A burgeoning interest in objects from the sixteenth, seventeenth, and eighteenth centuries in particular marked a departure from more traditional antiquarian collecting practices that privileged the fine and decorative arts of antiquity.[25] Coupled with this growing attention on objects from the more recent past were the expansion of the middle classes and the positioning of objects as cultural capital. For consumers who were not inheritors of significant family wealth, purchasing and owning antiques was a way to signify elite status and wealth.[26] During these decades, the popularity of revival styles in Britain and France that favored the Gothic, Louis XIII, and Louis XIV eras occurred in both fashionable interiors and women's dress. In this commercial context, Anthony Blackborne was able to take advantage of the trend for antique lace that was well established by the late 1850s.

In response to the demand for antique lace that was intended to be worn with or as part of a fashionable nineteenth-century ensemble, the Blackbornes often remodeled their pieces to make them more appealing to customers.[27] The Blackborne Collection includes numerous examples of refashioned historical lace. Although the three-dimensional needle laces of the late seventeenth century were particularly popular for this type of repurposing, a fine example of Flemish ecclesiastical bobbin lace dating to around 1700 featuring angels, orbs, and pierced hearts was altered into a deep bertha collar for the mid- to late nineteenth-century market (FIG. 12.13). The Blackborne Collection also includes examples in which the ground has been reworked, patterns reconfigured, and individual objects made up using fragments of antique lace. This was common practice at the time among lace merchants and women's fashion periodicals advised readers on how to update old lace in their possession to reflect current styles (FIG. 12.14).[28]

Technical expertise and taste were integral to the Blackbornes' success; they operated their business during a period when owning and appreciating historical lace connected people of wealth and status, particularly women of the upper classes.[29] Buying lace was a potentially fraught activity for the inexperienced customer, which necessitated assessing the authenticity and quality of the purchase.[30] To correctly identify antique lace, consumers needed a sophisticated understanding of its many refined techniques, and this appreciation was often rooted in privilege and social status that distinguished the pedigreed elite from the newly wealthy.[31]

Arthur Blackborne's clients relied on him for such assessments of their lace collections, and at the same time, they were one of his sources for antique lace. An article published in 1892 in *The Bazaar, the Exchange and Mart* makes it clear that Blackborne's evaluation services were well respected: "The Best place to have the lace valued is at Blackborne and Co. 35 South Audley Street, they make a small charge for doing it but I can tell you it's real value."[32] While working at Christie's auctioneers, which he advised for over fifty years, Arthur kept notebooks of lace evaluations for probate. These included, for example, the 1893 Douglas Labalmondiere estate.[33] Labalmondiere (1815–1893), who came from a wealthy family, worked for the Metropolitan Police in London as an inspecting superintendent. Among the Labalmondiere items that Arthur listed were

One small square of rose point
One cap trim of old veil with old Mechlin
One half lappet point de Venise
Four half pieces of Genoese
One old Flemish lappet

FIG. 12.9
Franz Xaver Winterhalter, *Duchess of Montpensier (Infanta Luisa Fernanda of Spain)*, 1847. Oil on canvas. Musée national des châteaux de Versailles et de Trianon, Versailles, MV5113.

Arthur used a discreet code of symbols and corresponding letters to make notes about the lace (FIG. 12.15).[34]

In a 1909 article in the *Whitehall Review*, Arthur conveyed how he had acquired some of his precious merchandise and related that, as a prominent laceman, he had entrée into exclusive homes, whose wealthy owners parted with their antique laces, sometimes unwillingly: "The most beautiful laces are to be found in England, hoarded away in old 'country seats,' having been laid up in lavender for generations, so you can imagine these treasures are parted with very reluctantly when bad times come and are bought and sold under the seal of profound secrecy. Many of these valuable specimens were acquired by squires and noblemen years ago or in past ages, traveling abroad on the 'grand tour.'"[35] The time Arthur spent inspecting these objects would have been advantageous for his collecting practice, particularly alongside his travels around Europe, where he could view and purchase different kinds of lace and connect with others involved in the antique lace trade.

A. Blackborne & Co. at International Exhibitions

In addition to their presence over a one-hundred-year period in Mayfair, the Blackbornes participated in several international exhibitions between 1855 and 1910. These events, the largest of which drew tens of millions of visitors to capital cities in Europe, were the most important venues for manufacturers and purveyors of all kinds to display—and sell—their most impressive goods to the public as well as to museums. Exhibition sites often stretched over hundreds of acres and included an array of purpose-built buildings realized on a monumental scale. Here hundreds of exhibitors from around the world mounted monthslong presentations showcasing everything from machinery to grains to textiles. In the second half of the nineteenth century, both hand- and machine-made laces were regularly included in the broader exhibition classification of textiles.[36] A. Blackborne & Co. was one of many lace exhibitors whose names appear in the official catalogues, and the firm presented and sold the finest examples of contemporary and antique handmade lace.

Three years after establishing the London shop, A. Blackborne & Co. exhibited at the 1855 Paris Exposition Universelle, officially called the Exposition Universelle des produits de l'agriculture, de l'industrie, et des beaux-arts. The event was staged on the Champs-Elysées and was visited by over five million people.[37] Blackborne displayed goods inside the Palais de l'Industrie alongside Jane Clarke in class 23, which included

FIG. 12.11 (ABOVE)
The Blackborne shop front, 35 South Audley Street, London, ca. 1905. The Bowes Museum, County Durham, the Blackborne Lace Collection Archive.

FIG. 12.12 (LEFT)
Bonnet veil with applied bobbin-lace pattern on handmade drochel net, Brussels, Batavian Republic, 1790–1810. Linen. The Bowes Museum, County Durham, the Blackborne Lace Collection, 2007.1.1.315.

FIG. 12.13 A,B (OPPOSITE)
Deep bertha collar, cut from an ecclesiastical bobbin-lace flounce, and detail, Flanders, Southern Netherlands, ca. 1700, reworked in the 19th century. Linen. The Bowes Museum, County Durham, the Blackborne Lace Collection, 2007.1.1.85.

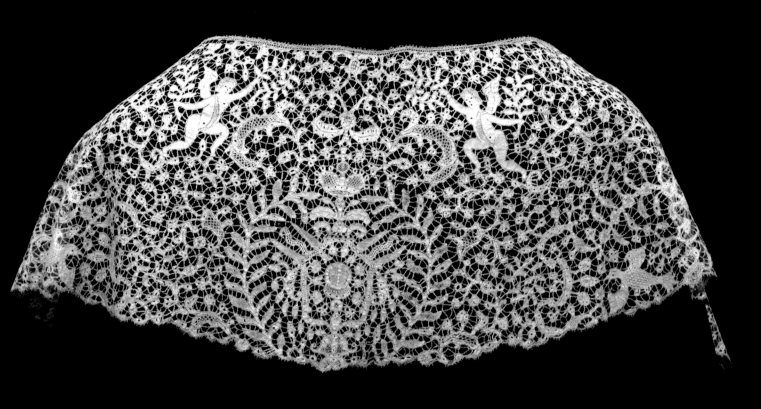
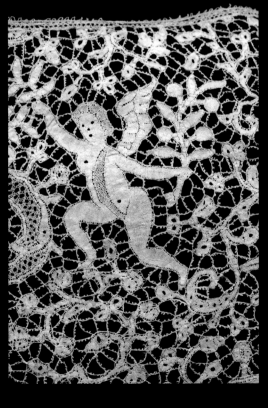

FIG. 12.14
Blackborne shop stock. The
Bowes Museum, County Durham,
the Blackborne Lace Collection.

Annabel Bonnin Talbot

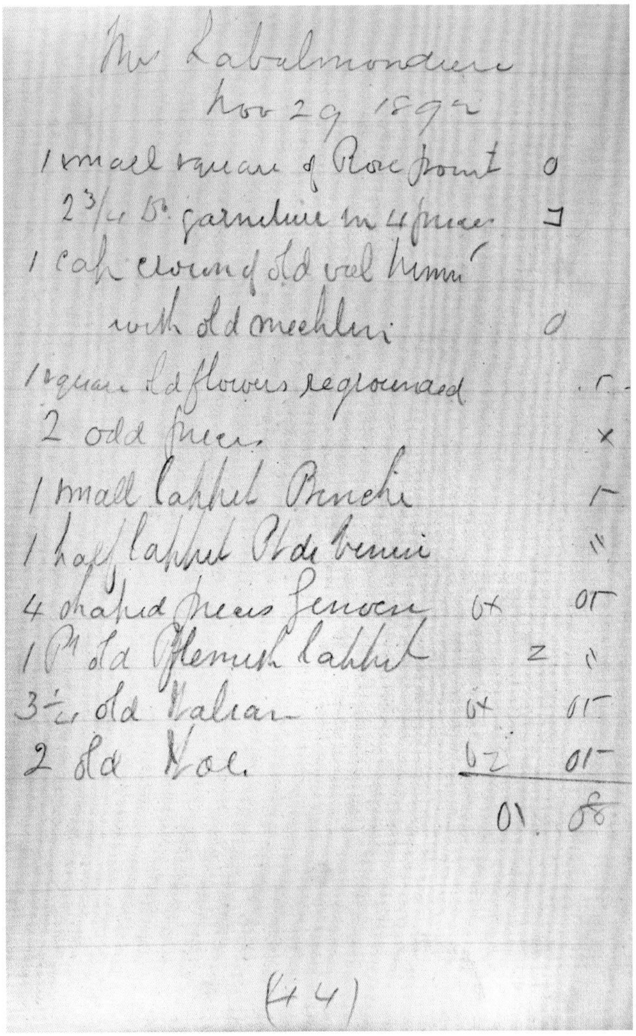

hosiery, carpets, and lace. Both firms would win a Second Class Medal at the event, Blackborne for Irish Guipure of "bonne fabrication" (good manufacture; FIGS. 12.16 AND 12.17).[38] Seven years later, Blackborne would show Irish, English, French, Spanish, and Brussels laces at the 1862 London International Exhibition of Industry and Art, held in South Kensington. The fair attracted 6.2 million visitors, and Blackborne was one of approximately thirty-five exhibitors in the category of tapestry, lace, and embroidery whose displays included lace.[39]

Blackborne again presented a selection of the firm's lace at South Kensington for two of the four London International Exhibitions in the early 1870s. Unlike previous international exhibitions, in which goods were displayed according to nationality of their exhibitor, these annual exhibitions, proposed to take place for ten years (but because of financial losses only ran between 1871 and 1874), were each focused on particular categories of objects and organized accordingly. The first of these events highlighted pottery, woolen and worsted fabrics, educational works, and appliances.[40] Here A. Blackborne & Co. exhibited contemporary English lace in the style of historic lace. An official catalogue published in conjunction with the exhibition notes that its authors aimed to describe in detail the more than eight thousand objects on display. Among those pieces of Blackborne's lace listed was sixteenth-century-style needle lace made by Mrs. Pearson (a well-known figure in the British lace industry) and work by Mrs. Garnham, which was described as bone-point lace inspired by lace from the period of Charles I (r. 1625–49).[41] Other pieces reflected the contemporary fashions of 1871, such as Spanish Chantilly lappets and a Belgium lace flounce and shawl (FIG. 12.18).[42]

In 1874, just two years after joining his father's company, Arthur Blackborne exhibited and judged at the fourth and final International Exhibition at the South Kensington Museum, which was focused on, among other things, lace, civil engineering, and foreign wines.[43] Blackborne was one of more than 170 exhibitors listed in the "Lace" category, which was separate from the "Lace, Embroidery, etc." grouping.[44] By this time, the Blackbornes were firmly placed within the high-end lace trade, consistently demonstrating their credentials and expertise as merchants dealing in desirable world-class luxury goods. In a review of the exhibition in the *Journal of the Society of Arts*, Blackborne's display is noteworthy:

FIG. 12.15
A page from Arthur Blackborne's probate evaluation booklet, entry "Mr. Labalmondiere," 1893. Graphite on paper. The Bowes Museum, County Durham, the Blackborne Lace Collection Archive.

Mr. A. [Arthur] Blackborne of South Audley-street, takes a prominent position. His collection includes valuable examples of the more remarkable varieties. Among these are some superb point de Venise coverlets of the time of Louis Quatorze, early specimens of Alençon (produced shortly after the establishment of that industry), a chalice veil of the same exquisite make of the time of the Empire, and a fine sample of d'Argentan, a lace in some respect akin to that of Alençon, but distinguished by a very bold style of design. Interesting as are these specimens, they are entirely dwarfed by a magnificent "bone point" coverlet, which once belonged to Louis XIV . . . it is two and a quarter yards square and is certainly the most important article in the entire collection.[45]

Of particular interest in this review is that compared to the display at the International Exhibition four years earlier, the wares A. Blackborne & Co. presented in 1874 focused on antique lace, reflecting the fashionable trend that had begun in midcentury. The presentation of lace goods was sanctioned by the involvement of Mrs. Bury Palliser, the author of the *History of Lace* (1865), who served on the selection committee.[46] In an 1874 article published in the *Art-Journal*, Palliser observed, "There is congratulatory recognition of Blackborne's display and retailing of the 'superb coverlet' of Rose Point. It states that the coverlet's provenance is connected to Louis XIV, valued at one thousand guineas." She further commented on Blackborne's display of handmade historical lace: "It has furnished the means of comparing the past with the present and of showing us how superior the simple, graceful designs of former times were to the crowded patterns of our modern productions. It would be well if the manufacturers of the present time would study the works of that of their predecessors."[47] Like many other specialists of historical lace, Mrs. Palliser encouraged the use of early models as a way to improve contemporary design (SEE CHAP. 14).

Another 1874 article also underscored the importance of the exhibit, noting that the "Public as well as those professionally interested in the subject, should have the means of studying the history of the art." Here again, Blackborne's display was mentioned, and the coverlet was highlighted as a key object: "In Mr. Blackborne's curiosities, we have a piece of bone point made by a lady in the time of Charles I., to say nothing of a grand Venetian point quilt, once the property of Louis XIV."[48] These numerous mentions of Blackborne and his exceptional pieces convey his position of authority within the field of lace.

At the 1889 Paris Exposition Universelle, which drew more than thirty million visitors, pieces on display from A. Blackborne & Co. were part of class 34, which included lace, net, embroidery, and trimmings. The catalogue of the British section of the exhibition specifies that Blackborne displayed "lace (real), modern and antique, of every description," a designation that suggests the wider ongoing tensions between "real" (handmade) lace and machine-produced lace (SEE CHAP. 11).[49]

In addition to showcasing A. Blackborne & Co. goods, Arthur also served on the juries of several of the major international design and trade exhibitions, including the one in London in 1874 and the Louisiana Purchase Exposition in Saint Louis, Missouri, in 1904, where he was a member of the organizing committee representing the British government.[50] Britain was particularly well represented at this event, and in this role

FIG. 12.16 (TOP)
Cut-Carrickmacross guipure flounce, Ireland, third quarter of the 19th century. Linen. The Bowes Museum, County Durham, the Blackborne Lace Collection, 2007.1.1.505.

FIG. 12.17 (BOTTOM)
Younghal needle-lace deep dress flounce, Ireland, 1860s. Linen. The Bowes Museum, County Durham, the Blackborne Lace Collection, 2007.1.1.493.

Arthur oversaw the categories of lace and embroidery and was a jury member for the clothing industries.[51] In an April 1904 article titled "Recent Developments in Devonshire Lace Making," Alan S. Cole explained that "The Royal Commission for the St. Louis Exhibition . . . decided to form a small representative collection of British Lace. . . . All have been made from fresh and carefully prepared designs."[52] While he was in the United States in 1904 acting as an agent for the British government, Arthur delivered an invitation-only lecture titled "A History of Lace and Its Uses" at the American Art Galleries in New York.[53] He clearly saw these activities as important for maintaining A. Blackborne & Co.'s visibility in the industry; when interviewed for the *Whitehall Review* in 1909, he recalled, "I was one of the judges of the Franco-British Exhibition, and also judged at the St. Louis Exhibition, America where I have lectured at New York, Newport, St. Louis and elsewhere."[54]

Arthur Blackborne and Historical Lace as Design Inspiration

As articles in the *Court Journal* and on the international exhibitions indicate, historical lace was often cited as an important source of inspiration for manufacturers of lace, especially machine made. From his position as a dealer of antique and new handmade lace, Arthur Blackborne became a leading pedagogical figure who generously shared his knowledge about historical lace, a focus which is evident from his professional activities. This aim contributed to and reflected the increasing recognition of the significance of antique lace in Britain as well as the United States, where the growing demand would lead to further success for the firm.[55] Arthur's collection was the subject of four

FIG. 12.18
Bobbin-lace flounce, Belgium, 19th century, inspired by 17th-century Flemish lace. Cotton. The Bowes Museum, County Durham, the Blackborne Lace Collection, 2007.1.1.485.

Annabel Bonnin Talbot

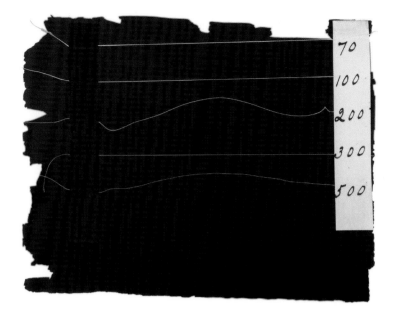

70
100
200
300
500

articles by prominent writer Margaret Jourdain (1876–1951) that appeared in the *Burlington Magazine* in 1904.[56] In her first article, she noted that "the collection of Mr. Blackborne is of greatest interest to the student of lace and design since it is peculiarly rich in rare types of lace."[57]

Arthur was committed to supporting the handmade lace industry, and he saw the company's collection as part of the potential solution: studying historical lace would enlighten manufacturers and designers and thereby raise the quality and desirability of their products. Arthur's understanding of both the manufacture of lace and its market, and his desire to disseminate knowledge about lace production, was—to a large extent—linked to his commercial activities, which would ultimately benefit. He shared his ideas about lace design at a meeting of the Royal Society of Arts in 1908, stating, "The designs of many artists were absolutely useless to the lace-maker because they displayed a lack of knowledge of the requirements of the trade. Fine designs were often made on paper, but it was impossible to interpret them into lace. . . . Good lace designers must have a technical knowledge of the subject." As he explained, "If an artist studied the question [of lace] for six or twelve months, he would be able to turn out good designs, but present-day artists would not devote their energies to the subject unless they were paid for it."[58] Knowledge of historical lace was in its infancy, and the Blackborne study collection was assembled both as a learning opportunity and in anticipation of the book Arthur was planning to write about the history of lace (FIG. 12.19).[59] Unfortunately, Arthur did not publish his book, and his impressive collection at the Bowes Museum along with its archival documents constitute his legacy.

Returning to New York: Arthur Blackborne and the Metropolitan Museum of Art

Blackborne's visit to New York in 1904 following the Louisiana Purchase Exposition was well timed. At the turn of the twentieth century, there was a growing interest in collecting antique lace on the part of wealthy society women, many of whom were connected to the city's museums, including the Metropolitan Museum of Art.[60] Although the museum had been acquiring antique lace since 1879 primarily through donations, their holdings were limited.[61] In 1906, however, the institution published a direct plea to "the ladies of New York" to donate or lend their lace pieces "to make the collection more complete."[62] The response was swift and unprecedented. Over the next five years, the Metropolitan Museum acquired over 2,500 lace objects through both donations and purchases that would ensure the world-class status of its collection.[63] As part of this

FIG. 12.19
Lace threads collected and added to the Blackborne Lace Study Collection. Linen and ink on paper. The Bowes Museum, County Durham, the Blackborne Lace Collection.

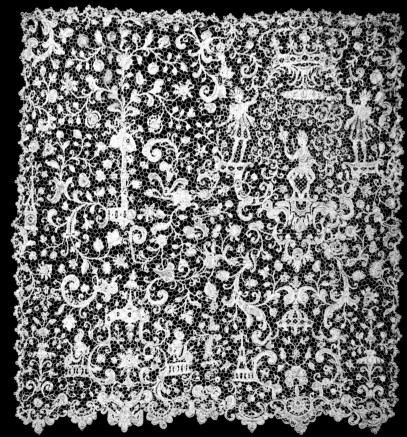

objective, the museum bought six hundred pieces from Arthur Blackborne's collection for $20,000 in 1909.[64]

The *New York Times* heralded this important addition in an article titled "Museum of Art Buys Blackborne Laces," which noted the amount the museum had paid for the collection "Representing All Periods for 400 Years" and indicated that "a number of prominent New Yorkers" had generously contributed funds for the purchase.[65] The article proclaimed that this acquisition "will make the Museum lace collection probably the finest in the world" and singled out the *punto in aria* Judith and Holofernes panel as "the most important in the collection" (SEE INTRODUCTION; FIG. I.16).[66] The museum quickly followed up with an article on this new acquisition in the May 1909 issue of the *Bulletin*, emphasizing that the Blackborne collection was "representative in itself of all periods of lace manufacture" and that "when added to the examples already the property of the Museum, places its collection in the first rank."[67] Further, the objects that were already on display in a dedicated lace gallery and arranged in chronological order afforded "an excellent opportunity for comparative study"—an aspect that would have pleased Blackborne, who was committed to promoting knowledge of historical lace design and techniques.[68] The article also highlighted the Judith and Holofernes piece and featured a full-page detail of one of the thirteen panels.[69] Although the Metropolitan Museum also received noteworthy donations from affluent female patrons during the five-year period that marked a highpoint in its acquisition of antique lace, the Blackborne collection was a significant addition that firmly placed the museum's holdings in the same league with important European institutions.[70]

Arthur continued to sell antique lace and textiles to an enthusiastic US market into the late 1920s. A *New York Times* article dated April 11, 1927, titled "Rare Laces to Be Sold," announced the upcoming auction of Arthur Blackborne's textile collection at the American Galleries and detailed important historical laces in the sale: "there are Brussels, Venetian, points de France, including point d'Alencon and d'Argentan. There are two Brussels point wedding robes, also flounces and borders and bridal veils, with minute semés designs. Point de Venise borders are supplemented by lace made in Venice for the Greek Market."[71] A few days later, the *Times* reported that the auction had realized $21,618 and listed a few of the lace buyers, their purchases, and the substantial amounts they paid for single pieces of lace:

W. Wadsworth—Point de Venise lace border—$1100
W. Wentworth—point d'Alencon flounce—$1100
James Crawford—point de France flounce—$875[72]

Prior to the donation of Arthur Blackborne's collection to the Bowes Museum in 2007, the only British museum to hold Blackborne material was the Victoria and Albert Museum, which had purchased a set of late seventeenth-century needle-lace ecclesiastical vestments in 1870.[73] Thus, the 1906 sale to the Metropolitan Museum of Art represented the largest acquisition by a museum of Blackborne material at the time. The six hundred objects not only added significantly to the museum's lace collection but also demonstrated the renown and reach of the Blackborne firm.

FIG. 12.20 (OPPPOSITE, TOP)
Cutwork and geometric needle-lace man's falling band, England, 1635. Linen. The Bowes Museum, County Durham, the Blackborne Lace Collection, 2007.1.1.28.

FIG.12.21 (OPPPOSITE, BOTTOM)
Point de France needle-lace panel, France, 1690s. Linen. The Bowes Museum, County Durham, the Blackborne Lace Collection, 2007.1.1.197.

Conclusion

The commercial activities of Anthony and Arthur Blackborne and the lace objects now in the collection of the Bowes Museum and other institutions allow unique insight into the handmade lace market from the second half of the nineteenth to the early twentieth century. The workings of the business also illustrate the complex societal relationships between elite consumers and leading tradespeople. The Blackbornes were trusted experts within the handmade lace market, and pieces of the finest nineteenth-century and antique lace passed through their hands (FIGS. 12.20 AND 12.21). Their dealings offer a clear picture of their clientele as well as how the firm positioned itself in this market. The company's diversification into antique lace and its rise in prominence among high-end lacemen interconnect with and reflect changes in fashion and commerce. Arthur Blackborne's comprehensive collection of handmade lace, now held at the Bowes Museum, which was significant even after selling six hundred pieces to the Metropolitan Museum, is an indication of his success as a collector. Although Arthur devoted substantial time and expertise to supporting the European handmade lace industry, it was in deep decline by the end of World War I (SEE CHAPS. 11 AND 15). The Blackborne Collection represents both the history of handmade lace over four hundred years and the business practices of a successful firm during a significant arc of the lace trade in Britain (FIG. 12.22).

FIG. 12.22
Oval furnishing "blonde" bobbin-lace panel or stole with an Art Nouveau design, provenance uncertain, ca. 1900. Silk. The Bowes Museum, County Durham, the Blackborne Lace Collection, 2007.1.1.2306.

Annabel Bonnin Talbot

1 The best known of these texts published in the second half of the 19th and early 20th centuries, which intended to educate readers about the history of lace and aid in identifying and caring for antique lace, include Mrs. Bury Palliser's *History of Lace* (London: S. Low, Son & Marston, 1865) and Ernest Lefébure's *Embroidery and Lace* (London: H. Grevel; Philadelphia: J. B. Lippincott, 1889). See also Elaine Freedgood, "'Fine Fingers': Victorian Handmade Lace and Utopian Consumption," *Victorian Studies* 45, no. 4 (Summer 2003): 625–47.

2 The number of merchants listed in the *Post Office London Directory* under the heading "Lacemen – Retail" decreased steadily between 1854 and 1921. There were more than one hundred lace retailers listed in the 1854 *Post Office London Directory*, fewer than thirty in 1900, and fewer than fifteen in 1921. "Lacemen – Retail" was a category separate from "Lace Manufacturers and Wholesale" and "Gold & Silver Lacemen." Up until 1895, Blackborne was included under the category of "Lacemen – Retail," and from that year the company seems to have been consistently listed under "Lace Manufacturer," although it is clear the firm was still dealing in lace until its closure.

3 Santina M. Levey, *Lace: A History* (Leeds, UK: W. S. Maney & Son; London: Victoria and Albert Museum, 1983).

4 Joanna Hashagen and Santina M. Levey, *Fine & Fashionable: Lace from the Blackborne Collection*, exh. cat. (Barnard Castle, UK: Bowes Museum, 2006). The donation to the Bowes Museum constituted Arthur's entire collection at the time of his death in 1952.

5 Jean Hemingway, email to Annabel Talbot, "Anthony Blackborne—Biographical Notes," May 4, 2011.

6 Hashagen and Levey, *Fine & Fashionable*, 7. In 1854 Anthony Blackborne was listed in the *London Post Office Directory* at 56A South Audley Street. A possible competitor, Mrs. A. C. La Chaier, was at 44 South Audley Street, while several other lace dealers also had premises in upscale shopping streets including Oxford Street, Regent Street, New Bond Street, and nearby Grosvenor Square. Levey, *Lace*, 98.

7 Eva Bright, "A Lace Expert Who Wishes to Found a Mediaeval Guild," *Whitehall Review*, April 1909, 62.

8 The *Court Journal* was a high-society publication that included coverage of activities at court and articles about literature, fine arts, theater, and social news, including one column called "Marriages in High Life."

9 *Court Journal: Gazette of the Fashionable World, Literature, Music, and the Fine Arts*, April 9, 1853, 238.

10 *Court Journal*, June 4, 1853, 375.

11 Hashagen and Levey, *Fine & Fashionable*, 7. Levey refers to lace dealers Daniel Biddle and Samuel Chick, who, during the same period as A. Blackborne & Co., successfully diversified into antique lace to mitigate problematic fluctuations in the market for new laces. Levey, *Lace*, 110–11.

12 *Court Journal*, January 1, 1859, 5.

13 *Court Journal*, March 5, 1859, 169.

14 A. Blackborne & Co. would occupy five locations on or around South Audley Street between 1853 and 1941. From 1853 to 1858, their address was 56A South Audley Street; from 1859 to 1887, they were located at 35 South Audley Street. In 1888 they moved to 51 and 52 Mount Street, which intersects with South Audley Street. In 1889 an advertisement noted that they were located at 70A South Audley Street, and later that year, they moved back to 35 South Audley Street. In late 1905 or 1906, they moved to 39 South Audley Street, where they remained until 1941.

15 *Court Journal*, May 28, 1859, 449.

16 Jean Hemingway, "Millinery and Old Lace: Miss Jane Clarke of Regent Street," *Textile History* 43, no. 2 (November 2012): 218.

Advertisements from this period used the words "antique" and "old" to refer to the type of lace A. Blackborne & Co. sold.

17 For further reading, see ibid. The three main buyers of her collection were Messrs. Grant and Gask (silk merchants on Oxford Street); Madame Elise, court dressmaker (who took over Jane Clarke's business premises after her death in 1859 and acquired some of her stock); and A. Blackborne & Co.

18 *Court Journal*, June 25, 1859, 544.

19 *Court Journal*, July 2, 1859, 563.

20 "Varieties," *Court Journal*, July 2, 1859, 563. The article reiterated Anthony's announcement about the transfer of Clarke's stock to Blackborne and ensured readers that it would soon be available to purchase at low prices. The journal noted that despite a telegram arriving from Germany to secure purchase of the gown, Blackborne gave preference to Lady Spencer, who ultimately bought it (ibid., 583).

21 *Court Journal*, July 9, 1859, 590.

22 *Court Journal*, November 26, 1859, 953.

23 *Census of England and Wales*, 1861, Ancestry (online database), http://www.ancestry.co.uk. A. Blackborne, 35 South Audley Street, London. Profession listed as Laceman.

24 Mark Wilfred Westgarth, "The Emergence of the Antique and Curiosity Dealer 1815–c. 1850: The Commodification of Historical Objects" (PhD diss., University of Southampton, 2006), 2–3. Between 1820 and 1840, the number of antiques dealers in London rose from under 10 to at least 155, a 1,500 percent increase.

25 Ibid., 10–12.

26 Ibid., 99.

27 Blackborne was not the only lace dealer during this period who altered antique lace to be sold, and, since demand outstripped availability, these laces were also remodeled with new grounds and additions. In England Mrs. Charlotte Treadwin, an important figure in the Devonshire lace industry, repaired and replicated lace as part of her lucrative business in contemporary manufacture (SEE CHAP. 11). Palliser, *History of Lace*.

28 Elena Kanagy-Loux, "Addicted to Frills: The Fervour for Antique Lace in New York High Society, 1840–1900," *Journal of Dress History* 4, no. 2 (Summer 2020): 60–63.

29 Clare Browne, *Lace from the Victoria and Albert Museum* (London: Victoria and Albert Museum, 2004), 16. This was also the case for American consumers. SEE CHAP. 13. See also Katie Marie Sabo, "Lace Collecting and Connoisseurship in New York City: 1870–1930," (MA thesis, SUNY Fashion Institute of Technology, 2013); and Kanagy-Loux, "Addicted to Frills."

30 Browne, *Lace from the Victoria and Albert Museum*, 16.

31 Identifying lace was a lost skill during this period. Individuals who had inherited large estates would have access to the family lace as a reference point, but otherwise, the customers were reliant on the lace traders. Kanagy-Loux, "Addicted to Frills," 57–58. This was often the case for dealers who sold antique decorative arts during this period as well. Westgarth, "Emergence of the Antique and Curiosity Dealer," 110–25.

32 "Dress and Fancy Work," *Bazaar, the Exchange and Mart*, July 1892, 19. Seventeen years later, in 1909, Arthur would again remark on his reputation for quality appraisals of lace: "Ladies consult me daily on the genuineness of laces—American ladies are great collectors and buy largely from me." Quoted in Bright, "A Lace Expert," 62.

33 Arthur Blackborne, notes on Labalmondiere lace, "Probate Notebook," 1893, Blackborne Lace Collection Archive, the Bowes Museum, Barnard Castle. Blackborne and Labalmondiere were neighbors on South Audley Street; in January 1868, the latter's address was listed at number 13. *Boyle's Fashionable Court & Country Guide and Town Visiting Directory* (London: 44, New Bond-Street, W., 1868), 240.

34 A. Blackborne's code is the expression "BE THANKFUL – 1, 2, 3, 4, 5, 6, 7, 8, 9, 10." Jean Hemingway solved the code in 2011 by comparing the valuations from Arthur's 1936 exercise book in the archive to the lappet collection labels.

35 Quoted in Bright, "A Lace Expert," 62. Other high-level lace dealers relied on this kind of access; the same *Court Journal* article that reported on Anthony Blackborne's purchase of the Clarke collection also noted, "The opportunities which Miss Clarke had of collecting from private sources, and purchasing when no other house would have been intrusted [sic] with the secret of the sale of rare family lace, enabled her complete her wishes [sic], and, consequently, in her choice stock, which has now come into the hands of her executors, there is a collection which is the most unique in the world, and it may be truly said that this is a fine-art cabinet of lace." *Court Journal*, July 2, 1859, 563.

36 In 1862, for example, the listing for A. Blackborne & Co. in the International Exhibition catalogue was included under "Tapestry, Lace, and Embroidery." *The International Exhibition of 1862: The Illustrated Catalogue of the Industrial Department*, vol. 1, *British Division* (London: Clay, Son, & Taylor; Clowes & Son; Petter & Galpin; and Spottiswoode & Co., 1862), 63. In 1889 Blackborne appeared in the category comprising "Lace, Net, Embroidery and Trimmings," which was part of the larger group "Textile Fabrics." *Paris Universal Exhibition, 1889: Official Catalogue of the British Section* (London: William Clowes & Sons, 1889), 37.

37 John E. Findling and Kimberly D. Pelle, ed., *Encyclopedia of World's Fairs and Expositions* (Jefferson, NC: McFarland, 2008), 26.

38 Hemingway, "Millinery and Old Lace," 200–222; and *Exposition Universelle de 1855, Rapports du Jury Mixte International, publiés sous la Direction de S.A.I le Prince Napoléon, Président de la Commission Impériale, Tome II* (Paris: Imprimerie Impériale, 1856), 438.

39 Findling and Pelle, *Encyclopedia of World's Fairs*, 30; and *The International Exhibition of 1862*, 63–74.

40 Findling and Pelle, *Encyclopedia of World's Fairs*, 44–45.

41 *London International Exhibition of 1871, Official Catalogue, Fine Arts Department, Under Revision* (London: J. M. Johnson & Sons, 1871), 177–78. The association of lacemaking with elite women that began in the late 16th and early 17th centuries with the emergence of needle and bobbin laces was reinforced in the second half of the 19th century. Considered a ladylike pursuit, lacemaking attested to leisure time and the creation of a product outside of the commercial market. Freedgood, "'Fine Fingers,'" 633–36.

42 *London International Exhibition of 1871*, 177–78.

43 Findling and Pelle, *Encyclopedia of World's Fairs*, 44–45.

44 *London International Exhibition of 1874, Official Catalogue, Under Revision* (London: J. M. Johnson & Sons, 1874), 119–29. Among the manufacturers included in the "Lace, Embroidery, etc." category was Iklé Frères of Switzerland, which showed "Embroidery by Machinery" (117) on muslin, cambric, linen, and silk (SEE CHAP. 14).

45 "Lace at the International Exhibition," *Journal of the Society of Arts* 22, no. 1120 (May 1874): 602–3.

46 Palliser, *History of Lace*. Originally published in 1865, the book was revised and enlarged in 1902 by Margaret Jourdain and Alice Dryden (repr., London: Sampson Low, Marston, Low and Searle 1910). *London International Exhibition of 1874*, xiv.

47 Mrs. Bury Palliser, "The International Exhibition, 1874," *Art-Journal* 36 (1874): 173.

48 "Lace, Ancient and Modern," *Victoria Magazine* 23 (May–October 1874): 145.

49 *Paris Universal Exhibition, 1889*, 37.

50 Hashagen and Levey, *Fine & Fashionable*, 7–8; and Bright, "A Lace Expert," 62. HRH the Prince of Wales was president of the Royal Commission for the Saint Louis International Exhibition. Sir Isidore

Spielmann, ed., *Royal Commission St. Louis International Exhibition* (London: Hudson and Kerns, 1904). In addition to 1874 and 1904, Arthur served on the juries of exhibitions in 1902, 1908, 1910, 1911, and 1912. Hashagen and Levey, *Fine & Fashionable*, 8.

51 *Report of His Majesty's Commissioners for the International Exhibition, Saint Louis, 1904* (London: William Clowes & Sons, 1904), 199–200.

52 Alan S. Cole, "Recent Developments in Devonshire Lace Making," *Journal of the Society of Arts* 52, no. 2680 (April 1904): 431. Alan Cole's father was Sir Henry Cole, who was instrumental in organizing London's Great Exhibition of 1851 and was the director of the South Kensington Museum, now the Victoria and Albert Museum, from 1857 to 1873.

53 "Among the Artists," *American Art News* 3, no. 53 (1904): 2.

54 Bright, "A Lace Expert," 62.

55 Ibid.

56 Margaret Jourdain wrote extensively on English furniture and interior decoration from the Elizabethan period through the eighteenth century. Margaret Jourdain, "Lace Collection of Mr. Arthur Blackborne: Part I," *Burlington Magazine* 5 (1904): 557–69; Margaret Jourdain, "Lace Collection of Mr. Arthur Blackborne: Part II, Later Punto in Aria," *Burlington Magazine* 6 (1904): 18–22; Margaret Jourdain, "Lace Collection of Mr. Arthur Blackborne: Part III, Rose Point," *Burlington Magazine* 6 (1904): 123–31; Margaret Jourdain, "Lace Collection of Mr. Arthur Blackborne: Part IV, Milanese Laces," *Burlington Magazine* 6 (1904): 384–92. Prior to these four pieces—and just three months after the *Burlington Magazine* first appeared—Jourdain published an article on Mabel Chermside's lace collection. "Margaret Jourdain and the *Burlington Magazine*," *Burlington Magazine Index Blog*, September 24, 2016, https://burlingtonindex.wordpress.com/2016/09/24/margaret-jourdain-and-the-burlington-magazine/.

57 Jourdain, "Lace Collection of Mr. Arthur Blackborne: Part I," 557.

58 A. Blackborne, in response to the paper read by Miss Ismonger, "Lace as a Modern Industry," *Journal of the Royal Society of Arts* 56, no. 2897 (May 1908): 715.

59 Hashagen and Levey, *Fine & Fashionable*, 8.

60 Sabo, "Lace Collecting and Connoisseurship," 17. Other American museums including the Smithsonian Institution were also acquiring large amounts of lace during this period. In 1907 Mrs. James W. Pinchot organized a donation of approximately 500 pieces of antique European lace to the museum. "Lace Collection," Smithsonian Institution, May 2022, https://www.si.edu/spotlight/lace-collection.

61 Prior to 1906, the Maccallum Collection of about 200 pieces of lace and the Astor Collection of about 60 pieces, bequests made in 1879 and 1888, respectively, had been the two largest acquisitions in the museum's lace collection of 700 objects. Sabo, "Lace Collecting and Connoisseurship," 1.

62 Ibid.

63 Ibid., 1–2.

64 The Blackborne collection was valued at $40,000 to $50,000 by the American Art Galleries when it was offered at auction in December 1908. After the collection failed to make its reserve price of $20,000, the Metropolitan Museum of Art decided to raise the money for its purchase.

65 "Museum of Art Buys Blackborne Laces," *New York Times*, May 11, 1909.

66 Ibid. The article also makes clear the importance of this piece for the study of lace techniques, noting that it would be of interest "to the novice in laces as well as to experts for the wonder of its construction."

67 Wilhelm R. Valentiner, "The Blackborne Collection of Lace," *Metropolitan Museum of Art Bulletin* 4, no. 5 (May 1909): 82.

Appointed in 1907, Valentiner was the first curator of the department of decorative arts at the Metropolitan Museum. The *Annual Report* of the Metropolitan Museum of Art for 1909 also noted the "very important acquisition in the Textile Department [of] the Blackborne collection of lace, one of the best private collections." *Metropolitan Museum of Art: Fortieth Annual Report; 1909* (New York, 1910), 32.

68 The *New York Times* article related that "the collection is on exhibition in Gallery E8, where it will remain for several months." "Museum of Art Buys Blackborne Laces." The Lace Room had opened at the museum that same year in order to display the lace collection. Kanagy-Loux, "Addicted to Frills," 54. Many museums established in the second half of the nineteenth century served as links between art and industry. Institutions including the South Kensington Museum in London (today the Victoria and Albert Museum), the Imperial Royal Austrian Museum of Art and Industry in Vienna (today the Museum für angewandte Kunst [Museum of Applied Arts], the Industry and Trade Museum in St. Gallen (today the Textilmuseum), and the Metropolitan Museum of Art were founded with the financial support of industrialists who encouraged—and expected—manufacturers to avail themselves of museum objects that offered exemplary design models.

69 Valentiner, "Blackborne Collection," 82, fig. 3.

70 For example, the *New York Times* reported on gifts of lace in July 1908 ("Art Needlework: New Acquisitions by Metropolitan Museum Show Many Rare Examples," *New York Times*, July 9, 1908); the *New York Tribune* announced a substantial donation by the English collector Magdalena Nuttall in November 1908 ("Gifts to the Museum: Painting from Mrs. Sage—Mrs. Nuttall Gives Collection of Laces," *New York Tribune*, November 7, 1908); and the same newspaper highlighted the bequest of lace to the Metropolitan Museum by Henrietta Seligman in 1910 ("Lace Treasures: Museum of Art Enriched by Mrs. Seligman's Bequest," *New York Tribune*, June 12, 1910).

71 "Rare Laces to Be Sold. Arthur Blackborne Collection to Be Auctioned Thursday," *New York Times*, April 11, 1927.

72 "Lace and Textiles Sold: Arthur Blackborne Collection Brings $21,618," *New York Times*, April 16, 1927. The value of $1,100 in 1927 is today approximately $17,000 or $18,000.

73 Blackborne had lent the pieces to the museum in 1868, and the purchase was made two years later. See accession numbers 743-1870, 744-1870, 745-1870, 746-1870. At the time, the museum was still known as the South Kensington Museum. *The Sixteenth Report of the Science and Art Department of the Committee of Council on Education, with Appendix: Presented to Both Houses of Parliament by Command of Her Majesty* (London: G. E. Eyre & W. Spottiswoode, 1869), 324.

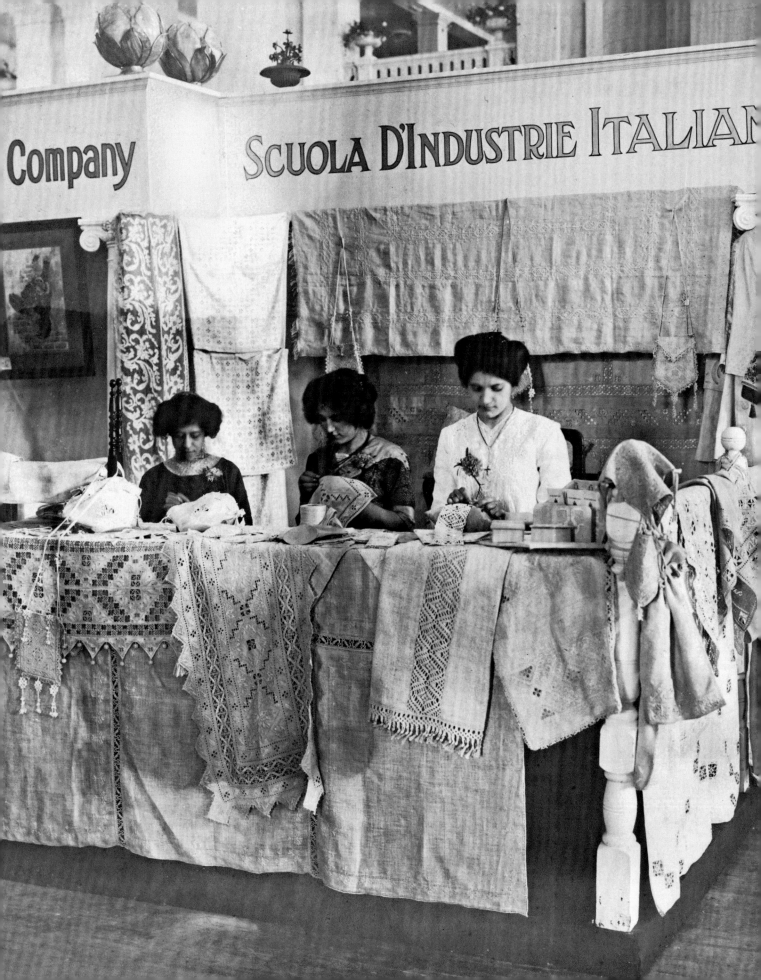

13 Italy to New York: Making Historic Textiles Modern at the Scuola d'Industrie Italiane

Emily Zilber

O PERATING BETWEEN 1905 AND 1927, the Scuola d'Industrie Italiane employed recent immigrants from Italy to New York City to create reproduction lace and embroidery, drawing on a variety of historical sources for their designs.[1] Many of these sources came from the personal collections of the Scuola's founders and included printed patterns published in sixteenth- and seventeenth-century Italy, historic textile collections, and contemporary examples of reproduction textiles manufactured by women in Italian lace and embroidery schools. This brief overview of the Scuola's history presents a look at the influences and personalities that prompted its founding; the scope of the school's vision, operations, and output; its eventual closure; and its broader legacy.

The Italian lace revival of the early 1870s was a direct result of Italy's incorporation as a modern nation-state. Artists and designers worked to localize historic Italian aesthetics, especially textile patterns, in the hopes of such designs becoming touchstones in the search for national identity; this was supported by the mass reprinting of historic lace and embroidery manuals, part of a broader initiative to increase accessibility to design manuals and photographs of antique objects for creative workers.[2] Renaissance and Baroque aesthetics were reframed so as to be quintessentially Italian, rather than the common heritage of Western civilization. For example, the 1872 reopening of the women's lace workshop on the island of Burano sought to reclaim Italian design and production from pan-European appropriation (FIG. 13.1). The Scuola Merletti di Burano specialized in needle and bobbin lace produced using Baroque patterns and enjoyed a decades-long trend of patronage by elite Italian women, a trend that mirrored similar backing of women's handicraft schools and workshops in greater Europe and the United States and occurred alongside the general growth of state and private schools for the study of design and the decorative arts (FIG. 13.2).[3] Among its production, lacemakers at Burano created direct copies of items in the private collections of its founding members and benefactresses as well as pieces from other well-known collections. Workers created copies of the historic lace collections of Pope Clement

FIG. 13.1
Scuola Merletti di Burano (Burano Lace School) poster, Venice, late 19th century. Ink on paper. Fondazione Musei Civici di Venezia - Fondazione Andriana Marcello.

292   Emily Zilber

XIII (1693–1769) and Crown Princess Margherita of Savoy (1851–1926), who became queen in 1878. Since both of these figureheads served as personifications of the ideal nation for nineteenth-century reformers, Burano-made copies of these objects had more meaning due to the provenance of their source material.⁴ By 1886 Burano was one of twenty-six government-subsidized schools across the peninsula that taught women to produce salable reproduction lace by hand using historical sources. Middle- and upper-class Italian consumers purchased these fashionable textiles.⁵

New textile workshops and organizations emerged alongside the revival of older institutions (FIG. 13.3). The Società Cooperativa Aemilia Ars was a design collective founded in Bologna in 1898 by the architect Alfonso Rubbiani, who modeled the group after the English Arts and Crafts movement. While the lace workshop did use contemporary designs—largely reflecting Stile Liberty, the Italian variant of Art Nouveau—its primary work was the mastery of sixteenth- and seventeenth-century *reticella* and *punto in aria* techniques (FIGS. 13.4 AND 13.5).⁶ As the textile scholar Elisa Ricci wrote in her introduction to a 1929 volume on Aemilia Ars lace and embroidery, the women of the lace workshop were encouraged to

FIG. 13.2 (ABOVE)

Henry Bacon, *Venice Lace Makers*, 1905. Watercolor on paper. The Museum of Fine Arts, Boston, Given in memory of the artist by his wife Mrs. Frederick L. Eldridge, 38.77.

FIG. 13.3 (RIGHT)

Teachers and pupils of the Sacred Heart School, where some of the lacemakers and embroiderers from the Società Cooperativa Aemilia Ars started, Bologna, Italy, ca. 1916. Private collection.

FIG. 13.4 (ABOVE)
Società Cooperativa Aemilia Ars,
punto in aria needle-lace trimmed
apron, Bologna, Italy, 1906–10. Linen.
Cooper Hewitt, Smithsonian National
Design Museum, Gift of Richard C.
Greenleaf Esq. in memory of his
mother, Adeline Emma Greenleaf,
1950-121-1.

FIG. 13.5 (RIGHT)
Società Cooperativa Aemilia Ars,
design for apron lace, Bologna, Italy,
early 20th century. Graphite on paper.
Cooper Hewitt, Smithsonian National
Design Museum, Gift of Anna Ferrarini,
1983-18-1.

familiarize themselves with textiles and patterns from "our best time, preparing the ground for a renaissance in the Italian decorative arts."[7] By 1908 both the Burano and Aemilia Ars workshops were affiliated with a larger cooperative formed in 1903: La Società Cooperativa Anonima per Azioni delle Industrie Femminili Italiane (IFI).[8] The IFI's first president was Countess Cora Ann Slocomb di Brazzà Savorgnan (1862–1944), an American married to an Italian who had published her own English-language guide to the lace-laden Italian Women's Pavilion at the 1893 World's Columbian Exposition in Chicago—a book familiar to the Scuola's founders—and in 1894 founded a lace school in Friuli (FIG. 13.6).[9] Under her direction, the IFI was to financially integrate, distribute, and market the work of handicraft schools. The group comprised thirty-two regional committees and associated enterprises with the express patriotic goal of giving "authentic" handicrafts a "certain stamp of national unity and sound solidarity."[10]

It seems fitting, then, that the Scuola's primary founders—Gino Speranza (1872–1927), the Italian American lawyer and immigration advocate, and Florence Colgate (1873–1951), daughter of the founder of the Colgate Company, who would marry Speranza in 1909—met and began planning the organization while on separate vacations to Italy in 1905.[11] Colgate was already a patron of the arts. She had no Italian ancestry herself but like many women of her class held a deep interest in Italian visual and literary culture.[12] Beginning in 1903, Colgate was a member of the Cooperative Society for Italian Female Industries, an IFI subsidiary marketing Italian textiles to a US clientele. Speranza and Colgate toured textile and handicraft schools in Florence, Rome, and Venice and lamented that such "talent should be lost upon box factories and sweatshops" should these women immigrate. They developed a plan "under the spell of the blue Italian sky" to open a school for lacemaking and textiles in New York City in collaboration with Carolina Amari (1866–1942), a philanthropist, textile collector, and scholar who ran the IFI's workshops in Rome.[13] Amari was, in Speranza's estimation, the "greatest expert of art embroidery in Italy."[14] She was quickly recruited as the Scuola's first artistic and educational director in the hopes of keeping "prominent Italian women" interested and involved despite the school's geographic separation from its closest predecessors (FIGS. 13.7 AND 13.8).[15] Once stateside, Colgate brought Marian Hague (1874–1971) into early planning. Hague, an American connoisseur and collector of lace and embroidery, was connected to the formation of the textile collections at both the Metropolitan Museum of Art and the Cooper Hewitt Museum and, in the late 1930s, donated samples of Italian lace (FIGS. 13.9 AND 13.10). Her

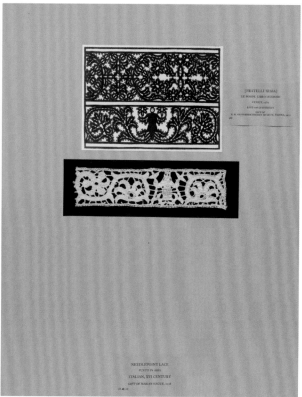

presence at the helm linked the Scuola to relevant museum collections and contemporary collectors of textiles and print designs in New York and across the United States.[16]

The Scuola opened in the fall of 1905 in two rooms on an upper floor of the Richmond Hill Settlement House in New York. Situated in the midst of Greenwich Village's large Italian immigrant community, it boasted a student body of six girls between the ages of fifteen and seventeen (FIG. 13.11). By the end of the first year of operation, women up to age twenty-one were accepted as students; the Scuola never employed more than twenty-five individuals at one time, inclusive of instructors.[17] Richmond Hill was involved only with the operations of the Scuola and not its product and was discussed as a landlord with a "suitable work room" rather than as an ideological partner.[18] Unlike in Italy, where

FIG. 13.10

Bobbin-lace sample book,
Pescocostanzo, Italy, 20th century.
Linen mounted on silk-covered pages.
Cooper Hewitt, Smithsonian National
Design Museum, Gift of Marian Hague,
1939-28-1-a.

there was government support for the IFI schools, the Scuola had to operate like other settlement house arts programs, seeking public support from the larger landscape of charitable giving.[19] Articles written early in the life of the Scuola convey an idealized atmosphere: the workroom was "comfortable and well warmed, clean, light and cheerful" with "childish chattering unchecked," all overseen by a daily instructor who "understands the girls' natures as well as their language."[20] A weekly exhibition of student work was displayed in the workrooms to remind the girls that their work was indeed art.[21] Illustrations from a 1907 article in the *Craftsman* further bolster this romantic vision.[22] Italian women "who might be sisters" gathered around a "cheery grate fire or near the big windows" in a "bright, homelike atmosphere, not stipulated by the labor commission." An "Italian instinct for creating the beautiful" found "full play, and full pay" at the Scuola (**FIGS. 13.12 AND 13.13**).[23] Scuola clientele purchased goods at small sales hosted by individuals in private homes, museum exhibitions, and, between 1908 and 1922, a small shop and gallery near Bryant Park (**FIG. 13.14**).[24] Sales were held in coastal resort towns in New England and major cities including Philadelphia and Milwaukee.[25] Prices for work produced by the Scuola were high; at the upper end, the Regina pillow retailed for $75 (approximately $2,100

"CHATTERING IN ITALIAN AS FAST AS THEIR FINGERS CAN FLY."

"TEEMING WITH SWARTHY BABIES AND THEIR GAILY ATTIRED MOTHERS."

FIG. 13.11 (ABOVE)

Group of Scuola d'Industrie Italiane workers, ca. 1910. Manuscripts and Archives Division, New York Public Library, MssCol 2844, Gino Speranza papers, Gino Speranza papers / III. Scuola d'Industrie Italiane.

FIG. 13.12 (LEFT)

Florence Scovel Shinn, *Chattering in Italian as Fast as Their Fingers Can Fly*, from Elisabeth R. Irwin, "Story of a Transplanted Industry: The Lace Workers in the Italian Quarter of New York," *Craftsman* 12 (1907): 405. Ink on paper. HathiTrust.org, University of Virginia.

FIG. 13.13 (RIGHT)

Florence Scovel Shinn, *Teeming with Swarthy Babies and Their Gaily Attired Mothers*, from Elisabeth R. Irwin, "Story of a Transplanted Industry: The Lace Workers in the Italian Quarter of New York," *Craftsman* 12 (1907): 407. Ink on paper. HathiTrust.org, University of Virginia.

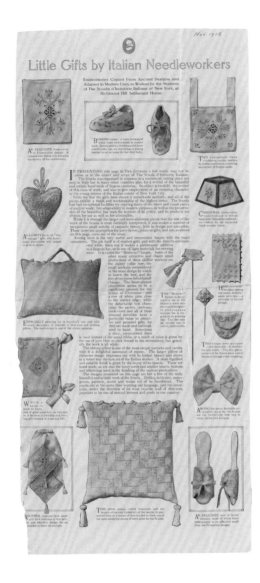

today; FIG. 13.15).[26] Nonetheless, sales of the Scuola's goods grossed over $1,700 in the first year, and wealthy, socially minded patrons invited Amari to establish similar schools in nearby locations such as Newark and New Haven.[27] As Amari saw it, the items produced by the Scuola filled a need for beauty that existed because US textiles were incapable of meeting that demand. Instead, the development, expression, and application of "artistic taste" at the Scuola was inherently connected to a worker's ability to learn from Italian sources, including the patterns, laces, and embroideries Amari brought with her on her journey from Italy to New York in 1905 (FIGS. 13.16–21).[28] The Scuola also ordered works from abroad for the duration of the school's existence; Speranza, Colgate, Hague, and Amari saw the acquisition of a large in-house collection as being integral to the school's mission.[29] Speranza noted in a 1908 letter that the Scuola held "examples of rare and or special artistic embroidery and laces loaned by friends and supporters and in other ways endeavor[ed] to create an artistic appreciation of a demand for a beautiful and too much neglected form of art" (FIGS. 13.22 AND 13.23).[30] In 1909 he embarked on a fundraising campaign expressly concerning the exhibition of this "patrimony," asking major players in the world of museums and philanthropy, including Andrew Carnegie, J. P. Morgan, and John D. Rockefeller, for financial support. Asking each for $5,000, Speranza's aim was to facilitate the purchase and display of "more frequent exhibitions of ancient and modern needle art, some few examples of which it owns and many rare and interesting examples of which it could secure as loans from friends of the *Scuola* and collectors . . . we should like to awaken interest in smaller places throughout the country, especially those communities where a certain civic and art spirit is manifest through the erection of libraries and small museums."[31]

Active interest in the work of the Scuola from overseas continued during its first years of operation, and in 1908 Amari reported to the board that Queen Margherita of Italy, acting patron of the IFI, had also agreed to be "patroness" of the Scuola.[32] Amari's frequent travel to Italy further cemented these connections, and she brought Scuola work to Italy as early as 1906 for L'Esposizione Internazionale del Sempione in Milan, a world's fair that received over four million visitors.[33] That display featured Scuola-made examples of the previously mentioned Regina pillow, a pattern based on historic precedents that had first been produced by IFI workshops for Queen Margherita. Amari brought an IFI Regina to New York on her initial trip to establish the Scuola in 1905. Based on that object, an American copy of an Italian pillow was ultimately displayed in Italy as the original work of the Scuola just one year later. The Scuola benefited from Amari's travel, which was actively covered by the press.[34] However, Amari's engagement with the Scuola was short-lived; by 1909 she

had returned to Italy in order to design the curriculum for a lacemaking school in Sicily. Amari was also highly sought after to develop schools with regionally focused specialties in Casalguidi (*punto riccio*), San Bartolo (net work), and Calabria.

Around the time of Amari's departure, Colgate wrote a draft pamphlet that attempted to more firmly argue for the Scuola using Arts and Crafts rhetoric. The text seems to be equal parts William Morris (1834–1896) and Karl Marx (1818–1883), perhaps as a way to increase ties to other settlement house craft schools.[35] Suggesting that in the "battle between the Machine and the Hand wherein the latter feebly struggled to save from the mighty invader at least the citadel of those industries which are truly the little brothers of the great arts," many immigrants have found themselves alienated from their labor, and forced to "sell-out" life and health, thereby squandering native artistic skill developed and perfected over generations. Saved from total annihilation only by reformers with an eye for craft, the "'joy-of-labor' philosophers and poets," Colgate proposes that handwork came to be "a sort of privileged occupation for a quasi-leisure class of men and women possessed of special opportunities for their work at home, in art colonies or in studio life." She championed the work as inherently modern, arguing that modernity was defined "in the sense that it should represent no hardship of the laborer; that the revival of an ancient craft should not mean a revival of ancient inadequate wages."[36]

The first strains of internal upheaval at the Scuola occurred shortly after, in 1910, when the board reorganized the daily management staff of the school and hired less

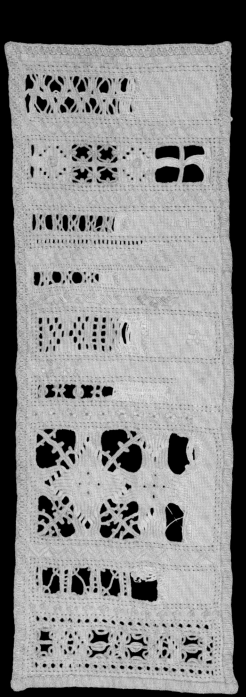

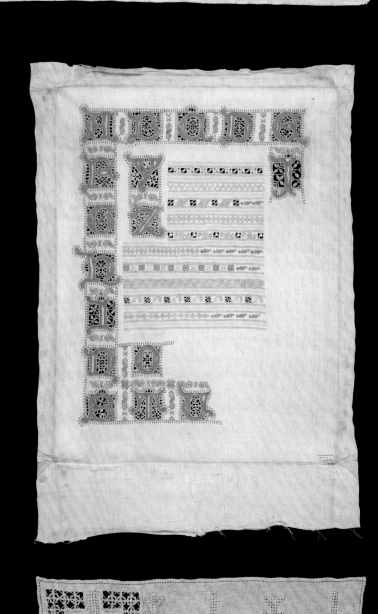

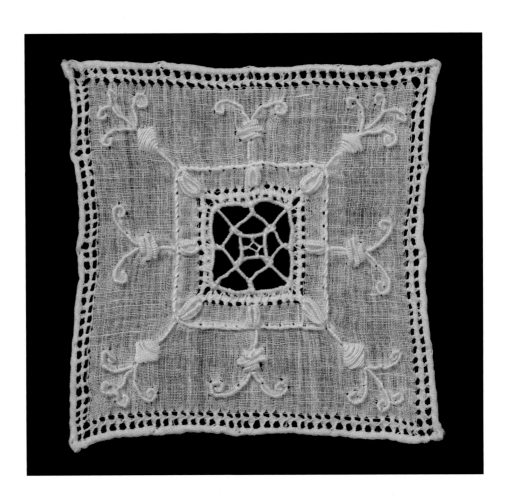

FIG. 13.20 (OPPOSITE, TOP)
Scuola d'Industrie Italiane, cutwork and embroidery cover, New York, ca. 1910. Linen. Cooper-Hewitt, Smithsonian National Design Museum, Bequest of Marian Hague, 1971-50-241.

FIG. 13.21 (OPPOSITE, BOTTOM)
Scuola d'Industrie Italiane, cutwork and embroidery cover, New York, early 20th century. Linen. Cooper-Hewitt, Smithsonian National Design Museum, Gift of Mrs. Gino Speranza, 1942-47-2.

FIG. 13.22 (ABOVE)
Scuola d'Industrie Italiane, cutwork and embroidery pin cushion cover, New York, early 20th century. Linen. Cooper-Hewitt, Smithsonian National Design Museum, Gift of Mrs. Gino Speranza, 1942.47.9.

costly workshop instructors.[37] An internal report of May 1911 assessed that there was insufficient worker supervision and a "lack of business method" in the daily administration of the school, with time cards so inaccurate that they were of "no practical use," all because students had grown accustomed to the atmosphere of "happy family life" without the pressure of working against a clock and chafed under regulatory suggestions from Scuola leadership.[38] Discontent continued despite pricing and production reforms, and in response, Hague offered her own funds to continue the Scuola, hosting sales at her home so that exhibitions for outside groups could be mounted at the Scuola gallery to help defray space rental costs.[39] Helen Pupke, a charity worker and founding member of the board, stated that she had entirely lost interest in the work because of the cost of the Scuola's goods.[40] While Colgate and Hague amassed an increasingly authentic body of design sources, a schism grew between board members more concerned about providing social welfare and those focused on building a functioning business. The Scuola's precarious financial situation almost forced its closure several times. The monthly operating cost was $600, but cash and orders for the month of April 1912 amounted to only $700, despite showing at a high-profile, heavily attended exhibition at the Women's

Industry Conference, where they expected significant sales. Speranza blamed the situation on the instructors' poor daily management of the workshops; subsequently, the board asked teachers to conduct fewer classes, fired three workers deemed "unable to learn," and sold goods at drastically reduced prices.[41] In contrast to strong statements made in 1908 declaring the Scuola to be fiscally self-supporting, by 1910 it was clear that idealism in design, workshop practice, and pricing weren't compatible with a coherent business model.[42]

At the start of World War I, a shortage of linen—among other larger political concerns—further reduced the Scuola's ability to produce and sell.[43] In 1915 Sarah Gore Flint, a curator of textiles at the Museum of Fine Arts, Boston, wrote to Colgate that a Christmas sale featuring Scuola work at the Society of Arts and Crafts was successful but required a great deal more work on the part of the gallerists to make sales; according to Flint, "People were much more particular, comparing articles and prices, before they made up their minds."[44] During the war, Colgate was largely absent from New York as she traveled with Speranza, who gave up his legal practice for a journalism career beginning

FIG. 13.23

Half of a needle-lace chalice cover, Italy, early 17th century. Linen. Cooper-Hewitt, Smithsonian National Design Museum, Estate of Mrs. Florence Colgate Speranza, Museum purchase from Au Panier Fleuri Fund, 1951-130-1.

in 1912.[45] The Scuola never recovered financially after the war, and few idealistic mission statements or design ideas survive in archives dating after 1914. Instead, bills, correspondence, sale arrangements, and practical items related to the day-to-day sales of goods fill the folders. The board paid such attention to Scuola finances with good reason: for the year 1921 the school posted a deficit of approximately $2,900, and throughout most of 1922 it operated at losses of $275 per month.[46] Colgate's written analysis of the situation suggested that the blame lay with "slackened and undisciplined production, lack of supervision in the workroom, insufficient advertising, and lack of initiative and vision on the part of the manager."[47] Attempts to re-interest Amari as an active participant in the work of the Scuola, and in potential expansion, do not seem to have been successful.

By 1922 attempts to hire a new manager at a lower salary had failed, which was made painfully clear through letters between Speranza and qualified applicants who balked once they learned of the compensation offered. Colgate became the full-time manager of the workrooms, and subsequently workers were cut, construction was stymied, and prices were reduced until all remaining stock was liquidated through the showroom of the Guild of Needle and Bobbin Crafts in New York.[48] Nonetheless, popular interest in the Scuola was still present during this period, evidenced by the school's participation in exhibitions at the Architectural League of New York and the Detroit Society of Arts and Crafts, both in 1923, at which the Scuola exhibited large-scale, multipiece altar sets (FIGS. 13.24-26). Customers and retailers still complained about the objects' prices but never their quality. One vendor wrote, "I am returning by express the goods sent to me as I consider the prices too high for selling to my customers. The work is beautifully done, but I have sold linens equally as good for less money, and even then my customers have considered the price high."[49] The final items of inventory produced by the school are listed on the last datable piece of archival material from January 21, 1927.[50]

The attraction of lace and embroidery outlasted the Scuola, with market prices for such textiles remaining high well into the 1940s. Even so, more traditional laces ceased to be highly fashionable for interiors and dress in the second decade of the twentieth century, considered by some to be hopelessly stodgy, over-ornamental, and incapable of reflecting modernity. Hazel Adler indirectly problematized the Scuola and similar organizations in *The New Interior: Modern Decoration for the Modern Home* (1916): "No textile renaissance, however, which is dependent for its existence upon whole or even partial handwork can ever be far-reaching in its results. . . . The great body of our manufactures of decorative textiles seem still laboring in the Dark Ages, continuing to copy fifteenth and sixteenth century designs that are a far cry to the modern spirit."[51] By 1916 many would have seen Scuola production as lacking innovation and incapable of revitalizing a stolid industry. Despite such harsh sentiments, those who organized and oversaw the work of the Scuola viewed themselves as participants in a transformative institution that was partaking in the development of a unique tradition, one simultaneously steeped in history *and* representative of the promise of the new: the new Italian nation, new levels of aesthetic taste and appreciation in cities like New York, and new opportunities for Italian immigrants.

The Italianization of both people and things makes explicit why collecting was so important in both the Italian and American contexts. Objects were acquired not only

for their beauty, economic value, and use as source material, but also for their ability to serve as material metonyms for larger faith in the authenticity of specific values. It therefore follows that collecting played an important role in grounding the Scuola as it adapted an Italian model to changing American surroundings. Board members were not only authority figures with links to collecting museums—perhaps the ultimate legitimating institutions for culture and citizenship in the late nineteenth and early twentieth centuries—but also reliant on these institutions collecting the works they cared about to validate the Scuola's own contribution. The status of Italian art and design in the museum canon, as well as the social function of the institution with regard to education and assimilation, provided support for the school.

Throughout the Scuola's twenty-two-year existence, this emphasis on authenticity never completely connected with the actual functioning of the organization. This conflict manifested itself in internal tensions: Was the Scuola a school or business? Did it make marketable, accessible products or museum pieces? Was it Italian or American, or both? This uniquely American translation of an Italian textile tradition ultimately exercised a decontextualized nationalistic faith in the value of historic sources and tradition while adapting to the standards of American expectations.

FIG. 13.24
Women working at a Scuola d'Industrie Italiane booth, ca. 1905–10. Cooper-Hewitt, Smithsonian National Design Museum, Scuola d'Industrie Italiane Folder.

FIG. 13.25 (ABOVE)

"Work of the Fiske Weaves: The Guild of Needle and Bobbin Crafts and the Scuola d'Industrie Italiane," plate 4 in "A Century of New York Needlework and Decorative Fabrics, 1820–1920," from *Bulletin of the Needle and Bobbin Club*, 1944. Antonio Ratti Textile Center and Reference Library, The Metropolitan Museum of Art, New York 156.2 N28.

FIG. 13.26 (RIGHT)

Scuola d'Industrie Italiane, cutwork and embroidery chalice veil from an altar set, New York, ca. 1920. Linen. Cooper Hewitt, Smithsonian National Design Museum, Gift of Scuola d'Industrie Italiane in New York through Florence Colgate Speranza, 1943-41-1.a-d.

1   The revival of textile handicrafts in the United States in the late 19th and early 20th centuries is addressed in a wide body of literature that discusses the renewed interest in disappearing craft techniques, as well as attempts to redevelop those that had already vanished. This revival also incorporated the patterns and techniques of new Americans—European immigrants—with differing traditions. Organizations were formed to save these handicraft skills while attempting to incorporate their possessors fully into American life, largely affiliated with settlement houses. Diana Greenwold's excellent PhD thesis on the topic, which uses the Scuola as a case study, looks specifically at sites in New York and Boston, including well-known examples like the Paul Revere Pottery. Diana Jocelyn Greenwold, "Crafting New Citizens: Art and Handicraft in New York and Boston Settlement Houses, 1900–1945" (PhD diss., University of California, Berkeley, 2016).

2   The publication series that encompasses most of these reprinted pattern books was coordinated by Ferdinando Ongania and titled *Raccolta di opere antiche sui disegni dei merletti di Venezia* (Collection of historic works on the design of Venetian lace [Venice: Ongania, 1872–1910]). The Metropolitan Museum of Art has a complete holding of Ongania lace design reprints and displayed them alongside actual 16th- and 17th-century copies. Margaret Harrington Daniels, "Early Pattern Books for Lace and Embroidery, Parts 1 and 2," *Bulletin of the Needle and Bobbin Club* 33, no. 3 (March 1938): 70–73.

3   This is detailed in Ilaria Porciani, ed., *Le donne a scuola: L'educazione femminile nell'Italia dell'Ottocento* (Siena, Italy: Palazzo Pubblico, 1987).

4   Elisa Ricci, "Revival of Needlework in Italy," *International Studio: An Illustrated Magazine of Fine and Applied Art* 61 (1914): 202.

5   The popularity of historically inspired patterns extended to the use of actual antique lace and embroideries in contemporary garments, a practice recommended to readers of Italian periodicals. An article in *Margherita*, a fashionable women's periodical named after the queen, noted that to attend an exhibition of Italian decorative arts in 1884, Margherita wore a gown entirely covered in lace that contained "all the ingenious ways antique lace can be used in modern style without making even a single cut to it." Quoted in Grazietta Butazzi, "The Abuse of the Renaissance: Elegance and Revival in Post-Unification Italy," in *Reviving the Renaissance: The Use and Abuse of the Past in Nineteenth-Century Art and Decoration*, ed. Rosanna Pavoni, trans. Adrian Belton (Cambridge: Cambridge University Press, 1997), 158–60.

6   Carla Bernardini and Marta Forlai, *Industriartistica bolognese: Aemilia Ars; Luoghi, materiali, fonti* (Milan: Silvana Editoriale, 2003), 60.

7   Their best-known project utilized workers to duplicate in lace every page in the 1591 design manual *Libro di lavorieri* (Workbook) by Aurelio Passerotti using both reprints and a period copy of the text. The manual was printed in Bologna, the hometown of the Aemilia Ars, and the use of this particular text served as an attempt to localize the history of textile design. The book contained thirty-three pages of patterns copied first onto paper using graphs and then translated into lace. The adaptation process is well documented, with the comprehensive collection of student designs featuring the coats of arms of famous Renaissance families currently housed in the Museo Davia Bargellini in Bologna. *Merletti e ricami della Aemilia Ars, con introduzione di Elisa Ricci* (Milan: Bestetti e Tumminelli, 1929), 1–4.

8   For primary source documents published by the IFI, see *Catalogo cooperativa nazionale industrie femminili Italiane Milan* (Milan: Pilade Rocco, 1906) and Industrie Femminili Italiane, Cooperativa Nazionale, Roma, *Le Industrie femminili Italiane, cooperativa Nazionale: Sede centrale via Marco Minghetti, Roma* (Milan: Pilade Rocco, 1906).

9   Countess Cora Ann Slocomb di Brazzà Savorgnan, *A Guide to New and Old Lace in Italy Exhibited at Chicago in 1893* (Chicago: W. B. Conkey, 1893).

10   Ricci, "Revival of Needlework in Italy," 205.

11   The son of a celebrated linguistics professor, Speranza was a second-generation Italian American who served as legal counsel to New York's Italian consulate general before founding two social service agencies—the Society for the Protection of Italian Immigrants (1901) and the Investigation Bureau for Italian Immigrants (1906)—that received direct support from the Italian government. Speranza also worked with the National Italian Labor Exchange, the Labor Information Office for Italians, the Prison Association of New York, and the Committee on Crime and Immigration of the American Institute of Law and Criminology. Speranza was concerned throughout his career with issues related to the Italian American immigrant experience and published texts on European immigration to and assimilation in the United States. More information on Speranza can be found in the Speranza papers at the New York Public Library, of which there are forty-five boxes of papers and notebooks, as well as in Speranza's own writings on race and immigration. Notably, Florence Colgate Speranza edited two volumes of her husband's diary that were published in 1941, fourteen years after his death in 1927. Gino Speranza, *The Diary of Gino Speranza, Italy 1915–1919*, ed. Florence Colgate Speranza, vols. 1–2 (New York: Columbia University Press, 1941).

12   For a history of the Colgate family, see Truman Abbe and Hubert Abbe Howson, *Robert Colgate, the Immigrant: A Genealogy of the New York Colgates and Some Associated Lines* (New Haven, CT: Tuttle, Morehouse & Taylor Co., 1941).

13   Elisabeth A. Irwin, "Story of a Transplanted Industry: Lace Workers of the Italian Quarter of New York," *Craftsman* 12 (1907): 405–6.

14   Gino Speranza to unidentified recipient, November 12, 1908, Gino Speranza Papers, box 14, folder 1908, New York Public Library (hereafter abbreviated as Speranza Papers).

15   Amari's "grand ambition" for the workshop was as follows: "mi per questa *Scuola* che spero avra la stessa fotuna pronta e prospera della consorelle Italiane. Nel recente mio giro nel Belgio in Inghilterra e Francia ho visto bensi un gran risveglio delle industrie artistiche ma null ache possa stare a paragone delle nostre dal punto di arte. Spero percio che col tempo questo primo tentative possa prendere la larghezza e l'importanza di una vera e propria *Scuola* professionale." (I hope that this school will have the same ready fortune and prosper like its Italian sisters. During my recent visits in Belgium and in England and France, I have seen well a great revival of the artistic industries, but it is not possible to stand them in comparison to ours from the point of artistic vision. I hope, therefore, that with time this first tentative venture will be able to hold the largesse and importance of a true and real professional school.) Carolina Amari to unidentified recipient (Gino Speranza), September 16, 1905, Speranza Papers, box 14, folder 1905.

16   A good overview of the collecting of Italian laces by American women, in both its historic and its reproduction forms, can be seen in Hague's heavily researched and engaging book in five parts, cowritten with Frances Morris, a textile curator at the Metropolitan Museum of Art, and titled *Antique Laces of American Collectors* (New York: Publication for the Needle and Bobbin Club by William Helbrun, 1920–26).

17   George E. Pozetta, "Immigrants and Craft Arts: *Scuola d'Industrie Italiane*," in *The Italian Immigrant Woman in North America*, ed. Betty Boyd Caroli et al. (Toronto: Multicultural History Society of Ontario, 1978), 144.

18   Elizabeth S. Williams to Florence Colgate Speranza, August 17, 1905, Speranza Papers, box 14, folder 1905.

19   Nominal assistance from groups in both Italy and the United States in the form of advisory board members was crucial to legitimating the project. Foreign interest proved to keep American investors and supporters involved in the work of the Scuola. As early as the fall of 1905, the following organizations pledged their support: Count

Raybandi Massiglia (the consul general of Italy in New York), the Italian Emigration Department of Rome, the Charity Organization Society, the Children's Aid Society, the Italian Chamber of Commerce, and the Italian Benevolent Institute, along with Speranza's own Society for Italian Immigrants. Speranza spent much of the period surrounding the Scuola's opening organizing a board of directors, which primarily included those associated with the settlement movement rather than those from the Italian interest groups who had pledged support or the Italian neighborhoods in the vicinity of the school. Funding was also gathered from organizations and individuals outside of groups explicitly involved with the plight of Italian immigrants. Speranza solicited the largest names in New York City concerned with general philanthropy and social reform in the period to raise the $20,000 needed to begin hiring and manufacture, sending letters on February 28, 1906, to John DeWitt Warner, George Foster Peabody, Charles T. Fairchild, Robert DeForest, Laurena T. Abbott, Algernon S. Frissel, Robert Hoe, and Oswald Garrison Villard. Speranza Papers, box 14, folder 1906.

20 Eva Lovett, "Italian Lace School in New York; Second Notice," *International Studio* 29 (1906): xiv.

21 Ibid., xiv–xv.

22 Irwin, "Story of a Transplanted Industry," 404.

23 Ibid., 405–6.

24 Scuola minutes detail the opening of the shop and gallery. Minutes, Scuola d'Industrie Italiane, September 8, 1908, Speranza Papers, box 14, folder 1908.

25 Minutes, Scuola d'Industrie Italiane, February 17, 1908, Speranza Papers, box 14, folder 1908; and Minutes, Scuola d'Industrie Italiane, July 13, 1909, Speranza Papers, box 14, folder 1909.

26 "Notice of Sale," *New York Times*, June 24, 1908.

27 Carolina Amari, contribution to the *Bolletino mensile della società cooperativa nazionale le industrie femminili italiane "la nationale" compagnia d'assicurazioni*, n.p.

28 Scuola d'Industrie Italiane certificate of incorporation, n.d. [1906], Speranza Papers, box 14, folder 1906.

29 For example, the expenses for January 1908 note that $54.50 was spent on duties on laces and linens ordered from abroad. Expense report, January 1908, Speranza Papers, box 14, folder 1908.

30 Gino Speranza to Howard F. Stratton, Esq., director of the School of Industrial Art in Philadelphia, November 12, 1908, Speranza Papers, box 14, folder 1908.

31 Gino Speranza to J. P. Morgan, Andrew Carnegie, and John Rockefeller, April 17, 1909, Speranza Papers, box 14, folder 1909.

32 Minutes, Scuola d'Industrie Italiane, June 1908, Speranza Papers, box 14, folder 1908.

33 The IFI produced a catalogue for the exhibition, which included the goods exhibited by all its member groups, including the Scuola. This text is also useful as a record of the IFI's exhibition, which was unfortunately destroyed by fire. Writing anonymously, the authors of the catalogue note: "We then present two particular schools that merit particular mention, centers of Italian women's work constituted outside Italy, which in diverse ways are in direct relation to the feminine industries: The school at Bucharest, cared for by a Romanian gentleman together with an Italian gentleman who helped in establishing, and the school of New York founded with the help of Miss Colgate by Miss Amari for the daughters of Italian immigrants." *Catalogo cooperativa nazionale industrie femminili Italiane*, 8–10. An extended catalogue from the same year noted that the New York school of the IFI made numerous works for display following Italian designs and models. Industrie Femminili Italiane, Cooperativa Nazionale, Roma, *Le industrie femminili Italiane*.

34 "Lace Expert Here: Miss Amari Arrives on the Cretic to Aid Italian Women," *New York Times*, June 14, 1908, 6; and "School for Immigrants: Effort to Revive Lace Industry Employing Many Italian Women," *New York Times*, June 24, 1908, 5.

35 Typewritten sheet by Florence Colgate, 1908, Speranza Papers, box 14, folder 1908.

36 Ibid.

37 Minutes, Scuola d'Industrie Italiane, February 17, 1910, Speranza Papers, box 14, folder 1910.

38 Second report on piece work, May 11, 1911, Speranza Papers, box 14, folder 1911.

39 Minutes, Scuola d'Industrie Italiane, July 25, 1912, Speranza Papers, box 14, folder 1912.

40 In her resignation letter, she stated, "I regret that no way has been found to lessen the great difference between the actual wages received by the workers and the final selling prices of the goods." Pupke to the Scuola d'Industrie Italiane board, February 12, 1912, Speranza Papers, box 14, folder 1912.

41 Minutes, Scuola d'Industrie Italiane, April 18, 1912, Speranza Papers, box 14, folder 1912.

42 Typewritten sheet by Florence Colgate. Ultimately, what allowed the school to continue was a reduction in daily expenses coupled with internal restructuring of staff; while the prices charged for goods were never formally reduced, merely placed periodically on sale, such markdowns were remarkably frequent. One such markdown sale is noted in Minutes, Scuola d'Industrie Italiane, April 18, 1912, Speranza Papers, box 14, folder 1912.

43 Pozetta, "Immigrants and Craft Arts," 148.

44 Sarah Gore Flint to Florence Colgate, February 12, 1915, Speranza Papers, box 14, folder 1915.

45 Speranza went to Italy in 1915 as a features correspondent for the *New York Evening Post* and the *Outlook* and later worked as an Italian correspondent for the *Atlantic Monthly* and special assistant to Ambassador Thomas Nelson Page at the United States Embassy in Rome. Francesca Pitaro, *Gino Speranza Papers*, online finding aid (June 1989), 2, https://www.nypl.org/sites/default/files/archivalcollections/pdf/speranza.pdf.

46 At the February 10, 1921, meeting a proposal was discussed to carry the goods of Hamilton House at the gallery. It was decided not to pursue a collaboration, because "this might further reduce the sales of the *Scuola* which already show a falling off, especially as the goods of Hamilton House would be mostly of a more inexpensive kind than the *Scuola* goods." Costs were met not through sales, but rather through new loans, the cashing of liberty bonds, and the cutting of staff and stock. Minutes, Scuola d'Industrie Italiane, February 10, 1921, Speranza Papers, box 14, folder 1921.

47 Minutes, Scuola d'Industrie Italiane, May 12, 1921, Speranza Papers, box 14, folder 1921.

48 In 1922 the staff of the guild showroom fielded a request from the *Ladies Home Journal* for the inclusion of Scuola needlework in an upcoming article. They also sent customers to the Scuola, referring parties interested in purchasing lace to the school if the piece in question might exist in the Scuola's stock. Minutes, Scuola d'Industrie Italiane, January 12, 1922, Speranza Papers, box 14, folder 1922; Florent Gritman, Guild of Needle and Bobbin Crafts Shop, to Florence Colgate, October 17, 1922, Speranza Papers, box 14, folder 1922.

49 Unnamed proprietor of the Forget Me Not Shop in Williamstown, Massachusetts, to Florence Colgate, September 20, 1922, Speranza Papers, box 14, folder 1922.

50 Stock inventory, Scuola d'Industrie Italiane, January 21, 1927, Speranza Papers, box 14, folder 1927. After this date, there is no further mention of the Scuola in contemporary periodicals or in the remaining papers in the archive, and one can reasonably consider the Scuola completely dissolved.

51 Hazel H. Adler, *The New Interior: Modern Decoration for the Modern Home* (New York: Century, 1916), 14–15.

14 A Source of Inspiration: The Leopold Iklé Collection in St. Gallen

Anne Wanner-JeanRichard and Ilona Kos

I N 1947 THE INFLUENTIAL AUSTRIAN ECONOMIST Joseph Alois Schumpeter (1883–1950) defined innovation as "the doing of new things or the doing of things that are already being done in a new way."[1] Although Schumpeter was referring broadly to economic development and cycles, his comment can be applied to lace production in St. Gallen in the late nineteenth and early twentieth centuries. At the height of its success at the turn of the century, the creation of "St. Gallen lace," which is actually a type of embroidery, was often based on historical models. Production of this so-called chemical lace, which is sometimes also referred to as "guipure," stretches back to the second half of the nineteenth century in eastern Switzerland where, at the time, it was customary for embroidery firms to build collections of historical textiles that served as models for new designs. In the late nineteenth century, St. Gallen–based embroidery manufacturer Leopold Iklé (1838–1922) sought out embroidery and lace from the sixteenth to the eighteenth century that would provide suitable sources of inspiration for the goods produced by his family-owned company, Iklé Frères. His professional interest in these textiles developed into a great passion, and Iklé created one of the world's most important collections of lace. In 1904 he gifted a significant portion of this collection to the Industry and Trade Museum in his hometown of St. Gallen, which is today the Textilmuseum. It was only much later, in 2014, that the museum acquired a set of pattern books from Iklé Frères. Some of the machine-produced embroidery samples compiled within make visual reference to the handmade versions in the same style.

The study presented here is an introduction to Leopold Iklé, his firm, and his collection. The invention of machine-embroidered imitation lace is retraced, shedding light on the importance of historical textiles as a source of inspiration for contemporary design.

Leopold Iklé and Iklé Frères

Leopold Iklé, the eldest of fifteen children, was born to a Jewish merchant family in Hamburg on May 9, 1838 (FIG. 14.1).[2] His parents, Moses Iklé (1803/1804–1864) and Sara (née Jonas, 1816–1886) traded in embroidery and lace, which provided a modest livelihood for the large family.[3] Despite these humble circumstances, Leopold later recalled a happy childhood with deeply harmonious family relations.[4] Extracts from his memoirs, which he recorded around the age of seventy-five, have been preserved for us through a commemorative volume that Adolf Fäh (1858–1932), a close friend of the then-elderly Leopold and a St. Gallen Abbey librarian, had composed.[5] Fäh reports that Leopold, at the age of fifteen, having completed secondary school, was interested in technical matters and would have liked to become a mechanic. Instead, he was obliged to follow his father's wishes and entered the family business in 1855, when he accompanied Moses for

FIG. 14.1
Leopold Iklé, ca. 1900–22.
Monika Frey-Iklé.

the first time on a business trip to purchase goods in St. Gallen. From then on, Leopold regularly traveled with his father to St. Gallen, until age nineteen, when he set off on his own for the first time. Several purchasing trips to Saxony, Germany, and France followed. Leopold was also sent to Denmark, Sweden, and Russia in order to take customer orders.[6] In 1861 his father acquired the right of establishment in St. Gallen for his two eldest sons (Leopold and Joseph) so that the young men could set up a business. The eastern Swiss town near Lake Constance became Leopold's new home, but his brother Joseph returned to Hamburg in the early 1870s, where he continued to run the parent company together with his mother and brother Julius (1842–1896) after Moses's death. The younger brother Adolf (1852–1923) entered the St. Gallen business around the same time and would be Leopold's valued partner for many years.[7]

In the nineteenth century, St. Gallen was a center of embroidery manufacture in Switzerland. Following the end of the American Civil War in 1865, machine-based embroidery, still in its infancy, experienced a boom. Exceptionally large orders came to Swiss exporters from North America.[8] Many merchants shifted to manufacturing, and the Iklé brothers set up their factory around the early 1870s under the name Iklé Frères. Leopold was one of eight factory owners to found the Industrial Association in St. Gallen on December 21, 1875.[9] Fäh names three early factory locations of the firm, all situated west of the city of St. Gallen in what was then the municipality of Straubenzell.[10] It was there in 1879 or 1880 that the Iklé Frères company set up the first shuttle embroidery machine in eastern Switzerland. The factory soon had to be expanded, and another factory was built between 1906 and 1907—an imposing, modern building based on plans by Swiss architect Wendelin Heene (1855–1913; FIG. 14.2). The building still stands today and is acknowledged as a unique example of factory architecture in Switzerland because of its internal functional structure.[11]

In addition to the businesses in Hamburg and St. Gallen, the Iklé Frères company opened other branches in various cities. Leopold's brother Ernst (1848–1936) ran a branch in Paris from 1871 onward, and Julius, who initially had remained in Hamburg, later joined him there. One acquaintance, Simon Israel, set up an office in Berlin. More Iklé Frères branches were opened in Vienna, Plauen, Germany, and New York. Initially, Julius Iklé was also responsible for business in New York, which his son Carl Felix Iklé (1879–1963) would eventually take over. Another nephew of Leopold Iklé, John Jacoby (1869–1953), worked as a young man in his uncle's company in St. Gallen and then opened a branch in London in 1895, which later continued under the name of John Jacoby-Iklé Ltd.[12]

FIG. 14.2
Iklé Frères factory, St. Gallen, Switzerland. Textilland Ostschweiz.

In the late nineteenth and early twentieth centuries, the production and distribution of machine embroidery from St. Gallen was a lucrative business despite the fact that it was subject to constant economic fluctuations.[13] The profitability of the Iklé Frères company is evident in the many new factory buildings and branches established. This favorable situation is also clear from Leopold's memoirs, which show that at an advanced age, he owned a villa in Rorschach on Lake Constance, where he spent his summers, in addition to his townhouse in St. Gallen.[14] Thanks to this success, the brothers were able to lead relatively prosperous lives, even after settling their father's debts following his death.[15] This wealth, in turn, also provided the basis for Leopold's collecting activities.

At the beginning of the twentieth century, Leopold retired from the family business, leaving his brother Adolf in charge. Adolf ran the St. Gallen business until 1923, and after his death, his son-in-law Felix German (1878–1943) took over the company.[16] At the time, the St. Gallen embroidery industry was already in the midst of an economic crisis that had begun shortly before the outbreak of World War I and continued throughout the 1920s.[17] In 1929 Iklé Frères merged with Reichenbach & Cie., a St. Gallen firm that also had subsidiaries in New York, Berlin, Paris, and Plauen. Iklé Frères was removed from the Swiss Commercial Register in 1931, but Fritz Iklé (1877–1946), Leopold's youngest son, remained registered until 1938.[18]

Leopold had married Selma Kugelmann from Kassel (1849–1906) in 1868 and went on to have three sons with her.[19] Their marriage was dissolved in 1902, though nothing is known of the circumstances. Correspondence from the time allows us to infer that Fritz was employed at the company until the mid-1930s, all while maintaining relations with his uncle Ernst in Paris.[20] Leopold died on February 26, 1922, at the age of eighty-four.[21] He devoted the last twenty years of his life to his collections and to the study of historical textiles.

Leopold Iklé as a Collector

"In 1888 or somewhat later, I was in Paris and struggling to find new patterns. Searching for inspiration in museums and shops with my brother Ernst, I saw a large cupboard with pieces of passementerie that had been collected by a Parisian, Mr. B., and donated to the city. 'You should build a collection like that of embroidery,' I said to myself."[22] This impulse apparently set off Leopold Iklé's activity as a collector. At the beginning, he acquired only inexpensive patterns, which he stored in small boxes and wooden frames. Then, after some years, closer to the end of the century, Iklé began to purchase selected, expensive collector's pieces.[23]

In 1904 Iklé gifted a considerable portion of his collection to the Textilmuseum St. Gallen. The museum's annual reports indicate that Leopold announced the donation as early as 1901 and that from 1902, he was entrusted with the task of arranging a room in the museum for pieces from his collection. Together with Emil Wild (1856–1923), the museum's director from 1882 to 1923, Iklé wrote an accompanying catalogue, printed in 1908, that lists all 1,467 objects.[24] In the introduction, Iklé explains his initial intentions for the collection, writing, "The present collection of embroidery and lace was originally created with the intention of serving as models for the industry. As time passed, historical

interest asserted itself along with the commercial aspect. Yet in view of the variety in the industry and changes in fashion, all good models are useful sooner or later."[25]

Embroidery, including items of clothing and household textiles, represented more than half the donated collection. Among the catalogue entries, there are 153 that describe openwork and net lace (FIG. 14.3) and another 474 that name lace from the sixteenth to the nineteenth century (FIGS. 14.4 AND 14.5; SEE FIG. 3.1).[26] Iklé's donation added more than six hundred handmade pieces of lace to the Textilmuseum, approximately forty of which are included in the *Threads of Power* exhibition and this publication.

Collecting had become a passion for Leopold, who continued to acquire historical textiles even after his generous donation to the Textilmuseum. He established a second collection, which was displayed in his houses in St. Gallen and Rorschach in the early twentieth century.[27] By then, Iklé had already become friends with Fäh, with whom he regularly met and corresponded.[28] The letters show that Fäh and Iklé engaged in intensive discussions on textile-related and historical issues. Together they studied books on such topics, and Fäh was sometimes invited to look at Iklé's latest pieces.[29] They collaborated to create a large-format volume of plates in which Iklé presented the developmental history of lace using objects from his collection.[30] In this 1919 publication, Leopold traces the origin of needle lace back to linen embroidery and to the various kinds of embroidery and looped stitching, which are worked "on to the canvas as if floating."[31]

After Iklé's death, his second collection was sold off at auction in 1923.[32] The auction catalogue comprises 835 lots, which include 268 "laces and lace-like fabric[s]."[33] A large number of the laces and embroidery for sale were acquired by Iklé's nephew John Jacoby, who, like his uncle, was a passionate collector and lace expert.[34] Following Jacoby's death, his wife, Edith, sold the collection to the St. Gallen Merchants' Association, and it, too, eventually reached the Textilmuseum and was accessioned in 1954. A second nephew of Leopold, Carl Felix "Charles" Iklé, who worked in New York, was also active as a collector, and much of his collection eventually entered the holdings of the Metropolitan

FIG. 14.3 (ABOVE)
Openwork border, Italy, second quarter of the 16th century. Linen. Textilmuseum St. Gallen, Gift of Leopold Iklé, 1904, 00832.

FIG. 14.4 (BELOW)
Bobbin-lace trimming, southern or western Europe, second half of the 16th century. Gold thread with silk core. Textilmuseum St. Gallen, Gift of Leopold Iklé, 1904, 00215.1-2.

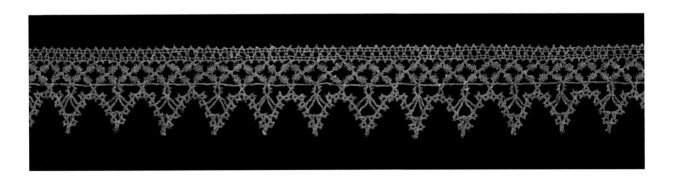

Museum of Art.[35] Iklé's brother Ernst was particularly interested in the development of machine embroidery, and in 1932, he published *La broderie mécanique*, which serves as an important source for the following section.[36]

The History of Embroidery in Eastern Switzerland

The discussion that follows is primarily devoted to regional and historical developments in lace and embroidery in eastern Switzerland, both of which were of great importance for the production of the Iklé Frères company. The mechanization of embroidery turned St. Gallen into the world leader in this sector throughout the nineteenth century.

From the Middle Ages onward, textile processing played an increasingly important role in eastern Switzerland. Early production of linen fabric in this region was later followed by the production of soft, lightweight cottons, which were sold on international markets. This prosperous trade led to proto-industrialization in the sense that many inhabitants earned their living entirely or in part from textile production, long before the first machines were invented. In the eighteenth century, the decoration of cotton fabrics by means of tambour-frame embroidery (a form of chain-stitch embroidery carried out

FIG. 14.5
Bobbin-lace border, Italy, second
quarter of the 17th century. Linen.
Textilmuseum St. Gallen, Gift of
Leopold Iklé, 1904, 00041. Cat. 31.

with a small hook) arose, and from this point on, embroidery was an important occupation for women, as lacemaking was elsewhere in Europe.[37]

The production of true needle and bobbin lace never played an important part in the textile industries in Switzerland. However, eastern Swiss embroiderers created delicate openwork effects in their pieces, as could frequently be seen in fashion around 1800. One example is a preserved baptismal blanket with chain-stitch embellishment (FIG. 14.6). As a decorative stitch, the recently introduced tambour-work technique appears in this embroidery with the finest pulled thread work. In these decorations, the loose fabric was pulled together in regular groupings, thus not detaching any threads. The technique may have been inspired by work from Saxony, where *point de Saxe* work had developed to a high level of perfection in the mid-eighteenth century. Similar techniques emerged at the same time in other areas, for example in Ayr in Scotland, Bourbonnais in France, and Dinant in what is now Belgium.[38]

Hand embroidery remained an important branch of the Swiss textile trade well into the twentieth century, and the embroiderers' repertoires expanded to include needlework, such as satin-stitch embroidery. The embroiderers of eastern Switzerland also became known in the mid-nineteenth century for their handmade lace inserts, such

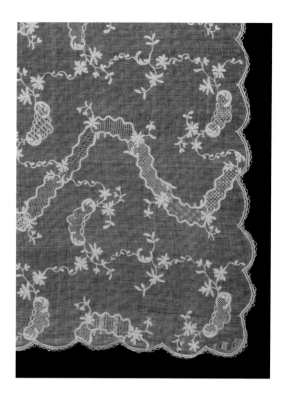

as on handkerchiefs, where they would cut small sections out of the base fabric and fill the gaps with needle lace (FIG. 14.7). It appears that embroiderers found inspiration for this technique in French lace; in many cases, Alençon lace of the second half of the eighteenth century features similar decorative forms.[39] Near the end of the century, however, the importance of hand embroidery waned as the machine-made embroidery industry advanced.

One of the first embroidery machines was developed as early as 1828 by Josué Heilmann (1796–1848) in Mulhouse, France (FIG. 14.8). The principle of this machine was based on a multiplication of the simple process of embroidering by hand. The embroiderer operated the machine using a pantograph, a mechanical instrument that transferred the template onto the embroidery. As the operator moved the pantograph, the embroidery base was pierced by numerous needles arranged in rows, each of which guided an embroidery thread. St. Gallen resident Franz Mange (1776–1846) acquired several embroidery machines in autumn 1829 from the André Koechlin & Cie. machine factory in Mulhouse. These recently introduced machines were not yet robust and accurate enough for industrial production. Nevertheless, Mange remained convinced of their advantages and hired mechanic Franz Anton Vogler (1806–1880), who gradually improved the machines starting in the 1840s while working with Franz Mange's son-in-law Jacob Bartholome Rittmeyer (1786–1848) and his grandson Franz Elisäus Rittmeyer (1819–1892). After a technical breakthrough in the mid-1840s, Rittmeyer was able to order reliably operating embroidery machines exclusively for himself according to his

FIG. 14.6 (ABOVE, LEFT)

Detail from an embroidered blanket, eastern Switzerland, ca. 1830. Cotton. Textilmuseum St. Gallen, 21357.

FIG. 14.7 (ABOVE, RIGHT)

Handkerchief with needle-lace inserts, Appenzell, Switzerland, mid-19th century. Linen. Textilmuseum St. Gallen, Acquired from the Estate of John Jacoby, 1954, 20332.

FIG. 14.8A (OPPOSITE, TOP)

Hand-embroidery machine, ca. 1890, on display at the Textilmuseum St. Gallen, 2015.

FIG. 14.8B (OPPOSITE, BOTTOM)

Technical drawing for embroidery machine, 1938–39. Ink on paper. Textilmuseum St. Gallen, 57478.

own design. From the early 1850s, a factory near St. Gallen also supplied these machines to other embroidery manufacturers in eastern Switzerland.[40]

The first products made on embroidery machines in Switzerland consisted of different types of ribbons for household linens. Inserts with hand-embroidered repeat patterns had already accounted for a large share of Swiss exports in the 1840s and 1850s, and the early mechanical products (FIG. 14.9) took these simple handmade works as their model and imitated them more efficiently and with greater uniformity.[41] Leopold Iklé recalled that his father had brought products of this kind from St. Gallen around 1854 and that members of his family had marveled greatly at them.[42]

In 1863 Isaak Gröbli (1822–1917) invented the shuttle embroidery machine (also known as the Schiffli machine), which, like the domestic sewing machine, relied on a two-thread system and was therefore significantly more efficient than the hand-embroidery machine. To transfer the pattern, an embroiderer operating the pantograph was still necessary, but the machine itself was powered by a variety of sources, including water, steam, and, eventually, electricity. As previously mentioned, it was the Iklé Frères company that equipped the first factory in eastern Switzerland with shuttle embroidery machines. Eighteen machines were acquired by the Iklé brothers in 1879 from the Winterthur-based machine builder Rieter.[43]

The next decisive step in embroidery machine technology was the invention of the automatic embroidery machine, which was fully mechanized and functioned without a human operator thanks to a control system based on punched cards. Initially, the technology was not directly accessible to Swiss manufacturers because the Feldmühle company in Rorschach held the Swiss monopoly until 1910. Iklé Frères circumvented this hurdle by having embroidery machines installed in their factories in Germany.[44] Alongside this evolution in machinery, manufacturers developed new design options for machine-based embroidery, and an increasingly larger variety of products appeared on the market from the 1870s onward.

Machine-Embroidered Lace

Lace was once again in high demand as machine embroidery made great strides forward. In the 1870s the need to be able to offer customers more products with lacelike open-work effects spread among embroidery producers. One fragment in the Textilmuseum's collection is evidence that the Iklé company made efforts in 1875 to produce net lace on the hand-embroidery machine. Embroiderers stretched threads vertically onto the embroidery base and then embroidered horizontal threads over it with the machine, producing a grid. They then separated the fabric by cutting it away from the thread grid, and in an additional step, the grid could be decorated with a needle and thread (FIG. 14.10).[45]

The manufacture of machine tulle had been possible from the beginning of the century thanks to John Heathcoat's (1783–1861) bobbinet machine (SEE CHAP. 11). It was on this bobbinet machine that, in 1808, an unpatterned tulle was first produced that was equal to handmade bobbin lace. The new net base could be decorated in various ways, and it was initially embellished with hand embroidery in basic stitches (FIG. 14.11).[46] However, tulle could also be embroidered with chain stitches by means of the chain or crank embroidery machine (Cornely machine), which was increasingly widespread from 1868 onward.[47] Nevertheless, the net frequently tangled during the process, and so manufacturers employed a special cutting technique in which the tulle was laid on muslin fabric and both layers were worked together. Subsequently, parts of the tulle or muslin were cut away, creating cutout (or *Spachtel*) work with the tulle.[48] In 1880 Theodor Bickel (1837–1903) from F. A. Mammen & Co. in Plauen succeeded in embroidering tulle by machine in satin stitch that did not require an auxiliary ground. The product was launched on the market as *dentelles de Saxe* or Saxon lace, and it was a sensational success.[49] In the years that followed, the St. Gallen companies also produced tulle embroidery, albeit with less success compared to their northern competitors in Plauen. In terms of design, the St. Gallen tulle embroiderers frequently looked to Alençon lace for inspiration and often used terms such as "Alençon embroidery" or *genre d'Alençon* for their products (FIG. 14.12).[50]

FIG. 14.9
Section of an entre-deux insert, early embroidery example created by a hand-embroidery machine, St. Gallen, Switzerland, ca. 1850. Cotton. Textilmuseum St. Gallen, Gift of Ernst Iklé, 30752.

The so-called cutout or Spachtel technique was not only used to produce embroidered tulle. With other forms of machine-produced embroidery, too, parts of the base fabric were cut away, resulting in lacelike formations. In particular, the outlines of the patterns that were to remain in place had to be embroidered and the individual pattern elements joined with threads (FIG. 14.13). The cutting away of the fabric base had to be done by hand because no alternative was available, and this task is still occasionally done by hand today. Ernst Iklé reports how, shortly before 1880, St. Gallen firms were able to sell large quantities of such cutout embroidery to consumers.[51]

In cutout embroideries, parts of the base fabric remained even after removal by hand. In the early 1880s, several producers searched for solutions to ensure that the embroidery base could be removed completely after the embroidery process without the tedious cutting-out process, so that, like lace, only the pattern-forming threads would remain. The earliest-known tests were carried out by Joseph Halter (1844–1914) in Rebstein, Switzerland (FIG. 14.14).[52] He experimented with a paper embroidery base, which he attempted to remove after the embroidering process by washing and scrubbing. This process provided less than satisfactory results, however, and his experiments were followed by those conducted by the manufacturer Charles Wetter-Rüesch (1857–1921), who also took note of and reported on experiments by J. Steiger-Meyer in Herisau, in which embroidery bases made of gelatin and muslin were treated by the so-called guncotton process.[53]

It was Wetter-Rüesch who eventually succeeded in developing a viable process that would come to be known as "chemical lace" after Swiss manufacturer Jakob Sutter described his accidental discovery that silk fabrics could be completely destroyed with a chlorine solution. However, this technique would not work on plant-based cotton, which is often bleached with chlorine. Wetter-Rüesch experimented and discovered in the early 1880s, through further research, that the hazardous chlorine could be replaced by sodium hydroxide (caustic soda). He was clearly fearful of mass industrial handling of the chlorine solution and was greatly relieved to find this alternative.[54]

In 1915 Wetter-Rüesch highlighted a related challenge: suitable embroidery patterns. Embroidery sturdy enough to survive without any base fabric at all had to meet special requirements. All stitches had to be interwoven so that the end product was firm and stable and would retain its shape. If this was not the case, the threads would fall apart after the base had been removed, resulting in formless balls of thread.[55] German competitors in Vogtland faced the same challenges, and as early as 1882, manufacturer Anton Falke

successfully created a template for the hand-embroidery machine that met the requirements for creating stable embroidered lace.[56] At the same time, Wetter-Rüesch engaged hand embroiderers who, as he later described, produced samples to his specifications that enabled him to experiment with removing the ground fabric through chemical processes. His experiments were ultimately successful, and Wetter Frères, his company, had the new process patented in the United States in June 1883, since there was still no patent protection in Switzerland at that time.[57]

In order to embark on his own production, Wetter-Rüesch once again set himself to the task of creating and then realizing patterns. As he stated:

> The heaviest stone to push was to make it clear to the illustrators and embroiderers that it was about lace and not about embroidery. These were all new creations; only with dogged testing and experimenting in stitch positioning and material did we manage to move a few steps further again. I soon discovered that my articles would be far too expensive if one wanted to create patterns like those that flowed from the pen of our embroidery artists. Thus, we had to create based on famous masters. I got the best lace works available at the time, still good today, I visited museums and collections, soon forming the view that for the time being our salvation could lie only in the imitation of the Irish hand lace, given that our embroiderers were not yet trained enough for all the others, although even then I nourished the hope that St. Gallen might one day have a say in lace manufacturing.[58]

FIG. 14.12 (LEFT)

Iklé Frères and Co., chemical-lace imitation of Alençon needle lace in a sample book (left page), St. Gallen, Switzerland, 1900–30. Paper, cardboard, leather, and cotton. Textilmuseum St. Gallen, STI IKL 3. Cat. 137.

FIG. 14.13 (RIGHT)

Example of cutout embroidery in a sample book, St. Gallen, Switzerland, 1878. Cotton. Textilmuseum St. Gallen, Gift of Ernst Iklé, 1930, 30750. Cat. 136.

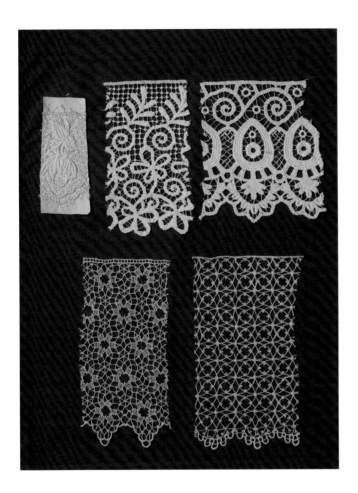

Wetter Frères also sent the talented illustrator Erwin Bernet to Ireland to understand the local production processes and gather patterns.[59] Several early chemical-lace patterns from Wetter Frères are preserved in the archive of the St. Gallen–based textile manufacturer Bischoff Textil AG, founded in 1927 (FIG. 14.15).

From 1889 onward, many patents for the manufacture of chemical lace were registered in Switzerland and Germany. These patents largely concern the fabric base and the search for new ways to remove it with as little effort as possible. Throughout the twentieth century, inventors and manufacturers would continue to develop processes using chemicals to etch away all or part of the fabric base after embroidering. Today it is possible to wash out a synthetic fiber ground with warm water. These new chemical technologies, combined with innovations in embroidery machines, soon made it possible for machines to imitate all kinds of handmade lace.[60]

Iklé Frères's Pattern Books and Pattern Design

Since the end of the nineteenth century, St. Gallen embroidery companies have kept pattern books. At least twice a year they have compiled new pattern collections, arranged corresponding samples in large pattern folios, and preserved them in special pattern rooms. Patterns by other companies were often also kept by the special staff looking after the collections, which were arranged according to an established numbering

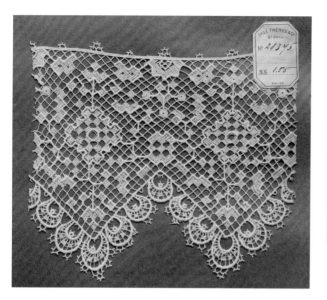

system. These archives often housed several versions of each book, with one example used as a demonstration copy for customers in the pattern room, another designated for the illustrator and for the firm's archives, and a third copy used by the shipping department. These books today form important source material recording the products of embroidery companies.[61]

Some four thousand pattern books are preserved in the collection of the Textilbibliothek St. Gallen (Textiles Library), including numerous examples compiled by important St. Gallen embroidery firms.[62] One hundred forty-seven books from the Iklé Frères company can also be found in the Textilmuseum's collection. Of interest are several folios with the labels Iklé Frères St. Gall, Iklé Frères New York, and Jacoby-Iklé London, all of which were donated to the museum in 2014.[63] Seven of these books offer insight into the production at Iklé Frères and include imitations of French lace (SEE FIG. 14.12), filet works (FIG. 14.16), Irish crochet works, and Sol lace from Paraguay (FIG. 14.17). A reticella imitation produced by the Iklé Frères company bears a particularly noticeable resemblance to a lace from Leopold's collection (FIGS. 14.18 AND 14.19).[64] The embroidered *gros point de Venise* enjoyed special success until the 1920s and was for a time the epitome of "St. Gallen lace" (FIG. 14.20).[65]

Although there are striking similarities between many embroidery patterns and their handmade counterparts, they are not exact copies. The production of all of the original handmade laces required a great deal of time, but a study of these pieces also reveals different qualities. Those items created at home for household linens in eastern Switzerland or Swabia, Germany, primarily in the eighteenth and nineteenth centuries, were relatively simple in their design, while the ornate handkerchiefs sometimes decorated with lace and the lace veils produced professionally for aristocratic ladies during the same period were far more complex. Machine-embroidered goods showed a similar range of quality in their design and execution; however, because of their mass production, they were lower priced and more widespread and so achieved high levels of recognition.[66]

FIG. 14.16 (LEFT)
Iklé Frères and Co., imitation filet embroidery from a sample book, St. Gallen, Switzerland, 1900–30. Paper, cardboard, cotton, and leather. Textilmuseum St. Gallen, Iklé Frères, RE 5.29, 28345.

FIG. 14.17 (RIGHT)
Iklé Frères and Co., imitation Sol lace (*ñanduti*) from Paraguay in a sample book, St. Gallen, Switzerland, 1900–30. Paper, cardboard, cotton, and leather. Textilmuseum St. Gallen, Iklé Frères, RE 5.31, 23190.

These machine-based works had their own limitations, and not every design could be realized. While the concept and inspiration for a pattern were important, designers also had to adapt their artistic ideas to what was possible on the machine. The repeat pattern and distance between the needles (which defined the size of the repeat) had to be considered, and the number of stitches had to be restricted to what was absolutely necessary. The price of the finished product depended on this number of stitches, which in turn determined the quality of the resulting embroidery. High-quality, luxury machine-made works were characterized by densely embroidered surfaces, which proved especially important for producing durable chemical lace.[67]

In order to train good designers for the eastern Swiss industry, a dedicated school was founded in St. Gallen in 1867. Depending on their needs and potential, students could take lessons in drawing and design, whether comprehensive or specific, to assist with their professional activities.[68] The school was subsequently integrated into the museum when the latter was built in 1886; it also housed the textile collection and library. This physical merger of the two institutions meant the students could benefit directly from the available models of historical textiles at their place of learning.[69] The designers trained at the school in St. Gallen found employment in embroidery firms, or they became self-employed embroidery designers. This training demanded more than the ability to imitate patterns, and the scope of products they were able to create expanded continuously over the years thanks to the technical possibilities of the increasingly complex machines. Creating new patterns was a key part of their job.

At the turn of the twentieth century, contemporary trends, such as Jugendstil, were absorbed into the students' repertoire of forms. The embroidery designer Ludwig Otto Werder (1868–1902) taught at the school in St. Gallen and published two books containing his own

embroidery patterns.[70] In the foreword to the first volume, published in 1898, Werder explains that he "makes it his duty not only to admire the historically conventional, but also to keep his heart and eye open for endeavors beyond that." Further, he does not wish "to give cause for copying and taking breaks," but rather "to place in the hand of specialists the key to starting independent thinking and creating."[71] However, Werder's new patterns initially attracted criticism. Generally, the industry in St. Gallen relied heavily on Baroque and Rococo forms, as these products sold especially well. Nonetheless, numerous Jugendstil patterns can be found among the museum's holdings, including one example produced by Iklé Frères (FIG. 14.21).[72]

Conclusion

It is clear that Leopold Iklé, whose carefully assembled collection was intended both for his own use and for that of the museum and school, exercised influence on the mass production of embroideries in eastern Switzerland in his lifetime. Leopold's collections demonstrate a return of those forms created by hand for many years, now produced under new mechanized conditions. Mass production as such has little to do with the individual motifs, enabling as it did only their simultaneous production in great numbers. Thus, it is not the process of work by hand or by machine, but rather technical factors combined with a creative, design-oriented mind that ensure a high-quality product in the end.

Martin Leuthold, former creative director of the St. Gallen–based company Jakob Schlaepfer, who is today one of Switzerland's most well-known textile designers, expressed the problem recently as follows: "ultimately, the world's archives and museum collections provide inspiration. . . . To create something entirely new is actually no longer possible. Everything is simply a re-interpretation of the existing."[73]

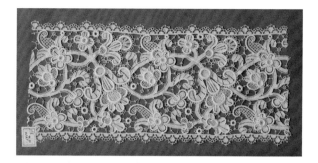

FIG. 14.20 (TOP)

Iklé Frères and Co., chemical-lace imitation of *point de Venise* needle lace in a sample book, St. Gallen, Switzerland, 1900–30. Paper, cardboard, leather, and cotton. Textilmuseum St. Gallen, STI IKL 1. Cat. 141.

FIG. 14.21 (BOTTOM)

Iklé Frères and Co., Jugendstil (Art Nouveau) design in a sample book, produced with a hand-embroidery machine and cutout work, St. Gallen, Switzerland, 1900–30. Paper, cardboard, leather, and cotton. Textilmuseum St. Gallen, RE 5.27, 2938.

This chapter takes as a starting point and draws upon Anne Wanner-JeanRichard, "'Das Alte auf eine neue Weise tun—das ist Innovation,'" in *Historische Spitzen: Die Leopold-Iklé Sammlung im Textilmuseum St. Gallen*, ed. Textilmuseum St. Gallen and Iklé-Frischknecht-Stiftung (Stuttgart, Germany: Arnoldsche, 2018).

The text (including quotations unless otherwise indicated) was translated from the German by Andrew Horsfield and Nils Schott.

1   Joseph Alois Schumpeter, "The Creative Response in Economic History," *Journal of Economic History* 7, no. 2 (November 1947): 151.
2   Adolf Fäh, ed., *Leopold Iklé 1838–1922: Gedenkblätter unter Zugrundelegung seiner Memoiren, zusammengestellt von Dr. Ad. Fäh Bibl.* (St. Gallen, Switzerland: Printed for Friends, by H. Tschudy, 1922), 8. On the origin of the family and the family name, see Gisela Graff-Höfgen, "Spitzen von Iklé und Jacoby," in *Hamburgische Geschichts- und Heimatblätter*, vol. 9, bk. 11 (October 1976): 274–81. All fifteen siblings are listed in an unpublished family tree. Leopold Iklé himself reports only twelve siblings, possibly because three died very early on. Fäh, *Leopold Iklé 1838–1922*, 8.
3   In a Hamburg business directory, the Firma Iklé, M. appears from 1836 onward and is described as a storehouse of French and Swiss manufactured goods. Graff-Höfgen, "Spitzen von Iklé und Jacoby," 274.
4   Fäh, *Leopold Iklé 1838–1922*, 8.
5   Ibid. Concerning the life of Leopold Iklé and his close friendship with Adolf Fäh, see also Anne Wanner-JeanRichard, *Leopold Iklé: Ein leidenschaftlicher Sammler* (St. Gallen, Switzerland: Textilmuseum St. Gallen, 2002). On Leopold himself with regard to the firm, see also Cristian Rusch, "Leopold Iklé (1838–1922): Ein St. Galler Unternehmer der Stickereizeit" (unpublished essay, Universität St. Gallen, 1998).
6   Fäh, *Leopold Iklé 1838–1922*, 11–13.
7   Ibid., 22–23; and Graff-Höfgen, "Spitzen von Iklé und Jacoby," 277. In 1882 Leopold received St. Gallen citizenship. Wanner-JeanRichard, *Leopold Iklé*, 6.
8   Eric Häusler and Caspar Meili, "Swiss Embroidery: Erfolg und Krise der Schweizer Stickerei-Industrie 1865–1929," *Neujahrsblatt: Historischer Verein des Kantons St. Gallen* 155 (2015): 11.
9   Ernest Iklé, *La broderie mécanique: 1828–1930; Souveniers et documents* (Paris: A. Calavas, 1931), 225–26.
10   Fäh, *Leopold Iklé 1838–1922*, 24.
11   Ibid.; and Peter Röllin, "Der Stickereihandelsplatz St. Gallen: Bemerkenswerte Fabrik- und Geschäftsbauten aus der Zeit der Stickereiblüte," *Unsere Kunstdenkmäler, Mitteilungsblatt für die Mitglieder der Gesellschaft für Schweizerische Kunstgeschichte* 34, no. 2 (1983): 229–31.
12   Wanner-JeanRichard, "'Das Alte auf eine neue Weise tun,'" 10–11; and Graff-Höfgen, "Spitzen von Iklé und Jacoby," 277–79. We extend thanks to Heino Strobel, who researched the company in Plauen, Germany.
13   For a more recent economic history of this time period, see Häusler and Meili, "Swiss Embroidery."
14   Fäh, *Leopold Iklé 1838–1922*, 25–27.
15   Graff-Höfgen, "Spitzen von Iklé und Jacoby," 275.
16   Wanner-JeanRichard, "'Das Alte auf eine neue Weise tun,'" 11; and Graff-Höfgen, "Spitzen von Iklé und Jacoby," 277.
17   Häusler and Meili, "Swiss Embroidery," 11–12.
18   Wanner-JeanRichard, "'Das Alte auf eine neue Weise tun,'" 11.
19   Martin Joseph Wilhelm (1869–1922), Louis Leopold (1875–1925), and Friedrich Arnold (known as Fritz), according to information in the unpublished family tree.
20   Wanner-JeanRichard, *Leopold Iklé*, 6; Anne Wanner-JeanRichard, *Kettenstich und andere Stickereien: Eine Sammlung von Stickbeispielen, die Fritz Iklé in den Jahren 1931 bis 1933 für Adolf Jenny-Trümpy zusammenstellte*, Edition Comptoir-Blätter 7 (Sent: Private edition by Reto D. Jenny, 2013), 34, 40; and unpublished letters from the private archive of Bartholome Jenny & Cie., Ennenda, Switzerland.
21   Fäh, *Leopold Iklé 1838–1922*, 62.
22   Ibid., 47. Fäh passes on an oral account here, which came to him via Fritz Iklé.
23   Ibid., 47–50.
24   Leopold Iklé and Emil Wild, *Industrie- und Gewerbemuseum St. Gallen: Textilsammlung Iklé, Katalog* (Zurich: Orell Füssli, 1908); Fäh, *Leopold Iklé 1838–1922*, 47–50; Industrie- und Gewerbemuseum, *Bericht über das Industrie- und Gewerbemuseum St. Gallen und über die Zeichnungsschule für Industrie und Gewerbe, Ateliers und Einzelkurse, 1. Mai. 1900–30 April 1901* (St. Gallen, Switzerland: Zollikofer'sche Buchdruckerei, 1901), 5; Industrie- und Gewerbemuseum, *Bericht über das Industrie- und Gewerbemuseum St. Gallen und über die Zeichnungsschule für Industrie und Gewerbe, Ateliers und Einzelkurse, 1. Mai. 1901–30 April 1902* (St. Gallen, Switzerland: Zollikofer'sche Buchdruckerei, 1902), 3; and Industrie- und Gewerbemuseum, *Bericht über das Industrie- und Gewerbemuseum St. Gallen und über die Zeichnungsschule für Industrie und Gewerbe, Ateliers und Einzelkurse, 1. Mai. 1908–30 April 1909* (St. Gallen, Switzerland: Zollikofer'sche Buchdruckerei, 1909), 4. Some years later, around 1920, Leopold donated Coptic textiles to the museum.
25   Iklé and Wild, *Industrie- und Gewerbemuseum St. Gallen*, 5.
26   Ibid., cat. nos. 249–402 (openwork and net lace), cat. nos. 403–784, 789–882 (16th- to 19th-century lace).
27   Fäh, *Leopold Iklé 1838–1922*, 55–54.
28   Anne Wanner-JeanRichard has been able to examine the correspondence preserved in the St. Gallen Abbey Archives. Wanner-JeanRichard, *Leopold Iklé*, 9 and 50n4.
29   Fäh mentions books including Ernest Lefébure, *Broderie et dentelles* (Paris: Maison Quantin, 1887); Moriz Dreger, *Entwicklungsgeschichte der Spitze: Mit bes. Rücksicht auf die Spitzen-Sammlung des K.K. Österreichischen Museums für Kunst und Industrie in Wien* (Vienna: Schroll, 1901); Marie Schuette, *Alte Spitzen: Nadel- und Klöppelspitzen; Ein Handbuch für Sammler und Liebhaber* (Berlin: R. C. Schmidt, 1914); Louis de Farcy, *La broderie du XIe siècle jusqu'à nos jours d'après des spécimens authentiques et les anciens inventaires*, 2 vols. (Angers, France: Belhomme, 1890–1919); and Joseph Braun, *Die liturgische Gewandung im Occident und Orient: Nach Ursprung und Entwicklung, Verwendung und Symbolik* (Freiburg im Breisgau, Germany: Herder, 1907).
30   Adolf Fäh and Leopold Iklé, *Beiträge zur Entwicklungsgeschichte der Spitze* (Zurich: Orell Füssli, 1919).
31   Ibid., 1, 2, 54; and Wanner-Jean Richard, *Leopold Iklé*, 7, 16, 32, 46.
32   The auction took place in Zurich on September 18, 1923.
33   Zunfthaus zur Meisen, *Sammlung Leopold Iklé, St. Gallen: Textilien*, 2 vols., auction cat., Zurich, September 18, 1923.
34   Graff-Höfgen, "Spitzen von Iklé und Jacoby," 279. Jacoby held lectures and organized exhibitions of his acquisitions, too. The author names exhibitions in London, Manchester, Rotterdam (1938), Amsterdam (after World War II), and Bristol (ca. 1951/52).
35   Graff-Höfgen, "Spitzen von Iklé und Jacoby," 279.
36   Iklé, *La broderie mécanique*.
37   Albert Tanner, *Das Schiffchen fliegt, die Maschine rauscht: Weber, Sticker und Fabrikanten in der Ostschweiz* (Zurich: Unionsverlag, 1985). In 1790, in its heyday, up to 50,000 embroiderers were working in the Lake Constance region (ibid., 23).

38 Wanner-JeanRichard, "'Das Alte auf eine neue Weise tun,'" 12–13; and Ruth Bleckwenn, *Dresdner Spitzen—Point de Saxe: Virtuose Weissstickereien des 18. Jahrhunderts* (Dresden, Germany: Staatliche Kunstsammlungen, 2000), 46.

39 Wanner-JeanRichard, "'Das Alte auf eine neue Weise tun,'" 13–14.

40 Heino Strobel and Patrick Schnetzer, *Die Handstickmaschine: Erfindungsgeschichte und erste Besitzer* (Plauen, Germany: Heino Strobel, 2021). This study yields new findings on the early history of the hand-embroidery machines, which at the time were described as "machine à broder Heilmann," and compares the data found in the St. Gallen literature with the accounting books of the company A. Koechlin & Cie.

41 Wanner, "'Das Alte auf eine neue Weise tun,'" 15.

42 Häusler and Meili, "Swiss Embroidery," 22–23; and Fäh, *Leopold Iklé 1838–1922*, 11.

43 Iklé, *La broderie mécanique*, 71–79.

44 Häusler and Meili, "Swiss Embroidery," 24, and remarks by Heino Strobel.

45 Ursula Karbacher, "Characteristics of the Ever-Reinvented Gros Point in St. Gallen Embroidery," in *Gros Point de Venise: The Most Important Lace of the 17th Century*, ed. Ursula Karbacher (St. Gallen, Switzerland: Textilmuseum St. Gallen, 2011), 160. The origin and dating of the fabric sample are derived from a handwritten note that is preserved with it. On the provenance of the sample and a double in the Comptoir Daniel Jenny & Cie. in Ennenda, see Wanner-JeanRichard, *Kettenstich und andere Stickereien*, 9, 22; and Anne Wanner-JeanRichard, "Frühe Stickereimuster mit Maschine ca. ab 1850 zu Inventarnummern 30'737 bis 30'883 des Textilmuseums St. Gallen und zum Werk von Ernest Iklé, *La broderie mecanique 1828–1930*, 1931," Anne Wanner's Textiles in History, last revised July 26, 2017, http://www.annatextiles.ch/machine%20embroidery/muster_eikle.htm.

46 Wanner-JeanRichard, "'Das Alte auf eine neue Weise tun,'" 14; and Anne Wanner-JeanRichard, "Die Kettenstichmaschine," Anne Wanner's Textiles in History, last revised July 19, 2014, http://www.annatextiles.ch/machine%20embroidery/chainstitch/geschichte.htm. The further development of machine-produced lace with the bobbinet machine, as well as the invention of the Raschel machine, are not considered here, as the article is focused on embroidery.

47 Pat Earnshaw, *Lace Machines and Machine Laces* (London: B.T. Batsford, 1986), 257.

48 Wanner-JeanRichard, "'Das Alte auf eine neue Weise tun,'" 14.

49 Katrin Färber, "Die vogtländische Stickerei- und Spitzenindustrie," in *Nouveautés: Kunstschule und Spitzenindustrie in Plauen*, ed. Staatliche Kunstsammlungen Dresden et al., exh. cat. (Dresden, Germany: Sandstein Verlag, 2020), 18.

50 Wanner-JeanRichard, "'Das Alte auf eine neue Weise tun,'" 14; Ursula Karbacher, "Imitation et réinterprétation du point d'Alençon à Saint-Gall," in *Dentelles: Quand la mode ne tient qu'à un fil*, ed. Alice Gandin and Julie Romain (Paris: Somogy; Caen, France: Musée de Normandie, 2012), 131–41.

51 Iklé, *La broderie mécanique*, 38, 43.

52 Halter had his process patented in the German Empire in 1881, Patent No. 17903. He also patented his process of embroidering on paper in the United States in 1881, US-251579-A. Heino Strobel has compiled the various patents for the development of chemical lace and was kind enough to send them to us, for which we thank him warmly.

53 Report by Charles Wetter-Rüesch, in *Schweizerische Landesausstellung in Bern 1914: Die Stickerei-Industrie; Eine Schilderung der Ausstellung verbunden mit einer Darlegung geschichtlicher Entwicklung und der gesamten Organisation dieser Industrie*, ed.

E. A. Steiger-Züst (Zurich: Orell Füssli, 1915), 37–40; and Albert Hempel, "50 Jahre stickmaschinengestickte Ätzspitze: Kritische Feststellungen in Wort und Bild aus dem industriellen Leben Plauens," *Vogtländischer Anzeiger und Tagblatt*, September 3, 1933, 21–23.

54 Report by Wetter-Rüesch, 37–40.

55 Ibid.

56 Hempel, "50 Jahre stickmaschinengestickte Ätzspitze."

57 Report by Wetter-Rüesch, 37–40. US Patent 280,094 is in the name of Frederick Suter and is assigned to the company Wetter Frères.

58 Technically, it was certainly embroidery, as the chemical lace was produced on the embroidery machine; however, due to the removal of the base, it had to be constructed differently from typical embroidery. Report by Wetter-Rüesch, 39.

59 Ibid.

60 Wanner-JeanRichard, "'Das Alte auf eine neue Weise tun,'" 16.

61 Ibid., 17.

62 For example, the collection includes pattern books of the companies Rittmeyer & Co., Tschumper, Otto Alder & Co., Grauer/Grauer-Frey, and many others.

63 It is no longer known how the books Iklé Frères 001–057 reached the museum. By the time they were recorded in 1992, none of the staff recalled that information. The books Iklé Frères New York (RE 4.1-32), Iklé Frères St. Gall (RE 5.1-37) and Jacoby-Iklé London (RE 7.1.-21) came to the museum in 2014, together with books from the company Reichenbach & Cie., as a donation from the Steinegg Stiftung Herisau (information from the library catalogue and unpublished reports).

64 The pattern books have not been systematically examined to date. A comparison with the Iklé Collection could yield further fascinating results.

65 Wanner-JeanRichard, "'Das Alte auf eine neue Weise tun,'" 17–20. Anne Wanner-JeanRichard compiled these embroidery patterns for her 2018 essay.

66 Ibid., 20.

67 Ibid.; and Iklé, *La broderie mécanique*, 132.

68 *Verwaltungsbericht des Kaufmännischen Directoriums an die kaufm: Corporation in St. Gallen* (St. Gallen, Switzerland: Zollikofer'sche Buchdruckerei, 1868), 22–23.

69 *IX. Bericht über das St. Gallische Industrie- und Gewerbemuseum 1886* (St. Gallen, Switzerland: Zollikofer'sche Buchdruckerei, 1887), 1; *Verwaltungsbericht des Kaufmännischen Directoriums an die kaufm: Corporation in St. Gallen* (St. Gallen, Switzerland: Zollikofer'sche Buchdruckerei, 1886), 16–17.

70 Wanner-JeanRichard, "'Das Alte auf eine neue Weise tun,'" 21. On Werder and St. Gallen, see also Anne Wanner-JeanRichard, *Von der Idee zum Kunstwerk: Stickereien aus der Sammlung des Textilmuseums St. Gallen und Tagebuchnotizen eines Stickereizeichners* (St. Gallen, Switzerland: Textilmuseum St. Gallen, 1999), 75; Anne Wanner-JeanRichard, "St.Galler Stickereispitze um die Jahrhundertwende," Anne Wanner's Textiles in History, last updated March 25, 2015, http://www.annatextiles.ch/publications/spitzen/spitzen_um_1900/spitz_1900.htm; Ludwig Otto Werder, *Neue Spitzen: Entwürfe für Spitzen, Stickereien, Gardinen in moderner Auffassung* (Zurich: N.p., 1898); and Ludwig Otto Werder, *Dentelles nouvelles: Types modernes pour dentelles, broderies et rideaux*, 2nd ed. (Plauen, Germany: C. Stoll, 1901).

71 Werder, *Neue Spitzen*, foreword.

72 Wanner-JeanRichard, "'Das Alte auf eine neue Weise tun,'" 21.

73 Menschen, *Migros Magazin*, January 15, 2018, 33.

INNOVATIONS IN LACE, 1900 TO TODAY

15 Fashion and Lace since 1900

Catherine Örmen

B Y THE TURN OF THE TWENTIETH CENTURY, the mechanization of the European lace industry was fully in place, and efforts to sustain the long-established handmade industries in France, Belgium, and England were ineffectual against this major shift in production, changing tastes, and the impact of World War I. The main centers of machine production were Calais and Caudry, both in the Nord-Pas-de-Calais region of France, and St. Gallen, in eastern Switzerland (SEE CHAPS. 11 AND 14). In the two French cities, Leavers machines from the late nineteenth century, measuring almost twenty feet long and weighing more than ten tons, are still in use today (FIG. 15.1).[1] These machines create both a net ground and motifs by intertwining 4,500 warp yarns with 10,000 weft yarns. In nineteenth- and twentieth-century Switzerland, the age-old tradition of hand embroidery was adapted for production on equally large embroidery machines that produced the region's highly successful "chemical lace" (FIG. 15.2).[2] In this process, cotton yarn was embroidered on a thin silk ground, which was then dissolved by submerging the fabric in a chemical solution so that only the embroidered motifs remained. Today Swiss manufacturers use water to dissolve a synthetic ground.[3] The resulting "lace" is generally called "guipure" (FIG. 15.3). This revolutionary technique allowed—and still allows—St. Gallen manufacturers to imitate any kind of traditional handmade lace, including extremely delicate ones.

1. - CALAIS. - L'industrie tullière. - Métiers à dentelles.

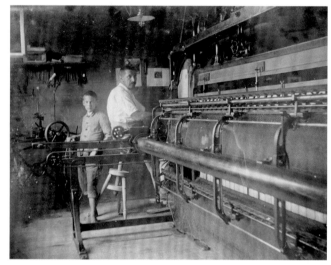

Lace as an embellishment for women's fashionable dress has transformed and developed over the course of the twentieth and twenty-first centuries alongside changing production methods that continue to be perfected.[4] Rather than presenting an overview of these innovations, however, the following panorama charts the uses of lace during this period, primarily in France, with special regard to St. Gallen production. Sometimes lace functions as simple decoration; sometimes it is the constitutive material of the garment. One important shift over the past 120 years has been the significant increase of lace in women's lingerie. Although prior to the late nineteenth century lace was often used as trimming on women's shifts, corset covers, and petticoats, these garments were of linen or cotton; since the early twentieth century, lace bras, girdles, slips, and nightdresses have enhanced the eroticism of what is known as intimate apparel. However it has been worn and wherever it has been made, lace in women's fashion is a consistent indicator of the tastes of an age.

FIG. 15.1 (TOP)

"1. - Calais. - L'industrie tullière. - Métiers à dentelles" postcard, Editions du Grand Bazar Lafayette, early 20th century. Cité de la dentelle et de la mode, Ville de Calais.

FIG. 15.2 (BOTTOM)

Home embroiderer at the pantograph of a hand-embroidery machine and a boy at a threading machine in an embroidery shop, Appenzell, Switzerland, ca. 1912. Gelatin silver print. Schweizerisches Nationalmuseum Zürich, LM-101938.225.

In the late nineteenth and early twentieth centuries, museums and private individuals throughout Europe collected old lace originally used as a decoration or accessory separate from the main garment, such as mantelets, flounces, veils, and shawls, on a large scale (SEE CHAPS. 11–14). At the time, these historical pieces—precious material witnesses of the past—were frequently combined with much cheaper mechanically produced items that were stained with tea to give them the appearance of being antique.[5] The infatuation with lace during this period was such that it was often used as the main fabric of the dress itself. The loose-fitting cotton voile tea gown with generous lace trimmings and insertions (ca. 1898) worn by the popular French stage actress Gabrielle Réjane (1856–1920) was intended for receiving guests at home, and it is likely that Réjane dispensed with a corset while wearing the gown—a daring thing to do (FIG. 15.4). The garment may have been designed by the leading couturier Jacques Doucet (1853–1929), who often dressed Réjane and who boasted an international clientele for his hyperfeminine gowns, or by Callot Sœurs, the four sisters renowned for the fineness of their creations, which often incorporated lace.[6] Worn beneath these delicate dresses, an abundance of silk and lace undergarments would have created a rustling sound that was particularly associated with Parisian women and referred to at the time as "froufrou."[7]

Twisted by their boned straight-front corsets into an S-shape that evoked the undulating lines of Art Nouveau, women of the Belle Époque wearing gowns that incorporated lace directly or whose pale colors were similar to old lace and broderie anglaise (a St. Gallen specialty) were often visually compared to flowers in advertising posters and decorative arts media.[8] However, this rarified world would collapse in the late summer of 1914 with the outbreak of World War I, and the profusion of new and old lace in French women's fashion disappeared.[9] Daytime wardrobes emphasized practicality, functionality, and understatement, and the war's toll was evident in fashion magazines' coverage of mourning dress.[10]

During the roaring twenties, earlier societal conventions governing what was perceived as proper female behavior were upended, and a narrower, shorter silhouette accompanied women's increasing visibility and independence. Lace reemerged in the wardrobes of the *garçonnes* and flappers who wore heavy makeup, bobbed their hair, smoked in public, and frequented jazz clubs and nightclubs. However, the European handmade lace industries had essentially collapsed by 1914, and in the following decades, the patient, time-consuming production of this textile art emigrated elsewhere, with European styles made in countries including Tunisia, Algeria, Madagascar, Vietnam, India, and China.[11] Instead, mechanical and chemical laces featured heavily in 1920s fashions. In daywear

FIG. 15.4
Tea gown belonging to the actress Gabrielle Réjane, France, ca. 1898. Cotton voile, machine-made lace insert, and cotton floral embroidery. Palais Galliera, musée de la Mode de la Ville de Paris, Gift of Mme Sieben, GAL 1957.77.1.

that continued to be characterized by casual simplicity, especially with the increasing emphasis on sports and *costumes de sport*, lace modesty panels and blouses were visible underneath dresses with open fronts or deep necklines, and lace skirts layered over contrasting-colored underskirts showed off large-scale patterns (FIGS. 15.5 AND 15.6).[12] Straight, loose evening dresses worn for performing the Charleston and other popular athletic dances were often embellished with lace, beading, or fringe. Lingerie also became more streamlined during this period and was often ornamented with delicate lace. In the mid-1920s, *Les Modes*, a leading French fashion magazine, promoted the products of St. Gallen that were used as trimming for slips and combinations (FIG. 15.7).[13]

Although the city's industry was in decline by this date, *Les Modes* gave extensive coverage to St. Gallen embroidery and lace. In November 1926 the fashion editor compared furriers' manufacture of faux fur and "ersatz" elegance to the products of St. Gallen, declaring that "lace . . . has become, thanks to the Saint Gall factories, one of the great elements of the feminine outfit and . . . offers such perfect samples of all the famous styles that these latter are often left to age in their boxes; preference is given to the perfect imitations that we find in the beige and ochre tones current fashion calls for, both in underwear and dresses."[14] Of particular interest in the illustration captions and text is the fashion editor's use of the terms "embroidery" and "lace" to refer to the two major creations of St. Gallen manufacturing. Although both were made on embroidery machines, the editor distinguished between them on the basis of their appearance (FIG. 15.8). The ground fabric in garments that incorporated embroidery is clearly visible, while the openwork of chemical lace and lace-trimmed dresses and lingerie mimics needle lace.[15]

FIG. 15.5 (LEFT)
Woman wearing a skirt made from Fritz Rau & Co. chemical lace at the Grand Prix de Paris, Paris, 1920. Photograph with inscription in ink. Textilmuseum St. Gallen, 55440. Cat. 165.

FIG. 15.6 (RIGHT)
Fritz Rau & Co., chemical-lace galloon samples, St. Gallen, Switzerland, ca. 1920s. Cotton. Textilmuseum St. Gallen, 55035. Cat. 164.

FIG. 15.7 (TOP)
"La Belle Lingerie s'orne de dentelle et de broderie de Saint-Gall," *Les Modes: Revue mensuelle illustrée des Arts décoratifs appliqués à la femme,* December 1926. Ink on paper. Bibliothèque nationale de France, département Sciences et techniques, FOL-V-4312.

FIG. 15.8 (BOTTOM)
"Les Dentelles et les broderies de Saint-Gall [. . .] cette année encore sur nos champs de courses," *Les Modes: Revue mensuelle illustrée des Arts décoratifs appliqués à la femme,* August 1926. Ink on paper. Bibliothèque nationale de France, département Sciences et techniques, FOL-V-4312.

MODÈLE DE BÉCHOFF — Mᵐᵉ T...E — Mᵐᵉ X... — Mᵐᵉ F...l — MODÈLE DE JACQUET — MODÈLE DE LA Mᵒⁿ AGNÈS

MODÈLE DE MARTIAL ET ARMAND — Mᵐᵉ ... — Mᵐᵉ ... — MISS ... — Mᵐᵉ ... — Mᵐᵉ ...

LES DENTELLES ET LES BRODERIES DE SAINT-GALL [...] CETTE ANNÉE ENCORE SUR NOS CHAMPS DE COURSES

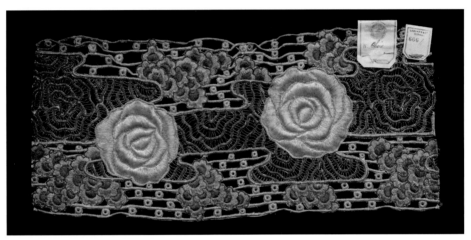

FIG. 15.9 (TOP)
Border of a machine-made Chantilly
lace veil, Europe, ca. 1920s. Matte silk.
Lacis Museum of Lace and Textiles,
Berkeley, California, L2014.2910.005.

FIG. 15.10 (BOTTOM)
Labhard & Co., chemical-lace
galloon, St. Gallen, Switzerland, first
third of the 20th century. Cotton.
Textilmuseum St. Gallen, 54086.
Cat. 163.

Whether for outerwear or underwear, lace patterns reflected major stylistic trends and topical influences: Egyptian motifs were popular after the discovery of Pharaoh Tutankhamun's treasures in 1922, and the orientalism and Japonisme evident in Art Deco design also appear in 1920s laces (FIGS. 15.9 AND 15.10).[16] Similarly, geometric patterns in lace complemented the dominant minimalist aesthetic and the overall simplicity of the cut and construction of women's dress in the 1920s. Designers such as Lucien Lelong (1889–1958) and Callot Sœurs employed lace discreetly as trimming or insertions or created dresses entirely in lace (FIG. 15.11).[17] The combination of tubular silhouettes and rich ornamentation culminated in the vogue for metallic yarns: lace and macramé in gold and silver and tulle embroidered all over in bronze thread. At night, evening dresses, coats, and oversized shawls sparkled and glittered (FIG. 15.12).

By 1920, however, the St. Gallen industry was in crisis: export figures had decreased by 75 percent compared with 1913, and in 1930 this figure reached 90 percent.[18] The war hampered trade, but above all, the products from St. Gallen began to go out of style as manufacturers were not able to keep up with rapid changes in fashion. After the market crash of 1929, the depression of the 1930s, and the disruption of World War II, Switzerland turned to producing synthetic textiles, to textile printing and upmarket embroidery, and, in the twenty-first century, to creating high-tech textiles (SEE CHAP. 16). In the postwar decades, however, the Swiss embroidery manufacturers that remained in business, such as Conrad Forster-Willi, maintained close relationships with fashion designers including Christian Dior (1905–1957), Cristóbal Balenciaga (1895–1972), and Hubert de Givenchy (1927–2018). Working collaboratively with couturiers helped manufacturers anticipate seasonal fashions.[19]

Shortly before the crisis of 1929, fashion underwent another change. The youthful androgyny of the flapper was replaced by a more mature feminine ideal with a shapely silhouette. Along with a renewed emphasis on ensembles that were intended for specific

FIG. 15.11 (LEFT)
Lucien Lelong, "Robe no. 188" sketch and swatches of black lace dinner dress, ca. 1925. Black ink and gouache on paper. Palais Galliera, musée de la Mode de la Ville de Paris, Paris, 1977.56.1.

FIG. 15.12 (RIGHT)
Callot Sœurs, evening dress, 1927. Silk satin and metallic lace. Musée des Arts décoratifs, Paris, UF 56-5-2.

times of day and occasions, women's garments became longer and accentuated the wearer's anatomy once again (FIG. 15.13). Floral motifs dominated the repertoire of lace designs, which were in keeping with fashions that reinforced traditional notions of femininity. Lace also adorned lingerie, which diversified again: dressing gowns, bed jackets, negligees, and long nightgowns—which were as sumptuous as evening dresses—as well as pajamas, corselettes, and slips (FIG. 15.14).

During the 1930s (especially from 1930 to 1935), classical antiquity was an important source of inspiration, especially for evening wear. However, rather than heavily boned corsets from the turn of the century that stiffly exaggerated female curves, women now had recourse to elasticized foundation garments that gently molded the body and created the illusion of an unsupported "natural" figure. Pleated or bias-cut silk satin or jersey gowns by French designers like Madeleine Vionnet (1876–1975) and Alix (later Madame Grès; 1903–1993) turned women into living sculptures. In the previous decade, garments were cut on the straight grain, which allowed for lace inlays and insertions. This construction, however, was more difficult in fabrics worked on the bias. Since the flexibility of these bias-cut materials differed from that of lace, the two were usually used separately (FIG. 15.15). Even Gabrielle Chanel (1883–1971), who had imposed an

FIG. 15.13 (LEFT)
Man Ray, *Tanja Ramm*, ca. 1930. Gelatin silver print. Musée National d'Art Moderne/Centre Georges Pompidou, Paris, AM1994-394(3534).

FIG. 15.14 (RIGHT)
Woman putting on stockings, 1937. Gelatin silver print. © Laure Albin Guillot/Roger-Viollet, RV-83862-16.

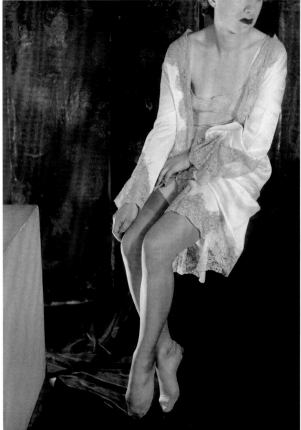

athletic style derived from men's apparel throughout the 1920s, made a stunning turn toward feminine grace at the end of the decade. In photographs dating to the 1930s, she staged herself in long dresses of white lace, and many of her designs for extremely delicate and light evening garments incorporating lace are fitted to the bust and widen from the hips to the hem (FIG. 15.16). Madeleine Vionnet used lace in large flared dresses, hinting at a body enclosed in a sheath, while Elsa Schiaparelli (1890–1973) made full use of lace's graphic potential (FIG. 15.17).[20] And for those who did not dress in haute couture, there was lace worked "in heavy cotton . . . worn over an underslip of contrasting colour," for example, or moderately priced lace gloves and mitts that made one's attire more sophisticated.[21]

World War II impacted the production and use of lace, which would not fully recover until the 1950s. The last European centers of handmade lace disappeared.[22] Despite the fact that Paris fashion houses were obliged from 1942 onward to include two designs in each collection featuring lace (one entirely in lace and another that incorporated lace), it was primarily seen on extravagant hats.[23] In the following decade, lace regained its former glory, and its widespread use visually reaffirmed the prescribed postwar role for women that insisted on their domestic responsibilities and femininity. Combined with

FIG. 15.15 (LEFT)
François Kollar, photograph of the linen maid at Callot Sœurs, Paris, 1931. © François Kollar/Bibliothèque Forney/Roger-Viollet, RV-34597-9.

FIG. 15.16 (RIGHT)
François Kollar, photograph of Coco Chanel at the Ritz Hotel in a flounced lace dress, seated in front of her Coromandel screen, 1937. Médiathèque de l'Architecture et du Patrimoine/Charenton-le-Pont/France, 71L00044.

FIG. 15.17 (OPPOSITE)
Boris Lipnitzki, photograph of a dress designed by Elsa Schiaparelli, 1934. © Boris Lipnitzki/Roger-Viollet, RV-9850-3.

cascades of tulle, it was the favorite material for wedding gowns such as that worn by Grace Kelly for her marriage to Prince Rainier III of Monaco on April 19, 1956 (FIG. 15.18).[24] This lavish use of lace recalled the similar ostentatious displays of the Second Empire. Haute couture deployed lace for the cocktail hour and the evening, where it became compulsory: black lace for Chanel (FIG. 15.19), bright and dense colors for Cristóbal Balenciaga (FIG. 15.20), and white for Pierre Balmain and Christian Dior (FIG. 15.21). In 1952 Dior, the most famous couturier of the 1950s, declared: "I love lace for evening dresses . . . for a cocktail frock . . . or for a blouse. . . . When a fabric is fancy in itself it needs simplicity of design to show it to its best advantage."[25] Corseted bustier-dresses with dramatically flared skirts gained popularity for evening wear in the late 1940s and 1950s, and elegant capes, bolero jackets, or vests were sometimes lined with lace (FIG. 15.22). Lace allowed for lightness in such garments and, at the same time, contributed to the opulence that characterized much of women's fashions of the decade.

Thanks to the development of synthetic materials—and nylon, in particular—lace was abundant throughout mainstream fashion as well as haute couture.[26] Nylon lace that was ubiquitous in the 1950s had neither the flexibility nor the feel of silk

FIG. 15.18 (LEFT)
Rainer III, Prince of Monaco, and Grace Kelly on their wedding day, April 19, 1956. MARKA/Alamy Stock Photo.

FIG. 15.19 (RIGHT)
Chanel, evening dress, ca. 1958. Lace over silk and net boned foundation. © Victoria and Albert Museum, London, Given by Sir Anthony Nutting, in memory of Anne, Lady Nutting, T.131-1990.

FIG. 15.20 (OPPOSITE)
Cristóbal Balenciaga, mid-length cocktail dress featuring Lesage embroidery, Winter 1953. Mechanical lace, silk embroidery, anthracite, sequins, and beads. Cité de la dentelle et de la mode, Ville de Calais, 97.48.3.

Catherine Örmen

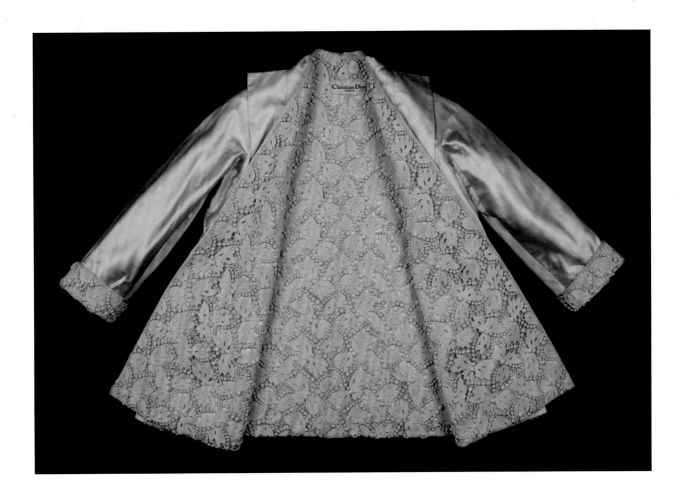

or cotton, but it was less fragile. The use of black lace in women's highly structured undergarments that emphasized the fullness of the bust and hips and the narrowness of the waist greatly increased their eroticism.[27] Thanks to the growth of prêt-à-porter in France in the postwar period that encompassed both outer garments and underwear, the *guêpière*, first launched by the couturier Marcel Rochas (1902–1955) in 1942, became affordable for a mass audience that followed the example of leading Hollywood stars, who were often photographed in black lingerie.[28] Dior's New Look, introduced at his first collection in February 1947, imposed a pinup girl's silhouette, which was obtainable thanks to guêpières, basques, bustiers, waist cinchers, push-up bras, and petticoats that were often decorated with lace.[29] This underwear could be washed without losing its color, dried quickly, and needed no ironing, which made it ideal for the busy housewife and working woman. Further, unlike silk, nylon could be dyed in colorfast black as well as other deep, rich shades such as red. In the 1950s this dye technology popularized underwear in darker colors, which affected tastes and attitudes toward lingerie. Although the use of white and pale-colored lace in underwear increased dramatically from the late nineteenth century through the 1930s, black was generally viewed as beyond the bounds of respectability since it was associated with immoral women. However, by midcentury, advertisements in French and American fashion periodicals attest to the acceptance of "sexy" black lingerie for upper- and middle-class women (FIG. 15.23).

In the 1960s a paradigm shift occurred: in London, in Paris, and on the East and West Coasts of the United States, young men and women became a powerful cultural force, and in the realm of women's fashion, a thin, adolescent body type and a whimsical, experimental approach to dressing swept away the previously dominant rich, sophisticated, conformist (and sometimes couture-clad) feminine ideal. In France the ready-to-wear industry that had lagged behind that of the United States expanded significantly in response to the demands of young consumers. As in the 1920s, the female silhouette became androgynous, emphasized by straight, body-skimming dresses, and under these minimally structured garments, lingerie also became simplified. In this environment, lace, a symbol of consummate femininity, disappeared from the body and was instead used primarily for furnishings, bedcovers, and curtains (FIG. 15.24).[30] Although rarely used even in lingerie, lace stockings sometimes covered the expanse of legs left visible under miniskirts (FIG. 15.25). Lace's partial comeback in the second half of this decade was due, in part, to the cinema: in *How to Steal a Million* (1966), Audrey Hepburn wore a dress of black Chantilly lace designed by Hubert de Givenchy, and in 1969 Yves Saint Laurent created a very simple short dress in white guipure and cotton voile for Catherine Deneuve for her role in *Mississippi Mermaid*, similar to those in fashion at the time (FIG. 15.26).[31] In 1970 Saint Laurent landed another coup, now legendary, with his World War II–inspired short black wool crepe evening dress that featured a large inset machine-made Chantilly lace panel at the back and demonstrated the ability of lace to simultaneously conceal and reveal (FIG. 15.27).[32]

The shift in attitudes toward dressing and the rise of streetwear that emerged in the 1960s persisted into the 1970s, dealing a nearly fatal blow to the French fashion industry's specialized artisans such as feather workers and embroiderers. This development was also directly related to the inexorable decline in activity of haute couture: between 1946 and 1967 the number of couture houses in operation in Paris decreased from 106 to 19.[33] Confronted with this dire economic situation and facing an increasingly global market, leading luxury brands including Louis Vuitton, Chanel, Hermès, and Cartier introduced campaigns to promote the cachet of their goods for both high- and middle-income consumers that were extremely successful.[34]

FIG. 15.23
Corselette by Warner's advertisement, *Vogue* 126, no. 6 (October 1955), page 110. Ink on paper. Courtesy PVH Archives.

At the same time, within this global fashion system, both French and Swiss manufacturers continued to produce lace. From the 1970s until the early 2000s, these firms regularly advertised in the front pages of French *Vogue* or the *Officiel de la couture*, presenting themselves in tandem with designers. To reinforce their connection to the historical manufacture of chemical lace in Switzerland and distinguish themselves from competitors in Asia, St. Gallen–based firms often added "St. Gall" after their company name in advertisements.[35] Since the 1970s they have affirmed their Swiss identity and their technical specialty (embroidery) with a variety of other marketing practices: Jakob Schlaepfer attach "Swiss embroidery" to their label, and Forster Willi, now Forster Rohner, even more radically, assert their ties with St. Gallen by using the slogan "St Gall embroidery." Manufacturing companies in both Calais and St. Gallen have to put their know-how on display, and communication is essential.[36]

In the 1980s the spread of Lycra and microfibers, synonymous with softness and comfort, resulted in a resurgence of lace with a new elasticity.[37] It smoothly encased legs and was widely incorporated into lingerie. The bodysuit exemplified the use of this innovative lace that acted as a form of support. Chantal Thomass, a leading French lingerie designer, selects her lace from firms in Calais but also turns to the St. Gallen manufacturers Forster Rohner AG, Jakob Schlaepfer AG, or Bischoff Textil AG for products to decorate her lingerie or embroider her lace.[38]

FIG. 15.24 (LEFT)
Film still of Mylène Demongeot in *Cherchez l'idole*, 1963. © BHVP/Roger-Viollet, RV-157292-23.

FIG. 15.25 (RIGHT)
Balmoral tights advertisement, *Parlons bas*, no. 7 (May–June 1967). Ink on paper. Private collection.

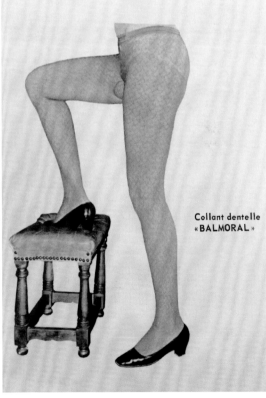

Collant dentelle «BALMORAL»

During this decade, fashion was characterized by both opulence and grunge; in service of the former, luxury and femininity took center stage. Boosted by a new clientele's demands for ostentation, haute couture—Chanel, Emanuel Ungaro, Jean-Louis Scherrer, Christian Lacroix—used copious amounts of lace that made powerful visual statements about women and their sartorial preferences (FIG. 15.28). Although Thierry Mugler, the inveterate showman, used traditional lace for his figure-hugging gowns (FIG. 15.29), he also experimented with spectacular rubber designs that were lace in name only.[39] Even menswear looked to lace; in his Spring–Summer 1997 collection the irreverent couturier Jean Paul Gaultier imagined men wearing lace again after a hiatus of two hundred years.

In the last decade of the twentieth century, what clothing signifies was dissected, analyzed, and commandeered, and the use of lace by couture and other high-end designers became marginal; for Martin Margiela, Hussein Chalayan, or Alexander McQueen, it was merely a vestige of cultural heritage.[40] European fashion—minimalist and sanitized—became globalized. Simultaneously, cocooning pushed the individual to refocus on the sphere of his or her immediate environment, and consumers demanded ever more comfort and protection from clothing. It was in the 1990s that women's lingerie

FIG. 15.26 (LEFT)
James Galanos, day dress, 1968. Manufactured as Galanos for Amelia Gray, Los Angeles. Cotton machine lace with applied cording and mother-of-pearl button. Fashion Institute of Design & Merchandising, Los Angeles, FIDM Museum Collection: Anonymous Donor, 2003.40.32.

FIG. 15.27 (RIGHT)
Yves Saint Laurent, evening dress, Look #117, Autumn/Winter 1970–71. Wool crepe by Gandini with machine-made silk Chantilly lace by Brivet. Palais Galliera, musée de la Mode de la Ville de Paris, GAL 1977.9.6.

JEAN-LOUIS SCHERRER

51 AVENUE MONTAIGNE
PARIS

FIG. 15.28
Lanel, Jean-Louis Scherrer
advertisement, 1987. Ink on paper.
Private collection.

became the principal source of demand for lace and embroidery manufacturers. Now, at the beginning of the twenty-first century, thanks to intelligent materials, shapewear is capable of softly sculpting the body while lace and embroidery, whose manufacture continues to be refined by innovative technology, can be included in encapsulation procedures designed to hydrate the skin or heal the body (FIG. 15.30).⁴¹ Over the last several years, designer brands including Burberry and Valentino have shown menswear with St. Gallen lace, heralding, perhaps, a new frontier for these manufacturers in a growing market of nonbinary dressing.⁴²

FIG. 15.29 (LEFT)

Thierry Mugler, evening gown, 1994. Silk satin, Chantilly lace, and velvet. Collection of The Museum at the Fashion Institute of Technology, 2016.114.2.

FIG. 15.30 (RIGHT)

Simon Frostick, Lars Neumann, W. Angus Wallace, and Alan McLeod (designers), Peter Butcher (textile designer), Ellis Developments Ltd. (developer), and Pearsalls Ltd. (manufacturer), bioimplantable device for reconstructive shoulder surgery, 1997–2003, textile designed 2004. Polyester. Cooper Hewitt, Smithsonian Design Museum, Gift of Ellis Developments, Ltd., 2004-15-1.

This chapter (including quotations unless otherwise noted) was translated from the French by Nils Schott.

1   There is now an official label protected by the Fédération Française des Dentelles et Broderies for Leavers lace produced in Calais and Caudry. "Le label: Découvrir l'histoire d'une marque iconique," Dentelle de Calais-Caudry, https://www.dentelledecalais caudry.fr/le-label/.
2   The procedure was discovered in Germany in 1883 and subsequently improved by the St. Gallen manufacturers. Although most Swiss manufacturers no longer use the original 19th-century embroidery machines, there is a surviving example of a hand-embroidery machine on display at the Textilmuseum St. Gallen.
3   In the late 19th century, chlorine was initially used for this solution, followed by caustic soda, while other chemicals were introduced in the 20th century (SEE CHAP. 14).
4   In 1948 in Germany, Karl Mayer introduced the first warp knitting machine. His company launched the first Raschel machine in 1953 and the first Multibar Raschel machine for the production of lace articles in 1956. Building on this procedure, their Jacquardtronic (debuted 1985) and Textronic (debuted 1990) machines brought technical improvements. And in St. Gallen the embroidery machines, too, have continually increased their output speed while maintaining the same quality as in 1900. Among the most important manufacturers of embroidery machines are Lässer and Saurer. See "History," Karl Mayer, https://www.karlmayer.com/en/corporate/history/; David Spencer, Knitting Technology, 3rd ed. (Cambridge: Woodhead Publishing, 2001), 340; and "Lässer übernimmt Saurer," Leader Digital, August 12, 2021, https://www.leaderdigital.ch/news /laesser-ueberimmt-saurer-6459.html.
5   Anne Kraatz, ed., Dentelles au Musée historique des tissus, exh. cat. (Lyon, France: Musée historique des tissus, 1983), 152. Kraatz notes that coffee and onion skins were also used to give what was deemed an appropriately "antique" look to laces at this time, in contrast to the 18th-century desire for white (linen) lace that attested to cleanliness achieved through laundering.
6   Emmanuelle Serrière, "The Invention of the Label," trans. Anna Hiddleston-Galloni, in Paris haute couture, ed. Olivier Saillard and Anne Zazzo (Paris: Skira, Flammarion, 2012), 27.
7   Farid Chenoune, Les dessous de la féminité: Un siècle de lingerie (Paris: Assouline, 1998), 17–18. Frou-frou, a play by Henri Meilhac and Ludovic Halévy, opened at the Gymnase Dramatique in Paris on October 31, 1869. In 1898 the review Paris qui marche published the lyrics to a song titled "Frou-Frou" that was first performed by Juliette Méaly at the Théâtre des Variétés in 1897. A copy of the score is available through BnF Gallica, https://gallica.bnf.fr/ark:/12148 /bpt6k318842n.r=henri%20chatau%20frou%20frou?rk=42918;4.
8   Regarding advertising posters and the connection between women and nature, see, for example, Paul Greenhalgh, Essential Art Nouveau (London: Victoria and Albert Museum, 2000), 151.
9   Lace was not entirely absent during this period. For example, in April 1916 Les Élégances Parisiennes showed lace blouses, and in August the fashion editor reported on the vogue for both Chantilly and metallic laces (ibid., 76). In March 1917 the same magazine illustrated lace tea dresses.
10 Lace was sometimes incorporated into mourning attire that primarily utilized black crepe. In April 1916 Les Élégances Parisiennes illustrated a half-mourning dress (fig. 68) with a bodice of white lace veiled with black silk chiffon and trimmed with soutache (corsage de dentelle blanche voilé de mousseline de soie noire avec applications d'ottoman soutaché). Just a few months before the outbreak of the war, an article on mourning in Les Modes described mourning lingerie that might be trimmed with black or mauve satin ribbons and black Chantilly. Marquise de Noy, "Le deuil, les nouveaux usages," Les Modes, April 1914. See also Maude Bass-Krueger, "Mourning," in French Fashion, Women, and the First World War, ed. Maude Bass-Krueger and Sophie Kurkdjian (New York: Bard Graduate Center; New Haven, CT: Yale University Press, 2019), 202–17.

During the war, many Paris couture houses relied on the American market to sustain their businesses, and evening garments made for this clientele included linen and metallic laces. In 1915 in the middle of World War I, thirteen fashion houses, including Paquin, Doucet, Callot Sœurs, Worth, and Lanvin, took part in the San Francisco International Exposition to promote French haute couture. For the French producer Darquer, it presented an occasion for finding new markets. "Notre histoire," Darquer, https://darquer.com/content/4-no-tre-histoire-darquer. See also Sophie Kurkdjian, "Restructuring French Couture, 1914–1918," in Bass-Krueger and Kurkdjian, French Fashion, Women, and the First World War, 383, 386–87.
11 According to Anne Kraatz, "Venetian lace [was] made in Tunisia, Algeria, Madagascar, and Vietnam; Cluny or Maltese lace in India; Irish Crochet lace, Milan, and Brussels lace in China." Anne Kraatz, Dentelles (Paris: Adam Biro, 1988), 165. For Algerian lace specifically, see Prosper Ricard, Dentelles algériennes et marocaines (Paris: Larose, 1928); and Marguerite A. Bel, Les arts indigènes féminins en Algérie (Algiers: Gouverneur Général de l'Algérie, 1939).
12 Nicky Albrechtsen, Vintage Fashion Complete (London: Thames & Hudson, 2014), 22.
13 A caption in the December 1926 issue of Les Modes refers to "beautiful lingerie adorned with Saint Gall lace and embroidery" (La belle lingerie s'orne de dentelle et de broderie de Saint-Gall). Les Modes, December 1926, 31, https://gallica.bnf.fr/ark:/12148/ bpt6k6106462s?rk=236052;4.
14 "La dentelle, qui est devenue, grâce aux fabriques de Saint-Gall, un des grands éléments de la toilette féminine et qui nous offre de si parfaits spécimens de tous les points célèbres, qu'on laisse souvent ceux-ci vieillir dans les cartons pour leur préférer les imitations parfaites qu'on trouve dans tous les tons beiges et ocrés demandés par la mode actuelle, aussi bien pour la lingerie que pour les robes." Les Modes, November 1926, 7, https://gallica.bnf.fr/ark:/12148 /bpt6k6106457g?rk=107296;4.
15 The fashion editor of Les Modes used various terms to describe lace from St. Gallen. See, for example, a voile dress by Maison Estelle with "guipure de St. Gall" (September 1925; https://gallica. bnf.fr/12148/bpt6k5731077c/f15.item); ensembles by Brandt that include "point d'Angleterre écru," "guipure," and "guipure Carrick Mac Cross" (July 1926; https://gallica.bnf.fr/ark:/12148/ bpt6k6106449x/f19.item); lingerie incorporating "dentelle crème fabriqué sur métier suisse" (cream lace manufactured on a Swiss loom; October 1926; https://gallica.bnf.fr/ark:/12148/ bpt6k61064547/f23.item); a dress of cream crêpe georgette with "dentelle de Venise du même ton" (Venetian lace of the same shade) by Maison Anna (July 1927; https://gallica.bnf.fr/ark:/12148/ bpt6k5726186z/f13.item); and an afternoon dress of black velvet by Béchoff with collar and cuffs of "dentelle de Venise" (October 1928; https://gallica.bnf.fr/ark:/12148/bpt6k5725695b/f12.item). For an example of embroidery, see a dress by Maison Estelle in "crêpe georgette blanc et noir garnie de broderie de St. Gall" (black and white crêpe georgette trimmed with St. Gall embroidery; May 1926; https://gallica.bnf.fr/ark:/12148/bpt6k6106446p/f12.item) and a two-piece ensemble of royal blue crêpe de chine trimmed with "broderies sur métier suisse" (July 1927; https://gallica.bnf.fr/ ark:/12148/bpt6k5726186z/f17.item). The term "métier suisse" refers to (Swiss) machine embroidery.

16 On these stylistic trends in art deco, see, for example, Christopher Frayling, "Egyptomania," and Anna Jackson, "Inspiration from the East," in *Art Deco 1910–1939*, ed. Charlotte Benton, Tim Benton, and Ghislaine Wood (London: Victoria and Albert Museum, 2003), 40–49, 66–77.

17 "The time might not be far off when the grande couture, creating a kind of sumptuous poverty, will shy away from its own work. It favors anyone capable of turning two ells of cloth into a double rectangle with holes for sleeves on which embroiderers, weavers, even painters"—and lacemakers, we might add—"then try to do their best. Every time dressmakers created too rigorous a type, and one so close to uniforms that only color, arabesque, and material bring any distinction, they carelessly renounced an important part of their prerogatives." (Le temps n'est peut-être pas très loin où la grande couture, créatrice d'une sorte d'indigence fastueuse, s'effraiera de son œuvre. Elle fait la part belle à toute main capable de prélever, sur deux aunes de tissu, un rectangle double percé de deux manches sur lequel le brodeur, le tisseur, voire le peintre [et le fabricant de dentelle, pourrait-on ajouter] s'évertuent après. Chaque fois que la couture a créé un type rigoureux, et si proche de l'uniforme que seule la couleur, l'arabesque, la consistance y interviennent en manière d'insignes, elle a résigné à la légère une partie importante de ses prérogatives.) Colette, "Printemps de demain," *Vogue*, February 1, 1925, 31, https://gallica.bnf.fr/ark:/12148/bpt6k6539893f/f3.item.r=Printemps%20de%20demain.

18 Cornel Dora, "Le berceau de la broderie," in *Secrets, sous le charme de la lingerie*, exh. cat. (St. Gallen, Switzerland: Textilmuseum St. Gallen, 2008), 146.

19 During a conversation with the author in July 2021, Tobias Forster relayed that just after World War II, Christian Dior saw a procession in Appenzell near St. Gallen and was struck by the women's wasp waists and the long pleated skirts—a silhouette very similar to that of his New Look presented in February 1947.

20 Gérard-Julien Salvy, *Mode des années 30* (Paris: Seuil, 1991), 126, 127.

21 Albrechtsen, *Vintage Fashion Complete*, 39. From 1930, the fashion magazine *Art goût beauté* announced the return of lace gloves and mitts. Guillaume Garnier, *Paris–couture–années trente* (Paris: Edition-Paris Musées: Société de l'histoire du costume, 1987), 189.

22 Kraatz, *Dentelles au Musée historique des tissus*, 12. In the 1920s there was still a small workshop in Tulle that employed war widows, but this closed in 1933, and the resurgence in production that began in 1982 was due to the efforts of an organization whose aim was to preserve these skills. Marie-Madeleine Bonneau-Pontabry, *La dentelle de Tulle: Une belle au bois dormant; Approche historique et sociale d'un artisanat d'art* (N.p.: À l'Enseigne du Griffon, 2005), 35–37. Handmade Alençon lace had all but disappeared by the mid-20th century. In order to maintain and promote this technique associated with the city since the 17th century, the Mobilier National created a specialized workshop for its production in 1976. Since 2010, the Alençon needle lace technique has been included on the Liste Représentative du patrimoine culturel immatériel de l'humanité. "Alençon: Atelier de dentelle," Mobilier National/Les Gobelins, http://www.mobiliernational.culture.gouv.fr/fr/nous-connaitre/les-manufactures/dentelle-alencon.

23 Tulle and embroidery were included in these regulations. Dominique Veillon, *Fashion Under the Occupation* (New York: Berg, 2002), 64–66, 91.

24 The American costume designer Helen Rose, who worked primarily for Metro-Goldwyn-Mayer, created the MGM star's wedding gown. Six years earlier, she designed the gown worn by Elizabeth Taylor in *Father of the Bride* (1950). Marilyn Monroe, another famous film star of the 1950s, wore a figure-hugging strapless dress designed by William Travilla with lace by Sophie Hallette at the premiere of *How to Marry a Millionaire* on November 4, 1953.

25 "Lace," in Christian Dior, *The Little Dictionary of Fashion* (1954; New York: Abrams, 2007), 71. The full entry reads: "Originally beautiful and expensive handwork; now machinery has made it possible for every woman to have it. I love lace for evening dresses . . . for a cocktail frock . . . or for a blouse. I am not so keen on it for trimmings—it easily looks old-fashioned. A little lace collar can look charming on a black frock but it must be chosen with discretion—you don't want to look like Little Lord Fauntleroy! Under a black suit or with a full skirt for parties, a lace blouse can look charming. But being a rich and elaborate material it should only be used for very simple styles. When a fabric is fancy in itself it needs simplicity of design to show it to its best advantage. It is the same with an evening dress—choose a style of great simplicity; no complicated drapes or complicated cutting."

26 See, for example, Susannah Handley, *Nylon: The Story of a Fashion Revolution; A Celebration of Design from Art Silk to Nylon and Thinking Fibres* (Baltimore: Johns Hopkins University Press, 1999), 43.

27 Shazia Boucher, Annette Haudiquet, and Philippe Peyre, *25 ans de lingerie: La dentelle sans dessus/dessous* (Calais, France: Musée des Beaux-Arts et de la Dentelle, 1997), 36–37.

28 In 1942 Marcel Rochas, inspired by Mae West, produced a very feminine collection in which he introduced "the famous bustier" (long-line strapless top) that became enormously influential in the late 1940s and throughout the 1950s. Veillon, *Fashion Under the Occupation*, 102. See also Françoise Mohrt, *Marcel Rochas: Trente ans d'élégance et de créations, 1925–1955* (Paris: Jacques Damase, 1983), 94. For contemporary press, see an advertisement for "'Le bustier et la guêpière' de Marcel Rochas" that appeared in *L'officiel de la mode*, no. 319–20 (1948): 17; reproduced in Denis Bruna, ed., *La mécanique des dessous: Une histoire indiscrète de la silhouette* (Paris: Les Arts Décoratifs, 2013), 236.

29 There were various terms for the all-in-one foundation garments. The 1948 advertisement with Rochas's bustier and *guêpière* shows a strapless long-line bra combined with a short girdle trimmed with a deep lace flounce. Similar-looking garments were also described as *justaucorps* and corselets. Farid Chenoune, *Beneath It All: A Century of French Lingerie* (New York: Rizzoli, 1999), 94–96. In English the guêpière was known as a "waspie." Charlotte Delory, "Brassieres, Girdles, Waspies, and Cami-Panties since 1900," in *Fashioning the Body: An Intimate History of the Silhouette*, ed. Denis Bruna (New York: Bard Graduate Center; New Haven, CT: Yale University Press, 2015), 235–36.

30 In a 1971 home decorating guide, the authors recommended "macramé and guipures that are much like lace" as well as contemporary ecru or colored nets, and cotton lace with large geometric motifs" for a large bay window. (Les macramés et les guipures, à aspect de dentelles, sont tissés sur des métiers très complexes. . . . Vous disposez d'une grande baie, la pièce est claire, votre mobilier moderne: vous avez le choix entre les tissages à mailles, les filets contemporains écrus ou colorés, la guipure de coton à grands motifs géométriques.) Michelle Mortier, Anne-Marie Pajot, and René-Jean Caillette, *Les guides pratiques de la redoute*, vol. 4, *Soyez décoratrice* (Paris: Librairie Jules Tallandier, 1971), 249.

31 The Yves Saint Laurent dress is preserved in the collection of the Palais Galliera, GAL1977.56.1. Saillard, *Anatomie d'une collection*, 54–55.

32 The dress, with black lace by Brivet, was photographed by Jean-Loup Sieff in 1970 for *Vogue France*. *Yves Saint Laurent et la photographie de mode*, preface by Marguerite Duras (Paris: Albin Michel, 1988), 71.

33 Didier Grumbach, *Histoires de la mode* (Paris: Éditions du Seuil, 1993), 57.

34 Vincent Bastien, "Parole d'expert: L'originalité du luxe à la française," *Vie publique*, November 20, 2019, https://www.vie-publique.fr/parole-dexpert/271890-loriginalite-du-luxe-la-francaise.
35 See, for example, advertisements for "Balmain/Union St. Gall (Switzerland)," *Vogue France*, September 1973; "Christian Dior Haute Couture/Forster Willi St Gall/Les Broderies Suisses," *Vogue France*, September 1978; "Emanuel Ungaro Couture/Jakob Schlaepfer & Co./ AG Broderies St Gall Suisse," *Vogue France*, September 1978.
36 Lace producers introduced the label "Dentelle de Calais" in 1967 and broadened it to "Dentelle de Calais-Caudry" in September 2015. These labels were intended, notably, to distinguish them from Chinese or Swiss manufacturers. For details, see the record on the French government website DATA INPI, https://data.inpi.fr/marques /WO1283273?q=dentelle%20de%20Calais-Caudry#WO1283273. However, in spite of this messaging on the part of the Forster Rohner company, for example, clients continue to refer to their "lace" products rather than using the term "embroidery." Personal communication, Miriam Rüthemann, executive assistant at Forster Rohner AG, 2021.
37 Bruno Noyon, manufacturer of lace in Calais, began in 1981 to look into the adaptation of elastane fiber for the "thin-bar" Leavers looms. These looms derived their name from the bars, 600 in number, that wove the lace ground in combination with the chariot-bobbins, independently of the 150–200 bars of thicker width that controlled the design. By 1982, with the technology mastered, two to three years were necessary to raise a stock of looms capable of responding to industrial demand. The first clients were the French company Barbara and the Italian company La Perla. Demand continually accelerated, and in five years, the corsetry-lingerie that had used 100 percent rigid lace swung toward 90 percent elastic lace. At the same time, the DuPont company improved the quality of its elastane thread,

Lycra, and a collaboration between DuPont and Noyon was firmly established. Author conversation with Olivier Noyon, former PDG (*president-dirécteur general*) of the Noyon Company, December 2021.
38 Chantal Thomass, conversation with the author, July 2021.
39 In his Spring/Summer 1992 collection, Thierry Mugler presented a sheath dress with long pagoda sleeves in black rubber. See Danièle Bott, *Galaxie Glamour, Collections et Créations* (Paris: Ramsay, 2009), 168.
40 Bruno Remaury, "Une mode entre deux décennies," in *Repères Mode et Textile 96: Visages d'un secteur*, ed. Bruno Remaury (Paris: Institut français de la mode, 1996), 60–70. One of Martin Margiela's designs includes a copy of an 18th-century man's shirt with lace trimmings that recall the historical import of the garment. *Martin Margiela: Collections femme, 1989–2009* (Paris: Paris Musées 2018), 47. See also Andrew Bolton, ed., *Alexander McQueen: Savage Beauty* (New York: Metropolitan Museum of Art, 2011), 125; and Hussein Chalayan, *Cartesia*, Autumn/Winter 1994, photographed by Chris Moore in *Hussein Chalayan*, ed. Robert Violette (New York: Rizzoli, 2011), 33.
41 Materials that incorporate Lycra Beauty technology offer different levels of support. For encapsulation, see Louise Roque, "Les tendances cosméto-textiles," *Le Monde*, October 18, 2000, https://www.lemonde.fr/archives/article/2000/10/18/les-tendances -cosmeto-textiles_3716795_1819218.html. On intelligent textiles, see Patricia Wilson, "Textiles from Novel Means of Innovation," in *Extreme Textiles: Designing for High Performance*, by Matilda McQuaid and Philip Beesley (New York: Princeton Architectural Press, 2005), 184.
42 Burberry used Forster Rohner guipure for menswear in its Spring 2016 and Spring 2017 collections, as did Valentino for its Resort 2022 collection. Hans Schreiber, creative director at Forster Rohner AG, email communication with the author and editors, April 2022.

16 Lace in St. Gallen Today: Tradition and Innovation at Forster Rohner and Jakob Schlaepfer

Introduction by Annina Dosch

Interview with Tobias Forster, Martin Leuthold, and Hans Schreiber

T HE HISTORY OF ST. GALLEN as a center of Swiss textile production stretches back to the mid-thirteenth century. Two hundred years later, the city was known throughout Europe for the production of high-quality linen, and it was in the second half of the nineteenth century that industrialization and several technological advancements developed by Swiss inventors enabled increased production and fueled the subsequent popularity of the region's specialty: chemical lace (SEE CHAP. 14).[1] This textile is often referred to as "guipure" as well as "St. Gall embroidery" or "Swiss embroidery" because it is made on an embroidery machine. Motifs are embroidered onto a thin fabric ground, which is then dissolved in a chemical bath. This process leaves only the embroidered threads behind, allowing manufacturers to imitate and re-create complicated styles of handmade lace.[2]

Like the European lace industries discussed in the previous chapters, the textile industry in eastern Switzerland relied on international markets that were often volatile. From the second half of the nineteenth century until 1914, the United States was a particularly important consumer of Swiss embroideries.[3] World War I drove the Swiss industry into crisis, and in this rapid decline, employment numbers fell dramatically, embroidery machines were destroyed, trade suffered, and manufacturers were forced to pivot to find other sources of income.[4] The country's textile industry would not recover until after World War II, when the European economy rebounded and high-end fashion designers once again sought out the goods from St. Gallen that had enjoyed great success earlier in the century. Clients in the United States were important in this period as well, and the American fashion press often reported on representatives from Swiss companies visiting to conduct market research or present new collections to buyers.[5] In the economic boom of the 1950s and 1960s, exports of Swiss embroidery products were once again on the rise. Technological improvements to the embroidery machines, including wider frames, enabled the decoration of greater surface areas of fabric at higher speeds. The expensive machinery, however, made this type of manufacturing a capital-intensive industry, and over the course of the 1960s, the number of companies and their employees in the industry declined.[6] The end of the decade also saw the introduction of computer technology, which not only made the patterning process more efficient but also improved the quality of the resulting products.[7]

Today, Forster Rohner AG and Jakob Schlaepfer AG are among those manufacturers continuing the rich textile history of St. Gallen and the surrounding region. For more than a century, both companies have proven themselves to be innovative, flexible, and creative. Both firms boast a devoted international clientele and a longstanding reputation for producing high-quality chemical lace and other textiles for fashion and interiors, with products that are especially popular among haute couture designers.[8]

Forster Rohner: Creativity, Innovation, and Tradition

Forster Rohner AG is a company built on tradition. The firm was founded in St. Gallen in 1904 by Conrad Forster-Willi (1870–1946) as Forster Willi & Co., and today it is led by Emanuel and Caroline Forster, the fourth generation of the Forster family.[9] The company's collaboration with high fashion designers in Paris, Milan, and New York began

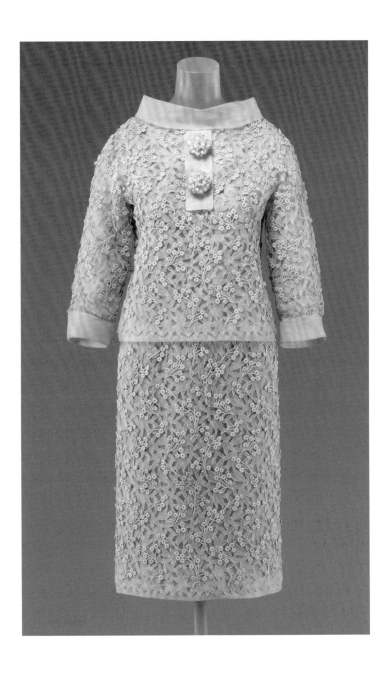

in the 1930s, and since then their range of products has adapted to changing markets. An emphasis on embroideries for blouses in the 1950s gave way to trimmings for bed linen in the 1960s, followed by embroideries for outerwear in the 1970s, and, increasingly, starting in the early 1980s, embroideries for lingerie. Since then, the company has grown larger and incorporated various other Swiss textile firms. In 1988 Forster Willi & Co. acquired textile firm Jacob Rohner AG, which specialized in embroidery for undergarments, and four years later the two would merge to form Forster Rohner AG. The newly consolidated company soon expanded beyond Switzerland, establishing the Forster Rohner Embroidery Co. Ltd. in Suzhou, China, in the mid-1990s.[10] Over the past two decades, Forster Rohner Group has been recognized worldwide for its contributions to the textile industry.[11]

At manufacturing sites in Switzerland, Romania, Bosnia-Herzegovina, and China, Forster Rohner Group produces a wide range of goods at different price points for a diverse international clientele. Their high-end products have been used by couture designers including Dior, Chanel, Givenchy, Yves Saint Laurent, Prada, Valentino, Akris, and Isabel Toledo, among others, for almost a century (FIGS. 16.1–3; SEE FIGS. I.2 AND 15.22). The company's headquarters houses an immense archive of textile samples and records that constitutes an important repository for contemporary couture houses who send design teams to St. Gallen for inspiration. Notable garments in the company's archive include those designs made for Doris Forster (1911–2008), who was married to Willy C. Forster (1899–1964; FIGS. 16.4–6). Forster Rohner also collaborates directly with designers to create custom fabrics for haute couture production; some designers pull directly from the archive and have historical textiles remade anew to then be fashioned into modern silhouettes. A large facet of the company's manufacturing for the commercial market is embroideries and lace for lingerie, including for brands such as Maison Lejaby and Chantelle.

FIG. 16.1
Yves Saint Laurent for House of Yves Saint Laurent (designer) and Forster Willi & Co. (now Forster Rohner AG; textile manufacturer), evening dress, Paris and St. Gallen, Switzerland, Spring/Summer 1963. Cotton, silk, pearl, and plastic. The Metropolitan Museum of Art, New York, Gift of Mrs. Charles B. Wrightsman, 1964, C.I.64.59.7a,b. Cat. 182.

Jakob Schlaepfer AG began as an embroidery firm established in 1904 in St. Gallen by Rudolf Vogel (1866–1937). Vogel would be joined four years later by an apprentice named Jakob Schläpfer (1892–1962), who was the sixth of seven children born to parents working in the home embroidery industry in Riemen, east of St. Gallen. In 1934 Schläpfer purchased the company (which at that point took on his name) and continued to run the business as a one-man operation. The firm was primarily an export business at this point, and sold goods commissioned from embroiderers working in the region. In an effort to be more easily legible to an international market, the company's name was changed that year from Schläpfer to Schlaepfer. Schläpfler's son Robert (1926–2015) joined the firm in 1945 and, in the following decades, it would grow steadily under his direction and that of his wife, Lisbet (1923–2015).[12]

The Jakob Schlaepfer company presented its first haute couture collection in Paris and Rome in 1964.[13] That same year, it purchased a patent for machine-embroidered sequins, and the production of sequined textiles has since remained a distinctive feature of the company's textile manufacturing. Another well-known facet of its production is rhinestone-embellished textiles; a collaboration with Swarovski jewelers for thermosetting rhinestones onto textiles began in 1975. In the 1980s Schlaepfer expanded globally, opening production sites and sales offices in Paris, New York, Los Angeles, London, Osaka, and Munich. Further technological developments followed. In 1983 the firm bought the worldwide patent for a transfer application machine and in 1985 developed the Marvel printing technique, a process that involves transferring pigment by rolling a wide metal cylinder covered in layers of colored plasticine over wet silk.[14] In 1993 the company partnered with Création Baumann, another Swiss textile company originally founded in 1886 in Langenthal, Switzerland, to design silk for furnishing and interiors and in the same year began to develop metal fabrics, also used for interior textiles such as curtains.[15] In 1995 Lisbet and Robert sold their business to von Meiss und Bolte investors, and in 1997 Jakob Schlaepfer AG was sold to Filtex AG in St. Gallen. Since 2016 Schlaepfer has been part of Forster Rohner Group, with headquarters in St. Gallen.

Schlaepfer is known for its creative designs and experimental combinations of different technologies.

FIG. 16.2

Miuccia Prada for Prada (designer) and Forster Rohner AG (textile manufacturer), ensemble, Italy and St. Gallen, Switzerland, Fall 2008. Cotton and polyester guipure lace, cotton poplin, leather, and silk knit. © The Museum at the Fashion Institute of Technology, New York, Gift of Prada, 2011.1.1. Cat. 184.

FIG. 16.3
Akris Prêt-à-Porter AG (designer)
and Forster Rohner AG (textile
manufacturer), guipure ensemble
(Look 13), St. Gallen, Switzerland, Fall/
Winter 2018. Cotton, wool guipure,
and cashmere. Akris Prêt-à-Porter AG.
Cat. 186.

Its products are highly regarded worldwide, and fabrics are selected by the leading fashion houses including Comme des Garçons, Iris van Herpen, Marc Jacobs, and Jean Paul Gaultier (FIGS. 16.7–12).[16] Combining industry and handcraft, Schlaepfer textiles are used in garments, accessories, and interiors, and with respect to contemporary lace, the company is particularly known for innovative designs that are laser-cut and 3D-printed in silicone (FIGS. 16.13–15; SEE FIG. I.30).[17] The fabrics are designed at the firm's headquarters in St. Gallen, which allows for fast and flexible implementation of client requests and the collaborative development of new ideas. Since 1995 Schlaepfer has earned recognition for excellence in its field, with awards including the 2009 and 2019 Première Vision Paris Fabrics Imagination Prize and a Highest Distinction Red Dot Design Award (Germany) in 2009. In 2013 the company received the Design Prize Switzerland, and creative director Martin Leuthold was honored with a Lifetime Achievement Award for his career spanning four decades, from 1973 to 2018.[18]

In the following interview, Tobias Forster, former creative director of Forster Rohner; Hans Schreiber, creative director of Forster Rohner; and Martin Leuthold, who was creative director at Jakob Schlaepfer until his retirement, respond to questions from Emma Cormack, Michele Majer, and Ilona Kos, discussing the long histories and continued successes of their companies during their tenure. Both Forster Rohner and Schlaepfer are highly attuned to an international market and constantly innovating to attract and maintain their worldwide clientele, continuing the position of St. Gallen at the forefront of the contemporary embroidery and lace industry.

Interview with Tobias Forster, Martin Leuthold, and Hans Schreiber

The future is split from the past, but still the
past shows us the future.
—Martin Leuthold

You have all enjoyed long careers in this industry.
How have you seen fashion change over the years?

MARTIN LEUTHOLD: Over fifty years many things have
changed. Fashion has shifted from textile wholesale and
retail to the couture business in the 1960s to the prêt-
à-porter business in the 1980s. When I started working
at Jakob Schlaepfer, our biggest market was northern
Europe, especially Denmark, Finland, and Sweden, which
had a new generation of designers in furniture and fashion like Marimekko. In the 1960s Schlaepfer developed
stitching sequins onto fabric with an embroidery machine,
which brought us to the couture labels in Paris. There were
almost two hundred couturiers in Paris in the 1960s and
1970s, but now there are only a few. During my period
in couture, we worked with Chanel, André Courrèges,
Christian Dior, Givenchy, Lacroix, Yves Saint Laurent,
and Emanuel Ungaro. In the 1980s there were many new
prêt-à-porter designers in Paris. We worked with Giorgio
Armani, Gianfranco Ferré, Jean Paul Gaultier, Romeo
Gigli, Thierry Mugler, and Vivienne Westwood. Italian
designers like Armani, Ferré, and Gianni Versace were
perhaps the most successful prêt-à-porter makers in terms
of industrial production. Donna Karan and Calvin Klein
from New York brought fashion into Europe in a new way
with their internationally successful brands. Calvin Klein,
still the leading name in the underwear world, made fashion more brand oriented through marketing. This was a
big shift. There are so many fashion labels around the
world now, and we can often buy the same clothes in Hong
Kong and New York and Switzerland.

TOBIAS FORSTER: The rise of the European ready-to-wear
market was a major change. In the 1960s when I started
at Forster Rohner (then called Forster Willi), the company was already collaborating with some of the New
York ready-to-wear designers such as Norman Norell
and Oscar de la Renta. In Paris, on the other hand,
we supplied couture houses, mainly Balenciaga, Dior,
Givenchy, and Yves Saint Laurent, but also designers like
André Courrèges and Emanuel Ungaro. I extended our
relationships to Rome and developed a close relationship
with Valentino.

Soon after, I met Karl Lagerfeld while he was still
designing for Chloé, which is where we took the first foray
into the European ready-to-wear market and saw instant
success. We designed dozens of chemical laces in the
reticella and Irish styles. Lagerfeld was fascinated by the
Rococo age, so we imitated feather-light Baroque needlework on the finest cotton net. Our collaboration continued after he was appointed design director of Chanel until
his death. Still today we are proud to maintain a close
relationship with that unique company. After a fabulous
introduction to the ready-to-wear market, it did not take
long before we started to design lace for Claude Montana,
Thierry Mugler, and Jean Paul Gaultier.

What have been the most important fashion trends
that have impacted your production? Do they stand
out clearly when looking back?

FORSTER AND HANS SCHREIBER: Guipure, what we call chemical lace, has always been a specialty of Forster Rohner.
Even when this type of lace was not particularly popular
with designers, we continued producing it, primarily to
keep our own designers and technicians trained. However, fashion designers created and responded to new
trends, pushing the product into whatever form was
fashionable at the time. In the 1960s and 1970s, Yves
Saint Laurent used a lot of the three-dimensional cotton lace in rather timeless designs, whereas Courrèges
and Cardin preferred to use lace in synthetic yarns and
geometrical designs like squares or circles. In the 1980s
fashion became more flamboyant. With designers like
Mugler and Montana, everything had to be bigger than
real life. Therefore, chemical lace had to incorporate large

three-dimensional patterns, often produced with thick yarns in cotton, wool, or even raffia. We also stitched diamonds the size of an egg onto lightweight tulle and glued thousands of rhinestones in cascades of fireworks.

LEUTHOLD: There has been a shift in material from natural to artificial fibers as well as the introduction of new

techniques. In garment production, there was a move from custom-made to wide-scale industrial manufacturing. I think it was also the symbiosis of fashion and fabric makers. How we developed and showed fabrics was a give-and-take process, with each industry encouraging the other to be creative. We began to understand that we had to vary our offerings, that we could not do the same

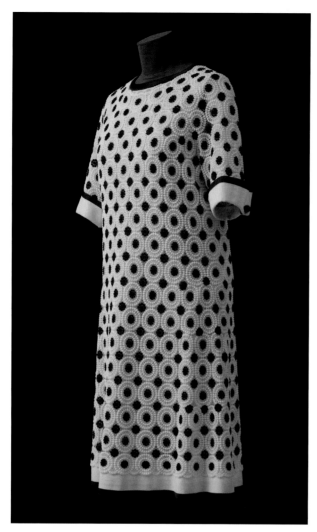

FIG. 16.6

Yves Saint Laurent for House of Yves Saint Laurent (designer) and Forster Willi & Co. (now Forster Rohner AG; textile manufacturer), dress made for Mrs. Doris Forster (1911–2008), Paris and St. Gallen, Switzerland, 1966–67. Cotton. Forster-Rohner-Collection, Koll. 217 1/2-C59. Cat. 179.

with different companies and techniques. Eventually, I found a company in Germany that was able to laser cut fabrics. In Paris the prêt-à-porter designers loved the technique and started to use the fabrics. But, out of all these new trends in techniques, silicone was the easiest thing to start working with because it comes in all colors and easily conveys a sense of three-dimensionality.

How has the use of your lace and other textiles for garment design changed?

FORSTER AND SCHREIBER: Our products are expensive and therefore were initially only used for haute couture, where garments are sewn completely by hand. Guipures were cut following even the most irregular patterns and pieced together without any visible seams to create garments that seemed magical. Thanks to modern machinery and different production facilities today, we are able to design products that are more attainable for the commercial ready-to-wear market. Additionally, aesthetic values have changed. Guipures are treated differently, more modern and experimental. They are combined in a mix of high and low, feminine and masculine, and playful combinations of patterns. Prime examples are the Winter 2008–09 and Summer 2012 collections of Miuccia Prada (SEE FIG. 16.2), for which we developed guipure, broderie anglaise, and *superposé* embroidery in very unusual combinations and materials.

LEUTHOLD: Our textiles, which are made using a variety of techniques, have always challenged designers to create new silhouettes. In the 1970s, 1980s, and 1990s, our fabrics were primarily "cutout" embroidery (*Spachtel*)—which was all done by hand—or guipure, and clients at the time understood the differences between the various lace and embroidery techniques. Now we have a new variety of interpretations of lace with the laser-cut techniques and silicone imitation laces. Young clients today also recognize the three-dimensional lace, the superposé, where there is raised embroidery on the fabric. I am sure there will be more to come in the future with the "burnout" technique, which I think is possible to further develop. We have known lace now for 550 years, and it has always followed changes in taste and techniques. This is true for

thing in successive seasons, a realization that prompted experimentation with new techniques. For example, in 1975 we started to work with Swarovski and developed a method for thermosetting a large number of small rhinestones onto fabric. Before that, we used big stones that had to be glued or sewn by hand. Laser cutting was a revolution for numerous industrial uses. We experimented

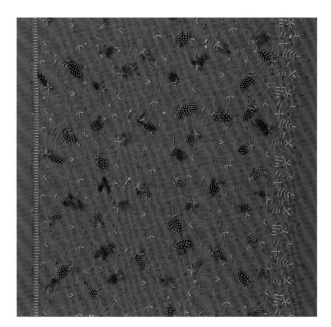

FIG. 16.7
Jakob Schlaepfer AG, sequined chemical-lace lurex with hand-appliquéd feathers, St. Gallen, Switzerland, 1998. Synthetic fibers, lamé, sequins, and feathers. Collection Martin Leuthold. Cat. 175.

FIG. 16.8
Jakob Schlaepfer AG, cutout lace with floral appliqué stitched with rubber bobbin (used by Emanuel Ungaro), St. Gallen, Switzerland, 1985. Silk. Collection Martin Leuthold. Cat. 177.

St. Gallen lace as well, and now the whole world is stitching chemical lace. Another possibility for the future is to use all this know-how and these different techniques to create a new fabric, one that is unrecognizable.

Can you speak to the different effects various materials have on the design process and the final product?

FORSTER AND SCHREIBER: Materials are key in our design and production. For guipure we have different supporting fabrics and procedures to ensure that every possible material can be used throughout production. Knowledge and testing are the basis for creating workable and wearable materials. In our creative process, we often change a technique from a common use of material to create a new look and completely different use. For Valentino Pre-Fall 2021, we created a luxurious three-dimensional, hand-cut embroidery on a sumptuous wool jersey. Traditionally, such a design in this technique would have been done in silk organza for an

evening or bridal dress, but this was made into beautiful short coats and styled with jeans and a pullover.

LEUTHOLD: For Jakob Schlaepfer, there is no limit when it comes to material. We love to surprise clients with various applications such as leather, glass, feathers, etc. In terms of yarn, we have experimented with stitching pure gold threads and flat lurex. In the late 1990s and early 2000s I was thinking about how nice it would be to have laser-cut fabrics. We had already developed the cutout techniques for embroideries in our field, so I tried with the metallic industry in St. Gallen to cut fabrics with a laser. Although it worked, it always burned away because the laser was too strong. Then I went to a hospital where they used a laser when operating on eyes or conducting other more difficult surgeries. But we needed something crafted for textiles. Finally, I read an article about cutting airbags with lasers for the automobile industry in Germany. We worked with them on the first laser-cut fabrics and eventually built our own machine to laser cut fabrics. Around the same time, I tried

FIG. 16.9
Jakob Schlaepfer AG, chemical lace (used by Balmain, Jean Paul Gaultier, Ralph and Russo, Philip Treacy, Valentino, and Versace), St. Gallen, Switzerland, 1987. Viscose. Collection Martin Leuthold. Cat. 192.

FIG. 16.10
Jakob Schlaepfer AG, chemical lace (used by Balmain, Jean Paul Gaultier, Ralph and Russo, Philip Treacy, Valentino, and Versace), St. Gallen, Switzerland, 1987. Viscose. Collection Martin Leuthold. Cat. 191.

putting fabrics in inkjet printers instead of photo paper. We found a company that had inkjet printing machines for the graphic industry and began to print on paper and then transfer the print onto fabric. This development brought us into the digital printing world. At the start, machines were printing half a meter of fabric per hour, making the product very costly. At Première Vision in 2002, the customers said, "You are crazy to sell your fabric for 200 Swiss francs a print; it should be no more than 30 Swiss francs." But they bought it! Luxury works like that. If it is new, fashionable, and desirable, then you buy it despite the cost.

What are the most meaningful sources of inspiration for Forster Rohner and Jakob Schlaepfer?

SCHREIBER: As Paul Smith famously said, "Inspiration can be found everywhere." Besides the obvious sources, like our own archive and the collection of the Textilmuseum in St. Gallen, we create mood boards for every season (twice a year) to capture essential directions for our collections. We find sources of inspiration in books, exhibitions, magazines and newspapers, movies, and social media—whatever fuels the imagination and captures the zeitgeist.

LEUTHOLD: Museums and their collections are a great source of inspiration. The antique is our future. This is the case for the Textilmuseum, where there are so many beautiful things. Also, paintings from all periods provide inspiration for colors, and forms are inspired by objects made of glass, ivory, and other materials. At Schlaepfer, working in a team, I used reference books of my own or from libraries. But, because it is hard to bring many books into the studio, I started to collect art postcards about forty years ago. I now have accumulated about four thousand, which I look at twice a year to pick out what I think resonates with what is currently in fashion. From there, I put together a collection of colors or themes that I would like to work with. I start with maybe five hundred or two hundred postcards and then narrow it down to fifty or twenty. Nature has also always been an important source of inspiration for me, in terms of both color and scale. I have a garden where the combinations of colors and forms are always different. Sometimes I am almost surprised to see how a pink is interesting next to a blue or a blue is interesting next to a yellow. This is still the biggest well of inspiration for me.

In this field, what does innovation look like? What is the relationship between traditional lace patterns and new, inventive ones?

SCHREIBER: Tradition is central to our company: "Fascination through tradition, creation, and innovation" is our leitmotif. Having an extensive archive with more than 600,000 textile samples offers us an ever-present source of inspiration, but we do not stop there. Innovation means that every season new ideas come from our selection of seasonal themes that influence the way we use techniques, colors, and materials. A little embroidered string of daisies, created twenty-five years ago as a bra strap for a lingerie company, is still a bestseller and is now redone in new colors, materials, and technical finishing effects every season.

Right now, innovation also means dealing with resources, sustainability, and creating change in the use of materials. Forster Rohner started to get Global Organic Textile Standard certification by 2010, which means that our products are developed at places that are under the strictest international standards regarding environmental effects and working conditions.

LEUTHOLD: We have what I would describe as classical Jakob Schlaepfer designs that are regularly presented in new combinations of color and material, including sequined lace in many variations.

Can you elaborate on the design process for working with a particular designer or company?

SCHREIBER: Forster Rohner creates two collections of one hundred designs a season every year. They include a mix of techniques, materials, designs, and colors to provide inspiration for the fashion market. As we serve clients across a wide range of aesthetics, it is of utmost importance for us to look for innovation on every level, while staying loyal to the DNA of our company. On the other hand, we often get requests from our clients to develop tailor-made solutions according to their design decisions. Often the creative teams of the important fashion houses visit our archives to get inspiration in order to initiate design developments. In the last couple of years, we have had very interesting and fruitful collaborations for innovative embroidery designs with the London-based designer Christopher Kane, whose brilliant ideas challenged us to utilize the various techniques that our company can offer.

LEUTHOLD: Jakob Schlaepfer is driven by its creativity to present a full story collection that surprises and inspires designers. Couture houses buy directly from the collection. Prêt-à-porter designers come up with their own ideas or source designs from our archive, which we then modify according to their request, reinventing as needed. It was

FIG. 16.11
Jakob Schlaepfer AG, chemical lace (used by Balmain, Jean Paul Gaultier, Ralph and Russo, Philip Treacy, Valentino, and Versace), St. Gallen, Switzerland, 1987. Viscose. Collection Martin Leuthold. Cat. 190.

FIG. 16.12
Jakob Schlaepfer AG, chemical lace with silver plating, St. Gallen, Switzerland, 1999. Synthetic fiber and silver plating. Collection Martin Leuthold. Cat. 176.

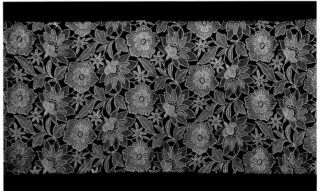

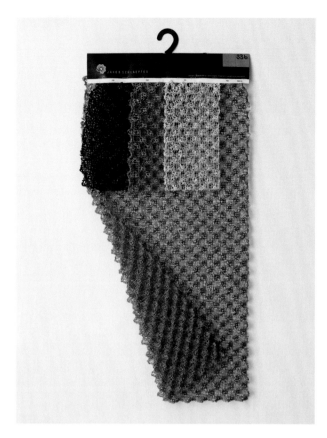

FIG. 16.13
Jakob Schlaepfer AG, sample of
hypertube guipure, St. Gallen,
Switzerland, 2019. Silicone. Collection
Jakob Schlaepfer AG. Cat. 194.

always nice to work with both older and younger designers. I worked with Givenchy from 1976 on; he loved the collections I showed in Paris. Montana, who was always intent on what he wanted to do, was the first designer to request stretch material with sequins, which was a very difficult thing to do.

What designer collaborations have been particularly successful or memorable for you?

LEUTHOLD: Marc Jacobs! We had great times together starting in 2005. He was one of the first designers to send employees to the Schlaepfer and other textile-related archives in St. Gallen. They found inspiration in the archives, taking the material that they found there and developing it for a new era, for today. Working with him was a creative and intense time for us. Jacobs was a creator. Something I learned very quickly in fashion is that there are only a few real creators. Dior, for example, was a creator.

When I began to work with Gaultier, he was young, like me, and said, "I love what you're doing, and I need all of it." After selecting fabrics, he asked, "You are sponsoring me? I'm young and fresh, and I believe in fashion." I told him, "I can only offer to sell you the fabrics. I cannot sponsor the fabrics." And he said, "Well, then, I have to look somewhere else. I don't have money." So then I told him, "Well, you only have to buy one piece from Schlaepfer. It's too expensive to do a whole collection." And so he bought two nine-meter lengths of nude tulle with clear sequins. That was a fortune for him to pay at that time—two thousand Swiss francs. But later, he said, "You were right. I just buy what I can afford."

FORSTER: The first designer that I used to work with on a regular basis was Karl Lagerfeld. I was introduced to him in the late 1960s by Francine Crescent, editor in chief of the Paris edition of *Vogue*. At that point he still had not used machine-made laces and embroideries but was fascinated by the possibilities that Forster Rohner presented. He told me that he wanted to study the technique and that I should come back in two weeks. When I met him again, he knew everything—all the effects and expressions. In the Spring 1977 collection, he used our embroideries and laces on virtually every garment that he designed. He also became my mentor, sending me to exhibitions and asking me to share my opinions. He sent me to his bookseller at Galignani's on the rue de Rivoli and told me what books to buy. Working with Lagerfeld was tough, but I learned more from him than any other designer.

Working for Valentino Garavani was wonderful. His love for beautiful material made the presentation of our collaborations a feast. His fashion shows in the 1960s and 1970s were sheer glamor. Once he called me, saying that he just completed a first garment with a silver-gray, thickly ruffled silk organza. He called out, "è un monumento" ("it's a monument"). In the end, he made three garments, all as glamorous as glamor can be—one modeled by Claudia Schiffer, one by Christy Turlington, and one by Naomi Campbell.

Finally, there were the rising stars of the 1980s like Claude Montana, Romeo Gigli, and Christian Lacroix. Working with each and every one of them was a rewarding experience. Don't we have a wonderful profession, where we have the opportunity to participate in the work of such incredibly talented people?

How important has the international market been, and how has it changed?

FORSTER AND SCHREIBER: Forster Rohner has never concentrated solely on the luxury outerwear market and has always maintained a strong presence in the worldwide market of women's lingerie. French and Italian couture, and subsequently the ready-to-wear markets of those countries, have also always been important for Forster Rohner, a development that started toward the end of World War II. We are a global company, and customers of other markets became increasingly important for its turnover. For a long time already, the core business was with Europe in countries like France, Italy, Germany, Britain, or Spain but also in the United States and Japan.

LEUTHOLD: Next to Paris, Italy, London, and New York, wholesale markets such as the Middle East and Japan were always very important. Japanese buyers came to St. Gallen until the year 2000 to select their fabrics. They always bought luxury fabrics in St. Gallen for a high-end market of daywear, not evening wear. They bought the most beautiful light fabrics, some more embellished than others, and in wintertime, cashmeres and wools. Other markets that came to St. Gallen were that of the Middle East and Southeast Asia. The Middle Eastern market preference was for shiny, glittery, and colorful fabrics. The royal families in countries like Malaysia favored bright colors, gold, and rhinestones. The princesses might wear entire outfits of one fabric, including shoes and scarves. In the 1980s and 1990s, we had big fabric fairs like Première Vision in Paris that were meeting points for fashion people to buy fabrics. It's also a bit changed now with the coronavirus pandemic. We try to do it online,

but it is difficult to show our fabrics over platforms like Skype. You can't feel them over a screen.

Have pattern rights and copyright concerns always been an aspect of working in this field? What concerns still persist today, and what steps do you take to combat them?

FORSTER: Forster Rohner designs have been copied since the company has existed, and they continue to be copied today, either by competitors or by customers who try to get our designs at a lower price, which is easy when you can avoid the cost of design. We, of course, try to protect ourselves against this type of unfair competition. Until some decades ago, the World Intellectual Property Organization in Geneva offered a fairly practical and inexpensive procedure to deposit new designs season after season. In the event that one of our designs was copied, it was simple to prove that we were the owner of a particular design. But then, as often happens with big bureaucracies, the system got so costly and, above all, so complicated that we

FIG. 16.14
Jakob Schlaepfer AG, sample of hypertube guipure used by Yang Li, St. Gallen, Switzerland, 2015–16. Silicone. Collection Jakob Schlaepfer AG.

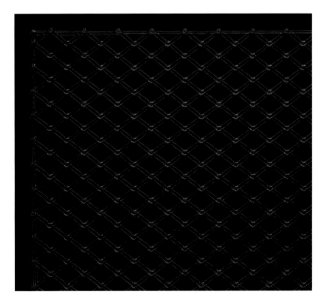

FIG. 16.15
Jakob Schlaepfer AG, sample of hypertube
guipure (used by Comme des Garçons),
St. Gallen, Switzerland, 2017. Silicone.
Collection Jakob Schlaepfer AG. Cat. 193.

practically do not use it any longer. Therefore, whenever we realize that we have been copied, it is a difficult decision whether it is worthwhile to pursue the case or not.

LEUTHOLD: Until the 1990s, all Jakob Schlaepfer designs were registered for copyright. Today, due to complicated international laws, we are more driven to let go and create something new. In Paris in the 1970s and 1980s, we were not able to show designs electronically. In the same season, we sold the same design to eight, ten, twelve couture people, all produced with the same fabric. Nobody asked for exclusivity because everyone thought, "I can make a better dress." Designers now want and need exclusivity. Fashion is online and instantaneous. If you see a print at Dior, then you do not want to see the same print at Armani. We have

to be fast with prints. When something is successful at the high end, then there are always people who produce it in a cheaper way. It is almost impossible and too expensive to secure protection of designs and techniques nowadays. If someone reproduces it quickly and cost efficiently, then you have to create something new.

What type of market fluctuations have you encountered in your careers? When those fluctuations did occur, what strategies have you used to work through them?

FORSTER: It is true that the embroidery and lace business is more volatile than other businesses. However, the market is huge, and Forster Rohner, with a worldwide staff of fewer than one thousand people, is a rather small player. We consider that if, even in a weaker year, we do not manage to make all of our production capacities work, then we have done something wrong. Either we did not understand a change of fashion, missed existing opportunities, or ultimately did not offer innovation that was convincing enough.

LEUTHOLD: It is a constant up and down because lace in fashion comes and goes. Therefore, it was always our aim at Jakob Schlaepfer to present various techniques in different fabrics. There have been many crises, but for me, it was clear: in a crisis, a door closes and another door opens. At one time, our biggest client was Japan. Three years later, it was Armani, and two years after that, Saudi Arabia, followed a year later by Lacroix. These changes are why you have to produce so much in order to meet the demands of a wide group of clients. You have to have the right fabrics at the right moment.

What changes have you seen in the fashion education system over the last several decades?

SCHREIBER: Traditionally, education in the fashion field took place in the ranks of the fashion houses. Outside that, we see two parallel tracks in fashion education programs: the very technical and practical training and the very creative and artistic training. Over the last few decades, our high fashion clients often scouted designers for their creative teams at Central Saint Martins in London or at the Royal Academy in Antwerp. These institutions, with their particular curriculums and sets of values, produce strong, creative individuals with distinctive design aesthetics.

LEUTHOLD: The big change in Switzerland regarding textile schools and education in this field of fabric design or fabric making is that with lecturing it has become more incorporated into the university system. When I was studying in this field, we always had instructors who worked in the industry, and we learned the craft directly from them. They understood how to produce fabric, how to create a design, how to look to nature for inspiration. I loved those instructors who helped me to learn this profession. Nowadays we have a lot of intelligent people who are professors, but they are not as strong in handcraft. It is more a field of study rather than that of a practitioner. When I look for talented people from these schools, I still have to train them. They have to learn for another year or two while working in a team from the business itself.

What do you see in the future for lace?

SCHREIBER: Embroidery is incredibly versatile, and the possibilities are endless. Our newest machines can combine multiple techniques like laser cutting, soutache, and sequins in one production step. Next to that, we find it important to work together with the most avant-garde design houses worldwide and with designers such as Rei Kawakubo, Miuccia Prada, Raf Simons, Gabriela Hearst, the Row, Cecilie Bahnsen, and many others. Thanks to them, embroidery will never be treated in a banal or boring way.

LEUTHOLD: Cheap production by our competitors challenges us to create to the limit. Handmade lace was produced from the sixteenth to the early twentieth century, but machine-made has only been around for about 150 years. We are still pulling from the roots of lace, from more than 550 years ago, and are not finished. There is much more innovation to come. Lace will be an inspiration forever.

The introduction to this chapter (including quotations unless otherwise noted) was translated from the German by Andrew Horsfield.

1   Cornel Dora, "St. Gallen's Textile Past," in *Textiles St. Gallen: Tausend Jahre Tradition, Technologie und Trends/A Thousand Years of Tradition, Technology and Trends*, ed. Cornel Dora, exh. cat. (St. Gallen, Switzerland: Amt für Kultur, 2004), 18–25.
2   Although this type of textile is made on an embroidery machine, it has historically been and continues to be referred to both as "lace" and "embroidery" alongside other names such as "guipure," "Swiss lace," "chemical lace," and "mechanical lace," primarily because the appearance of the final product is marked by distinctive holes forming the design (for more information, SEE THE EDITORS' NOTE).
3   Dora, "St. Gallen's Textile Past," in Dora, *Textiles St. Gallen*, 24–25.
4   Ibid., 86–87.
5   See, for example, *Women's Wear Daily* coverage in the late 1940s of St. Gallen–based firms visiting the United States: "Finishes, Dyeing, Printing Fabrics: Forster, of Swiss Cotton Firm, Arrives in U. S. Tomorrow," *Women's Wear Daily*, April 26, 1948, 25; and "A. Hufenus of St. Gall in U.S. Market," *Women's Wear Daily*, February 14, 1949, 14.
6   Albert Tanner, *Das Schiffchen fliegt, die Maschine rauscht: Weber, Sticker und Fabrikanten in der Ostschweiz* (Zurich: Unionsverlag, 1985), 204.
7   Forster Willi St-Gall brochure, 1982, S. 8. Before this technology was computerized, manufacturers in St. Gallen relied on Schiffli machines, originally invented 1863. Machines were initially controlled by an operator using a pantograph (SEE FIG. 14.8A), a role that would soon become obsolete with the incorporation of jacquard tape. This technology was state-of-the-art until the late 1970s. Designs developed digitally are translated into different stitching techniques on the computer today.
8   Textilmuseum St. Gallen, ed., *Stgall: Textilgeschichten aus acht Jahrhunderten*, exh. cat. (Baden, Switzerland: hier + jetzt, 2011), 148.
9   Tobias Forster, *Forster Rohner, St. Gallen: 100 Jahre Stickerei-Faszination* (Milan: Dimaprint, 2004), 6.
10   Among the other companies that have been incorporated into Forster Rohner are Inter-Spitzen AG, which joined in 2002. Inter-Spitzen was headquartered nearby in Oberbüren, Switzerland, along with its subsidiary in Lugoj, Romania, and was also active in the lingerie market. Since the 2000s Forster Rohner Textile Innovations, an independent branch of the Foster Rohner Group, has developed and produced electronic textiles for various markets in fashion as well as industry. Forster, *Forster Rohner*, 12.
11   Awards include the 2006 Créateur de l'année award for Tobias Forster, the Imagination Prize in 2011 at Première Vision Paris, and a nomination for the 2013 Design Prize Switzerland.
12   Martin Leuthold and Bernhard Duss, *Blendwerk: Inspiration und Kreation bei Jakob Schlaepfer*, vol. 2 (St. Gallen, Switzerland: Verlagsgemeinschaft, St. Gallen, 2004), timeline.
13   Two years after this first presentation in Paris, Schlaepfer was transformed into a joint stock company. The Textilmuseum St. Gallen recently acquired a large number of objects and records from the Schlaepfer archive, and research about these early collections is ongoing.
14   Jakob Schlaepfer pattern books from the company archives containing textiles printed with the Marvel technique were featured in *Kaleidoscopic Eye*, an exhibition by artist Mariana Castillo Deball at the Kunst Halle Sankt Gallen, St. Gallen, Switzerland, February 14–April 12, 2009. "Kaleidoscopic Eye," Mariana Castillo Deball, https://castillodeball.org/project/history-of-science/.
15   Leuthold and Duss, *Blendwerk*, 2:72.
16   Jost Hochuli and Michael Rast, *Freude an schöpferischer Arbeit* (St. Gallen, Switzerland: Typotron AG, 1992), 4.
17   Bettina Göttke Krogmann, ed., *Textildesign: Vom Experiment zur Serie* (Halle, Germany: Burg Biebichenstien Kunsthochschule, 2015), 152.
18   "Portrait," Jakob Schlaepfer, May 2022, https://jakob-schlaepfer.ch/portrait/.

Illustrated Checklist of the Exhibition

1

Judith and Holofernes bobbin-lace collar, commissioned by Bard Graduate Center for *Threads of Power: Lace from the Textilmuseum St. Gallen*
Elena Kanagy-Loux (American, b. 1986)
United States
2022
Silk
11¼ × 14¼ in. (28.6 × 36.2 cm)
Textilmuseum St. Gallen, 76004
SEE FIGS. I.14 AND I.15

2

In-process needle lace, including a design and pounced paper
Vienna or Brussels
Before 1882
Paper, cotton, and linen
3⅞ × 4¾ in. (10 × 12 cm) each
Textilmuseum St. Gallen, 00077.1–9

3

Unfinished *punto in aria* needle-lace border
Italy
ca. 1700
Parchment, paper, and linen
4⅞ × 7⅛ in. (12.5 × 18 cm)
Textilmuseum St. Gallen, Gift of Leopold Iklé, 1905, 01256
SEE FIG. 1.8

4

"Dentelle et façon du point," from *Recueil de Planches, sur les Sciences, Les Arts Libéraux, et Les Arts Méchaniques, avec leur explication: Troisième Livraison*, vol. 3
Denis Diderot (French, 1713–1784) and Jean Le Rond d'Alembert (French, 1717–1783)
Published by Briasson, Paris
1765
Engraving
15⅞ × 10⅝ × 3 in. (40.5 × 27 × 7.6 cm)
The Metropolitan Museum of Art, New York, Harris Brisbane Dick Fund, 1933, 33.23(3)
SEE FIG. 10.8

5

Lace pillow with bobbins and in-process torchon lace
Lauterbrunnen, Switzerland
1897
Cotton, paper, metal, and wood
17¾ × 17¾ × 4¾ in. (45 × 45 × 12 cm)
Textilmuseum St. Gallen, 40017
SEE FIG. 1.9

6

Sampler with openwork and needle lace
Western Europe
First third of the 17th century
Linen
27⅛ × 6⅜ in. (69 × 16 cm)
Textilmuseum St. Gallen, Gift of Leopold Iklé, 1908, 20138
SEE FIG. 1.5

7

Sampler with openwork and needle lace
Italy
1630–70
Linen
17¾ × 6½ in. (45 × 16.5 cm)
Textilmuseum St. Gallen, Gift of Leopold Iklé, 1908, 20135
SEE FIG. 1.6

8

Sampler with openwork and needle lace
England
17th century
Linen
22⅞ × 7⅞ in. (58 × 20 cm)
Textilmuseum St. Gallen, Acquired from the Estate of John Jacoby, 1954, 20120
SEE FIG. 1.7

9

Needle-lace insert
Italy
Second half of the 16th century
Linen
4⅜ × 14¼ in. (11 × 36 cm); repeat: 6⅛ in. (15.5 cm)

Textilmuseum St. Gallen, Gift of Fritz Iklé-Huber, 1996, 47515

10

Reticella needle-lace blanket or pillow cover
Italy
Second half of the 16th century
Linen
10⅞ × 18½ in. (27.5 × 47 cm)
Textilmuseum St. Gallen, Acquired from the Estate of John Jacoby, 1954, 00667

11

Reticella needle-lace insert
Italy
ca. 1600
Linen
6½ × 30 in. (16.5 × 76 cm)
Textilmuseum St. Gallen, Gift of Leopold Iklé, 1905, 00895
SEE FIG. 3.1

12

Reticella needle-lace border
Western Europe, possibly Great Britain
1590–1620
Linen
5½ × 76⅜ in. (14 × 194 cm); repeat: 6⅞ in. (17.5 cm)
Textilmuseum St. Gallen, Gift of Leopold Iklé, 1904, 00045

13

Embroidered and openwork border
Italy
16th century
Linen
4¾ × 17½ in. (12 × 44.5 cm)
Textilmuseum St. Gallen, 00833

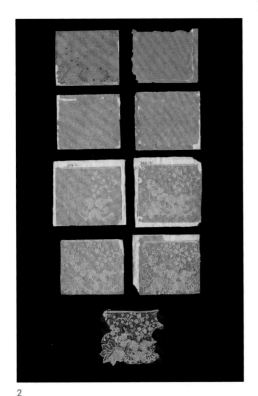

2

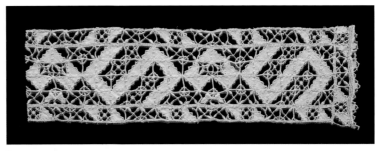

9

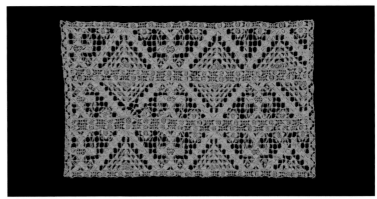

10

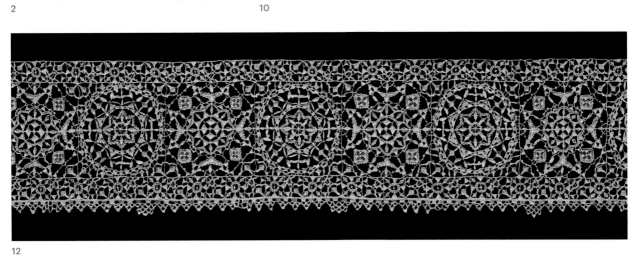

12

13

14

Illustrated Checklist of the Exhibition

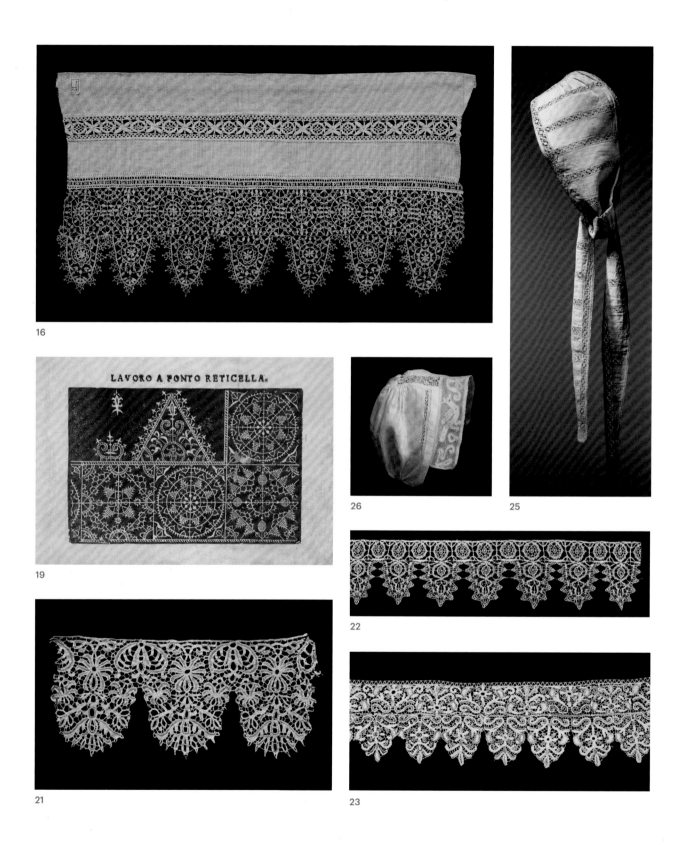

16

LAVORO A PONTO RETICELLA.

19

26   25

22

21   23

14
Bobbin-lace border
Northern or southern Europe
16th century
Linen and silk
1¾ × 28¾ in. (4.5 × 73 cm); repeat: 1⅛ in.
(2.8 cm)
Textilmuseum St. Gallen, 00803

15
Bobbin-lace trimming
Milan, northern Europe, or western Europe
1580–1620
Metal thread with silk core and gold sequins
2⅜ × 15⅜ in. (6 × 39 cm); repeat: 1⅝ in.
(4 cm)
Textilmuseum St. Gallen, Gift of Leopold
Iklé, 1904, 00096.1–2
SEE FIG. 3.4

16
Cloth with needle and bobbin lace
Probably France or Italy
ca. 1620
Linen
12¼ × 22 in. (31 × 56 cm)
Textilmuseum St. Gallen, 01073

17
Ein new Modelbuch . . .
Johann Schönsperger the Younger (German,
active 1510–30)
Zwickau, Germany
October 22, 1524
Woodcut
7⁵⁄₁₆ × 5⅜ in. (18.5 × 13.6 cm)
The Metropolitan Museum of Art, New York,
Gift of Herbert N. Straus, 1929, 29.71(1-31)
SEE FIG. 2.4

18
Bobbin-lace insert
Italy
16th century
Linen
1¾ × 10¼ in. (4.5 × 26 cm); repeat: 1 in.
(2.5 cm)
Textilmuseum St. Gallen, Acquired from
the Estate of John Jacoby, 1954, 00969
SEE FIG. 4.10

19
Gemma pretiosa della virtuose donne
Isabella Catanea Parasole (Italian, ca. 1575–
ca. 1625)
Published by Gugliemo Facciotti (Italian,
ca. 1560–1632), Rome
1625

Woodcut
5⁵⁄₁₆ × 7¹¹⁄₁₆ in. (13.5 × 19.5 cm)
The Metropolitan Museum of Art, New York,
Gift of Mary M. Greenwood, in memory of
Eliza Rudd Greenwood, 1953, 53.566.6(1-31)

20
Bobbin-lace border
Italy, probably Venice
1600–20
Linen
5 × 19¾ in. (12.5 × 50 cm); repeat: 8⅞ in.
(22.5 cm)
Textilmuseum St. Gallen, Gift of Leopold
Iklé, 1905, 01005
SEE FIG. 3.2

21
Needle-lace border
France or Great Britain
ca. 1630
Linen
4⅜ × 10⅜ in. (11 × 26.5 cm); repeat: 3½ in.
(9 cm)
Textilmuseum St. Gallen, Gift of Leopold
Iklé, 1902, 00112

22
Bobbin-lace border
Flanders, Southern Netherlands
Second quarter of the 17th century
Linen
4⅛ × 35 in. (10.5 × 89 cm); repeat: 2⅝ in.
(6.8 cm)
Textilmuseum St. Gallen, 00604

23
Punto in aria needle-lace border
England or western Europe
1620–40
Linen
4 × 31½ in. (10 × 80 cm); repeat: 4 in.
(10 cm)
Textilmuseum St. Gallen, Acquired from the
Estate of John Jacoby, 1954, 00111

24
Bobbin-lace border with scalloped edge
Venice
First quarter of the 17th century
Linen
13¾ × 80 in. (35 × 203 cm)
Textilmuseum St. Gallen, Acquired from the
Estate of John Jacoby, 1954, 01010
SEE FIG. I.10

25
Bonnet with needle-lace inserts
Italy
Second half of the 16th century
Linen
38⅝ × 7 ½ in. (98 × 19 cm)
Textilmuseum St. Gallen, Acquired from the
Estate of John Jacoby, 1954, 00813

26
Bonnet with reticella needle-lace and
bobbin-lace inserts
Netherlands or western Europe
1600–50
Linen
8¼ × 9⅛ in. (21 × 23 cm)
Textilmuseum St. Gallen, Acquired from the
Estate of John Jacoby, 1954, 23402

27
Bobbin-lace insert
Italy
Second half of the 16th century
Linen
2¾ × 51⅛ in. (7 × 130 cm); repeat: 2⅛ in.
(5.5 cm)
Textilmuseum St. Gallen, Gift of Leopold
Iklé, 1904, 00668
SEE FIG. 3.14

28
Needle-lace fragment, probably a chalice pall
Probably Venice
Last quarter of the 17th century
Linen
6 ⅛ × 6 ¼ in. (15.5 × 16 cm)
Textilmuseum St. Gallen, Acquired from the
Estate of John Jacoby, 1954, 00230

29
Needle-lace cover or chalice cover
Italy
ca. 1700
Silk and metal threads with silk core
25¾ × 25⅝ in. (65.5 × 65 cm)
Textilmuseum St. Gallen, Gift of Leopold
Iklé, 1908, 23963
SEE FIG. 1.13

30
Vari disegni di merletti
Bartolomeo Danieli (Italian, active Bologna
and Siena 1610–1643)
Published by Agostino Parisini (Italian,
active 1625–1637) and Giovanni Battista
Negroponte (Italian, active ca. 1633–),
Bologna
1639

Etching
13⅜ × 19⁵⁄₁₆ in. (34 × 49 cm)
The Metropolitan Museum of Art, New
York, Harris Brisbane Dick Fund, 1937,
37.47.2 (1–13)
SEE FIGS. 2.1 AND 2.24

31
Bobbin-lace border
Italy
Second quarter of the 17th century
Linen
5¾ × 40½ in. (14.5 × 103 cm); repeat:
9⅞ in. (25 cm)
Textilmuseum St. Gallen, Gift of Leopold
Iklé, 1904, 00041
SEE FIG. 14.5

32
Point de Venise needle-lace border
Venice; Orne, France; or Great Britain
1675–1715, with late 19th-century edgings
Linen
9⅝ × 26¾ in. (24.5 × 68 cm)
Textilmuseum St. Gallen, Acquired from
the Estate of John Jacoby, 1954, 01141
SEE FIG. 9.5

33
Needle-lace motif with tassels
Europe
17th–18th century
Linen
5⅜ × 4⅞ in. (13.5 × 12.5 cm)
Textilmuseum St. Gallen, Acquired from the
Estate of John Jacoby, 1954, 00781

34
*Kreüter Buch: Darinn Unterscheidt Namen
unnd Würkung der Kreutter . . .*
Hieronymus Bock (German, 1498–1554)
Published by J. and T. Rihel, Strassburg
1556
Book
7⁵⁄₁₆ × 17 × 13½ in. (18.6 × 43.2 × 34.3 cm)
The LuEsther T. Mertz Library, New York
Botanical Garden, f QK41 .B6 1556

35
*Opera quae extant omnia: Hoc est,
Commentarii in VI. libros Pedacii Dioscoridis
Anazarbei De medica materia . . .*
Pietro Andrea Mattioli (Italian, 1500–1577)
Published by Nicolaus Bassaeus (German,
ca. 1540–1601), Frankfurt
1598
Book
7⅞ × 19¹⁄₁₆ × 15⅜ in. (20 × 48.4 × 39 cm)

The LuEsther T. Mertz Library, New York
Botanical Garden, f QK 99 .D5 M3 1598
SEE FIG. 1.14

36
Punto in aria needle-lace border
Venice
1630–50, reworked in the 19th century
Linen and cotton
12⅝ × 49⅝ in. (32 × 126 cm); repeat:
8¼ in. (21 cm)
Textilmuseum St. Gallen, Acquired from the
Estate of John Jacoby, 1954, 00079
SEE FIG. 3.3

37
Punto in aria needle-lace border fragment
Venice
Second quarter of the 17th century
Linen
5⅞ × 7⅛ in. (15 × 18 cm)
Textilmuseum St. Gallen, Acquired from the
Estate of John Jacoby, 1954, 00063

38
*Neuw vollkommentlich Kreuterbuch, mit
schönen unnd künstlichen Figuren . . .*
Jacobus Theodorus Tabermontanus
(German, d. 1590)
Published by Paul Jacobi; Johann Dreutels,
Frankfurt
1625
Book
7⅞ × 18⅜ × 15 in. (20 × 46.7 × 38.1 cm)
The LuEsther T. Mertz Library, New York
Botanical Garden, f QK41 .T42 1625
SEE FIG. I.21

39
Punto in aria needle- and bobbin-lace cover
Italy, Greece, or Cyprus
First quarter of 17th century, reworked in
the 19th century
Linen, glass beads, and cotton
15¾ × 21⅝ in. (40 × 55 cm)
Textilmuseum St. Gallen, Gift of Leopold
Iklé, 1904, 00659

40
Needle-lace border depicting Judith and
Holofernes
Probably Italy for the Portuguese market
1600–25
Linen
7½ × 39 in. (19 × 99 cm)
Textilmuseum St. Gallen, Gift of Leopold
Iklé, 1904, 00040
SEE FIG. I.17

41
Needle-lace angel motif
Europe
1600–30
Linen and glass beads
9⅞ × 3⅞ in. (25 × 10 cm)
Textilmuseum St. Gallen, Gift of Leopold
Iklé, 1904, 04246

42
Cushion cover with needle lace, bobbin lace,
and openwork
Venice
ca. 1620, with later modifications
Linen
11⅜ × 18½ in. (29 × 47 cm)
Textilmuseum St. Gallen, Gift of Leopold
Iklé, 1905, 01066

43
Punto a fogliame needle-lace collar and cuffs
Italy
ca. 1600, reworked in the 19th century
Linen
Collar: 3¾ × 32⅜ in. (9.5 × 82 cm); cuffs:
3⅜ × 10⅝ in. (8.5 × 27 cm) each
Textilmuseum St. Gallen, Gift of Leopold
Iklé, 1904, 00402.1-3
SEE FIG. 3.5

44
Needle-lace chasuble
Venice
1650–75
Linen, silk, and silver threads
46 × 29⅛ × 4¾ in. (117 × 74 × 12 cm)
Textilmuseum St. Gallen, 51480
SEE FIG. 1.27

45
Point de Venise needle-lace motif, probably
a chalice pall
Venice
1700–30
Linen
4⅞ × 5½ in. (12.5 × 14 cm)
Textilmuseum St. Gallen, Acquired from the
Estate of John Jacoby, 1954, 00264

46
Needle-lace chalice pall depicting the
Annunciation
Italy or Spain
1700–1800
Linen and gold thread with silk core
5⅜ × 5⅜ in. (13.5 × 13.5 cm)
Textilmuseum St. Gallen, Gift of Leopold
Iklé, 1904, 00623

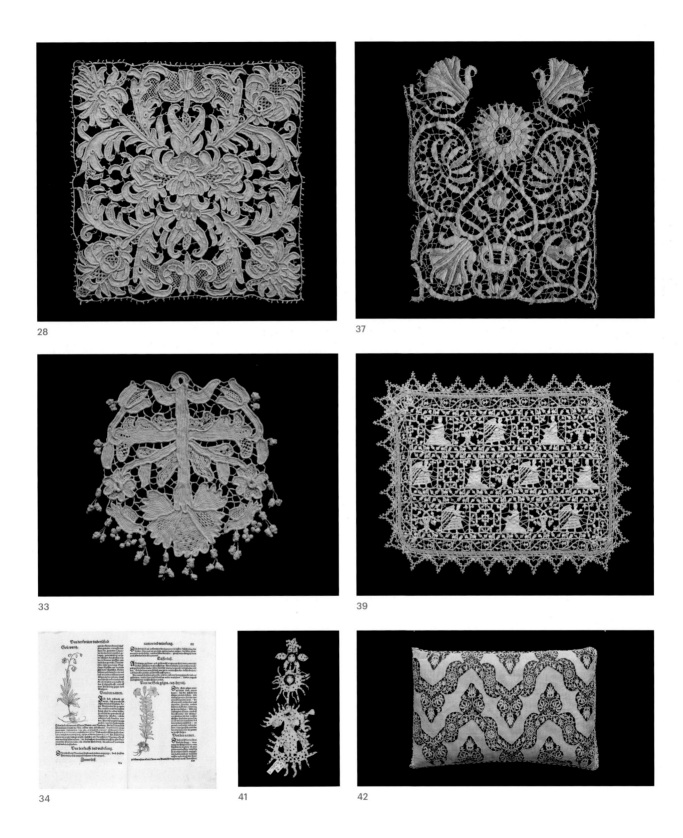

28

37

33

39

34

41

42

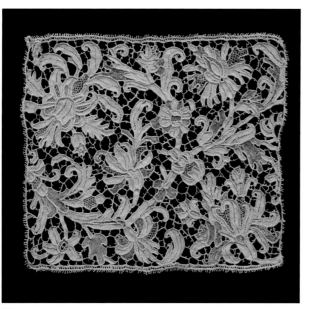

45

47

46

48

51

Portrait of Infanta Isabella Clara Eugenia
Frans Pourbus the Younger (Flemish,
1569–1622)
1599–1600
Oil on canvas
51 × 41⅝ in. (129.5 × 105.7 cm)
Williams College Museum of Art,
Williamstown, Massachusetts; Gift of
Prentis Cobb Hale, Jr., 64.31
SEE FIG. 1.11

52

Bobbin-lace border mounted as a millstone
collar
Northern Europe
1580–1620
Linen
5 × 30⅜ in. (12.5 × 77 cm); repeat: 2½ in.
(6.2 cm)
Textilmuseum St. Gallen, Gift of Leopold
Iklé, 1904, 00679
SEE FIG. 1.12

53

Punto in aria needle-lace cuff
Venice
ca. 1650, reworked in the 19th century
Linen
5¾ × 9⅞ in. (14.5 × 25 cm)
Textilmuseum St. Gallen, Acquired from the
Estate of John Jacoby, 1954, 00065
SEE FIG. 1.16

54

Upper part of a bobbin-lace glove
Probably Lombardy, Italy
Second half of the 17th century
Linen
14⅜ × 4⅝ in. (36.5 × 11.7 cm)
Textilmuseum St. Gallen, Gift of Leopold
Iklé, 1904, 00223
SEE FIG. 1.15

55

Bobbin-lace cuff
Lombardy, Italy
ca. 1700
Linen
9½ × 19 in. (24 × 48 cm)
Textilmuseum St. Gallen, Gift of Leopold
Iklé, 1904, 00202

56

Bobbin-lace fragment depicting Charles II
of Spain (1661–1700)
Flanders, Southern Netherlands, probably
Antwerp
1665
Linen
7¼ × 9¼ in. (18.5 × 23.5 cm)
Textilmuseum St. Gallen, Acquired from the
Estate of John Jacoby, 1954, 00696
SEE FIG. 4.13

49

55

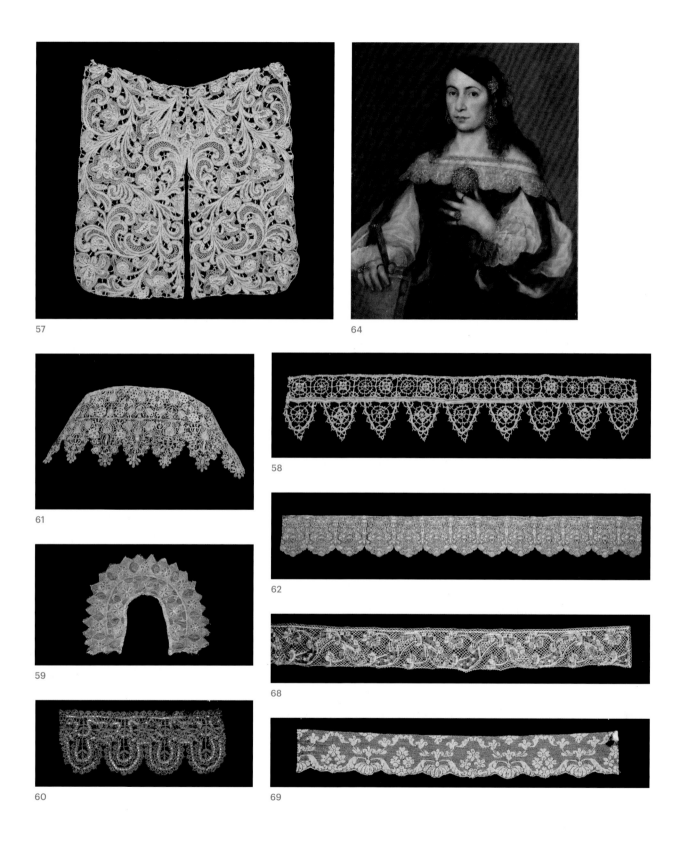

57

64

61

58

59

62

60

68

69

57
Bobbin-lace *rabat*
Flanders, Southern Netherlands
Fourth quarter of the 17th century
Linen
11 × 11¼ in. (28 × 28.5 cm)
Textilmuseum St. Gallen, Acquired from the
Estate of John Jacoby, 1954, 00692

58
Reticella needle-lace border
Italy or western Europe
1580–1620
Linen
2⅛ × 11⅞ in. (5.5 × 30 cm)
Textilmuseum St. Gallen, Acquired from the
Estate of John Jacoby, 1954, 00110

59
Filet-lace collar
Spain
ca. 1610
Linen and silk
13 × 17⅜ in. (33 × 44 cm)
Textilmuseum St. Gallen, Gift of Leopold
Iklé, 1905, 01944

60
Bobbin-lace border
Western or southern Europe
Second quarter of the 17th century
Metal thread with silk core and metal strip
3⅞ × 10⅝ in. (10 × 27 cm); repeat: 2½ in.
(6.5 cm)
Textilmuseum St. Gallen, 03996

61
Needle-lace collar
England
ca. 1635
Linen
11¾ × 23⅝ in. (30 × 60 cm)
Textilmuseum St. Gallen, 00684

62
Bobbin-lace border
Flanders, Southern Netherlands; or England
ca. 1640
Linen
5⅜ × 47⅝ in. (13.5 × 121 cm); repeat: 3⅝ in.
(9.3 cm)
Textilmuseum St. Gallen, Acquired from the
Estate of John Jacoby, 1954, 00676

63
Bobbin-lace border or bertha collar
Flanders, Southern Netherlands, probably
Antwerp

ca. 1660
Linen
5½ × 37⅜ in. (14 × 95 cm); repeat: 9⅝ in.
(24.5 cm)
Textilmuseum St. Gallen, Acquired from the
Estate of John Jacoby, 1954, 00691
SEE FIG. 4.24

64
Portrait of a Lady
Artist unknown
Spain
Late 17th century
Oil on canvas
31⅛ × 25 in. (79.1 × 63.5 cm)
Philadelphia Museum of Art, John G.
Johnson Collection, 1917, Cat. 815

65
Bobbin-lace coverlet, perhaps made for the
1649 wedding of Philip IV (1605–1655) and
Mariana of Austria (1634–1696)
Probably Italy
1625–50
Linen and glass beads
50⅜ × 50⅜ in. (128 × 128 cm)
Textilmuseum St. Gallen, Gift of Iklé-
Frischknecht Foundation, 2006, 52093
SEE FIG. I.12

66
Portrait of Simón de la Valle y Cuadra
Artist unknown
Peru
ca. 1760
Oil on canvas
38¾ × 32⅞ × 3¾ in. (98.4 × 83.5 × 9.5 cm)
Denver Art Museum, Funds from Jan &
Frederick R. Mayer, Carl & Marilynn Thoma,
Jim & Marybeth Vogelzang, Lorraine &
Harley Higbie, 2000.250.1
SEE FIG. 7.8

67
*Portrait of María del Carmen Cortés Santelizes
y Cartavio*
Artist unknown
Peru
ca. 1760
Oil on canvas
39 × 32⅞ × 3¾ in. (99.1 × 83.5 × 9.5 cm)
Denver Art Museum, Funds from Jan &
Frederick R. Mayer, Carl & Marilynn Thoma,
Jim & Marybeth Vogelzang, Lorraine &
Harley Higbie, 2000.250.2
SEE FIG. 7.15

68
Bobbin-lace border
Valenciennes, France
1730–60
Linen
2¼ × 69 in. (5.5 × 175 cm); repeat: 4½ in.
(11.3 cm)
Textilmuseum St. Gallen, Acquired from the
Estate of John Jacoby, 1954, 00683

69
Bobbin-lace border
Valenciennes, France
ca. 1770
Linen
2 × 14⅔ in. (5 × 37.5 cm); repeat: 3¼ in.
(8.3 cm)
Textilmuseum St. Gallen, 03253

70
Mixed Brussels needle-lace lappets
Brussels, Southern Netherlands
ca. 1735
Linen
4½ × 23⅞ in. (11.5 × 60.5 cm) each
Textilmuseum St. Gallen, Acquired from the
Estate of John Jacoby, 1954, 02341.1-2

71
Brussels or point d'Angleterre bobbin-lace
mantelet
Brussels, Southern Netherlands
ca. 1750, reworked in the 19th century
Linen
13⅜ × 52¾ in. (35 × 134 cm)
Textilmuseum St. Gallen, Acquired from the
Estate of John Jacoby, 1954, 02571

72
Point de Venise needle-lace mantelet or
frelange
Italy
ca. 1700
Linen
13¾ × 55⅛ in. (35 × 140 cm)
Textilmuseum St. Gallen, Acquired from the
Estate of John Jacoby, 1954, 01180
SEE FIG. I.26

73
Bobbin tape-lace border
Flanders, Southern Netherlands
Last quarter of the 17th century
Linen
9½ × 20⅞ in. (24 × 53 cm)
Textilmuseum St. Gallen, Gift of Leopold
Iklé, 1901, 02473

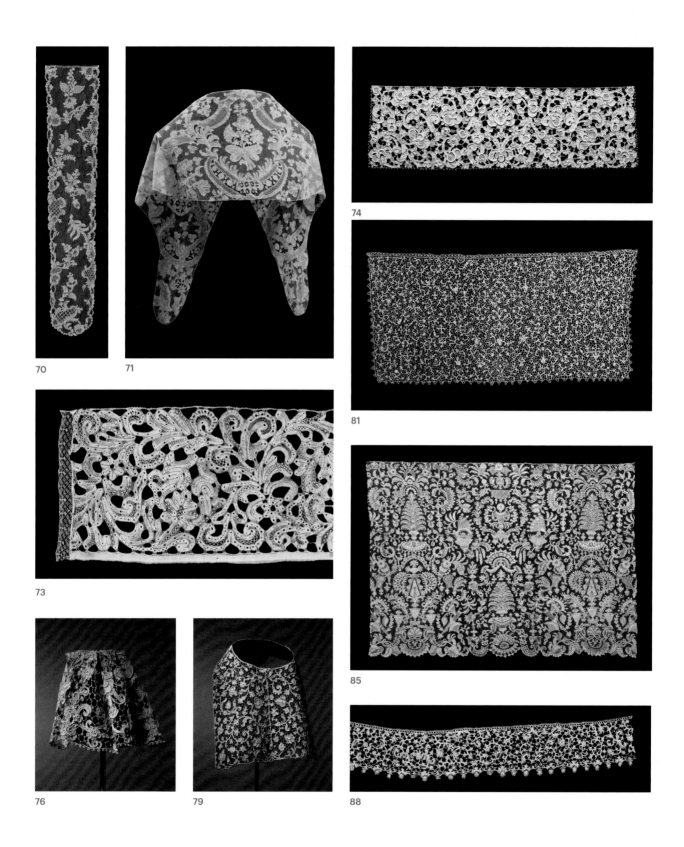

70

71

73

74

81

85

76

79

88

74

Point de Venise needle-lace border
Orne, France; or Venice
1680–1700
Linen
8⅝ × 30⅜ in. (22 × 77 cm)
Textilmuseum St. Gallen, Acquired from the
Estate of John Jacoby, 1954, 00606

75

Point plat de Venise needle lace mounted as
cravat ends
Venice
ca. 1690, reworked at the end of the 19th
century
Linen and cotton
7½ × 11½ in. (19 × 29 cm) each
Textilmuseum St. Gallen, Acquired from the
Estate of John Jacoby, 1954, 01226.1-2
SEE FIG. 1.19

76

Point de Venise needle-lace cuff or cravat end
France or Venice
ca. 1690
Linen and cotton
7½ × 15¾ in. (19 × 40 cm)
Textilmuseum St. Gallen, Gift of Leopold
Iklé, 1905, 01165

77

Point de Venise needle-lace border
Italy or France
ca. 1680, reworked in the 19th or 20th
century
Linen and cotton
16½ × 107¼ in. (42 × 272.5 cm)
Textilmuseum St. Gallen, 58760
SEE FIG. 1.21

78

Point de Venise needle-lace *rabat*
Probably Venice or Alençon, France
ca. 1670
Linen
11¾ × 15 in. (30 × 39 cm)
Textilmuseum St. Gallen, Gift of the Estate
of Isidor Grauer, 1983, 03914
SEE FIG. 1.20

79

Point de Venise needle-lace *rabat*
Venice or Orne, France
ca. 1690
Linen
6½ × 28¾ in. (16.5 × 73 cm)
Textilmuseum St. Gallen, Acquired from the
Estate of John Jacoby, 1954, 01194

80

*Marie Rinteau, Called Mademoiselle de
Verrières*
François Hubert Drouais (French, 1727–1775)
1761
Oil on canvas
45½ × 34⅝ in. (115.6 × 87.9 cm)
The Metropolitan Museum of Art, New York,
the Jules Bache Collection, 1949, 49.7.47
SEE FIG. I.25

81

Coraline needle-lace cravat end
Venice or France
ca. 1700
Linen
8⅞ × 18½ in. (22.5 × 47 cm)
Textilmuseum St. Gallen, Gift of Leopold
Iklé, 1905, 01214
SEE FIG. 7.3

82

Bobbin tape lace, mounted as a collar
Italy
1690–1725
Linen
14⅛ × 48⅞ in. (36 × 124 cm)
Textilmuseum St. Gallen, Gift of Leopold
Iklé, 1905, 00524
SEE FIG. I.29

83

Coraline needle-lace cravat end
Venice or France
ca. 1700
Linen
9¼ × 18¾ in. (23.5 × 47.5 cm)
Textilmuseum St. Gallen, Gift of Leopold
Iklé, 1905, 01213
SEE FIG. 7.3

84

Bobbin-lace cravat end
Flanders, Southern Netherlands
ca. 1700
Linen
13¾ × 17½ in. (35 × 44.5 cm)
Textilmuseum St. Gallen, Gift of Leopold
Iklé, 1904, 00286
SEE FIG. 1.22

85

Needle-lace border
Orne, France
ca. 1710
Linen
23 × 32⅛ in. (58.5 × 81.5 cm)
Textilmuseum St. Gallen, Gift of the Estate
of John Jacoby, 1955, 00700

86

Point de France needle-lace border
France
1695–1710
Linen
23⅝ × 142½ in. (60 × 362 cm); repeat:
21 in. (53.5 cm)
Textilmuseum St. Gallen, Acquired from the
Estate of John Jacoby, 1954, 01231
SEE FIG. 9.10

87

Point de France needle-lace *frelange* with
lappets
Orne, France
ca. 1695
Linen
4⅝ × 50½ in. (11.8 × 127.5 cm)
Textilmuseum St. Gallen, Acquired from the
Estate of John Jacoby, 1954, 01246
SEE FIG. 10.3

88

Needle-lace border
Venice
ca. 1700
Linen
3⅜ × 39⅜ in. (8.5 × 100 cm)
Textilmuseum St. Gallen, Gift of Leopold
Iklé, 1905, 01205

89

Needle-lace border
Venice
ca. 1700
Linen
3⅛ × 42⅛ in. (8 × 107 cm)
Textilmuseum St. Gallen, Acquired from the
Estate of John Jacoby, 1954, 01200

90

Lace-patterned silk
France
ca. 1720–25
Silk
22 × 41½ in. (55.9 × 105.4 cm)
Cora Ginsburg, LLC
SEE FIG. 1.24

91

Woman's dress (*robe à la française*) with
matching stomacher and petticoat
France
ca. 1755–60
Chinese export brocaded silk satin, trimmed
with silk chenille looped fringe
Length at center back: 63 in. (160 cm)
Philadelphia Museum of Art, Purchased
with the John D. McIlhenny Fund, the John

T. Morris Fund, the Elizabeth Wandell
Smith Fund, and with funds contributed by
Mrs. Howard H. Lewis and Marion Boulton
Stroud, 1988, 1988-83-1a–c
SEE FIG. I.23

92
Point d'Alençon needle-lace lappets
Alençon or Argentan, France
1750–60
Linen
3½ × 27½ in. (9 × 70 cm)
Textilmuseum St. Gallen, Acquired from the
Estate of John Jacoby, 1954, 02133.1-2
SEE FIG. 10.11E

93
Point d'Alençon needle-lace lappet
Alençon or Argentan, France
ca. 1750
Linen
4½ × 56⅞ in. (11.5 × 144.5 cm)
Textilmuseum St. Gallen, Acquired from the
Estate of John Jacoby, 1954, 02163

94
Needle-lace cap border
Alençon or Argentan, France
ca. 1760
Linen
2½ × 27⅛ in. (6.2 × 69 cm)
Textilmuseum St. Gallen, Acquired from the
Estate of John Jacoby, 1954, 02134

95
Point d'Argentan needle-lace border
Argentan or Alençon, France
1780–90
Linen
2¾ × 53⅞ in. (7 × 137 cm); repeat: 6⅛ in.
(15.4 cm)
Textilmuseum St. Gallen, 40158
SEE FIG. 10.29

96
Needle-lace border
Alençon or Argentan, France
ca. 1780
Linen
5½ × 83⅞ in. (14 × 213 cm)
Textilmuseum St. Gallen, Acquired from the
Estate of John Jacoby, 1954, 02145

97
Needle-lace trim
Alençon or Argentan, France
1780–90
Linen

1¾ × 65¾ in. (4.5 × 167 cm); repeat: 3¾ in.
(9.5 cm)
Textilmuseum St. Gallen, Acquired from the
Estate of John Jacoby, 1954, 02140

98
Point d'Argentan needle-lace border
Argentan or Alençon, France
ca. 1750
Linen
3½ × 64½ in. (9 × 164 cm); repeat: 16 in.
(40.5 cm)
Textilmuseum St. Gallen, Gift of Konrad
Huber-Iklé, 2000, 50130

99
Woman's dress (*robe à la française*) with
matching petticoat
France
ca. 1760–65
Brocaded silk twill, trimmed with self-fabric
and gimp
Length at center back: 61½ in. (156.2 cm)
Collection of Elaine J. Condon, Jane M.
Gincig, and Patricia L. Kalayjian

100
Brocaded silk taffeta with lace ribbon and
faux fur meander pattern
France
ca. 1760–65
Silk
19⅛ × 43½ in. (48.6 × 110.5 cm)
Cora Ginsburg, LLC, W3033a

101
Silk stomacher with metal-thread
embroidery, bobbin lace, and galloon
France or Italy
Second quarter of the 18th century
Silk and metal threads with silk core
16⅛ × 9⅞ in. (41 × 25 cm)
Textilmuseum St. Gallen, Gift of the Estate
of Leopold Iklé, 1923, 32287

102
Man's embroidered undress cap edged with
bobbin lace
France
ca. 1725–50
Silk and linen
9⅞ × 7⅞ in. (25 × 20 cm)
Textilmuseum St. Gallen, Gift of Leopold
Iklé, 1908, 59004

103
Stomacher with metallic bobbin lace
Graubünden, Switzerland
First quarter of the 18th century
Silk, paper, and metal threads with silk core
26 × 16½ in. (66 × 42 cm)
Textilmuseum St. Gallen, 58616

104
Man's silk-embroidered court suit with
needle-lace jabot
France
1780–90
Silk and linen
Coat length at center back: 49⅝ in. (126 cm)
Textilmuseum St. Gallen, Acquired from the
Estate of John Jacoby, 1954, 21500
SEE FIG. I.24

105
Mechlin bobbin-lace lappets
Mechlin, Southern Netherlands
Fourth quarter of the 18th century
Linen
3⅜ × 31⅜ in. (8.5 × 79.5 cm)
Textilmuseum St. Gallen, Acquired from the
Estate of John Jacoby, 1954, 02646.1-2

106
Needle-lace lappets
Brussels, Southern Netherlands
ca. 1780
Linen
3⅛ × 22⅝ in. (8 × 57.5 cm)
Textilmuseum St. Gallen, Acquired from the
Estate of John Jacoby, 1954, 00728.1-2

107
Point d'Alençon needle-lace lappets
Alençon or Argentan, France
ca. 1750
Linen
4½ × 26⅜ in. (11.5 × 67 cm)
Textilmuseum St. Gallen, Acquired from the
Estate of John Jacoby, 1954, 00729.1-2
SEE FIG. 10.11D

108
Valenciennes bobbin-lace lappet
Valenciennes, France; or Flanders, Southern
Netherlands
ca. 1745
Linen
3⅜ × 21¼ in. (8.5 × 54 cm)
Textilmuseum St. Gallen, Gift of Leopold
Iklé, 1904, 00744

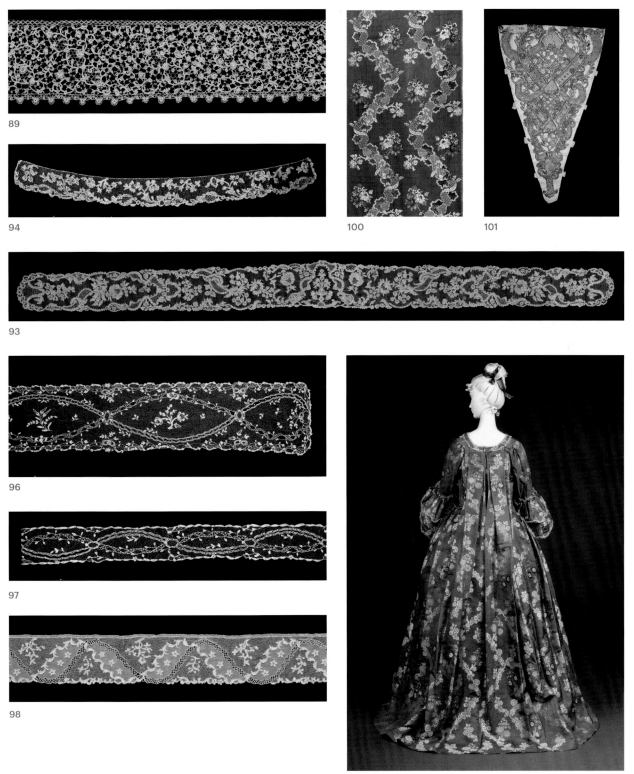

89

94

100

101

93

96

97

98

99

383   Illustrated Checklist of the Exhibition

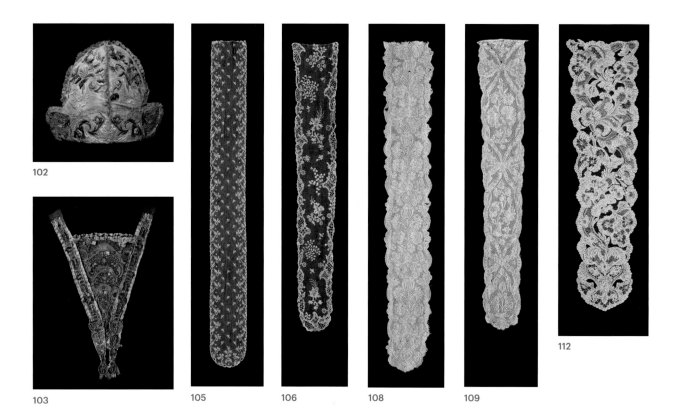

102

103

105

106

108

109

112

109
Mechlin bobbin-lace lappet
Mechlin, Southern Netherlands
ca. 1745
Linen
3⅜ × 20½ in. (8.5 × 52 cm)
Textilmuseum St. Gallen, Gift of Leopold
Iklé, 1901, 02585

110
Bobbin-lace lappet
Mechlin, Southern Netherlands
ca. 1740
Linen
3½ × 20½ in. (8.9 × 52 cm)
Textilmuseum St. Gallen, Acquired from the
Estate of John Jacoby, 1954, 03047
SEE FIG. 10.11C

111
Brussels or point d'Angleterre lappets or
neckpiece
Brussels, Southern Netherlands
ca. 1730
Linen
31¼ × 4¾ in. (79.5 × 12 cm)

Textilmuseum St. Gallen, Acquired from the
Estate of John Jacoby, 1954, 02552

112
Brussels needle-lace lappets
Brussels, Southern Netherlands
ca. 1720
Linen
22 × 6⅛ in. (56 × 15.5 cm)
Textilmuseum St. Gallen, Acquired from the
Estate of John Jacoby, 1954, 00727.1-2

113
Brussels or point d'Angleterre bobbin-lace
lappets
Brussels, Southern Netherlands
ca. 1720
Linen
4½ × 26½ in. (11.5 × 67.5 cm)
Textilmuseum St. Gallen, Acquired from the
Estate of John Jacoby, 1954, 00716.1-2
SEE FIG. 4.25

114
Brussels needle-lace lappet
Brussels, Southern Netherlands

First half of the 18th century
Linen
44⅞ × 3⅜ in. (114 × 8.5 cm)
Textilmuseum St. Gallen, Acquired from the
Estate of John Jacoby, 1954, 00721
SEE FIG. 10.11B

115
Point de France needle-lace lappet
Orne, France; or Venice
ca. 1700
Linen
3½ × 47⅝ in. (9 × 121 cm)
Textilmuseum St. Gallen, Acquired from the
Estate of John Jacoby, 1954, 01203
SEE FIG. 10.11A

116
Needle-lace sleeve ruffles (*engageantes*)
Alençon or Argentan, France
1780–90, reworked in the 19th century
Linen
6½ × 16⅞ in. (16.5 × 43 cm) each
Textilmuseum St. Gallen, Acquired from the
Estate of John Jacoby, 1954, 02143.1-2
SEE FIG. 10.6

117
Point de Sedan needle-lace sleeve ruffles
(*engageantes*)
Alençon or Argentan, France
ca. 1730
Linen
4 × 29⅛ in. (10 × 74 cm) each
Textilmuseum St. Gallen, Acquired from the
Estate of John Jacoby, 1954, 02131.1-2

118
Needle-lace cap back
Alençon or Argentan, France
ca. 1770–85
Linen
10¼ × 8⅝ in. (26 × 22 cm)
Textilmuseum St. Gallen, Gift of Leopold
Iklé, 1901, 02195

119
Brussels or point d'Angleterre bobbin-lace
cap back
Brussels, Southern Netherlands
ca. 1760
Linen
8⅝ × 10 in. (22 × 25.5 cm)
Textilmuseum St. Gallen, Acquired from the
Estate of John Jacoby, 1954, 03014
SEE FIG. 10.27

120
Brussels or point d'Angleterre bobbin-lace
cap back
Brussels, Southern Netherlands
ca. 1750
Linen
7½ × 9 in. (19 × 23 cm)
Textilmuseum St. Gallen, Acquired from the
Estate of John Jacoby, 1954, 00731
SEE FIG. 10.5

121
Brussels or point d'Angleterre bobbin-lace
cap back with lappets
Brussels, Southern Netherlands
ca. 1720
Linen
7⅛ × 26¾ in. (18 × 68 cm); lappets 4⅜ in.
(11 cm) each
Textilmuseum St. Gallen, Acquired from the
Estate of John Jacoby, 1954, 00627

122
Brussels or point d'Angleterre bobbin-lace
cap back
Brussels, Southern Netherlands
ca. 1720
Linen
11⅜ × 8¼ in. (29 × 21 cm)

Textilmuseum St. Gallen, Acquired from the
Estate of John Jacoby, 1954, 00717
SEE FIG. 4.26

123
Ball gown, presumably worn by Fanny
Appleton Longfellow (American, 1817–1861)
Probably France
ca. 1855–58
Yellow silk taffeta trimmed with black
Chantilly lace
Length at center back: 56½ in. (143.5 cm)
Courtesy National Park Service, Longfellow
House – Washington's Headquarters
National Historic Site, LONG 13493

124
Handmade Chantilly bobbin-lace shawl
France or Belgium
ca. 1860
Silk
117 × 57 in. (298 × 145 cm)
Textilmuseum St. Gallen, Acquired from the
Estate of John Jacoby, 1954, 00480
SEE FIG. 11.28

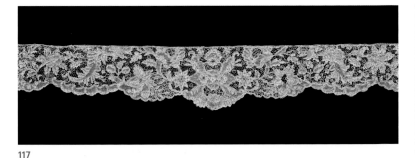
117

111

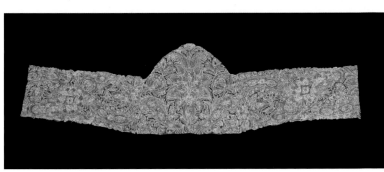
121

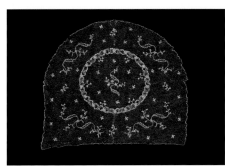
118

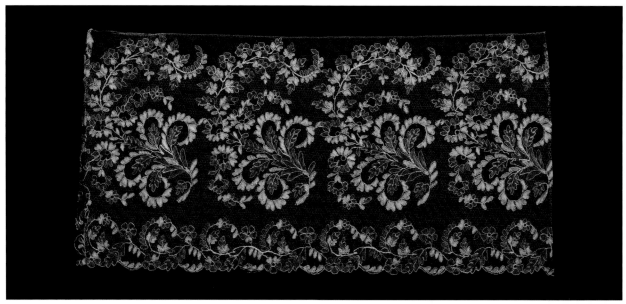

126

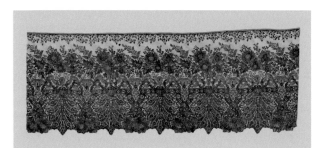

127

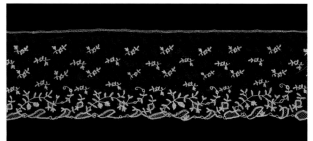

128

123

132

125
Handmade blonde bobbin-lace border
Probably Neuchâtel, France
ca. 1830
Silk
4⅛ × 24 in. (10.5 × 61 cm)
Textilmuseum St. Gallen, 03639
SEE FIG. 11.6

126
Handmade blonde bobbin-lace flounce
France
ca. 1850
Silk
11¼ × 23¼ in. (28.5 × 59 cm)
Textilmuseum St. Gallen, Acquired from the
Estate of John Jacoby, 1954, 03621

127
Handmade Chantilly bobbin-lace flounce
France or Belgium
Third quarter of the 19th century
Silk
14⅛ × 38⅛ in. (36 × 97 cm)
Textilmuseum St. Gallen, Acquired from the
Estate of John Jacoby, 1954, 00484

128
Brussels bobbin-lace border with machine
tulle
Brussels
ca. 1830
Cotton
5¼ × 150¾ in. (13 × 383 cm)
Textilmuseum St. Gallen, 40170

129
Handmade Chantilly bobbin-lace shawl
France or Belgium
1860–70
Silk
22½ × 77¼ in. (57.5 × 196 cm)
Textilmuseum St. Gallen, 00486
SEE FIG. 11.13

130
Brussels application lace flounce (handmade
needle and bobbin lace and machine lace)
Brussels
Mid-19th century
Cotton
8⅜ × 40½ in. (21.5 × 103 cm)
Textilmuseum St. Gallen, Acquired from the
Estate of John Jacoby, 1954, 58641
SEE FIG. 11.14

131
Handmade Honiton bobbin-lace stomacher
or vestee
Honiton, England
ca. 1860
Cotton
7⅞ × 13 in. (20 × 33 cm)
Textilmuseum St. Gallen, Acquired from the
Estate of John Jacoby, 1954, 03063
SEE FIG. 11.25

132
Tunic with appliquéd white linen birds,
fruits, and foliage on silk net ground
Europe
ca. 1910–11
Linen and silk
Length at center back: 36 in. (91.4 cm)
Cora Ginsburg, LLC

133
Handmade needle-lace collar
Mathilde Hrdlička (Austrian, 1859–1917),
lacemaker
Johann Hrdlička (Austrian, 1857–1907),
designer
Vienna
ca. 1900
Linen
8 × 16¼ in. (20.5 × 41.5 cm)
Textilmuseum St. Gallen, 03448
SEE FIG. 11.20

134
Sample and handwritten document,
"Experiment in Embroidering Lace"
St. Gallen, Switzerland
ca. 1875
Cotton and ink on paper
Embroidery sample: 4 × 7½ in. (10 × 19 cm);
document: 3¾ × 7½ in. (9.5 × 21.5 cm)
Textilmuseum St. Gallen, Gift of Ernst Iklé,
1930, 30743
SEE FIG. 14.10

135
Book with chemical-lace samples
Wetter Frères
St. Gallen, Switzerland
1881–82
Cardboard, paper, and cotton
18⅞ × 22¾ × 1⅛ in. (48 × 68 × 3 cm)
Bischoff Textil AG, Hufenus Collection
SEE FIG. 14.15

136
Samples of cutout lace and machine-made
openwork
St. Gallen, Switzerland

ca. 1878
Cotton
Samples: 4⅜–8⅝ × 4½–4⅞ in. (11–22 ×
11.5–12.5 cm); backing fabric: 19⅜ × 13¾ in.
(49 × 35 cm)
Textilmuseum St. Gallen, Gift of Ernst Iklé,
1930, 30750
SEE FIG. 14.13

137
Book with chemical-lace samples
Iklé Frères & Co. (1864–1931)
St. Gallen, Switzerland
1900–30
Paper, cardboard, leather, and cotton
24 × 16½ × 3⅞ in. (61 × 42 × 9 cm)
Textilmuseum St. Gallen, STI IKL 3
SEE FIG. 14.12

138
Point d'Angleterre or Brussels needle-lace
lappet
Brussels, Southern Netherlands
ca. 1770
Linen
42½ × 3½ in. (108 × 9 cm)
Textilmuseum St. Gallen, Acquired from the
Estate of John Jacoby, 1954, 00736
SEE FIG. 1.26

139
Point de Venise needle-lace border
Orne, France; or Venice
Third quarter of the 17th century
Linen
5⅜ × 14¾ in. (13.5 × 37.5 cm)
Textilmuseum St. Gallen, Gift of Leopold
Iklé, 1904, 01143
SEE FIG. 1.3

140
Point de Venise needle-lace border
Venice or France
ca. 1690
Linen
4½ × 12¼ in. (11.5 × 31 cm)
Textilmuseum St. Gallen, Gift of Leopold
Iklé, 1905, 01144
SEE FIG. 1.4

141
Book with chemical-lace samples
Iklé Frères & Co. (1864–1931)
St. Gallen, Switzerland
1900–30
Paper, cardboard, leather, and cotton
24 × 16½ × 3⅞ in. (61 × 42 × 9 cm)
Textilmuseum St. Gallen, STI IKL 1
SEE FIGS. 1.2 AND 14.20

142
Reticella needle-lace border
Western Europe
1590–1620
Linen
4⅞ × 18⅞ in. (12.5 × 48 cm)
Textilmuseum St. Gallen, Gift of Leopold
Iklé, 1905, 00935
SEE FIG. 14.19

143
Book with chemical-lace samples
Iklé Frères & Co. (1864–1931)
St. Gallen, Switzerland
1900–30
Paper, cardboard, leather, and cotton
24 × 16½ × 3⅞ in. (61 × 42 × 10 cm)
Textilmuseum St. Gallen, STI IKL 4
SEE FIGS 1.1 AND 14.18

144
Bird motif made on hand-embroidery
machine at the Textilmuseum St. Gallen
Jasmin Rigert, designer
Maria Weber, embroiderer
2016
Polyester and cotton
1½ × 3½ in. (3.8 × 8.9 cm)
Private collection

145
Dress with chemical lace and embroidery
Robert Heinrich Graf (Swiss, d. 1919),
embroiderer
Appenzell, Switzerland
ca. 1900–10
Cotton
Length at center back: 51⅛ in. (130 cm)
Textilmuseum St. Gallen, 48438
SEE FIG. 15.3

146
*Textilsammlung Iklé, Industrie- u.
Gewerbemuseum St. Gallen*
Published by Orell Füssli, Zurich
1908
Ink on paper
9⅞ × 14⅞ in. (25 × 38 cm)
Textilmuseum St. Gallen, TSP IKL.A

147
Chemical-lace insert with appliqués
Otto Alder & Co. (1874–1924)
St. Gallen, Switzerland
1904
Cotton
11⅜ × 23¼ in. (29 × 59 cm)

Textilmuseum St. Gallen, Acquired from
Otto Alder, 1931, 30128
SEE FIG. I.28

148
Thirty-five chemical-lace samples
St. Gallen, Switzerland
ca. 1883–90
Cotton
1⅛–10⅝ × 3⅛–11¾ in. (3–27 × 8–30 cm)
Textilmuseum St. Gallen, 56302.1-35

149
Chemical-lace galloon
Otto Alder & Co. (1874–1924)
St. Gallen, Switzerland
1900
Cotton
6⅛ × 26 in. (15.5 × 66 cm)
Textilmuseum St. Gallen, Acquired from
Otto Alder, 1931, 30122

150
Drawing of a dress with chemical-lace
inserts
St. Gallen, Switzerland
ca. 1910s
Pencil on paper
13 × 11⅞ in. (33 × 30 cm)
Textilmuseum St. Gallen, 54222

151
Two women at Longchamp
Paris
1911
Photograph with inscription in ink
9½ × 7⅛ in. (24 × 18 cm)
Textilmuseum St. Gallen, 55441

152
Chemical-lace sample
Stauder & Co. (1893–1911)
St. Gallen, Switzerland
Before 1911
Cotton, artificial silk, lamé, and cardboard
15 × 19¼ in. (38 × 49 cm)
Textilmuseum St. Gallen, 55555

153
Chemical-lace galloons imitating *point de
Venise* needle lace
Labhard & Co. (–1934)
St. Gallen, Switzerland
First third of the 20th century
Artificial silk and cardboard
18½ × 7⅛ in. (47 × 18 cm)
Textilmuseum St. Gallen, 55861

154
Woman wearing chemical-lace dress
Nathan Lazarnick (1879–1955), photographer
New York
ca. 1920
Photograph
10 × 8⅛ in. (25.5 × 20.5 cm)
Textilmuseum St. Gallen, 54433

155
Chemical-lace galloon imitating *point de
Venise* and *point de gaze* needle lace
Labhard & Co. (–1934)
St. Gallen, Switzerland
First third of the 20th century
Cotton
7⅞ × 23¼ in. (21 × 60 cm)
Textilmuseum St. Gallen, 54240

156
Woman wearing chemical-lace dress
Before 1913
Photograph mounted on cardboard
14⅛ × 11⅜ in. (36 × 29 cm)
Textilmuseum St. Gallen, 54331

157
Chemical-lace galloon
Labhard & Co. (–1934)
St. Gallen, Switzerland
First third of the 20th century
Cotton and lamé
11¾ × 7⅞ in. (30 × 20 cm)
Textilmuseum St. Gallen, 54239

158
Chemical-lace trimming with appliqués,
imitating *point de Venise* needle lace
Labhard & Co (–1934)
St. Gallen, Switzerland
First third of the 20th century
Cotton
16⅛ × 28 in. (39 × 71 cm)
Textilmuseum St. Gallen, 54202

159
Woman wearing dress with chemical-lace
inserts
Joel Feder (1890–1959), photographer
New York
ca. 1915
Photograph
7⅝ × 9⅝ in. (19.5 × 24.5 cm)
Textilmuseum St. Gallen, 55796

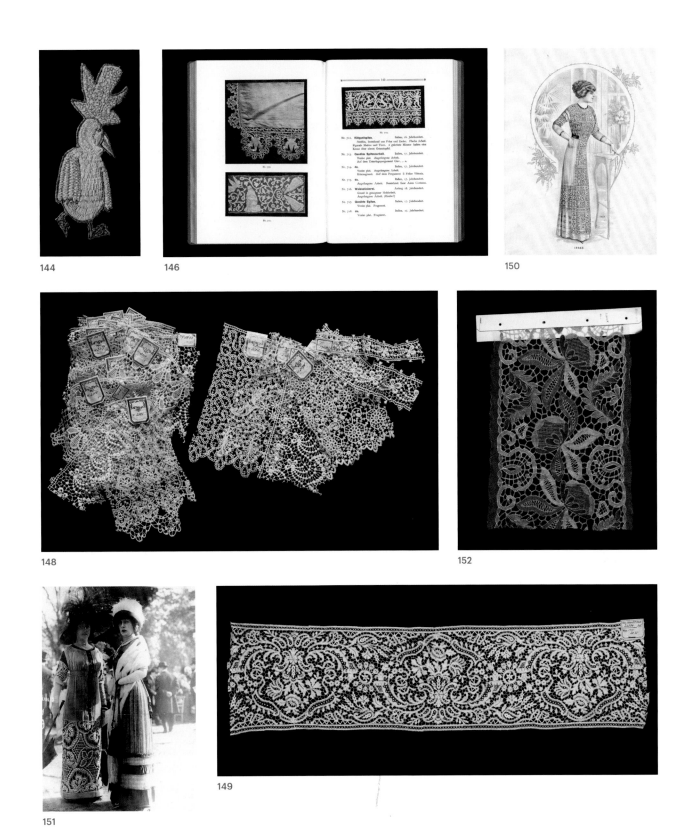

144

146

150

148

152

151

149

153

160

158

154

156

159

155

157

161

162

160
Chemical-lace border
Otto Alder & Co. (1874–1924)
St. Gallen, Switzerland
ca. 1900
Cotton and lamé
19¾ × 19¾ in. (50 × 50 cm)
Textilmuseum St. Gallen, Acquired from
Otto Alder, 1931, 30148

161
Drawing of a dress with chemical-lace
inserts
Probably St. Gallen, Switzerland
ca. 1925
Colored crayon and charcoal on tracing
paper on cardboard
10⅝ × 6⅞ in. (27 × 17.5 cm)
Textilmuseum St. Gallen, 54352

162
Drawing of a dress with chemical-lace
inserts
Location unknown
ca. 1925
Blueprint paper on cardboard
7¼ × 11 in. (18.5 × 28 cm)
Textilmuseum St. Gallen, 55893

163
Chemical-lace galloon samples
Labhard & Co. (–1934)
St. Gallen, Switzerland
First third of the 20th century
Cotton
6¾ × 15 in. (17 × 38 cm)
Textilmuseum St. Gallen, 54086
SEE FIG. 15.10

164
Chemical-lace galloon samples
Fritz Rau & Co. (1892–2012)
St. Gallen, Switzerland
ca. 1920s
Cotton
19⅝ × 19 in. (50 × 48 cm)
Textilmuseum St. Gallen, 55035
SEE FIG. 15.6

165
Woman wearing skirt made from Fritz Rau &
Co. chemical lace at the Grand Prix de Paris
Paris
1920
Photograph with inscription in ink
7⅛ × 5⅛ in. (18 × 13 cm)
Textilmuseum St. Gallen, 55440
SEE FIG. 15.5

166
Photograph with eyelet embroidery swatch
Robert Rigassi (active 1930s), photographer;
A. Hufenus & Cie (1880–ca. 1956), textile
manufacturer
France and St. Gallen, Switzerland
ca. 1935
Photograph and cotton
7⅛ × 9½ in. (18 × 24 cm)
Collection of Donna Ghelerter

167
Photograph with eyelet embroidery swatch
A. Hufenus & Cie (1880–ca. 1956), textile
manufacturer
France and St. Gallen, Switzerland
ca. 1932–35
Photograph and cotton
5¼ × 7¼ in. (13.5 × 18.5 cm)
Collection of Donna Ghelerter

168
Photograph with cutout lace and appliqué
swatch
Agence de presse Meurisse (French,
1909–1937), photographer
France and St. Gallen, Switzerland
1924
Photograph and cotton
5 × 7¼ in. (12.5 × 18.5 cm)
Collection of Donna Ghelerter

169
Photograph with chemical-lace swatches
Agence de presse Meurisse (French,
1909–1937), photographer
France and St. Gallen, Switzerland
1924
Photograph with inscription in ink and
cotton
5¼ × 7⅛ in. (13.5 × 18 cm)
Collection of Donna Ghelerter

170
Photograph with chemical-lace swatch
Seeberger Frères (French, 1909–1977),
photographer
France and St. Gallen, Switzerland
1924
5 × 7 in. (12.5 × 17.5 cm)
Photograph with inscription in ink and
cotton
Collection of Donna Ghelerter

171
Photograph with cutout lace and appliqué
swatch
A. Hufenus & Cie (1880–ca. 1956),

textile manufacturer
France and St. Gallen, Switzerland
ca. 1932–35
Photograph and cotton
5¼ × 7½ in. (13.5 × 19 cm)
Collection of Donna Ghelerter

172
2009 Presidential Inauguration ensemble
worn by First Lady Michelle Obama
Isabel Toledo (Cuban American, 1960–2019),
designer
Forster Rohner AG (1904–), textile
manufacturer
United States and St. Gallen, Switzerland
ca. 2008
Felted wool lace, silk radzimir, and silk
netting
Length at center back: 43¾ in. (123.8 cm)
Courtesy Barack Obama Presidential
Library, FL2011.1a-b
SEE FIG. I.2

173
Sketch and swatch of 2009 Presidential
Inauguration ensemble Isabel Toledo
designed for First Lady Michelle Obama
Ruben Toledo (Cuban American, b. 1961)
United States
2008
Ink on paper and felted wool lace
22⅜ × 15 in. (56.8 × 38.1 cm)
Ruben Toledo, courtesy Ruben and Isabel
Toledo Archives
SEE FIG. I.4

174
Guipure used to make First Lady Michelle
Obama's 2009 Presidential Inauguration
ensemble designed by Isabel Toledo
Forster Rohner AG (1904–)
St. Gallen, Switzerland
2008
Wool
34⅝ × 8 in. (88 × 20.5 cm)
Forster Rohner AG
SEE FIG. I.3

175
Sequined chemical-lace lurex with hand-
appliquéd feathers
Jakob Schlaepfer AG (1904–)
St. Gallen, Switzerland
1998
Synthetic fiber, lamé, sequins, and feathers
165⅜ × 30¾ in. (420 × 78 cm)
Collection Martin Leuthold
SEE FIG. 16.7

166

167

168

169

170

171

176
Chemical lace with silver plating
Jakob Schlaepfer AG (1904–)
St. Gallen, Switzerland
1999
Synthetic fiber and silver plating
14 × 30⅛ in. (35.5 × 76.5 cm)
Collection Martin Leuthold
SEE FIG. 16.12

177
Cutout lace with floral appliqué stitched
with rubber bobbin (used by Emanuel
Ungaro)
Jakob Schlaepfer AG (1904–)
St. Gallen, Switzerland
1985
Silk
63 × 43⅞ in. (160 × 111.5 cm)
Collection Martin Leuthold
SEE FIG. 16.8

178
"Tour Eiffel" coat from the *Trompe l'Œil* line
Christian Dior (French, 1905–1957) for
House of Dior (1947–), designer
Made in the *atelier tailleur* by Paul
Forster Willi & Co. (now Forster Rohner AG;
1904–), textile manufacturer
Paris and St. Gallen, Switzerland
Spring/Summer 1949
Silk satin lined in heavy cotton guipure
bobbin lace
Length at center back: 31⅜ in. (80 cm)
Royal Ontario Museum, Toronto, Gift of
Mrs. John David Eaton, 956.153.9
SEE FIG. 15.22

179
Dress made for Mrs. Doris Forster
(1911–2008)
Yves Saint Laurent (French, 1936–2008)
for House of Yves Saint Laurent (1961–),
designer
Forster Willi & Co. (now Forster Rohner AG;
1904–), textile manufacturer
Paris and St. Gallen, Switzerland
1966–67
Cotton
Length at center back: 39¾ in. (101 cm)
Forster-Rohner-Collection, Koll. 217 1/2-C59
SEE FIG. 16.6

180
Dress made for Mrs. Doris Forster
(1911–2008)
Hubert de Givenchy (French, 1927–2018) for

House of Givenchy (1952–), designer
Forster Willi & Co. (now Forster Rohner AG;
1904–), textile manufacturer
Paris and St. Gallen, Switzerland
1957–58
Silk
Length at center back: 39¾ in. (101 cm)
Forster-Rohner-Collection, Koll. 208 1/2-C12
SEE FIG. 16.5

181
Dress made for Mrs. Doris Forster
(1911–2008)
Christian Dior (French, 1905–1957) for
House of Dior (1947–), designer
Forster Willi & Co. (now Forster Rohner AG;
1904–), textile manufacturer
Paris and St. Gallen, Switzerland
1957
Silk
Length at center back: 44½ in. (113 cm)
Forster-Rohner-Collection, Koll. 208-C14
SEE FIG. 16.4

182
Evening dress
Yves Saint Laurent (French, 1936–2008)
for House of Yves Saint Laurent (1961–),
designer
Forster Willi & Co. (now Forster Rohner AG;
1904–), textile manufacturer
Paris and St. Gallen, Switzerland
Spring/Summer 1963
Cotton, silk, pearl, and plastic
Length at center back: 41 in. (104.1 cm)
The Metropolitan Museum of Art, New York,
Gift of Mrs. Charles B. Wrightsman, 1964,
C.I.64.59.7a, b
SEE FIG. 16.1

183
Cocktail dress
Marc Bohan (French, b. 1926) for House of
Dior (1947–), designer
France
Fall/Winter 1971–72
Cotton, silk, and leather
Length at center back: 41¾ in. (106 cm)
The Metropolitan Museum of Art, New York,
Gift of Bernice Chrysler Garbisch, 1977,
1977.108.7a-c

184
Ensemble
Miuccia Prada (Italian, b. 1949) for Prada
(1913–), designer
Forster Rohner AG (1904–), textile

manufacturer
Italy and St. Gallen, Switzerland
Fall 2008
Cotton and polyester guipure lace, cotton
poplin, leather, and silk knit
Length at center back: 46¾ in. (118.7 cm)
The Museum at the Fashion Institute of
Technology, New York, Gift of Prada, 2011.1.1
SEE FIG. 16.2

185
Chemical-lace wedding dress with bolero
St. Gallen, Switzerland
1970–75
Cotton
Length at center back: 39¾ in. (101 cm)
Textilmuseum St. Gallen, 59448.1-2

186
Ensemble (Look 13)
Akris Prêt-à-Porter AG (1922–), designer
Forster Rohner AG (1904–), textile
manufacturer
St. Gallen, Switzerland
Fall/Winter 2018
Cotton, wool, and cashmere
Jacket length at center back: 28 in. (71 cm)
Akris Prêt-à-Porter AG
SEE FIG. 16.3

187
Starched chemical-lace shoes
Designer/manufacturer unknown
Italy
ca. 1962
Probably silk
Length: 9½ in. (24 cm)
Textilmuseum St. Gallen, 52902.a-b

188
Chemical-lace dress
Textile designed by H. Andres for Union
(1759–)
Zurich and St. Gallen, Switzerland
ca. 1963–67
Cotton, silk, and nylon
Length at center back: 63⅜ in. (160.9 cm)
Textilmuseum St. Gallen, Gift of
Schweizerisches Baumwollinstitut/Textil-
und Modezentrum Zürich, 1983, 41100

189
Dress with chemical lace
Oscar de la Renta (Dominican, 1932–2014)
for House of Oscar de la Renta (1965–),
designer
Bischoff Textil AG (1927–), textile

183

185

187

189

188

manufacturer
United States and St. Gallen, Switzerland
Spring 2013
Synthetic fiber and cloque
Length at center back: 66 in. (167.6 cm)
Oscar de la Renta Archive

190
Chemical lace (used by Balmain, Jean Paul
Gaultier, Ralph and Russo, Philip Treacy,
Valentino, and Versace)
Jakob Schlaepfer AG (1904–)
St. Gallen, Switzerland
1987
Viscose
192 7/8 × 6 7/8 in. (490 × 17.5 cm)
Collection Martin Leuthold
SEE FIG. 16.11

191
Chemical lace (used by Balmain, Jean Paul
Gaultier, Ralph and Russo, Philip Treacy,
Valentino, and Versace)
Jakob Schlaepfer AG (1904–)
St. Gallen, Switzerland
1987
Viscose
291 3/8 × 53 1/8 in. (740 × 135 cm)
Collection Martin Leuthold
SEE FIG. 16.10

192
Chemical lace (used by Balmain, Jean Paul
Gaultier, Ralph and Russo, Philip Treacy,
Valentino, and Versace)
Jakob Schlaepfer AG (1904–)
St. Gallen, Switzerland
1987
Viscose
106 1/4 × 28 7/8 in. (270 × 73.5 cm)
Collection Martin Leuthold
SEE FIG. 16.9

193
Sample of hypertube guipure (used by
Comme des Garçons)
Jakob Schlaepfer AG (1904–)
St. Gallen, Switzerland
2017
Silicone
31 1/8 × 23 5/8 in. (79 × 60 cm)
Collection Jakob Schlaepfer AG
SEE FIG. 16.15

194
Sample of hypertube guipure
Jakob Schlaepfer AG (1904–)
St. Gallen, Switzerland
2019
Silicone
35 1/2 × 15 in. (90 × 38 cm)
Collection Jakob Schlaepfer AG
SEE FIG. 16.13

195
Hypertube guipure collar
Jakob Schlaepfer AG (1904–)
St. Gallen, Switzerland
ca. 2021
Silicone
16 1/8 × 18 7/8 in. (41 × 48 cm)
Private collection
SEE FIG. I.30

Selected Bibliography

Archives

Archives départementales du Rhône, Lyon, France

Archives nationales de France, Pierrefitte-sur-Seine, France

Archivio di stato di Firenze, Florence

Archivio di stato di Venezia, Venice

Archivo General de la Nación, Bogotá

Archivo General de Palacio de Madrid

Archivo Histórico Cipriano Rodríguez Santa María, Universidad de la Sabana, Chía, Colombia

Archivo Histórico Nacional del Ecuador, Quito

Archivo Histórico de Protocolos, Madrid

Bibliothèque nationale de France, Paris
	Cabinet des Estampes
	Département des manuscrits

Blackborne Lace Archive, the Bowes Museum, Barnard Castle, United Kingdom

Gilder Lehrman Institute of American History, New York

Gino Speranza Papers, New York Public Library

Plantin Archives, Museum Plantin-Moretus, Antwerp

Real Biblioteca del Palacio Real de Madrid

Vadianische Sammlung der Ortsbürgergemeinde, Kantonsbibliothek Vadiana, St. Gallen, Switzerland

Printed Sources

Abbe, Truman, and Hubert Abbe Howson. *Robert Colgate, the Immigrant: A Genealogy of the New York Colgates and Some Associated Lines.* New Haven, CT: Tuttle, Morehouse & Taylor Co., 1941.

Aceves, Gutierre. "Imagenes de la inocencia eterna." In "El arte ritual de la muerte niña." Special issue, *Artes de México*, no. 15 (1992): 26–49.

Adburgham, Alison. *Shops and Shopping, 1800–1914: Where, and in What Manner the Well-Dressed Englishwoman Bought Her Clothes.* London: George Allen & Unwin, 1964.

Alcega, Juan de. *Libro de geometria, pratica, y traça.* Álava, Spain, 1580. Reprinted Madrid, 1589.

Allerston, Patricia. "An Undisciplined Activity? Lace Production in Early Modern Venice." In *Shadow Economies and Irregular Work in Urban Europe: 16th to Early 20th Centuries*, edited by Thomas Buchner and Philip R. Hoffmann-Rehnitz, 63–71. Vienna: Lir Verlag, 2011.

Allgemeine merkantilische Erdbeschreibung auch Handlungs- und Fabriken Addressbuch. Leipzig, Germany: August Schumann, 1802.

Álvarez de Miranda, Pedro. *Palabras e ideas: El léxico de la ilustración temprana en España (1680–1760).* Madrid: Real Academia Española, 1992.

Amari, Carolina. Contribution to *Bolletino mensile della società cooperativa nazionale le industrie femminili italiane "la nationale" compagnia d'assicurazioni.* N.p.

Aristízabal García, Diana Marcela. *Poder y distinción colonial: Las fiestas del virrey presente y el rey ausente (Nueva Granada 1770–1800).* Bogotá: Universidad del Rosario, 2011.

Arizzoli-Clémentel, Pierre, and Pascal Gorguet Ballesteros, eds. *Fastes de cour et cérémonies royales: Le costume de cour en Europe, 1650–1800.* Exh. cat. Paris: Éditions de la Réunion des musées nationaux, 2009.

Armella de Aspe, Virginia, Teresa Castelló Yturbide, and Ignacio Borja Martínez. *La historia de México a través de la indumentaria.* México, DF: Inbursa, 1988.

Aubry, Félix. "Classe XXIV: Dentelles, broderie, passementerie, tapisserie." In *Exposition universelle de Londres de 1862: Rapports des membres de la section française du jury international sur l'ensemble de l'Exposition*, 203–20. Vol. 5, edited by M. Michel Chevalier. Paris: Imprimerie et Librairie Centrales des Chemins de Fer, 1862.

———. *Rapport sur les dentelles, les blondes, les tulles et les broderies: Fait à la Commission française du jury international de l'Exposition universelle de Londres.* Paris: Imprimerie Impériale, 1854.

Baker, Tabitha. "The Embroidery Trade in Eighteenth-Century Paris and Lyon." PhD diss., University of Warwick, 2019.

Bakewell, Peter. *A History of Latin America to 1825.* 3rd ed. Oxford: Blackwell, 2010.

Bambach, Carmen. "Leonardo, Tagliente, and Dürer: 'La scienza del far di groppi.'" *Achademia Leonardi Vinci: Journal of Leonardo Studies & Bibliographie Vinciana* 4 (1991): 72–98.

Bass, Laura R. *The Drama of the Portrait: Theater and Visual Culture in Early Modern Spain.* University Park, PA: Pennsylvania State University Press, 2008.

Bass-Krueger, Maude, and Sophie Kurkdjian, eds. *French Fashion, Women, and the First World War*. New York: Bard Graduate Center; New Haven, CT: Yale University Press, 2019.

Bayard, Françoise. *Vivre à Lyon sous l'Ancien Régime*. Paris: Perrin, 1997.

Beltrán-Rubio, Laura. "Cuerpos, moda y género en el Virreinato de la Nueva Granada: Un estudio a partir de la pollera y el faldellín." *Miradas* 5 (2022).

Benavente Velarde, Teófilo. *Pintores cusqueños de la colonia*. Lima: Municipalidad del Qosqo, 1995.

Bendel, Heinrich. *Erster Bericht über das St. Gallische Industrie- und Gewerbemuseum 1878*. St. Gallen, Switzerland: Zollikofer'sche Buchdruckerei, 1879.

Benhamou, Reed. *Public and Private Art Education in France, 1648–1793*. Oxford: Voltaire Foundation, 1993.

Bensimon, Fabrice. "The Emigration of British Lacemakers to Continental Europe (1816–1860s)." *Continuity and Change* 34, no. 1 (2019): 15–41.

———. "Women and Children in the Machine-Made Lace Industry in Britain and France (1810–60)." *Textile* 18, no. 1 (2020): 69–91.

Benson, Elizabeth P., et al. *Retratos: 2,000 Years of Latin American Portraits*. New Haven, CT: Yale University Press, 2009.

Berg, Maxine. "What Difference Did Women's Work Make to the Industrial Revolution?" *History Workshop Journal* 35, no. 1 (Spring 1993): 22–44.

Berguén, Juan. *Libro de geometria y traça*. Madrid: Guillermo Drouy, 1618.

Bernardini, Carla, and Marta Forlai. *Industriartistica bolognese: Aemilia Ars; Luoghi, materiali, fonti*. Milan: Silvana Editoriale, 2003.

Bernis, Carmen. *Indumentaria española en tiempos de Carlos V*. Madrid: Instituto Diego Velázquez, Consejo Superior de Investigaciones Científicas, 1962.

———. "Tejidos y guarniciones." In *El traje y los tipos sociales en El Quijote*, 281–92. Madrid: Ediciones El Viso, 2001.

———. *Trajes y modas en la España de los Reyes Católicos*. Vol. 1. Madrid: Instituto Diego Velázquez, Consejo Superior de Investigaciones Científicas, 1978.

Bernis, Carmen, and Amalia Descalzo. "El vestido femenino español en la época de los Austrias." In *Vestir a la española en las cortes europeas (siglos XVI y XVII)*, edited by José Luis Colomer and Amalia Descalzo, 39–75. Vol. 1. Madrid: Centro de Estudios Europa Hispánica, 2014.

Blanc, Charles. *L'art dans la parure et dans le vêtement*. Paris: Librairie Renouard, 1875.

Bleckwenn, Ruth. *Dresdner Spitzen—Point de Saxe: Virtuose Weissstickereien des 18. Jahrhunderts*. Dresden, Germany: Staatliche Kunstsammlungen, 2000.

Bleichmar, Daniela. *Visual Voyages: Images of Latin American Nature from Columbus to Darwin*. New Haven, CT: Yale University Press, 2017.

Bondois, Paul-Martin. "Colbert et l'industrie de la dentelle: Le 'Point de France' à Reims et à Sedan d'après des documents inédits." *Revue d'histoire économique et sociale* 13, no. 4 (1925): 367–408.

Bonneau-Pontabry, Marie-Madeleine. *La dentelle de Tulle: Une belle au bois dormant; Approche historique et sociale d'un artisanat d'art*. N.p.: À l'Enseigne du Griffon, 2005.

Borja Gómez, Jaime Humberto. *Los ingenios del pincel: Geografía de la pintura y la cultura visual en la América colonial*. Bogotá: Universidad de los Andes, 2021. https://losingeniosdelpincel.uniandes.edu.co/.

Boucher, Shazia, Annette Haudiquet, and Philippe Peyre. *25 ans de lingerie: La dentelle sans dessus/dessous*. Calais, France: Musée des Beaux-Arts et de la Dentelle, 1997.

Boyd-Bowman, Peter. "Spanish and European Textiles in Sixteenth Century Mexico." *Americas* 29, no. 3 (January 1973): 334–58.

Brading, D. A. *Miners and Merchants in Bourbon Mexico, 1763–1810*. Cambridge: Cambridge University Press, 1971.

Braun, Joseph. *Die liturgische Gewandung im Occident und Orient: Nach Ursprung und Entwicklung, Verwendung und Symbolik*. Freiburg im Breisgau, Germany: Herder, 1907.

Brazzà Savorgnan, Countess Cora Ann Slocomb di. *A Guide to New and Old Lace in Italy Exhibited at Chicago in 1893*. Chicago: W. B. Conkey, 1893.

Breskin, Isabel. "'On the Periphery of a Greater World': John Singleton Copley's 'Turquerie' Portraits." *Winterthur Portfolio* 36, no. 2/3 (Summer–Autumn 2001): 97–123.

Brook, Timothy. "Prologue: Coming onto the Map." In *Made in the Americas: The New World Discovers Asia*, edited by Dennis Carr, 9–17. Boston: MFA Publications, 2015.

Brown, Michael. "Image of an Empire: Portraiture in Spain, New Spain and the Viceroyalties of New Spain and Peru." In *Painting of the Kingdoms: Shared Identities; Territories of the Spanish Monarchy, 16th–18th Centuries*, edited by Juana Gutiérrez Haces, 446–503. Vol. 1. México, DF: Fomento Cultural Banamex, 2009.

———. "Portraits and Patrons in the Colonial Americas." In *Behind Closed Doors: Art in the Spanish American Home, 1492–1898*, edited by Richard Aste, 131–59. New York: Brooklyn Museum; New York: Monacelli Press, 2013.

Brulart, Madame de [pseud.]. *Discours sur le luxe et l'hospitalité: Considérés sous leurs rapports avec les mœurs et l'éducation nationale*. Paris: Onfroy, 1791.

Bruna, Denis, ed. *Fashioning the Body: An Intimate History of the Silhouette*. New York: Bard Graduate Center; New Haven, CT: Yale University Press, 2015.

———. *La mécanique des dessous: Une histoire indiscrète de la silhouette*. Paris: Les Arts Décoratifs, 2013.

Buck, Anne. *Thomas Lester: His Lace and the East Midlands Industry, 1820–1905*. Bedford, UK: Ruth Bean, 1981.

Burke, Peter. "Reflections on the Frontispiece Portrait in the Renaissance." In *Bildnis und Image: Das Portrait zwischen Intention und Rezeption*, edited by Andreas Köster and Ernst Seidl, 150–62. Cologne, Germany: Böhlau, 1998.

Butazzi, Grazietta. "The Abuse of the Renaissance: Elegance and Revival in Post-Unification Italy." In *Reviving the Renaissance: The Use and Abuse of the Past in Nineteenth-Century Art and Decoration*, edited by Rosanna Pavoni, translated by Adrian Belton, 149–76. Cambridge: Cambridge University Press, 1997.

Calderón de la Barca, Frances Erskine. *Life in Mexico during a Residence of Two Years in That Country*. Boston: Little and Brown, 1843.

Campagnol, Isabella. "Invisible Seamstresses: Feminine Works in Venetian Convents from the Fifteenth to the

Eighteenth Century." In *Women and the Material Culture of Needlework and Textiles, 1750–1950*, edited by Maureen D. Goggin and Beth F. Tobin, 167–82. Farnham, UK: Routledge, 2009.

Carrió de la Vandera, Alonso. *Lazarillo de ciegos caminantes*. 1775. Caracas: Biblioteca Ayacucho, 1985.

Catalogo cooperativa nazionale industrie femminili Italiane Milan. Milan: Pilade Rocco, 1906.

Charlot, Jean. *Mexican Art and the Academy of San Carlos, 1785–1915*. Austin: University of Texas Press, 1962.

Chenoune, Farid. *Beneath It All: A Century of French Lingerie*. New York: Rizzoli, 1999.

Chiozzotto, Marie. "Les apparences vestimentaires de Louis XV: La composition de la garde-robe du souverain pour l'année 1772." *Apparences* 4 (2012): pars. 27, 32.

Colomer, José Luis. "El negro y la image real." In *Vestir a la española en las cortes europeas (siglos XVI y XVII)*, 77–112. Madrid: Centro de Estudios Europa Hispánica, 2014.

Colomer, José Luis, and Amalia Descalzo, eds. *Spanish Fashion at the Courts of Early Modern Europe*. 2 vols. Madrid: Centro de Estudios Europa Hispánica, 2014.

Coppens, Marguerite. "'Au Magasin de Paris': Une boutique de modes à Anvers dans la première moitié du XVIIIe siècle." *Revue belge d'archéologie et d'histoire de l'art* 52 (1983): 81–107.

Cordey, Jean, ed. *Inventaire des biens de Madame de Pompadour, rédigé après son décès*. Paris: Francisque Lefrançois pour La société des bibliophiles françois, 1939.

Covarrubias Orozco, Sebastián de. *Tesoro de la lengua castellana o española*. Edited by Felipe C. R. Maldonado. 1611. Madrid: Editorial Castalia, 1995.

Croce, Giovanni. "Da Buranelle." In *Mascarate piacevoli et ridicolose per il carnevale a 4, 5, 6, 7 et otto voci: Di Giovanni Croce chiozotto; Libro primo*. Venice: Giacomo Vincenzi, 1590.

Croq, Laurence. "Les chemins de la mercerie, le renouvellement de la marchandise parisienne (années 1660–1760)." In *Mobilité et transmission dans les sociétés de l'Europe moderne*, online ed., 87–122. Rennes, France: Presses universitaires de Rennes, 2009.

Crowston, Clare Haru. *Fabricating Women: The Seamstresses of Old Régime France, 1675–1791*. Durham, NC: Duke University Press, 2001.

Dahrén, Lena. "Printed Pattern Books for Early Modern Bobbin-Made Borders and Edgings." *Konsthistorisk tidskrift* 82, no. 3 (2013): 169–90.

Daniels, Margaret Harrington. "Early Pattern Books for Lace and Embroidery, Parts 1 and 2." *Bulletin of the Needle and Bobbin Club* 33, no. 3 (March 1938): 70–73.

D'Aulnoy, Countess. *Relación del viaje de España*. Madrid: Akal, 1986.

Dean, Carolyn. *Inka Bodies and the Body of Christ: Corpus Christi in Colonial Cuzco, Peru*. Durham, NC: Duke University Press, 1999.

"Déclaration contre le luxe des habits, carrosses et ornemens." No. 357 in *Recueil général des anciennes lois françaises depuis l'an 420 jusqu'à la Révolution de 1789 [. . .]*. 17:384–85. Paris: Belin-Leprieur, 1829. BnF Gallica. https://gallica.bnf.fr/ark:/12148/bpt-6k517036?rk=557942.

DeJean, Joan. *The Age of Comfort: When Paris Discovered Casual and the Modern Home Began*. New York: Bloomsbury, 2010.

———. *The Essence of Style: How the French Invented High Fashion, Fine Food, Chic Cafés, Style, Sophistication and Glamour*. New York: Free Press, 2006.

———. *How Paris Became Paris: The Invention of the Modern City*. New York: Bloomsbury, 2015.

De La Croix, Jean. "Les images de Thérèse d'Avile et d'Anne de Jésus dans le couvre-pied de archiducs." *Bulletin van de Koninklijke Musea voor Kunst en Geschiedenis* 43–44 (1971–72): 89–98.

Descalzo, Amalia. "El traje masculino español en la época de los Austrias." In *Vestir a la española en las cortes europeas*, edited by José Luis Colomer and Amalia Descalzo, 15–38. Madrid: Centro de Estudios Europa Hispánica, 2014.

Descalzo Lorenzo, Amalia. "El retrato y la moda en España (1661–1746)." 3 vols. PhD diss., Universidad Autónoma de Madrid, Facultad de Filosofía y Letras, 2003.

———. "Spanish Foundation Garments in the Habsburg Period." In *Structuring Fashion: Foundation Garments through History*, 39–49. Munich, Germany: Bayerisches Nationalmuseum, 2019.

———. "Velázquez y la moda: Aproximación a la identidad de la dama del abanico." In *In sapientia libertas: Escritos en homenaje al profesor Alfonso Emilio Pérez Sánchez*, 435–40. Madrid: Museo Nacional del Prado; Seville, Spain: Fundación Focus-Abengoa, 2007.

———. "Vestirse a la moda en la España moderna." *Vínculos de historia*, no. 6 (2017): 105–34.

Descalzo Lorenzo, Amalia, and Carlos Gómez Centurión. "El Real Guardarropa y la introducción de la moda francesa en la corte de Felipe V." In *La herencia de Borgoña: La hacienda de la Reales Casas durante el reinado de Felipe V*, edited by Carlos Gómez-Centurión Jiménez and Juan A. Sánchez Belén, 159–87. Madrid: Centro de Estudios Políticos y Constitucionales, 1998.

Despierres, Gérasime Bonnaire. *Histoire du point d'Alençon, depuis son origine jusqu'à nos jours*. Paris: Librairie Renouard, 1886.

Diccionario de autoridades. 3 vols. 1732. Madrid: Editorial Gredos, 1990.

Diccionario panhispánico del español jurídico. Madrid: Real Academia Española, 2020. https://dpej.rae.es.

Dictionnaires d'autrefois: French Dictionaries of the 17th, 18th, 19th and 20th Centuries. Online database. ARTFL Project, University of Chicago. https://artfl-project.uchicago.edu/content/dictionnaires-dautrefois.

Diderot, Denis, and Jean le Rond d'Alembert, eds. *Encyclopédie, ou Dictionnaire raisonné des sciences et métiers*. Paris: Briasson, 1751–72.

Dora, Cornel. "Le berceau de la broderie." In *Secrets, sous le charme de la lingerie*. Exh. cat. St. Gallen, Switzerland: Textilmuseum, 2008.

———, ed. *Textiles St. Gallen: Tausend Jahre Tradition, Technologie und Trends/A Thousand Years of Tradition, Technology and Trends*. St. Gallen, Switzerland: Amt für Kultur, 2004.

Dreger, Moriz. *Die Wiener Spitzenausstellung*. Leipzig, Germany: K. W. Hiersemann, 1906.

———. *Entwicklungsgeschichte der Spitze: Mit bes. Rücksicht auf die Spitzen-Sammlung des K.K. Österreichischen Museums für Kunst und Industrie in Wien*. Vienna: Schroll, 1901.

Earnshaw, Pat. *A Dictionary of Lace*. Princes Risborough, UK: Shire Publications, 1982.

——. *Embroidered Machine Nets: Limerick and Worldwide*. Guildford, UK: Gorse Publications, 1993.

——. *The Identification of Lace*. Princes Risborough, UK: Shire Publications, 1980.

——. *Lace in Fashion: From the Sixteenth to the Twentieth Centuries*. London: B. T. Batsford, 1985.

——. *Lace Machines and Machine Laces*. London: B. T. Batsford, 1986.

Engel, Emily. *Pictured Politics: Visualizing Colonial History in South American Portrait Collections*. Austin: University of Texas Press, 2020.

Fäh, Adolf, ed. *Leopold Iklé 1838–1922: Gedenkblätter unter Zugrundelegung seiner Memoiren, zusammengestellt von Dr. Ad. Fäh Bibl*. St. Gallen, Switzerland: Printed for Friends, by H. Tschudy, 1922.

Fäh, Adolf, and Leopold Iklé. *Beiträge zur Entwicklungsgeschichte der Spitze*. Zurich: Orell Füssli, 1919.

Farcy, Louis de. *La broderie du XIe siècle jusqu'à nos jours d'après des spécimens authentiques et les anciens inventaires*. 2 vols. Angers, France: Belhomme, 1890–1919.

Felkin, William. *History of the Machine-Wrought Hosiery and Lace Manufactures*. London: Longmans, Green, 1867.

Ferguson, Samuel, Jr. *Histoire du tulle et des dentelles mécaniques en Angleterre et en France*. Paris: E. Lacroix, 1862.

Fertiault, François. *Histoire de la dentelle*. Paris: Au Dépot Belge, Maison Fragati, 1843.

Flores Ramos, Marlene. "The Filipina Bordadoras and the Emergence of Fine European-Style Embroidery Tradition in Colonial Philippines, 19th to Early-20th Centuries." MA diss., Mount Saint Vincent University, Nova Scotia, 2016. Wayback Machine. https://web.archive.org/web/20200212094914/https://pdfs.semanticscholar.org/4fda/da033e330b2bafcbe40f40dae90084c2d512.pdf.

Fontaine, Laurence. *History of Pedlars in Europe*. Cambridge: Polity Press, 1996.

Frauberger, Tina. *Handbuch der Spitzenkunde: Technisches und Geschichtliches über die Näh-, Klöppel- und Maschinenspitzen*. Leipzig, Germany: Verlag Seemann, 1894.

Freedgood, Elaine. "'Fine Fingers': Victorian Handmade Lace and Utopian Consumption." *Victorian Studies* 45, no. 4 (Summer 2003): 625–47.

Freyle, Diego de. *Geometría y traça para el oficio de los sastres*. Seville, Spain, 1588.

Frézier, Amédée-François. *A Voyage to the South-Sea and along the Coasts of Chili and Peru, in the Years 1712, 1713, and 1714 [. . .]*. London: Bowyer, 1717.

Fumi, Luigi. "La moda del vestire in Lucca dal secolo XIV al XIX." *Bollettino dell'Istituto Storico Artistico Orvietano* 54, no. 60 (2002–4), 527–85.

Gachard, L. P. "Arenberg (Jean de Ligne, comte d')." In *Biographie nationale publiée par l'Académie royale des sciences, des lettres et des beaux-arts de Belgique*. Vol. 1. Brussels: H. Thiry-Van Buggenhoudt, 1866.

Gage, Thomas. *The English American, His Travails by Sea and Land [. . .]*. London, 1677.

Gandin, Alice, and Julie Romain, eds. *Dentelles: Quand la mode ne tient qu'à un fil*. Paris: Somogy; Caen, France: Musée de Normandie, 2012.

Garzoni, Tommasso. *La piazza universale di tutte le professioni del mondo*. 1585. Venice: Giovanni Battista Somasco, 1587.

Gayot, Gérard. "La main invisible qui guidait les marchands aux foires de Leipzig: Enquête sur un haut lieu de la réalisation des bénéfices, 1750–1830." *Revue d'histoire moderne & contemporaine* 48, no. 2 (2001): 72–103.

Gering, Anne-Marie. "De Fundatie Terninck te Antwerpen (1697–1750)." MA thesis, Katholieke Universteit Leuven, 1990.

Glen, Jean Baptiste de. *Dv debvoir des filles: Traicte brief, et fort vtile, divise en devx parties; La premiere est, de la dignite de la femme [. . .] L'autre traicte de la virginité*. Liège, Belgium: Chez Jean de Glen, 1597.

Goldberg, Samuel L. *Lace, Its Origin and History*. [New York?]: Brentano's, 1904.

Gonzalbo Aizpuru, Pilar. "Lo prodigioso cotidiano en los exvotos novohispanos." In *Dones y promesas: 500 años de arte ofrenda (exvotos mexicanos)*, 47–63. México, DF: Centro Cultural/Arte Contemporáneo, Fundación Cultural Televisa, 1996.

González Marrero, María del Cristo. *La casa de Isabel la Católica: Espacios domésticos y vida cotidiana*. Ávila, Spain: Diputación Provincial de Ávila; Ávila, Spain: Institución Gran Duque de Alba, 2004.

Gorges, Édouard. *Revue de l'exposition universelle: Les merveilles de la civilisation*. Paris: Ferdinand Sartorius, 1856.

Graff-Höfgen, Gisela. "Spitzen von Iklé und Jacoby." *Hamburgische Geschichts- und Heimatblätter*, vol. 9, bk. 11 (October 1976): 274–81.

Greenwold, Diana Jocelyn. "Crafting New Citizens: Art and Handicraft in New York and Boston Settlement Houses, 1900–1945." PhD diss., University of California, Berkeley, 2016.

Grumbach, Didier. *Histoires de la mode*. Paris: Éditions du Seuil, 1993.

Guignet, Philippe. "The Lacemakers of Valenciennes in the Eighteenth Century: An Economic and Social Study of a Group of Female Workers under the Ancien Regime." *Textile History* 10 (1979): 96–113.

Gutierrez Usillos, Andrés. *La hija del virrey: El mundo femenino novohispano en el siglo XVII*. Madrid: Ministerio de Cultura y Deporte, 2019.

Hahn, H. Hazel. *Scenes of Parisian Modernity: Culture and Consumption in the Nineteenth Century*. New York: Palgrave Macmillan, 2009.

Haidt, Rebecca. *Women, Work and Clothing in Eighteenth-Century Spain*. Oxford: Voltaire Foundation, University of Oxford, 2011.

Harvey, John. *Des hommes en noir: Du costume masculin à travers les siècles*. Paris: Éditions Abbeville, 1998.

Hashagen, Joanna, and Santina M. Levey. *Fine & Fashionable: Lace from the Blackborne Collection*. Exh. cat. Barnard Castle, UK: Bowes Museum, 2006.

Häusler, Eric, and Caspar Meili. "Swiss Embroidery: Erfolg und Krise der Schweizer Stickerei-Industrie 1865–1929." *Neujahrsblatt: Historischer Verein des Kantons St. Gallen* 155 (2015): 11–101. https://www.hvsg.ch/pdf/neujahrsblaetter/hvsg_neujahrsblatt_2015.pdf.

Hemert, Maria van. *De handwerken van het eiland Marken*. Arnhem, Netherlands: Openluchtmuseum, 1960.

Hemingway, Jean. "Millinery and Old Lace: Miss Jane Clarke of Regent Street." *Textile History* 43, no. 2 (November 2012): 200–222.

Hempel, Albert. "50 Jahre stickmaschinenge-stickte Ätzspitze: Kritische Feststellungen in Wort und Bild aus dem industriellen Leben Plauens." *Vogtländischer Anzeiger und Tagblatt*, September 3, 1933, 21–23.

Hénon, Henri. *L'industrie des tulles & dentelles mécaniques dans Le Pas-de-Calais, 1815–1900.* Paris: Belin frères, 1900.

Hernández de Alba, Gonzalo. "El virreinato de la Nueva Granada." *Credencial historia* 20 (1991): https://www.banrepcultural.org/biblioteca-virtual/credencial-historia/numero-20/el-virreinato-de-la-nueva-granada.

Histoire de la vie de Mademoiselle Françoise Badar. Liège, Belgium: Jean-François Broncart, 1726.

Hohti, Paula. *Artisans, Objects and Everyday Life in Renaissance Italy: The Material Culture of the Middling Class.* Amsterdam: Amsterdam University Press, 2020.

———. "Dress, Dissemination and Innovation: Artisan Fashions in Sixteenth- and Early Seventeenth-Century Italy." In *Fashioning the Early Modern: Dress, Textiles, and Innovation in Europe, 1500–1800,* edited by Evelyn Welch, 143–65. Oxford: Oxford University Press/Pasold, 2017.

Honig, Elizabeth Alice. "The Art of Being 'Artistic': Dutch Women's Creative Practices in the 17th Century." *Woman's Art Journal* 22, no. 2 (Autumn 2001–Winter 2002): 31–39.

Hopkin, David. "Working, Singing, and Telling in the 19th-Century Flemish Pillow-Lace Industry." *Textile* 18, no. 1 (2019): 53–68.

Hôtel de la Monnaie. *Colbert 1619–1683.* Exh. cat. Paris: Archives nationales, 1983.

Hufton, Olwen. "Women and the Family Economy in Eighteenth-Century France." *French Historical Studies* 9, no. 1 (Spring 1975): 1–22.

Iklé, Ernest. *La broderie mécanique: 1828–1930; Souvenirs et documents.* Paris: A. Calavas, 1931.

Iklé, Leopold, and Emil Wild. *Industrie- und Gewerbemuseum St. Gallen: Textilsammlung Iklé, Katalog.* Zurich: Orell Füssli, 1908.

Indicateur alphabétique de Lyon. Lyon, France: Aimé Delaroche, 1788.

Industrie Femminili Italiane, Cooperativa Nazionale, Roma. *Le Industrie femminili*

Italiane, cooperativa Nazionale: Sede centrale via Marco Minghetti, Roma. Milan: Pilade Rocco, 1906.

Industrie- und Gewerbemuseum. *Bericht über das Industrie- und Gewerbemuseum St. Gallen und über die Zeichnungsschule für Industrie und Gewerbe, Ateliers und Einzelkurse.* St. Gallen, Switzerland: Zollikofer'sche Buchdruckerei, 1901; 1902; 1909.

Irwin, Elisabeth A. "Story of a Transplanted Industry: Lace Workers of the Italian Quarter of New York." *Craftsman* 12 (1907): 404–9.

Ismonger, Miss. "Lace a Modern Industry." *Journal of the Royal Society of Arts* 56, no. 2897 (May 1908): 715.

IX. Bericht über das St. Gallische Industrie- und Gewerbemuseum 1886. St. Gallen, Switzerland: Zollikofer'sche Buchdruckerei, 1887.

Jackson, Mrs. F. Nevill. *A History of Hand-Made Lace.* London: L. Upcott Gill, 1900.

Jacobs, Frederika Herman. *Defining the Renaissance Virtuosa: Women Artists and the Language of Art History and Criticism.* Cambridge: Cambridge University Press, 1997.

Jefferson, Thomas. *The Papers of Thomas Jefferson, Volume 11: 1 January to 6 August 1787.* Online ed. Princeton University Press, 1955. https://jeffersonpapers.princeton.edu/selected-documents/abigail-adams.

Johnstone, Pauline. *High Fashion in the Church: The Place of Church Vestments in the History of Art from the Ninth to the Nineteenth Century.* Leeds, UK: Maney, 2002.

Join-Lambert, Sophie, and Maxime Préaud, eds. *Abraham Bosse, savant-graveur: Tours, vers 1604–1676.* Exh. cat. Paris: BnF; Tours, France: Musée des Beaux Arts de Tours, 2004.

Jones, Ann Rosalind. "Labor and Lace: The Crafts of Giacomo Franco's *Habiti delle donne venetiane.*" *I Tatti Studies in the Italian Renaissance* 17, no. 2 (September 2014): 399–425.

Jones, Jennifer M. *Sexing la Mode: Gender, Fashion and Commercial Culture in Old Regime France.* New York: Berg, 2004.

Joubert de l'Hiberderie, Nicolas. *Le dessinateur pour les étoffes d'or, d'argent et de soie.* Paris: Jorry, 1765.

Jourdain, Margaret. "Lace Collection of Mr. Arthur Blackborne." Pts. 1–4. *Burlington Magazine* 5 (1904): 557; 6 (1904): 18–22; 6 (1904): 123–31; 6 (1904): 384–92.

———. *Old Lace: A Handbook for Collectors.* London: B. T. Batsford; New York: Charles Scribner's Sons, 1909.

Juan, Jorge, and Antonio de Ulloa. *Relación histórica del viage a la América Meridional hecho de orden de S. Mag. para medir algunos grados de meridiano terrestre y venir por ellos en conocimiento de la verdadera figura y magnitud de la Tierra con otras varias observaciones astronomicas y phisicas.* Madrid: Antonio Marín, 1748.

———. *A Voyage to South America, Describing at Large the Spanish Cities, Towns, Provinces, &c. on That Extensive Continent: Undertaken by Command of the King of Spain.* 1748. Translated by John Adams. London: J. Brookdale, 1806.

Kanagy-Loux, Elena. "Addicted to Frills: The Fervour for Antique Lace in New York High Society, 1840–1900." *Journal of Dress History* 4, no. 2 (Summer 2020): 42–74.

———. "The Disconnected Web: Making Lace by Hand in a Modern World." MA thesis, New York University, 2018.

Karbacher, Ursula. "Characteristics of the Ever-Reinvented Gros Point in St. Gallen Embroidery." In *Gros Point de Venise: The Most Important Lace of the 17th Century,* edited by Ursula Karbacher, 159–63. St. Gallen, Switzerland: Textilmuseum St. Gallen, 2011.

Katzew, Ilona. *Casta Painting: Images of Race in Eighteenth-Century Mexico.* New Haven, CT: Yale University Press, 2004.

Kiliaan, Cornelis. *Dictionarium Teutonic-Latinum.* Antwerp: Plantin, 1574.

Kisluk-Grosheide, Daniëlle, and Bertrand Rondot, eds. *Visiteurs de Versailles: Voyageurs, princes, ambassadeurs 1682–1789.* Exh. cat. Paris: Gallimard, 2017.

Klein, Kathryn. "Conservation and Cultural Identity." In *The Unbroken Thread: Conserving Textile Traditions of Oaxaca,* 1–21. Los Angeles: Getty Conservation Institute, 1997.

Konetzke, Richard. *Colección de documentos para la historia de la formación social de Hispanoamérica, 1493–1810*. Vol. 3. Madrid: Consejo Superior de Investigaciones Científicas, 1962.

Kraatz, Anne. *Dentelles*. Paris: Adam Biro, 1988.

———, ed. *Dentelles au Musée historique des tissus*. Exh. cat. Lyon, France: Musée historique des tissus, 1983.

———. *Die Kunst der Spitze: Textiles Filigran*. Frankfurt, Germany: Propyläen, 1989.

———. "The Eighteenth Century: Femininity." In *Lace: History and Fashion*, 71–104. London: Thames and Hudson, 1989.

———. "The Inventory of a Venetian Lace Merchant in the Year 1671." *Bulletin de liaison du Centre international d'étude des textiles anciens*, no. 55–56 (1982): 127–33.

———. "Lace at the Court of Louis XIV." *Magazine Antiques* (June 1981): 1368–75.

———. *Lace: History and Fashion*. Translated by Pat Earnshaw. New York: Rizzoli, 1989.

Ladd, Doris M. *The Mexican Nobility at Independence*. Austin: Institute of Latin American Studies, 1976.

Lahalle, Agnès. *Les écoles de dessin au XVIIIe siècle: Entre arts libéraux et arts mécaniques*. Rennes, France: Presses universitaires de Rennes, 2006.

Lara Romero, Héctor. *Fiestas y juegos en el Reino de la Nueva Granada: Siglos XVI–XVIII*. Bogotá: Universidad Distrital Francisco José de Caldas, 2015.

Lefébure, Ernest. *Broderie et dentelles*. Paris: Maison Quantin, 1887.

———. *Embroidery and Lace: Their Manufacture and History*. London: H. Grevel; Philadelphia: J. B. Lippincott, 1889.

Le Gouic, Olivier. *Lyon et la mer au XVIIIe siècle: Connexions atlantiques et commerce colonial*. Rennes, France: Presses universitaires de Rennes, 2011.

Lembré, Stéphane. "Les écoles de dentellières en France et en Belgique des années 1850 aux années 1930." *Histoire de l'éducation* 123 (2009): 45–70.

Lemire, Beverly. "Transforming Consumer Custom: Linens, Cottons and the English Market, 1660–1800." In *The European Linen Industry in Historical Perspective*, edited by Brenda Collins and Philip Ollerenshaw, 187–208. Oxford: Oxford University Press, 2003.

Lettres de Madame de Sévigné avec les notes de tous les commentateurs. Vol. 2. Paris: Firmin-Didot frères, 1853. BnF Gallica. https://gallica.bnf.fr/ark:/12148/bpt6k6101781m/f208.item.

Leuenberger, Hans Rudolf. *500 Jahre Kaufmännische Corporation St. Gallen, 1466–1966*. St. Gallen, Switzerland: Kaufmännisches Directorium, Zollikofer, 1966.

Levey, Santina M. *Lace: A History*. Leeds, UK: W. S. Maney & Son; London: Victoria and Albert Museum, 1983.

———. "Lace and Lace-Patterned Silks: Some Comparative Illustrations." In *Studies in Textile History: In Memory of Harold B. Burnham*, edited by V. Gervers, 184–201. Toronto: Royal Ontario Museum, 1977.

Leyder, Dirk, and Frédérique Johan. "Isabella's canten cleedt (1760): Meer dan een banaal huwelijksgeschenk uit Vlaanderen." *Archieflink: Driemaandelijkse nieuwsbrief van 't Archief* 9, no. 2 (April 2009): 4–5.

Lincoln, Evelyn. "The Jew and the Worms, Portraits and Patronage in a Sixteenth-Century How-to Manual." *Word & Image* 19, nos. 1 and 2 (January–June 2003): 86–99.

———. "Models for Science and Craft: Isabella Parasole's Botanical and Lace Illustrations." In "Illustrations as Visual Resources," edited by William B. MacGregor and Louis Marchesano, special issue, *Visual Resources* 17, no. 1 (2001): 1–35.

López-Bejarano, Pilar. "Maneras de trabajar Santafé de Bogotá (siglo XVIII)." *Illes i Imperis* 21 (2019): 15–40.

Lotz, Arthur. *Bibliographie der Modelbücher: Beschreibendes Verzeichnis der Stick- und Spitzenmusterbücher des 16. und 17. Jahrhunderts*. Leipzig, Germany: Karl W. Hiersemann, 1933. 2nd ed., Stuttgart, Germany: Anton Hiersemann; London: Holland Press, 1963.

———. "Die Spitzenmusterbücher des Bartolomeo Danieli." *Berliner Museen* 52, no. 3 (1931): 63–65.

Malotet, Arthur. *La dentelle à Valenciennes*. Paris: Jean Schemit, 1927.

Mangan, Jane E. *Trading Roles: Gender, Ethnicity, and the Urban Economy in Colonial Potosí*. Durham, NC: Duke University Press, 2005.

Mansell, Philip. *Dressed to Rule: Royal and Court Costume from Louis XIV to Elizabeth II*. New Haven, CT: Yale University Press, 2005.

Marchi, Neil de, and Hans J. Van Migroet. "Flemish Textiles Trade and New Imagery in Colonial Mexico (1524–1646)." In *Painting of the Kingdoms: Shared Identities; Territories of the Spanish Monarchy, 16th–18th Centuries*, edited by Juana Gutiérrez Haces, 878–924. Vol. 3. México, DF: Fomento Cultural Banamex, 2009.

Markey, Lia. "The Female Printmaker and the Culture of the Reproductive Print Workshop." In *Paper Museums: The Reproductive Print in Europe, 1500–1800*, edited by Rebecca Zorach and Elizabeth Rodini, 51–74. Chicago: David and Alfred Smart Museum of Art; Chicago: University of Chicago Press, 2005.

Marly, Diana De. *Louis XIV & Versailles*. London: B. T. Batsford, 1987.

Martínez del Río de Redo, Marita. "Teatro de maravillas: Magnificencia barroca." *Artes de México: Retrato novohispano* 25 (July–August 1994): 53–63.

Matos Moctezuma, Eduardo. *Textiles indígenas: Patrimonio cultural de México*. México, DF: Fundación Cultural Serafín, 1996.

May, Florence Lewis. *Hispanic Lace and Lace Making*. New York: Hispanic Society of America, 1939.

McHugh, Julia. "Andean Textiles." Heilbrunn Timeline of Art History, Metropolitan Museum of Art, June 2020. https://www.metmuseum.org/toah/hd/adtx/hd_adtx.htm.

Meléndez, Mariselle. *Raza, género e hibridez en El lazarillo de ciegos caminantes*. Studies in the Romance Languages and Literatures. Chapel Hill, NC: University of North Carolina Press, 1999.

———. "Visualizing Difference: The Rhetoric of Clothing in Colonial Spanish America." In *The Latin American Fashion Reader*, edited by Regina Root, 17–30. New York: Berg, 2005.

Méndez Silva, Rodrigo. *Diálogo compendioso de la antigüedad y cosas memorables de la noble y coronada villa de Madrid y recibimiento que en ella hizo su Magestad católica, con la grandeza de su Corte a la princesa de Cariñán, clarísima consorte del serenísimo príncipe Tomas,* con sus genealogías: Al señor don Alonso Pérez de Guzmán, patriarca de las Indias. Madrid: Viuda de Alonso Martín, 1637.

Mendiburu, Manuel de. Diccionario historico-biografico del Peru. Lima, 1885.

Mercier, Louis-Sébastien. Le tableau de Paris. Vols. 1 and 8. Hamburg, Germany: Virchaux et Compagnie; Neuchâtel, Switzerland: Samuel Fauche, 1781; Amsterdam, 1783.

Merletti e ricami della Aemilia Ars, con introduzione di Elisa Ricci. Milan: Bestetti e Tumminelli, 1929.

Middleton, James. "Reading Dress in New Spanish Portraiture." In New England/New Spain: Portraiture in the Colonial Americas, edited by Donna Pierce, 101–46. Denver: Mayer Center, Denver Art Museum, 2016.

———. "Their Dress Is Very Different: The Development of the Peruvian Pollera and the Genesis of the Andean Chola." In "Interwoven: Dress that Crosses Borders and Challenges Boundaries," edited by Jennifer Daley and Alison Fairhurst, special issue, Journal of Dress History 2, no. 1 (2018): 87–105.

Miller, Lesley Ellis. "Dressing Down in Eighteenth-Century Lyon: The Clothing of Silk Designers from Their Inventaires-après-décès." Costume 29, no. 1 (1995): 25–39.

———. "A Portrait of the 'Raphael of Silk Design.'" V&A Online Journal 4 (Summer 2012). http://www.vam.ac.uk/content/journals/research-journal/issue-no.-4-summer-2012/a-portrait-of-the-raphael-of-silk-design/.

Miller, Michael B. The Bon Marché: Bourgeois Culture and the Department Store, 1869–1920. Princeton, NJ: Princeton University Press, 1981.

Mohrt, Françoise. Marcel Rochas: Trente ans d'élégance et de créations, 1925–1955. Paris: Jacques Damase, 1983.

Moreno Rivera, Nathalie. "Circulación de efectos de Castilla en el Virreinato de la Nueva Granada a finales del siglo XVIII." Fronteras de la historia 18, no. 1 (2013): 211–49.

Moretti, Laura, and Sean Roberts. "From the Vite or the Ritratti? Previously Unknown Portraits from Vasari's Libro de' disegni." I Tatti Studies in the Italian Renaissance 21, no. 1 (2018): 105–36.

Morrall, Andrew. "Regaining Eden: Representations of Nature in Seventeenth-Century English Embroidery." In English Embroidery from The Metropolitan Museum of Art, 1580–1700: 'Twixt Art and Nature, edited by Andrew Morrall and Melinda Watt, 79–97. New York: Bard Graduate Center for Studies in the Decorative Arts, Design, and Culture, 2008.

Morris, Frances, and Marian Hague. Antique Laces of American Collectors. 5 vols. New York: Publication for the Needle and Bobbin Club by William Helbrun, 1920–26.

Mundt, Barbara. Die deutschen Kunstgewerbemuseen im 19. Jahrhundert. Munich, Germany: Prestel, 1974.

Museo Santa Clara. Catálogo Museo Santa Clara. Bogotá: Ministerio de Cultura, 2014.

Neu, Peter. Margaretha von der Marck (1527–1599): Landesmutter, Geschäftsfrau und Händlerin, Katholikin. Enghien, Belgium: Arenberg Stiftung, 2013.

"Novísima recopilación de las leyes de España." In Los códigos españoles concordados y anotados, tomo III, libro VI, título XIII, ley I (1847–51), 267–68. Biblioteca Jurídica Digital. https://www.boe.es.

Ochoa, Margarita R., and Sara Vicuña Guengerich, eds. Cacicas: The Indigenous Leaders of Spanish America, 1492–1825. Norman, OK: University of Oklahoma Press, 2021.

Ogilvie, Brian W. The Science of Describing: Natural History in Renaissance Europe. Chicago: University of Chicago Press, 2006.

Olausson, Magnus, and Xavier Salmon. Alexandre Roslin: Un portraitiste pour l'Europe. Paris: Éditions de la Réunion des musées nationaux, 2008.

Osorio, Alejandra B. Inventing Lima: Baroque Modernity in Peru's South Sea Metropolis. New York: Palgrave MacMillan, 2008.

Ovaere-Raudet, Nicole. Les manufactures de dentelle de Colbert: Alençon, Arras, Aurillac, Auxerre, Bourges, Montargis, Reims, Sedan, Sens. Bourges, France: Cercle généalogique du Haut-Berry, 2018.

Pagano, Matteo. Giardineto [sic] novo di punti tagliati et gropposi per exercitio & ornamento delle donne. Venice: Matteo Pagano, 1554. The Metropolitan Museum, New York, Rogers Fund, 1921 (21.15.1bis(1–48)).

Palliser, Fanny Bury. A History of Lace. 3rd ed. London: Sampson Low, Marston, Low, & Searle, 1875. Internet Archive. https://archive.org/details/historyoflace1875pall/.

———. History of Lace. London: S. Low, Son & Marston, 1865.

———. "The International Exhibition, 1874." Art-Journal 13 (1874): 173–74.

———. "Lace and Embroidery." In The Illustrated Catalogue of the Universal Exhibition, Published with the Art Journal, 107–20. New York: Virtue & Co., 1868.

Perrot, Phillipe. Fashioning the Bourgeoisie: A History of Clothing in the Nineteenth Century. Princeton, NJ: Princeton University Press, 1994.

Phipps, Elena. "Woven Silver and Gold: Metallic Yarns in Colonial Andean Textiles." In "Paradoxes and Parallels in the New World," edited by Georgia de Havenon, special issue, Notes in the History of Art 29, no. 3 (2010): 4–11.

Phipps, Elena, Johanna Hecht, and Cristina Esteras Martín, eds. The Colonial Andes: Tapestries and Silverwork, 1530–1830. Exh. cat. New York: Metropolitan Museum of Art; New Haven, CT: Yale University Press, 2004.

Plaideux, Hugues. "L'inventaire après décès de Claude Bourgelat." Bulletin de la Société français de l'histoire de la médecine et des sciences vétérinaires 10 (2010): 121–54.

Plebani, Tiziana. "I segreti e gli inganni dei libri di ricamo: Uomo con l'ago e donne virtuose." In "I liberi di colore nello spazio atlantico," edited by Federica Morelli and Clément Thibaud, special issue, Quaderni storici, 50, no. 1 (April 2015): 201–30.

Poisson, Raymond. Le baron de la Crasse. Paris: de Luyne, 1662. BnF Gallica. https://gallica.bnf.fr/ark:/12148/bpt6k83245v?rk=21459;2:.

Porciani, Ilaria, ed. Le donne a scuola: L'educazione femminile nell'Italia dell'Ottocento. Siena, Italy: Palazzo Pubblico, 1987.

Pozetta, George E. "Immigrants and Craft Arts: Scuola d'Industrie Italiane." In The Italian Immigrant Woman in North America: Proceedings of the Tenth Annual Conference of the American Italian Historical Association Held in Toronto, Ontario (Canada) October 28 and 29, 1977 in Conjunction with the Canadian Italian Historical Association, edited by Betty

Boyd Caroli, Robert F. Harney, and Lydio F. Tomasi. Toronto: Multicultural History Society of Ontario, 1978.

Las pregmáticas y capítulos que su magestad del Emperador y Rey nuestro señor hizo en las Cortes de Valladolid, el año de mil e quinientos e treinta y siete; Con la Declaración que sobre los trajes y sedas hizo. Medina del Campo, Spain: Pedro de Castro, 1545.

Puerta Escribano, Ruth de la. "Los tratados del arte del vestido en la España moderna." *Archivo español de arte* 74, no. 293 (2001): 45–65.

Raffel, Marta Cotterell. *The Laces of Ipswich: The Art and Economics of an Early American Industry, 1750–1840.* Hanover, NH: University Press of New England, 2003.

Rangström, Lena, ed. *Lions of Fashion: Male Fashion of the 16th, 17th, 18th Centuries.* Stockholm: Livrustkammaren, 2002.

Reade, Brian. *The Dominance of Spain.* London: Harrap, 1951.

Recopilación de las leyes de Indias. 3rd ed. Madrid: Imprenta de Don Bartholome Ulloa, 1774. 4th ed. Madrid: Viuda de Ibarra, 1791.

Remaury, Bruno. "Une mode entre deux décennies." In *Repères Mode et Textile 96: Visages d'un secteur,* edited by Bruno Remaury, 60–70. Paris: Institut français de la mode, 1996.

Report of Mr. Alan Cole, Commissioner from the South Kensington Museum, on the Present Condition and Prospects of the Honiton Lace Industry. London: Henry Hansard and Son, 1888.

Reynolds, Siân. *Marriage and Revolution: Monsieur & Madame Roland.* Oxford: Oxford University Press, 2012.

Ricci, Elisa. *Old Italian Lace.* 2 vols. London: William Heinemann; Philadelphia: J. B. Lippincott Company, 1913.

——. "The Revival of Needlework in Italy." Translated by C. Macfarlane. *International Studio: An Illustrated Magazine of Fine and Applied Art* 61 (1914): 197–206.

Richardson, Brian. *Women and the Circulation of Text in Renaissance Italy.* Cambridge: Cambridge University Press, 2020.

Riello, Giorgio. "Fashion in the Four Parts of the World: Time, Space and Early Modern Global Change." In *Dressing Global Bodies: The Political Power of Dress in World History,* edited by Beverly Lemire and Giorgio Riello, 41–64. New York: Routledge, 2020.

Riforma, e Prammatica sopra l'uso delle perle, gioie, vestire, et altro per la Città & Contado di Firenze. Florence: Massi e Landi, 1638.

Rinaldi, Furio. "The Roman Maniera: Newly Discovered Drawings." *Metropolitan Museum Journal* 52 (2017): 129–41.

Risselin-Steenebrugen, Marie. "Christophe Plantin, facteur de lingerie fine et en dentelles." *De Gulden Passer* 37 (1959): 74–111.

——. "Les débuts de l'industrie dentellière—Martine et Catherine Plantin." *De Gulden Passer* 39 (1961): 77–124.

——. "Une dentelle à l'effigie de Charles II d'Espagne." *Bulletin des Musées Royaux d'Art et d'Histoire* 23 (1951): 65–68.

——. "Martine et Catherine Plantin: Leur rôle dans la fabrication et le commerce de la lingerie et des dentelles au XVIe siècle." *Revue belge d'archéologie et d'histoire d'art* 26, nos. 3–4 (1957): 169–88.

——. *Trois siècles de dentelles aux Musées royaux d'art et d'histoire.* Brussels: Musées royaux d'art et d'histoire, 1980.

Rivas Pérez, Jorge F. "Domestic Display in the Spanish Overseas Territories." In *Behind Closed Doors: Art in the Spanish American Home, 1492–1892,* exh. cat. Edited by Richard Aste, 49–103. New York: Brooklyn Museum; New York: Monacelli Press, 2013.

Rizo-Patrón Boylan, Paul. *Linaje, dote y poder: La nobleza de Lima de 1700 a 1850.* Lima: Pontifica Universidad Católica del Perú Fondo Editorial, 2000.

RM. *New Pattern Book of All Kinds of Bobbin Laces (1561).* Edited by Helen Hough. Translated by Brad Gulliford and Helen Hough. Arlington, Texas: James G. Collins and Associates, 2018. Internet Archive. https://archive.org/details/NewModelbook1561/mode/2up.

——. *Nüw Modelbüch von allerley gattungen Däntelschnür.* Zurich: Christoph Froschauer, ca. 1561.

Robinson, Michele Nicole. "Dirty Laundry: Caring for Clothing in Early Modern Italy." *Costume* 55, no. 1 (2021): 3–23.

Rocha, Francisco de la. *Geometría y traça perteneciente al oficio de sastres.* Valencia, Spain: P. P. Mey, 1618.

Rodríguez Moya, Inmaculada. *La mirada del virrey: Iconografía del poder en la Nueva España.* Castellón de la Plana, Spain: Universitat Jaume I, 2003.

Rodríguez-Solís, Enrique. *Historia de la prostitución en España y en América.* 3rd ed. Madrid: Biblioteca Nueva, 1921.

Rolland, Christine, ed. *Autour des Van Loo: Peinture, commerce des tissus et espionnage en Europe (1250–1830).* Mont-Saint-Aignan, France: Publications des universités de Rouen et du Havre, 2012.

Röllin, Peter. "Der Stickereihandelsplatz St. Gallen: Bemerkenswerte Fabrik- und Geschäftsbauten aus der Zeit der Stickereiblüte." *Unsere Kunstdenkmäler, Mitteilungsblatt für die Mitglieder der Gesellschaft für Schweizerische Kunstgeschichte* 34, no. 2 (1983): 224–39.

——. *Stickerei-Zeit: Kultur und Kunst in St. Gallen, 1870–1930.* St. Gallen, Switzerland: Verlagsgemeinschaft St. Gallen, 1989.

Romero de Terreros, Manuel. *Bocetos de la vida social en la Nueva España.* Guadalajara, Mexico: Impenta de F. Jaime, 1919.

Rooses, Max. *Christophe Plantin, Imprimeur Anversois.* 2nd ed. Antwerp: Jos. Maes, 1896.

Root, Regina, ed. *The Latin American Fashion Reader.* New York: Berg, 2005.

Roquero, Ana. *Tintes y tintoreros de América: Catálogo de materias primas y registro etnográfico de México, Centro América, Andes Centrales y Selva Amazónica.* Madrid: Instituto del Patrimonio Histórico Español, 2006.

Rothstein, Natalie. "The Introduction of the Jacquard Loom to Great Britain." In *Studies in Textile History: In Memory of Harold B. Burnham,* edited by V. Gervers, 281–304. Toronto: Royal Ontario Museum, 1977.

Rusch, Cristian. "Leopold Iklé (1838–1922): Ein St. Galler Unternehmer der Stickereizeit." Unpublished essay, Universität St. Gallen, 1998.

Sabo, Katie Marie. "Lace Collecting and Connoisseurship in New York City: 1870–1930." MA thesis, SUNY Fashion Institute of Technology, 2013.

Salazar, José María. "Memoria descriptiva del reino de Santafé de Bogotá." *Semanario del Nuevo Reyno de Granada,* edited by Francisco José de Caldas. Bogotá: Editorial Kelly, 1942.

Salmon, Xavier, ed. *Madame de Pompadour et les arts.* Exh. cat. Paris: Réunion des musées nationaux, 2002.

Salvy, Gérard-Julien. *Mode des années 30.* Paris: Seuil, 1991.

Sandoval Villegas, Martha. "El huipil pre-cortesiano y novohispano: Transmutaciones simbólicas y estilísticas de una prenda indígena." In *Congreso Internacional Imagen y Apariencia: Universidad de Murcia, 19–21 noviembre 2008,* edited by María Concepción de la Peña Velasco and Manuel Pérez Sánchez. Murcia, Spain: Universidad de Murcia, Servicio de Publicaciones, 2009.

Sargentson, Carolyn. *Merchants and Luxury Markets: The Marchands Merciers of Eighteenth-Century Paris.* London: Victoria and Albert Museum; Los Angeles: J. Paul Getty Museum, 1996.

Saunders, Stephanie. *Fashion, Gender and Agency in Latin American and Spanish Literature.* Woodbridge, UK: Tamesis, 2021.

Savary des Bruslons, Jacques, and Philémon-Louis Savary. *Dictionnaire universel de commerce [. . .].* 4th ed. Paris: Chez la veuve Estienne, 1762.

Sayer, Chloe. *Costumes of Mexico.* Austin: University of Texas Press, 1985.

Schoenholzer Nichols, Thessy, and Raffaella Sgubin, eds. *I merletti del monas-tero di Sant'Orsola nelle collezioni dei Musei provinciali di Gorizia.* Gorizia, Italy: Musei provinciali, 2011.

Schöner, Friedrich. *Spitzen: Enzyklopädie der Spitzentechniken.* 2nd ed. Leipzig, Germany: Fachbuchverlag, 1982.

Schuette, Marie. *Alte Spitzen: Nadel- und Klöppelspitzen: Ein Handbuch für Sammler und Liebhaber.* Berlin: R. C. Schmidt, 1914.

Schumpeter, Joseph Alois. "The Creative Response in Economic History." *Journal of Economic History* 7, no. 2 (November 1947): 149–59.

Sciama, Lidia. "Lacemaking in Venetian Culture." In *Dress and Gender: Making and Meaning,* edited by Ruth Barnes and Joanne B. Eicher. New York: Berg, 1997.

Segovia, Baltasar. *Geometría y traças.* Barcelona, 1617.

Sgard, Jean. "L'échelle des revenus." *Dix-huitième siècle* 14 (1982): 425–33.

Sheridan, Geraldine. *Louder Than Words: Ways of Seeing Women Workers in Eighteenth-Century France.* Lubbock: Texas Tech University Press, 2009.

"6 mars–21 avril 1744 Inventaire-après-décès Hyacinthe Rigaud." Transcribed by Ariane James-Sarazin. 2nd ed. (Paris, 2003). Mediterranées, managed by Agnès and Robert Viñas. Last modified March 5, 2019. https://mediterranees.net/art _roussillon/rigaud/inventaire.html.

Sorber, Frieda. "Het Windesel van het miraculeuze Beeld van Onze-Lieve-Vrouw in Zand in de Sint-Waldetrudiskerk te Herentals." *Historische Jaarboek van Herentals* 24 (2017): 72–81.

Sorber, Frieda, Wim Mertens, Marguerite Coppens, Kaat Debo, and Romy Cockx, eds. *P.LACE.S: Looking through Flemish Lace.* Tielt, Belgium: Lannoo, 2021.

Speelberg, Femke. "Fashion & Virtue: Textile Patterns and the Print Revolution, 1520–1620." *Metropolitan Museum of Art Bulletin* 73, no. 2 (Fall 2015): 1, 4–48.

Spenceley, Geoff. "The Lace Associations: Philanthropic Movements to Preserve the Production of Hand-Made Lace in Late Victorian and Edwardian England." *Victorian Studies* 16, no. 4 (June 1973): 433–52.

Spencer, David. *Knitting Technology.* 3rd ed. Cambridge: Woodhead Publishing, 2001.

Speranza, Gino. *The Diary of Gino Speranza, Italy 1915–1919.* Edited by Florence Colgate Speranza. Vols. 1–2. New York: Columbia University Press, 1941.

Spielmann, Sir Isidore, ed. *Royal Commission St. Louis International Exhibition 1904.* London: Hudson and Kerns, 1904.

Staatliche Kunstsammlungen Dresden et al., eds. *Nouveautés: Kunstschule und Spitzenindustrie in Plauen.* Exh. cat. Dresden, Germany: Sandstein Verlag, 2020.

Stanfield-Mazzi, Maya. *Clothing the New World Church: Liturgical Textiles of Spanish America, 1520–1820.* Notre Dame, IN: Notre Dame University Press, 2021.

———. "The Possessor's Agency: Private Art Collecting in the Colonial Andes." *Colonial Latin American Review* 18, no. 3 (2009): 339–64.

Staniland, Kay. "Queen Victoria's Wedding Dress and Lace." *Costume* 17, no. 1 (1983): 1–32.

Steiger-Züst, E. A. *Schweizerische Landesausstellung in Bern 1914: Die Stickerei-Industrie; Eine Schilderung der Ausstellung verbunden mit einer Darlegung geschichtlicher Entwicklung und der gesamten Organisation dieser Industrie.* Zurich: Orell Füssli, 1915.

Stone-Miller, Rebecca, ed. *To Weave for the Sun: Andean Textiles in the Museum of Fine Arts, Boston.* Boston: Museum of Fine Arts, 1992.

Strobel, Heino, and Patrick Schnetzer. *Die Handstickmaschine: Erfindungsgeschichte und erste Besitzer.* Plauen, Germany: Heino Strobel, 2021.

Tagliente, Giovanni Antonio. *Essempio di recammi.* 3rd ed. Venice: Giovanni Antonio di Nicolini da Sabio e i Fratelli, 1530. The Metropolitan Museum of Art, New York, Harris Brisbane Dick Fund, 1935 (35.75.3(1–55)).

Tanner, Albert. *Das Schiffchen fliegt, die Maschine rauscht: Weber, Sticker und Fabrikanten in der Ostschweiz.* Zurich: Unionsverlag, 1985.

Textilmuseum St. Gallen and Iklé-Frischknecht-Stiftung, eds. *Historische Spitzen: Die Leopold-Iklé-Sammlung im Textilmuseum St. Gallen.* Stuttgart, Germany: Arnoldsche, 2018.

Thépaut-Cabasset, Corinne, ed. *L'esprit des modes au Grand Siècle.* Paris: CTHS, 2010.

Thijs, A. K. L. "Aspecten van de opkomst der textieldrukkerij als grootbedrijf te Antwerpen in de achttiende eeuw." *Bijdragen en Mededelingen betreffende de Geschiedenis der Nederlanden* 86, no. 2 (1971): 200–17.

Thompson, Victoria E. *The Virtuous Marketplace: Women and Men, Money and Politics in Paris, 1830–1870.* Baltimore: John Hopkins University Press, 2000.

Thunder, Moira. "Deserving Attention: Margaretha Helm's Designs for Embroidery in the Eighteenth Century." *Journal of Design History* 23, no. 4 (2010): 409–27.

Todd, Leslie E. "Intertextual Intimacy: An Investigation of the Relationship between Word and Image in Eighteenth-Century Quito." *Hemisphere: Visual Culture of the Americas* 10 (2017): 6–30.

Toledo, Isabel. *The Roots of Style: Weaving Together Life, Love & Fashion.* New York: New American Library, 2012.

Tomasini, Silvio, and Thessy Schönholzer Nichols. *Merletti a Gandino: La collezione in oro, argento e lino del Museo della Basilica.* Vol. 3 of *Quaderni del Museo.* Gandino, Italy: Museo della Basilica di Gandino, 2012.

Tonna, Charlotte Elizabeth. *The Wrongs of Woman.* New York: John S. Taylor, 1844.

Treadwin, C. E. *Antique Point and Honiton Lace.* London: Ward, Lock and Tyler, 1873.

Trionfo di virtu: Libro novo. Venice: Matteo Pagano, 1563. The Metropolitan Museum of Art, New York, Harris Brisbane Dick Fund, 1937 (37.47.1(8)).

Truyens-Bredael, C. L. *Het Kantwerk van de Ommegang.* Antwerp: De Standaard Boekhandel, 1941.

Twinam, Ann. *Public Lives, Private Secrets: Gender, Honor, Sexuality, and Illegitimacy in Colonial Spanish America.* Stanford, CA: Stanford University Press, 1999.

Valentiner, Wilhelm R. "The Blackborne Collection of Lace." *Metropolitan Museum of Art Bulletin* 4, no. 5 (May 1909): 82–84.

Van Overloop, Eugène. *Matériaux pour servir à l'histoire de la dentelle en Belgique, 1ère série: Une dentelle de Bruxelles de 1599.* Brussels: H. Lamertin, 1908.

Vargas Murcia, Laura Liliana. "De Nencatacoa a San Lucas: Mantas muiscas de algodón como soporte pictórico en el Nuevo Reino de Granada." *UCOARTE* 4 (2015): 25–43.

Veillon, Dominique. *Fashion Under the Occupation.* New York: Berg, 2002.

Verhaegen, Pierre. *La dentelle et la broderie sur tulle.* Vol. 4 of *Les industries à domiciles en Belgique.* Brussels: Société Belge de librairie and J Lebègue & Cie., 1902.

Verwaltungsbericht des Kaufmännischen Directoriums an die kaufm. Corporation in St. Gallen. St. Gallen, Switzerland: Zollikofer'sche Buchdruckerei, 1868; 1886.

Vinciolo, Federico de. *Les secondes œuvres et subtiles inventions de lingerie.* Paris: Jean Le Clerc, 1594.

Voet, Leon. *Christophe Plantin and the Moretuses: Their Lives and their World.* Vol. 1 of *The Golden Compasses: The History of the House of Plantin-Moretus.* Amsterdam:

Vangendt; London: Routledge & Kegan Paul; New York: Abner Schram, 1969.

Walker, Tamara. *Exquisite Slaves: Race, Clothing, and Status in Colonial Lima.* Cambridge: Cambridge University Press, 2017.

Wanner-JeanRichard, Anne. "Frühe Stickereimuster mit Maschine ca. ab 1850 zu Inventarnummern 30'737 bis 30'883 des Textilmuseums St. Gallen und zum Werk von Ernest Iklé, *La broderie mecanique 1828–1930,* 1931." Anne Wanner's Textiles in History. Last revised July 26, 2017. http://www.annatextiles.ch/machine%20embroidery/muster_eikle.htm.

———. "Die Kettenstichmaschine." Anne Wanner's Textiles in History. Last revised July 19, 2014. http://www.annatextiles.ch/machine%20embroidery/chainstitch/geschichte.htm.

———. *Kettenstich und andere Stickereien: Eine Sammlung von Stickbeispielen, die Fritz Iklé in den Jahren 1931 bis 1933 für Adolf Jenny-Trümpy zusammenstellte.* Vol. 7 of *Edition Comptoir-Blätter.* Sent: Private edition by Reto D. Jenny, 2013.

———. *Leopold Iklé: Ein leidenschaftlicher Sammler.* St. Gallen, Switzerland: Textilmuseum St. Gallen, 2002.

———. "St. Galler Stickereispitze um die Jahrhundertwende." Anne Wanner's Textiles in History. Last updated March 25, 2015. http://www.annatextiles.ch/publications/spitzen/spitzen_um_1900/spitz_1900.htm.

———. *Von der Idee zum Kunstwerk: Stickereien aus der Sammlung des Textilmuseums St. Gallen und Tagebuchnotizen eines Stickereizeichners.* St. Gallen, Switzerland: Textilmuseum St. Gallen, 1999.

Wanner-JeanRichard, Anne, Marianne Gächter-Weber, and Cordula Kessler-Loertscher. *Leopold Iklé: Ein leidenschaftlicher Sammler.* St. Gallen, Switzerland: Textilmuseum St. Gallen, 2002.

Wardle, Patricia. *Victorian Lace.* New York: Frederick A. Praeger, 1969.

Werder, Ludwig Otto. *Dentelles nouvelles: Types modernes pour dentelles, broderies et rideaux.* 2nd ed. Plauen, Germany: C. Stoll, 1901.

———. *Neue Spitzen: Entwürfe für Spitzen, Stickereien, Gardinen in moderner Auffassung.* Zurich: N.p., 1898.

Westgarth, Mark Wilfred. "The Emergence of the Antique and Curiosity Dealer 1815–c. 1850: The Commodification of Historical Objects." PhD diss., University of Southampton, 2006.

Wilson, Patricia. "Textiles from Novel Means of Innovation." In *Extreme Textiles: Designing for High Performance,* edited by Matilda McQuaid and Philip Beesley, 183–213. New York: Princeton Architectural Press, 2005.

Winter, Anne. *Migrants and Urban Change: Newcomers to Antwerp, 1760–1860.* London: Taylor & Francis, 2015.

Woodcroft, Bennet. *Titles of Patents of Invention, Chronologically Arranged: From March 2, 1617 (14 James I.) to October 1, 1852 (16 Victoriae).* 2 vols. London: G. E. Eyre & W. Spottiswoode, 1854.

Wright, Thomas. *The Romance of the Lace Pillow: Being the History of Lace-Making in Bucks, Beds, Northants and Neighbouring Counties, Together with Some Account of the Lace Industries of Devon and Ireland.* Olney, UK: H. H. Armstrong, 1919.

Yonan, Michael. "Materializing Empire in an Eighteenth-Century Lace Gown." *Textile: The Journal of Cloth & Culture* 14, no. 3 (2016): 376–93.

Zola, Émile. *The Ladies' Paradise.* Translated by Brian Nelson. 2nd ed. Oxford: Oxford University Press, 2008.

Zunfthaus zur Meisen. *Sammlung Leopold Iklé, St. Gallen: Textilien.* 2 vols. Auction cat. Zurich: Orell Füssli, September 18, 1923.

Glossary

Compiled by Kenna Libes

This compiled glossary draws on groundbreaking works in the field including Pat Earnshaw's *The Identification of Lace* (1980) and Santina M. Levey's *Lace: A History* (1983), which expand on the significant contributions that Fanny Bury Palliser, Alice Dryden, Margaret Jourdain, Emily Jackson, and Ernest Lefébure, among others, made more than a century ago. The inclusion of several glossary terms is thanks to the generous help of many textile experts, particularly Denis Bruna and Elena Kanagy-Loux, who provided clarification on the French entries; Ilona Kos, who shared her knowledge of German; and Laura Beltrán-Rubio, Amalia Descalzo Lorenzo, Mariselle Meléndez, Tanya Melendez, and Amanda Wunder, who weighed in on the Nahuatl, Quechua, and Spanish words.

abanillo
Spanish; each of the folds in the linen that make up a ruff or *lechuguilla*. 16th century.

Alençon
A lacemaking center in Normandy, France, from the 17th century onward. The name is also associated with a light looped net. See also *point d'Alençon*.

application lace
Any lace in which the additional decorative pieces are attached to the surface of a machine net or bobbin *réseau* ground via needle and thread.

Argentan
A lacemaking center in Normandy, France, from the 17th century onward. The name is associated with heavy, hexagonal mesh grounds (*brides bouclées* and *brides tortillées*).

Argentella
An 18th-century needlepoint lace (usually regarded as a form of **Argentan**) distinguished by its elaborate ground of solid hexagons within skeletal hexagons (*réseau rosace*).

basquiña
Spanish; the overskirt in a Spanish *guardainfante* ensemble, worn over the *pollera*. 17th century.

bavaro
Italian; a type of modesty cover (partlet) often made of lace and worn by Venetian women with decolleté gowns. The word can also refer to other kinds of collars or capes about the neck. Plural: *bavari*. 16th century.

blonde
Lace made of silk. In the 18th century the name was applied to a large group of bobbin laces made originally of undyed silk from Nanjing, China, but later it was used for any lace made of silk, leading to confusing terms like "black blonde." *Blonde de Caen* was a 19th-century version with threads of varying textures and colors and bold floral patterns with large open or colored areas in the centers of flowers.

bobbin lace
The generic term for lace made by plaiting and twisting together a number of threads wound on small bobbins and secured at the upper ends to a hard pillow. Dutch: *kloskant, gespeldewerkte kant, spellewerk kant*. French: *dentelle aux fuseaux*. German: *Klöppelspitze*. Italian: *opere a mazette, pizzi a fuselli, merletti a piombino*. Spanish: *encaje, bolillos de randa, punto de bolillos*.

bobbinet
Originally, any form of mesh ground made with bobbins, but after the invention of the bobbinet machine, the term was confined to machine-made net, which mimics handmade **twist net**. The bobbinet machine was invented by John Heathcoat in 1809 and is also called the "Old Loughborough."

bobbins
Handheld tools (usually elongated and made of wood or bone) used to manipulate the threads in **bobbin lace** by hand. Bobbins vary in size according to the quality and weight of the lace; the threads are wound around their centers to provide tension.

braccio
Italian; an old unit of length used in Italy, usually about 26 or 27 inches (66 or 68 centimeters), but varying between 18 and 28 inches (46 and 71 centimeters). Plural: *braccia*.

brides
French; bars, bridges. Narrow bobbin- or needle-made threads linking the individual motifs of a lace design. Also used in describing the mesh grounds of French needle laces.

Brussels bobbin lace
A name especially associated with a fine 18th-century **part lace** grounded with **Drochel** net. See also **point d'Angleterre** and **rosaline**.

Brussels needle lace
A name associated with a flat lace made with very fine thread and decorated with elaborate fillings. See also *point de gaze*.

Burano

A name applied to two groups of needle lace made in Burano, Italy: one dating from the late 18th century and one from the late 19th century. It is made with a mesh (*réseau*) ground and fine thread and resembles **Alençon** and **Brussels needle laces**.

buttonhole stitch

The basic stitch of all needle laces. French: *bouclette, point de boutonnière*. Italian: *punto a feston*. German: *Knopflochstich, Schlingstich*.

Chantilly lace

Name for black silk bobbin laces produced in Chantilly, France, from the second half of the 18th century. Designs of flowers and flowing ribbons are made in half stitch for delicacy with untwisted *cordonnet* outlines on mesh *fond chant* (see **point de Paris**). In the 19th century Chantilly broadened to include cotton and linen fibers and could also be made by machine. It was especially desirable for shawls and *mantillas*. In this period, the black silk used was called *grenadine*.

chemical lace

A form of machine embroidery developed in the 1880s in which the pattern was worked in a vegetable fiber (usually cotton) on a silk ground; the latter was then burnt out or dissolved with caustic soda or chlorine. Today chemical lace is made from many other combinations of materials and the ground fabric can be dissolved with warm water. Key to production is a difference in the material of the ground fabric and the threads of the embroidery. It is generally used to produce imitation needle lace and crochet. French: *métier suisse, dentelle suisse*. See also **guipure**.

Cirsaka

French; an Indian textile woven with a silk warp and cotton filling, usually ornamented with metal stripes in silver or gold. Predecessor (in both textile and terminology) to seersucker. 18th century.

continuous lace

See **straight lace**. French: *dentelle à fils continus*.

coraline

Name given to a late 17th-century Venetian flat point needle lace featuring a pattern of short, branching stems and a minimal amount of raised work. The name is said to refer to its appearance, resembling coral.

cordon/cordonnet

French; an outline of the motifs of lace, made of single thicker thread (**gimp**), several thinner strands, or a padded wreath oversewn with buttonhole stitch. Also called "trolly" and, in French, *brode*.

Cornely machine

An embroidery machine with a hooked needle moved about following the outlines of the pattern by means of a handle mounted beneath the machine. The single needle and thread produced a chain stitch in imitation of **tambour work**. It was patented by Antoine Bonnaz in 1865 but is named after Ercole Cornely, who purchased the patent and innovated the hooked needle.

cotilla

Spanish; stays, corset. 18th–19th century.

crieur/crieuse

French; crier, as in "town crier" or a person making a public announcement. Hawker. 17th–18th century.

crochet

1. French name for the hooked needle used in a number of textile trades, including lacemaking.
2. Form of openwork in which a single length of thread is manipulated with a fine hook to form a series of loops, chains, and knots.

cumbi

Quechua; a finely woven Andean textile made from the highest-quality alpaca fibers. 16th–18th century.

cutwork

An embroidery technique in which holes are cut in linen, embroidered with thread, and decorated with buttonhole-stitch **bars**. Often considered the precursor to true needle lace. 16th century. French: *point coupé*. German: *aussgeschnittene Arbeit, Ausschneidestickerei*. Italian: *punto tagliato*.

dentelle

French; from *dents*, "teeth." It originally referred to any indented edging, but by the late 16th century became the generic term for all lace: *dentelle à l'aiguille* (needle lace) and *dentelle aux fuseaux* (bobbin lace).

drawn-thread work

Selected warp or weft threads are drawn out and cut off, the raw edges stitched over, and the remaining threads decorated with buttonhole or other stitches in a variety of designs. Extensive use of this technique could result in **cutwork**, and it is sometimes combined with **pulled-fabric work**. Requires a tightly woven fabric. Italian: *punto tirato*.

Drochel

A **bobbinet** ground most commonly associated with 18th-century **Brussels bobbin lace** and made without pins except along the outer edges. It is a hexagonal mesh with two sides of four threads plaited four times and four sides of two threads twisted twice. The name is thought to have derived from the Flemish word *Draadsel*, meaning "mesh of threads." Also called Droschel, drossel, *vrai réseau*, and Flemish *réseau*.

ell

An old measure of length often used for textiles. Equivalent in England to about 45 inches (114.3 centimeters); in Scotland, 37 inches (94 centimeters); in Belgium, 27 inches (68.6 centimeters); in France, 54 inches (137.2 centimeters; the *aune*).

engageantes

French; the gathered and shaped ruffles of lace or muslin that were attached to women's sleeve cuffs in the late 17th and 18th centuries.

entretoile

French; openwork created or lace inserted between two pieces of linen. Also known as insertion work or insertion lace.

falbala

French; a gathered piece of fabric used as a decorative edging. English: furbelows.

faldellín

Spanish; a wrapped A-line skirt with a side-front opening that became fashionable to use as an outer skirt among the women of the Viceroyalties of New Granada and Peru in the 18th century. An early 18th-century source describes it as having three rows of lace with the middle row of gold and silver.

fillings
Composite stitches used to form decorative patterns in the centers of both needle- and bobbin-lace motifs to fill space. They are essentially ornamental and usually varied, as opposed to the ground, which serves the practical purpose of holding the design in place and is of uniform appearance. French: *jours*, *modes*.

fleuron
French; a flower-shaped ornament used in series or at the end of a piece of lace.

fond
French; see *réseau*.

à la francesa
Spanish; a catchall term for Mexican clothing in the international 18th-century style, distinct from the *robe à la française*.

frelange
French; a high headdress usually made of linen and lace worn by women between 1680 and 1720. Often mistakenly called a *fontange*, which refers only to the silk ribbons sometimes worn behind the lace.

fustán
Spanish; in 18th-century Peru, a white underskirt or petticoat, sometimes with a deep flounce of lace at the hem.

galerilla
Spanish; a woman's fitted gown cut without a waist seam. 16th–17th century.

Genoese lace
Refers to both bobbin and needle laces made in Genoa, Italy, in a variety of materials but usually indicates the noncontinuous scalloped linen bobbin laces decorated with wheat ears (small oval and square motifs worked in basket stitch) popular in the first half of the 17th century. French: *point de Gênes*.

gimp
1. A silk or metal-wrapped cord.
2. Baroque bobbin lace incorporating such cords.
3. The thick outlining threads used in English Midland county laces, also known as *cordonnet* or trolly.

goffering
Crimping; goffering irons were used to set starched linen ruffs in the late 16th and early 17th centuries and also to set flounces and ruffles in linen into the 19th century.

golilla
A misnomer for the *valona*, a wide, flat, starched linen collar worn at the Spanish court in the 17th century. The term actually refers to the pasteboard undercollar used for support.

grand habit
Also called a *robe de cour*; the official court dress for French women, 1682–1789. An elaborate gown that comprised a boned bodice with back lacing, multitiered lace sleeves, a skirt, and a train. The skirt was worn over a wide pannier for most of the 18th century. Spanish: *traje de corte*.

gros point (de Venise)
French; a 19th-century misnomer for the largest of the raised Venetian needle laces of the second half of the 17th century. Characterized by spacious, scrolling flowers and leaves with heavily padded borders. The padding was made of a bundle of flax or wool thread covered with buttonhole stitches and extended into crowns of spines and other intricate embellishments. It was also sometimes known as *punto tagliato a fogliami* (**cutwork** with foliage). See also *point de Venise*.

ground
The background bars or net supporting the pattern in a piece of lace. French: *fond*. See also *réseau*.

guardainfante
Spanish; the extremely wide hoop skirt worn in the Spanish court in the 17th century. The full ensembles are sometimes called "*infanta* dresses," after the princesses who wore them in portraits by Diego Velázquez.

guarniciones
Spanish; trims.

guipure
1. French; originally a lace of narrow parchment tapes whipped round with silk or gold or silver thread; later, a lace made of bobbin or woven tapes filled with bobbin or needle

stitches and linked by *brides*.
2. Generic term for any lace where the parts of the *toilé* are joined by *brides* rather than a mesh or net ground.
3. Swiss **chemical lace** made on embroidery machines from the late 19th century; the term continues to be used today for lace from St. Gallen, Switzerland.

hand-embroidery machine
A hand-guided embroidery machine that initially could produce several identical satin-stitched designs simultaneously. It was the predecessor to the **Schiffli machine** and was invented in France in 1828 by Josué Heilmann.

Honiton lace
A term for bobbin lace of the **Brussels** type in Devonshire and parts of Dorset, Somerset, and Wiltshire, United Kingdom. 18th–20th century.

huipil
Spanish; a shirt or tunic of cotton, silk, or wool and often embroidered, worn by Indigenous women of any social rank in Mesoamerica prior to the arrival of the Spanish in the Americas. Traditionally, a large square of cotton with a center opening for the head; it is worn over the shoulders and seamed on the sides with arm holes at the fold. A luxury version was made entirely of imported lace and cut like an ecclesiastical surplice in the 18th century. From Nahuatl *huīpīlli*.

hypertube
A term for the lacelike textiles produced by textile manufacturer Jakob Schlaepfer AG (St. Gallen, Switzerland, 1904–) through a computerized process that applies silicone pigments to fabric (3D printing). The resulting textile is based on traditional embroidery patterns used by the company and imitates the use of **gimp** in handmade lace.

infanta dress
Spanish; see *guardainfante*.

jabot
French; a decorative ruffle attached to the front opening on a man's shirt. 17th–18th century.

júbon
Spanish; doublet. 16th–17th century.

lace
Originally a term meaning a narrow tape or braid. By the late 16th century, it had become the generic term for all forms of nonwoven, bobbin- and needle-made openwork. Dutch: *kant*. French: *dentelle*. German: *Spitze*. Italian: *pizzo, merletto*. Spanish: *encaje*.

lappets
Two strips of lace or linen hanging from the back or sides of a woman's cap. Popular in the late 17th and 18th centuries and again in the middle of the 19th century. Also called *barbes* (French), pinners, and streamers.

Leavers machine
A versatile variant of the 1809 **bobbinet** machine. Because it held more bobbins in a single row, it was able to make patterned laces more easily and did not need to traverse the net. It was invented in 1813 by John Levers in the United Kingdom.

lechuguilla
Spanish; ruff.

Lille
A lacemaking center in northern France that primarily produced lace of the **Mechlin** and **Valenciennes** types, though it is now associated with a fine **twist net** ground decorated with delicate, thin patterns.

listas
Spanish; ribbons.

lliclla
Quechua; a traditional Andean shawl or shoulder cloth, usually rectangular or square, worn since at least the 16th century.

macramé
A kind of lace formed by hand-knotting hanging yarns or strings, which has been practiced in various forms for thousands of years. Often seen in the form of decorated fringe on the edge of linen cloths.

Maltese lace
A 19th-century heavy cream or black silk bobbin lace based on 17th-century **Genoese** needle lace. Made in Malta, it often sports the Maltese cross, and it inspired the English style of Bedfordshire Maltese.

mantelet
A short mantle, cloak, or shawl.

mantilla
Spanish; a traditional lace or silk veil worn by Spanish and Mexican women that covers the head and shoulders but leaves the face visible. In 16th- and 17th-century Spain, a shorter version of the *manto*.

manto
Spanish; cloak, cape. In 16th- and 17th-century Spain, a cloak for women and girls that also covered the head. French: *manteau*.

marchandes lingères
French; female merchants and makers of linen and lace goods who worked within the guild system. 16th–18th century.

marchands merciers
French; dealer-decorators who specialized in contracting artists and craftsmen to create *objets d'art* for interiors. 17th–18th century.

Mechlin
English name for Mechelen, Belgium. The name is particularly associated with a straight bobbin lace made with a soft linen thread and a silky **gimp** with a hexagonal mesh ground. French: Malines.

mesh
Basic element of a piece of net. The shape and construction of the mesh ground is the distinguishing feature of many laces. Dutch: *masche*. French: *mailles*. Italian: *maglia*. See also *réseau*.

mignonette
French; inexpensive, narrow **Lille** thread bobbin lace with a delicate pattern and mesh ground. Also known as *blond de fil* and *point de tulle* and can be spelled alternatively *minuit* and *mennuet*. 18th century.

Milanese lace
A name associated with the heavy Baroque bobbin laces of the second half of the 17th century, often featuring large lilies with spreading petals. By 1700, the designs became precise and elaborate floral sprays within a round **Valenciennes** ground with varied fillings.

needle lace / needlepoint
A generic term covering all forms of openwork constructed with buttonhole stitches using a needle and thread. See also **cutwork**.

Dutch: *naaldkant*. French: *point à l'aiguille, point coupé vélin*. German: *Nadelspitze*. Italian: *punto in aria, trina ad ago*.

needle-run
A method of decorating machine net by darning an embroidery thread in and out of the meshes with a hand needle.

net
A machine-made mesh, though the term is also used in modern hand-worked lacemaking, e.g., net stitch (Honiton), and net ground (Bucks point).

part lace
Any bobbin lace in which the individual motifs or sections of the pattern or *toilé* are made separately and are joined by hooking or by **bars** or a mesh ground. Also called noncontinuous lace.

pearls
See *picots*.

pelerine
A woman's short shoulder cape. 19th century.

picots
French; the small projecting loops or tiny knobs that decorate both needle and bobbin laces. Also called pearls and purls.

pillow lace
An alternative term for bobbin lace that refers to the pillow upon which bobbin lace is worked (although some needle laces are also worked using a pillow).

point
French; stitch. Used first to describe early needle lace (*point à l'aiguille*) and then to describe certain types of needle lace (*point d'Alençon*), etc. By the late 17th century, it was also being used inaccurately to describe some bobbin laces, notably **point d'Angleterre**. In the 19th century it became a more generic term applied to many needle, bobbin, tape, and embroidered "laces."

point Colbert
French; a 19th-century French needle lace originally made in imitation of *point de Venise* (see *gros point*) with a design of flowers, leaves, and scrolls ornamented with high raised work and a **bar**-and-*picot* ground. Named in honor of French minister

Jean-Baptiste Colbert, who promoted lace-making in the 17th century.

point d'Alençon
French; an 18th-century meshed lace with architecturally arranged flowers and swags neatly and precisely suspended in the **Alençon** ground. It had a sharp, clear, firm texture, achieved by the hard rim of *cordonnet* supporting every piece of the design, which often extended into *picots* made over horsehair. There are multiple types of Alençon grounds:
1. *Réseau ordinaire* (ordinary *réseau*), a mesh ground made of twisted buttonhole stitches worked from left to right with the thread carried back from right to left. It has a light and delicate appearance and is the only one used in the earlier forms;
2. *Brides tortillées* (twisted *réseau*): this is *réseau ordinaire* (1) with the meshes twisted around with thread to make it look like **Argentan**;
3. *Réseau mouché* (fly *réseau*), a clear ground with scattered spots like tiny insects. See also *semé*;
4. The *petit réseau* (little *réseau*) is not used as a ground but as a filling. It is *réseau ordinaire* (1) on a smaller scale.

point d'Angleterre
French; "English stitch," though it has no connection to England. A very fine noncontinuous bobbin lace (see **part lace**), occasionally with needlepoint fillings or motifs, made in Brussels from the mid-17th to late 18th centuries. The earlier floral designs were similar to the *gros points* with crowded hexagonal **Drochel** grounds. In the late 19th century the term referred to a Belgian lace made of fine-quality bobbin sprigs linked by a *point de gaze* ground and with delicate needle-made fillings.

point d'Espagne
1. French; name given to gold and silver bobbin lace produced mainly in France and exported in great quantities to Spain and Spanish America in the 17th and 18th centuries.
2. A later name sometimes applied to one 17th-century Venetian needle lace with curving lines of raised work elaborately decorated with *picots*. There is no evidence that lace of this type was made in Spain. Spanish: *puntos de España*.
3. Though *point d'Espagne* translates as

"Spanish lace," the English version of the phrase references an entirely different set of laces. See **Spanish lace**.

points de France
French; all needle and bobbin laces made under the direction of Colbert following the establishment of the French lace industry in 1665 and meant to compete with Venetian work (*points de Venise*). The name came to be associated with French needle lace of the late 17th and early 18th centuries decorated with delicate symmetrical floral, foliate, and figurative designs, including **Alençon**, **Argentan**, **Argentella**, and *point de Sedan*.

point de gaze
French; a mid-19th-century form of **Brussels needle lace** with a gauze ground of buttonhole stitches and naturalistic floral patterns, especially roses. Also called *gase point*, *gauze point*, *point à l'aiguille gazée*, **rosaline**, Brussels rose point, and *point de Bruxelles*.

point de Paris
French; a type of bobbin *réseau*, variously called "six-point star," from its shape; *fond chant*, from its forming the ground of 18th-century **Chantilly** laces; *fond double*, because its technique of working is like a whole stitch; "Kat stitch"; "French ground"; and "wire ground," because the intertwining of the stretched threads looks like a wire mesh.

point de raccroc
French; a stitch used to invisibly join the strips of **straight lace** made in Chantilly and other French centers in the 19th century. Also applied to the different linking stitch used to join strips of **Drochel** net. Literally, "hitch stitch."

point de Venise
1. French; an umbrella term for all laces made in Venice or in the Venetian style, including **rosaline** and **coraline**. In 17th-century French documents, the phrase used for lace made in Venice is the literal *points qui se font à Venise*.
2. *Point de Venise à réseau*; 19th-century misnomer for fine, flat, mesh-grounded needle lace made in Brussels in the 18th century.

pollera
1. Spanish; a padded skirt worn between the *guardainfante* and *basquiña* in Spain. 17th century.

2. In the Viceroyalties of New Granada and New Spain, a gathered skirt that could be worn as the top layer in domestic settings and was usually calf-length. The term also refers to a mode of dress that consisted of a very full, relatively short skirt (the *pollera*) that revealed the lacy flounce of an underskirt, a chemise lavishly decorated with lace, and a short lace-trimmed waistcoat and shawl. 18th century. *Polleras* were adapted by Indigenous women and women of Indigenous descent in colonial Spanish America after the arrival of the Spaniards. Today, they are associated mostly with Indigenous cultures and worn in festive celebrations.

potten kant
Dutch; "flowerpot lace." A continuous, dense Flemish bobbin lace usually patterned with a pot-of-flowers motif set in a Kat stitch (*point de Paris*), *cinq trous*, or round-meshed ground. Features a silky *cordonnet* and a straight heading and is similar to **Mechlin** but heavier and sturdier. Also called Antwerp lace. 17th–19th century.

pricking
The marking of a pinhole pattern on a card or parchment used for bobbin-lace work.

pulled-fabric work
A technique in which the threads of a woven fabric are pulled and stitched together to form decorative holes in an openwork pattern. It does not entail cutting or removing threads and requires a loosely woven fabric. Distinct from (but often combined with) **drawn-thread work**.

puntas
Spanish; serrated edgings. Any work that formed waves or points on the edges of a textile. 16th–17th century.

punto
Italian; stitch. Like the French *point*, it came to be applied to both needle and bobbin laces and to the stitches used in their construction.

punto in aria
Italian; "stitches in the air." A needle-lace technique of detached embroidery worked in buttonhole stitch on a network of foundation threads anchored on a parchment or textile, which is afterward detached. Considered one of the first true laces. 16th century.

punto riccio

Italian; "curled stitch." An embroidery stitch used to create curved decorations, like tendrils, found especially in Tuscan filet or Modano. A variety of *punto scritto*.

Pusher machine

A variant of the **bobbinet** machine (1809) invented in 1812, in which each bobbin was controlled by a long implement called a pusher. It made close copies of **blonde** and **Chantilly** bobbin laces, though they still had to be finished by hand.

quesquémel

Spanish; an Indigenous Mexican garment worn by the Nahuatl elite in pre-Hispanic times. The triangular form consists of a cloth with a neck hole cut in the center that is pulled on over the head and usually falls to a point in front and back. It was worn by noblewomen and priestesses in ceremonies and used over a *huipil*. From Nahuatl *quechquemitl*.

rabat

French; a man's broad, flat white linen collar, often trimmed with lace, fitting around the base of the throat and stretching across the shoulders and to some extent over the back and chest. 16th–17th century. English: falling band.

raised work

Any three-dimensional detail in needle or bobbin lace.

randas

Spanish; a generic word denoting lace, though originally it was a kind of openwork lacis (embroidered knotted net) involving embroidery on a square woven mesh.

rengos

Spanish; likely refers to needle laces created using techniques similar to the original *randas*.

réseau

French; network. The uniform mesh background of a lace design (as opposed to **bar**-based grounds) in both needle and bobbin laces. Also called the *fond*, mesh, or ground.

reticella

Italian; "little net." A geometric **cutwork** technique of the late 16th century in which large squares of woven linen are removed and the edges are covered in buttonhole stitches; it also refers to needle lace built up on a ground of laid threads (***punto in aria***). A precursor to true lace.

robe à l'anglaise

French; "English gown." A late 18th-century front-opening women's gown with a fitted bodice and attached, pleated skirt that opened in the front to display the petticoat (in this case, an overskirt and not an undergarment). English: English nightgown, close-bodied gown. Spanish: *vaquero a la inglesa*.

robe à la française

French; "French gown." An 18th-century open-front gown with stomacher and voluminous loose pleats of fabric at back, commonly called "sack-back" or referred to by the later term "Watteau pleats." Considered informal dress early in the century but worn for formal occasions after midcentury. English: sack gown.

ropilla

Spanish; a short Spanish overgarment with sleeve caps surrounded by a fold (*brahón*) and hanging sleeves, worn over a doublet. 16th–17th century.

rosaline

1. Italian; a term for English *point de neige*, often used for later Burano lace rather than for the 17th-century Venetian styles;
2. Rose point, which is a 19th-century name for medium-sized raised Venetian needle lace of the later 17th century (*gros point* being the largest and *point de neige* the smallest);
3. Brussels *point de gaze*;
4. A late 19th-century **Brussels bobbin lace** with crinkly edges to the motifs and a suggestion of button roses in the design;
5. A late 19th- or 20th-century Italian bobbin lace with boldly curling stems terminating in half-stitch buds, associated today with the town of Cantù. Also spelled "roselline."

runners

1. An alternative name for worker bobbins.
2. Term for the embroiderers who worked the **needle-run** patterns on machine net.

saya

Spanish; a two-piece ensemble worn by Spanish women in the 16th and 17th centuries that included a cone-shaped overskirt (*basquiña*) and a bodice (*cuera*). In some later contexts, it simply denotes the skirt of the ensemble.

Schiffli machine

An embroidery machine invented by Isaak Gröbli in Switzerland in 1863 that applied the shuttle, continuous thread, and lockstitch innovations of the sewing machine to embroidery. Until this point, such machines could work only with short lengths of thread. It can reproduce the same design many times over at once and imitate the patterns of **needle-run** laces. The design was originally controlled by a pantograph: as the course of the threads was traced stitch by stitch on a master design, the net itself was moved and the hundreds of needles embroidered in tandem along the width of the textile.

semé

French; a delicate allover motif of spots, sprigs, stars, or other figures.

Spachtel-Stickerei

German; an embroidered fabric in which parts of the ground are cut away to create a lacelike textile.

Spanish lace

1. Spanish bobbin lace, Spanish **blonde**: a **continuous lace** using two thicknesses of soft, lustrous silk thread and a dense design ideal for draped white or black *mantillas* and flounces. 18th–19th century.
2. Machine net with **needle-run** embroidery in a floral repeat design worked in a heavy silk thread along the border with smaller sprigs scattered through the ground. Made in black and white. 19th century.
3. Machine "Spanish lace" of varying qualities made on the **Leavers** and other machines, always heavily patterned with flowers.
4. See also *point d'Espagne* for the seventeenth-century laces under that name.

straight lace

Any bobbin lace that is made all in one piece, both pattern (*toilé*) and **bars** or ground, as opposed to **part lace**. Also called **continuous lace**.

superposé
French; a term for the three-dimensional embroidered appliqué motifs, often applied to **chemical lace**.

Swiss lace
See **chemical lace**.

tambour work
A chain-stitch embroidery technique done with a hooked needle. Commonly used to decorate machine net.

tape lace
Any lace constructed using tape (plain, narrow textiles resembling ribbons), whether loom-woven or made by needle or bobbins. Tape is often used similarly to **gimp**, to create thick outlines and border effects, or to split up motifs.

toilé
French; clothwork. The term can refer to:
1. As a technique, the bobbin-lace whole stitch, which looks exactly like woven linen. Also clothwork, clothing, cloth stitch, linen stitch.
2. Generally, the denser, patterned parts of the lace including motifs, trails, and fillings, as distinct from the ground.

traje de corte
Spanish; court costume. See also **grand habit**.

trencillas
Spanish; braid. *Trencillas de oro*, gold braid. In some cases it refers to bobbin or insertion lace (see **entretoile**).

Tulle
Small town on the edge of the Massif Central (France) that produced a fine silk net, either knotted or made with bobbins, decorated with embroidery. The name was applied by the French to the first machine-knitted nets and was subsequently used internationally to describe machine-made net of all types.

twist net
Simple form of **bobbinet** made with two pairs of bobbins. Also called *fond simple*, *fond clair*; Lille, *point*, or net ground; two-twist net; and tulle mesh. Found in Bucks, **Lille**, **Chantilly**, Spanish bobbin, and **blonde** lace. This is the net that Heathcoat sought to mimic with the bobbinet machine.

underpropper
The metal wire or pasteboard under-support for a ruff or other standing linen collar. Also called a *supportasse* or *rebato*. 16th–17th century.

Valenciennes
A lacemaking center in territory contested between the Southern Netherlands and France (from 1678, part of France). In the 18th century Valenciennes referred to a high-quality **straight lace** in which clearly defined patterns are grounded with a round or square plaited mesh. In the 19th century it evolved to include extensive *fil coupé* and *fil attaché* techniques to create lace of variable quality with exceptionally dense, white patterns and a square mesh. It is related to Binche and **Mechlin** laces.

valona / valonas llanas
Spanish; the linen collars that replaced *lechuguillas* for both men's and women's dress. These *valonas* were part of shifts and shirts usually trimmed with lace. 17th century.

vaquero
1. Spanish; a coat-like garment with a fitted waist and long skirts worn by women and children in Spain in the late 16th and early 17th centuries.
2. Colloquial name of the *robe à l'anglaise* style in New Spain, 18th century.

verdugado
Spanish; farthingale. The boned hoop-petticoat used in the 16th century to support women's skirts.

Contributors

Laura Beltrán-Rubio specializes in the history of art and fashion in Latin America and the early modern Spanish world. She is a PhD candidate at the College of William and Mary, Williamsburg, Virginia, and received her MA in fashion studies from Parsons School of Design, New York. She is currently assistant professor of design at the Universidad de los Andes, Bogotá. Her work explores the constructions of identity through fashion and the legacy of colonialism in contemporary fashion systems.

Denis Bruna holds a PhD from the Sorbonne University, Paris, and joined the Musée des Arts décoratifs, Paris, as chief curator of the pre-nineteenth-century fashion and textile collections in 2011. He is also professor in the history of fashion, costume, and textiles at the École du Louvre, Paris. His research has focused on the history and iconography of fashion, sartorial customs, and the body. At the Musée des Arts décoratifs, he has curated several exhibitions including *La Mécanique des dessous* (2013), which was also presented at the Bard Graduate Center Gallery, New York, in 2015.

Emma Cormack is an associate curator at Bard Graduate Center, New York. Her research specialties include the history of fashion and consumer culture in late nineteenth- and early twentieth-century France with a particular interest in department stores and print advertising. At Bard Graduate Center, she was assistant curator of the exhibition *French Fashion, Women, and the First World War* (2019) and curatorial and editorial assistant for the exhibition *Eileen Gray* (2020).

Amalia Descalzo Lorenzo holds a PhD in art history from the Universidad Autónoma of Madrid. She is currently a professor of the history of fashion for masters' courses at the University of Alcalá and the ISEM Fashion Business School, University of Navarra, both in Madrid. Previously she was a curator at the Museo del Traje, Madrid, and a member of the curatorial committee for the founding of the Museo Cristóbal Balenciaga, Getaria, Spain. She has published extensively about Spanish fashion, including *Spanish Fashion at the Courts of Early Modern Europe* (2014).

Annina Dosch is an art historian with a focus on historical textiles and handicrafts. She studies art history and archaeology of the Mediterranean and received an MA in art history with special qualification of textile arts at the University of Bern, Switzerland. She is the curator for the textile collection at the Raetien Museum, Chur, Switzerland, and is a research assistant at the Textilmuseum St. Gallen, Switzerland, where she is currently head of a project that will integrate the Lisbet and Robert Schläpfer Collection into the museum's collection.

Tobias Forster was creative director of Forster Rohner AG from 1967 until 2006. He has worked with high-fashion designers in Paris and Rome as well as leading ready-to-wear designers all over the world. In 2006 he was awarded Designer of the Year by the Mayor of Paris. Since 2011 he has been president of the Textilmuseum St. Gallen, Switzerland.

Paula Hohti is a professor of art and culture history at Aalto University, Espoo, Finland. Her research focuses on Italian Renaissance dress and material culture, with a special focus on their role and function within the classes of artisans and shopkeepers. She earned a PhD from the University of Sussex, Brighton, UK, and has held research positions at Bard Graduate Center, New York; European University Institute, Florence; Helsinki Collegium for Advanced Studies; and the University of Copenhagen. She has been a principal investigator in two major international research projects: Fashioning the Early Modern, led by Evelyn Welch, and the Material Renaissance.

Barbara Karl's interdisciplinary research spans the sixteenth to the nineteenth century and focuses on art and textile history and museological themes. An art historian by training, she received her PhD from the University of Vienna in 2004 and Habilitation from the University of Innsbruck in 2020. In her work for the Institute for Iranian Studies at the Austrian Academy of Sciences and the MAK-Museum für angewandte Kunst, both in Vienna, and the Textilmuseum St. Gallen, Switzerland, she focused on the formation of their collections and the history of collecting by the Austrian Habsburgs and the Medici in Florence. Another facet of Karl's research focused on global art and textile history through an examination of the arts of the Portuguese expansion to Asia.

Ilona Kos is curator at the Textilmuseum St. Gallen, Switzerland. As an art historian and archaeologist, she studies handicraft and industrial products, especially textiles. She was assistant curator of the Textilmuseum's exhibition *Circus Knie Fashion* (2019–20) and co-curator of *Material Matters: From Fibre to Fashion* (2020–21). Recent publications include her essay "A puzzling cope from Lausanne Cathedral," published in *Velvets of the Fifteenth Century* (2020).

Martin Leuthold is a textile designer and the former creative director at Jakob Schlaepfer, St. Gallen, Switzerland, where he worked for more than forty years before retiring in 2018. During his time at the company, he led a small creative team that was known for innovative and experimental fabrics used by couturiers around the world. Today Leuthold continues to work in his private atelier, partnering with various artists, institutions, and companies on projects ranging from theater productions to exhibitions, including an installation at the Textilmuseum St. Gallen titled *"Good": At the Beginning Is White Gold* (2022–23), which explores more than seven hundred years of linen production in the St. Gallen region.

Kenna Libes is a PhD candidate at Bard Graduate Center, New York. She holds an MA in public humanities from Brown University, Providence, as well as an MA in fashion and textile studies from the Fashion Institute of Technology, New York. Her current areas of research include size bias in museum collections and fat fashion in historic dress, and she brings experience in making and conservation to all of her projects. She has published in the journal *Dress* and has contributed to exhibitions internationally.

Michele Majer is assistant professor at Bard Graduate Center, New York, where she teaches courses on American and European fashion and textile history from the eighteenth through the twentieth century. Her work draws on social, cultural, art, economic, and political history as well as literature. In 2012 she curated the exhibition *Staging Fashion, 1880–1920: Jane Hading, Lily Elsie, Billie Burke* at Bard Graduate Center and contributed to and edited the accompanying catalogue. Her recent publications include chapters in the exhibition catalogues *French Fashion, Women, and the First World War* (2019) and *Boldini e la moda* (2019).

Mariselle Meléndez is a professor of colonial Latin American literatures and cultures and LAS Alumni Distinguished Professorial Scholar at the University of Illinois, Urbana-Champaign. She is the author of *Deviant and Useful Citizens: The Cultural Production of the Female Body in Eighteenth-Century Peru* (2011; reprinted in 2021) and *Raza, género e hibridez en El lazarillo de ciegos caminantes* (1999) and is the co-editor of *Mapping Colonial Spanish America: Places and Commonplaces of Identity, Culture, and Experience* (2002). Her articles have appeared in journals such as *Colonial Latin American Review*, *Latin American Research Review*, and *Revista Iberoamericana*, among others.

James Middleton is an independent scholar of dress and material culture in colonial Spanish America. He came to scholarly work after twenty-five years as a stage director and designer, primarily of baroque opera. He has published, given presentations, and led workshops in Colombia, England, Mexico, Panama, and the United States, at venues including the Association of Dress Researchers, London; Museo Nacional de Arte and Museo Nacional de Historia, Mexico; the Los Angeles County Museum of Art; and the Metropolitan Museum of Art in New York.

Lesley Ellis Miller has been professor of dress and textile history at the University of Glasgow since 2013. From 2005 to 2021, she was senior curator of textiles and fashion (before 1800) at the Victoria and Albert Museum, London, where she led the curatorial team that redeveloped the Europe 1600–1815 galleries (2010–15). Her main publications are *Selling Silks: A Merchant's Sample Book 1764* (2014) and *Balenciaga: Shaping Fashion* (2017).

Catherine Örmen received degrees from the École du Louvre and the École Nationale du Patrimoine, both in Paris. She was the founding curator of the Musée de la Mode de Marseille, France, which opened in 1989. In 1995 she became the curator in charge of the twentieth-century collections at the Musée de la Mode et du Textile, Paris. Since 2000 she has worked as an independent curator. She has published several books on the history of fashion and teaches courses on this topic.

Hans Schreiber has been creative director at the St. Gallen–based textile manufacturer Forster Rohner AG since 2006. Following his studies in fashion design at the Royal Academy of Fine Arts Antwerp, he was design assistant for Romeo Gigli in Milan. Before coming to Forster Rohner, he was a creative consultant for different companies in fashion and textiles.

Frieda Sorber holds degrees in art history, archeology, and textile technology. Starting in 1976 she worked as curator for the Textielmuseum Vrieselhof, Belgium, and since 2001 has been the curator of historical collections at the Fashion Museum Antwerp, where she recently curated the exhibition *P.LACE.S: Looking through Flemish Lace* (2021–22). Sorber's scholarly practice has included fieldwork studying textile technology in China, Japan, Mexico, Morocco, Peru, and Uzbekistan. She has organized several exhibitions and publications based on this research, which has also inspired her own textile production, resulting in several solo exhibitions in Belgium.

Femke Speelberg is curator in the department of drawings and prints at the Metropolitan Museum of Art, New York. She oversees the drawings, prints, and illustrated books related to the subjects of ornament, design, and architecture. In her exhibitions and research she explores the role that these works play in the artistic process, as a means to generate ideas, to find and provide inspiration, to advertise skill, and as records in the workshop.

Annabel Bonnin Talbot is a freelance artist, teacher, and researcher with a particular interest in enhancing community well-being through the decorative arts. She began working with the Blackborne Lace Collection in preparation for the exhibition *Fine and Fashionable: Lace from the Blackborne Lace Collection* at the Bowes Museum, Barnard Castle, UK (2006–7).

Anne Wanner-JeanRichard was curator at the Textilmuseum St. Gallen, Switzerland, for twenty-two years. After her retirement in 2000, she became a member of the Iklé-Frischknecht Foundation, St. Gallen, and later its president. In 2018 the foundation collaborated with the Textilmuseum to publish a catalogue of the museum's historic lace collection: *Historische Spitzen: Die Leopold-Iklé-Sammlung im Textilmuseum St. Gallen*. Wanner Jean-Richard's contribution, "'Das Alte auf eine neue Weise tun—das ist Innovation,'" is one of numerous articles and publications that she has authored on the topic of textiles, many with a focus on embroidery.

Emily Zilber is a curator and consultant working with artists, museums, and organizations to champion modern and contemporary craft and design. She has held administrative, curatorial, and educational roles at the Cranbrook Academy of Art and Art Museum, Bloomfield Hills, MI; Wharton Esherick Museum, Malvern, PA; Museum of Fine Arts, Boston; Renwick Gallery of the Smithsonian American Art Museum, Washington, DC; and Tyler School of Art and Architecture, Philadelphia.

Index

Photographic Credits

Photographs were taken or supplied by the lending institutions, organizations, or individuals credited in the picture captions and are protected by copyright; many names are not repeated here. Individual photographers are credited below. Permission has been sought for use of all copyrighted illustrations in this volume. In several instances, despite extensive research, it has not been possible to locate the original copyright holder. Copyright owners of these works should contact Bard Graduate Center, 18 West 86th Street, New York, NY 10024.

akg-images / Cameraphoto: Fig. 3.16
Album / Alamy Stock Photo: Fig. 7.10
Album / Art Resource, NY: Figs. 5.17, 5.19
© Alinari Archives / Nicola Lorusso / Art Resource, NY: Fig. 3.11
Photo © Raffaello Bencini / Bridgeman Images: Fig. 3.6
By permission of Biblioteca Apostolica Vaticana, with all rights reserve: Fig. 6.13
bpk Bildagentur / Herzog Anton Ulrich-Museum / C. Cordes / Art Resource, NY: Fig. 10.21
Reproduced by permission of Chatsworth Settlement Trustees/Bridgeman Images: Fig. 5.12
C. Choffet: Figs. 10.25, 10.26
© Christie's Images/Bridgeman Images: Fig. 5.20
Digital Image © CNAC/MNAM, Dist. RMN-Grand Palais / Art Resource, NY / Guy Carrard: Fig. 15.13
© Fréderic Collier | Ville de Calais: Fig. 15.20
© Cooper Hewitt, Smithsonian Design Museum: Fig. 9.16
© Cooper Hewitt, Smithsonian Design Museum / Art Resource, NY: Figs. 13.5, 13.10, 13.24
© Cooper Hewitt, Smithsonian Design Museum / Art Resource, NY / Matt Flynn: Figs. 13.4, 13.16, 13.18, 13.19, 13.21, 13.22, 13.26
© Cooper Hewitt, Smithsonian Design Museum / Matt Flynn: Figs. I.19, 15.30
Erik Cornelius / Nationalmuseum: Fig. 10.7
Stany Dederen: Fig. 4.17
Photograph courtesy of the Denver Art Museum: Figs. 7.8, 7.11–13, 7.15–17
© Christian Devleeschauwer: Fig. 9.2
Rafael Doniz: Fig. 7.7
© Eric Emo / Paris Musées, Palais Galliera / Roger-Viollet: Fig. 15.27
Julia Featheringill: Cat. 123
HIP / Art Resource, NY: Fig. 3.7
Christoph Hirtz: Figs. 8.1, 8.7, 8.8, 8.12
Photo courtesy of the Institute of Valencia de Don Juan: Fig. 5.18
Meredith E. Keffer: Fig. 8.14
© KU Leuven – foto Bruno Vandermeulen: Fig. 4.4
Gerardo Landa: Fig. 7.23
© Les Arts Décoratifs / Jean Tholance: Fig. 15.12
Erich Lessing / Art Resource, NY: Fig. 4.14

Livrustkammaren (The Royal Armoury) / Göran Schmidt / CC BY-SA: Fig. 3.8
© MAD, Paris / Christophe Dellière: Fig. 9.17
Hugo Maertens: Fig. 4.2
The Metropolitan Museum of Art, New York: Figs. I.16, I.22, I.25, 2.1–6, 2.9–24, 3.15, 3.18, 4.7, 4.16, 5.11, 5.15, 9.12, 9.14, 10.4, 10.8–10, 10.14, 11.7, 11.12, 11.17–19, 13.7, 13.9; Cat. 30
Image copyright © The Metropolitan Museum of Art, New York. Image source: Art Resource, NY: Figs. 2.25, 13.25, 16.1; Cat. 183
Photo © Ministère de la Culture / Médiathèque du Patrimonie, Dist. RMN Grand-Palais / Art Resource, NY; © François Kollar – RMN: Fig. 15.16
© Collectie Modemuseum Antwerpen: Figs. 4.12, 4.22, 4.23
Oscar Monsalve: Fig. 8.17
Creative Commons CC BY– MRAH/KMKG: Figs. 4.6, 4.8, 4.11
© Musée d'art et d'histoire, Ville de Genève, photographer: Jean-Marc Yersin: Fig. 4.9
© Musée des Beaux-Arts de Dijon / François Jay: Fig. 10.18
Musée des Beaux-Arts Orléans © François Lauginie: Fig. 9.3
Musée des Beaux-Arts Orléans © Mathieu Lombard: Fig. 9.15
© Museo Colonial / Oscar Monsalve: Figs. 8.4–6, 8.10, 8.11
Copyright of the image Museo Nacional del Prado / Art Resource, NY: Figs. 5.1–3, 5.5–9, 5.13, 5.21, 7.9
© Museo Santa Clara / Oscar Monsalve: Fig. 8.9
© Museum Associates / LACMA Conservation, by Yosi A. R-Pozeilov: Fig. 6.8
Michael Myers: Fig. I.18
© National Gallery, London / Art Resource, NY: Fig. 10.1
Nationalmuseum, Stockholm / Bridgeman Images: Fig. 10.20
National Museum of the American Indian, Smithsonian Institution (05/3773). Photo by NMAI Photo Services: Fig. 7.1
Joaquín Otero: Fig. 8.2
© Paris Musées, Palais Galliera, Dist. RMN-Grand Palais / image ville de Paris / Art Resource, NY: Fig. 15.11

Paris Musées / Palais Galliera, musée de la Mode de la Ville de Paris: Fig. 15.4
Michael Rast: Cover; Endpapers; Page VIII; Figs. I.3, I.10–12, I.17, I.24, I.26, I.28–30, 1.1–9, 1.12, 1.13, 1.15, 1.16, 1.19–22, 1.26, 1.27, 3.1–5, 3.14, 4.10, 4.13, 4.19, 4.20, 4.24–26, 7.3, 9.5, 9.10, 9.11, 10.3, 10.5, 10.6, 10.11a–e, 10.27, 10.29, 11.6, 11.13, 11.14, 11.20, 11.25, 11.27, 11.28, 14.4–21, 15.6, 15.10, 16.4–15; Cats. 2, 9, 10, 12, 14, 16, 21, 25, 26, 28, 33, 37, 39, 42, 45–49, 55, 57–62, 70, 71, 74, 76, 79, 85, 89, 93, 98, 102, 103, 105, 106, 108, 109, 111, 117, 118, 121, 126, 128, 148, 149, 152, 153, 155, 157, 158, 160, 185, 187, 188
© RMN-Grand Palais / Art Resource, NY: Figs. 11.8, 11.9, 12.9
© RMN-Grand Palais / Art Resource, NY / Gérard Blot: Figs. 1.17, 9.09, 11.1
© RMN-Grand Palais / Art Resource, NY / Christophe Foin: Figs. 9.7, 10.24
© RMN-Grand Palais / Art Resource, NY / Stéphane Maréchalle: Fig. 1.23
© RMN-Grand Palais / Art Resource, NY / René-Gabriel Ojéda: Figs. 9.4, 11.15
© RMN-Grand Palais / Art Resource, NY / Michel Urtado: Fig. 11.3
Javier Rodríguez Barrera: Figs. 6.3–5, 6.7, 7.19
© Yves Saint Laurent: Figs. 15.27, 16.1, 16.6
Scala/Ministero per i Beni e le Attività culturali / Art Resource, NY: Fig. 3.10
Courtesy of SFO Museum: Fig. 15.9
Susanne Stauss: Fig. I.13
Donat Stupan, Schweizerisches Nationalmuseum: Fig. I.9
© Tate: Fig. 11.16
Pat Verbruggen: Fig. 4.21
Cedric Verhelst: Fig. 4.15
Waddesdon Image Library, University of Central England Digital Services: Figs. 10.13, 10.15
Bruce M. White: Fig. I.15; Cat. 144
Michel Wuyts: Fig. 4.1